DENALI
FLORA

Moss-campion (*Silene acaulis*, p. 110)

An Illustrated Guide to the Plants of
Denali National Park and Preserve

STEVE CHADDE

NOTE: ♦ preceeding a species name indicates that the species is illustrated.

DENALI FLORA
An Illustrated Guide to the Plants of Denali National Park and Preserve

STEVE CHADDE

ISBN 978-1-951682-69-9

A Pathfinder Field Guide
Published by ORCHARD INNOVATIONS
Mountain View, Arkansas
info@orchardinnovations.com

VER. 1.0 12/2022

CONTENTS

4

INTRODUCTION

Denali National Park and Preserve, located in Alaska's interior, encompasses over six million acres (9,446 square miles, 24,464 square km). This Park, larger than the state of New Hampshire, supports boreal forests and taiga, dwarf-shrub and wetland communities, alpine tundra, and more. Each community or habitat is home to an array of plant species, and to date, over 800 vascular plant species have been recorded for the Park and surrounding area. In addition, about 400 species of moss, 459 lichens and 124 liverwort species are known to occur in the area. *Denali Flora* includes descriptions for all vascular plant species known from the park (as of 2022), a number of species known from the region and likely to occur in the Park, and also a handful of the the most common mosses and lichens (see page 323). The majority of species are illustrated with a color photograph, and keys for each species within a genus are provided to assist in identification of unknown plants.

Using the Flora

Begin identification of a completely unknown plant by first determining which major group the specimen in question belongs to (see Family Synopses, page 7): either a fern or clubmoss, a conifer (gymnosperm), or a 'dicot' or 'monocot' (angiosperms). Within these major groups, family descriptions and photographs of representative species are provided. Once a likely family is identified, refer to the genera and species included in that family (the body of the *Flora* is also arranged in this order, with families arranged alphabetically within each group). Use the provided habitat information as well to see if the plant in question is likely to be found in the habitat supporting the plant. With experience, plant families will be recognized more easily, and determination of unknown plants becomes much easier. Remember, all plants are protected in the Park, and should not be carelessly picked or removed from the ground.

Each species is described in a fairly standard format: its scientific name and most commonly used common name are provided, followed by any important synonyms (other formerly applied scientific names). Accepted scientific names can vary somewhat depending on the authority used, but by and large, scientific names used here conform to those presented by the Plants of the World Online database maintained by the Royal Botanical Gardens (see *powo.science.kew.org*). Next, each plant's habit (growth form), leaves, flowers, fruit, and habitat where typically found are described; all plants are considered native to the Denali region unless otherwise noted in the description. Flowering period is only given for species blooming very early (soon after snowmelt) or very late, as the growing season is short in Denali. Many plants of the region have had traditional medicinal or food uses, and these features are included where known. Note however that these uses are provided for information purposes only (some of Denali's plants are quite toxic), and no plant should be consumed or applied to the skin without proper guidance or tutelage under an experienced teacher.

Technical terminology has been kept to a minimum, and a glossary is provided on page 331. A list of additional references to the Denali flora is given on page 344, followed by an index to first the common names (page 345), followed by an index of scientific or latin names (page 357).

Acknowledgments

A work of this scope could not be completed without acknowledging the field work and publications of dozens of botanists and explorers of the Denali region conducted over the past 100 years. The author is especially indebted to the Denali National Park Botany

Program who have made available their *Ecological Atlas of Central Alaska's Flora* (see *ecologicalatlas.uaf.edu*). The Botany Program also has a smartphone app available for download which provides information on over 350 vascular plants, plus common mosses and lichens present in the Park. Photographs were used under Creative Commons commercial-use licenses; the photographer name is provided for each photograph.

Mount Denali, North America's highest peak (20,310 feet, 6,190 m), with low-elevation forests and taiga in the foreground, and alpine tundra and barren rock, ice, and snow at higher elevations.

FAMILY SYNOPSES

In lieu of a lengthy key to the families of vascular plants found in Denali National Park, below are brief descriptions of the plant families present in the region's flora; family characteristics refer to plants present in the Park. Once one is able to recognize plant families in the field, identification of unknown plants becomes much easier.

Key to the Major Groups

1   Plants without true flowers or seeds, reproduction by spores; plants always herbaceous ....**FERNS AND LYCOPHYTES**
1   Plants with true flowers bearing stamens and carpels (or sometimes only stamens or carpels); reproduction by seeds (Spermatophytes) 2
2   Trees or shrubs with needlelike or scalelike leaves; flowers mostly single sex, sepals and petals absent; ovule naked, not enclosed in an ovary ....**GYMNOSPERMS**
2   Trees, herbs, or shrubs with leaves of diverse form; flowers bisexual or unisexual, sepals and petals usually present; ovule completely enclosed in an ovary (Angiosperms) 3
3   Leaves net-veined, usually pinnately or palmately so, often toothed or lobed; flowers with sepals, petals and stamens mostly in multiples of 4 or 5; usually with differentiated sepals and petals ....**DICOTYLEDONS** ('Dicots')
3   Leaves usually parallel-veined, often strap-shaped, mostly alternate and entire; flowers with sepals, petals and stamens mostly in multiples of 3; usually with undifferentiated sepals and petals ('tepals') ....**MONOCOTYLEDONS** ('Monocots')

Ferns and Lycophytes

(13 families)

ATHYRIACEAE
Lady Fern Family, p. 23
Medium to large, tufted, deciduous ferns.

CYSTOPTERIDACEAE
Bladder Fern Family, p. 23
Small to medium deciduous ferns, leaves (fronds) tufted or singly along a rhizome.

DRYOPTERIDACEAE
Wood Fern Family, p. 25
Medium to large deciduous or evergreen ferns; rhizomes short, stout and scaly; sori round, on underside veins of pinnae; indusia round to kidney-shaped.

EQUISETACEAE
Horsetail Family, p. 26
Rushlike herbs with dark rhizomes; stems annual or perennial, grooved, usually with large central cavity and smaller outer cavities, unbranched or with whorls of branches at nodes; leaves reduced to scales, united into a sheath at each node.

ISOETACEAE
Quillwort Family, p. 30
Perennial aquatic or emergent herbs; leaves simple, linear, from a corm; outer fertile leaves with a pocketlike structure (sporangia) bearing whitish spores (megaspores; about 0.5 mm in diameter); inner fertile leaves have numerous small microspores.

LYCOPODIACEAE
Clubmoss Family, p. 30
Low, trailing, evergreen herbs resembling large mosses; leaves needlelike or scalelike; spore-bearing leaves (sporophylls) similar to vegetative leaves or in conelike clusters at tips of upright stems.

ONOCLEACEAE
Sensitive Fern Family, p. 33
Large coarse ferns of moist to wet places; sterile and fertile fronds very different.

OPHIOGLOSSACEAE
Adder's-Tongue Family, p. 34
Small perennial herbs from short, erect rhizomes having several fleshy roots; spores in numerous round sporangia.

POLYPODIACEAE
Polypody Fern Family, p. 36
Evergreen, colony-forming ferns.

PTERIDACEAE
Maidenhair Fern Family, p. 36
Deciduous or evergreen ferns, leaves

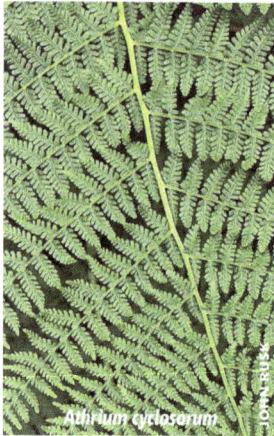
Athirium cyclosorum

ATHYRIACEAE
Lady Fern Family, p. 23

Cystopteris fragilis

CYSTOPTERIDACEAE
Bladder Fern Family, p. 23

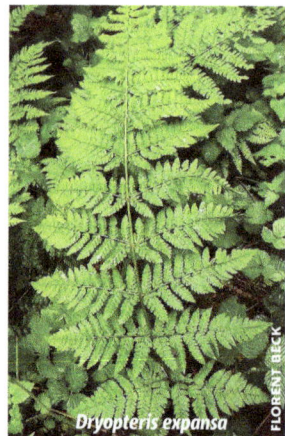
Dryopteris expansa

DRYOPTERIDACEAE
Wood Fern Family, p. 25

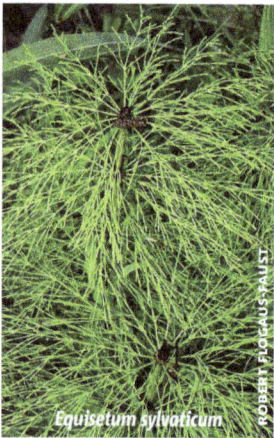
Equisetum sylvaticum

EQUISETACEAE
Horsetail Family, p. 26

Isoetes echinospora

ISOETACEAE
Quilwort Family, p. 30

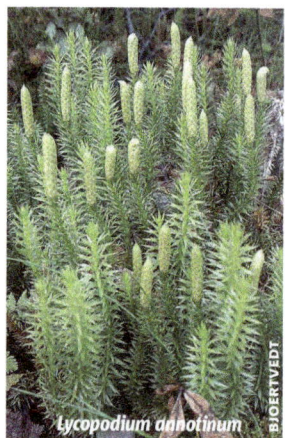
Lycopodium annotinum

LYCOPODIACEAE
Clubmoss Family, p. 30

Matteuccia struthiopteris

ONOCLEACEAE
Sensitive Fern Family, p. 33

Botrychium lunaria

OPHIOGLOSSACEAE
Adder's-Tongue Family, p. 34

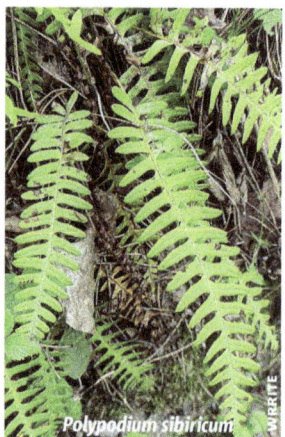
Polypodium sibiricum

POLYPODIACEAE
Polypody Family, p. 36

tufted or single from a rhizome; sori marginal, or borne along the veins and lacking an indusium.

SELAGINELLACEAE
Spike-Moss Family, p. 37

Trailing, evergreen herbs with branched, leafy stems, rooting at branching points. Leaves small and overlapping.

THELYPTERIDACEAE
Maiden Fern Family, p. 38

Small deciduous ferns, spreading by rhizomes to form colonies; sterile and fertile fronds alike.

WOODSIACEAE
Cliff Fern Family, p. 38

Small tufted ferns arising from compact rootstocks; indusium of thread-like or plate-like segments, more or less arched over the round sori.

Conifers

(2 families)

CUPRESSACEAE
Cypress Family, p. 39

Shrubs; leaves awl-shaped, whorled; fruit becoming fleshy and berry-like.

PINACEAE
Pine Family, p. 40

Resinous trees with evergreen or deciduous, needlelike leaves; male and female cones separate but borne on same tree.

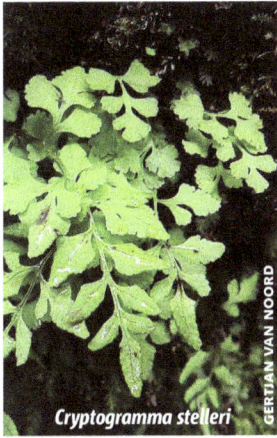

PTERIDACEAE
Maidenhair Fern Family, p. 36

Cryptogramma stelleri

SELAGINELLACEAE
Spike-Moss Family, p. 37

Selaginella selaginoides

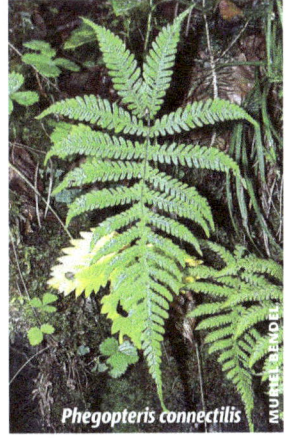

THELYPTERIDACEAE
Maiden Fern Family, p. 38

Phegopteris connectilis

WOODSIACEAE
Cliff Fern Family, p. 38

Woodsia alpina

CUPRESSACEAE
Cypress Family, p. 39

Juniperus communis

PINACEAE
Pine Family, p. 40

Picea mariana

Angiosperms—Dicots
(48 families)

AMARANTHACEAE
Amaranth Family, p. 42
Annual herbs; leaves simple, alternate; flowers small, aggregated into spikes or heads, in some species with conspicuous colored bracts; sepals usually 5; petals absent; fruit a 1-seeded utricle. Amaranthaceae now includes former members of the Chenopodiaceae.

APIACEAE
Carrot Family, p. 43
Biennial or perennial aromatic herbs with usually hollow stems, some very toxic; leaves alternate and sometimes also from base of plant, mostly compound; petioles sheathing stems; flowers small, perfect, in flat-topped or rounded umbrella-like clusters (umbels); petals 5, white or greenish; fruit 2-chambered.

ARALIACEAE
Ginseng Family, p. 47
Coarse, thorny shrub (*Oplopanax*); leaves lobed; flowers small, in an elongate inflorescence; fruit a red berry.

ASTERACEAE
Aster Family, p. 47
Annual, biennial or perennial herbs; leaves simple or compound, opposite, alternate, or whorled; flowers perfect or single-sexed (sometimes sterile) and of 2 types: ray (or ligulate) and disk (or tubular); ay flowers joined at base and have a long, flat, segment above (the ray); disk flowers tube-shaped with 5 lobes or teeth at tip; flowers clustered in 1 of 3 types of heads resembling a single flower and attached to a common surface (receptacle): ray flowers only (as in dandelion, *Taraxacum*); disk flowers only (discoid, as in sagebrush, *Artemisia*); and heads with both ray and disk flowers (radiate), the ray flowers surrounding the disk flowers (as in fleabane, *Erigeron*).

BALSAMINACEAE
Jewel-Weed Family, p. 74
Thin-leaved plants with watery juice and pendent, brightly colored irregular flowers; seedpod, when ripe, pops open when touched to eject the seeds.

BETULACEAE
Birch Family, p. 75
Small to medium trees, or shrubs; leaves deciduous, alternate; fruit a small, 1-seeded, winged nutlet.

BORAGINACEAE
Borage Family, p. 78
Annual or perennial herbs with often bristly stems and alternate, bristly leaves; flowers typically in a spirally coiled, spike-like head that uncurls as flowers mature.

BRASSICACEAE
Mustard Family, p. 81
Annual, biennial, or perennial herbs; leaves simple or compound, alternate on stems or basal; flowers with 4 sepals and 4 yellow, white, pink or purple petals; fruit a cylindrical (silique) or round (silicle) pod with 2 chambers.

CAMPANULACEAE
Bellflower Family, p. 102
Perennial herbs; leaves simple, alternate; flowers in racemes at ends of stems or single from upper leaf axils, perfect, 5-parted, funnel-shaped; petals blue or purple.

CAPRIFOLIACEAE
Honeysuckle Family, p. 103
Low trailing shrubs (*Linnaea*); or perennial herbs (*Valeriana*), with basal and opposite leaves; flowers in a terminal pair or cluster; perfect, 5-parted; fruit a dry capsule or achene. Family now includes members of the former Valerianaceae (*Valeriana*).

CARYOPHYLLACEAE
Pink Family, p. 104
Annual or perennial herbs; leaves simple, entire, mostly opposite but sometimes alternate or whorled; stems often swollen at nodes; flowers perfect or imperfect, in open or compact heads at ends of stems or from leaf axils; fruit a few- to many-seeded capsule.

CELASTRACEAE
Bittersweet Family, p. 115
Perennial herbs; leaves basal; flowers white, 5-parted, single at end of stem; fruit a dry capsule.

CERATOPHYLLACEAE
Hornwort Family, p. 116
Aquatic perennial herbs; roots absent, but plants usually anchored to substrate by modified leaves; leaves in whorls, with more than

Blitum capitatum — DEREK RAMSEY

AMARANTHACEAE
Amaranth Family, p. 42

Heracleum maximum — NPS · JACOB FRANK

APIACEAE
Carrot Family, p. 43

Oplopanax horridus — ROBERT FLOGAUS-FAUST

ARALIACEAE
Ginseng Family, p. 47

Erigeron humilis — USFWS

ASTERACEAE
Aster Family, p. 47

Impatiens noli-tangere — ALPSDAKE

BALSAMINACEAE
Jewel-Weed Family, p. 74

Betula pumila — LOUIS-M. LANDRY

BETULACEAE
Birch Family, p. 75

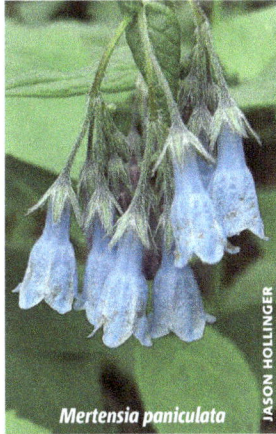
Mertensia paniculata — JASON HOLLINGER

BORAGINACEAE
Borage Family, p. 78

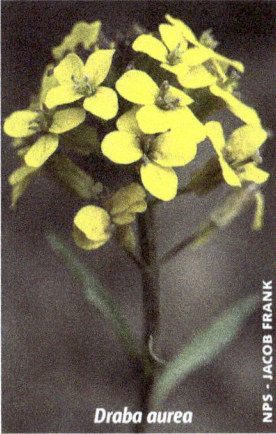
Draba aurea — NPS · JACOB FRANK

BRASSICACEAE
Mustard Family, p. 81

Campanula lasiocarpa — NPS · JACOB FRANK

CAMPANULACEAE
Bellflower Family, p. 102

Linnaea borealis
BRIAN GRATWICKE

CAPRIFOLIACEAE
Honeysuckle Family, p. 103

Cherleria arctica
ALFRED COOK

CARYOPHYLLACEAE
Pink Family, p. 104

Parnassia palustris
NPS · JACOB FRANK

CELASTRACEAE
Bittersweet Family, p. 115

Ceratophyllum demersum

CERATOPHYLLACEAE
Hornwort Family, p. 116

Cornus canadensis
RYAN HODNETT

CORNACEAE
Dogwood Family, p. 116

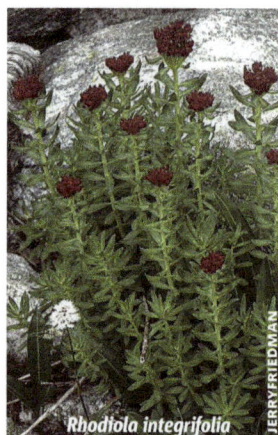
Rhodiola integrifolia
JERRY FRIEDMAN

CRASSULACEAE
Stonecrop Family, p. 118

Diapensia lapponica
ALPSDAKE

DIAPENSIACEAE
Pincushion-Plant Family, p. 118

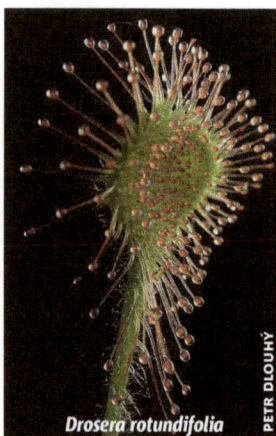
Drosera rotundifolia
PETR DLOUHÝ

DROSERACEAE
Sundew Family, p. 119

Shepherdia canadensis
ROBERT FLOGAUS-FAUST

ELAEAGNACEAE
Oleaster Family, p. 120

4 leaves per node, whorls crowded at ends of stems, dissected 2–3 times into narrow segments; flowers small, inconspicuous in leaf axils, staminate and pistillate flowers separate on same plant.

CORNACEAE
Dogwood Family, p. 116
Shrubs or perennial herbs (woody at base); flowers 4- or 5-parted. Fruit a drupe.

CRASSULACEAE
Stonecrop Family, p. 118
Plants succulent; leaves simple; flowers deep red, in a dense terminal cluster.

DIAPENSIACEAE
Pincushion-Plant Family, p. 118
Dwarf subshrub; leaves evergreen, thick and shiny, in whorls along stem; flowers single at end of stem, white.

DROSERACEAE
Sundew Family, p. 119
Small insectivorous bog plants; leaf blades round or spatulate, covered with sticky glands or hairs; flowers white, 5- petaled, in a slender cluster on a separate stalk.

ELAEAGNACEAE
Oleaster Family, p. 120
Shrubs or trees; leaves opposite or alternate, covered with small scales (lepidote); flowers small, solitary or clustered, perfect or unisexual, petals none.

ERICACEAE
Heath Family, p. 120
Ericaceae now includes former members of Pyrolaceae. Traditional Ericaceae are shrubs; leaves evergreen or deciduous, mostly alternate, simple; flowers urn- or vase-shaped, mostly white, pink, or cream-colored; fruit a berry or dry capsule. Former Pyrolaceae (*Moneses, Orthilia, Pyrola*) are perennial herbs or half-shrubs, most dependent on wood-rotting fungi (mycotrophic); leaves alternate to sometimes opposite or nearly whorled, often shiny, evergreen or deciduous; flowers 5-parted, waxy and nodding; fruit a capsule.

FABACEAE
Pea Family, p. 135
Biennial to perennial herbs; leaves alternate, pinnately divided, the terminal leaflet sometimes modified as a tendril (*Vicia*); flowers in simple or branched racemes, irregular; ovary maturing into a pod.

GENTIANACEAE
Gentian Family, p. 143
Annual, biennial or perennial herbs; plants usually glabrous; leaves simple, entire, opposite or whorled; flowers often showy, single at end of stems or in clusters; petals 4-5, blue, purple, white or green, joined for at least part of their length; fruit a 2-chambered, many-seeded capsule enclosed by the withered, persistent petals.

GERANIACEAE
Geranium Family, p. 147
Perennial herbs; leaves opposite, palmately lobed; Flowers in a terminal cluster, petals 5, pink to purple; fruit a 4-parted capsule.

GROSSULARIACEAE
Currant Family, p. 148
Shrubs; stems smooth, or with spines at nodes and sometimes also with bristles between nodes; leaves alternate, palmately veined and palmately lobed; flowers one to several in clusters, or few to many in racemes; green to white or yellow; fruit a many-seeded berry, usually topped by persistent, dry flower parts.

HALORAGACEAE
Water-Milfoil Family, p. 150
Perennial aquatic herbs; leaves alternate, opposite, or whorled, finely dissected; flowers small, stalkless in axils of leaves or bracts.

LAMIACEAE
Mint Family, p. 150
Perennial, often aromatic, herbs; stems 4-angled; leaves opposite; flowers solitary in leaf axils; corolla blue, 2-lipped.

LENTIBULARIACEAE
Bladderwort Family, p. 151
Insectivorous herbs; leaves in a basal rosette (*Pinguicula*), or floating, or in muck, or wet soil (*Utricularia*); flowers 2-lipped, sometimes with a spur, 1 to several on an erect stem; fruit a capsule.

LINACEAE
Flax Family, p. 152
Annual or perennial herbs; leaves simple, alternate or opposite, narrow, petioles absent; flowers regular, perfect, 5- parted, petals yellow or blue; fruit a 10-chambered capsule.

MENYANTHACEAE
Buckbean Family, p. 153
Perennial wetland herb; leaves palmately

Empetrum nigrum
ERICACEAE
Heath Family, p. 120

Lupinus nootkatensis
FABACEAE
Pea Family, p. 135

Gentianella propinqua
GENTIANACEAE
Gentian Family, p. 143

Geranium erianthum
GERANIACEAE
Geranium Family, p. 147

Ribes triste
GROSSULARIACEAE
Currant Family, p. 148

Myriophyllum verticillatum
HALORAGACEAE
Water-Milfoil Family, p. 150

Scutellaria galericulata
LAMIACEAE
Mint Family, p. 150

Pinguicula vulgaris
LENTIBULARIACEAE
Bladderwort Family, p. 151

Linum lewisii
LINACEAE
Flax Family, p. 152

divided into 3 leaflets; flowers in a racemes on a leafless stalk; petals white, bearded with white hairs on inner surface.

MONTIACEAE
Candy-Flower Family, p. 153

Now includes *Claytonia,* formerly within Portulacaceae; plants from tubers; petals 5, white to pink, often with pink veins.

MYRICACEAE
Bayberry Family, p. 154

Dioecious shrub, with alternate simple leaves; leaves resinous-dotted and fragrant; flowers solitary in the axils of small bracts, grouped into rounded to cylindric catkins.

NYMPHAEACEAE
Water-Lily Family, p. 155

Aquatic perennial herbs; stems long and fleshy, from rhizomes rooted in bottom mud; leaves large, leathery, mostly floating or emergent above water surface, heart-shaped to shield-shaped, notched at base; flowers showy, single on long stalks and borne at or above water surface, white or yellow; petals numerous; fruit a many-seeded, berrylike capsule, opening underwater when mature.

ONAGRACEAE
Evening-Primrose Family, p. 155

Perennial herbs; leaves opposite to alternate; flowers usually large and showy, in leaf axils or in heads at ends of stems; petals 4, white, yellow, or pink to rose-purple; fruit a 4-chambered capsule; seeds many, with or without a tuft of hairs (coma).

OROBANCHACEAE
Broom-Rape Family, p. 160

Annual to perennial herbs; often at least partially parasitic on roots of other plants; leaves opposite, alternate, or reduced to scales; flowers single or few from leaf axils, or numerous in clusters at ends of stems or leaf axils, usually with a distinct upper and lower lip; fruit a capsule; now includes many former members of Scrophulariaceae.

PAPAVERACEAE
Poppy Family, p. 166

Annual, biennial, or perennial herbs, with watery, milky, or colored juice; leaves basal or alternate on stem, dissected; flowers regular (*Papaver*), petals 4 or more, showy; fruit a capsule. The Fumariaceae, now included as a subfamily of Papaveraceae, differ in bilateral symmetry of the flowers and stems with watery juice.

PHRYMACEAE
Lopseed Family, p. 169

Perennial herbs; corolla yellow, funnel-shaped and 2-lipped; calyx tubular, 5-lobed; fruit a capsule.

PLANTAGINACEAE
Plantain Family, p. 169

Perennial herbs; leaves simple, entire, all from base of plant, and flowers perfect in a narrow spike (*Plantago*). Plantaginaceae now includes not only the plantains, but also many genera formerly placed in Scrophulariaceae (such as *Veronica*), and several aquatic genera, such as *Hippuris* (Hippuridaceae) and *Callitriche* (Callitrichaceae).

POLEMONIACEAE
Phlox Family, p. 174

Perennial herbs; leaves opposite (*Phlox*) or pinnately divided (*Polemonium*); flowers single or in clusters at ends of stems and from leaf axils; sepals and petals 5-parted and joined for part of length; fruit a 3-chambered capsule, with usually 1 seed per chamber.

POLYGONACEAE
Buckwheat Family, p. 175

Annual or perennial herbs; leaves alternate, simple, sometimes wavy-margined, otherwise entire, the nodes usually enlarged; stipules joined to form a membranous or papery sheath (ocrea) around stem at each node; flowers in spike-like racemes or small clusters from leaf axils, or in crowded panicles at ends of stems, petals absent; in *Rumex,* sepals green to brown, in inner and outer groups, each group with 3 sepals, the 3 inner enlarging after flowering, becoming broadly winged, persisting to enclose the achene; in other genera of family, sepals more or less petal-like, white to pink or yellow.

PRIMULACEAE
Primrose Family, p. 181

Annual, biennial, or perennial herbs; leaves mostly basal (opposite or whorled in *Lysimachia*); flowers regular, mostly in clusters at ends of stems; petals mostly 5, colors varying from pink, to white or yellow; fruit a capsule.

RANUNCULACEAE
Buttercup Family, p. 185

Mostly perennial, aquatic or terrestrial herbs, leaves usually alternate, sometimes opposite or whorled, or all at base of plant;

Menyanthes trifoliata
KRZYSZTOF ZIARNEK
MENYANTHACEAE
Buckbean Family, p. 153

Claytonia sarmentosa
NPS
MONTIACEAE
Candy-Flower Family, p. 153

Myrica gale
STEN
MYRICACEAE
Bayberry Family, p. 154

Nymphaea tetragona
ALPSDAKE
NYMPHAEACEAE
Water-Lily Family, p. 155

Epilobium angustifolium
MIKE LEHMANN
ONAGRACEAE
Evening-Primrose Family, p. 155

Pedicularis lanata
ELMI ALASKA
OROBANCHACEAE
Broom-Rape Family, p. 160

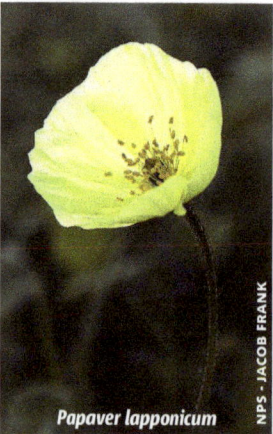
Papaver lapponicum
NPS - JACOB FRANK
PAPAVERACEAE
Poppy Family, p. 166

Erythranthe guttata
AGNIESZKA KWIECIEN
PHRYMACEAE
Lopseed Family, p. 169

Veronica wormskjoldii
WALTER SIEGMUND
PLANTAGINACEAE
Plantain Family, p. 169

flowers mostly white or yellow, usually with 5 (occasionally more) separate petals and sepals, stamens usually numerous; pistils several to many, ripening into beaked achenes or dry capsules (follicles).

ROSACEAE
Rose Family, p. 198

Small tree (*Sorbus*), shrubs (sometimes dwarf shrubs as in *Dryas*), and annual to perennial herbs; leaves evergreen or deciduous, mostly alternate and simple or compound; flowers regular, with 5 sepals and petals; stamens numerous; fruit an achene, capsule, or fleshy fruit with numerous embedded seeds (drupe), or a fleshy fruit with seeds within (pome).

RUBIACEAE
Madder Family, p. 211

Perennial herbs; leaves simple, whorled; flowers small, perfect, white to green, single or several in loose or round clusters; fruit a capsule.

SALICACEAE
Willow Family, p. 212

Deciduous trees or shrubs with alternate leaves; both staminate and pistillate flowers in catkins (aments); fruit a capsule; seeds with a dense coma of long, mostly white, silky hairs (these aid in wind-dispersal).

SANTALACEAE
Sandalwood Family, p. 227

Perannial herbs, parasitic on roots of other plants; leaves simple, alternate; flowers perfect or unisexual, in small axillary clusters; fruit a berry-like orange drupe.

SAXIFRAGACEAE
Saxifrage Family, p. 228

Perennial herbs, with many species found in alpine areas; leaves alternate, opposite or basal; inflorescence various, flowers regular, sepals and petals mostly 5 (4 in *Chrysosplenium*).

URTICACEAE
Nettle Family, p. 239

Perennial herbs with stinging hairs; leaves opposite, simple, with petioles; flowers small, green, in branched clusters from leaf axils, staminate and pistillate flowers usually separate, on same or separate plants; fruit an achene.

VIBURNACEAE
Viburnum Family, p. 239

A musk-scented perennial herb, *Adoxa moschatellina*, from a scaly rhizome; family now also includes shrubby genera, *Sambucus* and *Viburnum*, previously in Caprifoliaceae.

VIOLACEAE
Violet Family, p. 241

Perennial herbs; leaves simple, basal and sometimes alternate along stem; flowers irregular, axillary or basal, usually nodding; lower petal usually spurred or larger than the others; fruit a capsule.

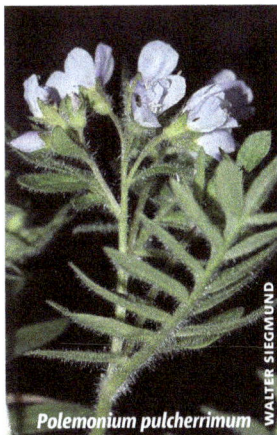

Polemonium pulcherrimum

POLEMONIACEAE
Phlox Family, p. 174

Bistorta plumosa

POLYGONACEAE
Smartweed Family, p. 175

Primula cuneifolia

PRIMULACEAE
Primrose Family, p. 181

Ranunculus eschscholtzii
RANUNCULACEAE
Buttercup Family, p. 185

Dryas integrifolia
ROSACEAE
Rose Family, p. 198

Galium boreale
RUBIACEAE
Madder Family, p. 211

Salix reticulata
SALICACEAE
Willow Family, p. 212

Geocaulon lividum
SANTALACEAE
Sandalwood Family, p. 227

Micranthes nelsoniana
SAXIFRAGACEAE
Saxifrage Family, p. 228

Urtica dioica
URTICACEAE
Nettle Family, p. 239

Viburnum edule
VIBURNACEAE
Viburnum Family, p. 239

Viola epipsila
VIOLACEAE
Violet Family, p. 241

Angiosperms—Monocots

(16 families)

AMARYLLIDACEAE
Daffodil Family, p. 243

Perennial herb, from an onion-like bulb; leaves basal, linear; flowers in a tightly clustered pink-purple head.

ARACEAE
Arum Family, p. 244

Perennial aquatic herbs; ours tiny and floating (*Lemna*), or larger and rooted, with a conspicuous white spathe subtending a cylindric spike of flowers (*Calla*).

ASPARAGACEAE
Asparagus Family, p. 244

Perennial herb (*Maianthemum*); leaves alternate in two rows; flowers white, in a terminal cluster; fruit a round berry, blue-black when mature.

CYPERACEAE
Sedge Family, p. 245

Mostly perennial, grasslike, rushlike or reedlike plants; stems 3-angled, or more or less round in section, solid or pithy; leaves 3-ranked or reduced to sheaths at base of stem; leaf blades, when present, grasslike, parallel-veined, often keeled; sheaths mostly closed around the stem; flowers small, perfect, or single-sexed, each flower subtended by a bract (scale); perianth of 1 to many (often 6) small bristles, or a single perianth scale, or absent; in *Carex*, ovary within a saclike covering (perigynium), maturing into an achene, stigmas 3 or 2; flowers arranged in spikelets (termed spikes in *Carex*), the spikelets single as a terminal or lateral spike, or several to many in various types of heads, the head often subtended by 1 to several bracts.

HYDROCHARITACEAE
Tape-Grass Family, p. 278

Aquatic herbs; leaves opposite; flowers either staminate or pistillate and borne on separate plants; fruit an achene.

IRIDACEAE
Iris Family, p. 278

Perennial herbs spreading by with rhizomes; leaves parallel-veined, narrow, 2-ranked, the margins joined to form an edge facing the stem (equitant); flowers with 6 petal-like segments, single or in clusters at ends of stem; fruit a 3-chambered capsule.

JUNCACEAE
Rush Family, p. 279

Distinguished from grasses and sedges by the presence of a true perianth of 6 tepals and a 3–many-seeded capsule rather than a 1-seeded grain (grasses) or achene (sedges); no ligule (as in grasses) is present at junction of leaf blade and sheath, however an auricle (an earlike appendage) may occur at top of leaf sheath.

JUNCAGINACEAE
Arrow-Grass Family, p. 285

Grasslike perennial herbs, often in brackish habitats; stems slender, leafless; leaves all from base of plant, slender, linear, round or somewhat flattened in section; flowers on short stalks in a spike-like raceme at end of stem.

LILIACEAE
Lily Family, p. 286

Perennial herbs, from bulbs or rhizomes; leaves linear to ovate, usually from base of plant, sometimes along stem, opposite or whorled; flowers regular; sepals and petals of 6 petal-like tepals; fruit a capsule or round berry. Many former genera in the Liliaceae have been placed into various new families.

MELANTHIACEAE
False Hellebore Family, p. 288

Perennial herbs (ours toxic if eaten); leaves all basal or numerous along the stem, linear to broadly oval; flowers white or greenish, in a branched or unbranched inflorescence; fruit a capsule.

ORCHIDACEAE
Orchid Family, p. 289

Perennial herbs, from fleshy or tuberous roots, corms, or bulbs; leaves simple, along the stem and alternate, or mostly at base of plant, stalkless and usually sheathing the stem, parallel-veined; flowers irregular, showy in some species, in heads of 1 or 2 flowers at ends of stems, or with several to many flowers in a spike, raceme or panicle, each flower usually subtended by a bract; fruit a many-seeded capsule, opening by longitudinal slits (remaining closed at tip and base); seeds minute.

POACEAE
Grass Family, p. 297

Perennial or annual plants, clumped, or spreading by rhizomes; stems (culms) usually hollow, with swollen, solid nodes; leaves

Allium schoenoprasum

AMARYLLIDACEAE
Daffodil Family, p. 243

Calla palustris

ARACEAE
Arum Family, p. 244

Maianthemum stellatum

ASPARAGACEAE
Asparagus Family, p. 244

Carex lasiocarpa

CYPERACEAE
Sedge Family, p. 245

Najas flexilis

HYDROCHARITACEAE
Tape-Grass Family, p. 278

Iris setosa

IRIDACEAE
Iris Family, p. 278

Juncus filiformis

JUNCACEAE
Rush Family, p. 279

Triglochin maritima

JUNCAGINACEAE
Arrow-Grass Family, p. 285

Fritillaria camschatcensis

LILIACEAE
Lily Family, p. 286

linear, parallel-veined, alternate in 2 ranks or rows, sheathing the stem, with a membranous or hairy ring (ligule) at top of sheath between blade and stem (or ligule sometimes absent), a pair of projecting lobes (auricles) sometimes present at base of blade; flowers (florets) small, usually perfect, or sometimes either staminate or pistillate, the staminate and pistillate flowers separate on the same or different plants; florets grouped into spikelets, each spikelet with one to many florets, with a pair of small bracts (glumes) at base of each spikelet, the glumes usually of different lengths, the lowermost (or first) glume usually smaller, the upper (or second) glume usually longer; each floret subtended by 2 bracts, the larger one (lemma) containing the flower, the smaller one (palea) covering the flower; ovary superior, never enclosed in a sac (as in sedges); spikelets grouped in a variety of heads, most commonly in branching heads (panicles), or stalked along an unbranched stem (rachis) in a raceme, or the spikelets stalkless along an unbranched stem in a spike.

POTAMOGETONACEAE
Pondweed Family, p. 314

Aquatic perennial herbs, with only underwater leaves, or with both underwater and floating leaves, sometimes reproducing and overwintering by free-floating winter buds; stems long, wavy, anchored to bottom by roots and rhizomes; leaves alternate, or becoming opposite upward in some species, simple, with an open or closed sheath at base; underwater leaves usually linear and threadlike, sometimes broader, margins often wavy, usually stalkless; floating leaves, if present, oval or ovate, with a waxy upper surface; flowers perfect, regular, green to red, in stalked spikes at ends of stems or from leaf axils, usually raised above water surface, the spikes with few to many small flowers.

SCHEUCHZERIACEAE
Scheuchzeria Family, p. 318

A single species, *Scheuchzeria palustris*, a perennial rushlike herb, from creeping rhizomes, found in wetlands; leaves alternate, several from base and 1–3 along stem; flowers perfect, regular, green-white, in a several-flowered raceme.

TOFIELDIACEAE
Featherling Family, p. 318

Perennial herbs with smooth or glandular-hairy stems; leaves basal and sometimes also along stem, sword-shaped; flowers 6-parted, white or greenish, in terminal clusters; fruit a rounded capsule.

TYPHACEAE
Cat-Tail Family, p. 321

In addition to *Typha* (Cat-tail), family now includes genus *Sparganium* (Bur-reed). *Typha* are large reedlike perennials, from fleshy rhizomes and forming colonies; stems erect, unbranched, round in section, sheathed for most of length by overlapping leaf sheaths; leaves mostly near base of plant, alternate in 2 ranks, erect, linear, spongy; flowers tiny, either staminate or pistillate, separate on same plant; heads with staminate flowers above pistillate in a single, dense, cylindric spike, the staminate and pistillate portions of the spike unalike. *Sparganium* are perennial sedgelike herbs, floating or emergent in shallow water, from rhizomes and forming colonies; stems stout, erect or floating, unbranched, round in section; leaves long, broadly linear, sheathing stem at base; flowers crowded in round heads, the heads with either staminate or pistillate flowers; fruit a beaked, nutlet-like achene.

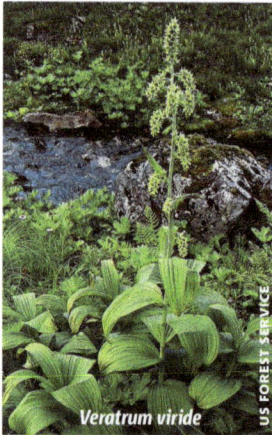
Veratrum viride
US FOREST SERVICE

MELANTHIACEAE
False Hellebore Family, p. 288

Cypripedium guttatum
OKSANA SERIKOVA

ORCHIDACEAE
Orchid Family, p. 289

Arctagrostis latifolia
NINA NESTEROVA

POACEAE
Grass Family, p. 297

Potamogeton gramineus
JASON HOLLINGER

POTAMOGETONACEAE
Pondweed Family, p. 314

Scheuchzeria palustris

SCHEUCHZERIACEAE
Scheuchzeria Family, p. 318

Tofieldia coccinea
NINA NESTEROVA

TOFIELDIACEAE
Featherling Family, p. 318

Sparganium angustifolium
BARBARA STUDER

TYPHACEAE
Cat-Tail Family, p. 321

FERNS AND LYCOPHYTES

ATHYRIACEAE
Lady Fern Family

Athyrium LADY FERN
(Greek, shield-less, perhaps for the absent indusium in some species.)

1 Smallest segments of leaf very narrow and separate from one another; indusium absent . . . . *A. americanum*
1 Smallest segments of leaf broad and close together; indusium present, curved or horseshoe-shaped . . . . *A. cyclosorum*

◆*Athyrium americanum* (Butters) Maxon
ALPINE LADYFERN
Athyrium alpestre subsp. *americanum* (Butters) Lellinger
  Habit tufted deciduous fern, leaves (fronds) to about 80 cm long, at ends of stout, scaly rhizomes; stipe short, sparsely scaly; blades glabrous, somewhat leathery, linear to oblong-lanceolate, twice pinnate-pinnatifid; smallest segments narrow and distant; indusium absent; sori round.
  Where Found uncommon in moist, rocky subalpine and alpine slopes and meadows.

Athyrium cyclosorum (Rupr.) Maxon
WESTERN LADYFERN
Athyrium filix-femina var. *cyclosorum* (Rupr.) Ledeb.
  Habit tufted deciduous fern, leaves to about 1 m long, erect-spreading from a stout,

chaffy rhizome; stipe scaly near base; blades narrowly to broadly lanceolate, bipinnate; pinnae lanceolate; indusium curved or horseshoe-shaped, attached by their inner side to a veinlet on pinna underside; sori oblong to horseshoe-shaped.
  Where Found occasional in moist meadows, thickets, streambanks.

CYSTOPTERIDACEAE
Bladder Fern Family

1 Pinnae alternate; leaves lanceolate or triangular-lanceolate in outline, longer than wide . . . . *Cystopteris*
1 Pinnae opposite; leaves triangular in outline, about as long as wide . . . . *Gymnocarpium*

Cystopteris BLADDER FERN
(Greek, bladder-fern.)

1 Leaves lanceolate in outline, stipe shorter than blade . . . . *C. fragilis*
1 Leaves triangular in outline, stipe twice as long as blade . . . . *C. montana*

◆*Cystopteris fragilis* (L.) Bernh.
BRITTLE BLADDERFERN
  Habit small, tufted, deciduous fern, leaves 10–30 cm long, from a stout dark rhizome; leaf stalks mostly without scales, with only a few scales at base; leaves lanceolate, twice-pinnately divided, leaflets pinnately lobed; almost all leaves fertile; leaf underside with oval-shaped, white indusia, covering sporangia; indusium often shed, exposing the clusters of brown sporangia.
  Where Found occasional at low- to high-elevations (mostly in alpine areas), in rock crevices, steep scree-slopes, forests, and

Athyrium americanum ALPINE LADYFERN

Cystopteris fragilis BRITTLE BLADDERFERN

thickets.

Similar Species the other *Cystopteris* in Denali, *C. montana,* has leaves triangular in outline, nearly as wide as long, not lanceolate in outline as in *C. fragilis;* other lanceolate ferns lack the hood-shaped indusium unique to *Cystopteris.*

♦ **Cystopteris montana** (Lam.) Bernh.
MOUNTAIN BLADDERFERN

Habit deciduous fern, leaves to 40 cm long, growing singly from a thin, long-creeping black rhizome; leaf stalk longer than blade, darker at base, with a few scales; leaves 3× pinnate-pinnatifid, the smallest leaflets pinnately lobed; blade broad, triangular in outline, wider than long; lowest pinnae pair much longer than other pairs; all leaves fertile, leaf underside with white indusia covering the sporangia.

Where Found uncommon in subalpine meadows, shrub thickets, rocky outcrops, woodlands; soils moist, often calcareous.

Similar Species fronds of *Cystopteris fragilis* twice as long as wide; *Gymnocarpium dryopteris* also similar, but indusia absent in that species.

Gymnocarpium OAK FERN

(Greek *gymnos,* naked, and *karpos,* fruit, referring to the absence of indusia).

1 Leaf blade firm and somewhat stiff, the 2 lower divisions about half as long as terminal division; rachis with glands, especially conspicuous at base of pinnae; underside of leaf blade glandular ...... *G. continentale*

1 Leaf blade membranous, the 2 lower divisions nearly as long as terminal division; rachis without glands; leaf blade without glands .... *G. dryopteris*

♦ **Gymnocarpium dryopteris** (L.) Newman
WESTERN OAK FERN

Habit colony-forming, deciduous perennial fern, arising individually at intervals from a long creeping rhizome; stipes smooth or with a few scales; all leaves fertile, light green, the blades triangular in outline, to about 25 cm long and about same width, 2-pinnate, pinnae broadly triangular, the lowest pair typically much larger than the others; sporangia on leaf underside, brown, not covered by an indusium (unlike similar looking *Cystopteris montana*); sori round, located near leaf margins.

Where Found occasional at low- to moderate-elevations, in thickets, moist forests, rock outcrops, and meadows (most common south of Alaska Range crest).

Gymnocarpium continentale (Petrov) Pojark.
ASIAN OAK FERN
Gymnocarpium jessoense subsp. *parvulum* Sarvela

Habit colony-forming, deciduous perennial fern, arising individually at intervals from a long creeping, blackish rhizome; stipes wiry, with many glandular hairs near attachment of pinnae; leaf blades triangular in outline, to about 15 cm long and about same width, 2-pinnate; ultimate segments lobed, with glands on the lower surface; indusium absent; sori small, near margins.

Where Found uncommon in calcareous rocky places and moist rocky woods.

Cystopteris montana MOUNTAIN BLADDERFERN

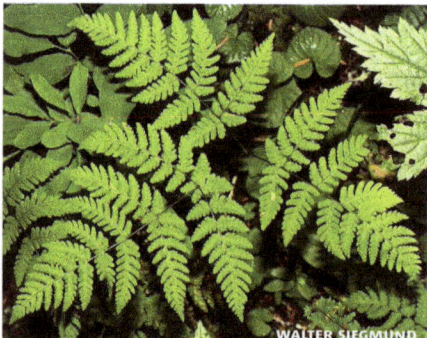
Gymnocarpium dryopteris WESTERN OAK FERN

DRYOPTERIDACEAE
Wood Fern Family

---

1   Pinnae margins thin and green; indusia laterally attached, kidney-shaped. . . . . *Dryopteris*
1   Pinnae margins thick and pale; indusia centrally attached, shield-shaped . . . . *Polysticum*

Dryopteris WOOD FERN
(Greek *drys*, tree, and *pteris*, fern.)

---

1   Leave blade covered with stalked glands; margin of indusia glandular; plants aromatic . . . .
  . . . . *D. fragrans*
1   Leaf blade and indusia without glands; plants not aromatic . . . . *D. expansa*

♦ *Dryopteris expansa* (C. Presl) Fraser-Jenk. & Jermy SPREADING WOOD FERN

Habit deciduous fern, leaves 20–70 cm long, in vase-like clusters, from a stout, ascending rhizome; leaves twice pinnately divided, the pinnae themselves pinnatifid; lowest pinnae more or less the same length as next highest pair, but broader than all other pinnae; these pinnae also asymmetrical: leaflets on the lower half conspicuously longer than the upper leaflets; indusia white, horseshoe-shaped and about 1 mm wide, covering the brown sori.

Where Found occasional in lowland forests through subalpine meadows and sheltered alpine sites, preferring humid, shaded places; much more common south of Alaska Range than north.

Similar Species dissimilar in outline to the narrow *Dryopteris fragrans;* the horseshoe-shaped indusium separates it from any other fern genus in Denali.

Traditional Uses fiddleheads edible, collected in early spring before they unfurl; rhizomes also edible and were eaten by Natives as a survival food (Turner et al. 1992).

♦ *Dryopteris fragrans* (L.) Schott
FRAGRANT WOOD FERN

Habit evergreen fern, in dense clusters arising from a short rhizome; plants sweet-smelling, with many persistent, curled dead leaves; stem (stipe) short, with many papery brown or rust-brown scales; leaves leathery, typically small but to 30 cm long in sheltered sites, long-elliptic and broadest at the middle, 2–3 pinnate, pinnae slightly angled upwards; leaves all fertile, the backs dotted with rust-brown sori; indusium kidney-shaped, white, turning brown and early deciduous.

Where Found occasional on steep rocky slopes and rock outcrops mostly in subalpine and alpine areas.

Similar Species can be mistaken for *Woodsia ilvensis*, which has similarly shaped fronds and is also found in rocky places, but *Dryopteris fragrans* coarser, stouter, and has kidney-shaped indusia while *W. ilvensis* only has dissected hairs around its sori.

Dryopteris expansa SPREADING WOOD FERN

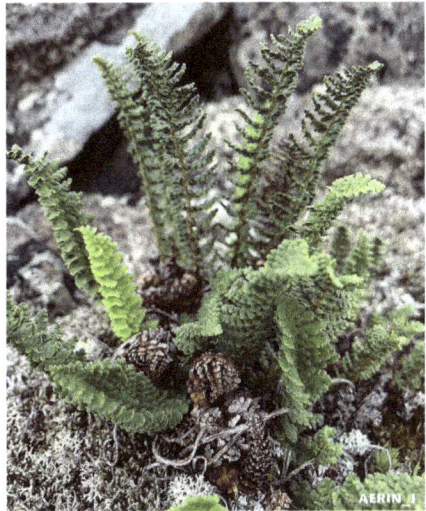

Dryopteris fragrans FRAGRANT WOOD FERN

Polystichum
HOLLY FERN, SWORD FERN
(Greek, many rows.)

1	Leaf blade once-pinnate . . . . *P. lonchitis*
1	Leaf blade twice-pinnate. . . . . *P. braunii*

♦ *Polystichum braunii* (Spenn.) Fée
BRAUN'S HOLLY FERN

Habit evergreen perennial fern, arising from a short, stout rhizome; stipe and rachis chaffy with both broad and narrow bright-brown scales; leaves in a crown, broadly lanceolate in outline, gradually narrowed toward base, 20–60 cm long, 10–20 cm wide, 2-pinnate; marginal teeth spine-tipped; indusia round, small, nearly entire.

Where Found uncommon in woods and thickets.

♦ *Polystichum lonchitis* (L.) Roth
NORTHERN HOLLY FERN

Habit evergreen perennial fern, arising from a short, stout rhizome; leaves rigidly ascending in a crown, 10–50 cm tall, with pinnae almost to base of stipe, densely chaffy at base, leaves lanceolate in outline, broadest near the middle, 1-pinnate; pinnae oblong, densely toothed with small spines, glabrous above, somewhat chaffy beneath; indusia orbicular, nearly entire; sori usually in two rows.

Where Found uncommon in woods, thickets, rocky slopes, outcrops.

EQUISETACEAE
Horsetail Family

Equisetum
HORSETAIL, SCOURING-RUSH
(Latin, *Equus*, horse, and *setum*, bristle.)

1	Stems with terminal cones 2
1	Stems sterile, without terminal cones 9
2	Fertile and sterile stems different; fertile stems (with terminal cones) pinkish or brown, unbranched or sparsely branched; fertile stems appear in spring before sterile shoots 3
2	Fertile and sterile stems similar; fertile green, branched or unbranched, appearing at about same time as sterile stems (or later), cones appearing in summer 6
3	Cone-bearing stems usually not branched, fleshy, pinkish or brown, not persistent. . . . *E. arvense*
3	Cone-bearing stems branched and green, persistent (although cones and tips of stems soon wither) 4

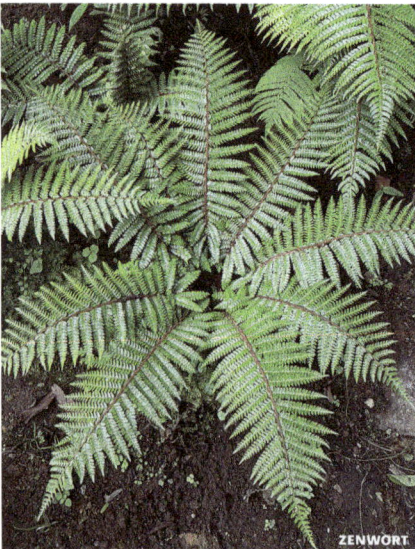

Polystichum braunii BRAUN'S HOLLY FERN

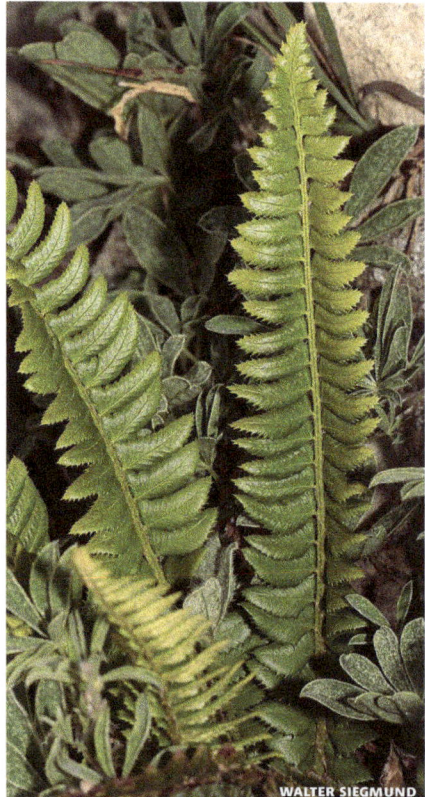

Polystichum lonchitis NORTHERN HOLLY FERN

4 Stem branches usually branched again; stem sheaths with teeth fused into broad lobes .... *E. sylvaticum*

4 Stem branches not branched again; stem sheaths with distinct teeth; 5

5 Teeth of stem sheaths with broad whitish membranaceous margins; branches fine, solid, rectangular in cross section; branch sheaths with 4 teeth .... *E. pratense*

5 Teeth of stem sheaths with brownish-green teeth (whitish membranaceous margin absent); branches coarse, hollow, triangular in cross section; branch sheaths with 3 teeth... *E. arvense*

6 Cones rounded at top 7

6 Cones with an abruptly sharp-pointed tip 8

7 Stems with deep grooves, the central cavity less than 1/4 of stem diameter; stem sheaths with 5–10 teeth; teeth black with conspicuous white margins .... *E. palustre*

7 Stems without deep grooves, the central cavity more than 3/4 of stem diameter; stem sheaths with 15–30 teeth; teeth with obscure, narrow white margins or early deciduous . *E. fluviatile*

8 Stems straight or slightly curved, usually more than 15 cm long and more than 0.6 mm in diameter, hollow, the central cavity about 1/3 of stem diameter .... *E. variegatum*

8 Stems curved, contorted, usually less than 15 cm long and less than 0.6 mm in diameter; stems solid, without a central cavity .... *E. scirpoides*

9 Stems branched, with branches in whorls... 10

9 Stems not branched, or with irregular branches (not in whorls)......................... 14

10 Teeth of stem sheaths joined in 3–6 lobes; most branches branched again .... *E. sylvaticum*

10 Teeth of stem sheaths distinct; branches not branched again (or with occasional branches) 11

11 Stems not grooved, the central cavity about 4/5 of stem diameter; branches in a single (or very few) whorl .... *E. fluviatile*

11 Stems grooved, the central cavity not more than 2/3 of stem diameter; branches in many regular whorls 12

12 Branches delicate; teeth of stem sheaths about 1/2 total length of sheaths; stems with a central cavity more than 1/2 of stem diameter .... *E. pratense*

12 Branches coarse; teeth of stem sheaths 1/4–1/3 total length of sheaths; stems with a central cavity less than 1/2 of stem diameter13

13 Stems with a central cavity about 1/5 of stem diameter; teeth of branch sheaths 2–4 times longer than wide .... *E. arvense*

13 Stems with a central cavity about 1/3 of stem di-

ameter; teeth of branch sheaths as wide as long .... *E. palustre*

14 Stems with a large central cavity about 4/5 of stem diameter .... *E. fluviatile*

14 Stems with a central cavity less than 2/3 of stem diameter, or central cavity absent.......... 15

15 Stem sheaths with 3–14 teeth; stems straight or slightly curved, hollow, with central cavity about 1/3 of the stem diameter ...... *E. variegatum*

15 Stem sheaths with 3 teeth; stems curved and contorted, solid, without a central cavity...... .... *E. scirpoides*

◆*Equisetum arvense* L.
FIELD HORSETAIL

Habit deciduous horsetail, from dark brown to black, felt-covered rhizomes; stems of two types: fertile stems unbranched, 10-15 cm tall, pale brown and fleshy, without chlorophyll, appearing in early spring before the sterile stems, cones 1-3 cm long, long-stalked; sterile stems variable, upright to 50 cm tall or prostrate, but usually with regular whorls of ascending branches; central cavity about ¼ stem diameter; first internode of branch longer than the closest stem sheath, sheath teeth lance-shaped.

Where Found abundant on gravel bars, shrub thickets, and lowland forests to scree, subalpine meadows and alpine tundra; sites often somewhat disturbed.

Similar Species *Equisetum pratense* similar, with spreading branches and triangular sheath teeth, but first internode of branch same or shorter than length of corresponding stem sheath.

Traditional Uses (for all Denali *Equisetum*) used as a tool, food, dye and medicine; used as a medicine by North American indigenous

Equisetum arvense FIELD HORSETAIL

people wherever it occurred; the Dena'ina used the ashes of burned stems and leaves on sores and heated the root to treat aching teeth; as a food, the first green sprouts were eaten in early spring by the Lower Chinook, the Hesquiat, and the Saanich; the Dena'ina and Eskimos of Alaska ate the tubers and nodules in the spring; other peoples ate the cones boiled or pickled; mature stems with their high silica content were used as a sandpaper for cleaning and for polishing wood and metal.

◆ *Equisetum fluviatile* L.
WATER HORSETAIL
Habit deciduous horsetail, from shiny, light brown rhizomes; fertile and sterile stems, similar, to 1 m tall and 3–8 mm thick, central stem-cavity more than 4/5 stem diameter; stems may be unbranched or have a few whorled branches; stem sheaths with 15–20 dark brown teeth; cones to 2 cm long, short-stalked.

Where Found occasional in shallow water of lake and rivers, marshes, bogs, ditches.

Equisetum arvense FIELD HORSETAIL

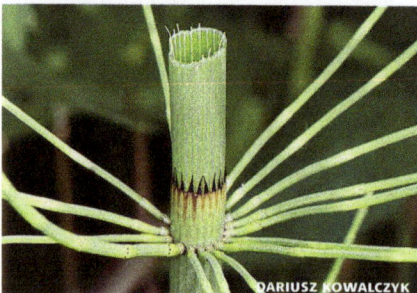
Equisetum fluviatile WATER HORSETAIL

Similar Species *Equisetum palustre*, but its central stem-cavity only one-sixth the stem-diameter, its stems more likely branched, and its sheaths with 10 or less white-margined teeth.

◆ *Equisetum palustre* L.
MARSH HORSETAIL
Habit deciduous horsetail, from shiny, black to brown rhizomes; fertile and sterile stems similar, 15–60 cm tall, 1–3 mm thick, central cavity about one-sixth stem diameter, unbranched or branched with irregular whorls; the first internode of the branch shorter than the corresponding sheath; cones 1–2 cm long, rounded at tip and short-stalked.

Where Found occasional in standing water in ponds, marshes, swamps, ditches, stream-banks, wet forests; mostly at low-elevations.

Similar Species *Equisetum fluviatile* similar but larger and with much larger stem-cavity, and its stem sheaths with dark brown margins versus white margins in *E. palustre*.

◆ *Equisetum pratense* Ehrh.
MEADOW HORSETAIL
Habit deciduous horsetail, from a dull black rhizome; sterile and fertile stems of two kinds: sterile stems whitish green and branched, 10–50 cm long, central cavity one-half diameter of stem; branches whorled, horizontal to drooping, stem sheaths with brown teeth and a blackish midrib; fertile stems to 40 cm tall; when young, unbranched, without chlorophyll, and not fleshy; when mature, becoming green and may develop a few short branches; sheaths light green to yellowish white, with pale teeth and dark midribs; cones stalked, to 1–2 cm long, rounded at tip.

Equisetum palustre MARSH HORSETAIL

Where Found common in moist to wet forests, meadows, bog margins, river terraces; in sun or partial shade.

Similar Species *Equisetum arvense* and *E. palustre,* but in those species branches ascending and stiff, not spreading or drooping as in *E. pratense.*

◆ *Equisetum scirpoides* Michx.
DWARF SCOURING-RUSH

Habit low-growing, wiry perennial, evergreen scouring-rush, from a slender brown rhizome; sterile and fertile stems same, central cavity absent; stems unbranched, to 15 cm long and to 1.5 mm thick, tipped with a small, pointed, black cone 3–5 mm long.

Where Found common in dry to wet conifer forests, bogs, fens, swamps, tundra, from lowlands to alpine; often in moss.

Similar Species *Equisetum variegatum* also evergreen and unbranched, but has a central stem-cavity and is taller (up to 50 cm).

◆ *Equisetum sylvaticum* L.
WOODLAND HORSETAIL

Habit deciduous horsetail, from a light brown rhizome; sterile and fertile stems of two kinds: sterile stems 15–50 cm tall, central cavity one-half stem diameter; sheaths inflated, reddish brown; branches compound, the smaller branchlets arched and drooping; fertile stems shorter, with stalked cones 1–3 cm long.

Equisetum pratense MEADOW HORSETAIL

Where Found common in low-elevation forests, meadows and bogs; shade tolerant.

Similar Species separated from *Equisetum pratense* and *E. arvense* by its twice-branched drooping branches (the only horsetail in Denali with compound branches).

◆ *Equisetum variegatum* Schleich. ex F. Weber & D. Mohr VARIEGATED SCOURING-RUSH

Habit evergreen, often tufted scouring-rush, from a smooth rhizome; sterile and fertile stems same; central cavity of stem one-quarter stem diameter; stems 10–40 cm tall and 2–3 mm in diameter, usually ascending but may be decumbent, mostly unbranched (though there may be a few

Equisetum sylvaticum WOODLAND HORSETAIL

Equisetum scirpoides DWARF SCOURING-RUSH

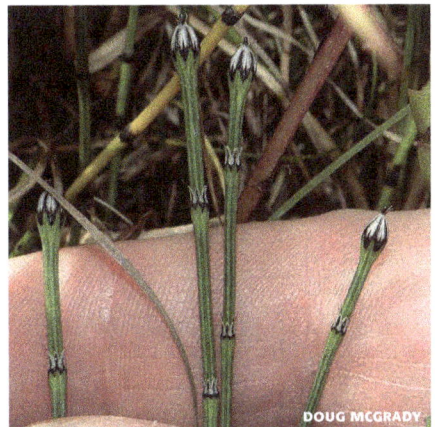
E. variegatum VARIEGATED SCOURING-RUSH

branches at base); cones to 1 cm long, pointed with a sharp tip.

Where Found common in moist meadows, gravel bars and moist sandy riverbanks, wet lakeshores, fens, ditches, roadsides, muskegs, tundra, scree-slopes.

Similar Species *Equisetum scirpoides*, but that species smaller and lacks a central stem-cavity.

ISOETACEAE
Quillwort Family

Isoetes QUILLWORT
Spores of two kinds, the inner sporangia bearing the microspores, the outer leaves enclosing sporangia with macrospores. (Greek, equal at all seasons.)

1 Leaves flaccid; megaspores with long spines; microspores smooth or with very fine thread-like spines . . . . *I. echinospora*
1 Leaves stiff; megaspores with blunt spines, these sometimes merged into ridges; microspores with coarse pronounced spines . . . . *I. maritima*

♦ *Isoetes echinospora* Durieu
SPINY-SPORE QUILLWORT
Habit perennial aquatic herb, rooted in sediments; from a 2-lobed corm; leaves grasslike, 7–25 or more, usually erect, soft, bright green to yellowish green; sporangia in a hollow at expanded base of leaves and more or less covered by thin edge of the hollow (velum); spores dimorphic; megaspores (female) borne in spherical, white megasporangia, covered with sparse to dense spines; microspores (male) borne in microsporangia, kidney-shaped, usually smooth or with fine threadlike spines.

Isoetes echinospora SPINY-SPORE QUILLWORT

Where Found uncommon in small lakes or ponds.

Isoetes maritima Underw.
MARITIME QUILLWORT
Habit perennial aquatic herb from a 2-lobed corm; leaves grasslike, 8–15, erect, rigid or somewhat recurved, dark green, mostly 2–5 cm long, 1.5 mm wide; sporangia oval, 4 mm long, 2.5 mm wide, covered one-third to one-half by the velum; megaspores spherical, white, covered with blunt spines that are sometimes joined into ridges or plates; microspores (male) kidney-shaped, white, with short sharp spines.

Where Found may be present in Denali's lakes and ponds.

LYCOPODIACEAE
Clubmoss Family

1 Sporangia in the axils of ordinary green leaves, not grouped into a cone . . . . *Huperzia*
1 Sporangia grouped into a cone . . . . *Lycopodium*

Huperzia FIR-MOSS
(Named in honor of Johann Peter Huperz (d. 1816), a German fern horticulturist.)

1 Stems with weak annual constrictions; gemmae-producing branchlets and gemmae (vegetative buds) formed in 1 pseudo-whorl at end of annual growth . . . . *H. miyoshiana*
1 Stems without annual constrictions; gemmae-producing branchlets and gemmae produced throughout mature portion of shoot . . . . *H. continentalis*

♦ *Huperzia continentalis* Testo, A. Haines & A.V Gilman FIR CLUBMOSS
Huperzia haleakalae auct. non (Brack.) Holub, *Lycopodium selago* L.

Habit perennial clubmoss, with strobili borne along the stem in axils of its needle-like, fertile, spore-producing leaves (not in terminal 'cones' as in *Lycopodium*); stems 8–12 cm tall, covered in triangular leaves.

Where Found alpine tundra and openings in shrub tundra areas (particularly in mossy places dominated by heath species), snowbed sites, often on north-facing slopes.

Huperzia miyoshiana (Makino) Ching
FIR CLUBMOSS

Huperzia selago L., *Lycopodium selago* subsp. *miyoshianum* (Makino) Calder & Taylor

Habit Evergreen perennial clubmoss from a short rhizome; stems dark olive-green, 5 to 25 cm long; shoots single or in loose clusters of 2 to 5, without noticeable annual constrictions; leaves crowded, lanceolate awl-shaped, less than 1 mm wide, 5–10 mm long, spreading to loosely ascending.

Where Found common in moist to wet places from lowlands to alpine areas.

Lycopodium CLUBMOSS

Spores very numerous, powdery, yellow and, being highly inflammable, formerly used in the manufacturing of fireworks. (Greek, wolf's foot.)

---

1 Leaves in 4 or 5 ranks, less than 4 mm long . . 2
1 Leaves in 6 to 10 ranks, usually more than 4 mm long 4
2 Plants with creeping underground rhizomes; stems strongly flattened and winged; leaves on concave side of stem noticeably narrower than leaves on margins or convex side. . . . .
. . . . *L. complanatum*
2 Plants with aboveground rhizomes; stems round or slightly flattened, not winged; all leaves similar in size. 3
3 Cones unstalked; vegetative branches flattened; plants usually bluish-green . . . . *L. alpinum*
3 Cones stalked; vegetative branches round; plants usually light green. . . . . *L. sitchense*
4 Stems upright, branched and tree-like. . . . .
. . . . *L. dendroideum*
4 Stems decumbent or ascending, but not branched and tree-like 5
5 Cones unstalked, one on each fertile branch; leaves without whitish hairs . . . . *L. annotinum*

5 Cones stalked, one or several on each fertile branch; leaf midrib extends into a long whitish hair 6
6 Plants with one cone on each fertile branch . . .
. . . . *L. lagopus*
6 Plants with two or more cones on each fertile branch . . . . *L. clavatum*

♦*Lycopodium alpinum* L. ALPINE CLUBMOSS
Diphasiastrum alpinum (L.) Holub

Habit evergreen perennial clubmoss, with unstalked strobili (cone-like reproductive structures), from horizontal stems on soil (or rock) surface or shallowly buried; upright shoots to 10 cm tall, branched, square in cross-section, bluish green, with flattened branches and overlapping, 4-ranked leaves.

Where Found occasional in alpine heaths and meadows in snowbed areas.

Similar Species the strobili not stalked and solitary at branch tips (along with habitat differences) separates *Lycopodium alpinum* from the other common clubmoss found in Denali, *L. complanatum;* it could also be confused with the rare *L. sitchensis* (known only from south side of Alaska Range in Denali) which has 5-ranked leaves all the same shape, and a stem round in cross-section.

Traditional Uses various clubmosses were used by the Dena'ina to make an eye wash (Kari 1995).

Huperzia continentalis FIR CLUBMOSS

Lycopodium alpinum ALPINE CLUBMOSS

◆*Lycopodium annotinum* L.
STIFF CLUBMOSS
Spinulum annotinum (L.) A. Haines

Habit evergreen perennial clubmoss, with unstalked strobili; stems horizontal, long-creeping, branched, with erect branches 5–20 cm tall with numerous leaves; stems increase in height each year, with each year's growth marked by a leafless patch on the stem that looks like a constriction; leaves needle-like, with toothed margins, thin compared to leaves of other clubmosses; protruding away from stem, giving it a bottlebrush-like appearance.

Where Found abundant in forest, bogs, shrublands and alpine heaths.

Similar Species the sessile strobili (without a naked stalk) on tips of vertical branches, separates *L. annotinum* from the similar *Lycopodium lagopus*, which has stalked strobili.

◆*Lycopodium clavatum* L.
RUNNING CLUBMOSS

Habit evergreen perennial clubmoss; stems long-creeping, branched, horizontal on ground surface, rooting at intervals; erect branches, 10–25 cm tall, at first simple, later forking; leaves linear, 3–5 mm long, usually tipped with a soft white hairlike bristle, typically ascending or appressed; strobili 2–6 cm long, single or several on short peduncles on fertile branches.

Where Found common in dry woods.

◆*Lycopodium complanatum* L.
GROUND-CEDAR
Diphasiastrum complanatum (L.) Holub

Habit evergreen perennial clubmoss, with stalked strobili, from shallowly buried horizontal stems; upright shoots 6–25 cm tall, branched several times more or less in one plane; branches flattened; leaves flattened, arranged in four rows, sometimes darker green on convex side, lighter on the concave side.

Where Found occasional in well-drained areas in lowlands to subalpine zone, from deciduous and mixed woodlands and shrublands to open dry, grassy sites; ground-cedar is shade tolerant, often on poor, acidic soils having a thick organic layer.

Similar Species *Lycopodium alpinum*, but that species found in the alpine and its strobili unstalked; the other clubmoss in Denali with stalked strobili is *Lycopodium clavatum*, but that species has tapering linear leaves with hair-like tips.

◆*Lycopodium dendroideum* Michx.
TREE GROUNDPINE
Dendrolycopodium dendroideum (Michx.) A. Haines

Habit evergreen perennial clubmoss; stems horizontal, underground; upright branches branched similar to a tree; leaves needle-like, 1–4 mm long, spreading; cones terminal 1–5 cm long.

Lycopodium clavatum RUNNING CLUBMOSS

Lycopodium complanatum GROUND-CEDAR

Lycopodium annotinum STIFF CLUBMOSS

Where Found uncommon at mostly lower elevations, in dry to moist forests, rocky or sandy places.

♦ *Lycopodium lagopus* Zinserl. ex Kuzen.
ONE-CONE CLUBMOSS
Lycopodium clavatum var. *lagopus* Laest. ex C. Hartm.

Habit evergreen perennial clubmoss; stems horizontal, long-creeping; erect branches 10–25 cm tall, tipped with a solitary stalked strobili; leaves numerous, narrow, appressed and overlapping on stem, tipped with a white hair.

Where Found occasional in subalpine woodlands, shrublands, heaths, and dry open slopes. Similar Species the stalked strobilii distinguish it from *Lycopodium annotinum; L. complanatum* is another clubmoss with stalked strobilii, but that species more highly branched and the strobilii often several to a stem.

Lycopodium sitchense Rupr.
SITKA CLUBMOSS
Diphasiastrum sitchense (Rupr.) Holub

Habit evergreen perennial clubmoss, from horizontal stems creeping on ground surface or shallowly underground; upright shoots branched, 5–15 cm tall, bright green and shiny; branches 4–5 ranked, not flattened; leaves all alike, 3–5 mm long, lanceolate, stiff.

Where Found uncommon on the south side of Alaska Range in Denali, in subalpine and alpine heath communities, open woods, and tundra.

ONOCLEACEAE
Sensitive Fern Family

Matteuccia OSTRICH FERN
(Named in honor of Italian physicist Carlo Matteucci, 1800-1863.)

♦ *Matteuccia struthiopteris* (L.) Tod.
OSTRICH FERN
Onoclea struthiopteris (L.) Roth

Habit large perennial fern, from a stout rootstock, bearing a circle of sterile fronds with fertile ones in the center; sterile leaves deciduous, in vase-like clusters, light green, 30–120 cm long, 15–30 cm wide, broadest in upper 1/4, 1-pinnate, pinnae deeply cut in 30–80 segments; fertile fronds overwinter-

Lycopodium dendroideum TREE GROUNDPINE

Lycopodium lagopus ONE-CONE CLUBMOSS

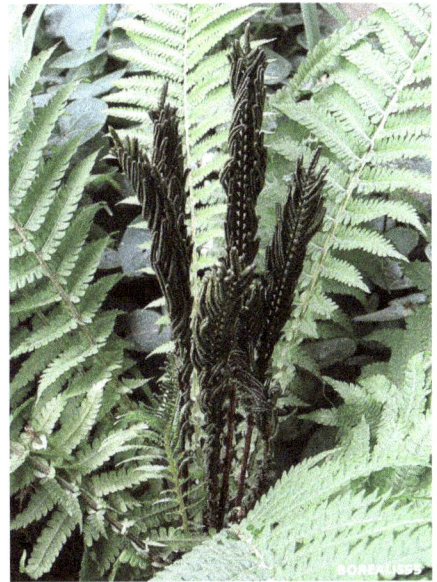

Matteuccia struthiopteris OSTRICH FERN

ing, rolled into necklace-like or berry-like segments, dark brown, about 60 cm long, 5–10 cm wide, with linear, obtuse pinnae; sori round, borne on the back of the veins; indusium delicate, fixed at the inferior side of the sorus.

Where Found uncommon in moist woods.

OPHIOGLOSSACEAE
Adder's-Tongue Family

Botrychium MOONWORT

Small perennial ferns divided into two parts: the sporophore, a modified leaf bearing grape-like sporangia, and the trophophore, which bears the single frond (leaf). Members of this genus have undergone significant taxonomic revision (and splitting into new species) and correct identification can be difficult. (Name in allusion to the grapelike arrangement of the sporangia.)

1 Trophophore (leaf) 4- to 5- pinnate . . . .
. . . . *B. virginianum*
1 Trophophores less than 4-pinnate 2
2 Trophophore 1-pinnate or simple. 3
2 Trophophore 2-pinnate 5
3 Basal pinnae broadly fan-shaped, semicircular in shape. . . . . *B. lunaria*
3 Basal pinnae narrowly fan-shaped, wedgelike 4
4 Pinnae strongly ascending . . . . . . *B. ascendens*
4 Pinnae spreading or only moderately ascending . . . . *B. minganense*
5 Trophophore triangular in outline; sporophore stalk 1/3–1/4 as long as sporophore; pinna pairs 3 or 4; basal pinna pair 2 x as wide as the adjacent pinna pair. . . . . *B. lanceolatum*
5 Trophophore ovate to triangular in outline; sporophore stalk 1/2–1/3 as long as sporophore; pinna pairs 5–7; basal pinna pair equal to or slightly larger than the adjacent pair. 6
6 Trophophores mostly ovate to triangular in outline; pinnae somewhat irregularly incised, bright green; pinna bases forming an angle of about 40–90 degrees from main stalk. . . *B. alaskense*
6 Trophophores mostly ovate; pinnae very regularly incised, dark (olive) green; pinna bases forming an angle of about 120–140 degrees from main stalk . . . . *B. pinnatum*

Botrychium alaskense W.H. Wagner & J.R. Grant ALASKA MOONWORT
Habit deciduous perennial moonwort; trophophore (leaf) bright green, leathery, oblong-deltate, 1-pinnate, up to 6 cm long and wide; pinnae up to 6 pairs, horizontal to slightly ascending; sporophore (fertile segment) 2-pinnate, with 3 major branches.

Where Found in somewhat recently disturbed open places including sandbars, lakeshores, ditches, highway edges.

Botrychium ascendens W.H. Wagner
TRIANGLE-LOBE MOONWORT
Habit deciduous perennial moonwort, 5–13 cm tall; trophophore (leaf) lanceolate, short stalked; blades 1-pinnate; pinnae in 3 to 5 well-separated pairs, strongly ascending with minutely toothed margins, often shallowly incised; sporophore (fertile segment) 2-pinnate, 1.5–2 times the length of trophophore.

Where Found moist meadows in lowland and montane zones.

♦***Botrychium lanceolatum*** (S.G. Gmel.) Ångstr.
LANCE-LEAF MOONWORT
Habit deciduous perennial moonwort, 3–25 cm tall; leaves 20 cm long or longer, stout,

JASON HOLLINGER

Botrychium lanceolatum LANCE-LEAF MOONWORT

succulent, blade broadly triangular in outline, green to pale yellow-green, 1–2-pinnate with up to 5 pairs of pinnae, the first pair of pinnae longest, margins with distinct lobes; sporophore (fertile segment) 1–2.5 times length of trophophore.

Where Found alpine meadows and grassy places.

♦ *Botrychium lunaria* (L.) Sw.
DAINTY MOONWORT

Habit deciduous, perennial, somewhat fleshy moonwort, 5–15 cm tall; trophophore (leaf) green, oblong, once-pinnate with 4–9 pairs of pinnae; pinnae fan-shaped, symmetrical, usually overlapping one another (but not the rachis); sporophore (fertile segment) branched, to 2 times length of trophophore at time of spore release.

Where Found well-drained to moist sites in open soil or meadows, on slopes and floodplains at all elevations; the most common moonwort in Denali and interior Alaska.

♦ *Botrychium minganense* Vict.
MINGAN MOONWORT

Botrychium lunaria var. *minganense* (Vict.) Dole

Habit deciduous perennial moonwort, with fan-shaped leaflets; trophophore (leaf) linear to oblong in outline, pinnately divided into as many as 10 pairs of pinnae; pinnae do not overlap one another as in *B. lunaria;* sporophore (fertile segment) once-pinnate, distinctly stalked.

Where Found in meadows and open sandy to gravelly soil in mountainous regions of Denali, on both sides of Alaska Range crest.

Similar Species Plants a dull yellowish green, unlike deep green of *Botrychium lunaria;* other *Botrychium* species in Denali have pinnatifid leaves.

♦ *Botrychium pinnatum* H. St. John
NORTHERN MOONWORT

Habit deciduous perennial moonwort, to 15 cm tall, from a few yellow to brown roots; trophophore (vegetative leaf) shiny, broadly triangular or ovate, 1–2-pinnate, to 8 cm long; fertile segment pinnae up to 8 pairs, sporangium nearly completely exposed, borne in 2 rows on pinnate sporophore branches.

Where Found Moist or wet, mostly open places at fairly high elevations.

♦ *Botrychium virginianum* (L.) Sw.
RATTLESNAKE FERN

Botrypus virginianus (L.) Michx.

Habit deciduous perennial from a few fleshy roots, to about 60 cm tall; trophophore (leaf) to 30 cm long or longer, glabrous or nearly so; leaf blade leathery, broadly triangular in outline, 2-pinnate, attached above middle of stipe; ultimate segments oblong-lanceolate, usually overlapping; sporophore 2-pinnate, 0.5–1.5 times length of trophophore.

Where Found uncommon in conifer woods, thickets.

Botrychium lunaria DAINTY MOONWORT

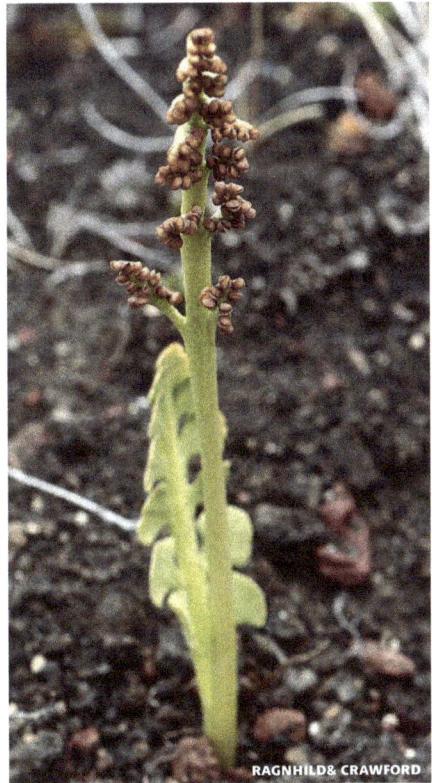

Botrychium minganense MINGAN MOONWORT

POLYPODIACEAE
Polypody Fern Family

Polypodium POLYPODY

(Greek, many, and foot, alluding to the knoblike prominences of the rhizome).

⧫ ***Polypodium sibiricum*** Sipliv.
SIBERIAN POLYPODY

Habit evergreen, perennial fern, arising singly or in small clusters along a creeping, branching, scaly rhizome; leaves leathery, oblong, 4–20 cm long, 1–4 cm wide, jointed to rhizome, pinnately cleft with broad, rounded sinuses and narrow, entire segments; stipe scales often with dark central stripe, rachis smooth throughout; sori round, naked, situated midway between midvein and margin, located on upper segments.

Where Found uncommon in shallow humus on rocks.

PTERIDACEAE
Maidenhair Fern Family

Cryptogramma ROCKBRAKE

(Greek, in allusion to the hidden sori.)

1   Leaves scattered along a slender rhizome; sterile leaves ovate to lanceolate in outline . *C. stelleri*
1   Leaves tufted; sterile leaves broadly ovate to triangular in outline 2
2   Sterile leaves 2- to 3-pinnate, coarsely dissected . . . . *C. acrostichoides*
2   Sterile leaves 2- to 4- pinnate, finely dissected . . . . *C. sitchensis*

⧫ ***Cryptogramma acrostichoides*** R. Br.
AMERICAN ROCKBRAKE

Cryptogramma crispa (L.) R. Br. var. *acrostichoides*

Habit densely tufted, evergreen, perennial fern from a compact rhizome; stipes of old leaves persisting at base of plant; leaves numerous, dimorphic; fertile leaves erect, 10–30 cm long (over-topping the short-stalked sterile leaves), long-stalked, narrowly triangular, with linear segments about 2 mm wide, margins of segments broadly reflexed (often to midrib), but opening as sporangia mature; sterile leaves spreading, oblong-triangular in outline, 5–20 cm long, 2–3-pinnate, stipes straw-colored.

Where Found rocky outcrops, talus slopes.

Botrychium virginianum RATTLESNAKE FERN

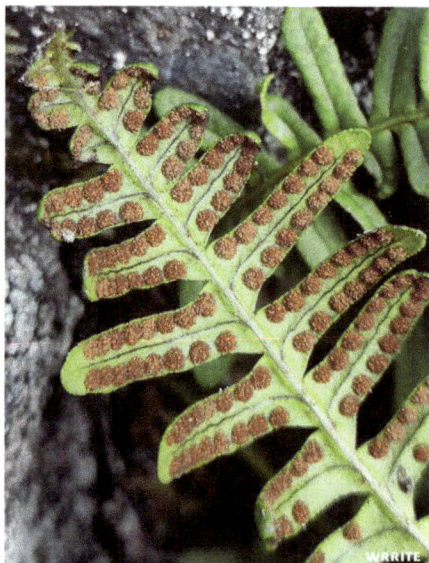

Polypodium sibiricum SIBERIAN POLYPODY

Cryptogramma sitchensis (Rupr.) T. Moore
SITKA ROCKBRAKE
Cryptogramma acrostichoides var. *sitchensis* (Rupr.) C. Chr., *Cryptogramma crispa* (L.) R. Br. var. *sitchensis*

Habit densely tufted, evergreen, perennial fern from a compact rhizome; stipes of old leaves persisting at base; leaves in clumps; sterile leaves spreading, broadly triangular in outline, 5–20 cm long, 3–4-pinnate; fertile leaves erect, narrowly triangular in outline.

Where Found rock outcrops, thickets, woods.

♦ ***Cryptogramma stelleri*** (S. G. Gmel.) Prantl
SLENDER CLIFFBRAKE

Habit deciduous perennial fern; leaves scattered, arising singly from a slender creeping rhizome; stipes pale to purplish; leaves thin, 3–15 cm long, from deeply pinnately lobed to 2-pinnate, dimorphic, fertile leaves only slightly differentiated from sterile ones (their segments stiffer and narrower than in sterile leaves); sori situated around margins of fertile pinnules; the inrolled margin forming a false indusium.

Where Found uncommon on usually calcareous crevices and cliffs, where moist and shaded.

Cryptogramma acrostichoides
AMERICAN ROCKBRAKE

Cryptogramma stelleri SLENDER CLIFFBRAKE

SELAGINELLACEAE
Spike-Moss Family

Selaginella SPIKE-MOSS
(Diminutive of *Selago*, ancient name of some *Lycopodium*).

---

1 Cones stalked, circular in cross-section; leaves flat without grooved midveins, midvein not extended into a bristle . . . . *S. selaginoides*
1 Cones unstalked, rectangular in cross-section; leaves with grooved midveins, midvein extended into a bristle . . . . *S. sibirica*

♦ ***Selaginella selaginoides*** (L.) P. Beauv. ex Schrank & Mart. LOW SELAGINELLA

Habit evergreen perennial, sending up erect, annual, deciduous fertile branches, 1–7 cm long; leaves broadly lanceolate, 1–3 mm long; cones unstalked, cylindrical, 0.5–1.5 cm long.

Where Found uncommon on moist banks and shores, bogs and boggy woods, heathlands.

Selaginella sibirica (Milde) Hieron.
NORTHERN SELAGINELLA

Habit evergreen perennial, forming long-spreading, dense mats; fertile branches ascending or erect, 1–5 cm tall; leaves densely overlapping, 1–2 mm long; cones unstalked, 4-angled in cross-section, 5–20 mm long.

Where Found uncommon on dry rock outcrops and ridgelines.

Selaginella selaginoides LOW SELAGINELLA

THELYPTERIDACEAE
Maiden Fern Family
Phegopteris BEECH FERN
(Greek *phegos*, beech, and *pteris*, fern.)

◆*Phegopteris connectilis* (Michx.) Watt
NARROW BEECH FERN
Thelypteris phegopteris (L.) Sloss.

Habit perennial fern, with single leaves scattered along a slender, widely creeping rhizome; leaves on scaly stipes usually longer than the blade; blades long-triangular, 10–25 cm long and 3–15 cm wide, pinnate; sori submarginal, naked.

Where Found occasional on rocky slopes and in woods and thickets.

WOODSIACEAE
Cliff Fern Family
Woodsia CLIFF FERN
(In honor of Joseph Woods, 1776–1864, English architect and botanist.)

1 Leaves glabrous; stipes straw-yellow to yellow-ish-green, dark brown only at base *W. glabella*
1 Leaves with hairs or scales on the lower surface; stipes and rachis reddish brown to dark purple
. 2
2 Stipes and lower surfaces of pinnae chaffy with a few, often light scales; primary segments about as wide as long . . . . *W. alpina*
2 Stipes and lower surfaces of pinnae with numerous reddish-brown scales; primary segments longer than wide. . . . . *W. ilvensis*

◆*Woodsia alpina* (Bolton) Gray
ALPINE WOODSIA
Habit deciduous, tufted, perennial fern, from a short rhizome; all leaves fertile, to 20 cm long; leaves narrowly elliptic or obovate in shape, once pinnately divided; leaflets pin-

nately lobed, broadly triangular or diamond-shaped; sori round, found on either side of the leaflet midvein; indusium of long white hairs.

Where Found occasional at high-elevations on dry gravelly slopes, dry tundra, rock outcrops.

Similar Species two other *Woodsia* species, separated by: *Woodsia ilvensis*, with stipe scaly throughout (not just at base), and *Woodsia glabella*, which lacks hairs and scales above the joint at the base.

◆*Woodsia glabella* R. Br.
SMOOTH WOODSIA
Habit deciduous, tufted, perennial fern, from a short rhizome; leaves 4–10 cm long, narrowly lanceolate in outline and barely over a centimeter wide; pinnae fan-shaped, three-five lobed, lower pinnae widely spaced on underside of pinnae, with several sori; the small indusium dissected into white hairs; stipes persistent, leaves without hairs or scales above the joint on the stipe.

Woodsia alpina ALPINE WOODSIA

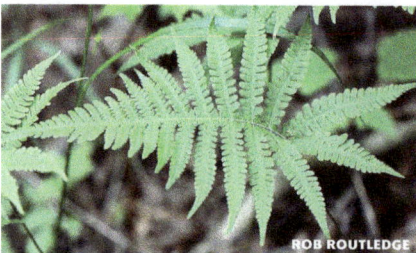
Phegopteris connectilis NARROW BEECH FERN

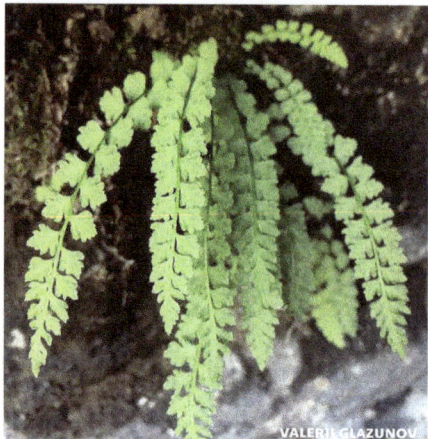
Woodsia glabella SMOOTH WOODSIA

Where Found occasional in alpine and sub-alpine areas, on tundra, gravelly slopes, and rocky outcrops, preferring calcareous substrates.

Similar Species smooth woodsia is green-stemmed and hairless, whereas other woodsia species have brown or purplish, variably hairy stems.

♦ *Woodsia ilvensis* (L.) R. Br. RUSTY WOODSIA

Habit deciduous tufted perennial fern (Denali's largest woodsia), from a short rhizome; stems with red-brown scales and coarse hairs, base of stem dark brown or purplish; leaves 5–15 cm long, lanceolate or elliptic in outline; 2–3 pinnate-pinnatifid (more divided than other *Woodsia* species); pinnae longer than wide, ovate or triangular, tapering at ends; sori light brown on underside of pinna near margins, surrounded by hairs.

Where Found occasional on dry rocky slopes and outcrops from the lowlands to the alpine zone; often on very steep slopes.

Similar Species the very scaly stems, and pinnae twice as long as wide distinguish rusty woodsia from other *Woodsia* species; the similarly narrow, *Dryopteris fragrans* has horseshoe-shaped indusia covering the sori.

Woodsia ilvensis RUSTY WOODSIA

CUPRESSACEAE
Cypress Family

Juniperus JUNIPER
(Latin *juniperus,* name for juniper.)

♦ *Juniperus communis* L.
COMMON JUNIPER

Habit sprawling, mat-forming, evergreen shrub, to 60 cm tall, from a taproot; bark very thin, reddish brown, shredding and scaly; entire plant with a characteristic aromatic smell. Leaves in whorls of 3, 5–15 mm long, awl-shaped, sharp to the touch. Flowers either a male or female cone and on separate plants (dioecious); cones in whorls along the branches, in-between leaves; male cones yellow-brown, 2–3 mm long, and shed after releasing pollen in spring; female cones mature in the second season, maturing into a hard, bluish black, berry-like fruit, with one seed.

Similar Species common juniper is the only mat-forming conifer in Denali, and the only one with fruits similar in appearance to a berry.

Where Found occasional in open, dry, rocky or gravelly slopes (usually with a southerly aspect), river terraces.

Traditional Uses the Dena'ina and Inupiat made teas from twigs containing berries or just berries, to be drunk as treatment for urinary, respiratory, and digestive problems, and also to fight or prevent colds (Garibaldi 1999); the Inupiat toasted leaves in the presence of sick people to prevent disease spread.

Juniperus communis COMMON JUNIPER

PINACEAE
Pine Family

1 Leaves (needles) solitary . . . . *Picea*
1 Leaves (needles) borne in clusters of 7 or more
. . . . *Larix*

Larix TAMARACK
(Latin *larix*, name for larch.)

◆ *Larix laricina* (Du Roi) K. Koch TAMARACK
Habit coniferous tree to about 10 m tall, with a single unbranched trunk with many secondary horizontal branches (or the branches sweeping slightly upward), overall appearance is conical to slightly pear-shaped; bark scaly, rough, brown-gray; twigs light brown, with many short spur twigs, covered in leaf scales. Leaves needlelike, pale blue-green, three-angled in cross-section, 1–2.5 cm long and very narrow, soft, 12–20 in a bundle from short spur twigs; in fall, needles turn golden-yellow before being shed. Flowers either male or female in different cones on same tree, often on same branches; male cones inconspicuous, made up of yellow pollen sacs attached to the side of the leaf-bearing twigs; female cones round to ovate, 1–1.5 cm long, with rounded, finely toothed scales, attached on short curved stems; seeds 2–3 mm long, with a slightly winged covering.
Where Found occasional in wet lowland areas (often intermingled with black spruce), and in wet, cold upland soils.
Similar Species tamarack almost never grows in pure stands, and trees usually found mixed with black spruce (less often with white spruce); the soft needles arranged in bundles distinguish it from both white spruce (*Picea glauca*) and black spruce (*P. mariana*); in winter, needle-less tamarack

can be distinguished from dead spruce trees by the presence of short, knoblike, spur twigs.
Traditional Uses the wood is brown, dense, and highly resin-filled making it rot-resistant and useful as lumber.

Picea SPRUCE
(Latin *picis*, pitch, name of a pitchy pine.)

1 Cones 1.5–3 cm long, ovate to almost spherical, persistent on tree for many years; cone scales purplish to dark brown; young twigs densely hairy with short rusty hairs . . . . *P. mariana*
1 Cones generally slightly longer (2.5–3.5 cm), cylindric, seldom persisting; cone scales brown when mature; young twigs glabrous or sparsely hairy . . . . *P. glauca*

◆ *Picea glauca* (Moench) Voss WHITE SPRUCE
Picea laxa (Münchh.) Sarg.
Habit evergreen tree; bark silvery-brown to blackish, scaly, thin; branches droop from their point of attachment to the trunk; twigs hairless (in contrast to the minutely red-haired twigs of black spruce); wood nearly white; on favorable sites in Denali, can grow to more than 30 m in height, with basal diameters to 70 cm; however, because of De-

NIC MCPHEE

ALBERT HERRING

Larix laricina TAMARACK

Picea glauca WHITE SPRUCE

nali's location near the northern edge of this species' range, white spruce trees often much smaller, especially in cold, wet, exposed, or high-elevation sites. Leaves stiff, blue-green, four-angled, needlelike, with whitish lines on underside; needles extend in all directions (like a bottlebrush) from the twig, each needle borne on a small peg-like pedicel, which persists once the needle falls, giving twigs a rough texture. Flowers either male or female in different cones on same tree; male cones borne lower in canopy, and wither and fall soon after pollen released in spring; female cones cylindrical, light brown, hang downward from branches, usually positioned near branch ends and clustered near top of tree; seed-bearing cones open in late August and September while on the tree, and the winged seeds fall to the ground after cones open.

Where Found abundant in moist to dry sites, sometimes also in poorly-drained areas; prefers better drained, permafrost free uplands and alluvium.

Similar Species the best characters to separate white spruce from black spruce are absence of red hairs on young twigs, and cylindrical cones borne at branch ends (instead of ovoid cones borne close to the bole); trees of white spruce may be much large than black spruce, but that relates more to environmental conditions than genetics of the tree.

Traditional Uses white spruce is a softwood commonly used as lumber, its bark in roofing, and its long roots for twine or in baskets; it is the preferred tree for cabin logs in interior and northern Alaska, due to its size and usually straight boles; white spruce is also used as pulpwood and cut into lumber for use in construction. Tea brewed from the soft growth tips can be consumed for colds or pleasure; the Dena'ina use spruce roots, pitch, bark and tips for a variety of medicinal purposes (Kari 1995); pitch is used to help heal cuts, and is converted into a healing salve by mixing with fat (or wax) for use on skin injuries and infections by the Inupiat, Yup'ik and Tlingit (Garibaldi 1999, Jernigan et al. 2015); the pitch can be chewed like gum.

♦ *Picea mariana* (Mill.) Britton, Sterns & Poggenb.
BLACK SPRUCE

Habit evergreen tree, to about 10 m tall; bark thin, gray-brown, often shedding from trunk, leading to a shaggy appearance; smallest twigs with minute red-brown hairs; trees often lopsided, with irregular bulges or many dead branches along the trunk due to shifts in permafrost or poor growing conditions; however, on well-drained, productive sites, black spruce can have the symmetrical, strongly conical form typical of spruce, and be superficially indistinguishable from white spruce. Leaves four-angled, needlelike, radiating in all directions from the twig, with stomata (appearing as white lines) on each side of needle. Flowers either male or female, in different cones on same tree; female cones short and ovoid, 1.5–3 cm long, often found close to trunk; cones curve downward from upper branches of tree, and often remain closed for several years until heated by fire, when they open and disperse their seeds.

Where Found abundant (and often the dominant tree in Denali) in cold, wet habitats, at low-elevations, particularly in bogs, where trees are highly stunted (100-year-old trees can be as short as a black spruce sapling found in warmer, better-drained conditions).

Similar Species black spruce trees have minute hairs on the smallest twigs, which are absent in white spruce; cones of white spruce

Picea mariana BLACK SPRUCE

are longer and borne near branch tips, in contrast to the shorter, darker cones of black spruce borne near trunk of tree.

Traditional Uses black spruce used in the same medicinal ways as white spruce; spruce roots are harvested by interior Natives to make baskets. Because of its small size, black spruce little used for lumber; the most important consideration for black spruce in Alaska is its role as a fuel for wildfires.

ANGIOSPERMS – DICOTS

AMARANTHACEAE
Amaranth Family

1 Sepals 1, stamen 1 . . . . *Blitum*
1 Calyx-lobes 3–5, stamens usually 5 . . . .
. . . . *Chenopodium*

Blitum POVERTY-WEED
(Ancient name for a type of spinach.)

1 Perianth a single bractlike segment, smaller than the fruit and not enclosing it; seeds vertical . . .
. . . . *B. nuttallianum*
1 Perianth 3- to 5-lobed; fruit at least partially enclosed by perianth or by large subtending bracts; seeds often horizontal. . . . . *B. capitatum*

♦*Blitum capitatum* L. STRAWBERRY-BLITE
Chenopodium capitatum (L.) Aschers.
Habit annual herb from a stout taproot; stems erect, several, green and glabrous, 20–60 cm tall. Leaves alternate, triangular-hastate, to 10 cm long, somewhat fleshy, margins irregularly toothed. Flowers in dense globose clusters along the stem, petals absent, some with 3-4 stamens, others with one or none; sepals fleshy and bright red when mature, covering the fruit, and having the appearance of an aggregate berry.
Where Found uncommon in moist to somewhat dry open places at low-elevations, often where soil has been disturbed; considered adventive in Alaska.
Similar Species the hastate (arrow-shaped) leaves and bright red round clusters of fruit along stem are distinctive.
Traditional Uses leaves edible when boiled, breaking down the oxalic acid; fruit edible but with little flavor; Fort Yukon natives used plants as a dye (Garibaldi 1999).

Blitum nuttallianum Schult.
POVERTY-WEED
Monolepis nuttalliana (Schult.) Greene
Habit annual herb from a taproot; stems prostrate to ascending, 10–25 cm long, branched from near the base, glabrous, or somewhat mealy when young. Leaves alternate, hastate-lanceolate with 2 spreading lobes near middle, short-petioled or the upper sessile and sometimes entire, rather succulent, reduced upward to leafy bracts. Flowers in dense stalkless, axillary clusters, reddish; sepal 1, green and bract-like, about 2 mm long. Fruit a dark brown seed within a thin, membranous envelope.
Where Found uncommon on dry, disturbed soil; native to western North America, considered adventive in Alaska.

Chenopodium GOOSEFOOT
(Greek, goose and foot, from the shape of the leaves of some species.)

1 Fruit pitted (visible at 20×) . . . . . *C. berlandieri*
1 Fruit smooth, not pitted. . . . . *C. album*

♦*Chenopodium album* L.
LAMB'S-QUARTERS
Habit annual herb, stems erect, to about 60 cm tall, branched (if not crowded). Leaves ovate-lanceolate, 2-8 cm long, mealy to nearly glabrous; margins mostly toothed.

ROBERT FLOGAUS-FAUST
Blitum capitatum STRAWBERRY-BLITE

Flowers small, in terminal and axillary spikes, usually compound and often panicle-like. Fruit a black, shiny, flattened seed.
  Where Found uncommon weed of disturbed places, considered adventive in Alaska.

Chenopodium berlandieri Moq.
PIT-SEED GOOSEFOOT
  Habit annual herb, from a taproot; stems erect, solitary, branched, 0.2–1 m tall, greenish to grayish mealy, often reddish tinged with age. Leaves alternate, somewhat succulent, broadly lanceolate, ovate or diamond-shaped, 2–10 cm long, often with a few teeth, sparsely to densely mealy. Flowers small, in densely clustered terminal or axillary spikes, greenish, mealy; with or without bracts. Fruit a black, shiny, flattened seed.
  Where Found uncommon weed of moist, disturbed places.

APIACEAE
Carrot Family

1 Basal leaves entire . . . . *Bupleurum*
1 Basal leaves compound. 2
2 Fruit clavate, bristly-hairy. . . . . *Osmorhiza*
2 Fruit less than 3 times as long as broad, not bristly-hairy 3
3 Ultimate segments of leaves linear or lanceolate . . . . *Cicuta*
3 Ultimate segments of leaves not long and linear-lanceolate. 4
4 Ultimate segments of leaves large, ovate to ovate-lanceolate, entire or deeply lobed or toothed. 5
4 Ultimate segments of leaves smaller, deeply cleft, divided or simple 6

Chenopodium album LAMB'S-QUARTERS

5 Stem and leaves pubescent . . . . *Heracleum*
5 Stem and leaves glabrous . . . . *Angelica*
6 Plants with naked flower stems . . . . . *Podistera*
6 Plants with leafy flower stems . . . . *Cnidium*

Angelica ANGELICA
(Named for supposed medicinal virtues.)

1 Leaf rachis bent downward; leaflets lanceolate to narrowly ovate, mostly 2–3 times as long as wide . . . . *A. genuflexa*
1 Leaf rachis straight; leaflets ovate to lanceolate, mostly 1–2 times as long as wide . . . . *A. lucida*

Angelica genuflexa Nutt.
BENT-LEAVED ANGELICA, KNEELING ANGELICA
  Habit stout perennial herb, from a taproot; stems to about 2 m tall, hollow, often purple, glabrous, arising from a tuberous, chambered stem-base. Leaves compound, with 3 major divisions that are again divided; primary divisions strongly deflexed; leaf axis bent; leaflets reflexed, oblong to lanceolate, 4–10 cm long; margins irregularly sharply serrate. Flowers many, in a terminal umbel; flowers white or pinkish; involucral bracts absent. Fruit an oblong schizocarp, 3–5 mm long, glabrous, with broadly winged ribs.
  Where Found uncommon in moist meadows and thickets.

♦*Angelica lucida* L.
SEACOAST ANGELICA, WILD CELERY
  Habit stout perennial herb, from a strong taproot and partitioned stem-base; stems erect, single or less often branched, 30–60 cm tall. Leaves large, not bent downwards, pinnately or bipinnately divided, the leaflets ovate with narrow tips, margins serrate and white-tipped; petiole with a conspicuous inflated sheath at base. Flowers in one to a few terminal, compound umbels (an umbel of umbels), with 20–45 rays of unequal length; the overall appearance is flat-topped or slightly rounded or uneven; each smaller umbel contains many tiny flowers; petals five, greenish white to white; stamens five, white, much longer than petals. Fruit an oval schizocarp, flat on one side and ribbed on the other.
  Where Found common in moist meadows from the lowlands to the subalpine and alpine.

Similar Species cow parsnip (*Heracleum max-imum*), but that plant is much larger (growing to 1.5 m high), and has pubescent leaves and stems; Jakutsk snow-parsley (*Cnidium cnidi-ifolium*) also has many small white flowers in an umbel and divided leaves, but leaf segments much more finely divided, and tends to grow in drier sites as compared to the moist sites preferred by *Angelica lucida*.

Traditional Uses Young stems can be peeled and eaten raw; the root is toxic if eaten, but was used by the Aleut, Yup'ik and Dena'ina to treat cuts, infections, pain or ill-health (Garibaldi 1999).

Bupleurum THOROW-WAX

(Greek, ox-ribbed, from the veining of the leaves, not evident in our species.)

◆*Bupleurum americanum* J.M. Coult. & Rose
AMERICAN THOROW-WAX
Bupleurum triradiatum subsp. *arcticum* (Regel & Tiling) Hultén

Habit slender perennial herb; stems 10–30 cm tall, from a branching stem-base. Leaves alternate, simple, parallel veined, narrowly lanceolate, 2–25 cm long, with a whitish blush. Flowers in compound umbels, each head with 1–8 rays, the terminal umbels compact and rounded, with one or several leafy

bracts below umbel, and smaller bracts beneath each secondary umbel; petals yellow with the margin inrolled. Fruit a schizocarp, about 5 mm long, with short ribs.

Where Found uncommon on warm, dry, gravelly slopes in foothills and mountains north of Alaska Range crest.

Similar Species the only species in Denali with umbels of yellow flowers and linear leaves; leaves similar to those of *Anticlea elegans* (found in similar habitats) but the flowers very different.

Cicuta WATER-HEMLOCK
(The ancient Latin name.)

1 Bulblets present in leaf axils; leaflets with narrowly linear segments . . . . *C. bulbifera*
1 Bulblets absent; leaflets broader, lanceolate . . 2
2 Fruit slightly wider than long; midvein on upper leaflet surface rough-hairy . . . . *C. virosa*
2 Fruit from as wide as long or longer; midvein on upper leaflet surface glabrous 3
3 Leaflets 3–4 times longer than wide, lanceolate to narrowly oblong or elliptic; fruit with a narrow raised border along edge . . . . *C. douglasii*
3 Leaflets more than 5 times longer than wide, linear to narrowly lancelolate; fruit without a raised border along edge . . . . *C. maculata*

Angelica lucida SEACOAST ANGELICA

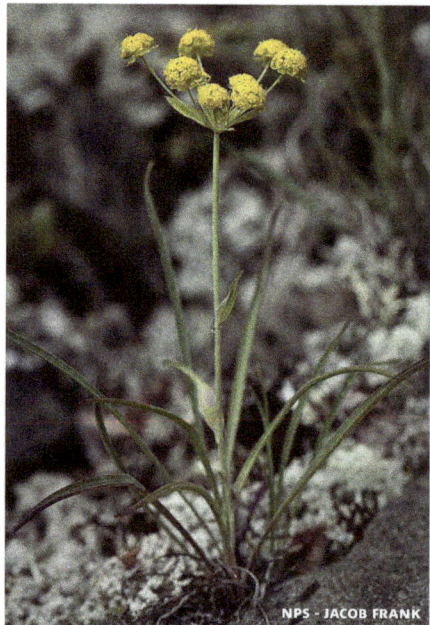
Bupleurum americanum
AMERICAN THOROW-WAX

Cicuta bulbifera L.
BULBLET-BEARING WATER-HEMLOCK

   Habit stout perennial herb, from a cluster of tuberous roots; stems single, not thickened at base, erect, to about 80 cm tall. Leaves compound, divided 1–3 times; the middle and lower leaves dissected, narrowly linear; upper leaves smaller, with fewer segments, many with pea-like bulblets clustered in their axils. Flowers in a terminal compound umbel, white to greenish; calyx saw-toothed. Fruit a small schizocarp, about 2 mm long, constricted where the carpels join, ribs broad.

   Where Found uncommon in marshy places, lakeshores.

Cicuta douglasii (DC.) J.M. Coult. & Rose
WESTERN WATER-HEMLOCK

   Habit stout perennial herb, from a cluster of tuberous roots; stems solitary or few together from a tuberous-thickened and chambered base, leafy, glabrous, 0.5–2 m tall. Leaves basal and along stem; divided 1–2 times, leaflets 3–10 cm long, 3–4 times as long as broad, lanceolate to narrowly oblong or elliptic, these sharply pointed and toothed; veins prominent on underside, lateral veins ending at base of the teeth. Flowers of several to many small, compact clusters forming several compound umbels; flowers white to greenish; involucral bracts mostly absent. Fruit an ovate to orbicular, glabrous schizocarp, 2–3 mm long and wide; ribs unequal, with a narrow raised border on edge of dark intervals.

   Where Found shores, marshy areas.

◆ *Cicuta virosa* L.
MACKENZIE'S WATER-HEMLOCK
Cicuta mackenzieana Raup

   Habit stout perennial herb, from a cluster of tuberous roots; stems single erect, to about 1 m tall. Leaves compound, divided 1–2 times,; leaflets linear to narrowly lanceolate, 2–10 cm long, midvein on upper leaflet surface rough-to-touch; margins with forward-pointing teeth; axils without bulblets (as in *C. bulbifera*). Flowers in a terminal compound umbel; flowers white to greenish or pinkish. Fruit an orbicular, glabrous schizocarp, to 2 mm long and slightly broader than long.

   Where Found occasional in marshes, edges of lakes and ponds.

Cnidium SNOW-PARSLEY
(Ancient name for a potherb.)

◆ *Cnidium cnidiifolium* (Turcz.) Schischk.
JAKUTSK SNOW-PARSLEY
Conioselinum cnidiifolium (Turcz.) Schischk.

   Habit glabrous perennial herb from a short, stout base, with a cluster of fleshy roots or a taproot, sometimes glaucous; stems solitary, to 60 cm or more tall, loosely branched. Leaves 2–3 times pinnately divided into fine segments, shiny dark green; lower leaves

Cicuta virosa MACKENZIE'S WATER-HEMLOCK

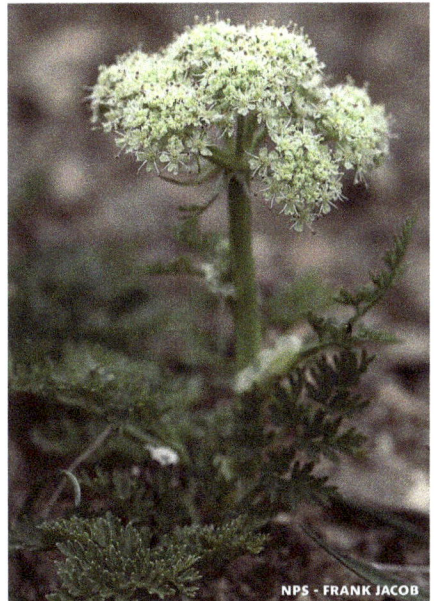
Cnidium cnidiifolium JAKUTSK SNOW-PARSLEY

long-petioled, upper leaves sessile and smaller; leaf base sheaths stem, broadly inflated with dark veins. Flowers in compound umbels, each smaller head a rounded cluster of flowers; terminal umbels surrounded by a few small, linear-lanceolate bracts; flowers deep purple-red in bud, turning white to yellow. Fruit a schizocarp; each half tan-colored, flat on one side with 5 winged ribs on the other.

Where Found uncommon on dry gravelly slopes and floodplains, primarily in the subalpine and on steep south-facing slopes.

Similar Species *Angelica* also with pinnately divided leaves and umbels of white flowers, but leaf segments of *Angelica* much broader and less finely divided.

Heracleum COW-PARSNIP
(Named for Hercules of mythology.)

♦ *Heracleum maximum* W. Bartram
COMMON COW-PARSNIP
Heracleum lanatum Michx.

Habit Large biennial to perennial herb, from a thick taproot; stems to 1.5 m tall, ridged, densely covered with short white hairs; one of the largest herbaceous plants in Denali's flora; entire plant with a strong, skunk-like smell. Leaves 20–50 cm across, palmately divided into 3 leaflets, these segments further lobed and with serrate margins; petioles forming an inflated sheath around the stem. Flowers in umbels from leaf axils and termi-

nally; umbels 10–20 cm wide; plants with either all male (staminate) flowers or the flowers with both male and female parts; in both cases, petals five, white. Fruit a flattened schizocarp, ovate to heart-shaped, 7–12 mm long, with a strong center vein and raised margins, papery and transparent otherwise.

Where Found common in moist meadows and openings, primarily in the subalpine, becoming more common south of Alaska Range.

Similar Species While other members of the Apiaceae look similar, none are as large as cow-parsnip.

Traditional Uses Cow-parsnip can irritate the skin from a potentially photo-toxic oil produced on its leaves and stem surface. The Dena'ina used boiled roots as a poultice or to make a tea for drinking or as a wash, apparently with antibiotic and numbing effects (Kari 1995); the root could be chewed as a preventative medicine and toothaches were dealt with by placing a raw root on the offending tooth until it disintegrated; the Yup'ik eat the peeled stem raw (Jernigan et al. 2015).

Osmorrhiza SWEET-CICELY
(Greek, a scent and root.)

♦ *Osmorhiza depauperata* Phil.
BLUNT-FRUIT SWEET-CICELY

Habit perennial herb, from a well-developed, aromatic taproot, sometimes below a slightly branched stem-base; stems solitary or sometimes 2–3, 15–60 cm tall, branching. Leaves basal and along stem, round in outline, twice divided into 3's; basal leaves several, with long petioles; stem leaves 1–3, petioles short; leaflets coarsely toothed, more or less hairy. Flowers in loose compound umbels, with 3–5 strongly ascending rays; petals greenish white, sometimes pink or purple,

Heracleum maximum COMMON COW-PARSNIP

Osmorhiza depauperata
BLUNT-FRUIT SWEET-CICELY

inconspicuous. Fruit a club-shaped schizocarp, 10–15 mm long.

Where Found uncommon in wet meadows.

Podistera WOODROOT

(Greek, solid foot, probably referring to its tight, compact growth pattern.)

♦ *Podistera macounii* (J.M.Coult. & Rose) Mathias & Constance MACOUN'S WOODROOT

Habit small perennial herb, from a taproot; stems 5–20 cm tall, stout, green or purplish, leafless; stem-base sheathed with older leaves. Leaves all basal, shiny and dark green, long-petioled, oblong to rounded in outline, pinnately divided; leaflets deeply lobed, 3–12 mm long. Flowers many, small, in usually one (sometimes a few), compact, terminal umbels; umbels with 5–20 rays, and several bracts below; petals purple or yellow. Fruit a cylindric-ovate schizocarp, with thick ribs, red-green in color. Flowering early, shortly after snowmelt.

Where Found occasional in rocky alpine tundra.

Similar Species Denali's only alpine plant with pinnate leaves and small purple or yellow flowers in small, compact umbels; leaves similar to those of *Thalictrum alpinum*, but that plant has very different flowers arranged in a long raceme.

ARALIACEAE
Ginseng Family
Oplopanax DEVIL'S-CLUB
(Greek, *hoplon*, meaning weapon, and *panakos*, meaning panacea or "all-heal"—referring to the medicinal qualities.)

Podistera macounii MACOUN'S WOODROOT

♦ *Oplopanax horridus* (Sm.) Miq.
DEVIL'S-CLUB

Habit tall, deciduous shrub; stems 1–3 m tall, coarse, thick, strongly armed with spines 5–10 mm long. Leaves orbicular in outline, palmately 3–7-lobed, cordate at base, 10–40 cm wide, with prickles on petioles and veins; margins doubly serrate. Flowers in small, headlike umbels in an elongate inflorescence to 25 cm long; petals 5, greenish white, stamens 5. Fruit a bright red berry, 2–3 seeded, 5–8 mm wide.

Where Found occasional in woods, alder thickets, rocky slopes and outcrops.

ASTERACEAE
Aster Family

Perennial, biennial, or annual herbs (*Artemisia* somewhat woody). Flowers small, aggregated on a receptacle, in a head resembling a single large flower, surrounded by an involucrum of one to several rows of bracts (phyllaries); flowers of head either all alike, or those in center differing from those at margin; head termed *discoid* when all flowers with regular tubular corollas (as in a thistle), *ligulate* when corollas irregular and one-sided and straplike (as in a dandelion), and *radiate* when central flowers discoid or tubular with radial flowers ligulate (as in a daisy).

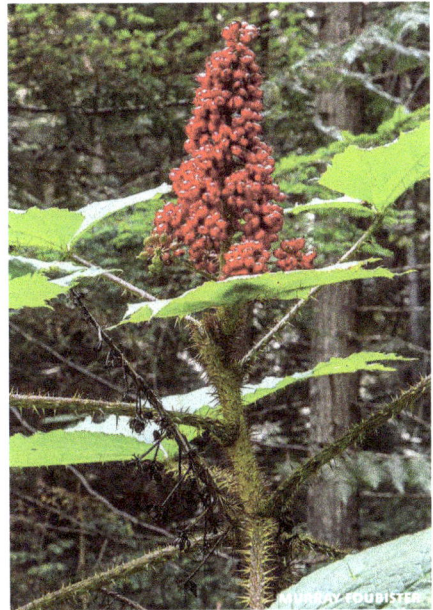

Oplopanax horridus DEVIL'S-CLUB

KEY TO ASTERACEAE GROUPS

1 Flowers all ligulate (strap-shaped) and perfect; stems and leaves with milky juice ..... Group I
1 Flowers not all ligulate; ray flowers marginal (if present); juice watery 2
2 Heads radiate (with disk and ray flowers) 3
3 Ray flowers yellow or orange .... Group II
3 Rayflowers white or pink or purple, never yellow or orange .... Group III
2 Heads discoid (without ray flowers)......... 4
4 Pappus of numerous hairlike (sometimes feathery) bristles...................... Group IV
4 Pappus of scales, awns, very short chaffy bristles, or a small crown (or sometimes pappus absent) .... Group V

GROUP I Flowers all ligulate (strap-shaped) and perfect; juice milky.

1 Leaves all basal; heads solitary on erect naked stalks; achenes beaked.......... *Taraxacum*
1 Plants more or less leafy-stemmed (upper leaves often reduced to bracts); heads mostly several; achenes beaked or beakless............... 2
2 Achenes flattened; flowers yellow .... *Sonchus*
2 Achenes not flattened; flowers yellow....... 3
3 Pappus sordid or brownish; roots fibrous .... *Hieracium*
3 Pappus white; with a taproot.............. 4
4 Introduced annual weed with a single leafy stem; leaves auriculate, mainly along stem ... *Crepis*
4 Native perennials with numerous stems, not weedy; leaves not auriculate, mainly basal.... ....*Askelia*

GROUP II
Heads with ray and disk flowers; ray flowers yellow or orange.

1 Pappus of firm awns; receptacle chaffy . *Bidens*
1 Pappus of capillary bristles; receptacle naked. 2
2 Leaves opposite .... *Arnica*
2 Leaves alternate, or all basal 3
3 Involucral bracts overlapping, in several series. ....*Solidago*
3 Involucral bracts in one series....... Group VI

GROUP III
Heads with ray and disk flowers; ray flowers white, pink, purple, or blue, not yellow or orange.

1 Pappus, or at least in part, of capillary bristles; receptacle naked 2
1 Pappus of scales or awns or flattened, chaffy bristly, or a mere crown, or none.......... 5
2 Basal leaves cordate or sagittate..... *Petasites*
2 Basal leaves not cordate or sagittate 3
3 Involucral bracts nearly equal or more or less overlapping, often green in part, but not definitely leafy, nor with papery base and herbaceous green tip .... *Erigeron*
3 Involucral bracts either nearly equal with outer leafy, or more often overlapping, with papery or distinctly green tips, or sometimes papery throughout............................. 4
4 Involucral bracts usually with purple tips and margins; leaves rough at least beneath *Eurybia*
4 Involucral bracts without purple tips and margins; leaves not rough beneath ....*Symphyotrichum*
5 Leaves toothed or entire.................. 6
6 Leaves entire, mainly basal .... *Hulteniella*
6 Leaves pinnately lobed or toothed, only the uppermost entire .... *Leucanthemum*
5 Leaves all pinnately dissected.............. 7
7 Heads small and numerous; rays about 5 in number, 2–3 mm long .... *Achillea*
7 Heads few, larger; rays numerous, 5–13 mm long ....*Tripleurospermum*

GROUP IV
Heads discoid (without ray flowers); pappus partly or wholly of numerous hairlike (sometimes feathery) bristles.

1 Receptacle densely bristly .... *Saussurea*
1 Receptacle naked........................ 2
2 Flowers perfect, yellow or orange 3
2 At least some flower heads pistillate only.... 5
3 Leaves mainly opposite .... *Arnica*
3 Leaves alternate......................... 4
4 Involucral bracts essentially in a single series .. ..*Packera*
4 Involucral bracts in more than one series ....*Erigeron*
5 Basal leaves cordate or sagittate..... *Petasites*
5 None of leaves cordate or sagittate 6
6 Plants more or less white-woolly; involucral bracts mostly with dry, papery, thin, white or yellowish tips 7

6   Plants not white-woolly (see also **Group III**) . . 8

7   Basal leaves soon deciduous but otherwise similar to stem leaves . . . . *Anaphalis*

7   Basal leaves persistent. . . . . *Antennaria*

8   Involucral bracts in a single row . . . . . *Erigeron*

8   Involucral bracts overlapping 9

9   Involucral bracts usually with purple tips and margins; leaves rough at least beneath *Eurybia*

9   Involucral bracts without purple tips and margins; leaves not rough beneath . . . .
. . . . *Symphyotrichum*

GROUP V

Heads discoid (without ray flowers); pappus of scales, awns or very short papery bristles, or reduced to a crown (or sometimes absent).

1   Somewhat woody, usually aromatic plants, from branching base . . . . *Artemisia*

1   Herbaceous plants. . . . . *Matricaria*

GROUP VI

Senecio and former *Senecio* now classified as *Packera* or *Tephroseris*.

1   Leaves all on the stem (basal rosette absent) . 2

1   Leaves mainly in basal rosettes, and always larger and wider than those of stem 3

2   Perennial herb. . . . . *Senecio triangularis*

2   Annual or biennial herb . . . .
. . . . *Tephroseris palustris*

3   Heads solitary (or occasionally with 1 or 2 small, lateral heads). 4

3   Heads one to many, all about same size 7

4   Involucral bracts glabrous. . . . .
. . . . *Packera cymbalaria*

4   Involucral bracts hairy (at least at base). 5

5   Heads solitary or often with two smaller lateral heads; leaves, stem and involucrum prominently white floccose-tomentose. . . . .
. . . . *Tephroseris lindstroemii*

5   Heads always solitary 6

6   Involucral bracts and upper third of stem densely woolly with brown hairs . . . .
. . . . *Tephroseris kjellmanii*

6   Involucral bracts with purplish hairs (sometimes partly covered by white-woolly pubescence). . .
. . . . *Tephroseris integrifolia*

7   Plants with a well-developed ascending rhizome
. . . . 8

7   Plants with fibrous roots; basal leaves with petioles. 10

8   Basal leaves sessile, oblanceolate, entire, or their

margins finely denticulate; involucral bracts prominently black-tipped . . . . . *Senecio lugens*

8   Basal leaves with petioles; involucral bracts not black-tipped. 9

9   Stems delicate, 4–15 cm high; basal leaves entire, irregularly lobed or toothed . . . .
. . . . *Packera ogoturukensis*

9   Stems stouter, 10–35 cm high; basal leaves oblanceolate to oblong or elliptic, entire to finely toothed. . . . . *Tephroseris yukonensis*

10   Stems slender; basal leaves oval, nearly entire to serrate . . . . *Packera paupercula*

10   Stems stout; basal leaves oblong-ovate, mostly deeply toothed . . . . *Packera pauciflora*

Achillea YARROW
(Named for Achilles of mythology.)

1   Leaves pinnately dissected, the divisions again dissected . . . . *A. millefolium*

1   Leaves linear, incised, the divisions toothed, not dissected. . . . . *A. alpina*

♦*Achillea alpina* L. SIBERIAN YARROW
Achillea sibirica Ledeb.

Habit perennial, aromatic herb, usually rhizomatous; stems erect, 20–80 cm tall densely hairy, simple or branched above. **Leaves** linear-lanceolate, slightly toothed to almost divided, sessile. **Flowers** in a rounded to flat-topped corymb, usually with several borne on each plant; heads with white ray flowers 1–3 mm long, and white disk flowers,

NPS- JACOB FRANK

Achillea alpina SIBERIAN YARROW

each head 5–8 mm across. Fruit an achene, with an attached, winged calyx.

Where Found occasional in low-elevation moist to wet meadows and woods.

Similar Species very similar to common yarrow (*Achillea millefolium*), but leaves of that species finely divided.

♦*Achillea millefolium* L. COMMON YARROW
Achillea borealis Bong.

Habit perennial, aromatic herb, usually rhizomatous; stems erect, slender, 20–60 cm tall; stems unbranched to few-branched above, hairy; plants have a distinctive smell when crushed. Leaves in a basal rosette and alternate on stem; 3–15 cm long, lanceolate in outline and twice-divided into very fine segments. Flowers many, small, in a flat-topped, branched, terminal inflorescence (corymb); each head composed of several tiny flowers; about 5 white ray flowers and 10–20 white disk flowers. Fruit an achene, with a persistent calyx with wings 1–2 mm long.

Where Found Dry meadows, roadsides and other disturbed places.

Similar Species Siberian yarrow (*Achillea alpina*), but its leaves not as finely divided as in common yarrow; A. alpina also found in wetter habitats.

Traditional Uses widely used as a medicinal plant, owing to its variety of biologically active compounds; all parts used for numerous ailments, either as a tea or a poultice.

Anaphalis PEARLY-EVERLASTING
(Greek, name of some similar plant.)

♦*Anaphalis margaritacea* (L.) Benth. & Hook.
f. PEARLY-EVERLASTING

Habit white-tomentose or woolly perennial herb, from rhizomes; stems usually unbranched, 20–50 cm tall, leafy, white-woolly. Leaves basal and alternate along stem; basal leaves few, deciduous; stem leaves alternate, narrowly lance-shaped with a conspicuous mid-vein, 2–15 cm long, greenish above, white-woolly beneath, margins often rolled under. Flowers many, in small heads in dense flat-topped clusters, of yellowish disk flowers only; involucral bracts dry, pearly white, sometimes with a dark basal spot. Fruit an achene, to about 1 mm long; pappus hairs white.

Where Found uncommon in open woods, talus slopes.

Antennaria PUSSYTOES
Antennaria can be difficult to identify, because many plants are part of asexually-reproducing swarms that are different in appearance from plants that rely on sexual reproduction. (Latin *antenna*, and *-aria*, connection to or possession of, alluding to simi-

Achillea millefolium COMMON YARROW

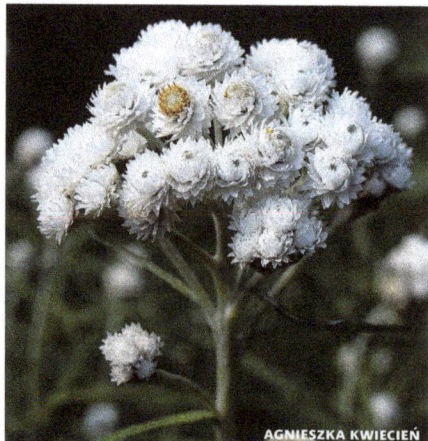

Anaphalis margaritacea PEARLY-EVERLASTING

larity of staminate pappus bristles to insect antennae.)

1 Basal leaves 3- to 5-nerved, similar to lower stem leaves; pistillate plants 30–65 cm high . . . .
. . . . *A. pulcherrima*

1 Basal leaves 1-nerved (sometimes with two obscure lateral veins); stem leaves smaller and different shape than basal leaves; pistillate plants less than 30 cm high 2

2 Flowering stalks with a single head. . . . .
. . . . *A. monocephala*

2 Flowering stalks with more than one head . . . 3

3 Plants tufted, not mat-forming, with crowded sessile or subsessile rosettes from a short rhizomatous stem-base; upper stem stems always with glandular hairs . . . . *A. friesiana*

3 Plants mat-forming, with rosettes at ends of well-developed leafy stolons; upper stem leaves with or without glandular hairs 4

4 Membraneous portion of phyllaries green-black or black. . . . . *A. alpina*

4 Membraneous portion of phyllaries a gradient from white, pink, rose, to light brown . *A. rosea*

♦ *Antennaria alpina* (L.) Gaertn.
ALPINE PUSSYTOES

Habit small mat-forming perennial herb, with only female flowers, from a creeping, branched underground stem; stems short, 3–

Antennaria alpina ALPINE PUSSYTOES

15 cm tall, leafy, densely gray-hairy. Leaves basal in a tight rosette, and along stem; oblanceolate, 0.5–2.5 cm long, abruptly sharp-pointed, green to gray, hairless to slightly hairy above, gray tomentose below; middle and upper stem leaves with dark brown papery tips. Flowers in 2–5 heads in rounded clusters, surrounded by many narrow bracts, the tip dark and papery (similar to tips of stem leaves); petals fused, purple, 3–5 mm long, over-topped by the white, hair-like pappus (modified sepals); plants of this clonally reproducing species produce only female flowers. Fruit an achene, pappus a tuft of white hairs about 4 mm long; overall, flowers with a soft, white appearance due to the pappus.

Where Found occasional in alpine tundra and gravelly meadows, usually in swales and other moist places.

Similar Species *Antennaria friesiana* also with several heads per stem but it has gland-tipped hairs on its leaves and stems.

♦ *Antennaria friesiana* (Trautv.) Ekman
FRIES' PUSSYTOES

Habit tufted perennial herb; stems 3–12 cm high, covered in fine white to purple, gland-tipped hairs. Leaves basal and along stem; basal leaves narrowly oblanceolate, stem leaves linear with papery brown tips; upper surface green-hairless to gray-tomentose, underside gray, hairy; margins entire. Flowers in heads surrounded by several layers of

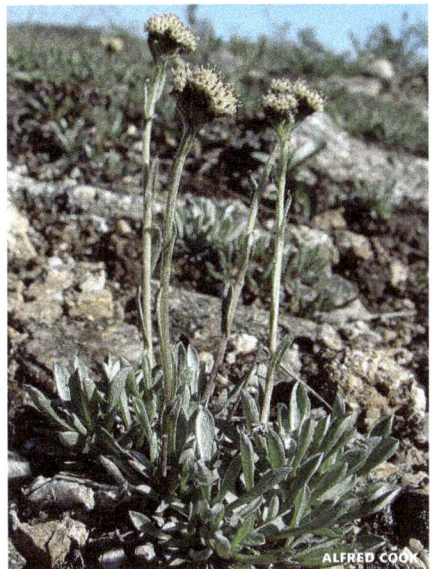

Antennaria friesiana FRIES' PUSSYTOES

dark, narrow bracts, tips a papery brown similar to that found on stem leaves. Fruit an achene, 1–2 mm long, with persistent pappus of yellowish long hairs.

Where Found occasional in dry alpine tundra, gravelly sites, and fellfields.

Similar Species Separated from the more common *Antennaria monocephala* as it has multiple heads per stem; the bracts of *A. friesiana* are brown-margined vs. pink-margined in *A. rosea*.

♦ *Antennaria monocephala* DC.
PYGMY PUSSYTOES

Habit loosely cushion-forming perennial herb, from a slender, branching rhizome with stolons; stems erect, 5–12 cm tall, few, simple, glandular. Leaves in a basal rosette and along stem; basal leaves spatulate or narrowly oblanceolate, 1–2 cm long, upper side green-hairless or occasionally sparsely pubescent, underside densely hairy; stem leaves with similar pubescence, alternate, linear, with papery brown tips. Flowers in solitary heads (less often 2–3); heads subtended by several layers of dark, papery-margined bracts, narrow and just shorter than the flowers. Fruit an achene, pappus hairs 3–4 mm long, giving heads a distinctive fuzzy look (but plants primarily spread vegetatively).

Where Found common at mid- and especially high-elevations in tundra, moist meadows, and snowbeds.

Similar Species the only *Antennaria* in Denali with a single head per stem.

Antennaria pulcherrima (Hook.) Greene
SHOWY PUSSYTOES

Habit dioecious perennial herb, from a short, branched woody base or rhizome; stems erect, 20–50 cm tall, solitary or few, branched above, densely woolly-hairy. Leaves basal and along stem; basal leaves erect to ascending, narrowly spoon-shaped to oblanceolate, 4–15 cm long, densely woolly-hairy, 3–5-nerved; stem leaves narrower, becoming sessile and smaller upwards. Flowers male or female and on separate plants; in 4–20 heads; corolla 3–5 mm long Fruit a glabrous achene, 1–2 mm long; pappus white with hairlike bristles 4–6 mm long.

Where Found uncommon in open woods, floodplains, terraces, and mountain slopes.

♦ *Antennaria rosea* Greene
ROSY PUSSYTOES

Habit mat-forming perennial herb, with numerous leafy, branching stolons; stems erect, 5–20 cm tall, several, branched above, densely woolly-hairy, sometimes glandular above, the glands with reddish crosswalls. Leaves basal and along stem; basal leaves oblanceolate, gray to white woolly-hairy above and below, 6–25 mm long, with a sharp, slender tip; stem leaves 8–10, linear to lanceolate, abruptly sharp-pointed, without papery tips. Flowers in several to many heads in a compact, rounded cluster; female flowers 3–4 mm long. involucral bracts lanceolate, the upper papery portion some

Antennaria monocephala PYGMY PUSSYTOES

Antennaria rosea ROSY PUSSYTOES

combination of white, pink, rose, green, pale yellow or light brown. Fruit a glabrous achene, about 1 mm long; pappus dirty white, of hair-like bristles 3–6 mm long.

Where Found occasional in open woods, floodplains, terraces.

Arnica ARNICA
(Ancient Latin or Greek name.)

1 Stem leaves mostly 5–12 pairs. . . . *A. lanceolata*
1 Stem leaves mostly 1–4 pairs 2
2 Anthers purplish-black . . . . *A. lessingii*
2 Anthers yellow. 3
3 Pappus somewhat feathery, tawny or straw-colored . . . . *A. ovata*
3 Pappus finely-barbed, usually white or nearly so 4
4 Leaves broad, basal leaves 1–2.5 times longer than wide. . . . . *A. latifolia*
4 Leaves narrow, basal leaves 3–10 times longer than wide. 5
5 Achenes usually glabrous toward base, or glabrous throughout. . . . . *A. griscomii*
5 Achenes usually short-hairy throughout . . . . *A. angustifolia*

♦*Arnica angustifolia* Vahl
NARROWLEAF ARNICA
Arnica alpina (L.) Olin
Habit perennial herb, from a fibrous-rooted rhizome or stem-base; stems leafy, erect or ascending, to 40 cm tall, simple or branched

Arnica angustifolia NARROWLEAF ARNICA

only in inflorescence, sparsely to densely hairy or sometimes glandular in upper portion. Leaves basal and along stem; basal leaves narrowly lanceolate, simple, with entire margins, more or less densely hairy; stems leaves similar to basal leaves, opposite, in 2–4 pairs, becoming smaller upwards. Flowers usually in a single flowering head per stem (or sometimes several); ray and disk flowers yellow, the rays (petals) oblong and toothed at tip. Fruit a narrow achene, pappus a tuft of white hairs.

Where Found occasional in floodplains, rocky slopes, and tundra, especially on warmer, south-facing slopes.

Similar Species distinguished from other arnicas by its narrow basal leaves, upright (not nodding) flowering heads, and white pappus.

Traditional Uses The Gwich'in people used arnica flowers to make tea for stomach ailments (Andre and Fehr 2000 in Aiken et al. 2003); however, this use contraindicated by research on the European *Arnica montana* which has negative side effects from internal use (Blumenthal 2000, Moore 1993).

♦*Arnica griscomii* Fernald SNOW ARNICA
Arnica frigida subsp. *griscomii* (Fernald) S.R. Downie
Habit perennial herb, from a short, branched stem-base; stems erect or ascending, to 30 cm tall (but usually shorter), solitary or occasionally a few clustered together, rarely branched above; sparsely long-hairy and sometimes glandular. Leaves mainly basal; basal leaves lanceolate to oblanceolate, 3–5 veined, 1–8 cm long, simple, more or less densely hairy and occasionally glandular, margins entire to toothed; stem leaves opposite, 1–4 pairs, to 10 cm long. Flowers in 1–3 heads per stem, heads nodding when young; ray and disk flowers yellow; the rays oblong, notched at tip. Fruit a narrow achene; pappus a tuft of white hairs.

Arnica griscomii SNOW ARNICA

Where Found common on river floodplains, meadows, rocky slopes, and alpine tundra.

Similar Species Most similar to *Arnica lessingii*, which also has a single nodding flower head, but in that species the pappus brown and the anthers black to dark purple.

Arnica lanceolata Nutt. CLASPING ARNICA
Arnica amplexicaulis Nutt.

Habit perennial herb, from creeping rhizomes; stems leafy, erect, 15–70 cm tall, branched only in inflorescence, usually somewhat hairy and glandular at least in upper portion. Leaves basal and along stem; basal leaves small, often deciduous by flowering time; stem leaves opposite, all but lowermost sessile, usually in 4–10 pairs, lance-shaped to oblanceolate, 2–12 cm long, nearly glabrous to glandular-hairy, margins sharply toothed. Flowers in 1–5 heads with ray and disk flowers, on stalks with yellowish hairs and often stalked glands; ray flowers 8–14, pale yellow, 1–2 cm long, conspicuously toothed at tip; disk flowers yellow; involucral bracts lance-shaped, hairy. Fruit an achene, 4–6 mm long, sparsely hairy, sometimes glandular; pappus brownish, somewhat feathery.

Where Found uncommon on mountain slopes, woods.

♦ *Arnica latifolia* Bong. BROADLEAF ARNICA

Habit perennial herb, from a stout rhizome; stems usually simple, 20–40 cm tall, sparingly hairy below, more densely hairy in inflorescence. Leaves 2–5 pairs along the stem, the lower ovate to elliptic-lanceolate and petioled, the upper sessile; margins toothed. Flowers in usually single heads (or up to 5); rays 8–15, yellow; involucral bracts lanceolate to oblanceolate, brownish hairy. Fruit a dark brown achene, 5–9 mm long; pappus white.

Where Found occasional in open woods, meadows, heathlands.

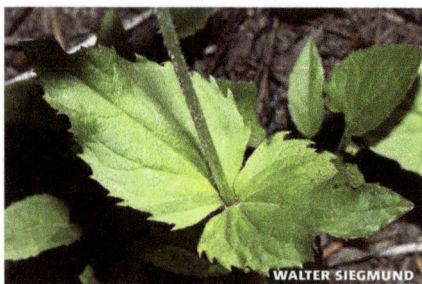

Arnica latifolia BROADLEAF ARNICA

♦ *Arnica lessingii* Greene NODDING ARNICA

Habit perennial herb, from a rhizome; stems solitary, to 30 cm tall, sometimes branched above, densely pubescent. Leaves mainly basal, lanceolate or elliptic, entire or toothed, pubescent above; stem leaves opposite, close to base of stem. Flowers in solitary, usually nodding heads; ray and disk flowers yellow; rays oblong and toothed at tip; anthers dark purplish; involucral bracts long-hairy with brown hairs. Fruit a narrow achene, topped with a tuft of brown or tawny hairs (pappus).

Where Found common in cool, moist alpine areas, especially in mossy ericaceous dwarf shrub tundra.

Similar Species the nearly black anthers and brown pappus distinguish nodding arnica from other members of the genus.

Arnica ovata Greene STICKY-LEAF ARNICA
Arnica diversifolia Greene

Habit perennial herb, from a freely rooted rhizome; stems erect, solitary or occasionally a few clustered together, 15–40 cm tall, simple, sparsely long-hairy and often glandular. Leaves basal and along stem; basal leaves smaller than stem leaves and often deciduous by flowering time; stem leaves opposite, usually 3 pairs, the middle pair the largest, ovate to elliptic, short-stalked below, sessile above; uppermost leaves reduced. Flowers in usually 3–5 heads with ray and disk flowers,

Arnica lessingii NODDING ARNICA

ray flowers 12–15, yellow, inconspicuously toothed; disk flowers yellow; involucral bracts lanceolate, long-hairy and often fringed with glandular hairs. Fruit an achene, 5–6 mm long, glabrous or sparsely hairy; pappus tawny to brownish, more or less feathery.

Where Found uncommon in open woods.

Artemisia SAGEBRUSH

(Greek Artemis, goddess of the hunt and namesake of Artemisia, Queen of Anatolia.)

1 Stems 4–15 cm high; inflorescence a rounded head . . . . *A. globularia*
1 Stems usually higher; inflorescence spikelike, racemose or paniculate 2
2 Plants mat-forming, with a stout woody and much-branched crown . . . . *A. frigida*
2 Plants tufted or spreading by rhizomes, with a taproot or a woody stem-base 3
3 Leaves mainly along stem . . . . *A. tilesii*
3 Leaves mainly basal 4
4 Basal leaves 2- to 3-pinnate 5
4 Basal leaves once or twice 3-parted or palmately divided 7
5 Flowering heads nodding, to 10 mm in diameter . . . . *A. norvegica*
5 Flowering heads spreading to nodding, smaller, ... 6
6 Leaves glandular-dotted; corolla hairy . . . . *A. laciniata*
6 Leaves not glandular-dotted; corollas glabrous. . . . . *A. borealis*
7 Flowering stems from woody branches of previous season; lower leaves usually once or twice 3-parted . . . . *A. kruhsiana*
7 Flowering stems directly from stem-base 8
8 Stems 4–8 cm tall; leaves with short, appressed hairs on both sides . . . . *A. furcata*
8 Stems 10–50 cm tall; leaves with short to long silky hairs . . . . *A. borealis*

◆*Artemisia borealis* Pallas
NORTHERN WORMWOOD
Artemisia campestris subsp. *borealis* (Pallas) H.M. Hall & Clem.

Habit biennial, or more often perennial herb, scarcely aromatic, from a taproot; stems erect, 1–several, 1–3 dm tall, glabrous to hairy, often reddish. Leaves mostly basal, 2–3 times pinnately cut or 3-parted, 2–12 cm long, the segments linear, to 2 mm wide, glabrous to more often long-hairy; becoming

smaller upwards on stem. Flowers many, in a narrow, spikelike, purplish to green inflorescence, of 10–25 disk flowers only; involucral bracts glabrous to densely long-hairy. Fruit a glabrous achene.

Where Found occasional in alpine tundra, heathlands, open woods.

◆*Artemisia frigida* Willd.
PRAIRIE SAGEWORT

Habit perennial herb, from a stout stem-base or woody crown; stems ascending to erect, 10–40 cm tall, whole plant white or tawny, woolly-hairy. Leaves basal and along stem; basal leaves few, soon deciduous; stem leaves silvery-silky hairy, small, 2–3 times divided into fine-linear segments, the segments 1 mm wide or less, often with a pair of 3-parted, stipule-like divisions at base. Flowers several to many, in a simple or branched inflorescence, nodding; disk flowers 25–50, yellow or reddish tinged; involucral bracts hairy, green at center, brown on margins. Fruit a glabrous achene, pappus absent.

Where Found uncommon on steep, open slopes, lakeshores, floodplains, sandy terraces.

◆*Artemisia furcata* M. Bieb.
FORKED WORMWOOD

Habit perennial aromatic herb, with a stout taproot and a simple to branched woody base with persistent leaf bases; stems ascending

Artemisia borealis **NORTHERN WORMWOOD**

to erect, 5–20 cm tall, glabrate to hairy. Leaves gray-green, short-hairy, primarily in basal rosettes but also with smaller leaves on stem; basal leaves 1–3 times palmately divided into linear-lanceolate segments; stem leaves alternate, lower stem leaves similar to basal leaves, upper leaves linear. Flowers in globe-shaped, erect or nodding heads clustered in a loose raceme or spike; of disk flowers only; corolla yellow or sometimes reddish; involucral bracts ovate, pubescent, with brown papery margins. Fruit an achene; pappus absent.

Where Found uncommon on well-drained rubble slopes, fellfields, and tundra, often on steep, south-facing slopes.

Similar Species distinguished from most other species of *Artemisia* in Denali by its simple, linear stem leaves, and small flowering heads (3–4 mm in diameter).

Traditional Uses wormwood is a medicinally important plant throughout the range of the genus, though it is also poisonous, and was therefore mostly used externally only.

Artemisia globularia Cham. ex Besser
PURPLE WORMWOOD

Habit tufted perennial herb, with a short woody stem-base; stems 1 or more, erect, 4–15 cm tall, light green to purplish, densely hairy, especially upwards. Leaves basal and along stem; leaves of basal rosettes 1–3 cm long, 1- or 2-divided, segments oblong to linear, petioles broad, flat; stem leaves few, usually 1-divided. Flowers in several heads; of disk flowers only; corolla purplish or less often yellow, often glandular, glabrous; involucral bracts with green centers, and narrow brownish papery margins. Fruit a

glabrous achene.

Where Found uncommon on dry rocky rubble on steep alpine slopes.

♦ *Artemisia kruhsiana* Besser
ALASKA WORMWOOD
Artemisia alaskana Rydb.

Habit tufted perennial subshrub from a stout, woody, branching base; stems erect or

Artemisia furcata FORKED WORMWOOD

Artemisia frigida PRAIRIE SAGEWORT

Artemisia kruhsiana ALASKA WORMWOOD

ascending, 15–50 cm tall, clustered, simple or branched above, white-woolly. Leaves basal and along stem, woolly above and below; basal leaves 1–5 cm long, once or twice 3-parted; segments oblong to linear, blunt-tipped; stem leaves becoming reduced and entire upwards. Flowers in numerous heads in a branched or narrow inflorescence; of disk flowers only; involucral bracts with matted, woolly hairs and brownish, thin, dry, papery margins. Fruit a glabrous achene.

Where Found gravelly floodplains, scree and gravelly slopes.

Artemisia laciniata Willd.
SIBERIAN WORMWOOD

Habit perennial herb, with a thick stem-base and taproot; stems 20–60 cm high, greenish to reddish purple, pubescent to glabrate. Leaves basal and along stem; basal leaves 5–20 cm long, 2–3-times pinnately divided, pubescent especially below, and glandular-dotted; stem leaves smaller, 1–2-times pinnately divided, or uppermost leaves simple. Flowers several to many, in nodding heads, in a panicle-like to spike-like inflorescence; of disk flowers only; corolla hairy, yellowish; involucral bracts with greenish centers, and dark to light brown translucent margins. Fruit a glabrous achene.

Where Found may occur in Denali's alpine tundra.

Artemisia norvegica Fr.
BOREAL SAGEBRUSH
Artemisia arctica Less.

Habit perennial herb, from a short, branched, somewhat woody stem-base; stems erect-ascending, solitary or sometimes several, 10–40 cm tall, glabrous to sparsely or densely hairy. Leaves mostly basal, bipinnately divided into 5–7 pairs of narrow leaflets; leaves usually (but not always) glabrous. Flowers in a spikelike inflorescence, heads typically nodding; disk flowers yellow, often reddish tinged; involucral bracts with papery, dark margins. Fruit an achene.

Where Found common in meadows, rocky slopes, peaty places, and shrub tundra, usually at high-elevations.

Similar Species boreal sagebrush is not aromatic, unlike other sagebrushes and wormwoods.

◆*Artemisia tilesii* Ledeb.
TILESIUS' WORMWOOD

Habit perennial aromatic herb, from a tough rhizome; stems erect, several, 15–80 cm tall, woolly-hairy to nearly hairless. Leaves mostly on stem, 2–10 cm long, pinnately divided into 3–5 lanceolate lobes, margins toothed; green and glabrous above, gray and hairy to tomentose below. Flowers in a spikelike inflorescence of several nodding flower heads; of disk flowers only; corolla yellowish to pink-

Artemisia norvegica BOREAL SAGEBRUSH

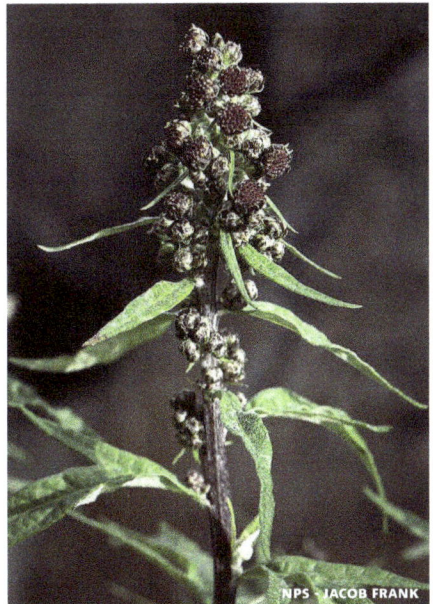

Artemisia tilesii TILESIUS' WORMWOOD

ish; involucral bracts green to white tomentose, with a brown papery margin. Fruit an achene.

Where Found common on gravel bars, meadows, and occasionally in tundra and rocky alpine places; in Denali, also common in disturbed soil around ground squirrel colonies.

Similar Species distinguished from other wormwoods by its large, broad stem leaves (in contrast to the narrow or finely divided leaves of other *Artemisia*).

Askellia HAWK'S-BEARD

(In honor of Icelandic botanist Áskell Löve, 1916-1994.)

1 Stems 2–8 cm high; alpine species; achene beakless or short-beaked . . . . *A. pygmaea*
1 Stems 8–25 cm high; lowland species; achene beaked . . . . *A. elegans*

♦ *Askellia elegans* (Hook.) W.A. Weber
ELEGANT HAWK'S-BEARD
Crepis elegans Hook.

Habit perennial herb, from a taproot and a simple or slightly branched woody base; stems several to many, 8–25 cm tall, freely branched, glabrous. Leaves basal and along stem; basal leaves numerous, spoon-shaped to orbicular or ovate, 3–10 cm long, glaucous and purplish, margins entire to coarsely toothed; stem leaves linear, somewhat reduced upwards. Flowers many, in an open inflorescence; ray flowers yellow, 6–8 mm long; disk flowers absent; involucral bracts glabrous, outer bracts 7–8, very short; inner bracts 8–10, 2-ranked, broadly papery-mar-

gined, purple at tip. Fruit a golden brown achene, about 4 mm long; pappus white, of very fine, soft deciduous bristles.

Where Found occasional on streambanks, gravel bars, lakeshores.

♦ *Askellia pygmaea* (Ledeb.) Sennikov
DWARF ALPINE HAWK'S-BEARD
Crepis nana Richards.

Habit densely tufted perennial herb, from a stout taproot and woody base; stems spreading, several to many, 4–10 cm tall, simple or more often branched, glabrous. Leaves mostly basal, in a tight circular rosette, glabrous, purplish, elliptic to oblanceolate, margins toothed to pinnatifid. Flowers in numerous heads borne among the leaves, the heads yellow and compact; each head with 9–12 reduced flowers; corolla yellow, strap-shaped and toothed at tip, 9–12 mm long. Fruit a ribbed achene, 4–7 mm long; pappus a tuft of white hairs.

Where Found occasional in dry alpine talus, gravelly floodplains, lakeshores.

Bidens BEGGARTICKS

(Latin, 2-toothed, from the achene.)

1 Leaves, except sometimes the lowermost, sessile; outer involucral bracts mostly spreading or reflexed . . . . *B. cernua*
1 Leaves with petioles; outer involucral bracts ascending to erect. . . . . *B. tripartita*

♦ *Bidens cernua* L. **NODDING BUR-MARIGOLD**

Habit annual herb, from a fibrous root; stems erect, simple or branched, 10–60 cm tall, sparsely spreading-hairy to glabrous. Leaves opposite, linear-lanceolate to lanceo-

Askellia elegans ELEGANT HAWK'S-BEARD

Askellia pygmaea DWARF ALPINE HAWK'S-BEARD

late, 1.5–20 cm long, sessile, sometimes joined at the stem, coarsely saw-toothed to nearly entire, glabrous. Flowers in several to many hemispheric heads, nodding at maturity; ray flowers 6–8 (or sometimes absent), yellow, about 1.5 cm long; disk flowers yellow; involucral bracts in 2 dissimilar series, outer bracts 5–8, green, leafy, spreading or reflexed, inner bracts erect, greenish brown. Fruit a 4-angled tan achene with 3–4 retrorsely-barbed awns.

Where Found uncommon in moist places, considered adventive in Alaska.

Bidens tripartita L.
THREE-LOBE BEGGARTICKS

Habit annual herb, from a fibrous root; stems erect, simple or branched, 20–80 cm tall. Leaves mostly deeply incised or 3-lobed, saw-toothed, to 20 cm long; petioles short, winged. Flowers in heads of disk flowers only, ray flowers usually lacking; disk flowers yellow, about 3 mm long; involucral bracts linear, spreading, outer bracts 1–3 cm long, inner bracts shorter. Fruit a 4-angled achene with 3–4 retrorsely-barbed awns.

Where Found uncommon in moist places, considered adventive in Alaska.

Crepis HAWK'S-BEARD
(Greek slipper or sandal, possibly alluding to shape of achene.)

Crepis tectorum L.
NARROW-LEAF HAWK'S-BEARD

Habit annual herb, from a short taproot; stems erect, solitary, 20–50 cm tall (sometimes taller), branched, glabrous or hairy. Leaves basal and along stem; basal leaves lanceolate or oblanceolate, 2–15 cm long, entire to toothed or pinnately parted, petioles short, often soon deciduous; stem leaves sessile, clasping, more or less linear, margins often inrolled. Flowers several to many, in a flat-topped inflorescence; ray flowers yellow, to 13 mm long; disk flowers absent; involucral bracts awl-like, short woolly-hairy and sometimes glandular-hairy. Fruit a purplish brown achene, 3–4 mm long; pappus white, of fine, hairlike bristles, deciduous.

Where Found uncommon in disturbed places; introduced from Eurasia.

Erigeron FLEABANE
(Greek, early old, in allusion to the pappus.)

1	Basal leaves slightly 3-lobed or once or more 3-parted. 2
1	Leaves entire or serrate. 3
2	Leaves spatulate, 2–4 mm wide, margins entire or shallowly 3-lobed at tip; phyllaries densely woolly-hairy. . . . . *E. denalii*
2	Leaves linear to narrowly oblanceolate, 1–3 mm wide, margins entire or early leaves with 1 or 2 shallow lobes; phyllaries sparsely hairy to smooth . . . . *E. purpuratus*
3	Upper stem leaves clasping . . . . . *E. peregrinus*
3	Upper stem leaves not clasping 4

Bidens cernua NODDING BUR-MARIGOLD

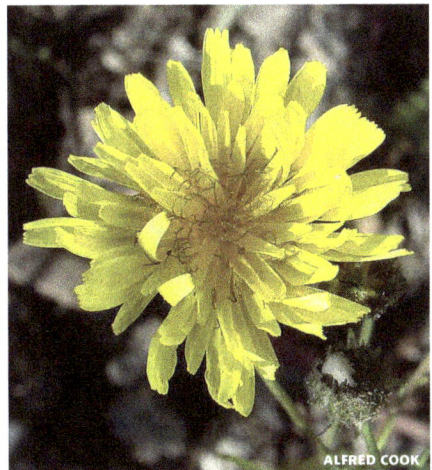

Crepis tectorum NARROW-LEAF HAWK'S-BEARD

4 Rays conspicuous, about twice as long as pappus (or longer) 5
4 Rays shorter 7
5 Heads several (or sometimes solitary) . . . . *E. glabellus*
5 Heads always solitary 6
6 Involucral bracts glandular . . . . . *E. hyperboreus*
6 Involucral bracts not glandular . . . . . *E. porsildii*
7 Stems unbranched 8
7 Stems branched 10
8 Pappus white, brownish, or sordid . . *E. humilis*
8 Pappus purplish 9
9 Leaves spatulate, 2–4 mm wide, margins entire or shallowly 3-lobed at tip; phyllaries densely woolly-hairy . . . . *E. denalii*
9 Leaves linear to narrowly oblanceolate, 1–3 mm wide, margins entire or early leaves with 1 or 2 shallow lobes; phyllaries sparsely hairy to smooth . . . . *E. purpuratus*
10 Inflorescence raceme-like; peduncles erect; stem leaves linear . . . . *E. lonchophyllus*
10 Inflorescence in a more or less flat-topped head; peduncles spreading; stem leaves wider 11
11 Involucre glandular; heads few to many *E. acris*
11 Involucre not glandular or nearly so; heads few or sometimes one . . . . *E. elatus*

◆ *Erigeron acris* L. BITTER FLEABANE

Habit biennial or short-lived perennial herb, from a taproot; stems solitary to several, erect, 20–60 cm tall, branched above, often with spreading stiff hairs. **Leaves** both basal and along stem, stem leaves oblanceolate to lanceolate, to about 12 cm long; margins entire or irregularly toothed. **Flowers** in an open, much branched inflorescence (corymb), peduncles spreading or ascending; ray flowers white to purplish, the petals not much longer than the central yellow disk flowers. **Fruit** a plumed achene; pappus white to pinkish.

Where Found on river bars and terraces, occasionally in open woods.

Similar Species distinguished from other *Erigeron* in Denali by the branched, flat-topped inflorescence, and glandular hairs on the involucre.

Erigeron denalii A. Nelson
DENALI FLEABANE
Erigeron purpuratus var. *dilatatus* B. Boivin
Habit perennial herb, with usually well-developed, horizontal stem-base branches and taproot; stems 2–10 cm tall, spreading-hairy and finely glandular. **Leaves** mostly basal, narrowly oblanceolate to oblong or spatulate, 1–

3.5 cm long, margins entire or 3-toothed; stem leaves much smaller. **Flowers** heads solitary, the peduncles variously curved or straight; rays mostly 60–90, pink or white, 4–6 mm long, to 1 mm wide; involucral bracts lance-linear, mostly purplish throughout, hairy with long, multicellular hairs, at least some with purplish black cross-walls. **Fruit** a hairy to nearly glabrous achene; pappus pinkish or purplish.

Where Found open alpine and subalpine habitats, tundra slopes, openings in spruce-fir woods, gravelly and shaley scree.

◆ *Erigeron elatus* Greene
SWAMP BOREAL-DAISY
Habit biennial or short-lived perennial herb; stems erect, 10–40 cm tall, more or less spreading-hairy. **Leaves** basal and along stem; basal leaves narrowly oblanceolate or spatulate, to 10 cm long; stem leaves similar. **Flowers** solitary or few, in heads with ray and disk flowers; peduncles and involucres glandless or nearly so, more or less spreading-hairy; rays about 5 mm long, white or pink; involucral bracts linear-lanceolate. **Fruit** a hairy achene; pappus white to pinkish.

Where Found floodplain meadows, open boggy woods.

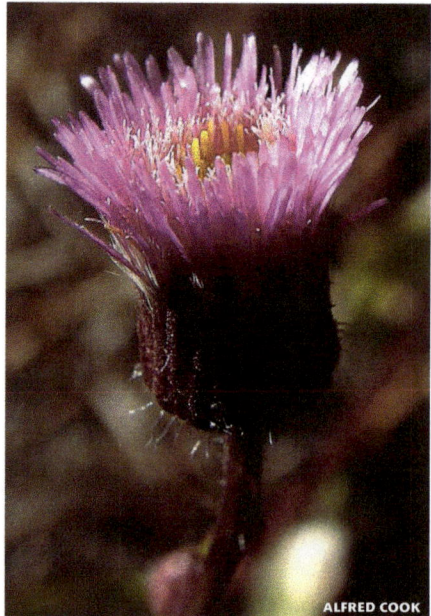
ALFRED COOK
Erigeron acris BITTER FLEABANE

Erigeron glabellus Nutt.
STREAMSIDE FLEABANE

Habit biennial or perennial herb, from fibrous roots; stems erect or somewhat curved at base; 15–60 cm tall, usually branched, sparsely to densely hairy with bristly hairs. Leaves basal and along stem; basal leaves oblanceolate, 1–15 cm long (including the petiole), with stiff hairs, margins entire to irregularly toothed; stem leaves similar to basal, becoming linear to bractlike upwards. Flowers solitary to many, usually on long, nearly naked stalks; heads with ray and disk flowers; ray flowers 125–175, white to pinkish purple, 8–15 mm long, about 1 mm wide; disk flowers 4–5 mm long; involucral bracts nearly equal or slightly graduated, linear, with long-pointed tip, stiffly hairy, not glandular, often with a brownish midvein. Fruit a hairy achene; pappus tan.

Where Found uncommon on river gravel bars and terraces, meadows, open woods.

♦ *Erigeron humilis* Graham
ARCTIC ALPINE FLEABANE

Habit perennial herb; from a short taproot or a short, brittle, woody stem-base, and often some fibrous roots; stems generally lax, erect or ascending, 2–25 cm tall, densely long-hairy, the hairs, especially on upper stem, usually with some purple cross-walls. Leaves mainly in a basal rosette, obovate to spatulate, long-hairy; stem leaves alternate, somewhat smaller. Flowers in solitary heads; ray flowers white or pale purple, 4–6 mm long and less than 1 mm wide; disk flowers yellow; involucral bracts densely covered with purple-black hairs. Fruit a singled-seeded achene; pappus of white or tawny bristles.

Where Found common in alpine meadows, snowbeds, tundra, along streams; sites often steep and moist.

Similar Species *Erigeron humilis* distinguished by its solitary heads, pale pappus, dark purple-black involucral hairs, and narrow ray flowers.

Erigeron hyperboreus Greene
TUNDRA FLEABANE
Erigeron alaskanus Cronq.

Habit perennial with a simple or branched stem-base and taproot; stems 5–10 cm high, erect or somewhat arched, conspicuously spreading-hairy. Leaves basal and along stem; basal leaves narrowly oblanceolate, 1–5 cm long, spreading hairy, tapering to a short petiole or nearly sessile; stem leaves few, reduced, linear to oblong. Flowers in solitary heads with ray and disk flowers; rays 40–60, 8–12 mm long, 1–2 mm wide, 2-toothed at tip, blue to pale purple; involucral bracts lance-oblong, purplish, with long multicellular hairs in which crosswalls clearly purplish black; bracts and involucre more or less viscid or glandular. Fruit a hairy achene; pappus whitish.

Where Found may occur in Denali on alpine heath slopes and rocky places.

Erigeron elatus SWAMP BOREAL-DAISY

Erigeron humilis ARCTIC ALPINE FLEABANE

♦*Erigeron lonchophyllus* Hook.
SHORT-RAY FLEABANE

Habit biennial or short-lived perennial herb; stems erect, 10–40 cm tall, solitary to several, simple or more usually few-branched above, sparsely to densely stiff-hairy. **Leaves** basal and along stem; basal leaves oblanceolate or sometimes spoon-shaped, stalked, to 15 cm long including the petiole, sparsely to densely stiff-hairy or nearly glabrous, margins often stiff-hairy; stem leaves similar, becoming linear and reduced upwards. **Flowers** in heads with ray and disk flowers, borne on the single stem or more often on nearly erect branches; ray flowers numerous, white or sometimes pinkish, 2–3 mm long, slightly longer than the disk flowers; involucral bracts lanceolate, light green, stiffly hairy, commonly purplish near tips. **Fruit** an oblong achene, sparsely stiff-hairy; pappus whitish.

Where Found wet meadows, open slopes, gravel bars and terraces.

♦*Erigeron peregrinus* Greene
SUBALPINE FLEABANE, WANDERING FLEABANE

Habit perennial herb, from a rhizome or short, stout stem-base; stems erect, 10–50 cm tall, simple, glabrous to moderately long-hairy below, usually densely long-hairy beneath the heads. **Leaves** basal and along stem; basal leaves oblanceolate to spatulate, 2–15 cm long, glabrous or somewhat pubescent on undersurface; margins fringed with hairs; stem leaves lanceolate to oblanceolate, becoming smaller and sessile upwards. **Flowers** in mostly solitary heads, with ray and disk flowers; ray flowers 30–80, purplish to lavender, 1 cm or more long, 2–4 mm wide; disk flowers 4–6 mm long; involucral bracts lance-oblong, glandular, more or less pubescent with white hairs. **Fruit** a sparsely hairy achene; pappus tawny.

Where Found uncommon in open woods, moist meadows.

♦*Erigeron porsildii* G.L. Nesom & D.F. Murray
PORSILD'S FLEABANE

Erigeron grandiflorus subsp. *arcticus* A.E. Porsild

Habit Perennial herb, from a taproot; stems erect, decumbent at base, 5–25 cm tall, simple, solitary, sparsely to moderately soft-hairy. **Leaves** basal and along stem; basal leaves oblanceolate, 1–11 cm long, conspicuously long-hairy; stem leaves several, lanceolate to ovate, reduced upwards. **Flowers** Heads with ray and disk flowers, solitary, the disks 10–20 mm wide; involucres 8–10 mm tall; involucral bracts densely long-hairy, the tips sometimes glandular, not graduated; ray

Erigeron lonchophyllus SHORT-RAY FLEABANE

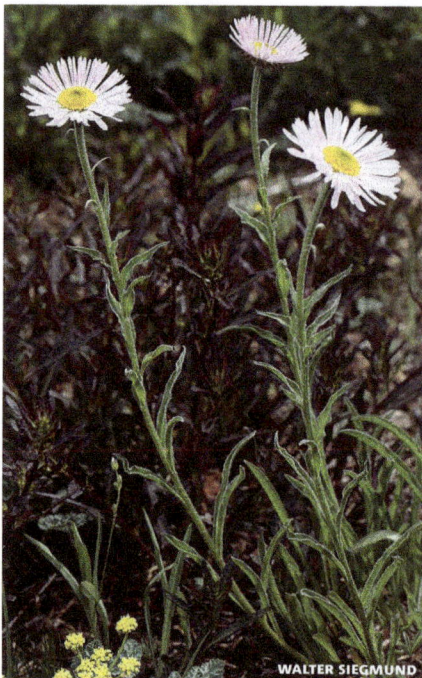

Erigeron peregrinus SUBALPINE FLEABANE

flowers 60–125, blue, 10–15 mm long, 1–2 mm wide; disk flowers mostly 3–5 mm long. Fruit a densely stiff-hairy achene; pappus tan.

Where Found uncommon on dry alpine tundra, talus slopes.

◆ *Erigeron purpuratus* Greene
PURPLE FLEABANE

Habit tufted perennial herb, with a loosely branched stem-base; stems 2–9 cm tall, more or less glandular, usually thinly pubescent. Leaves mostly basal, narrowly oblanceolate, 1–4 cm long, 1–2 mm wide toward tip, hairy, glandular; early leaves sometimes deeply parted into narrow lobes at tip. Flowers heads solitary, rays 60–90, white or pink, 4–8 mm long, less than 1 mm wide; involucral bracts purplish at least towards tip, with spreading, multicellular hairs, with crosswalls usually clearly dark purple. Fruit a short-hairy achene; pappus pinkish to purplish.

Where Found sand and gravel bars, floodplain terraces.

Eurybia WOOD-ASTER

◆ *Eurybia sibirica* (L.) G.L. Nesom **ARCTIC ASTER**
Aster sibiricus L.

Habit perennial herb, from a slender rhizome; stems to 50 cm tall, several to many, ascending to decumbent, sparsely to densely short-hairy, simple to branched above. Leaves basal and along stem; basal leaves deciduous; stem leaves elliptic to oblong, to 10 cm long, densely short-hairy on lower surface, margins with small teeth; lower stem leaves usually smaller than upper stem leaves. Flowers solitary or several; ray flowers 10–25, white to pale violet or purple; disk flowers

yellow, becoming purplish; involucral bracts usually green-tipped and purple-margined. Fruit a hairy achene; pappus dark cinnamon or reddish tan.

Where Found common in floodplains but also in subalpine and alpine meadows, occasionally in dry tundra.

Similar Species distinguished from other asters in having pubescent, purple tipped involucral bracts without glands.

Hieracium HAWKWEED

(Greek, hawk, from the supposition that hawks used the plants to strengthen their eyesight.)

1 Heads large, 1–2 cm in diameter; stems leafy . . . . *H. umbellatum*
1 Heads smaller, less than 1 cm in diameter; stems with a few small leaves . . . . *H. triste*

◆ *Hieracium triste* Willd. ex Spreng.
WOOLLY HAWKWEED

Habit perennial herb, from a short, often stout rhizome; stems erect, 10–30 cm tall, simple or sometimes branched, few to several, sparsely to moderately short or long soft-hairy, sometimes sparsely glandular-hairy above, exuding milky juice when bro-

Erigeron pupuratus PURPLE FLEABANE

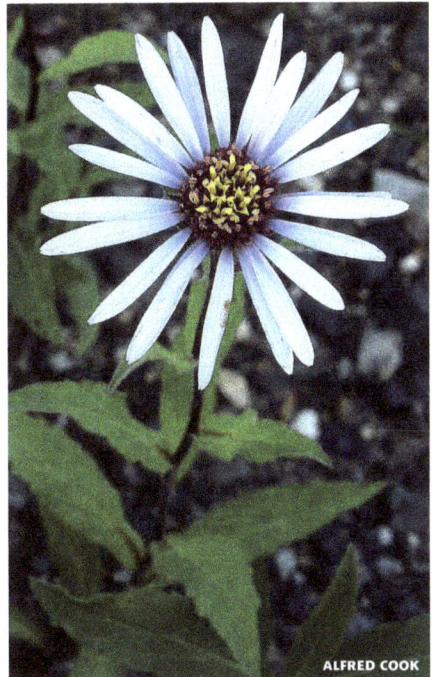

Eurybia sibirica ARCTIC ASTER

ken. Leaves mostly basal; basal leaves persistent, tufted, narrowly elliptic, 1–16 cm long, 0.4–3 cm wide, entire or nearly so; stem leaves few or absent, small and bractlike. Flowers solitary or several, in heads of yellow ray flowers only; involucral bracts linear-lanceolate, nearly equal, long soft-hairy. Fruit an black achene, 2–3 mm long; pappus tawny or sometimes white.

Where Found occasional in alpine meadows, streambanks, talus slopes.

◆*Hieracium umbellatum* L.
NARROW-LEAF HAWKWEED

Habit perennial herb, from a short, stout rhizome; stems erect, 20–60 cm tall, branched above, solitary or several, glabrous or nearly glabrous below, with starlike hairs above, exuding milky juice when broken. Leaves basal and along stem; basal and lower stem leaves small, deciduous around flowering time; middle stem leaves lanceolate to narrowly oblong, sessile, 6–10 cm long; margins entire to somewhat toothed, rough-hairy to nearly glabrous; upper stem leaves reduced. Flowers few, in heads 1–2 cm in diameter, on arched-ascending stalks; of yellow ray flowers only; bracts conspicuously overlapping, essentially glabrous, black or greenish. Fruit a reddish-brown achene, about 3 mm long; pappus tawny.

Where Found openings in woods, roadsides.

Hulteniella ENTIRE-LEAF DAISY
(In honor of Swedish botanist Eric Hultén, 1894–1981.)

◆*Hulteniella integrifolia* (Richardson) Tzvelev
ENTIRE-LEAF DAISY
Chrysanthemum integrifolium Richardson, *Leucanthemum integrifolium* DC.

Habit Perennial herb, from a creeping rhizome or with a well-developed woody stem-base; stems erect, solitary to few, 5–12 cm tall, simple, glabrous or soft-hairy. Leaves

mostly basal, linear to narrowly oblong, entire, 1–2 cm long, 1–2 mm wide, margins long-hairy; stem leaves single or few, similar to basal leaves but smaller, often with brownish translucent margin near leaf tip. Flowers solitary, heads with ray and disk flowers; ray flowers white, 5–12 mm long, 3–4 mm wide; disk flowers yellow; involucral bracts oblong, the centers greenish, with papery, brownish black margins. Fruit a nearly cylindric achene; pappus absent.

Where Found uncommon in alpine tundra and heathlands.

Leucanthemum OX-EYE DAISY
(Greek *leuco-*, white, and *anthemon*, flower.)

Leucanthemum vulgare Lam. OX-EYE DAISY
Chrysanthemum leucanthemum L.

Habit perennial herb, from a creeping rhizome; stems erect, 20–80 cm tall, solitary to several, sparingly branched, usually glabrous, with a sage-like odor. Leaves basal and along stem; basal leaves alternate, ovate to spoon-shaped, stalked, pinnately lobed or toothed, 4–15 cm long; stem leaves smaller, becoming sessile and nearly entire upwards.

Hieracium umbellatum NARROW-LEAF HAWKWEED

Hulteniella integrifolia ENTIRE-LEAF DAISY

Hieracium triste WOOLLY HAWKWEED

Flowers in heads with ray and disk flowers, solitary on long stalks at ends of branches; ray flowers white, 12–20 mm long; disk flowers yellow; involucral bracts narrowly lanceolate, dark-brown near margins. Fruit a black, cylindric achene; pappus absent.

Where Found uncommon in disturbed places; introduced native of Eurasia.

Matricaria MAYWEED

(Greek *matrix*, womb, and *-aria*, alluding to reputed medicinal properties.)

♦ *Matricaria discoidea* DC.
PINEAPPLE-WEED
Chamomilla suaveolens (Pursh) Rydb.

Habit pineapple-scented annual herb, from a fibrous root; stems erect, 1–4 dm tall, much-branched, glabrous. Leaves basal and along stem; basal leaves soon deciduous; stem leaves alternate, 1–5 cm long, 1–3 times divided into short, very narrow segments. Flowers several to many, in heads with disk flowers only; disk flowers yellowish green, 4-toothed, 1–1.5 mm long; receptacles conic, 4–6 mm tall; involucral bracts broadly oblong to ovate, with broad, pale margins and a central brownish to greenish area. Fruit a glabrous achene; pappus a short, membranous crown.

Where Found native weed of disturbed soils.

Packera GROUNDSEL

Previously included in the genus *Senecio*. (Named in honor of John G. Packer, born 1929, Canadian botanist.)

1 Heads solitary (or less often with 1 or 2 small lateral heads) . . . . *P. cymbalaria*
1 Heads 1 to many, all about same size 2
2 Plants with a well-developed ascending rhizome, basal leaves petioled. . . . . *P. ogotorukensis*
2 Plants with fibrous roots; basal leaves petioled 3
3 Stems slender; basal leaves oval, margins nearly entire to sharply toothed . . . . *P. paupercula*
3 Stems stout; basal leaves oblong-ovate, margins mostly deeply toothed . . . . *P. pauciflora*

♦ *Packera cymbalaria* (Pursh) W.A. Weber & Á. Löve **DWARF ARCTIC RAGWORT**
Packera heterophylla (Fisch.) E.Wiebe, *Senecio cymbalaria* Pursh, *Senecio resedifolius* Less.

Habit perennial herb, from a fibrous-rooted short rhizome; stems solitary, erect or ascending, 5–20 cm tall, simple or rarely branched above, glabrous, purplish. Leaves basal and along stem, dark green; basal leaves long-petioled, varying from spatulate to elliptic, entire margined to deeply pinnatifid; stem leaves opposite and sessile, lower stem leaves often deeply pinnatifid; upper stem leaves typically smaller, linear, with entire to toothed margins. Flowers in a single terminal flower head (rarely two), with both ray and disk flowers; ray floret petals 7–14 mm

Matricaria discoidea PINEAPPLE-WEED

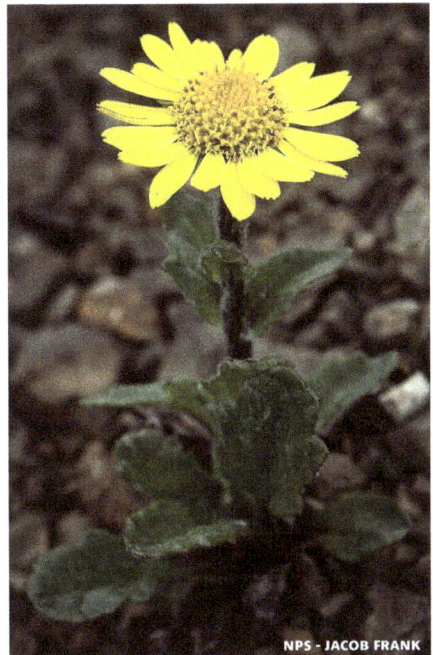

Packera cymbalaria DWARF ARCTIC RAGWORT

long, yellow; disk flowers yellow to orange; involucral bracts dark red or green with red tips. Fruit a single-seeded achene; pappus a tuft of white hairs.

Where Found an alpine species of well-drained tundra, rocky places, gravel bars.

Similar Species *Packera ogoturukensis* has woolly-hairy leaf undersides, and does not have the highly variable leaf shape typical of *P. cymbalaria*.

Packera ogoturukensis (Packer) Á. & D. Löve
OGOTORUK CREEK RAGWORT
Senecio ogoturukensis Packer

Habit perennial herb, from a fibrous-rooted rhizome; stems ascending to erect, 5–20 cm tall, solitary to several, simple to few-branched, sparsely to densely white woolly-hairy. Leaves basal and along stem; basal leaves with petioles, elliptic to oblanceolate; woolly on underside, variable above; margins entire to pinnately-lobed; stem leaves similar but smaller and more or less sessile. Flowers in 1–3 heads, with both disk and ray flowers; ray petals yellow, 8–12 mm long; involucral bracts often green-purple and woolly. Fruit a glabrous achene; pappus with white hairs.

Where Found uncommon in warm, dry, open gravelly floodplains; and alpine slopes, these often south-facing.

Similar Species long, woolly, cobwebby hairs on both sides of leaves and on stems distinguish this species from the similar (but mostly glabrous) *Packera cymbalaria* of similar habitats.

Packera pauciflora ALPINE GROUNDSEL

♦ *Packera pauciflora* (Pursh) Á. & D. Löve
ALPINE GROUNDSEL
Senecio discoideus Britt., *Senecio pauciflorus* Pursh

Habit perennial herb, from a fibrous-rooted, simple or slightly branched woody stem-base; stems erect, 10–50 cm tall, solitary or several, simple or few-branched above, glabrous. Leaves basal and along stem; basal leaves thick, fleshy, elliptic, ovate or nearly round, 1.5–6 cm long including the petiole, glabrous to sparsely white woolly-hairy, margins toothed; stem leaves similar, lanceolate, variously toothed, cleft or lobed, progressively reduced upwards, becoming sessile. Flowers in heads with disk flowers only, solitary to several at tips of stems or branches; disk flowers orange or reddish; involucral bracts linear-lanceolate, reddish purple throughout or at least above the middle, glabrous or sparsely hairy. Fruit a plump, glabrous achene; pappus of white hairlike bristles.

Where Found uncommon in alpine meadows, open woods, river terraces, shores.

♦ *Packera paupercula* (Michx.) Á. & D. Löve
BALSAM GROUNDSEL
Senecio pauperculus Michx.

Habit perennial herb, from a fibrous-rooted short, simple or slightly branched woody stem-base, occasionally with a few short slender stolons; stems erect, 10–60 cm tall, solitary or sometimes several, few-branched upwards. Leaves basal and along the stem; basal leaves oblanceolate to elliptic or oblong, stalked, 2–20 cm long including the petiole, nearly entire to toothed, glabrous; stem leaves lanceolate, deeply toothed or lobed, progressively reduced upwards and becoming sessile. Flowers few to several, in a clustered, flat-topped inflorescence, with ray and disk flowers; ray flowers yellow, mostly 5–10 mm long; disk flowers yellow; involucral bracts lanceolate, green or purplish

Packera paupercula BALSAM GROUNDSEL

tipped, glabrous to moderately woolly-hairy, margins translucent. Fruit an oblong, ribbed achene, glabrous or sometimes finely hairy; pappus of white hairlike bristles.
Where Found uncommon in meadows, open woods.

Petasites SWEET COLT'S-FOOT

(Greek *petasos*, broad-brimmed hat, alluding to large basal leaves.)

♦ *Petasites frigidus* (L.) Fr.
ARCTIC SWEET COLT'S-FOOT

Habit perennial herb, with a single basal leaf and small heads of white to purplish flowers, from a much branched rhizome; stems thick, erect, 10–50 cm tall, branched above, more or less white woolly-hairy, with parallel-veined bracts 2.5–6 cm long (reduced upwards); flowering stems appearing before leaves. Leaves basal and along stem; basal leaves appear after flowering stem, highly variable in shape: heart-shaped to triangular to kidney-shaped, petioles to 30 cm long, margins variably lobed or toothed; leaves green and glabrous above, white-hairy below; stem leaves smaller, alternate, sheathing, lanceolate, margins entire. Flowers in few to many heads in a rounded raceme, with white to purplish flowers. Fruit a glabrous achene, pappus of soft white bristles. Flowering very early in the season; flowering stalk appearing before the leaves.

Petasites frigidus ARCTIC SWEET COLT'S-FOOT

Where Found common at mid-elevations in moist to wet places including white spruce, willow, and alder communities.
Traditional Uses all parts edible, either raw or cooked, though plants contain pyrrolizidine alkaloids and should not be consumed in large quantities. The Alutiiq and Athabascans chewed roots, and made tea of the roots for colds, coughs and tuberculosis (Garibaldi 1999).

Saussurea SAW-WORT

(In honor of Nicolas (1767–1845) and Horace (1740–1799) de Saussure, Swiss naturalists.)

♦ *Saussurea angustifolia* (L.) DC.
NARROW-LEAF SAW-WORT

Habit perennial herb, from a rhizome; stems erect, solitary or few, branched above, dark purple, glabrous or hairy, 10–40 cm tall. Leaves all from stem, dark green, linear to lanceolate, often covered in white woolly hairs, margins entire or irregularly toothed. Flowers 2–10, in a branched, flat-topped inflorescence (corymb); heads with purple disk flowers only; stigmas dark purple, exserted from the petals. Fruit a single-seeded achene, with a tuft of tawny hairs (pappus).
Where Found wide-ranging, from low- to high-elevations in muskegs to alpine tundra.
Similar Species the combination of linear leaves and purple aster-like flowering heads is distinctive. Var. *yukonensis* is also present in Denali, which differs from the typical variety by its tufted, low-growing habit, broader leaves, and its habitat of alpine scree-slopes and tundra.

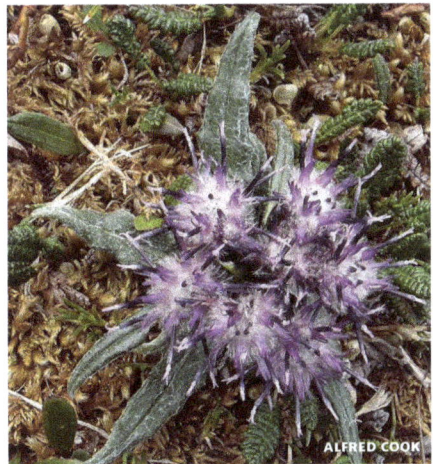

Saussurea angustifolia var. **yukonensis**
NARROW-LEAF SAW-WORT

Senecio RAGWORT

(Reputedly from Latin *senex,* old man or woman, alluding to white pappus bristles resembling white hair of an elderly person.)

---

1 Leaves all on stem (basal rosette absent), leaves triangular-hastate . . . . *S. triangularis*
1 Leaves mainly in basal rosettes, always larger than stem leaves, oblanceolate to elliptic . . . . .
. . . . *S. lugens*

◆*Senecio lugens* Richardson
SMALL BLACKTIP RAGWORT

Habit perennial herb, from a fibrous-rooted, short, thick, ascending or horizontal rhizome; stems erect, 5–35 cm tall, solitary, branched above, glabrous or sparsely woolly-hairy. **Leaves** basal and along stem; basal leaves variable, sessile (petiole absent), usually oblanceolate to elliptic, hairless to sparsely hairy, margins entire or finely toothed; stem leaves similar, smaller. **Flowers** in 2–12 heads in a branched, corymb-like inflorescence; with ray and disk flowers; ray flowers yellow; disk flowers yellow; involucral bracts below the head in two rows, these tipped with black or purple. **Fruit** a glabrous achene.

Where Found common in moist to dry subalpine meadows, dwarf shrub communities, and open forests.

Similar Species distinctive are the black- or purple-tipped involucral bracts arranged in two rows, the multiple flowering heads, and sessile basal leaves.

◆*Senecio triangularis* Hook.
ARROW-LEAF RAGWORT

Habit perennial herb, from a fibrous-rooted, woody stem-base or rhizome; stems erect, 20–100 cm tall, solitary or several from the same clump, branched above, glabrous to sparsely short-hairy above, leafy to the top of stem. **Leaves** basal and along stem; basal leaves triangular to heart-shaped, squared-off at base; strongly toothed, stalked, 5–15 cm long, hairless except for short hairs on underside veins, sometimes deciduous by flowering time; stem leaves similar, larger, 5–25 cm long, gradually reduced upwards, becoming sessile. **Flowers** few to many, on sparsely hairy stalks, in a short, flat-topped inflorescence; with ray and disk flowers; ray flowers yellow, 7–14 mm long; disk flowers yellow; involucral bracts lanceolate, conspicuously black-tipped. **Fruit** an achene, oblong, faintly ribbed, glabrous; pappus of white hairlike bristles.

Where Found uncommon in alpine and subalpine meadows, thickets.

Senecio lugens SMALL BLACKTIP RAGWORT

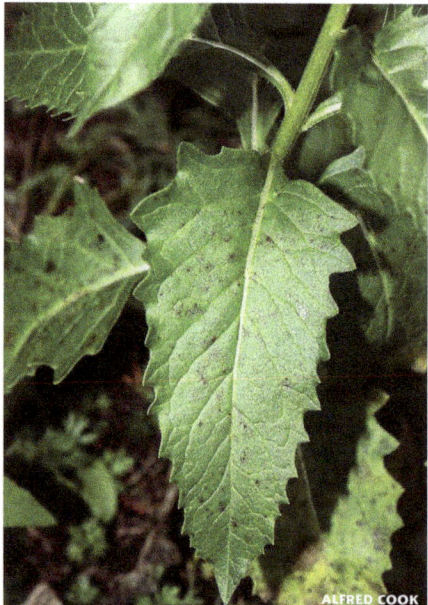

Senecio triangularis ARROW-LEAF RAGWORT

Solidago GOLDENROD

(Latin *solidus,* whole, and *-ago*, resembling or becoming, probably alluding to healing properties.)

---

1   Stems usually more than 35 cm high, from well-developed rhizomes; involucres usually less than 4 mm high . . . . *S. lepida*

1   Stems usually less than 35 cm high, from short rhizomes or a stem-base; involucres usually more than 4 mm high . . . . *S. multiradiata*

Solidago lepida DC.
WESTERN CANADA GOLDENROD
Solidago canadensis var. *lepida* (DC.) Cronquist

Habit perennial herb, from a short rhizome; stems 3–10 dm tall, leafy. **Leaves** oblong to lanceolate, to 1 dm long, margins coarsely and sharply toothed. **Flowers** in a rather compact and spikelike inflorescence, to 1 dm long, sometimes but little exceeding the leaves; heads 5–6 mm long; ray and disk flowers yellow.

Where Found uncommon in meadows, open woods.

◆ Solidago multiradiata Aiton
ARCTIC GOLDENROD

Habit perennial herb, from a short rhizome or branching woody stem-base; stems erect, 5–40 cm tall, solitary, branched above, long-hairy (at least in inflorescence). **Leaves** basal and along stem; basal leaves stalked, linear-oblanceolate in shape, underside net-veined, margins ciliate; stem leaves smaller, alternate, sessile or partially clasping stem. **Flowers** in numerous heads arranged in a dense corymb, sometimes with additional single heads lower on stem; flower heads yellow, with both disk and ray flowers; petals of ray flowers 4–7 mm long. **Fruit** a single-seeded, hairy achene.

Where Found common in a variety of habitats from floodplains, meadows, and open forest in the boreal zone, to meadows and tundra in the alpine.

Similar Species distinguished by its conspicuously net-veined leaf underside.

Traditional Uses plants of various *Solidago* have been used for a variety of ailments: inflammation reduction, as a diuretic, to treat gout, arthritis, eczema, and many others.

Sonchus SOW-THISTLE

(Greek *sonchos,* ancient name for a kind of thistle.)

◆ Sonchus arvensis L. FIELD SOW-THISTLE

Habit perennial herb, with long horizontal roots; stems erect, 4–10 dm tall, solitary, few-branched above, glabrous below, usually glandular-bristly above, hollow, exuding milky juice when broken. **Leaves** basal leaves absent; stem leaves alternate, deeply lobed or pinnately cut, 5–40 cm long, clasping at base, margins prickly; upper leaves smaller

Solidago multiradiata ARCTIC GOLDENROD

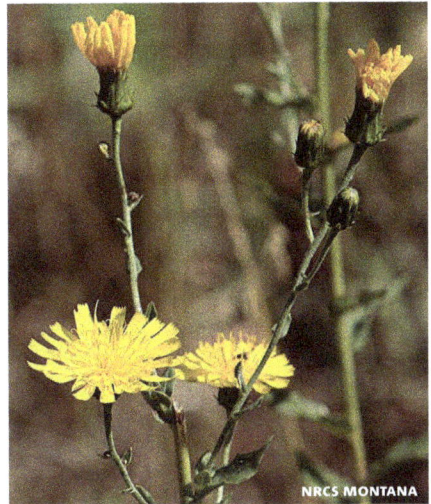

Sonchus arvensis FIELD SOW-THISTLE

and less lobed. Flowers several, relatively large (3–5 cm wide), on glandular stalks in an open, flat- or round-topped inflorescence, of yellow ray flowers only; involucral bracts lanceolate, woolly-hairy or more or less densely covered with coarse, spreading, gland-tipped hairs. Fruit a ribbed achene, 2.5–3.5 mm long; pappus of white hairlike bristles.

Where Found weed of roadsides and waste places; introduced from Europe.

Symphyotrichum
AMERICAN-ASTER
Our species formerly treated within genus *Aster.* (Greek *symphysis*, junction, and *trichos*, hair.)

1   Leaves oblong to lanceolate, usually more than 10 mm wide; ray flowers blue, purple, or pink . . . . *S. subspicatum*
1   Leaves linear, less than 10 mm wide; ray flowers white (less often pale purplish). . . . . *S. boreale*

◆ *Symphyotrichum boreale* (Torr. & A.Gray) Á. & D. Löve **NORTHERN BOG ASTER**
Aster borealis Prov., *Aster junciformis* Rydb.

Habit perennial herb from a slender rhizome; stems erect, 20 to 60 cm tall, simple or branched above, glabrous below becoming hairy above. Leaves basal leaves reduced

Symphyotrichum boreale **NORTHERN BOG ASTER**
ALFRED COOK

and soon deciduous; stem leaves linear-lanceolate, 2–7 cm long, sessile or somewhat clasping, glabrous, margins usually inrolled, entire or inconspicuously toothed, becoming smaller upwards on stem. Flowers in heads, with ray and disk flowers, solitary (in reduced plants) to many in a short, usually broad inflorescence; ray flowers 20–50, white or rarely pale violet, 12–20 mm long; disk flowers yellow; involucral bracts more or less abruptly sharp-pointed, glabrous, often with purplish tips or margins. Fruit a hairy achene; pappus white.

Where Found uncommon in bogs, wet meadows, damp mossy openings in muskeg forest.

Symphyotrichum subspicatum (Nees) G.L. Nesom **LEAFY-BRACT ASTER**
Aster subspicatus Nees.

Habit perennial herb, from a fibrous-rooted, creeping rhizome; stems ascending to erect, 3–9 dm tall, branched above, smooth below, pubescent above. Leaves basal and along stem, basal leaves soon deciduous; stem leaves oblanceolate and stalked below, linear or lanceolate and unstalked above, 3–15 cm long, mostly glabrous, entire. Flowers in heads, with ray and disk flowers, solitary to many in an open, round-topped inflorescence; ray flowers 20–50, blue to violet or purple, 10–15 mm long; disk flowers yellow; involucral bracts abruptly sharp-pointed, glabrous, margins fringed with small hairs, often green to the base. Fruit a hairy achene; pappus whitish.

Where Found uncommon in moist woods, meadows.

Taraxacum **DANDELION**
In addition to the familiar introduced common dandelion, several other *Taraxacum* species are native to Alaska. In Denali, native species are found most often in alpine tundra and on streamside gravel bars at lower elevations. (Arabic or Persian talkh chakok, a bitter herb.)

1   Flowers pinkish or flesh-colored (uncommon native species) . . . . *T. carneocoloratum*
1   Flowers yellow. 2
2   Coarse weedy plants; outer bracts lance-acuminate, reflexed (non-native) . . . . *T. officinale*
2   Plants smaller; outer bracts appressed or ascending (or sometimes reflexed in *T. erythrospermum*) 3

3　Inner involucral bracts usually swollen or with appendage at tip; achenes straw-colored to olive-drab or brownish (native species) . . . .
. . . . *T. cerataphorum*

3　Inner involucral bracts usually not swollen or with appendage at tip; achenes red to brownish red to black 4

4　Achenes black or grayish black (native species) . . . . *T. holmenianum*

4　Achenes red or brownish red (introduced species) . . . . *T. erythrospermum*

◆ ***Taraxacum carneocoloratum*** A. Nelson
PINK DANDELION

Habit small perennial herb, from a branched taproot; flower stem 4–9 cm tall, purplish, glabrous. **Leaves** basal, oblanceolate, 3–8 cm long; margins shallowly lobed or toothed; tapered at base to a narrowly winged petiole. **Flowers** (rays) pink or flesh-colored. **Fruit** an achene; pappus yellowish.

Where Found uncommon on alpine ridges, scree slopes, gravelly floodplains; often on calcareous substrates.

◆ ***Taraxacum ceratophorum*** (Ledeb.) DC.
HORNED DANDELION

Habit perennial herb, with a simple or branched stem-base and a taproot; flower stem to 20 cm or more tall, somewhat hairy below the head. **Leaves** basal, 4–20 cm long, nearly entire or toothed to pinnately lobed or pinnatifid, tapered at base to a winged petiole. **Flowers** (rays) yellow; outer bracts ovate to lanceolate, usually appressed, appendaged; inner bracts dilated or appendaged at tip; rays yellow. **Fruit** a straw-colored to olive-drab or brownish achene; pappus white.

Where Found alpine heath and tundra.

Taraxacum erythrospermum Andrz. ex Besser **RED-SEED DANDELION**
Taraxacum laevigatum (Willd.) DC.

Habit perennial herb, with a simple or branched stem-base; flower stem 1–40 cm tall, glabrous to somewhat hairy. **Leaves** basal, 5–25 cm long, deeply pinnatifid, tapered at base to a more or less winged petiole; terminal lobe narrow and similar to lateral lobes. **Flowers** (rays) yellow; outer bracts ovate to lanceolate, usually appressed to ascending; inner bracts usually without appendages. **Fruit** a red or brownish red, spiny achene; pappus white.

Where Found introduced weed of waste places.

Taraxacum holmenianum Sahlin
NORTHERN DANDELION
Taraxacum alaskanum Rydb., *Taraxacum phymato-carpum* J. Vahl.

Habit perennial herb, with a simple or branched stem-base, and with a taproot; flower stem 3–10 cm or more tall, glabrous or nearly so. **Leaves** basal, mostly 2–8 cm long, usually pinnately lobed to pinnatifid with terminal lobe wider than lateral lobes, tapered at base to a more or less winged petiole. **Flow-**

Taraxacum carneocoloratum **PINK DANDELION**

Taraxacum ceratophorum **HORNED DANDELION**

ers (rays); outer bracts lanceolate to ovate, appressed to ascending; inner bracts usually without appendages. Fruit a black or grayish black achene; pappus white.

Where Found alpine tundra.

Taraxacum officinale G.H. Weber ex Wiggers
COMMON DANDELION

Habit coarse perennial herb; flower stem to 40 cm or more tall, somewhat hairy to nearly glabrous, often densely hairy below the head. Leaves to 30 cm or more long, nearly entire to pinnately lobed or pinnatifid, terminal lobe wider than lateral lobes, tapered at base to a winged petiole; leaves often somewhat pubescent on lower surface and on midvein. Flowers (rays) yellow; outer bracts reflexed; inner bracts rarely with an appendage. Fruit a straw-colored to olive-drab achene; pappus white.

Where Found roadsides and waste places; introduced from Eurasia.

Tephroseris GROUNDSEL

Our species formerly included within *Senecio*. (Greek *tephros,* ashlike or ash-colored, and *seris,* endive or chicory, presumably alluding to color of the densely woolly leaves.)

1   Leaves all on stem; basal rosettes absent . . . . .
. . . . *T. palustris*
1   Leaves mainly in basal rosettes, always larger than stem leaves 2
2   Heads one to many, all about same size . . . . . .
. . . . *T. yukonensis*
2   Heads solitary (or occasionally with 1 or 2 small, lateral heads) 3
3   Heads solitary or often with two smaller lateral heads; leaves, stem and involucrum white-woolly hairy. . . . . *T. lindstroemii*
3   Heads always solitary 4
4   Involucral bracts and upper third of stem densely woolly with brown septate hairs. . *T. kjellmanii*
4   Involucral bracts blackened by distinctly purplish septate hairs (sometimes partly covered by white hairs) . . . . *T. integrifolia*

♦ ***Tephroseris integrifolia*** (L.) Holub
ARCTIC GROUNDSEL

Senecio atropurpureus (Ledeb.) B. Fedtsch., *Senecio integrifolius* (L.) Clairv., *Tephroseris atropurpurea* (Ledeb.) Holub

Habit perennial herb; stems upright, 10–30 cm tall, from a slender underground rhizome. Leaves basal and along stem, linear-lanceolate to ovate, sparsely covered with purplish hairs, margins wavy. Flowers in solitary heads, yellow, and usually (not always) with both ray and disk flowers; involucral bracts with greenish tips and covered in brown woolly hairs. Fruit an achene, with attached white hairs (pappus).

Where Found common in a variety of moist to wet habitats in the subalpine and alpine: black spruce muskegs, alpine meadows.

♦ ***Tephroseris kjellmanii*** (A.E. Porsild) Holub
KJELLMAN'S GROUNDSEL

Senecio kjellmanii Porsild

Habit perennial herb; stems 7–15 cm tall from creeping rhizomes; when first emerging, whole flowering stalk covered in brown, cobwebby fuzz; a few hairs remain on leaves the whole season. Leaves basal and along stem, green-purple; basal leaves few, ovate, fleshy; stem leaves few, sessile, elliptic, margins weakly toothed. Flowers in one (rarely

NPS - JACOB FRANK

Tephroseris integrifolia ARCTIC GROUNDSEL

ALFRED COOK

Tephroseris kjellmanii KJELLMAN'S GROUNDSEL
Young flower buds.

two) heads per stem; buds densely brown-hairy; flowering heads with both ray flowers (with petals 7–12 mm long) and disk flowers (lacking prominent petals); both with yellow corolla. Fruit an achene, with attached white hairs (pappus).

Where Found occasional at high-elevations, on barren alpine slopes, solifluction lobes, and moist gravelly places.

Similar Species differentiated from other *Tephroseris* by its covering of dense, brown, cobwebby hairs.

♦ *Tephroseris lindstroemii* (Ostenf.) Á. & D. Löve FUSCATE GROUNDSEL
Senecio lindstroemii (Ostenf.) Porsild

Habit perennial herb, from a short, rhizome-like woody stem-base; stems erect, solitary or few, 3–30 cm tall, simple or rarely few-branched above, white or yellowish woolly or long-hairy. Leaves basal and along stem; basal leaves oblanceolate to ovate, somewhat thick; stem leaves similar but smaller, alternate. Flowers in solitary heads, sometimes with two smaller heads alongside the central head; petals of ray florets to 2 cm long, distinctively yellow-orange; disk florets orange to reddish; bracts below inflorescence purplish. Fruit a single-seeded achene, with a tuft of white hairs.

Where Found uncommon in well-drained tundra and gravelly places on north side of the Alaska Range.

Similar Species fuscate groundsel has much longer ligules (ray petals) than other *Tephroseris,* and is white-hairy rather than with brown or purple pubescence.

♦ *Tephroseris palustris* (L.) Schrenk ex Rchb. MARSH FLEABANE, MASTODON FLOWER
Senecio congestus (R. Br.) DC.

Habit robust annual or biennial herb, from fibrous roots; stems solitary, 20–100 cm tall, erect, hollow, branched above, with long (over 1 mm) whitish or yellowish hairs. Leaves alternate, large, sessile, lanceolate to linear-oblong, margins wavy and toothed (or shallowly pinnatifid). Flowers in an open, branched head (corymb-like); flower heads with both ray and disk florets; petals yellow. Fruit a single-seeded achene, with a tuft of white hairs.

Where Found uncommon in marshes, lakeshores, and other wetlands in the boreal zone.

Similar Species distinguished from other *Tephroseris* species by absence of basal leaves.

Traditional Uses young leaves and stems edible, and may be used raw in salads or cooked as a potherb.

♦ *Tephroseris yukonensis* (A.E.Porsild) Holub YUKON GROUNDSEL
Senecio alaskanus Hultén, *Senecio yukonensis* A.E. Porsild

Habit perennial herb, from a rhizome; stems erect, solitary, 10–30 cm tall, few-branched above; nearly glabrous to sparingly

Tephroseris lindstroemii FUSCATE GROUNDSEL

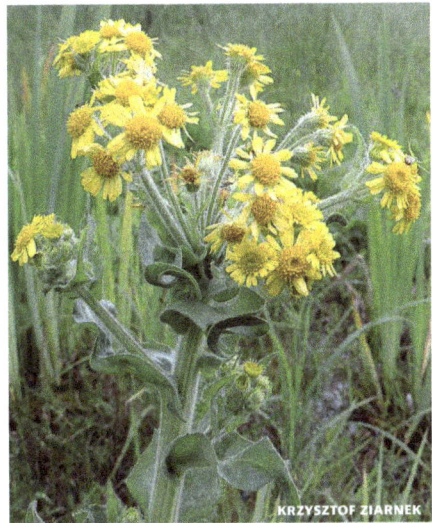
Tephroseris palustris MARSH FLEABANE

long-hairy below, becoming densely woolly around the flowers. Leaves basal and along the stem; basal leaves with a long petiole, oblanceolate to lanceolate, 2–5 cm long, margins entire (occasionally toothed), often withering before flowering; stem leaves smaller, linear, clasping stem. Flowers 3–6; ray florets with a pale yellow corolla, about 10 mm long; disk florets white; involucral bracts purplish at tip; flowering heads covered in woolly hairs. Fruit a ribbed achene, with a white pappus (tuft of hairs).

Where Found uncommon in moist to well-drained places in shrub and alpine tundra north of Alaska Range; most sites calcium-rich.

Similar Species *Tephroseris palustris*, but that species lacks basal leaves and has sharply serrate leaf margins; and *Senecio lugens*, which is not densely white-hairy and has much longer petals.

Tripleurospermum MAYWEED
(Greek *tri-*, three-, *pleuro-*, ribbed, and *sperma*, seed, alluding to 3-ribbed achene.)

Tripleurospermum inodorum (L.) Sch.Bip.
SCENTLESS MAYWEED
Matricaria inodora L.

Habit annual, biennial or sometimes perennial scentless herb, from a fibrous root; stems erect, 5–50 cm tall, simple or branched, glabrous. Leaves alternate, 2–8 cm long, 1–3 times divided into short, threadlike segments, glabrous; basal leaves deciduous by flowering time. Flowers in several to many heads with ray and disk flowers, mostly terminal on upper branches; ray flowers white, 10–25, 4–13 mm long; disk flowers yellow, many, about 1 mm long, 5-toothed; receptacles hemispheric. Fruit an achene, 1–2 mm long, with 3 light-colored ribs on inner face.

Where Found Waste places; introduced from Europe.

BALSAMINACEAE
Jewel-Weed Family

Impatiens TOUCH-ME-NOT
(Latin *impatiens*, impatient, in reference to valves of seed pods, which discharge forcibly at a slight touch.)

◆ Impatiens noli-tangere L.
WESTERN TOUCH-ME-NOT

Habit annual succulent herb; stems erect to ascending, 20–60 cm tall, often branched, hairy. Leaves alternate, stalked, elliptic to ovate, thin, 3–12 cm long; margins coarsely saw-toothed. Flowers one to several in leaf axils, pale yellow, flecked with brownish purple; sepals pouched, the upper sepal a spurred sac, curved or deflexed forward. Fruit a capsule, elastically dehiscent, bursting open when touched, 1–2 cm long, many-seeded.

Where Found uncommon in moist woods, streambanks, seeps.

Tephroseris yukonensis YUKON GROUNDSEL

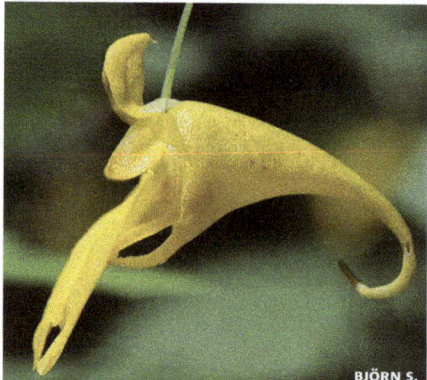
Impatiens noli-tangere WESTERN TOUCH-ME-NOT

BETULACEAE
Birch Family

---

1 Female catkin conelike, hardened and persistent after release of nutlets . . . . *Alnus*
1 Female catkin cylindric, shed with release of nutlets. . . . . *Betula*

Alnus ALDER
(Ancient Latin name.)

---

1 Leaves finely once or twice sharply toothed; axillary buds unstalked, pointed; male catkins unstalked; female catkins on stalks as long as or longer than catkins; nutlets with broad wings . . . . *A. alnobetula*
1 Leaves coarsely to irregularly round-toothed; axillary buds pedunculate, blunt or short-pointed; male catkins stalked; female catkins on stalks shorter than catkins; nutlets without membranous wings. . . . . *A. incana*

◆*Alnus alnobetula* (Ehrh.) K. Koch
GREEN ALDER
Alnus crispa (Ait.) Pursh, *Alnus viridis* A. Gray

Habit shrub or small tree, 1–5 m tall; with unstalked pointed axillary buds; bark smooth when young, yellowish brown or gray, with small horizontal pinkish openings (lenticels). Leaves deciduous, ovate or elliptic, shiny dark green on upper surface, pale and shiny green below, margins finely serrate; leaves resin-coated when young. Flowers in separate male and female catkins, usually borne on same branch; male catkins long, narrow and drooping; female catkin a long-stalked ovate cone, with long brown scales overlapping the two-styled flowers. Fruit a

winged nutlet, the wings wider than body. Flowering May and early June; flowers opening before leaf buds.

Where Found abundant and sometimes forming dense thickets on slopes and in valleys, from lowlands into the subalpine, where it dominates large areas.

Similar Species separated from thinleaf alder (*Alnus incana*) by its conspicuously shiny leaves, long-stalked female catkins, and the nutlet wings broader than the body.

Traditional Uses thinleaf and green alder have been used for a variety of medicinal ailments; tea brewed from inner bark used by the Dena'ina to address stomach problems, tuberculosis, induce vomiting, and break fevers (Kari 1995); the wood is used to smoke salmon, and occasionally as firewood. Alder species have root nodules which support symbiotic nitrogen-fixing bacteria; as a result, they can survive on nutrient-poor soils.

◆*Alnus incana* (L.) Moench THINLEAF ALDER
Alnus tenuifolia Nutt.

Habit shrub or small tree, thicket-forming, to 2–5 m tall, new growth short-hairy; axillary buds on short stalks; stems many, much-branched; bark gray when young, maturing to reddish brown, marked with many horizontal lines (lenticels). Leaves deciduous, thin and ovate, dull gray-green above, paler below, the lower surface hairy or almost hairless, margins coarsely doubly serrate. Flowers in separate male and female catkins, usually borne on same branch; male catkins long and drooping with yellow-green scales; female catkins ovate and cone-like, 0.5–2.5 cm long, with dark brown scales, in clusters of 3–9; the catkin stalks shorter than the catkins. Fruit an unwinged nutlet. Flowering May and early

Alnus alnobetula GREEN ALDER

Alnus incana THINLEAF ALDER

June; flowers opening before leaf buds.

Where Found common along low-elevation rivers and floodplain terraces.

Similar Species distinguished from green alder by the doubly-serrate leaf margins, the dull, (not shiny as in green alder) leaves, and the peduncles (catkin stalks) shorter than the catkins.

Betula BIRCH

The different species seem to hybridize freely and a large proportion of the birches in the region are probably hybrids. (The Latin name.)

1   Low, spreading shrubs with rounded leaf tips. **2**
1   Trees, leaf tips acute **3**
2   Leaves wedge-shaped at base, longer than wide
    . . . . ***B. glandulosa***
2   Leaves truncate or heart-shaped at the base, often wider than long. . . . . ***B. pumila***
3   Leaves ovate, doubly serrate . . . B. occidentalis
3   Leaves with truncate or wedge-shaped base. . **4**
4   Leaves with prolonged tip. . . . .
    . . . . ***B. pendula*** subsp. ***mandshurica***
4   Leaves without prolonged tip. . . . ***B. papyrifera***

◆ *Betula glandulosa* Michx. RESIN BIRCH

Habit shrub, 1–2 m tall; bark becoming reddish brown, not peeling; twigs densely glandular and covered with a thin waxy layer. Leaves deciduous, alternate, leathery; blades usually oval or oblong-elliptic, 1–2 cm long, longer than wide, glandular on both surfaces, bright green and glabrous above, paler and usually pubescent below; petioles pubescent; margins finely serrate. Flowers in separate male and female catkins; male catkins elongate and pendulous, 1–4 per cluster; female

catkins erect, 1–2.5 cm long and 3–5 mm thick, the naked flowers subtended by a 3-lobed bract, the middle lobe narrower and longer than the other two. Fruit a samara, oval in outline, the wings very narrow.

Where Found abundant in tundra, heathlands. open woods, terraces, bogs, streambanks, sand and gravel bars.

◆ *Betula occidentalis* Hook. WATER BIRCH

Habit small tree or large shrub, with several trunks, typically 3–4 m tall; bark dark reddish brown to black. Leaves deciduous, ovate to round, with a broad to narrow wedge-shaped base, margins coarsely toothed; leaf size intermediate between dwarf birch and paper birch, 2–5 cm long. Flowers in separate male and female catkins on same twig; male flowers of two stamens surrounded by a brown-green calyx; female flowers an ovary with styles, protected by a scalelike bract. Fruit a nutlet with papery brown wings. Flowering late spring, before leaves open.

Where Found common in moist to wet places, mostly at mid-elevations.

Similar Species distinguished from its parent species by differences in leaf shape and size.

Traditional Uses an important browse species for moose and snowshoe hare.

Note *Betula occidentalis* is a hybrid between Alaska birch (*B. pendula*) and bog birch (*B. pumila*); as a result, its size and morphology are intermediate between these two species, and show considerable variation, sometimes with greater similarity to resin birch, sometimes more closely resembling dwarf birch.

Betula glandulosa RESIN BIRCH

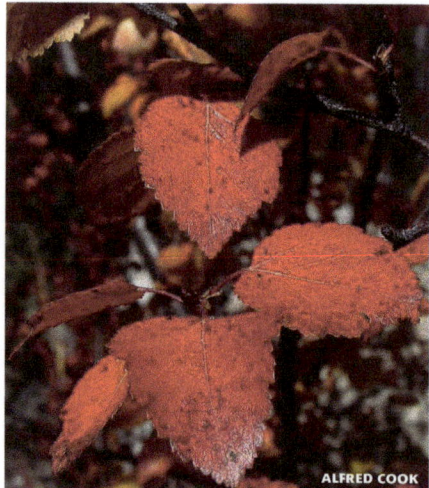

Betula occidentalis RESIN BIRCH

♦ *Betula papyrifera* Marshall
PAPER BIRCH, KENAI BIRCH
Betula kenaica W.H. Evans, *Betula papyrifera* var. *kenaica* (W.H. Evans) A. Henry

Habit small to medium tree, 10–20 m tall, trunk usually single; bark white, yellowish to reddish brown or dark gray, often peeling, marked with horizontal lenticels; twigs hairy with both short and long hairs. Leaves alternate, deciduous, broadly ovate in outline, the tips sharp-pointed, hairy below, rarely glandular, 4–8 cm long, petioles more than 1 cm long; margins usually doubly serrate. Flowers male and female flowers in separate catkins on same tree, 2–4 cm long; flowers emerging before or with leaves; catkins breaking apart when mature. Fruit a broad-winged nutlet, the wing wider than body.

Where Found lower elevation woods, streambanks, slopes, terraces.

♦ *Betula pendula* subsp. *mandshurica*
(Regel) Ashburner & McAll. **ALASKA BIRCH**
Betula alaskana Sarg., *Betula neoalaskana* Sarg., *Betula papyrifera* var. *neoalaskana* (Sarg.) Raup., *Betula resinifera* Britt.

Habit tree, to 15 m tall; young twigs with yellowish, wartlike resin glands and brown-pink bark; older trees with silver-white or cream-pink papery bark marked with faint horizontal lines (lenticels); trees with slender crowns in forests, or more branched and rounded in open places. Leaves deciduous, deltoid-ovate, the base round to wedge-shaped, with doubly serrate teeth and a long, narrow tip; back of leaf dotted with glands, lower veins typically hairy. Flowers in separate, drooping male and female catkins on same twig; male catkins 2.5–4 cm long, each flower a calyx and two stamens; female catkins short (1–2 cm long) and cylindrical (0.5–1 cm wide), with numerous tiny flowers, each with one ovary and two styles. Fruit a small seed, with two papery wings, wings wider than body. Flowering late spring, before the leaves open.

Where Found the most abundant deciduous tree in Alaska, occurring across forested regions of Denali (especially after fires), and, rarely, into the subalpine.

Similar Species Young birch trees can be confused with alder (*Alnus*), but alder bark not papery and peeling; alder leaves larger, ovate (not deltoid), and its twigs not dotted with resin glands; trees of black cottonwood and quaking aspen also never have papery and peeling bark.

Traditional Uses slabs of the papery, waterproof bark have long been used in making boats and baskets. Wood used for fuel, and in cabinetry, furniture, bowls, and other

Betula papyrifera PAPER BIRCH

Betula pendula ALASKA BIRCH

handcrafts. Birch leaf tea is used for its aspirin-like effect, the sap is used as a tonic or wash on skin problems, and the bark is brewed in tea or chewed for fighting fevers and colds (Garibaldi 1999). Birch leaves can be eaten when very young, and the sap can be tapped in early spring and boiled to make a sweet syrup.

♦ *Betula pumila* L. BOG BIRCH
Betula glandulifera (Regel) E. J. Butler, *Betula nana* L.
   Habit shrub, 0.5–2 m tall, with one to several trunks to about 10 cm diameter; young twigs covered with yellowish resin dots. Leaves deciduous, alternate, orbicular, dark green above, paler below, margins round-toothed. Flowers in separate male and female catkins on same plant; male catkins 10–25 mm long; female catkins 6–10 mm long. Fruit a winged nutlet, with wings half as broad as the body. Flowering early spring, before leaf buds open.
   Where Found abundant, particularly in the subalpine zone, and a dominant shrub along much of the Park Road.
   Similar Species Denali's only shrub with round leaves having round-toothed margins.
   Traditional Uses less used medicinally than B. pendula, however young leaves consumed as food or used to make a tea with properties similar to aspirin by the Yup'ik (Lantis 1958, 1959 in Garibaldi 1999).

Note this shrub can form hybrids with Alaska birch; hybrid plants (named *Betula occidentalis*) intermediate between parent's leaf size and shape, and bark characteristics.

BORAGINACEAE
Borage Family

Amsinckia FIDDLENECK
(Amsinck was a burgomaster of Hamburg.)

♦ *Amsinckia menziesii* (Lehm.) A. Nelson & J.F. Macbr. SMALL-FLOWER FIDDLENECK
   Habit coarse annual herb, from a taproot; stems 20–80 cm tall, usually branched with sparse, rough, hairs. Leaves basal and along stem; basal leaves not persistent; stem leaves alternate, lance-oblong or elliptic, 2–12 cm long and 0.5–2.5 cm wide, with sparse stiff hairs; margins entire. Flowers in a coiled cluster (scorpioid cyme); petals yellow, fused into a tube 5–8 mm long, opening at top 2–4 mm wide, with 5 shallow lobes; calyx lobes 5, with both silky and longer stiff hairs. Fruit a group of 4 nutlets clustered together, 2–4 mm long, ovate, warty or pimply and often wrinkled.
   Where Found may occur in Denali in disturbed places.

Betula pumila BOG BIRCH

Amsinckia menziesii SMALL-FLOWER FIDDLENECK

Eritrichium
ALPINE-FORGET-ME-NOT
(Greek, wool, and small hairs.)

1 Flowers about 10 mm wide; leaves linear to narrowly oblanceolate, densely strigose with mostly appressed hairs . . . . *E. splendens*
1 Flowers about 6 mm wide; leaves ovate to ovate-lanceolate, with straight, more or less spreading hairs 2
2 Flowers scarcely exceeding leaves; leaves ovate, thickly covered with blister-like hairs . . . . *E. chamissonis*
2 Flowering stems 5–10 cm high; leaves ovate-lanceolate to oblanceolate; hairs occasionally blister-like . . . . *E. aretioides*

♦ *Eritrichium aretioides* (Cham.) DC.
MANY-FLOWER ALPINE-FORGET-ME-NOT
Eritrichium nanum var. aretioides (Cham.) Herder
  Habit cushion-forming perennial herb; stems 5-10 cm tall from a branched stem-base; base of stem with many persistent gray dead leaves. **Leaves** basal and along stem; ovate-lanceolate, densely covered in white hairs, overlapping on stem. **Flowers** in a short, dense terminal raceme; corolla 5-lobed, sky-blue, about 6 mm long; sepals fused at base, linear; stamens 5, carpel 5-parted. **Fruit** a small brown nutlet with teeth at top.
  Where Found uncommon in rocky places, and on dry, gravelly alpine tundra.

Eritrichium aretioides
MANY-FLOWER ALPINE-FORGET-ME-NOT

Similar Species plants have smaller flowers (less than 1 cm long) and are lower-growing than other *Eritrichium* (such as *E. splendens*, which has stiff hairs parallel to the leaf (the hairs of *E. aretoides* are less stiff and more spreading).

Eritrichium chamissonis A. DC.
ARCTIC ALPINE-FORGET-ME-NOT
Eritrichium nanum var. *chamissonis* (DC.) Herder
  Habit densely long-hairy perennial herb, from a branching stem-base covered with persistent leaves; flower stems barely longer than leaves. **Leaves** ovate to oblong, to about 1 cm long, dense and overlapping, thickly covered with gray blister-like hairs. **Flowers** few to many, in terminal clusters barely longer than the leaves, blue; limb of corolla about 6 mm wide. **Fruit** a nutlet, with a crown of jagged teeth.
  Where Found uncommon on alpine tundra, limestone barrens.
  Similar Species flowers and nutlets much as in *Eritrichium aretioides,* but bristles at tip of nutlet teeth often divergent or reflexed.

Eritrichium splendens Kearney
SHOWY ALPINE FORGET-ME-NOT
  Habit tufted perennial herb, from a much branched stem-base, forming a mat of numerous short, sterile, leafy shoots; flowering stems few, to about 10 cm tall. **Leaves** mostly basal, narrowly oblanceolate, 15-20 mm long, 2-3 mm wide, densely appressed-hairy; stem leaves few, sessile. **Flowers** few, in an open raceme; corolla tubular, 5-lobed, bright blue, 5-8 mm long, limb of corolla about 10 mm across. **Fruit** a nutlet about 2 mm long, with a crown of spine-like teeth.
  Where Found uncommon on alpine slopes.

Lappula STICKSEED
(Latin, *lappa,* bur, in reference to the bur-like fruit.)

♦ *Lappula squarrosa* (Retz.) Dumort.
EUROPEAN STICKSEED
Lappula echinata Gilih, *Lappula myosotis* Moench
  Habit annual or biennal herb, from a tap-root; rough-hairy throughout; stems 10-40 cm tall, usually branched. **Leaves** basal and along stem; basal leaves oblanceolate, to 8 cm long, often deciduous; stem leaves alternate, linear to narrowly oblong or oblanceolate, reduced upwards to the leafy, lanceolate bracts of the inflorescence, sessile, entire. **Flowers** in narrow, elongating clusters with

bracts throughout; flower stalks ascending to erect when in fruit; petals blue (sometimes white), fused at base into a small tube that flares at top to 5 lobes, with 5 yellow bulges in the throat; sepals hairy, about 3 mm long. Fruit a group of 4 clustered nutlets, 3–4 mm long, with 2–3 marginal rows of slender, barb-tipped prickles.

Where Found uncommon weed of roadsides, dry hillsides; native of Eurasia.

Mertensia BLUEBELLS
(In honor of German botanist C. F. Mertens.)

Mertensia paniculata (Aiton) G. Don
TALL BLUEBELLS

Habit perennial herb, from a taproot and stout rhizome or branched base; stems several, erect or ascending, glabrous or hairy, 20–60 m tall. Leaves many along stem; basal leaves few (but these sometimes the only leaves to appear in a given year); long ovate, to 15 cm long, with stiff white hairs and deeply impressed with a branching network of veins; lower leaves with long petioles, upper leaves short-petioled or sessile. Flowers in an open, loosely branched, nodding panicle, each branch bearing a row of flowers; heads; petals bell-shaped, 10–20 mm long, with five short lobes at tip, pink in bud, becoming blue; calyx short, white-hairy, Fruit a group of 4 nutlets per flower, each with a single wrinkled seed. Flowering early; the flowers in a panicle maturing sequentially.

Where Found common in floodplains, meadows, and open forest in the boreal zone, extending into subalpine meadows and shrublands, and occasionally to alpine tundra; absent from acidic bogs and heaths.

Similar Species No other plant in Denali has similar panicles of drooping blue bell flowers.

Myosotis FORGET-ME-NOT
(Greek, mouse ear.)

1 Calyx with spreading hairs, some of which are hooked . . . . *M. asiatica*
1 Calyx with appressed hairs, hooks absent . . . . *M. scorpioides*

♦ *Myosotis asiatica* (Vestergr.) Schischk. & Serg.
MOUNTAIN FORGET-ME-NOT, ASIAN FORGET-ME-NOT
Myosotis alpestris subsp. *asiatica* Vesterg.

Habit perennial herb, from fibrous roots and a branching stem-base or short rhizome, spreading-hairy throughout; stems erect to ascending, 5–40 cm tall, several to many. Leaves basal and along stem; basal leaves oblanceolate to lanceolate, with long petioles; stem leaves similar but sessile. Flowers in a terminal, compact, few-branched inflorescence, with several to many heads; corolla 5-lobed, flat, with a narrow throat, 4–10 mm wide, lobes bright blue, yellow at center; sepals 5, hairy, fused at base; stamens 5, surrounding one pistil. Fruit 4 black, shiny nutlets, each with one seed.

Where Found common in subalpine meadows, moist swales, and alpine tundra.

Similar Species similar to *Eritrichium*, another genus in the Borage family, but taller and with stem leaves; *Eritrichium* form dense cushions of basal leaves.

Note *Myosotis asiatica* is the Alaska state flower.

Lappula squarrosa EUROPEAN STICKSEED
ROLF ENGSTRAND

Myosotis asiatica MOUNTAIN FORGET-ME-NOT
ALFRED COOK

♦*Myosotis scorpioides* L.
TRUE FORGET-ME-NOT
Habit perennial herb, from fibrous roots, frequently stoloniferous as well; stems decumbent to ascending, 15–60 cm long, mostly unbranched, angled, inconspicuously appressed-hairy. Leaves alternate, lower stem leaves oblanceolate, narrowed at base; middle and upper leaves more oblong or elliptic to lance-elliptic; 2.5–8 cm long, 7–20 mm wide, nearly glabrous or with short appressed hairs, entire. Flowers in a lax, coiled, elongating terminal cluster, not much longer than leafy part of stem; petals sky-blue, fused at base into a 5-lobed tube that spreads flat (4–10 mm wide) at top; calyx 2–4 mm long, appressed-hairy. Fruit 4 nutlets clustered together, about 2 mm long, blackish, smooth, shining.
Where Found weed of waste places, introduced from Europe.

Myosotis scorpioides **TRUE FORGET-ME-NOT**

BRASSICACEAE
Mustard Family

GROUP I KEY

1 Fruit short, not more than three times longer than wide. 2
1 Fruit more than three times longer than wide 17
2 Plants essentially glabrous 3
2 Plants pubescent 6
3 Petals yellow. . . . . *Draba*
3 Petals white 4
4 Fruit broadly winged . . . . *Noccaea*
4 Fruit wingless. 5
5 Leaves subulate; small submerged aquatic plant . . . . *Subularia*
5 Leaves elliptic-oblong. . . . . *Draba*
6 Hairs simple. 7
6 Hairs forked, branched or stellate, sometimes mixed with simple hairs 10

7 Petals purple . . . . *Parrya*
7 Petals white or yellow. 8
8 Basal leaves entire or toothed . . . . *Draba*
8 Basal leaves pinnatifid or pinnate 9
9 Valves of fruit winged; seeds solitary in each locule . . . . *Lepidium*
9 Valves not winged; seeds several in each locule . . . . *Rorippa*
10 Petals deep purple; fruit ovoid, oblong or terete . . . . *Smelowskia*
10 Petals white or yellow. 11
11 Petals white 12
12 Fruit obcordate-triangular . . . . *Capsella*
12 Fruit not obcordate-triangular 13
13 Plant densely pubescent. . . . . *Smelowskia*
13 Plant not densely pubescent. 14
14 Fruit with constrictions . . . . *Braya*
14 Fruit without constrictions . . . . *Draba*
11 Petals yellow (creamy white in *Smelowskia porsildii*). 15
15 Plant short gray-hairy. . . . . *Smelowskia*
15 Plant not densely gray-hairy. 16
16 Fruit flat. . . . . *Draba*
16 Fruit globular . . . . *Lesquerella*
17 Stems and leaves glabrous 18
17 Stems and leaves pubescent, with simple, forked, branched, or stellate hairs 24
18 Petals purplish. 19
18 Petals white, pale lavender or yellowish 21
19 Leaves pinnate; valves of fruit veinless . . . . *Cardamine*
19 Leaves not pinnate; valves veined 20
20 Fruit terete; style long . . . . *Parrya*
20 Fruit linear, flat; style short . . . . . . Group II Key
21 Leaves pinnate, digitate or 3-parted *Cardamine*
21 Leaves simple. 22
22 Basal leaves sessile or nearly so . . Group II Key
22 Basal leaves long-petioled 23
23 Low, densely tufted alpine-arctic plants. . . . . *Cardamine*
23 Tall, not densely tufted plants. . . . . . . *Eutrema*
24 Hairs all simple 25
24 Hairs forked or branched or stellate (star-shaped), sometimes mixed with simple hairs 36
25 Petals purplish. 26
25 Petals white or yellow. 31
26 Stems about 2 cm high; stem leaves crowded below inflorescence . . . . *Aphragmus*
26 Stems longer 27

27 Basal leaves lyrate (lobed near base) or pinnate or simple 28

27 Basal leaves simple, entire, toothed or sinuate. 29

28 Valves of fruit veined; leaves simple or lyrate . . . . *Cardamine*

28 Valves of fruit veinless; leaves pinnate . . *Arabis*

29 Fruit 4–5 mm broad . . . . *Parrya*

29 Fruit narrower 30

30 Fruit torulose (swollen and constricted at intervals) . . . . *Braya*

30 Fruit not twisted. . . . . Group II Key

31 Petals white . . . . Group II Key

31 Petals yellow or yellowish 32

32 Stems about 2 cm high; stem leaves crowded below inflorescence . . . . *Aphragmus*

32 Stems longer 33

33 Lower leaves bi- or tri-pinnate . . . . *Descurainia*

33 Leaves not bi- or tri-pinnate 34

34 Stem angular; lower leaves lyrate . . . *Barbarea*

34 Stem terete. . . . . *Rorippa*

35 Petals purplish 36

35 Petals white or yellow. 37

36 Stem scapose or 1- to 3-leaved; fruit twisted. . . . . *Braya*

36 Stem with several leaves; fruit not twisted . . . . Group II Key

37 Petals white 38

37 Petals yellow; lower leaves pinnate 43

38 Stem leaves clasping 39

38 Stem leaves not clasping. 40

39 Stems erect, simple . . . . Group II Key

39 Stems much-branched, spreading . . . . *Crucihimalaya*

40 Plant densely pubescent, with short grayish hairs . . . . *Smelowskia*

40 Plant not densely pubescent, with short grayish hairs 41

41 Fruit torulose . . . . *Braya*

41 Fruit not torulose, flat 42

42 Fruit less than 15 mm long . . *Draba stenoloba*

42 Fruit longer. . . . . Group II Key

43 Stems with appressed forked hairs attached in the middle. . . . . *Erysimum*

43 Stems without such hairs 44

44 Fruit linear, terete . . . . *Descurainia*

44 Fruit flat, inflated . . . . *Smelowskia*

GROUP II KEY
Arabis, Arabidopsis, Boechera.

1 Mature siliques drooping . . *Boechera grahamii*

1 Mature siliques erect or angled upward 2

2 Stem leaves neither clasping nor ear-like at base . . . . *Arabidopsis kamchatica*

2 Stem leaves clasping stem, with ear-like lobes at base 3

3 Mature siliques erect but somewhat spreading away from axis of the inflorescence. . . . . *Arabis eschscholtziana*

3 Mature siliques tightly appressed against the axis of the inflorescene 4

4 Stems glabrous or sparsely stiff-hairy at base; siliques 2–3 mm thick; seeds with wings to 1 mm wide . . . . *Boechera drummondii*

4 Stems densely stiff-hairy at base; siliques 1–2 mm thick; seeds minutely winged . . . . *Arabis pycnocarpa*

Aphragmus ALEUTIAN-CRESS
(Latin, referring to lack of a septum.)

♦ *Aphragmus eschscholtzianus* Andrz. ex DC.
ALEUTIAN-CRESS

Habit small perennial herb, from a short rhizome and stolons; stems ascending, 2–5 cm tall, glabrous or minutely hairy, naked below, but with an 2–4 small leafy bracts below inflorescence. **Leaves** basal and along stem; basal leaves simple, spoon-shaped, 1.5–4 cm long, 4–8 mm wide; stem leaves crowded below raceme, oblanceolate, 5–10 mm long. **Flowers** in a short, clustered raceme; petals 2–3 mm long, longer than sepals, white or purple. **Fruit** an oblong-elliptic silicle, 6–12 mm long.

Where Found uncommon in alpine tundra and heath, often where wet.

Aphragmus eschscholtzianus
ALEUTIAN-CRESS

Arabidopsis THALECRESS
(Genus Arabis and Greek opsis, resembling.)

♦*Arabidopsis kamchatica* (Fisch. ex DC.) K.
Shimizu & Kudoh KAMCHATICA ROCKCRESS
Arabidopsis lyrata subsp. *kamchatica* (Fisch. ex DC.)
O'Kane & Al-Shehbaz, *Arabis kamchatica* (Fisch. ex DC.)
Ledeb.

Habit Biennial or short-lived perennial herb
with white flowers, from a simple or
branched stem-base; stems one to several, to
30 cm tall, simple or branched, glabrous
throughout or sparsely stiff-hairy near base.
Leaves basal and along stem; basal leaves to 6
cm long, in a rosette, lyrate-shaped and pinnately cleft with one large terminal ovate
lobe; stem leaves alternate, not clasping the
stem. Flowers in a raceme, compact early in
season, elongating as it matures; petals white
(occasionally pink), to 5.5 mm long. Fruit an
ascending silique, 2–4 cm long.

Where Found occasional along river floodplains or in other disturbed areas, especially
in subalpine and alpine areas.

Similar Species distinguished from Arabis by
its lyrate basal leaves, and the absence of
clasping stem-leaves.

Traditional Uses one of the mustards traditionally used as a salad green or cooked veg-
etable (along with *Brassica juncea, B. rapa,
Barbarea orthoceras, Lepidium densiflorum,*
and *Thlaspi arvense*) (Moerman 1998).

Arabidopsis kamchatica
KAMCHATICA ROCKCRESS

Arabis ROCKCRESS
(Latin, Arabia.)

1 Petals small, 3–5 mm long; siliques to 1 mm
   wide, erect and appressed to rachis. . . . .
   . . . . *A. pycnocarpa*
1 Petals larger, 7–9 mm long; siliques 1–2 mm
   wide, somewhat divergent from rachis . . . .
   . . . . *A. eschscholtzii*

Arabis eschscholtziana Andrz. ex Ledeb.
ESCHSCHOLTZ'S HAIRY ROCKCRESS
Arabis hirsuta var. *eschscholtziana* (Andrz. ex Ledeb.)
Rollins

Habit biennial or short-lived perennial herb,
usually from an unbranched stem-base;
stems 1-few, 20–80 cm tall, stiff-hairy
basally, glabrous above. Leaves basal and
along stem; basal leaves oblanceolate, 2–8
cm long, 0.5–2 cm wide, narrowed to a slender, fringed petiole; stem leaves broadly
ovate to oblanceolate, with clasping base and
often toothed margins. Flowers few to many
in a raceme; petals 6–9 mm long, white to
pale pink; sepals bulging on one side at base.
Fruit an erect to slightly spreading silique,
straight or slightly curved, 5–8 cm long.

Where Found uncommon in moist meadows,
gravelly floodplains.

♦*Arabis pycnocarpa* M. Hopkins
CREAM-FLOWER ROCKCRESS
Arabis hirsuta var. *pycnocarpa* (M. Hopkins) Rollins

Habit biennial or short-lived perennial herb,
from a simple stem-base; stems usually unbranched, 20–60 cm tall, strongly stiff-hairy
at base, usually glabrous above. Leaves basal
and along stem; basal leaves oblanceolate, 2–
8 cm long, 1–1.5 cm wide, often purplish beneath; narrowed to a fringed, winged petiole;
stem leaves broadly ovate, 2–10 cm long, 1–3
cm wide, usually ear-like at base and clasping stem. Flowers few to many, in a raceme;
petals 4–9 mm long, white to cream or pale
pink; outer sepals bulging on one side at
base. Fruit an erect silique, tightly appressed
to axis of inflorescence or angled slightly
outward, 4–8 cm long.

Where Found uncommon in gravelly floodplains, rocky outcrops.

Barbarea WINTERCRESS
(For Saint Barbara, fourth-century, or perhaps alluding to being only plants available
for food on Saint Barbara's Day, December,
4th.)

♦ *Barbarea orthoceras* Ledeb.
WINTERCRESS, YELLOW-ROCKET

Habit Biennial (occasionally perennial) herb, from a taproot and a simple stem-base; stems branched, erect, 20–60 cm tall, angled. **Leaves** basal and along stem; basal leaves pinnately lobed, less than 12 cm long, with 1–5 pairs of lateral lobes (terminal lobe largest), margins entire or irregularly toothed; stem leaves often clasping stem, becoming smaller upwards. **Flowers** in a raceme, terminal or more often in small racemes from lower leaf axils; petals pale yellow, broadly spoon-shaped, 3–5 mm long; sepals pale yellow-green, about 2 mm long. **Fruit** an erect to spreading-ascending silique, 2.5–5 cm long, straight.

Where Found Moist streambanks, seeps, and shores.

Boechera ROCKCRESS

Formerly included in the genus *Arabis*, but now separated from *Arabis* based on genetic and cytological data. (In honor of Tyge Wit-

trock Böcher, 1909-1983, Danish geneticist who studied subarctic plants.)

1 Mature siliques mostly erect or angled upward
.... *B. drummondii*
1 Mature siliques drooping downward.........
.... *B. grahamii*

♦ *Boechera drummondii* (A. Gray) Á. & D. Löve
DRUMMOND'S ROCKCRESS
Arabis drummondii A. Gray, *Boechera stricta* Al-Shehbaz

Habit short-lived perennial herb; stems 1–several, branched, 30–80 cm tall, glabrous throughout, or with simple or 2-branched hairs at base. **Leaves** basal and along stem; basal leaves oblanceolate to elliptic, entire, 2–7 cm long, 3–15 mm wide; stem leaves overlapping, unstalked, ear-like at base, oblong-lanceolate to linear-lanceolate, 1.5–3 cm long. **Flowers** few to many, in a raceme; petals 7–12 mm long, white; outer sepals slightly bulging on one side at base. **Fruit** a stiffly erect silique, straight or slightly curved, glabrous, 3–9 cm long.

Where Found Uncommon in disturbed areas along streams.

♦ *Boechera grahamii* (Lehm.) Windham & Al-Shehbaz **HOELBELL'S ROCKCRESS**
Arabis holboellii var. *brachycarpa* (Torr. & A. Gray) S.L. Welsh

Habit tall biennial or short-lived perennial herb; stems 1–several, simple or branched, to 1 m tall, hairy at base, usually glabrous

Arabis pycnocarpa **CREAM-FLOWER ROCKCRESS**

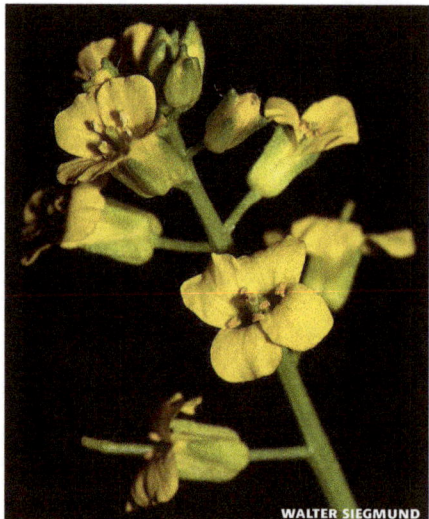

Barbarea orthoceras **WINTERCRESS**

above. Leaves basal and along stem; basal leaves in a tight rosette, oblanceolate, covered with minute stellate hairs; stem leaves opposite, clasping, oblong to linear. Flowers many, in a raceme; petals 6–10 mm long, white to purplish. Fruit a downward-hanging silique, 3–8 cm long, straight or slightly curved.

Where Found uncommon at low-elevations; in dry, rocky or sandy places such as riverbanks and open slopes.

Similar Species the decumbent, strongly appressed siliques help separate this species from other members of the Mustard family with erect or spreading fruits.

Braya NORTHERN-ROCKCRESS
(Count F. G. deBray, botanist and French ambassador to Bavaria.)

1 Flowering stem with 1 or more leaves; silique linear, about 1 mm wide . . . . *B. humilis*
1 Flowering stems leafless, or with a single leaf or bract subtending lowermost flower; silique wider 2
2 Silique lanceolate, widest near base; mature fruiting inflorescence loosely elongated . . . . *B. glabella*
2 Silique oblong, widest near middle; mature fruiting inflorescence usually densely compact . . . . *B. purpurascens*

♦ *Braya glabella* Richardson
SMOOTH NORTHERN-ROCKCRESS
Habit perennial herb, from a thick taproot; stems 5–15 cm tall, green or purplish, loosely pubescent with 2-branched hairs. Leaves basal, narrowly spatulate, 1–5 cm long, glabrous; margins fringed with hairs. Flowers in a head-like raceme in flower, elongating to 2–5 cm long in fruit; petals 5 mm long, white,

Boechera drummondii DRUMMOND'S ROCKCRESS

Braya glabella SMOOTH NORTHERN-ROCKCRESS

purplish at base; sepals shorter. Fruit a pubescent silique, 6–12 mm long.

Where Found alpine tundra.

Braya humilis (C.A. Mey.) B.L. Rob.
ALPINE NORTHERN-ROCKCRESS

Habit perennial or biennial from a taproot; stems several, erect or spreading, 5–30 cm long, simple or branched, more or less hairy with forked hairs, purplish. Leaves basal and along stem; basal leaves thick, linear-oblanceolate, 1–4 cm long, entire to somewhat toothed or wavy-margined, glabrous or somewhat hairy; stem leaves smaller, lanceolate or linear, clasping at base. Flowers in a head-like raceme in flower, elongating in fruit; petals white or purplish, 3–4 mm long; sepals about half as long as petals, deciduous. Fruit a finely hairy, cylindric silique, 1–3 cm long, erect or ascending, somewhat constricted between seeds.

Where Found may occur in Denali, on alpine slopes, open woodlands.

♦ *Braya purpurescens* (R. Br.) Bunge ex Ledeb.
SMOOTH NORTHERN-ROCKCRESS
Braya glabella subsp. *purpurascens* (R. Br.) Cody

Habit perennial herb, from a taproot; stems one to several, 4–10 cm tall, pubescent. Leaves basal, fleshy, spatulate, hairy, usually entire, arising directly from the stem-base. Flowers in a head-like raceme in flower, elongating somewhat in fruit; petals white or purplish; sepals purplish, 2 mm long. Fruit a somewhat pubescent silique, 8–10 mm long.

Where Found alpine tundra or heathlands, gravelly slopes, rock outcrops.

Capsella SHEPHERD'S-PURSE
(Latin, little box, from shape of pod.)

♦ *Capsella bursa-pastoris* (L.) Medik.
SHEPHERD'S-PURSE

Habit erect, summer or winter annual, often forming a rosette over winter, from a taproot; stems simple to branched, 10–50 cm long, with simple and starlike hairs. Leaves basal and along stem; basal leaves in rosettes, 3–6 cm long, oblanceolate, more or less entire to pinnately lobed or dissected; stem leaves few, unstalked and clasping, lanceolate to oblong-oblanceolate, with earlike lobes at base. Flowers many in a raceme; flower stalks slender, spreading, 7–15 mm long; petals white, with a distinctly stalked base, 2–4 mm long; sepals shorter than petals. Fruit a, heart-shaped to triangular silicle, 6–8 mm long, 3–5 mm wide, strongly flattened, tip broad and squared-off to slightly notched; pedicels spreading.

Where Found uncommon weed of disturbed places, native of Europe.

Cardamine BITTERCRESS
(Greek name of a cress.)

1	Dwarf plant; leaves ovate, entire. *C. bellidifolia*
1	Taller plants; leaves pinnate 2
2	Petals 4 mm long or less . . . . *C. umbellata*
2	Petals 5 mm long or longer 3
3	Stem leaves with 9–17 leaflets . . . .
	. . . . *C. polemonioides*
3	Stem leaves with 1–3 leaflets . . . . . *C. purpurea*

Braya purpurescens SMOOTH N.-ROCKCRESS

Capsella bursa-pastoris SHEPHERD'S-PURSE

Cardamine bellidifolia L.
ALPINE BITTERCRESS

Habit tufted, perennial herb, from a taproot and often branched stem-base; stems several, few-leaved, to 15 cm high (usually much smaller), glabrous. Leaves mostly in a basal rosette, ovate, entire and simple, fleshy, to 30 mm long; leaf bases often persistent. Flowers in an umbel-like raceme; petals white (rarely pale purple), 3–5 mm long; sepals to 2 mm long. Fruit an erect silique, to 3.5 cm long.

Where Found occasional in the alpine zone in rocky places.

Similar Species other species of *Cardamine* in Denali have somewhat dissected leaves, not simple as in *C. bellidifolia; Eutrema edwardsii,* also has four-petaled white flowers and ovate leaves, but that species lacks the compact basal rosette of leaves and is usually larger and found in moister places than *Cardamine bellidifolia.*

Traditional Uses plants of *Cardamine* known for juicy, succulent leaves high in vitamin C.

Cardamine polemonioides Rouy
CUCKOO BITTERCRESS
Cardamine pratensis var. *angustifolia* Hook.

Habit perennial herb, from a rhizome; stems to 30 cm tall when in flower; stems and leaves without hairs. Leaves basal and along stem; basal leaves in a rosette, pinnate, with 9–17 orbicular to lanceolate leaflets, usually shed early in season; stem leaves with linear to oblanceolate leaflets. Flowers in a raceme; petals pink to pink-purple (rarely white), 8–12 mm long; flowers typically all similar height due to lower flowers with longer pedicels. Fruit an erect, glabrous silique, to 3 cm long.

Where Found occasional at low- to mid-elevations in wet meadows, poorly drained areas, seepage slopes, and along streams, often in moss or wet sands and gravels.

Similar Species distinguished from other species of *Cardamine* by its larger flowers (petals longer than 4 mm) and glabrous stems.

Traditional Uses leaves edible.

Cardamine purpurea Cham. & Schlect.
PURPLE BITTERCRESS

Habit tufted perennial herb, from a long rhizome; stems unbranched, pubescent, to 12 cm tall. Leaves mostly basal, shiny, lyrate-pinnate (terminal segment much larger than lower segments), spatulate or obovate in outline, pubescent margins entire; stem leaves 1–3, similar to basal leaves or occasionally simple. Flowers in a raceme, with ascending pedicels; petals four, pink to purple (rarely white), 5–8 mm long. Fruit a linear silique, to 20 mm long.

Where Found occasional in moist alpine tundra and herb-mats, and on moist scree-slopes.

Similar Species distinguished from other *Cardamine* by its low-growing, tufted form, lyrate basal leaves, and pubescent stems and leaves.

Cardamine bellidifolia ALPINE BITTERCRESS

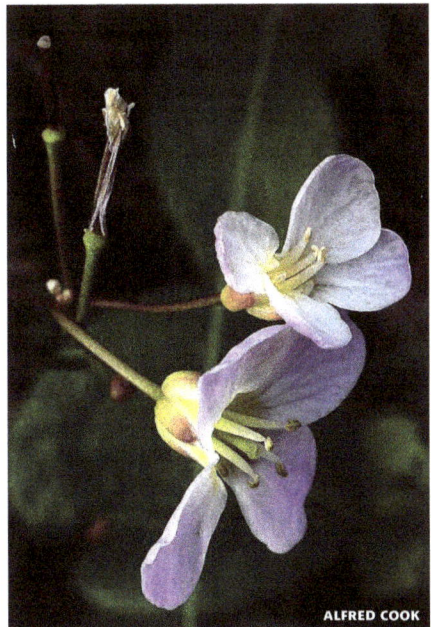

Cardamine polemonioides CUCKOO BITTERCRESS

♦*Cardamine umbellata* Greene
UMBEL BITTERCRESS
Cardamine oligosperma subsp. *kamtschatica* (Regel)
Cody

Habit glabrous perennial herb, from a tap-root; stems erect to ascending, one or more, freely branched, to 30 cm tall. Leaves both basal and along stem; basal leaves pinnately divided into 1-3 lateral pairs of ovate leaflets, with a single large 3-lobed terminal leaflet; stem leaves similar but smaller. Flowers in an umbel-like cluster; petals white, 3-4 mm long. Fruit a linear, erect silique, 15-30 mm long.

Where Found occasional in at low- to mid-elevations, in meadows, thickets, and moist places, most commonly south of Alaska Range crest.

Similar Species *Cardamine purpurea* also has pinnate leaves with a large terminal segment, but is smaller, with a more tufted habit, longer petals, and shorter siliques, and its stems are hairy.

Traditional Uses like many mustards, edible either raw or cooked, with a spicy flavor.

Crucihimalaya
FALSE FISSUREWORT
(Refers to presence in Himalayan Mountains.)

Crucihimalaya bursifolia (DC.) D.A. German &
A.L. Ebel ARCTIC FALSE FISSUREWORT
Arabidopsis mollis (Hook.) O.E. Schulz, *Arabis hookeri* Lange, *Halimolobos mollis* (Hook.) Rollins, *Transberingia bursifolia* (DC.) Al-Shehbaz & O'Kane

Habit Coarse weedy biennial herb; stems 1 to several, erect-ascending, 10-50 cm high, simple or branched, more or less glabrous above, hairy below. Leaves basal and along stem; basal leaves 3-6 cm long, oblanceolate, densely hirsute with forked hairs, margins wavy-toothed; stem leaves 1-3 cm long, sessile, auricled or sagittate, margins toothed to entire. Flowers in at first capitate, soon elongating; petals small, white; sepals and pedicels hairy. Fruit a glabrous silique, 3-5 cm long.

Where Found uncommon in disturbed places, rocky outcrops, riverbanks.

Descurainia TANSY-MUSTARD
(Francis Descurain was a friend of the botanist Jussieu.)

1 Stems sparsely to densely covered with stalked glands; racemes clustered at top of stem; upper leaves simply pinnate..........*D. sophioides*
1 Stems not covered with with stalked glands; racemes elongated; all leaves 2-3-pinnate ....
................................*D. sophia*

ALFRED COOK
Cardamine purpurea PURPLE BITTERCRESS

WALTER SIEGMUND
Cardamine umbellata UMBEL BITTERCRESS

Descurainia sophia (L.) Webb ex Prantl
HERB-SOPHIA

Habit annual or biennial herb, from a taproot; stems 20–60 cm tall, usually branched above, occasionally from base; finely star-like-hairy, often grayish, sometimes with some simple hairs. Leaves basal and along stem; basal leaves few; stem leaves very deeply 2–3× pinnately lobed or compound, ultimate lobes of leaves more or less linear. Flowers in an elongate raceme; flower stalks slender, ascending, 7–14 mm long, less than half the length of siliques; petals pale yellow, spoon-shaped, about length of sepals; sepals 2–3 mm long, greenish or yellowish. Fruit a nearly erect silique, distinctly curved, 15–30 mm long, inconspicuously constricted between seeds.

Where Found Waste places, roadsides; introduced European weed.

◆*Descurainia sophioides* (Fisch. ex Hook.) O.E. Schulz NORTHERN TANSY-MUSTARD

Habit annual or sometimes biennial herb, from a taproot; stems 10–90 cm tall, simple or branched above, finely hairy, often glandular. Leaves basal and along stem, nearly glabrous; basal leaves few; stem leaves pinnate or bipinnate, 2–12 cm long, segments oblong to oblanceolate, 1–2 mm wide. Flowers in a raceme, elongating when fruiting; flowers stalks spreading-ascending, often curved, 4–8 mm long, less than half the length of siliques; petals yellowish, about

Descurainia sophioides N. TANSY-MUSTARD

length of sepals; sepals 1.5–2 mm long, yellowish. Fruit a silique, 12–30 mm long

Where Found gravel bars, riverbanks, disturbed places; native but somewhat weedy.

Draba WHITLOW-GRASS

A complicated and confusing group of plants; the following key adapted from Flora of Alaska Project (*floraofalaska.org*). (Greek name for some member of this family.)

1 Flowering stem without leaves; flowers without subtending bracts; stems unbranched 2

1 Flowering stem with one to many leaves; flowers with or without subtending bracts; stems branched or unbranched. 19

2 Leaf underside either glabrous or with simple to 2–6 rayed hairs; fruit flattened or inflated at base; fruit straight 3

2 Leaf underside mostly pubescent with stellate, 6–12 rayed; fruit flattened and not inflated; fruit straight to slightly twisted 13

3 Leaf underside glabrous, or with both simple and multi-branched hairs; flowering stem pubescent or glabrous. 4

3 Leaf underside without simple hairs, only with 2–6 rayed hairs; flowering stem pubescent. . 11

4 Flowers white 5

4 Flowers yellow. 6

5 Leaf underside glabrous, or with simple and 2-rayed hairs; petals 2–2.5 mm long. . . . .
 . . . . *D. fladnizensis*

5 Leaf underside glabrous, or with multi-branched hairs mostly toward leaf tip; petals 3–5 mm long
 . . . . *D. lactea*

6 Flowering stem, rachis, and pedicels glabrous 7

6 Flowering stem, rachis, and pedicels hairy . . 10

7 Upperside of leaf glabrous except for ciliate margins. 8

7 Upperside of leaf hairy 9

8 Cusion-forming; fruit hairy with simple or 2–5-rayed hairs; petals 2–5 mm long; leaves not fleshy . . . . *D. densifolia*

8 Not cushion-forming; fruit glabrous; petals 1.5–2.5 mm long; leaves fleshy. . . . . . . *D. crassifolia*

9 Leaves with simple and 2 rayed hairs; petals 1.5–2.5 mm long; fruit glabrous . . . . . *D. crassifolia*

9 Leaves with simple and 2–4 rayed hairs; petals 3.5–6 mm long; fruit hairy or glabrous *D. pilosa*

10 Midvein prominent and thickened on underside of leaves . . . . *D. pilosa*

10 Midvein not prominent or noticeable and not persistent . . . . *D. stenopetala*

11 Fruit surface hairy . . . . *D. corymbosa*

11 Fruit surface glabrous 12
12 Lowest fruit pedicels 1.5–4.5 mm; ovules 10–14; fruit inflated near base; petals pale yellow . . . . *D. macounii*
12 Lowest fruit pedicels 5–17 mm; ovules 16–30; fruit not inflated; petals pale yellow to creamy white . . . . *D. juvenilis*
13 Fruit hairy. 14
13 Fruit glabrous, without hairs, or if present then only on replum (partition between segments) 16
14 Flowers yellow. . . . . *D. ruaxes*
14 Flowers white 15
15 Fruit hairs simple and 2-rayed; fruit 6–15 mm long; petal 2–3.5 mm long; stem glabrous to pubescent. *D. lonchocarpa*
15 Fruit hairs 2–15-rayed; fruit 4–8 mm long; petals 3.5–5 mm long; stem pubescent. . . . *D. cinerea*
16 Flowering stem and pedicels pubescent with stellate hairs; fruit slightly twisted or straight . . 17
16 Flowering stem and pedicels glabrous or pubescent toward the base; fruit straight 18
17 Fruit elliptic to oblong-elliptic; fruit 3.5–9 mm long; fruit surface glabrous, but sometimes with 3–6-rayed hairs on the replum . . . . . . *D. nivalis*
17 Fruit narrowly lanceolate or oblong; fruit 9–15 mm long. . . . . *D. lonchocarpa*
18 Underside of older basal leaves with a prominent or thickened midvein . . . . *D. lactea*
18 Midvein not prominent on underside of basal leaves . . . . *D. lonchocarpa*
19 Underside of leaf glabrous, or with simple to mostly 2–6-rayed hairs 20
19 Underside of leaf hairy, with predominately stellate, or 6–12-rayed hairs. 25
20 Fruit hairy. 21
20 Fruit glabrous. 22
21 Rachis glabrous; petals yellow . . . *D. nemorosa*
21 Rachis hairy; petals white. . . . . *D. borealis*
22 Flowers white, creamy white, or very faint pale yellow. 23
22 Flowers yellow. 24
23 Flowering stem glabrous; leaf underside usually glabrous or with simple hairs if present; lowest pedicel 2–6 mm long . . . . *D. fladnizensis*
23 Flowering stem pubescent; leaf underside with cruciform or 2-rayed hairs; lowest pedicel 5–18 mm long . . . . *D. juvenilis*
24 Fruiting pedicels long (7–28 mm), longer than fruit. . . . . *D. nemorosa*
24 Fruiting pedicels short (3–14 mm), nearly equal to or shorter than fruit . . . . *D. stenoloba*
25 Lowest flowers with subtending bracts 26

25 Flowers without subtending bracts 28
26 Fruit surface glabrous. . . . . *D. glabella*
26 Fruit surface hairy 27
27 Rachis pubescent; flowers 15–47; lowest pedicel 2–5 mm long; sepals 1.5–2 mm long . . *D. cana*
27 Rachis glabrous; flowers 3–9; lowest pedicel 3–10 mm long; sepals 2–3.5 mm long *D. glabella*
28 Fruit glabrous. 29
28 Fruit hairy, or valve surface glabrous but with hairs present on replum 30
29 Petals 4–5.5 mm long; stem leaves 2–17; stembase simple or branched . . . . *D. glabella*
29 Petals 2–4 mm long; stem leaves usually 1; stembase branched . . . . *D. lonchocarpa*
30 Fruit with hairs 2–5 rayed, or if surface glabrous then with 3–6-rayed hairs on the replum . . . 31
30 Fruit with both simple and 2–5-rayed hairs. . 32
31 Fruit glabrous except for hairs on the replum; petals 2.5–3.5 mm long; lowest pedicel 1–4 mm long. . . . . *D. nivalis*
31 Fruit covered with dense stellate hairs; petals 3.5–4.5 mm long; lowest pedicel 4–7 mm long . . . . *D. cinerea*
32 Leaf margins finely toothed; stem leaves 2–17; fruit straight . . . . *D. glabella*
32 Leaf margins entire; stem leaves 1–2; fruit straight or slightly twisted . . . . *D. lonchocarpa*

⬧ ***Draba aurea*** Vahl ex Hornem.
GOLDEN ROCKCRESS
Habit perennial herb, from a taproot; stems simple or branched, erect or decumbent at base, 10–50 cm tall, hairs long and simple or often branched. Leaves basal and along stem; basal leaves oblanceolate, 1–4 cm long; stem leaves mostly 10–20, ovate to lanceolate or oblanceolate, 0.5–3 cm long; densely hairy, lower leaf surface with mostly starlike hairs. Flowers 5–50, in a raceme, occasionally with solitary flowers or lateral racemes in upper leaf axils; flower stalks 3–20 mm long, appressed to axis of inflorescence, hairy; petals pale to deep yellow, rounded, 4.5–6 mm long; sepals 2–3.5 mm long, soft-hairy. Fruit a silique, 7–20 mm long, pubescent, usually contorted.
Where Found uncommon on gravelly slopes, rock outcrops.

Draba borealis DC. NORTHERN ROCKCRESS
Habit loosely tufted perennial herb, from a taproot and a simple or branched stem-base; stems branched, often decumbent decumbent at base, 5–40 cm tall, hairy with some long, simple or occasionally branched hairs;

often purplish (under the hairs). Leaves basal and along stem; basal leaves oblanceolate, 0.6–5 cm long; stem leaves 3–8, similar to basal leaves but slightly smaller; leaves hairy with starlike hairs and also straight, simple or branched hairs. Flowers several to many, in a raceme, occasionally with solitary flowers in axils of upper leaves; petals white to cream, 4–6 mm long; sepals 2–3 mm long, soft-hairy. Fruit a sparsely hairy silique, to 10 mm long, about half as wide, often somewhat twisted.

Where Found uncommon in alpine tundra, heath, gravelly banks and shores.

♦ *Draba cana* Rydb. HOARY WHITLOW-GRASS
Draba breweri var. *cana* (Rydb.) Rollins

Habit loosely tufted perennial herb, from a taproot and a simple or branched stem-base; stems branched, erect or decumbent at base, 5–25 cm tall, densely hairy with simple and starlike hairs. Leaves basal and along stem; basal leaves oblanceolate, 1–4 cm long, 1–4 mm wide, margins entire or with 1–2 teeth near tip; stem leaves 5–8, lanceolate; leaves densely hairy with simple or branched hairs. Flowers several to many (less than 60), in a raceme, usually some in leaf axils; petals white, 3–5 mm long; sepals about 2 mm long, sparsely soft-hairy. Fruit a lanceolate silique, to 12 mm long, often twisted; usually soft-hairy.

Where Found gravelly river terraces and slopes.

♦ *Draba cinerea* Adams
GRAY-LEAF WHITLOW-GRASS

Habit tufted perennial herb, from a taproot and a simple or branched stem-base; stems branched, erect, 6–20 cm tall, starlike-hairy, mixed with simple or branched hairs. Leaves basal and along stem; basal leaves oblanceolate, 0.5–3 cm long, 2–6 mm wide; stem leaves absent, or 1–4, lanceolate to ovate, to 1.5 cm long; hairy with overlapping starlike

Draba cana HOARY WHITLOW-GRASS

Draba aurea GOLDEN ROCKCRESS

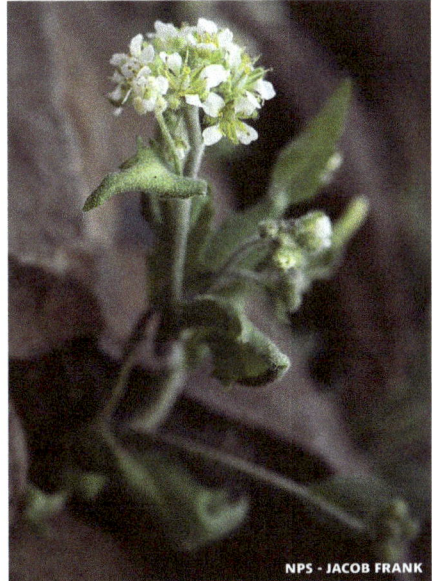

Draba cinerea GRAY-LEAF WHITLOW-GRASS

hairs, or nearly glabrous. Flowers several to many, in a long raceme, sometimes with solitary flowers in upper leaf axils; flower stalks 3–8 mm long (or more), spreading to semierect, hairy; petals white to cream, notched at tip, 3–4 mm long; sepals about 2 mm long, densely hairy. Fruit a silique, 6–8 mm long, flat, often densely hairy with appressed branched hairs.

Where Found uncommon in alpine tundra, heath, and rocky slopes.

♦ *Draba corymbosa* R. Br. ex DC.
FLAT-TOP WHITLOW-GRASS
Habit densely tufted perennial herb, from a taproot and much-branched stem-base, forming compact, rounded tussocks; stems 1–5 cm tall, hairy with simple and branched hairs. Leaves basal, withering but persistent, in a densely crowded rosette, long-hairy on upper surface with simple and branched hairs, lower surface with branched, crosslike and starlike hairs. Flowers 2–8, in a raceme; petals pale yellow. Fruit a silique, rarely twice as long as wide, pubescent ith short, simple and once-forked hairs.

Where Found uncommon on alpine slopes.

Draba crassifolia Graham
SNOWBED WHITLOW-GRASS
Habit biennial or perennial herb, from a taproot and a simple or branched stem-base; stems branched, erect, 2–12 cm tall, glabrous or nearly so. Leaves basal, ovate to oblanceolate, to 2 cm long, 1–6 mm wide, usually glabrous or with a few simple and branched hairs; margins glabrous or fringed with simple or branched hairs; stem leaves absent or rarely one. Flowers 2–12, in an open raceme; petals 2 mm long, pale yellow, fading to white; sepals shorter, often suffused with purple, glabrous. Fruit an elliptic silique, 4–10 mm long, glabrous or nearly so.

Where Found uncommon in alpine tundra, rocky outcrops.

♦ *Draba densifolia* Nutt.
DENSE-LEAF WHITLOW-GRASS
Habit tufted perennial herb, from a taproot and a usually branched stem-base; stems erect, 1–5 cm tall, glabrous to hairy with simple and branched hairs. Leaves basal, linear to linear-oblanceolate, to 1.5 cm long, upper surface usually glabrous, lower surface with simple and branched hairs; margins fringed with stiff simple hairs. Flowers 3–15, in a raceme; flower stalks 2–5 mm long, hairy; petals yellow, 2–6 mm long; sepals 2–3 mm long, soft-hairy. Fruit an ovate or orbicular, 2 silicle, 2–7 mm long, 2–4 mm wide, more or less pubescent.

Where Found uncommon in alpine tundra.

Draba fladnizensis Wulfen
AUSTRIAN WHITLOW-GRASS
Habit tufted perennial herb, from a taproot and a simple or branched stem-base; stems erect, 2–10 cm tall, glabrous. Leaves usually all basal, oblanceolate, 0.3–1 cm long, 1–2 mm wide, somewhat hairy with simple and some branched hairs; margins fringed with long, simple hairs; stem leaves absent or sometimes one. Flowers 3–12, in a raceme; flower stalks 2–10 mm long, glabrous; petals white, 2–3 mm long; sepals about 1 mm long, sparsely long-hairy. Fruit a silique, 3–6 mm long, usually glabrous to finely hairy.

Where Found rocky alpine slopes.

Draba corymbosa FLAT-TOP WHITLOW-GRASS

Draba densifolia DENSE-LEAF WHITLOW-GRASS

♦ *Draba glabella* Pursh
SMOOTH WHITLOW-GRASS

Habit loosely tufted perennial herb, from a taproot and a simple or branched stem-base; stems erect, 10–40 cm tall, with stellate hairs, rarely with a few simple hairs below. Leaves basal and along stem; basal leaves oblanceolate, 1–4 cm long, 2–10 mm wide; stem leaves 2–10, ovate to lanceolate, 1–3 cm long, sessile; leaves pubescent with simple and branched hairs; margins fringed with simple or branched hairs. Flowers several to many, in a raceme, occasionally with solitary flowers in upper leaf axils; flower stalks 2–15 mm long, ascending, straight, sparsely soft-hairy to glabrous; petals white, occasionally cream to yellow, notched at the tips, 4–5 mm long; sepals 2–3 mm long, sparsely soft-hairy.

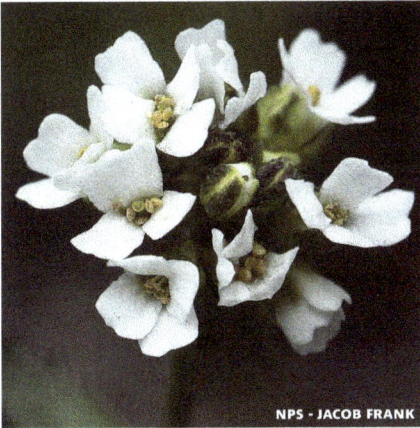

Draba glabella SMOOTH WHITLOW-GRASS

NPS - JACOB FRANK

Draba juvenilis LONG-STALK DRABA

UNKNOWN

Fruit a silique, 5–15 mm long, glabrous or nearly so.
Where Found occasional in alpine tundra, heath.

♦ *Draba juvenilis* Komarov LONG-STALK DRABA
Draba longipes Raup

Habit loosely tufted perennial herb, from a taproot; stems decumbent at base, 10–15 cm tall, sparsely hairy with branched or starlike hairs, sometimes with a few long simple hairs near base. Leaves mostly basal in a loose rosette, lanceolate to oblanceolate, to 2.5 cm long, pubescent with branched hairs, margins entire or slightly toothed; stems often with a few small leaves, or leaves absent. Flowers 3–15, in a terminal raceme; petals 3–5 mm long, white to light yellow. Fruit a silique, 5–11 mm long, usually glabrous, flattened and not twisted.
Where Found occasional in wet to well-drained alpine sites; on gravel bars, meadows, scree-slopes, snowbeds, and tundra, primarily north of Alaska Range crest.
Similar Species one of the most common alpine species of *Draba* in Denali; *Draba nivalis* is another common, white-flowered *Draba*, but it has tiny leaves in dense basal rosettes.

♦ *Draba lactea* Adams MILKY WHITLOW-GRASS

Habit loosely tufted perennial herb from a taproot and a usually branched stem-base; stems erect, 5–10 cm tall, glabrous. Leaves usually all basal, linear-oblong, 0.5–2 cm long, 1–5 mm wide, pubescent with at least some branched or starlike hairs; midribs persistent; margins fringed with stiff hairs; stem leaves absent or one. Flowers 3–5, in a raceme; flower stalks 1–8 mm long, glabrous or sometimes starlike short-hairy; petals creamy white, 3–4 mm long; sepals about 2 mm long, sparsely soft-hairy. Fruit a dark green silique, 5–10 mm long, glabrous.
Where Found alpine tundra, snowbeds.

♦ *Draba lonchocarpa* Rydb.
LANCE-POD WHITLOW-GRASS

Habit tufted perennial herb from a taproot; stems tufted, 2–10 cm tall, glabrous to finely feltlike and woolly with starlike hairs. Leaves usually all basal, linear to oblanceolate, 0.5–1.5 cm long, 1–5 mm wide, densely covered with feltlike and woolly branched hairs; midribs firm, withering but persistent; margins toothed; stem leaves absent or sometimes 1–2. Flowers 3–12, in a raceme; petals white, 3–4 mm long. Fruit a silique, 5–10 mm long, somewhat twisted.

Where Found alpine turf, talus slopes, rock outcrops.

Draba macounii O.E. Schulz
MACOUN'S WHITLOW-GRASS

Habit tufted perennial herb from a taproot and a branching stem-base; stems 2–3 cm tall, sparsely hairy with simple and branched hairs. Leaves basal, oblanceolate, 0.5–1 cm long, 2.5–5 mm wide, pubescent with tangled

Draba lactea MILKY WHITLOW-GRASS

Draba lonchocarpa LANCE-POD WHITLOW-GRASS

simple and branched hairs; margins fringed with hairs. Flowers 4–8, in a raceme; petals pale yellow, drying white, 3–5 mm long. Fruit a silique, 5–7 mm long, about half as wide, glabrous, dark green.

Where Found uncommon in alpine turf, talus.

♦ *Draba nemorosa* L.
WOODLAND WHITLOW-GRASS

Habit annual herb from slender taproot; stems simple or branched, 5–25 cm tall, hairy with both branched and starlike hairs, sometimes with some simple hairs or nearly glabrous. Leaves basal and along stem; basal leaves few; stem leaves on lower third of stem, narrowly ovate or spoon-shaped; 1–3 cm long, pubescent with simple and branched hairs. Flowers 10–40, in a raceme, long and lax; petals light yellow, 2–3 mm long; sepals 2 mm long, sparsely soft-hairy to glabrous. Fruit a silique, 4–10 mm long, glabrous.

Where Found somewhat weedy, usually where disturbed; considered adventive in Alaska and throughout its North American range.

♦ *Draba nivalis* Lilj. **ARCTIC DRABA**

Habit small, tufted perennial herb, from a taproot; stems branched, 3–15 cm tall, with

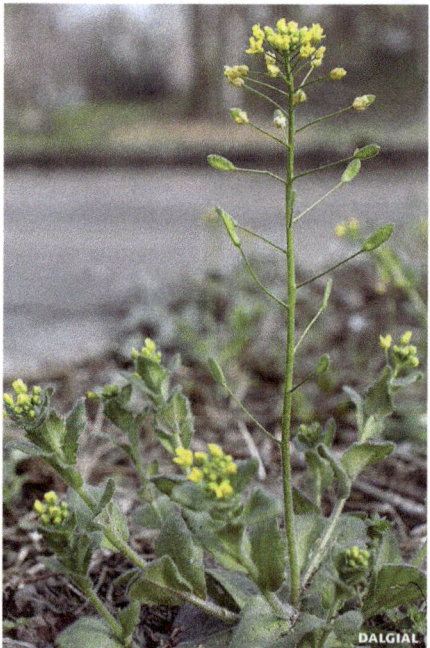
Draba nemorosa WOODLAND WHITLOW-GRASS

gray stellate (star-like) hairs. Leaves in a basal rosette, oblong-obovate, densely covered with gray stellate hairs; margins entire. Flowers 3–12, in a raceme elongating with age; petals 3–4 mm long, white; sepals about 2 mm long. Fruit a flattened, linear-elliptic silique, 6–9 mm long, glabrous to pubescent.

Where Found Alpine scree, rock outcrops, dry gravelly tundra.

Similar Species *Draba longipes* another common, white-flowered *Draba,* but it has larger, oblanceolate leaves, and the pedicels longer than the siliques.

◆ *Draba pilosa* Adams ex DC.
ALPINE ROCKCRESS
Draba alpina var. *pilosa* (Adams ex DC.) O.E. Schulz

Habit tufted perennial herb, stem-base with thick covering of withered leaves; stems 3–10 cm tall, pubescent. Leaves basal (rarely with one stem leaf), oblanceolate to oblong or elliptic, 5–20 mm long, pubescent with simple and branched hairs; margins conspicuously fringed with long hairs. Flowers 4–12, in a raceme; flower stalks 3–10 mm long; petals yellow, about 5 mm long; sepals 2–3.5 mm long. Fruit a silique, 5–9 mm long, glabrous or finely hairy.

Where Found alpine tundra, heathlands, snowbeds.

Note formerly treated as *Draba alpina* L., that species now considered absent in Alaska.

Draba ruaxes Payson & H.St. John
RAINIER WHITLOW-GRASS

Habit tufted perennial herb, from a taproot and a branched stem-base, often clothed with dried remains of old leaves; stems 2–6 cm tall, hairy with simple and branched hairs. Leaves basal, ovate to elliptic or oblanceolate, 5–12 mm long, pubescent with simple and branched hairs; margins entire. Flowers 3–10, in a short raceme; petals yellow, 4–5 mm long; sepals 2–2.5 mm long, soft-hairy. Fruit a silique, 5–8 mm long, oval to ovate, densely soft-hairy with simple and branched hairs; fruiting stalks almost as long as silicles.

Where Found uncommon on alpine scree, often on limestone.

◆ *Draba stenoloba* Ledeb.
ALASKA WHITLOW-GRASS

Habit biennial or short-lived perennial herb, from a slender taproot and a usually simple stem-base; stems simple or branched, 3–32 cm tall, pubescent below mainly with cross-like branched hairs, commonly glabrous above. Leaves basal and along stem; basal leaves 10–25 in a rosette, ovate to oblanceolate, to 3 cm long; stem leaves one to several; with simple and branched hairs. Flowers few, in an often compound raceme; flower stalks ascending, 3–15 mm long, usually glabrous, seldom hairy; petals 3–4 mm long, yellow, often fading to white; sepals 1–2 mm long,

Draba nivalis ARCTIC DRABA

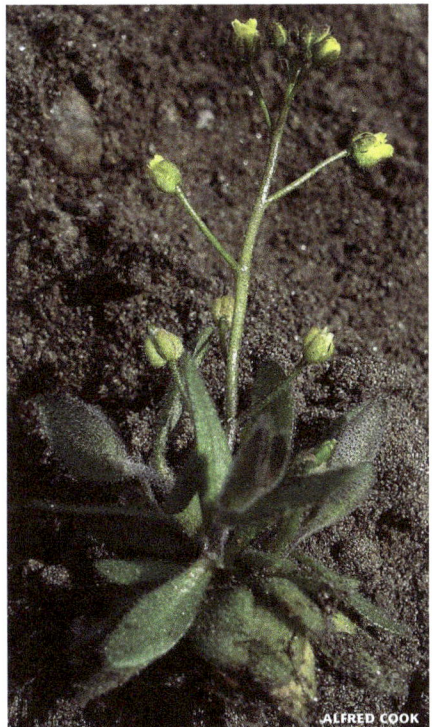

Draba pilosa ALPINE ROCKCRESS

soft-hairy. Fruit a silique 10–15 mm long; narrowly elliptic to narrowly ovate, glabrous or rarely hairy.

Where Found uncommon in alpine tundra and meadows.

◆ *Draba stenopetala* Trautv.
ANADYR DRABA, STAR-FLOWERED DRABA

Habit small tufted perennial herb, from a taproot and a branched stem-base densely clothed with persistent leaves; stems short, only 0.5 –2 cm above the leaves, with simple to 3-branched hairs. Leaves basal, spatulate, to 3 mm long, pubescent with simple and branched hairs. Flowers 2–4, in a very short-stalked raceme; petals yellow (rarely purple), very narrow; sepals reflexed and covered with simple and branched hairs. Fruit a silique, 3–4 mm long, glabrous or sometimes hairy.

Where Found uncommon on high-elevation gravelly or rocky scree-slopes, tundra, meadows, and fell-fields.

Similar Species the combination of small, rosette forming leaves, and flowers with four narrow, yellow petals is diagnostic for *Draba stenopetala;* it could possibly be confused with cushion saxifrage (*Saxifraga eschscholtzii*) based on the leaves, but in that species the flowers are five-parted, and the fruit a two-beaked capsule, not a round silique.

Draba stenoloba ALASKA WHITLOW-GRASS

Erysimum WALLFLOWER

(Greek *eryso,* to ward off or to cure, alluding to supposed medicinal properties of some species.)

1 Petals pink to pinkish-purple . . . . *E. pallasii*
1 Petals yellow to deep orange 2
2 Petals 3–5 mm long; siliques 1.5–3 cm long . . . . *E. cheiranthoides*
2 Petals 5–10 mm long; siliques 2.5–5 cm long . . . . *E. inconspicuum*

Erysimum cheiranthoides L.
WORM-SEED WALLFLOWER

Habit annual or biennial herb, from a taproot; stems simple or branched, 3–10 dm tall, leafy, sparsely hairy with 2-pronged hairs. Leaves lanceolate, 2–8 cm long, finely hairy with 3-pronged hairs; margins entire or finely toothed. Flowers in a raceme; flower stalks 4–15 mm long, spreading or spreading-ascending; petals pale yellow, 3–5 mm long; sepals yellowish or greenish, 2–3 mm long. Fruit an ascending to erect silique, 2–3 cm long, 1 mm wide, round in cross section, finely appressed-hairy; beak 0.5–1 mm long.

Where Found uncommon in disturbed places; introduced from Eurasia.

Draba stenopetala ANADYR DRABA

♦ *Erysimum inconspicuum* (S. Watson)
MacMill. SHY WALLFLOWER

Habit biennial or short-lived perennial herb,
from a short taproot and a usually unbranched stem-base; stems erect, 3–10 dm
tall, simple or branched, hairy throughout
with appressed, 2-pronged hairs. Leaves basal
and along stem; basal leaves linear to linear-
oblanceolate, entire or with a few teeth, 2–7
cm long, 2–6 mm wide; stem leaves becoming smaller and unstalked upwards. Flowers in
a raceme; flower stalks 3–6 mm long, ascending; petals pale to bright yellow, 5–10
mm long; sepals narrow, often purplish, 4–6
mm long, densely hairy. Fruit a silique, 2–5 cm
long, 1–2 mm wide, ascending to erect,
densely hairy with 2-pronged hairs; beak 1–2
mm long.

Where Found uncommon on dry slopes,
gravelly streambanks, open woods.

Erysimum inconspicuum SHY WALLFLOWER

Erysimum pallasii PALLAS' WALLFLOWER

♦ *Erysimum pallasii* (Pursh) Fernald
PALLAS' WALLFLOWER

Habit perennial or biennial herb, from a
thick taproot and branched or unbranched
stem-base; flowering stems short, elongating
in fruit to 20 cm tall, hairy. Leaves in a basal
rosette, grayish, linear to oblong, margins
entire or irregularly toothed. Flowers with
four purple or pink petals, 1–2 cm long. Fruit
an elongate, sometimes curved silique 3–9
cm long, ascending from the stem.

Where Found uncommon in dry gravelly tundra and calcareous rubble and scree.

Similar Species the only species in Denali
with a cluster of four-petaled purple flowers
and linear leaves; wallflowers also with distinctive two-parted hairs attached at their
middle.

Eutrema MOCK WALLFLOWER
(Greek, well, and opening, referring to the in-
complete septum.)

♦ *Eutrema edwardsii* R. Br.
EDWARDS' MOCK WALLFLOWER

Habit perennial herb, from a slender taproot and a simple or branching stem-base;

Eutrema edwardsii
EDWARDS' MOCK WALLFLOWER

stems 1-20, decumbent-ascending to erect, glabrous; this is a tiny, easily overlooked alpine plant. Leaves both basal and along stem; basal leaves with long petioles; stem leaves opposite, elliptic to lanceolate. Flowers in a dense raceme, elongating in fruit; petals 4, white, spatulate, longer than the sepals. Fruit an elliptic-cylindric silique (long, thin seedpod).

Where Found uncommon in moist to wet alpine meadows, tundra, and dwarf scrub.

Similar Species *Cardamine bellidifolia,* but that plant with a basal rosette of leaves, not stem leaves.

Lepidium PEPPERGRASS
(Greek, a little scale, from the shape of the pod.)

♦ *Lepidium densiflorum* Schrad.
COMMON PEPPERGRASS

Habit annual herb, from a slender taproot; stems usually single, erect, 10-50 cm tall, branched above, short-hairy. Leaves basal and along stem; basal leaves usually absent by flowering time; stem leaves 3-10 cm long, entire to saw-toothed or pinnately divided into toothed segments, reduced upwards. Flowers numerous, in an elongate raceme; flower stalks slightly ascending, 2-4 mm long; petals absent; sepals about 1 mm long. Fruit a round to ovate silicle, 3-3.5 mm long; beak absent.

Where Found uncommon in disturbed places; weedy, but considered native in western and central North America.

Noccaea PENNYCRESS
(In honor of Domenico Nocca, 1758-1841, Italian clergyman, botanist, and director of botanic garden at Pavia.)

♦ *Noccaea arctica* (A.E.Porsild) Holub
ARCTIC PENNYCRESS
Thlaspi arcticum A.E. Porsild

Habit glabrous perennial herb, with a many-branched stem-base; stems one to several, simple, at anthesis 3-5 cm long, in fruit to 15 cm tall. Leaves basal and along stem; basal leaves spatulate, 10-25 mm long, somewhat fleshy, entire, the midrib prominent; stem leaves 3-5, linear, sessile Flowers in a short raceme (elongating in fruit); petals white, 4-5 mm long; Fruit a silicle, 6-7 mm long.

Where Found uncommon in alpine tundra turf.

Parrya FALSE WALLFLOWER
(In honor of William E. Parry, 1790-1855, arctic explorer during whose first expedition to the North American arctic specimens of the genus were first collected.)

♦ *Parrya nudicaulis* (L.) Regel
NAKED-STEM FALSE WALLFLOWER

Habit perennial herb, from a stout taproot and stem-base; flowering stem single, leaf-less, hairless, to 20 cm tall. Leaves basal, simple, glabrous, ovate-lanceolate to spatulate, margin with gland-tipped hairs. Flowers 3-20, in a dense raceme; petals 4, purple or pink (rarely white), 1.5-2 cm long. Fruit an elongate silique, 2-5 cm long. Flowering early, shortly after snowmelt.

Where Found occasional in alpine tundra, snow beds, mossy streambanks, seeps, wet meadows, and sandy slopes.

Similar Species the flower's large size and

Lepidium densiflorum COMMON PEPPERGRASS

Noccaea arctica ARCTIC PENNYCRESS

purple or pink petals distinguish it from other members of the mustard family.

Physaria BLADDERPOD

(Greek *physa,* bladder, alluding to inflated fruitsof some species.)

Parrya nudicaulis
NAKED-STEM FALSE WALLFLOWER

♦ *Physaria arctica* (Wormsk. ex Hornem.) O'Kane & Al-Shehbaz ARCTIC BLADDERPOD
Lesquerella arctica (Wormsk. ex Hornem.) S. Watson

Habit perennial herb, with stellate pubescence, from a short taproot and woody stembase; stems decumbent to erect, 4–15 cm tall, usually simple. Leaves basal and along stem; basal leaves in a rosette, ovate to oblanceolate, stalked, entire, 2–8 cm long; stem leaves much smaller, unstalked or short-stalked, densely hairy, the hairs starlike. Flowers in a loose raceme; flower stalks ascending to erect, 5–20 mm long; petals yellow, 5–6 mm long; sepals shorter, hairy, the hairs starlike. Fruit a nearly round silicle, 5–7 mm long, with a short beak, glabrous or hairy, the hairs starlike.

Where Found uncommon on rocky slopes and cliffs, gravelly streambanks, and often where calcareous.

Physaria arctica ARCTIC BLADDERPOD

Rorippa YELLOWCRESS
(Saxon *rorippen*, name cited by Euricius Cordus, 1515-1544.)

1 Fruit globose to pear-shaped, with 4–6 segments
. . . .*R. barbareifolia*
1 Fruit elliptic to cylindric, with 2 segments. . . . .
. . . . *R. palustris*

Rorippa barbareifolia (DC.) Kitag.
HOARY YELLOWCRESS
Habit annual herb, from a taproot; stems erect, 30–70 cm tall, usually single, branched above, densely long-hairy toward base, long-hairy to glabrous above. **Leaves** both basal and along stem; basal leaves compound, lyrate-pinnate, margins irregularly serrate; stem leaves sessile, lanceolate in outline, irregularly serrate, lower stem leaves typically pinnate, becoming lobed upward on stem. **Flowers** in racemes, terminal and from axils of stem leaves; petals yellow, 2–4 mm long. **Fruit** a round, glabrous silicle (short pod), 4–6 mm long.
Where Found low-elevation wet places such as streambanks and lakeshores.
Similar Species *Barbarea orthoceras,* another tall yellow-flowered mustard with lyrate leaves, but that plant has seedpods that are long and narrow, not round.
Traditional Uses leaves edible, with a spicy flavor.

♦ Rorippa palustris (L.) Besser
BOG YELLOWCRESS
Habit annual, biennial, or short-lived perennial herb, from a slender taproot; stems erect, 10–40 cm tall, simple to much branched from base, glabrous to stiffly hairy. **Leaves** both basal and along stem, oblong to elliptic in outline, margins varying from irregularly toothed to pinnatifid; stem leaves alternate, becoming smaller upward on stem. **Flowers** many, in a branched terminal raceme; petals four, short, yellow. **Fruit** an elliptic silique (elongated seedpod), 4–8 mm long.
Where Found open peaty soil, wet places at low-elevations.
Similar Species *Rorippa barbareifolia* has lyrate-pinnatifid leaves and a round silique.
Traditional Uses like many mustards, leaves edible, with a spicy flavor.

Smelowskia FALSE CANDYTUFT
(In honor of Timotheus Smielowsky, 1769-1815, Russian botanist and pharmacist from St. Petersburg.)

1 Flowers creamy white; stems mostly branched from near base. . . . .*S. porsildii*
1 Flowers white or purple; stems simple or branched 2
2 Basal leaves palmately 3–5-lobed; petals purple; silique ovate to oblong or linear . . . .
. . . . *S. borealis*
2 Basal leaves pinnately divided to midrib, 7–9-lobed; petals white; silique pear-shaped. . . . . . .
. . . . *S. pyriformis*

♦ Smelowskia borealis (Greene) W.H. Drury & Rollins NORTHERN FALSE CANDYTUFT
Habit densely short-hairy perennial herb; stems several, drooping, 6–30 cm long; plants growing with a long, woody, pliable taproot, allowing it to move as rocks shift in its typical habitat of loose rock. **Leaves** mostly

ANDREY ZHARKIKH
Rorippa palustris BOG YELLOWCRESS

in a basal rosette, fuzzy, often surrounded by withered leaves of previous years at base of stem; leaves oblong to wedge-shaped with a 3-lobed tip, grayish green and pubescent; stem leaves similar, but smaller and without petioles. Flowers 20–40, in a raceme; petals pink-purple, larger than sepals; sepals persistent and purplish. Fruit an oblong to ovate silique, 8–10 mm long.

Where Found uncommon at high-elevations on calcareous, loose scree-slopes and gravelly tundra.

Similar Species No other plant in Denali is densely woolly, with several flattened stems, bearing clusters of pink-purple flowers.

Smelowskia porsildii (W.H. Drury & Rollins) Jurtzev ALPINE FALSE CANDYTUFT
Smelowskia calycina subsp. *integrifolia* (Seem.) Hultén

Habit densely tufted perennial herb, from an elongate rhizome and a branched stem-base, covered with withered and persistent leaf bases; stems 1.5–20 cm tall, few to numerous, simple, sparsely to densely hairy with branched and simple hairs. Leaves basal and along stem; basal leaves linear to wedge-shaped or ovate, to 10 cm long, entire to pinnately divided, sparsely to densely hairy with branched hairs, petioles slender, conspicuously fringed with hairs near their base; stem leaves several, reduced, nearly sessile. Flowers in a rounded head, elongating in fruit to 10 cm long; flower stalks ascending to spreading, 5–10 mm long, hairy with gener-

ally simple hairs; petals white to purplish tinged, 5–7 mm long; sepals often pinkish or purplish tinged, 2–3 mm long, soft-hairy, deciduous just after anthesis. Fruit a linear to narrowly oblong silique, 5–12 mm long, glabrous (rarely hairy), slightly flattened or nearly round in cross section.

Where Found uncommon in alpine tundra, scree slopes.

Smelowskia pyriformis W.H. Drury & Rollins
PEAR-FRUIT FALSE CANDYTUFT

Habit perennial herb, from a stout stem-base covered with old leaf bases; stems 5–15 cm long, branched from near base, pubescent with branched and simple hairs. Leaves basal and along stem; basal leaves 25–40 mm long, oblong to ovate in outline, pinnately divided into 7–9 segments, densely pubescent; stem leaves smaller upwards. Flowers in a raceme, on spreading to ascending, pubescent pedicels, 3–7 mm long; petals about 3 mm long, white or cream. Fruit a pear-shaped, glabrous silique, 5–8 mm long.

Where Found may occur in Denali on rocky slopes; endemic to Alaska.

Subularia WATER-AWLWORT
(Latin, an awl, from the shape of the leaves.)

Subularia aquatica L. WATER-AWLWORT
Habit small, tufted, annual aquatic herb from fibrous roots; stems erect, 1–10 cm tall, glabrous. Leaves basal and along stem; basal

Smelowskia borealis NORTHERN FALSE CANDYTUFT

leaves erect, linear and awl-like, 1–5 cm long, about 1 mm wide, entire; stem leaves similar, few, reduced. Flowers few, in an open raceme-like inflorescence elongating to 5–10 cm long; petals white, to 1 mm long; sepals green, erect, glabrous. Fruit an elliptic or obovoid silicle, 2–3 mm long, to 2 mm wide, inflated, glabrous.

Where Found uncommon in shallow ponds, where rooted in silty soil.

CAMPANULACEAE
Bellflower Family

1 Leaves entire; corolla funnel-shaped, with lobes as long as the tube . . . . . *Melanocalyx uniflora*
1 Leaves toothed; corolla bell-shaped, shallowly lobed . . . . *Campanula lasiocarpa*

Campanula BELLFLOWER
(Latin, *campana*, a bell.)

♦*Campanula lasiocarpa* Cham.
MOUNTAIN HAREBELL
Habit tiny perennial herb, with a solitary vi-olet-blue bell-shaped flower, from a thin, branching rhizome; stems single to several, erect or ascending, 5–10 cm tall, smooth or slightly hairy. Leaves primarily in a basal rosette 1–3 cm wide; elliptic to oblanceolate, margins coarsely serrate, petioles long; stem leaves alternate, sessile, reduced. Flowers usu-ally solitary, petals fused into a large blue to purple corolla, 1.5–3.5 cm long, with ovate lobes shorter than the tube; calyx lobes lin-ear to lanceolate, toothed, with white hairs.

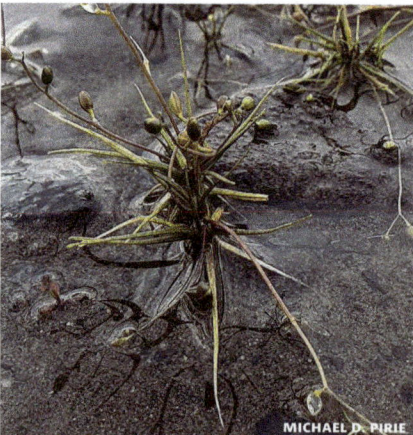

Subularia aquatica WATER-AWLWORT

Fruit a many-seeded, oblong capsule, opening by pores.

Where Found common in well-drained alpine sites such as sandy or rocky tundra and rock outcrops, primarily on non-calcare-ous soil.

Similar Species Arctic-bellflower (*Melanoca-lyx uniflora*) lacks dentate leaves and toothed sepals, and its floral tube is much narrower and only slightly longer than the calyx.

Traditional Uses the stems are edible.

Melanocalyx
ARCTIC-BELLFLOWER
(From the Greek *mélās*, black, Greek *kalyx*, seed pod or husk.)

♦*Melanocalyx uniflora* (L.) Morin
ARCTIC-BELLFLOWER
Campanula uniflora L.
Habit perennial herb, with a narrow funnel-like blue flower, from a taproot and slenderly branched stem-base or rhizome; stems sin-

Campanula lasiocarpa MOUNTAIN HAREBELL

gle or several, lax, 3–30 cm tall, glabrous except for a few long, loose hairs. Leaves primarily along stem, alternate, dark green and somewhat leathery, glabrous, margins entire; lower leaves with petioles, elliptic, oblong, or spatulate; upper leaves sessile, linear to lanceolate. Flowers solitary, slightly nodding; petals fused into a narrow blue corolla, 7–11 mm long, with ovate lobes as long as tube; calyx lobes lance-shaped, with white hairs and almost as long as the corolla; narrow teeth (as in *Campanula lasiocarpa*) absent. Fruit a capsule.

Where Found occasional at high-elevations on dry, sandy to rocky tundra and grassy areas, scree and rock outcrops, stream terraces.

Similar Species *Campanula lasiocarpa* has dentate leaves, toothed sepals, and a larger, bell-shaped corolla, much longer than the calyx.

CAPRIFOLIACEAE
Honeysuckle Family

1   Low, trailing, dwarf shrub; fruit a capsule . . . . .
. . . . *Linnaea*
1   Perennial herb; fruit an achene . . . . . *Valeriana*

Melanocalyx uniflora ARCTIC-BELLFLOWER

Linnaea TWINFLOWER
(In honor of Swedish botanist Carl von Linné, 1707-1778.)

♦*Linnaea borealis* L. TWINFLOWER
Habit evergreen, creeping, semi-woody herb or subshrub; stems long, slender, weakly rooting, thinly hairy and often also glandular, with numerous short (less than 10 cm tall), upright, leafy stems, evenly forked at top to support two pink, bell-shaped flowers. Leaves in opposite pairs along the horizontal stems, leathery, round-obovate, slightly toothed at tip, sparsely hairy. Flowers dark pink in bud, maturing to medium pink or pinkish white; corolla 6–12 mm long and funnel-shaped, hairy on inside, with five rounded lobes flaring slightly outward at tip; flowers nod downwards, the single style protruding and the 4 stamens enclosed. Fruit a tiny rounded capsule, 1.5 - 3 mm long, covered in sticky glandular hairs, with a single seed.

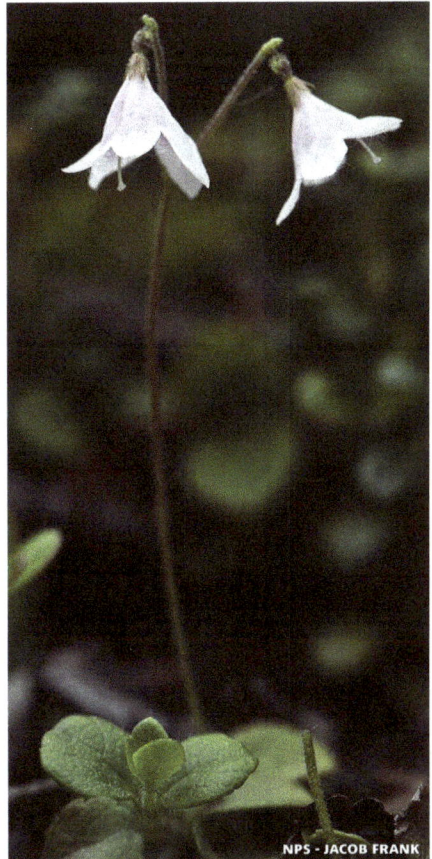

Linnaea borealis TWINFLOWER

Where Found common, and characteristic of Alaska's boreal forest.

Similar Species the combination of round, opposite leaves on creeping runners, and paired pink bell-like flowers are unique to twinflower.

Traditional Uses used by the Dena'ina to treat headache by tying a vine around a sufferer's head (Kari 1995).

Valeriana VALERIAN

(Latin, *valere*, to be strong or healthy, generally thought to refer to its medicinal use, though may also refer to the strong odor.)

♦ *Valeriana capitata* Pall. ex Link
CLUSTERED VALERIAN

Habit perennial herb; stems single, 30–70 cm tall, from a creeping rhizome. Leaves basal and along stem; basal leaves elliptic to ovate, with long petioles, margins entire; stem leaves opposite, sessile, 3-lobed. Flowers in a rounded, terminal cluster, subtended by lobed bracts; flower buds purple; petals 5, fused at base, initially pink, becoming white. Fruit an achene; sepals becoming plumose to aid in wind dispersal.

Where Found common in moist floodplains, meadows, shrublands and tundra, especially at higher elevations.

Similar Species distinguished by its manyflowered terminal cluster of white-pink flowers and opposite stem leaves.

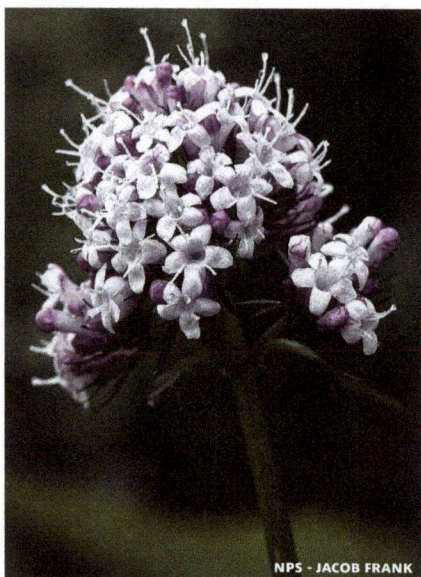

Valeriana capitata CLUSTERED VALERIAN

Traditional Uses was used medicinally as a sedative, anti-depressant, diuretic, and antispasmodic (Garibaldi 1999); plants contain valerine and chatinine, similar to valium.

CARYOPHYLLACEAE
Pink Family

1 Sepals united into a tube; petals free, pink or white . . . . *Silene*

1 Sepals and petals free, not united below; petals white 2

2 Petals deeply cleft, notched, or absent 3

2 Petals entire or shallowly notched 4

3 Styles usually 3; capsule ovoid or ellipsoid . . . . *Stellaria*

3 Styles usually 5; capsule cylindrical . *Cerastium*

4 Leaves broad, oval or oblong; styles 3 5

4 Leaves linear, acute; styles 3–5 7

5 Capsule inflated, 3–4-chambered . . *Wilhelmsia*

5 Capsule 1-chambered 6

6 Seeds shiny, with a pale spongy appendage; leaves elliptic or lanceolate . . . . *Mohringia*

6 Seeds dull, without a spongy appendage; leaves lanceolate-oblanceolate. . . . . *Arenaria*

7 Styles 4 or 5; flower buds spherical . . . . *Sagina*

7 Styles normally 3; flower buds oblong. 8

8 Capsules opening by 6 teeth. 9

8 Capsules opening by 3 teeth. 10

9 Stems 10–25 cm high; leaves threadlike, 5–8 cm long. . . . . *Eremogone*

9 Stems low, tufted or matted; leaves overlapping, lanceolate or oblanceolate, 3–5 mm long . . . . *Arenaria longipedunculata*

10 Leaves stiff, prominently 3-nerved (most visible on dried leaves of previous season). . . . . *Sabulina rubella*

10 Leaves 1-nerved, or appearing nerveless (obscurely 3-nerved in *Pseudocherleria macrocarpa*) 11

11 Stems and leaves glabrous . . . . *Sabulina*

11 Stems and leaves pubescent, or leaves at least ciliate-margined 12

12 Leaves very narrow, 7–8 times longer than wide, distinctly ciliate-margined *Cherleria yukonensis*

12 Leaves wider, 4–5 times longer than wide . . 13

13 Petals narrowly oblong, rarely much longer than sepals; seeds smooth . . . . *Cherleria biflora*

13 Petals spatulate or clawed, much longer than sepals; seeds rough. 14

14 Leaves narrowly linear, stiff . . . . *Cherleria obtusiloba*

14 Leaves soft 15
15 Leaves obscurely 3-nerved, ciliate; flowers short-stalked; capsules more than three times longer than calyx . . . . . . *Pseudocherleria macrocarpa*
15 Leaves 1-nerved; flowers long-stalked; capsule not much longer than calyx . . *Cherleria arctica*

Arenaria SANDWORT
(Latin *arena,* sand, a common habitat of these plants.)

Arenaria longipedunculata Hultén
LONGSTEM SANDWORT
Habit perennial herb, from a taproot and branching stem-base, rhizomatous; forming mats to 10 cm across; flowering stems erect, 2-4 cm tall. Leaves basal and along stem; basal leaves oblanceolate to elliptic, 3-8 mm long, 1-2 mm wide, sharp-pointed; stem leaves opposite, 1-4 pairs, 3-5 mm long. Flowers solitary, erect; petals 5, white, narrowly oblong, 3-4 mm long; sepals 5, ovate, 3-4 mm long, more or less glandular-hairy. Fruit an ovate capsule, 4-6 mm long.
Where Found uncommon on gravelly floodplains.

Cerastium CHICKWEED
(Greek, horn, referring to shape of capsule.)

♦ *Cerastium beeringianum* Cham. & Schltdl.
BERING CHICKWEED
Habit delicate, alpine perennial herb, with deeply cleft white petals, from a taproot and prostrate stems; forming mats to about 30 cm wide; stems erect to decumbent, 3-25 cm long, glandular-hairy, slender (less than 1

Cerastium beeringianum BERING CHICKWEED

mm in diameter). Leaves basal and along stem, pubescent; stem leaves opposite, sessile, lanceolate to oblong or elliptic, margins entire. Flowers 3-6, in a cyme; petals five, white, twice as long as sepals, deeply dissected and appearing separate; stamens 10; styles 5. Fruit a capsule.
Where Found common on sandy or rocky slopes, meadows, and alpine tundra in the mountains (primarily north of Alaska Range crest); less often on low-elevation gravel bars, cliffs, dry slopes, and lakeshores.
Similar Species can be confused with *Stellaria,* also with opposite leaves and dissected white petals, but plants of that genus have 3 styles, not five (visible with a hand lens).

Cherleria SANDWORT
Includes former species of *Arenaria* and *Minuartia.* (In honor of Swiss physician J. H. Cherler, 1570-1610.)

1 Leaves with blunt or truncate tips; rounded in cross-section. *C. arctica*
1 Leaves with tips acute or obtuse, but not truncate; triangular or flat in cross-section. 2
2 Leaves ± flat in cross-section . . . . *C. biflora*
2 Leaves strongly keeled and triangular in cross-section 3
3 Leaves straight, less than 1 mm wide, with sharply pointed tips . . . . *C. yukonensis*
3 Leaves generally curved, more than 1 mm wide, tips acute, but often not sharply pointed. . . . . *C. obtusiloba*

♦ *Cherleria arctica* (Steven ex Ser.) A.J. Moore & Dillenb. **ARCTIC SANDWORT**
Arenaria arctica Steven ex Ser., *Minuartia arctica* (Steven ex Ser.) Graebn.
Habit semi-evergreen alpine perennial, forming small mats or loose cushions with disproportionately large white flowers; stems 3-10 cm tall, glandular-hairy, growing from a stout taproot. Leaves basal and along stem; basal leaves opposite, tightly-packed, linear; stem leaves shorter, more loosely spaced. Flowers solitary; petals 5, white to pinkish, 10 mm long, twice as long as sepals; sepals 3-nerved and purple-margined. Fruit a capsule, the calyx persisting.
Where Found common on rocky slopes and well-drained subalpine and alpine tundra.
Similar Species distinguished from related species by its one-nerved leaves and petals twice as long as sepals.

Cherleria biflora (L.) A.J. Moore & Dillenb.
TWO-FLOWERED SANDWORT
Arenaria biflora L., *Minuartia biflora* (L.) Schinz & Thell.

Habit tufted perennial herb, from a taproot and branching stem-base; forming mats to 15 cm across; flowering stems erect, 4–10 cm tall, simple to few branched, glandular. Leaves basal and along stem; basal leaves linear, 4–10 mm long, less than 1 mm wide, 1-nerved, glabrous to slightly hairy; stem leaves opposite, 2–3 pairs, linear, 4–8 mm long. Flowers solitary or paired; petals 5, white, narrowly oblong, 2–4 mm long; sepals 5, linear-oblong, sometimes purplish at tip, prominently 3-nerved, about same length as petals. Fruit a cylindric capsule, 3–5 mm long.

Where Found uncommon in alpine tundra, snowbeds.

♦*Cherleria obtusiloba* (Rydb.) A.J. Moore & Dillenb. **ALPINE SANDWORT**
Arenaria obtusiloba (Rydb.) Fern., *Minuartia obtusiloba* (Rydb.) House

Habit tufted perennial herb, from a taproot and branching stem-base; forming mats to 40 cm across; stems prostrate to ascending or erect, 3–8 cm tall, hairy and more or less glandular above; lower part of stem covered with old leaves. Leaves basal and along stem; basal leaves oblong to linear, crowded and overlapping, 1-nerved, 4–8 mm long, less than 1 mm wide, rather rigid, glabrous or glandular-hairy or hairy margined; stem leaves opposite, 1–2 pairs or occasionally lacking, similar to basal leaves but usually wider. Flowers usually solitary; petals 5, white, ovate to spoon-shaped, 4–10 mm long; sepals 5, often purplish, especially at tip, shorter than petals and capsules, mostly 3-nerved, usually glandular-hairy. Fruit an ovate-cylindric capsule, 4–8 mm long.

Where Found uncommon on dry alpine tundra.

Cherleria yukonensis (Hultén) A.J. Moore & Dillenb. **LARCH-LEAVED SANDWORT**
Arenaria laricifolia (L.) B.L. Robins. p.p., *Minuartia yukonensis* Hultén

Habit tufted perennial herb, from a branched taproot; stems decumbent below, erect or ascending above, 5–15 cm long, repeatedly branched, glandular-pubescent, with several pairs of bracts. Leaves linear, awl-like, fresh green, to about 15 mm long, 0.5 mm wide, in dense clusters; Flowers 1–4, in a cyme; petals white, about 1 cm long; sepals oblong, 3-nerved, 5–7 mm long; Fruit a capsule, slightly longer than the calyx.

Where Found uncommon on alpine slopes.

Eremogone
MATTED SANDWORT
(Greek *eremo-*, solitary or deserted, and *gone*, seed or offspring, allusion uncertain.)

♦*Eremogone capillaris* (Poir.) Fenzl
BEAUTIFUL SANDWORT
Arenaria capillaris Poir.

Habit tufted perennial herb, from a taproot and slender, branched stem-base; stems numerous, erect to ascending, 5–20 cm tall, usually glaucous, glabrous below and glandular-hairy on upper stems and in inflorescence. Leaves basal and along stem; basal leaves many, grasslike, erect or ascending to somewhat lax, 2–6 cm long, about 1 mm wide, margins toothed; stem leaves opposite, 2–5 pairs, grasslike, reduced upwards. Flowers

Cherleria arctica ARCTIC SANDWORT

Cherleria obtusiloba ALPINE SANDWORT

1-3, in small open clusters; petals 5, white, ovate, 5-9 mm long; sepals 5, ovate, 3-5 mm long, the margins membranous and often violet-tinged. Fruit an ovate, sparsely glandular capsule, 5-8 mm long.

Where Found uncommon on gravelly floodplains, rocky slopes.

Moehringia GROVE-SANDWORT
(In honor of Danzig naturalist P. H. G. Moehring, 1710-1791.)

♦ *Moehringia lateriflora* (L.) Fenzl
BLUNTLEAF SANDWORT
Arenaria lateriflora L.

Habit Small matted perennial herb, from a branched stem-base and slender rhizomes or stolons; stems ascending to erect, 5-20 cm tall, several, usually branched, short-hairy (rarely glabrous. Leaves opposite, simple, elliptic to oblong; margins fringed with hairs. Flowers single or in a cluster of up to five; pedicels from lower leaf axils; petals five,

Eremogone capillaris BEAUTIFUL SANDWORT

Moehringia lateriflora BLUNTLEAF SANDWORT

white, twice as long as the ovate or obovate, glabrous sepals. Fruit a rounded capsule, 3-5 mm long.

Where Found common in open woods, forest edges, meadows, gravel bars, at mostly mid-elevations.

Similar Species *Wilhelmsia physodes,* but that species has inflated capsules.

Pseudocherleria
WESTERN SANDWORT
(*Pseudo-*, false, and genus *Cherleria*.)

♦ *Pseudocherleria macrocarpa* (Pursh) Dillenb. & Kadereit LONG-POD SANDWORT
Arenaria macrocarpa Pursh, *Minuartia macrocarpa* (Pursh.) Ostenf.

Habit mat-forming alpine perennial, with disproportionately large white flowers; stems erect to ascending, 10-50 cm tall; mats sometimes 50-100 cm wide. Leaves semi-evergreen, basal and along stem; basal leaves tightly packed, stem leaves less so; leaves linear to oblong, 5-15 mm long, prominently three-veined, margins fringed with hairs. Flowers solitary, petals 5, white, about twice as long as sepals; sepals 3-veined, the tip often purple. Fruit a capsule, 10-15 mm long.

Where Found common in moist alpine tundra, snowbeds, and rocky places.

Similar Species separated from related species by its flat, 3-nerved, ciliate leaves, and larger fruit.

Sabulina MOCK SANDWORT
Includes former species of *Arenaria* and *Minuartia*.

1 Leaves stiff, prominently 3-nerved (easiest to see in dried leaves of previous season) .. *S. rubella*
1 Leaves 1-nerved, or appearing nerveless..... 2

Pseudocherleria macrocarpa
LONG-POD SANDWORT

2 At least some stems 2–several-flowered . . . . . .
. . . . *S. dawsonensis*
2 Stems only with 1-flower 3
3 Plants cushion-forming or densely tufted; sepals
oblong-ovate, obtusish, 1.5–2.5 mm long, 1-
nerved . . . . *S. rossii*
3 Plants loosely tufted; sepals lanceolate, acute, 3–
3.5 mm long, often 3-nerved . . . . . . *S. elegans*

Sabulina dawsonensis (Britt.) Rydb.
ROCK STITCHWORT
Arenaria stricta (Sw.) Michx., *Arenaria dawsonensis*
(Britt.) Maguire, *Minuartia dawsonensis* (Britt.) House

Habit short-lived tufted perennial herb,
from a weak taproot and branching stem-
base; stems erect, 10–20 cm tall, several,
simple to 2–4-branched, glabrous. **Leaves**
basal and along stem; basal leaves linear, 5–
15 mm long, to 1 mm wide, 1-nerved,
glabrous; stem leaves opposite, 2–6 pairs, to
14 mm long, often with sterile axillary
branches. **Flowers** 2–7, in a loose cluster, rarely
solitary; petals 5, white, oblanceolate to oblong, 2–3.5 mm long; sepals 5, ovate, slightly
longer than petals, 3-nerved, margins
translucent. **Fruit** an oblong capsule, longer
than the sepals.
Where Found uncommon on dry rocky tundra, sandy slopes.

♦ *Sabulina elegans* (Cham. & Schltdl.) Dillenb. &
Kadereit **ELEGANT SANDWORT**
Arenaria elegans Cham. & Schltdl., *Minuartia elegans*
(Cham. & Schltdl.) Schischk.

Habit short-lived, tufted perennial herb,
from a taproot and branching stem-base;
forming loose mats to 30 cm across; stems
erect, to 8 cm tall, several, branched, glabrous.
Leaves linear, blunt-tipped, tightly overlapping,
to 3 mm long. **Flowers** solitary, on short stalks;
petals 5, white, about same length as sepals;
sepals ovate to lanceolate, 3-veined, sometimes purplish. **Fruit** a dry capsule.

Where Found uncommon on alpine tundra
and rocky places.
Similar Species distinguished from related
species by its glabrous stems and very short
leaves.

Sabulina rossii (R. Br. ex Richardson) Dillenb. &
Kadereit **ROSS SANDWORT**
Minuartia rossii (R. Br. ex Richardson) Graebn.

Habit cushion-forming or tufted perennial
herb; cushions to 10 cm in diameter. **Leaves** 3-
angled, 2–4 mm long, blunt or rounded at tip,
glabrous, overlapping on stem. **Flowers** solitary, on pedicels 5–20 mm long (or flowers
absent, vegetatively reproducing by small
fascicles of leaves in leaf axils); petals obovate to spatulate, white, longer than sepals;
sepals oblong-ovate, 1.5–2.5 mm long, purple, keeled. **Fruit** a dry capsule.
Where Found uncommon in dry gravelly or
sandy places, alpine tundra.

♦ *Sabulina rubella* (Wahlenb.) Dillenb. &
Kadereit **REDDISH SANDWORT**
Arenaria rubella (Wahlenb.) Sm., *Minuartia rubella*
(Wahlenb.) Graebn.

Habit tiny, cushion-forming perennial herb,
from a small taproot and branched crown;
stems several to many, slender, ascending,
2–8 cm tall, simple to few branched, glandular-hairy; cushions 4–20 cm across. **Leaves** opposite, linear, distinctly 3-nerved, 3–6 mm
long, somewhat hairy, persistent on the stem
for several years. **Flowers** 2–7, in an open
cyme; petals white, oblanceolate, 2.5–5 mm
long; sepals lanceolate, 3-veined, slightly
longer than petals, green to purple; stamens
10; styles 3. **Fruit** a light brown capsule, 3-
toothed upon opening.
Where Found occasional on open slopes and
gravel bars from lowlands to the alpine, most
commonly north of Alaska Range crest.
Similar Species distinguished from related
species by its three-nerved leaves.

Sabulina elegans **ELEGANT SANDWORT**

Sabulina rubella **REDDISH SANDWORT**

Sagina PEARLWORT
(Ancient name of the spurry.)

1　Cushion-forming plant; stem leaves subulate (awl-shaped); margins of sepals purple . . . .
. . . . *S. nivalis*
1　Mat-forming plant; stem leaves linear or some-times linear-subulate; margins of sepals white (rarely purple) . . . . *S. saginoides*

Sagina nivalis (Lindblad) Fr.
SNOW PEARLWORT
Spergella intermedia (Fenzl) Á. & D. Löve

Habit perennial herb, from a taproot and much-branched woody stem-base; forming low cushions to 10 cm across; stems decumbent to erect, 1–8 cm long, numerous, branched, glabrous. **Leaves** basal and along stem; basal leaf rosette present in first season only, the leaves linear, 4–8 mm long, less than 1 mm wide, glabrous; stem leaves opposite, 1–8 pairs, awl-like, usually with clusters of secondary leaves in axils. **Flowers** 1–3, on short stalks; petals 4 or 5, white, narrowly elliptic, to 1.5 mm long; sepals 4 or 5, with violet margins, ovate, to 2 mm long. **Fruit** a capsule 2–3 mm long, dull greenish or whitish yellow, on pedicels 3–10 mm long.

Where Found uncommon on sandy or gravelly lakeshores, moist alpine tundra.

◆ *Sagina saginoides* (L.) H. Karst.
ARCTIC PEARLWORT
Spergella saginoides (L.) Rchb.

Habit biennial or more usually perennial herb (sometimes flowering the first year), from a taproot and slender branching stem-base; forming mats to 20 cm wide; stems decumbent to ascending, 3–10 cm long, several, simple to few-branched, glabrous. **Leaves** basal and along stem; basal leaves linear, abruptly sharp-pointed, 5–15 mm long,

Sagina saginoides ARCTIC PEARLWORT

less than 1 mm wide, glabrous; stem leaves opposite, 2–6 pairs, linear, mostly 3–8 mm long. **Flowers** usually solitary, terminal; petals 5, white, rounded, 1–2 mm long; sepals usually 5 (sometimes 4), ovate, greenish with a white margin, as long as or slightly longer than petals. **Fruit** an ovate capsule, 3 mm long.

Where Found uncommon on moist gravelly lakeshores and streambanks, alpine meadows, rocky outcrops.

Silene CATCHFLY
(Greek, *saliva*, in allusion to the viscid secretion of some species.)

1　Plant a dense cushion; flowers solitary, pink. . .
. . . . *S. acaulis*
1　Plant not forming dense cushions 2
2　Flowers nodding in anthesis; petals purple, short-exserted . . . . *S. uralensis*
2　Flowers upright; petals white or pink, exserted
. . . . 3
3　Calyx purple or green 4
3　Calyx with broad striped veins 6
4　Calyx purple, sometimes with faint stripe . . . . .
. . . . *S. repens*
4　Calyx green 5
5　Calyx bell-shaped, 5–7 mm long . . *S. menziesii*
5　Calyx urn-shaped to cylindric, about 12 mm long
. . . . *S. williamsii*
6　Biennial or usually perennial native herb; basal leaves 1–5 cm long . . . . *S. involucrata*
6　Annual introduced herb; basal leaves 5–12 cm long . . . . *S. noctiflora*

◆ *Silene acaulis* (L.) Jacq.
MOSS-CAMPION

Habit cushion-forming perennial herb, with pink flowers, from a woody root and a branched stem-base; forming thick cushions to about 30 cm or more wide; stems erect, only 3–6 cm tall, solitary, simple, glabrous. **Leaves** densely crowded, linear, a characteristic bright grass-green color, margins fringed with stiff white hairs. **Flowers** numerous, solitary at end of short stalk and held just above cushion of leaves; petals 5, pink to lavender, free, notched; sepals fused into a tubular calyx. **Fruit** a cylindric capsule, about as long as calyx.

Where Found common on well-drained, sandy to rocky soils in alpine tundra, cliffs, slopes, ridges, and stream terraces.

Similar Species distinguished from other

cushion-forming, pink-flowered alpine plants by the linear, ciliate leaves.

Note Called 'moss campion' due to its moss-like growth habit.

◆*Silene involucrata* (Cham. & Schltdl.) Bocquet
ARCTIC CATCHFLY
Silene tayloriae (B.L. Robins.) Hultén
Habit biennial or more usually perennial herb, from a taproot and branching stem-base; stems more or less erect, 5–30 cm tall, several, simple or sometimes branched, lower stem white-hairy below, becoming glandular-hairy above. Leaves basal and along stem; basal leaves oblanceolate to narrowly elliptic, 1–5 cm long, 2–8 mm wide, margins fringed; stem leaves opposite, 2–3 pairs, reduced upwards. Flowers usually solitary or sometimes 2 or 3, erect to spreading; petals 5, white to pink or purple, 2-cleft; sepals 5, united, forming a bell- to urn-shaped tube 10–17 mm long, hairy, purple-nerved. Fruit a capsule, 12–18 mm long.
Where Found moist sandy or gravelly places.

◆*Silene menziesii* Hook. MENZIE'S CAMPION
Habit perennial herb, from a long, slender, branched rhizome; stems decumbent to ascending, 10–40 cm long, usually much branched, hairy and usually glandular above. Leaves basal and along stem; basal leaves usually deciduous by flowering time; stem leaves opposite, lanceolate to narrowly ovate, acute at both ends, 2–10 cm long,

more or less pubescent on both surfaces. Flowers several, in a leafy bracted, open cluster, or, less commonly, solitary; petals 5, white, blades 2–3 mm long, lobed halfway or more; sepals 5, purplish or greenish, united, forming a glandular-hairy tube 5–8 mm long.

ALFRED COOK
Silene involucrata ARCTIC CATCHFLY

JÖRG HEMPEL
Silene acaulis MOSS-CAMPION

Fruit an oblong capsule, 5–8 mm long; seed black, shiny.

Where Found open slopes, open woods of aspen or spruce, can be weedy on disturbed sites.

Silene noctiflora L.
NIGHT-FLOWERING CATCHFLY

Habit annual herb, from a taproot; stems erect, 20–80 cm tall, branched, hairy, becoming sticky-hairy above. Leaves basal leaves spoon-shaped, 5–12 cm long, short-stalked; stem leaves opposite, lanceolate to elliptic, 2–10 cm long, to 4 cm wide, unstalked, hairy above and below. Flowers 2-many, in a cluster, opening at night, fragrant; petals 5, yellowish beneath and rosy above, glabrous; blades 7–10 mm long; sepals 5, greenish to pinkish, forming a woolly, glandular-hairy tube 12–25 mm long. Fruit an ovate capsule, 1.5–2.5 cm long.

Where Found on disturbed soils, introduced from Europe.

♦ *Silene repens* Patrin PINK CAMPION

Habit matted perennial herb, from a branched stem-base and short rhizome; stems erect, 10–35 cm tall, several, simple or branched, densely crinkled-hairy. Leaves opposite, linear-lanceolate, margins fringed with hairs. Flowers 5–20, in several branched cymes subtended by bracts; corolla fused at base; petals 5, pale pink to white, bilobed; calyx tubular, purple, finely hairy and conspicuously inflated. Fruit an ovate capsule.

Where Found uncommon on dry, rocky or grassy slopes of the subalpine and lower alpine zones, north of Alaska Range crest.

Similar Species other plants with opposite leaves and cleft white petals (including several *Stellaria* species) are present in Denali, but they lack a purple, fused calyx below the petals.

♦ *Silene uralensis* (Rupr.) Bocquet
APETALOUS CATCHFLY
Silene macrosperma (A.E. Porsild) Hultén

Habit perennial herb, with conspicuously inflated purple-striped flowers, from a branched stem-base; stems ascending to erect, 5–30 cm tall, usually simple, finely white-hairy below, becoming glandular above. Leaves both basal and along stem; basal leaves linear to oblanceolate, more or less pubescent with ciliate margins; stem leaves similar but smaller and arranged in 1–5 pairs. Flowers solitary and nodding; petals purple, inconspicuous; calyx large, 10-veined, inflated, purplish, 1–2 cm long. Fruit a capsule.

Where Found occasional at high-elevations in sandy to rocky soils of tundra, meadows, lakeshores, streambanks, and fell-fields, primarily north of Alaska Range crest.

Similar Species no other plant in Denali has inflated, striped flowers with reduced petals.

Silene williamsii Britt. WILLIAMS' CAMPION

Habit perennial herb, from a branched rootstock, with white, notched petals, and covered with sticky-viscid glands (making it

Silene menziesii MENZIE'S CAMPION

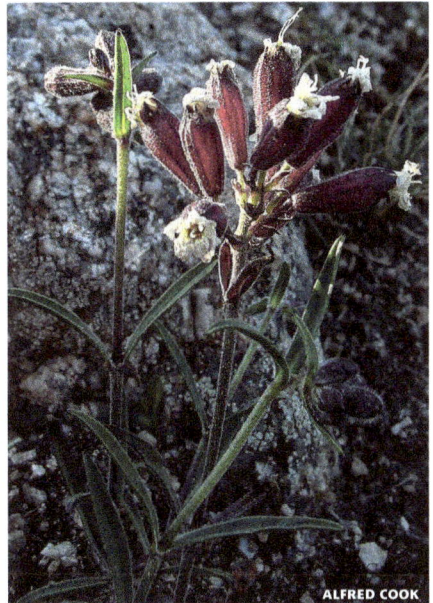

Silene repens PINK CAMPION

112 Caryophyllaceae • *Pink Family*

easy to recognize); stems 5–30 cm tall, branched. Leaves mostly along stem, opposite, lanceolate, hairy on both sides. Flowers in a terminal cyme; petals white, notched, shorter than the calyx; calyx urn-shaped, green, about 12 mm long. Fruit a light brown capsule.

Where Found occasional on gravelly floodplains and dry slopes in the northern foothills of Denali; endemic to Alaska and Yukon Territory.

Similar Species distinguished from other *Silene* by its much branched habit, the plants sticky due to viscid glands, and its large, green, urn-shaped calyx.

Stellaria
CHICKWEED, STARWORT
(Latin, star, with reference to the star-shaped flower.)

Silene uralensis APETALOUS CATCHFLY

1   Plants forming dense cushions, with a central taproot . . . . *S. dicranoides*
1   Plants upright or matted. 2
2   Leaves firm, keeled, green or often glaucous . . . . *S. longipes*
2   Leaves soft, not prominently keeled, fresh green 3
3   Flowers in axils of small scarious bracts or scarious-margined leaves 4
3   Flowers in axils of green leaves, or if in cymes, with leafy bracts 6
4   Flowers in umbel-like clusters; petals shorter than sepals or absent . . . . *S. irrigua*
4   Flowers not in umbel-like clusters 5
5   Flowers solitary or sometimes 2; leaves lanceolate to elliptic, entire . . . . *S. alaskana*
5   Flowers in open cymes; leaves linear to elliptic, finely toothed . . . . *S. longifolia*
6   Plants forming mats; leaves somewhat fleshy . . . . *S. crassifolia*
6   Plants not forming mats; leaves not fleshy. . . . 7
7   Leaves lanceolate to linear-lanceolate, to 6 cm long; leaf veins other than midrib usually not visible; stems usually more or less covered with small bumps . . . . *S. borealis*
7   Leaves ovate, ovate-lanceolate to elliptic, mostly less than 2.5 cm long, net-veined; stems never with small bumps . . . . *S. calycantha*

Stellaria alaskana Hultén
ALASKA STARWORT
Habit delicate alpine perennial herb, from elongate rhizomes, forming diffuse to compact clumps among rocks in alpine zone; stems unbranched, 3–10 cm tall. Leaves opposite, relatively thick, compressed at base, lanceolate-elliptic, glabrous. Flowers 1–2 from axils of membranous bracts; petals five, white, cleft nearly to base (appearing like 10 petals); sepals linear-lanceolate, prominently veined and longer than petals; stamens 10; styles 3. Fruit a capsule, opening by six-valves.

Where Found uncommon on alpine rocky slopes, scree, and talus, mostly north of Alaska Range crest.

Similar Species distinguished from other *Stellaria* by its short habit, unbranched inflorescence, and the flower stalks emerging from membranous bracts instead of green leaves.

Stellaria borealis Bigelow
BOREAL STARWORT
Habit matted perennial herb, from a long

rhizome; stems prostrate to ascending, 10–35 cm long, freely branched above middle nodes. Leaves opposite, linear-lanceolate to elliptic, to 6 cm long. Flowers either solitary and terminal, or in leaf axils; small, with five deeply cleft petals (or petals absent), shorter than the green, 2–5 mm long sepals. Fruit an ovoid capsule opening by three valves.

Where Found occasional in boreal to lower alpine, in moist to wet places, shrub thickets.

Similar Species distinguished from other *Stellaria* by its ascending habit, lanceolate to elliptic leaves, and lack of papery bracts.

Stellaria calycantha (Ledeb.) Bong.
NORTHERN BOG STARWORT

Habit clumped perennial herb, from a slender rhizome; stems weak, 10–30 cm tall; Leaves ovate-lanceolate to linear-lanceolate, 5–25 mm long, 2–6 mm wide; Flowers few-many, in a terminal cyme; petals often absent, if present, shorter than sepals; sepals lanceolate, about 2–3 mm long. Fruit a nearly round capsule.

Where Found alpine meadows, lakeshores, streambanks, thickets.

♦ *Stellaria crassifolia* Ehrh.
FLESHY STARWORT

Habit perennial herb, from a slender rhizome; stems weak and slender, decumbent

Stellaria crassifolia FLESHY STARWORT

to erect, to about 25 cm long, branched, often matted. Leaves opposite, unstalked, lanceolate to lance-linear, 5–15 mm long, 1–3 mm wide, thin. Flowers, solitary in leaf axils, occasionally several flowers in an open terminal cluster; petals 5, white, deeply 2-cleft, 2–5 mm long; sepals 5, oblong-lanceolate, shorter than petals and capsule, inconspicuously 1-nerved. Fruit a straw-colored, narrowly ovate capsule, 4–5 mm long, 6-valved.

Where Found moist to wet meadows, muskegs, lakeshores, often in shallow water.

Stellaria dicranoides (Cham. & Schltdl.) Fenzl
MATTED STARWORT
Arenaria chamissonis Maguire, *Cherleria dicranoides* Cham. & Schlect.

Habit cushion-forming, dioecious, perennial herb, from a branching stem-base; branches densely covered in withered old leaves; flowering stems erect, to 1 cm long. Leaves lanceolate, 4–5 mm long, overlapping, glabrous. Flowers solitary, at ends of stems; male flowers with 10 stamens; female flowers with a single pistil, 3 styles, and 10 sterile stamens; petals absent; sepals five, acute, green, 2–4 mm long. Fruit (in female plants) a small, ovate capsule, opening by three valves.

Where Found uncommon in alpine tundra and barrens, north of Alaska Range crest.

Similar Species the only cushion-forming plant in Denali with green flowers.

Stellaria irrigua Bunge
COLORADO STARWORT
Stellaria umbellata Turcz. ex Kar. & Kir.

Habit perennial herb, from a slender rhizome; forming small clumps or mats; stems erect or ascending, 5–20 cm tall, several, branched, glabrous. Leaves opposite, oblong to linear-lanceolate, 5–25 mm long, 2–5 mm wide, unstalked, glabrous or sometimes fringed at base. Flowers 2 to many, in terminal and axillary umbel-like clusters; petals usually absent; sepals 5, lanceolate, 2–3 mm long, 3-nerved. Fruit a straw-colored, ovate capsule, 3–4 mm long, 6–8-valved.

Where Found uncommon on moist alpine slopes.

♦ *Stellaria longifolia* Muhl. ex Willd.
LONG-LEAF STARWORT

Habit perennial herb, from slender rhizomes; stems decumbent to ascending, 10–40 cm long, several, branched, matted, sharply 4-angled, glabrous except minutely rough-hairy above. Leaves basal and along stem; basal leaves few, reduced, soon deciduous; stem leaves opposite, unstalked, linear to linear-lanceolate, 2–5 cm long, 2–4 mm wide, glabrous or with a few basal hairs on margins. Flowers solitary or several in an open cluster; petals 5, white, 2-cleft, about as long as sepals; sepals 5, narrowly-elliptic to lanceolate, 2–3 mm long, 3-nerved. Fruit a greenish yellow, oblong capsule, 4–6 mm long, 6-valved.

Where Found uncommon in moist to wet meadows, marshes, muskegs.

◆ *Stellaria longipes* Goldie
LONG-STALK STARWORT

Habit small to medium perennial herb, from a slender rhizome; stems decumbent to more usually erect, 3–30 cm long, several, branched, matted, 4-angled, glabrous to slightly hairy near base. Leaves opposite, sessile, linear to lanceolate, glossy-green to glaucous blue-green with a prominent keel; leaf hairiness variable. Flowers solitary or few, in terminal cymes; petals 5, white, 5–7 mm long, longer than sepals, deeply lobed (appearing as 10); sepals purple-tinged, 3–5 mm long; stamens 10; styles 3. Fruit a brown capsule with 6 teeth, containing numerous seeds.

Where Found common in a variety of boreal to alpine habitats: black spruce muskegs, floodplains, meadows, shrublands, rocky places, tundra.

Similar Species distinguished from other *Stellaria* species by the prominent keel of the leaf.

Wilhelmsia ARCTIC-FLOWER

(Possibly in honor of Christian Wilhelms, plant collector in the Caucasus region.)

◆ *Wilhelmsia physodes* (Fisch ex Ser.) McNeill
ARCTIC-FLOWER
Arenaria physodes Fisch.

Habit creeping perennial herb, with white flowers and purple, inflated capsules; stems 2–10 cm tall, freely branching, covered in glandular purple hairs. Leaves opposite, elliptic-lanceolate, sessile, margins ciliate. Flowers solitary, terminal at stem ends; petals 5, white, 5–6 mm long; sepals 5, often purple and shorter than petals. Fruit a round, inflated capsule, with 3 reddish leathery valves.

Where Found uncommon on sandy lakeshores, streambanks, and gravel bars, at low-elevations north of Alaska Range crest.

Similar Species *Moehringia lateriflora* is another creeping, opposite-leaved herb of similar habitats, but it does not have inflated capsules.

Stellaria longipes LONG-STALK STARWORT

Stellaria longifolia LONG-LEAF STARWORT

CELASTRACEAE
Bittersweet Family

Parnassia
GRASS-OF-PARNASSUS
(Name from Mount Parnassus in Greece.)

1 Petals barely as long as sepals, 3-veined . . . . . .
   . . . . *P. kotzebuei*
1 Petals nearly twice as long as sepals, 5–9-veined
   . . . . *P. palustris*

◆ *Parnassia kotzebuei* Cham. ex Spreng.
KOTZEBUE'S GRASS-OF-PARNASSUS
Habit perennial herb, from a short rootstock and fibrous root; stems erect, solitary or sometimes several, simple, 5–15 cm tall. Leaves in a basal rosette, cordate to broadly ovate; stem leaf absent or sometimes present, but not much above basal leaves. Flowers single at end of stem; petals white, with 3–5 impressed veins; sepals 5, as long as or slightly shorter than petals; stamens 5, white; pistil one, with two sessile stigmas; behind the stamens are 5 'staminodes', each staminode dissected into 4–6 filaments (these do not produce pollen). Fruit a dry capsule, splitting along 4 seams, releasing over many small, winged seeds.

Where Found high-elevation gravel bars, moist meadows, tundra, often on steep slopes.

Similar Species may be confused with *Parnassia palustris*, in *P. kotzebuei* petals about same length as sepals, in *P. palustris* petals much longer than sepals; also, stem leaf often absent, or otherwise close to basal leaves, in *P. palustris,* stem leaf always present, borne higher on stem.

Wilhelmsia physodes ARCTIC-FLOWER

◆ *Parnassia palustris* L.
MARSH GRASS-OF-PARNASSUS
Habit perennial herb, from a short rootstock and fibrous roots; stems ascending to erect, usually solitary, simple, 10–25 cm tall. Leaves basal, heart-shaped or blunt at base, tapering at tip; with a leafy bract on flowering stem. Flowers solitary, cup-shaped, facing upward; petals 5, white, ovate, with 7–13 veins, longer than sepals; stamens 5, white; below are 5 'staminodes' (sterile stamens divided into slender, yellowish filaments). Fruit a dry capsule, splitting along 4 seams to release seeds.

JIM MOREFIELD

Parnassia palustris
MARSH GRASS-OF-PARNASSUS

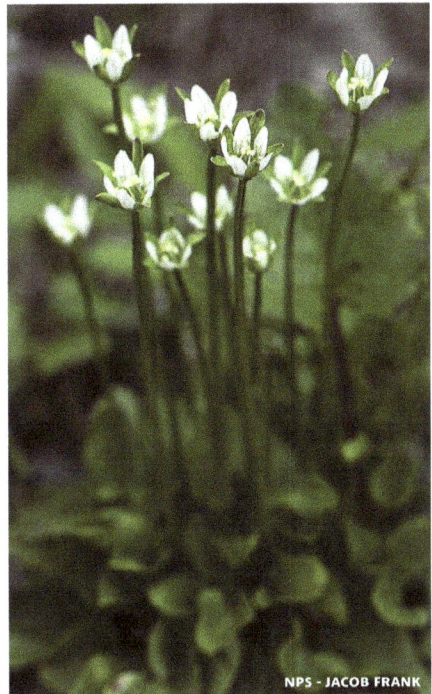

NPS - JACOB FRANK

Parnassia kotzebuei
KOTZEBUE'S GRASS-OF-PARNASSUS

Where Found mid-elevation wet, marshy areas and riparian zones.

Similar Species *Parnassia kotzebuei* lacks the large leafy stem bract, and petals and sepals are same length.

CERATOPHYLLACEAE
Hornwort Family

Ceratophyllum HORNWORT
(Greek *ceratos*, horn, and *phyllon*, leaf.)

Ceratophyllum demersum L.
HORNWORT, COONTAIL
Habit mat-forming, aquatic herb, usually without roots; stems freely branching, 1 m long or more. Leaves in whorls of 5–12, 2–3 times forked into linear or threadlike segments, these stiff and spiny-toothed. Flowers solitary, tiny, from leaf axil; petals absent; sepals 3–15, sometimes petal-like. Fruit a flattened achene (but usually absent), 4–6 mm long, elliptic, with a persistent style and 2 basal spines.

Where Found uncommon in ponds and small lakes.

CORNACEAE
Dogwood Family

Cornus DOGWOOD
(Greek, horn, from the toughness of the wood of some species.)

1 Shrub, with open cymes of small white flowers; bracts absent................*C. stolonifera*
1 Herbs; flowers subtended by 4 petal-like, whitish bracts, surrounding a tight cluster of small flowers....................................2
2 Petals cream or yellowish green and purple ... .*C. unalaschkensis*
2 Petals cream or yellowish green...........3
3 Leaves sessile, ovate to elliptic, lateral veins arising from base of leaf (or nearly so); petals and sepals dark purplish ....*C. suecica*
3 Leaves with a short petiole, obovate to diamond-shaped, lateral veins arising from midvein in lower third of leaf; petals and sepals usually yellowish or greenish, sometimes purplish-tinged but never dark purplish ....*C. canadensis*

◆ *Cornus canadensis* L.
BUNCHBERRY DOGWOOD
Habit low, trailing perennial herb, somewhat woody at base, from a rhizome; stems erect, solitary, to 15 cm tall, greenish to reddish, leafless or with bracts on the lower part. Leaves 4–7 in the upper whorl, elliptic to ovate, with deeply impressed parallel veins; with a pair of opposite smaller leaves below them; leaves turning dark purple-red in fall. Flowers with four white ovate bracts; true flowers tiny, in a cluster; petals tiny, white, recurved; calyx green; stamens four, white. Fruit a round, berry-like red drupe, favored by birds.

Where Found abundant in low-elevation forests, alder and willow thickets, often forming large colonies; and in heathlands with *Arctous alpina, Vaccinium uliginosum,* and *Empetrum nigrum.*

Similar Species *Cornus suecica* similar but not as common, with several pairs of usually smaller opposite leaves along stem (in *C. canadensis* only one pair of leaves present below the upper whorl of large leaves).

Traditional Uses fruit edible, but flavorless. The Yup'ik sometimes use it in akutaq ('Eskimo icecream'), mixed with other berries, but it is not preferred (Jernigan et al. 2015). The dwarf dogwoods, were used by the Dena'ina for stomach troubles and eye problems as a tea brewed from the berrylike drupes (Andrews 1975 in Garibaldi 1999). The leaves of bunchberry have also been used for burns and cataracts by the Tlingit (de Laguna 1972 in Garibaldi 1999) and cuts by the Alutiiq (Wennekens 1985 in Garibaldi 1999).

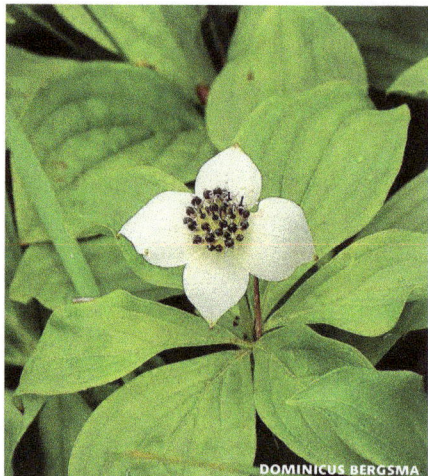

Cornus canadensis BUNCHBERRY DOGWOOD

♦ *Cornus sericea* L.
RED-OSIER DOGWOOD
Cornus alba L., *Cornus stolonifera* Michx.
Deciduous shrub; stems 1–3 m tall, spreading by layering of prostrate stems; young branches opposite, reddish, later turning grayish green. Leaves opposite, oval, pointed, 4–12 cm long, greenish above, slightly paler below, finely hairy, with 5–7 prominent parallel veins converging at leaf tip; turning reddish in fall. Flowers small, in flat-topped terminal clusters 2–4 cm wide; white to greenish white, petals 4, about 3 mm long; bracts inconspicuous. Fruit a berrylike drupe, 7–9 mm long, white sometimes blue-tinged, each with a flattened stone about 5 mm long.
Where Found uncommon in moist thickets, moist open woods.

♦ *Cornus suecica* L.
LAPLAND CORNEL, DWARF BOG BUNCHBERRY
Habit perennial herb, somewhat woody at base, from a rhizome; stems erect, 10–20 cm tall. Leaves elliptic to ovate, with pronounced parallel veins, margins entire; with several pairs of opposite leaves below the upper cluster of whorled leaves and flowers; often branching towards the top, these side shoots ending in clusters of four leaves; leaves turning dark purple-red in fall. Flowers with 4 conspicuous white bracts (modified leaves); true flowers tiny, in a cluster between bracts, dark purple, as opposed to white flowers of *Cornus canadensis*. Fruit a round, bright red, berry-like drupe, the dark style remaining attached.
Where Found common across a wide elevational range in woodlands, moist meadows, shrub tundra.
Similar Species very similar in appearance to the more common *Cornus canadensis*, but

that has only one small pair of leaves below the upper whorl of large leaves; *C. suecica* has several pairs of large opposite leaves on the stem.
Traditional Uses see *Cornus canadensis*.

♦ *Cornus unalaschkensis* Ledeb.
ALASKAN BUNCHBERRY
Habit perennial herb, somewhat woody at base; stems erect, less than 20 cm tall. Leaves elliptic to ovate, 2–8 cm long, in a whorl of 4–6 below inflorescence, plus a pair of small leaves near middle of stem. Flowers in a head, 2–4 cm wide, surrounded by 4 conspicuous, white, petal-like bracts, to 2 cm long; petals 1–2 mm long, cream-colored to yellowish green, with purple tip. Fruit a red spherical drupe, 6–8 mm wide, with 1–2 smooth seeds.
Where Found occasional on streambanks, moist meadows.

Cornus suecica LAPLAND CORNEL

Cornus sericea RED-OSIER DOGWOOD

Cornus unalaschkensis ALASKAN BUNCHBERRY

Similar Species Differing from *Cornus canadensis* by its somewhat taller size and larger pairs of lower leaves, and petals cream-colored to yellowish green.

CRASSULACEAE
Stonecrop Family

Rhodiola ROSEROOT
(Greek *rhodon*, rose, alluding to odor of rootstock.)

♦ *Rhodiola integrifolia* Raf. ROSEROOT
Sedum rosea var. *integrifolium* (Raf.) Berger

Habit perennial mat-forming, dioecious herb, from a thick, branched rhizome; stems erect to decumbent, 5–30 cm tall, branched above, glabrous. Leaves fleshy, alternate, glaucous gray-green, spatulate to oblong, margins toothed. Flowers either male or female,

Rhodiola integrifolia ROSEROOT

on separate plants, in a dense terminal cluster; petals fleshy, deep red, 2–3 mm long, oblong with acute tips; sepals shorter (1–2 mm). Fruit a dry capsule.

Where Found common in alpine meadows, talus, tundra, and late-lying snow areas.

Similar Species roseroot the only succulent present in the region.

Traditional Uses edible and high in vitamin A and C; traditional uses include chewing the leaves and flowers for pain (Yup'ik), and drinking a tea made from leaves and roots for childbirth, colds, sore throats and sore eyes (Dena'ina).

DIAPENSIACEAE
Pincushion-Plant Family

Diapensia PINCUSHION-PLANT
(Greek *dia-*, composed, and *pente*, five, alluding to number of sepals, petals, and stamens.)

♦ *Diapensia lapponica* L. PINCUSHION-PLANT
Habit dwarf subshrub, with showy white flowers; stems prostrate, 5–10 cm long, much branched, forming compact cushions. Leaves evergreen, obovate to oblong, 5–12 mm long, leathery, thick and shiny with a revolute margin, overlapping in circular whorls along the stem. Flowers single, atop a short stem, subtended by 3 small bracts; corolla 5-lobed, lobes 7–10 mm long, white or cream colored; sepals 5, red-purple. Fruit a brown capsule, 3–4 mm wide.

Diapensia lapponica PINCUSHION-PLANT

Where Found common in rocky alpine tundra and fellfields.

Similar Species Denali's only alpine, cushion-forming plant having white flowers and leaves with a revolute margin. Similar to alpine-azalea (*Kalmia procumbens*), but that species often with multiple, not single, flowers atop the stem.

DROSERACEAE
Sundew Family

Drosera SUNDEW
(Greek, dewy, from the appearance of the leaves.)

1 Leaf-blade rounded, usually wider than long; petiole hairy . . . . *D. rotundifolia*
1 Leaf-blade linear to spoon-shaped, much longer than wide; petiole glabrous. . . . . *D. anglica*

◆*Drosera anglica* Huds. ENGLISH SUNDEW
Habit small insect-eating perennial herb with white flowers (but plants often without flowers); stems erect, 5–15 cm tall. Leaves in a basal rosette, held upright, paddle-shaped, at end of a long petiole (2–3 times length of blade), margins entire; upper surface covered in long red hairs, each tipped with a transparent dot of mucous; this sticky substance—the source of the name 'sundew'—serves to both attract and entrap insects; when an insect that lands on a leaf moves, it

triggers a response in the leaf: other gland-tipped hairs bend toward it, further entangling the insect, and the leaf slowly curls around the insect and releases digestive enzymes to help break down the insect body, releasing nutrients for the plant. English sundew is fully photosynthetic, and gains most of its energy (carbon) from the sun; capturing insects allows the plant to acquire limiting nutrients such as nitrogen. Flowers several, on a slender leafless stem above the basal rosette; petals 5, white, to 5 mm long; sepals 5, green, with glandular hairs. Fruit a many-seeded capsule, opening to release seeds.

Where Found uncommon in low-elevation bogs in mats of peatmoss (*Sphagnum*).

Similar Species the leaf-shape (spatulate instead of round) and habit (leaves ascending, rather than flat on the ground) distinguish English sundew from roundleaf sundew.

◆*Drosera rotundifolia* L. ROUNDLEAF SUNDEW
Habit tiny insect-eating perennial herb (see *D. anglica* for details); stems erect, leafless, 5–20 cm tall. Leaves in basal clusters, only a few centimeters long, on long pedicels with a round blade; margin entire; upper surface covered in dark pink hairs tipped with glandular droplets. Flowers white, in a one-sided raceme; petals 5, white, rounded-ovate, surrounded by 5 green sepals. Fruit a many-seeded dehiscent capsule.

Where Found common in sphagnum moss in acidic bogs and black spruce muskegs at low-elevations.

Similar Species distinguished from *Drosera anglica* by its round leaf blade, and its leaves lying close to the ground rather than upright.

Drosera anglica ENGLISH SUNDEW

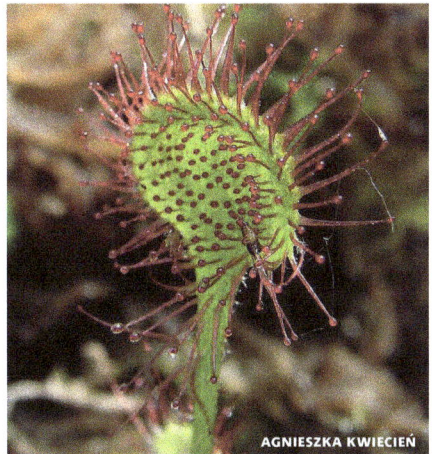
Drosera rotundifolia ROUNDLEAF SUNDEW

ELAEAGNACEAE
Oleaster Family

1 Leaves opposite, dark green above, silvery green below; stamens 8 . . . . *Shepherdia*
1 Leaves alternate, silvery on both sides; stamens 4 . . . . *Elaeagnus*

Elaeagnus SILVERBERRY
(Uncertain, may refer to Greek, *elaia*, olive tree, and *agnos*, chaste tree.)

♦ *Elaeagnus commutata* Bernh. ex Rydb.
SILVERBERRY
Habit medium shrub, from a strong rhizome; stems ascending, 1–2 m tall, with silvery- to brownish scales, old branches dark grayish red, young twigs brown or green. **Leaves** deciduous, alternate, lanceolate to oblanceolate, 2–7 cm long, silvery-scaly on both surfaces, underside with rusty-brown hairs. **Flowers** 1–4, nodding, almost sessile in axillary clusters; corolla yellow within, silvery outside, funnel-shaped with 4 lobes, 6–14 mm long, sweet-scented; stamens 4. **Fruit** a single achene enclosed in an ovate silvery-scurfy berry, about 1 cm long.
Where Found uncommon along rivers, on sandy shores, open woods, thickets.

Shepherdia BUFFALOBERRY
John Shepherd, 1764–1836, curator of Liverpool Botanic Garden.)

♦ *Shepherdia canadensis* (L.) Nutt.
RUSSET BUFFALOBERRY
Habit dioecious shrub; stems erect to spreading, to about 1 m tall, with brownish scales. **Leaves** deciduous, opposite, elliptic to ovate, covered with silvery stellate hairs, underside with rusty-brown scurfy scales; margins entire. **Flowers** yellow-brown, 2–3 mm

long, in small clusters in branch axils. **Fruit** an inedible bitter red berry (drupe) held closely along stem, with many ovoid achenes. **Flowering** immediately after snowmelt in spring, flowers opening before or during leaf-out; berries mature in late-July.
Where Found common on floodplain terraces, lakeshores, rocky alpine slopes, glacial moraines, old burns, open rocky woods, mostly at low- to mid-elevations; considered an early successional species, and able to fix nitrogen.
Similar Species *Viburnum edule* also has opposite leaves and red berries but its leaves not elliptic, and without rusty brown scales on stems and leaf undersides.
Traditional Uses the red berries are bitter, and one common name 'soapberry' comes from their unappetizing flavor, although bears eat them with abandon; traditionally used as a tonic or as a poultice for skin abrasions (Garibaldi 1999); the bitter berries are easily whipped into a creamlike froth for the traditional akutaq, or 'Eskimo icecream'.

ERICACEAE
Heath Family

1 Ovules and seeds 1 to 2 per carpel; stamens 3 . . . . *Empetrum*
1 Ovules and seeds many; stamens 5 to 12, generally 10 2
2 Plants woody; leaves on stem, alternate or opposite 3

Elaeagnus commutata SILVERBERRY

Shepherdia canadensis RUSSET BUFFALOBERRY

2 Plants barely woody; leaves basal or on short stems, alternate to whorled 15

3 Fruit a berry, ovary inferior . . . . *Vaccinium*

3 Fruit fleshy or dry, ovary superior. 4

4 Leaves densely rusty-tomentose below . . . . *Rhododendron*

4 Leaves not rusty-tomentose below. 5

5 Fruit a drupe 6

5 Fruit a dry capsule 7

6 Leaves deciduous, thin, conspicuously veined, margins with rounded teeth; branchlets glabrous; fruits juicy. . . . . *Arctous*

6 Leaves evergreen, leathery, not conspicuously veined, margins entire; branchlets hairy; fruits dry and mealy. . . . . *Arctostaphylos*

7 Leaves opposite 8

7 Leaves alternate. 10

8 Stamens 5 . . . . *Kalmia procumbens*

8 Stamens 10. 9

9 Corolla white; anthers awned . . . . *Cassiope*

9 Corolla pink; anthers not awned . . . . . . *Kalmia*

10 Leaves linear or linear-oblanceolate 11

10 Leaves wider 12

11 Leaves 2.5–4.5 mm long; leaf margins entire, somewhat scarious. . . . . *Cassiope*

11 Leaves 3–10 mm long; leaf margins glandular-serrate . . . . *Phyllodoce*

12 Flowers 4-parted. . . . *Rhododendron menziesii*

12 Flowers 5-parted 13

13 Anthers awned . . . . *Andromeda*

13 Anthers not awned 14

14 Corolla broadly cup-shaped, purple . . . . *Rhododendron*

14 Corolla urn-shaped or cylindric, white . . . . *Chamaedaphne*

15 Flower solitary . . . . *Moneses*

15 Flowers in a raceme 16

16 Inflorescence 1-sided . . . . *Orthilia*

16 Inflorescence cylindrical. . . . . *Pyrola*

Andromeda BOG-ROSEMARY

(In mythology, Andromeda was a daughter of Cassiope.)

♦ *Andromeda polifolia* L. BOG-ROSEMARY

Habit creeping evergreen shrub, with pink flowers; stems red-brown, 10–50 cm tall. Leaves alternate, thick-leathery, linear 12–25 mm long, dark green above and white below, both surfaces hairless; margin inrolled. Flowers 1–4 terminal on twigs, nodding at end of thick pink pedicels; petals pink, fused, constricted at tip with a few small lobes. Fruit an

inedible fleshy pink capsule.

Where Found common in black spruce muskeg, bogs, wet sedge meadows (and rarely in alpine tundra on limestone).

Similar Species distinguished from other Ericaceae by its rosemary-like linear leaves, and urn-shaped, bright pink flowers.

Traditional Uses Although called 'bog rosemary' plants should not be eaten as they contain a neurotoxin.

Arctostaphylos
BEARBERRY, KINNIKINNICK

(Greek, bear and bunch of grapes, alluding to common name for *A. uva-ursi*.)

♦ *Arctostaphylos uva-ursi* (L.) Spreng.
BEARBERRY, KINNIKINNICK

Habit creeping evergreen shrub, with white to light pink flowers, sometimes forming mats several meters wide; bark reddish to brownish, peeling off; stems ascending at tip, 5–15 cm tall, minutely hairy, sometimes glandular. Leaves alternate, leathery, oblanceolate to obovate, noticeably net-veined, dark green above and light green below; margins entire. Flowers one to several in a raceme; urn-shaped, white to light pink, constricted at tip with five small lobes. Fruit a red, mealy berry (drupe).

Andromeda polifolia BOG-ROSEMARY

Where Found common in dry, open places and aspen forests, from low- to high elevations.

Similar Species distinguished from the closely related red-fruit bearberry and alpine bearberry by the smaller, leathery leaves without ciliate margins, and the mealy fruit, not juicy as in *Arctous*.

Traditional Uses dried leaves were smoked by Native Americans; fruit generally tasteless, but important for some mammals and birds, and berries have been used as an extender in seasons when more desirable berry crops produced poorly; fruit was chewed or eaten for colds and flu, constipation, and stomach troubles (Garibaldi 1999).

Arctous ALPINE BEARBERRY

(Greek *arktous*, northern, alluding to distribution.)

1 Fruit purplish black; leaves to 5 cm long, margins hairy at base of leaf and on petioles; dead leaves of previous years persisting . . . . *A. alpina*
1 Fruit scarlet; leaves to 9 cm long, leaf margins and petioles not hairy, stalks glabrous; leaves of previous years not persisting . . . . *A. rubra*

♦*Arctous alpina* (L.) Nied.
ALPINE BEARBERRY
Arctostaphylos alpina (L.) Spreng.

Habit mat-forming, deciduous shrub, with whitish flowers and rhizomatous stems; branches erect, to 15 cm tall, with shedding bark, leading to a shaggy appearance; many dead leaves persistent along the trailing

branches. Leaves alternate, tightly clustered along stem; obovate to oblanceolate, thick and strongly net-veined, dark green in summer, sometimes reddish; leaf base and the winged petiole fringed with hairs; margins with small rounded teeth; leaves turn bright red in fall and tend to overwinter on the plant. Flowers 2–3, clustered at end of stem; petals fused into an urn-shape, white or pale yellow-green, transparent at base; stamens 10. Fruit a shiny black berry. Flowering before the leaves develop in late-spring; fruit produced in July.

Where Found common in alpine tundra and open conifer forests.

Similar Species very similar to the red-fruited *Arctous rubra*, and before the black berries develop (berries red in *A. rubra*), *A. alpina* can be distinguished by its somewhat thicker, rounder and more densely ciliate leaves, and its habitat of dry gravelly, exposed sites (in contrast to more protected, moist, and shady sites at lower elevation preferred by *A. rubra*).

Traditional Uses fruit can be eaten, but is rather flavorless; berries have been used as an extender in seasons with a shortage of more desirable berries; leaves were widely used as a medicinal tea by Native peoples, serving as an astringent and used for urinary and kidney ailments; fruit from bearberries were chewed or eaten raw by Athabascans for colds and flus, and by the Tsimshian for constipation, stomach troubles and symptoms from ulcers (Garibaldi 1999).

♦*Arctous rubra* (Rehder & E.H. Wilson) Nakai
RED-FRUIT BEARBERRY
Arctostaphylos rubra (Rehd. & E.H. Wilson) Fern.

Habit prostrate deciduous shrub, with whitish flowers, forming large patches. Leaves

Arctostaphylos uva-ursi BEARBERRY

Arctous alpina ALPINE BEARBERRY

alternate, obovate to oblanceolate, leathery green, often with reddish veins in summer, turning scarlet in fall, margins more or less finely toothed and sparsely fringed with hairs, especially towards tip. Flowers 2–5, in a terminal cluster; urn-shaped, gradually narrowing to a constriction, with small lobes at tip; white to cream, slightly translucent at base. Fruit a bright red, juicy berry. Flowering when leaves developed (early summer); berries ripen in July-August.

Where Found common in forests and shrub thickets at low- to mid-elevations in Denali.

Similar Species when in fruit, separating *Arctous rubra* and *A. alpina* is straightforward: the berry of *A. rubra* is bright red, in *A. alpina*, black; leaves of *A. alpina* are typically smaller and thicker and persist for several years; those of *A. rubra* are larger, thinner, and do not persist, and when shed, they leave conspicuous areas of leafless stems.

Traditional Uses few people eat the berries due to lack of flavor, but it is an important wildlife food; berries have been used as an extender in seasons when the crop of more desirable berries is poor; fruits were used medicinally by the Dena'ina and Tsimshian for a variety of ailments (Garibaldi 1999).

Cassiope MOUNTAIN-HEATHER

(Cassiope of Greek mythology was mother of Andromeda.)

1	Leaves alternate	*C. stelleriana*
1	Leaves opposite	2
2	Leaves prominently grooved on back	*C. tetragona*
2	Leaves not prominently grooved on back	*C. lycopodioides*

Arctous rubra RED-FRUIT BEARBERRY

♦ *Cassiope lycopodioides* (Pall.) D. Don.
CLUBMOSS MOUNTAIN-HEATHER

Habit dwarf, mat-forming shrub; stems prostrate or decumbent, 5–20 cm long, about 2 mm wide including appressed leaves. Leaves evergreen, opposite, 4-ranked but not in four distinct rows, appressed to stem, ovate to lance-shaped, 2–3 mm long, thinly papery-margined, often fringed and long-hairy at tip, the concave upper surface often hairy, the convex lower surface not grooved; unstalked. Flowers solitary in leaf axils, nodding on glabrous stalks to 10 mm long, longer than the subtending leaves; corolla cream to white, bell-shaped, the lobes shorter than the tube, 5–7 mm long; calyx 2–3 mm long, papery-margined. Fruit a globe-shaped capsule, about 3 mm wide, slightly longer than the calyx.

Where Found uncommon in heath and alpine tundra.

♦ *Cassiope stelleriana* (Pall.) DC.
ALASKAN MOUNTAIN-HEATHER
Harrimanella stelleriana (Pall.) Coville

Habit dwarf, mat-forming shrub; stems prostrate to decumbent, 5–20 cm long, minutely hairy. Leaves evergreen, alternate, spreading, linear- to lance-shaped, 3–5 mm long, upper surface flat, lower surface convex and slightly keeled (not grooved), glabrous, margins often somewhat irregular; short-stalked. Flowers solitary and terminal, nod-

Cassiope lycopodioides
CLUBMOSS MOUNTAIN-HEATHER

ding; flower stalks 3–10 mm long, finely hairy; corolla white or pinkish, broadly bell-shaped, 5–7 mm long, lobed about half way to base; calyx reddish. Fruit a nearly globe-shaped, erect capsule, about 5 mm wide.

Where Found occasional in alpine heath.

♦ *Cassiope tetragona* (L.) D. Don
WHITE ARCTIC MOUNTAIN-HEATHER

Habit coarse, dwarf, mat-forming shrub; stems 4-angled, stiff, ascending to erect, to 25 cm long, finely hairy. Leaves evergreen, opposite one other in four rows, leathery, ovate to lanceolate; outer leaf surface short-hairy, margins fringed with hairs. Flowers 2–6, nodding, on an upright, reddish pedicel curved at tip; corolla bell-shaped, white, tipped with 5 flared, semi-triangular lobes; calyx yellow-green or reddish, appressed to the corolla, five-toothed. Fruit a dry globose capsule, splitting open to release small seeds.

Where Found abundant, especially near snowbeds and in alpine areas on north-facing slopes of heath tundra.

Similar Species distinguished from *Cassiope lycopodioides* by the deeply grooved leaf underside.

Traditional Uses because it burns well when still green, *C. tetragona* has long been used as a fire starter in arctic or alpine regions.

Note at first glance, *Cassiope tetragona* looks like a clubmoss due to its spreading habit and stems obscured by lowermost bract scalelike leaves, but the white urn-shaped flowers place it within the heath family; the square shape of the stem is the source of the scientific name 'tetragona', meaning four-angled.

Chamaedaphne LEATHERLEAF
(Greek *chamai*, dwarf, and *daphne*, laurel, alluding to low habit and persistent leaves.)

♦ *Chamaedaphne calyculata* (L.) Moench
LEATHERLEAF

Habit low shrub; stems much-branched, mostly 20–60 cm tall, white-hairy, sometimes scaly; twigs yellow-brown. Leaves evergreen, alternate, thick and leathery, pointing upwards from branch, elliptic to oblanceolate, dark green above, much lighter gray-green below, with white scales; margin finely toothed. Flowers several, in a one-sided, leafy raceme, pendant at end of branch; white, urn-shaped, constricted below the 5 small terminal corolla lobes. Fruit a brown capsule, 3–5 mm long, splitting open to release many seeds. Flowering early to late-May, one of Denali's earliest flowering plants.

Where Found abundant in low-elevation wetlands and black spruce muskeg, sometimes growing in shallow water.

Similar Species no other medium-sized shrub in Denali has white bell-flowers and leathery, oblong leaves.

Cassiope tetragona
WHITE ARCTIC MOUNTAIN-HEATHER

Cassiope stelleriana
ALASKAN MOUNTAIN-HEATHER

Chamaedaphne calyculata LEATHERLEAF

Empetrum CROWBERRY
(Greek in, and rock, alluding to habitat.)

♦ *Empetrum nigrum* L. BLACK CROWBERRY
Habit dwarf, mat-forming shrub; stems somewhat decumbent, 15–30 cm long, freely branching, more or less woolly-hairy. Leaves evergreen, needle-like, whorled, to 7 mm long. Flowers small, solitary in leaf axils; petals 3 or more, purple, 3 mm long; sepals 3. Fruit a black, globe-shaped, fleshy drupe, to 9 mm in diameter, with 2–9 white seeds. Flowering early, just after snowmelt; ripe berries can be found in mid-June.

Where Found abundant in a variety of habitats from low- to high- elevations: shrub thickets, open woods, bogs, swamps, heathlands, tundra.

Similar Species **Alpine bearberry** (*Arctous alpina*) the only other shrub in Denali with black berries, but leaves of that species large and net-veined, not needle-like as in *Empetrum.*

Traditional Uses Used as a food, dye plant, and medicinally; berries, although not tasty when fresh, improve with cooking or preservation; the berries may have been an important survival food (especially when other berries were scarce), since it is common, the berries form early, last throughout the winter, and preserve well. The Yup'ik commonly use these berries in akutaq ('Eskimo ice-cream'); all parts of the plant have been used in traditional remedies (Garibaldi 1999, Kari 1995, Moerman 1998).

Kalmia MOUNTAIN-LAUREL
(In honor of Peter Kalm, 1715-1779, Swedish botanist, pupil of Linnaeus, and plant collector in eastern North America.)

♦ *Kalmia procumbens* (L.) Gift & K.A. Kron
ALPINE-AZALEA
Loiseleuria procumbens (L.) Loisel.
Habit low, mat-forming, alpine shrub, with star-shaped pink flowers; stems 5–30 cm long but only rising several cm above the ground, glabrous or minutely hairy. Leaves evergreen, opposite, small (3–8 mm long), leathery, oblong, green above, whitish and minutely hairy below; margins inrolled. Flowers star-shaped, 2–6 in clusters at ends of branches, on narrow pedicels 1-10 mm long; petals fused at base into a bell shape, separated midway into five triangular sections, deep to light pink; sepals dark red with ciliate margins, remaining attached to the fruit; stamens 5 with dark red anthers. Fruit a rounded capsule, 2–3 mm long, held upright from the pedicel; seeds winged, numerous, about 1 mm long. Flowering early in season.

Where Found common in alpine areas with *Dryas* and on heath tundra, dry gravelly slopes and ridges; most often on steep, south-facing slopes.

Empetrum nigrum BLACK CROWBERRY

Similar Species no other cushion-forming alpine plant has star-shaped pink flowers and oblong leaves with inrolled margins.

Moneses SINGLE-DELIGHT

(Greek *monos,* single, and *hesis,* delight, alluding to the attractive solitary flower.)

♦ *Moneses uniflora* (L.) A. Gray SINGLE-DELIGHT

Habit perennial, slightly woody herb, from a slender, rhizome-like root; stems erect or nearly so, to 15 cm tall, hairless, curved at tip. Leaves evergreen, basal and sometimes whorled around the stem a few centimeters up from the base of the stem; round or ovate with blunt tip, thin, dark green, conspicuously veined; margins toothed. Flowers single, initially nodding, turning upwards in fruit; corolla flat to broadly cup-shaped; petals 5, white, ovate, entire or finely fringed, 8–12 mm long; sepals small, pale green and rounded, reflexed in fruit; stamens 10; style with a large toothed stigma. Fruit a globe-shaped capsule, 6–10 mm long.

Where Found common in moist woods and shrub thickets at mid-elevations.

Similar Species no other species in Denali has a solitary, white, downward-facing flower.

Traditional Uses leaves and roots were prepared as teas for coughs and sore throats (Garibaldi 1999).

Orthilia SIDEBELLS

(Greek, straight, and side or flank, possibly alluding to the one-sided inflorescence.)

♦ *Orthilia secunda* (L.) House SIDEBELLS
Pyrola secunda L.

Habit perennial, slightly woody herb, from a rhizome, often forming colonies; stems usually single, 5–15 cm tall. Leaves evergreen, basal (sometimes leaves also on lower stem); ovate, with a sharp-pointed tip, green and shiny, petiole short, margins finely serrated. Flowers 5–25, in a raceme on one side of the stem ('secund'); petals 5, whitish green and translucent at tip, 4–6 mm long, overlapping to form a nodding bell; style long, protruding from the flower, stigma five-lobed; anthers 10, inverted at maturity and releasing pollen by two pores. Fruit a slightly flattened globe-shaped capsule; seeds minute, numerous.

Where Found abundant in mid-elevation forests and shrublands, occasional in alpine tundra.

Similar Species the single-sided raceme separates *Orthilia secunda* from the closely related genus *Pyrola.*

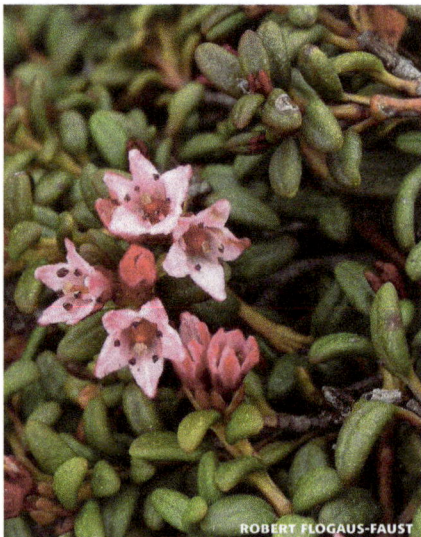

Kalmia procumbens ALPINE-AZALEA

ROBERT FLOGAUS-FAUST

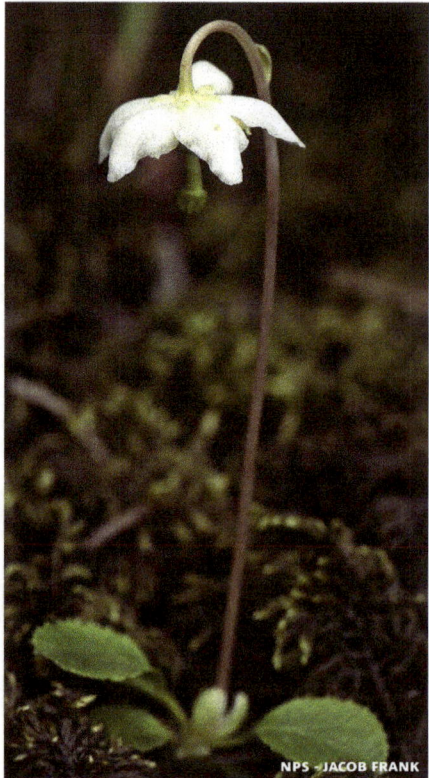

Moneses uniflora SINGLE-DELIGHT

NPS –JACOB FRANK

Phyllodoce MOUNTAIN-HEATH
(Greek, a sea nymph.)

1 Flowers pink to purplish . . . . *P. caerulea*
1 Flowers yellowish 2
2 Corolla glandular-hairy . . . . *P. glanduliflora*
2 Corolla glabrous . . . . *P. aleutica*

♦ *Phyllodoce aleutica* (Spreng.) A. Heller
  ALEUTIAN MOUNTAIN-HEATH
  Habit low, matted shrub; stems ascending to erect, to 20 cm tall Leaves evergreen, linear, 5–11 mm long, margins finely toothed. Flowers few to several, on pedicels mostly less than 1 cm long in flower, longer in fruit; corolla yellowish or greenish yellow, urn shaped; calyx lobes linear to lanceolate with gland-tipped hairs. Fruit a hairy capsule.
  Where Found uncommon in heath and alpine tundra.

♦ *Phyllodoce caerulea* (L.) Bab.
  BLUE MOUNTAIN-HEATH
  Habit low, matted shrub; stems erect to ascending, 8–20 cm tall, glandular; Leaves evergreen, needlelike, 4–10 mm long, less than 2 mm wide, dark green, shiny above; with a deep groove in middle and a pale groove beneath; margins rough or small-toothed. Flowers 2-several at stem ends, borne singly on glandular pedicels from leaf axils; corolla urn-shaped, pink to purple; calyx lobes lanceolate, reddish. Fruit a usually hairy capsule, about 3–4 mm long and about as broad.
  Where Found uncommon in heath and alpine tundra.
  Note hybridizes with *Phyllodoce aleutica*.

♦ *Phyllodoce glanduliflora* (Hook.) Coville
  YELLOW MOUNTAIN-HEATH
  Habit low, matted shrub; stems erect or ascending, 10–40 cm tall, finely glandular-

Phyllodoce aleutica ALEUTIAN MOUNTAIN-HEATH

Orthilia secunda SIDEBELLS

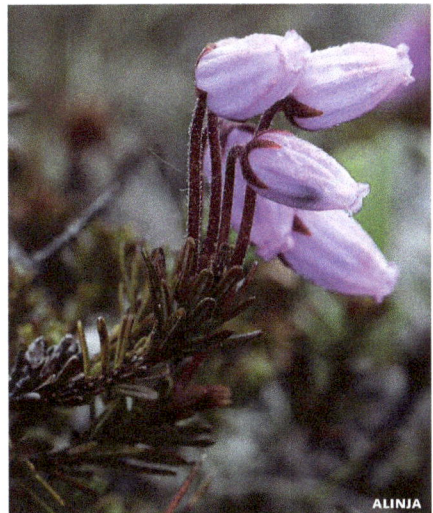
Phyllodoce caerulea BLUE MOUNTAIN-HEATH

hairy. Leaves evergreen, alternate, spreading-ascending, linear, 4–12 mm long, 1–2 mm wide, with a narrow groove above and a light, minutely hairy line below; margins appearing rolled under. Flowers several to many, nodding to erect in terminal clusters; flower stalks, calyx and corolla glandular-pubescent; flower stalks 2–3 cm long; corolla yellowish to greenish white, narrowly urn-shaped, 5–9 mm long, the lobes spreading; calyx lobes greenish, narrowly lance-shaped, 3–5 mm long; filaments hairy, anthers purplish. Fruit a globe-shaped capsule, 3–5 mm long, nearly as wide, glandular-hairy.

Where Found uncommon in heath and alpine tundra.

Pyrola WINTERGREEN
(Latin, diminutive of *Pyrus*, the pear, in reference to the leaves.)

1 Petals and anthers crimson to pale pink . . . . . .
. . . . *P. asarifolia*
1 Petals white, greenish white, or pinkish; anthers yellow. 2
2 Style short, included; petals white or pinkish . .
. . . . *P. minor*
2 Style longer, exserted 3
3 Flowers small, greenish white; leaves small, rounded . . . . *P. chlorantha*
3 Flowers large, creamy white or pinkish; leaves larger, blades 3–5 cm long. . . . . . *P. grandiflora*

♦*Pyrola asarifolia* Michx. PINK WINTERGREEN
Habit perennial herb, from a rhizome; stems leafless, smooth, often reddish, 15–30 cm tall. Leaves evergreen, basal, long-petioled, heart-shaped to round, the base sometimes indented, shiny dark green on upper

MATT LAVIN
Phyllodoce glanduliflora
YELLOW MOUNTAIN-HEATH

side; margins entire to slightly crenate; a few bracts present below the flowers. Flowers 5–25, in a spikelike raceme; petals 5, red to white-pink, usually lighter at base and darker at tip, overlapping in a bowl-shaped flower; style curves downwards (like an elephant's trunk), exserted, with a ring below the stigma; anthers curled over. Fruit a globose capsule, with many tiny seeds. Flowering early in the season.

Where Found common in moist to somewhat dry forests, woodlands, shrub thickets at low- to mid-elevations.

Similar Species similar to other *Pyrola* species, but distinguished by its pink flowers and anthers; *Pyrola minor* can sometimes have pink flowers, but its anthers are yellow, and the style is straight, and not exserted from the flower.

Pyrola chlorantha Sw.
GREEN-FLOWER WINTERGREEN
Habit perennial herb from a slender rhizome; flowering stems 10–20 cm tall, single, with 1 to several leaves at base or sometimes naked. Leaves evergreen, basal, somewhat

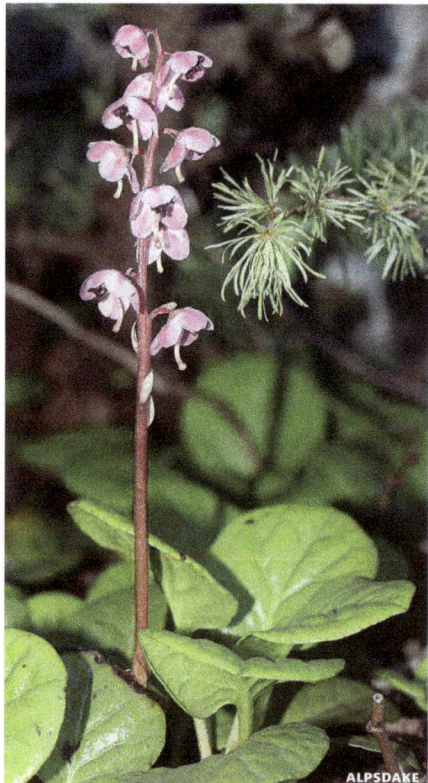

ALPSDAKE
Pyrola asarifolia PINK WINTERGREEN

leathery, more or less elliptic to oblong-ovate or circular, blades 1–3.5 cm long, pale green above, deep green below; margins finely toothed. Flowers 3–10 in an open terminal raceme; petals pale yellowish to greenish white, 5–6 mm long; styles curved downward, exserted, with a distinct collar below the lobed stigma. Fruit a depressed globe-shaped capsule, to about 6 mm wide.

Where Found woods and thickets.

♦ *Pyrola grandiflora* Radius
ARCTIC WINTERGREEN,
LARGE-FLOWER WINTERGREEN

Habit perennial herb, with white flowers, from a slender rhizome; flowering stems 5–20 cm tall, single. Leaves evergreen, leathery, basal, broadly ovate to rounded, with a blunt, round or cordate base, petioles longer than the blade; margins with small rounded teeth; leaves turning dark red from fall until early spring. Flowers 4–12, spiraled around a reddish unbranched stem, flat to cup-shaped, the petals spread apart; petals 5, large (6–10 mm long by 4–6 mm wide), white, often pinkish at base; sepals reddish; style long-exserted from the flower and curved, with a ring below the stigma lobes; flowers face outward and slightly downwards. Fruit a globose capsule, 4–6 mm wide, containing many tiny seeds.

Where Found common in low- to mid-elevation forests, and in meadows and tundra at higher elevations, sometimes on steep slopes.

Similar Species distinguished from other *Pyrola* species by its relatively large white flowers.

♦ *Pyrola minor* L. SMALL-FLOWER PYROLA

Habit perennial herb, from slender rhizomes; flowering stems usually single, leafless, 6–25 cm tall. Leaves evergreen, basal, leathery, broadly elliptic or ovate, turning dark red-purple in fall, margins crenulate. Flowers 3–11, spirally arranged on stem; petals five, white or pink, overlapping, forming downward facing bells; style short (not exserted from flower), with a five-lobed stigma, the lobes curving back towards the style; flowers often closed-up like a ball. Fruit a globose capsule, 4–5 mm wide, containing many tiny seeds.

Where Found alpine meadows and tundra, mid-elevation moist forests.

Similar Species Unlike other *Pyrola* species, the style is straight and does not protrude from the flower.

Pyrola grandiflora ARCTIC WINTERGREEN

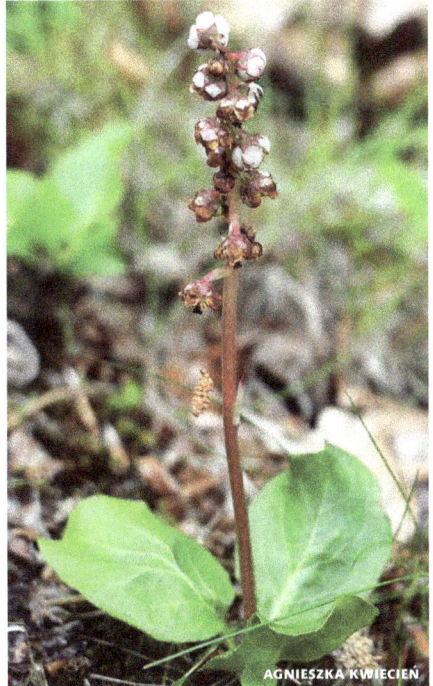

Pyrola minor SMALL-FLOWER PYROLA

Rhododendron
AZALEA, LABRADOR-TEA
(Greek, from a plant now placed in a different family; *Cistus ledon,* the Rock Rose.)

1 Leaves densely rusty-tomentose below 2
1 Leaves not rusty-tomentose below. 3
2 Leaves linear; stamens about 10 . . . .
. . . . *R. tomentosum*
2 Leaves oblong, stamens 5–10. . . . .
. . . . *R. groenlandicum*
3 Flowers 4-parted . . . . *R. menziesii*
3 Flowers 5-parted 4
4 Flowers 3–6, in an umbel; leaves about 1 cm
long, covered on both sides with resin dots . . .
. . . . *R. lapponicum*
4 Flowers usually solitary; leaves larger, resin dots
absent . . . . *R. camtschaticum*

◆ *Rhododendron camtschaticum* Pall.
KAMCHATKA RHODODENDRON
Therorhodion camtschaticum (Pall.) Small
  Habit low shrub; stems decumbent to erect, to about 20 cm tall. **Leaves** deciduous, spatulate to obovate, 2–5 cm long, underside veins long-hairy; margins fringed with hairs. **Flowers** solitary, borne at ends of new growth on hairy pedicels 1–4 cm long; corolla rose-purple, 3–4 cm across, the lobes ovate with finely hairy margins; sepals ovate or elliptic, green, with glandular hairs. **Fruit** a hairy capsule 5–10 mm long.
  Where Found uncommon in alpine tundra, heathlands.

◆ *Rhododendron groenlandicum* (Oeder) Kron & Judd **BOG LABRADOR-TEA**
Ledum groenlandicum Oeder
  Habit erect shrub; stems 30–80 cm tall, rusty soft-hairy. **Leaves** evergreen, leathery and thick, aromatic, lanceolate-ovate, 5–12 mm wide (broader than the leaves of R. tomentosum), rounded at tip; upper surface dark green, lower surface covered with rusty-brown hairs, margins inrolled; in fall, leaves turn reddish brown and bend downwards. **Flowers** many in a terminal rounded cluster; petals five, white, 5–7 mm long; stamens typically 8 (varies from 5–10); pedicels curve downward in fruit (not abruptly bent as in R. tomentosum). **Fruit** a capsule, which splits open from bottom into five parts, releasing many seeds **Flowering** mid-summer, fruiting in fall; fruits remain attached to the plant most of the winter.
  Where Found abundant in low-elevation spruce and mixed deciduous-conifer forests.
  Traditional Uses like the more common northern labrador-tea, leaves of *R. groenlandicum* were boiled in water to make a beverage or a medicinal tea.

◆ *Rhododendron lapponicum* (L.) Wahlenb.
LAPLAND ROSEBAY
  Habit dwarf, mat-forming, much-branched shrub, with striking magenta blossoms; stems prostrate to ascending, 5–30 cm long.

Rhododendron camtschaticum
KAMCHATKA RHODODENDRON

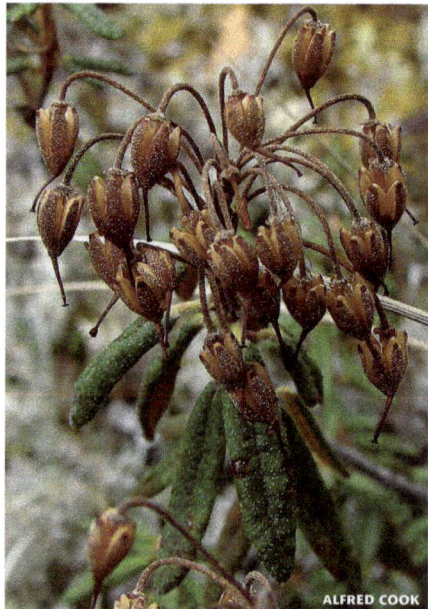
Rhododendron groenlandicum
BOG LABRADOR-TEA

Leaves evergreen, leathery, broadly elliptic with an impressed central vein; upper surface dark green, underside rusty brown, both surfaces flecked with white scales; margins slightly inrolled; leaves turning red-brown from fall to spring. Flowers 3–6, fragrant, in clusters in branch axils; corolla magenta, broadly cup-shaped, 5-lobed, the margins slightly wavy; each flower with 5–10 stamens, often as long as or longer than the petals, anthers pink or yellow; style dark pink. Fruit a dry ovoid capsule, covered with sessile glands.

Where Found uncommon in subalpine and alpine heath and shrub tundra, often on steep-slopes.

Similar Species Denali's only shrub with broadly open pink flowers and white-spotted leaves.

Traditional Uses leaves and flowers are toxic and should not be eaten.

♦ *Rhododendron menziesii* Craven
FOOL'S-HUCKLEBERRY, RUSTY MENZIESIA
Menziesia ferruginea Smith

Habit erect to spreading, straggly shrub; stems 0.5–2 m tall, finely hairy; older branches with loosely shredding bark, often glabrous. Leaves deciduous, alternate, clustered at stem tips, thin, elliptic to broadly ovate, 2–6 cm long, glandular-hairy on both surfaces, pale beneath, margins fine-toothed and fringed with hairs. Flowers 2–10 in a terminal cluster on shoots of previous year; flower pedicels short-hairy to conspicuously glandular-hairy, curved downward in flower,

erect in fruit; corolla coppery pink, urn-shaped, 4-lobed; calyx saucer-shaped, indistinctly 4-lobed, to 1 mm long. Fruit an ovate capsule, 5–7 mm long.

Where Found moist woods and thickets.

Note plants have a somewhat skunky odour when crushed.

♦ *Rhododendron tomentosum* Harmaja
NORTHERN LABRADOR-TEA,
NARROW-LEAF LABRADOR-TEA
Ledum decumbens (Ait.) Lodd. ex Steud.

Habit shrub; stems decumbent to ascending, mostly 10–50 cm long, rusty soft-hairy.

Rhododendron menziesii FOOL'S-HUCKLEBERRY

Rhododendron lapponicum LAPLAND ROSEBAY

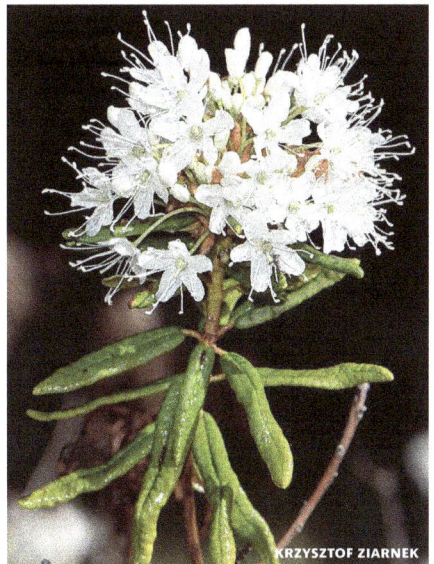

Rhododendron tomentosum
NORTHERN LABRADOR-TEA

Leaves evergreen, leathery, alternate, linear, 0.3–2 cm long, with a strong midvein, margins inrolled; upper surface dark green, underside with rust-brown hairs; leaves with a strong, characteristic smell. Flowers 10–35, in an umbel-like terminal cluster; petals 5, white, 2–8 mm long; stamens 10; in fruit the pedicels bent sharply downwards. Fruit a capsule, splitting into 5 segments from its base, remaining attached at tip of the fruit, releasing many seeds.

Where Found abundant in black spruce muskegs, bogs, heaths, shrub and alpine tundra.

Similar Species *Rhododendron groenlandicum* has strap-shaped, wider leaves, and usually 8 stamens; *R. tomentosum* has narrow, linear, inrolled leaves, and 10 stamens.

Traditional Uses leaves made into a tea, and used by Native peoples for treating a variety of ailments (Garibaldi 1999); Labrador-tea leaves traditionally burnt as a purifying incense by the Yup'ik.

Vaccinium
BLUEBERRY, CRANBERRY
(Latin name for the blueberry.)

1 Corolla divided nearly to base; stems threadlike . . . . *V. oxycoccus*
1 Corolla urn- or cup-shaped; stems wider 2
2 Leaves evergreen, shiny; berries red, shiny . . . . *V. vitis-idaea*
2 Leaves deciduous; berries blue, purplish or black 3
3 Flowers in axillary clusters; calyx lobes triangular, persistent in fruit . . . . *V. uliginosum*
3 Flowers single in leaf axils; calyx lobes blunt, deciduous in fruit. 4
4 Margin of leaves finely toothed throughout . . . . *V. cespitosum*
4 Margin of leaves not finely toothed throughout 5
5 Leaf margins entire or finely toothed only in lower part. . . . . *V. ovalifolium*
5 Leaf margins finely toothed to tip, but not completely to leaf base . . . . *V. membranaceum*

◆ *Vaccinium cespitosum* Michx.
DWARF BLUEBERRY
Habit low, spreading, mat-forming shrub; stems 10–30 cm tall, much-branched, yellowish green to reddish, usually finely hairy. Leaves deciduous, alternate, thin, prominently net-veined below, obovate, 1–3 cm

long, 5–15 mm wide, light green on both surfaces; margins finely toothed in upper half, the teeth usually gland-tipped. Flowers solitary in leaf axils, nodding; flower stalks short, curved downward; corolla whitish to pink, narrowly tubular urn-shaped, 4–6 mm long, twice as long as wide; calyx obscurely lobed, the lobes very short, deciduous in fruit; filaments glabrous, longer than anthers; anthers awned, with slender terminal tubes. Fruit a round berry, 5–8 mm wide, light blue to blackish blue with a pale gray bloom; sweet and palatable.

Where Found uncommon in subalpine and alpine meadows, bogs.

◆ *Vaccinium ovalifolium* Sm.
ALASKA BLUEBERRY, OVAL-LEAF BLUEBERRY
Vaccinium alaskensis Howell
Habit erect, spreading shrub; stems 5–15 dm tall, angled; glabrous; young twigs brownish to yellowish or reddish; old branches grayish. Leaves deciduous, alternate, oval to broadly ovate, 1–5 cm long, 0.7–3 cm wide, blunt at both ends, entire or sometimes very slightly toothed, glabrous; underside pale and glaucous. Flowers solitary in leaf axils, appearing before leaves have reached half their mature

Vaccinium cespitosum DWARF BLUEBERRY

Vaccinium ovalifolium ALASKA BLUEBERRY

size; flower stalks 1–8 mm long, strongly curved downward in fruit, not enlarged immediately under the berry; corolla pinkish, tubular urn-shaped, about 4–7 mm long, usually longer than wide, widest just below mid-length; calyx shallowly lobed, the lobes deciduous (rarely persistent) in fruit. Fruit a round berry, 6–10 mm wide, purplish to bluish black, mostly with distinct bluish bloom; pleasantly tart.

Where Found occasional in woods and thickets, subalpine heath.

◆ *Vaccinium oxycoccos* L. SMALL CRANBERRY
Oxycoccus microcarpus Turcz. ex Rupr.

Habit Small, creeping, dwarf shrub; stems very slender, 15–40 cm long, to 1 mm thick, glabrous to finely hairy; the stems trailing through moss, rooting at nodes, with reddish

QWERT1234

LFRED COOK

Vaccinium oxycoccos SMALL CRANBERRY

flowering stems only a few cm high; flowering stems short-hairy, with a few scalelike bracts below middle of stem. Leaves evergreen, leathery, waxy, 4–5 mm long, ovate to elliptic, green above, white below, margins inrolled. Flowers single, nodding downward from tip of stem; petals 5, pale pink, 5–7 mm long, completely curled back; stamens 8, filaments fused, forming a red to orange tube with anthers at top, and the style protruding. Fruit a tart, juicy red berry, 5–7 mm wide, disproportionately large compared to the rest of the plant; berries develop behind the petals, the remnant of their bases present on top of fruit. Flowering spring.

Where Found abundant in boggy wetlands on mats of Sphagnum moss.

Similar Species separated from other *Vaccinium* by its habitat of peatmoss wetlands, its tiny revolute ovate leaves, trailing stems, reflexed pink petals, and oversized red berries.

Traditional Uses people eat the tart berries, but in the Denali region these usually not abundant enough to be collected in quantity. Cooked powdered leaves were used by the Yup'ik to treat nausea and as a laxative; past-season berries were boiled in water as a spring tonic (Garibaldi 1999).

◆ *Vaccinium uliginosum* L. BOG BLUEBERRY
Habit spreading shrub, from rhizomes, often forming large thickets; stems to 60 cm tall, not angled; young branches yellowish green, minutely hairy; old branches grayish red. Leaves deciduous, alternate, obovate or elliptic, light green, 6–25 mm long, margins entire. Flowers 4–5, in a terminal cluster, peduncles red; petals pink, urn-shaped, 3–4 mm long, with four or five small upturned white lobes at tip; calyx with five red teeth. Fruit a round juicy berry, 5–8 mm wide, blue-black with a paler bloom, and bright purple flesh. Flowering June, fruit ripe in August and September.

Where Found abundant and found in nearly every vegetated habitat in Denali; especially common in open upland forest and shrub tundra in the subalpine zone in northern portion of the park.

Similar Species distinguished by its pale green, entire-margined, obovate leaves, even when the pink flowers or blueberries are absent.

Traditional Uses berries have a sweet, tart flavor and are widely used for food. Native peo-

ples picked them and mixed them with animal fat for long term storage; today, they are eaten fresh, frozen, or turned into preserves; bog blueberries are also commercially harvested in Alaska.

♦ *Vaccinium vitis-idaea* L.
LOWBUSH CRANBERRY, LINGONBERRY

Habit low, mat-forming shrub; stems decumbent or ascending, 5–20 cm long, rounded or slightly angled, minutely hairy. **Leaves** evergreen, leathery, oblong to elliptic, with a rounded tip and impressed midvein, glossy green above, paler below, dotted with glandular brown hairs; margins often inrolled. **Flowers** one to several, in a cluster at ends of twigs; corolla bell-shaped with 4 (or 5) lobes; flowers dark pink in bud, becoming whiter; calyx red, 4-lobed, persisting on tip of fruit. **Fruit** a red berry, 8–10 mm wide, with 3–15 yellow seeds. **Flowering** mid- to late-June and July; fruits form in August, often persisting over winter.

Where Found abundant in lowland bogs and forests to high alpine tundra; one of Denali's most common and widespread species.

Similar Species the glossy, revolute leaves with a deeply impressed central vein are distinctive.

Vaccinium uliginosum BOG BLUEBERRY

Vaccinium uliginosum BOG BLUEBERRY

Traditional Uses lowbush cranberry is a ubiquitous evergreen groundcover in Alaskan forests, producing an abundance of cranberries (also referred to as lingonberries); the berries are widely harvested, and eaten fresh or turned into jams, jellies, syrups, or juice; berries traditionally used as a tonic for congestion, coughing, colds, flus (Garibaldi 1999). Plants are browsed by hares, moose, caribou and black bears; bears, spruce grouse, ravens and other birds eat the fruit.

FABACEAE
Pea Family

1   Leaves with a slender terminal tendril . . . . *Vicia*
1   Leaves without tendrils. 2
2   Leaflets 3 (also see *Oxytropis mertensiana*). . . 3
2   Leaflets more than 3 (except *Oxytropis mertensiana*) 4
3   Inflorescence globose . . . . *Trifolium*
3   Inflorescence spikelike . . . . *Melilotus*
4   Legume articulated and jointed . . . *Hedysarum*
4   Legume not articulated. 5
5   Leaves palmately lobed . . . . *Lupinus*
5   Leaves pinnately divided. 6
6   Stems usually leafy; keel of corolla blunt. . . . . .
. . . . *Astragalus*
6   Stems usually not leafy; keel of corolla tipped with an erect point . . . . *Oxytropis*

Astragalus MILK-VETCH
(Greek name of some legume.)

1   Flowers yellow, without any trace of purple . . .
. . . . *A. umbellatus*
1   Flowers whitish or yellowish with purple-tipped keel, or purplish. 2
2   Pods sessile or short-stalked, in densely hairy, short, compact racemes, with erect flowers . . .
. . . . *A. laxmannii*
2   Pods sessile or short-stalked, at maturity not in compact, headlike inflorescence. 3
3   Plants decumbent, more or less matted, with short racemes 4
3   Plants taller, erect or ascending, with elongate racemes (at least in fruit) 6
4   Raceme usually 9- to 15-flowered; leaflets large
. . . . *A. alpinus*
4   Raceme 2–5-flowered; leaflets smaller, to 5 mm long 5

5   Pod sessile, ovate and inflated when ripe . . . . .
. . . . *A. polaris*
5   Pod with a long stalk above calyx, forming a distinctive semi-circle when ripe . *A. nutzotinensis*
6   Pods about 1 cm long, sessile or nearly so . . . .
. . . . *A. eucosmus*
6   Pods longer, stalked 7
7   Petals yellowish white or pale purplish; legumes about 1.5 cm long, glabrous . . . . . . *A. australis*
7   Petals whitish with keel tip purple; legumes 2–2.5 cm long, with minute black or white hairs .
. . . . *A. robbinsii*

♦*Astragalus alpinus* L. ALPINE MILK-VETCH
Habit low mat-forming perennial herb, from a taproot and rhizomes; stems few to several, decumbent to ascending, 5–25 cm long, branched, with short, black, appressed hairs. **Leaves** pinnately compound, with 8–11 pairs of leaflets; margins entire. **Flowers** 5–30, in a spreading raceme; petals pale blue to violet. **Fruit** a drooping pod (legume), 10–17 mm long, with obvious black hairs.

Where Found common on gravel bars, open soil, rocky places, and meadows, from low-elevations to the alpine.

Similar Species distinguished from other *Astragalus* by its prostrate habit (instead of upright), its many-flowered inflorescence, and its stalked seedpods.

♦*Astragalus australis* (L.) Lam.
INDIAN MILK-VETCH
Habit tufted perennial herb, from a woody taproot and much-branched stem-base;

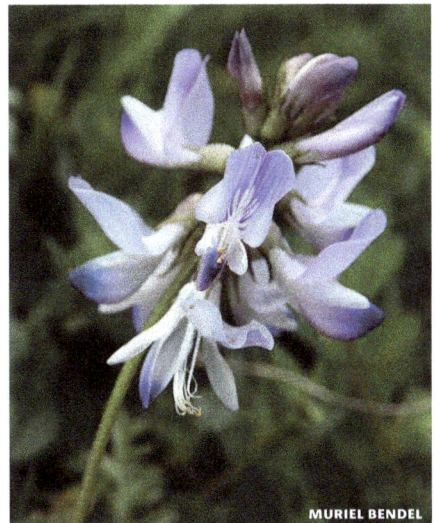

MURIEL BENDEL

Astragalus alpinus ALPINE MILK-VETCH

stems few to several, decumbent to ascending, 15–40 cm long, hairy to nearly glabrous. Leaves pinnately compound, 2–10 cm long; leaflets 7–15, hairy on both surfaces or glabrous above. Flowers 6–30 in a short, axillary raceme, the racemes compact at first, later elongating; corolla yellowish white, often tipped or tinged with purple; calyx usually black-hairy. Fruit a narrowly elliptic pod, somewhat sickle-shaped, 2–3 cm long, spreading to drooping.

Where Found alpine tundra, heathlands, woods, streambanks; soils often sandy or gravelly.

Astragalus eucosmus B.L. Rob.
ELEGANT MILK-VETCH

Habit perennial herb, from a taproot and branching stem-base; stems solitary to few, ascending to erect, 20–50 cm tall, unbranched, with short, appressed, unbranched hairs. Leaves pinnately compound; leaflets usually 13 or 15, hairless above, hairy below. Flowers 10–30 in an axillary raceme, the racemes compact and 2–3 cm long initially, elongating in age to 20 cm; flowers nodding and becoming oriented to one side; corolla purplish, 6–9 mm long; calyx black- or gray-hairy. Fruit a drooping, elliptic pod, rigid-pointed at tip, densely gray-black-hairy, 8–12 mm long, straight, membranous-papery.

Where Found heathlands, woods, thickets, river floodplains; soils often sandy or gravelly.

◆ Astragalus laxmannii Jacq.
LAXMANN'S MILK-VETCH

Astragalus adsurgens var. *tananaicus* (Hultén) Barneby

Habit tufted perennial herb, from a taproot and short-branching stem-base; stems several to many, 10–40 cm long, decumbent to

erect. Leaves pinnately compound; leaflets 9 to 23, appressed-hairy. Flowers 15–50 in a dense, head-like or spikelike, axillary raceme; corolla white to purplish, 12–18 mm long, the banner 1–3 mm longer than the wings, which are 2–3 mm longer than the keel; calyx 5–10 mm long, appressed-hairy with mixed black and white hairs. Fruit an erect, cylindric pod, 7–12 mm long, densely appressed-hairy, deeply grooved on one side.

Where Found sandy or gravelly soils, floodplains.

◆ Astragalus nutzotinensis J. Rousseau
NUTZOTIN MILK-VETCH

Habit mat-forming perennial herb from a branching stem-base and taproot; stems few to several, slender, prostrate along the ground, 10–30 cm long, to 6–10 cm high, finely appressed-hairy with white and black hairs. Leaves pinnately compound, leaflets 7–

Astragalus laxmannii LAXMANN'S MILK-VETCH

Astragalus australis INDIAN MILK-VETCH

Astragalus nutzotinensis NUTZOTIN MILK-VETCH

15. Flowers 2–4 in a terminal raceme; petals pale purple to pink, 12–18 mm long; calyx black-hairy. Fruit a large pod, highly curved and nearly circular at maturity, 3–5 cm long; the distinctive sickle-shaped pods allow the wind to roll them along gravel bars, dispersing their seed.

Where Found occasional at mid- to high-elevations in gravelly soil of glacial river floodplains; also in steep, rocky places in the alpine.

Astragalus polaris (Seem.) Benth.
POLAR MILK-VETCH

Habit tiny, loosely matted perennial herb; stems from a central rhizome. Leaves pinnately compound; leaflets 7–17, to 5 mm long. Flowers 1–3 in a raceme; petals pale purple; calyx covered in black or white hairs. Fruit a pod, becoming inflated and papery when mature (a distinguishing feature of this species). Flowering early to mid-summer.

Where Found occasional in moist alpine areas in tundra and gravelly and sandy places, often associated with limestone bedrock.

Astragalus robbinsii (Oakes) A. Gray
ROBBINS' MILK-VETCH

Habit perennial herb from a taproot and branching stem-base; stems usually ascending to erect but decumbent at base (or sometimes prostrate in harsh environments), 20–50 cm long, with short, stiff, appressed, unbranched hairs to nearly glabrous. Leaves pinnately compound; leaflets 7–19, glabrous above, paler and hairy below. Flowers 6–25 or more, in a loose, axillary raceme, mostly on one side of the axis; corolla whitish or yellowish to pale purple, fading bluish; calyx short-black-hairy. Fruit a narrowly elliptic pod, spreading to drooping, short-stalked, black-hairy, about 15 mm long.

Where Found on sandy or gravelly soils in woods and along streams and rivers; talus slopes.

♦ Astragalus umbellatus Bunge
TUNDRA MILK-VETCH

Habit perennial herb from a buried stem-base and rhizome-like branches; stems solitary or few together, erect to ascending, 5–30 cm tall, unbranched, long-soft-hairy. Leaves pinnately compound; leaflets 7–11, glabrous above, sparsely white-hairy beneath. Flowers 1–10, crowded in a short, headlike raceme; petals bright yellow with white margins. Fruit

an ovate to elliptic, black-hairy pod, 20–25 mm long.

Where Found common in alpine heath tundra, snowbeds, moist meadows.

Similar Species distinct from other milk-vetches by having yellow flowers in an umbel (radiating from a single attachment point) and a black-hairy seedpod.

Hedysarum SWEET-VETCH
(Greek, sweet.)

1 Leaflets thin, with prominent lateral veins; calyx teeth triangular, shorter than the tube . . . . *H. alpinum*
1 Leaflets thick, lateral veins usually not evident; calyx teeth awl-shaped, longer than the tube . . . . *H. boreale*

♦ Hedysarum alpinum L.
ALPINE SWEET-VETCH

Habit perennial herb, from a brown, scaly stem-base and large, fleshy or woody taproot; stems usually several, erect or decumbent-ascending, 20–35 cm tall, often branched above, short-stiff-hairy. Leaves alternate, pinnately compound with 15–20 ovate to elliptic leaflets, with obvious lateral veins. Flowers 10–20 in a raceme; petals pink, 2.5–3 cm long. Fruit a dry loment (constricted pod), with 2–3 segments.

Where Found abundant at low- to mid-elevations in rocky places, meadows and tundra,

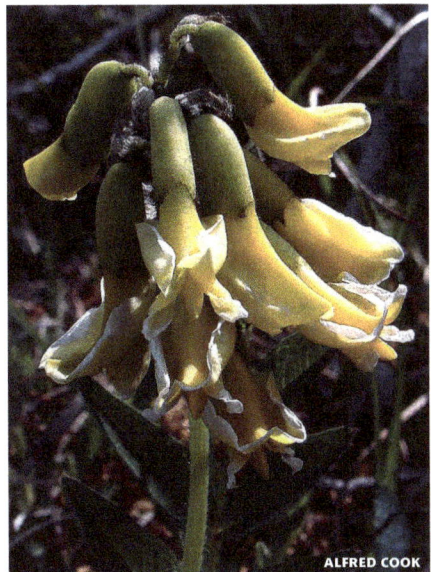

ALFRED COOK

Astragalus umbellatus TUNDRA MILK-VETCH

and on sandy to rocky river bars and lakeshores; it can also persist in the understory of floodplain forests.

Similar Species Hedysarum boreale lacks visible veins on leaflet underside, and has somewhat larger flowers.

Traditional Uses roots, stems and leaves edible and have been a traditional food source for Alaskan natives either raw, cooked, roasted or fried; also an important early season food for grizzly bears, who dig the roots while plants still dormant.

♦ *Hedysarum boreale* Nutt.
NORTHERN SWEET-VETCH

Habit perennial herb, from a branched, woody stem-base and thick, fibrous taproot; stems decumbent to ascending, 10–30 cm long, sometimes branched above, grayish stiff-hairy. **Leaves** alternate, pinnately compound with 7–15 ovate to elliptic leaflets and no obvious lateral veins. **Flowers** in a raceme of 5–15; petals pink, 2.5–3 cm long. **Fruit** a dry loment (constricted pod) with 3–6 segments, the joints of the pod winged.

Where Found at low- to mid-elevations on open gravel bars and early successional habitats; in some years, it can be seen covering large areas along the Thorofare River gravel bar below Eielson Visitor Center.

Similar Species *Hedysarum alpinum* differs by having a visible vein on leaflet underside, and a pod without wing-margined joints.

Lupinus LUPINE
(Latin, *lupus*, a wolf.)

1	Leaflets 10-18; basal leaves 15-20 cm in diameter . . . . *L. polyphyllus*
1	Leaflets fewer; leaves smaller. 2
2	Basal leaves with short petioles; petioles usually about as long as diameter of leaf; leaflets blunt, tipped with a short sharp point *L. nootkatensis*
2	Basal leaves with long-petioles; petioles usually 2 to several times longer than diameter of leaf; leaflets acute . . . . *L. arcticus*

♦ *Lupinus arcticus* S. Watson
ARCTIC LUPINE

Habit perennial herb, from a branched, woody stem-base; stems several, erect to ascending, to 50 cm tall, with appressed to spreading, silky hairs. **Leaves** mostly basal, palmately compound, with 4–9 oblong-elliptic leaflets, petioles at least twice as long as leaf blade; stem leaves few, small; all leaves glabrous above, woolly-hairy below. **Flowers** in a raceme to 15 cm long; petals blue to purple (rarely white), 1.5–2 cm long. **Fruit** a hairy pod, 2–4 cm long.

Where Found common at mid-elevations in well-drained floodplains, open forests, shrub tundra and open tundra; very common along the Park Road.

Similar Species *Lupinus nootkatensis,* found primarily on south side of the park, has short petioles, and the whole plant is densely woolly.

Note Arctic lupine is associated with symbiotic nitrogen-producing bacteria (*Rhizobium*) that occur in nodules in its roots, helping it to colonize rocky, nutrient-poor soils.

Hedysarum alpinum **ALPINE SWEET-VETCH**

Hedysarum boreale **NORTHERN SWEET-VETCH**

♦ *Lupinus nootkatensis* Donn ex Sims
NOOTKA LUPINE

Habit perennial herb, from a woody stem-base; stems few to several, erect or ascending, to 1 m tall (but barely 10 cm in exposed areas), often hollow, soft-shaggy (especially when young) or with short, stiff hairs. Leaves palmately compound; leaflets 5–8, broadly oblanceolate, blunt to rounded at tip, 2–6 cm long; generally glabrous above, shaggy-soft-hairy below. Flowers a stalked, terminal raceme, to 25 cm long; corolla bluish, often tinged with white or pink. Fruit a silky-hairy pod, 3–5 cm long; seeds 7–11.

Where Found common on alpine slopes and meadows, gravel bars.

Note seeds poisonous, and can cause inflammation of the stomach if eaten.

Lupinus polyphyllus Lindl.
BIG-LEAF LUPINE

Habit perennial herb from a branched, somewhat rhizomatous stem-base; stems erect, to 1 m or more tall, generally unbranched, cylindric-hollow at base, usually nearly glabrous but sometimes hairy. Leaves basal (a few) and alternate along stem, palmately compound; petioles of basal leaves often much longer than those of stem leaves; leaflets 9–17, 3–12 cm long, glabrous

above, sparsely stiff-hairy below. Flowers in a dense, terminal raceme, to 40 cm long; corolla bluish to violet. Fruit a curved, densely soft-hairy pod, 3–5 cm long; seeds 6–10.

Where Found uncommon on streambanks and moist places in general.

Melilotus SWEET-CLOVER

(Greek meli, honey, and lotos, a leguminous plant.) White and yellow-flowered forms are now sometimes grouped into a single species: *M. officinalis* (L.) Lam.

1 Flowers white . . . . *M. albus*
1 Flowers yellow . . . . *M. officinalis*

Melilotus officinalis (L.) Lam.
YELLOW SWEET-CLOVER

Habit biennial or annual herb, from a strong taproot, sweet-scented in drying; stems erect, 1 m or more tall, freely branched, glabrous to sparsely short-hairy. Leaves alternate, pinnately compound; leaflets 3, margins fine-toothed to near the base. Flowers 20–50 or more in a slender, spikelike, axillary raceme; corolla yellow or white. Fruit an ovate, somewhat flattened, nodding pod, 3–5 mm long; seeds 1 or 2.

Where Found uncommon in disturbed places, roadsides; European introduction.

Lupinus arcticus ARCTIC LUPINE

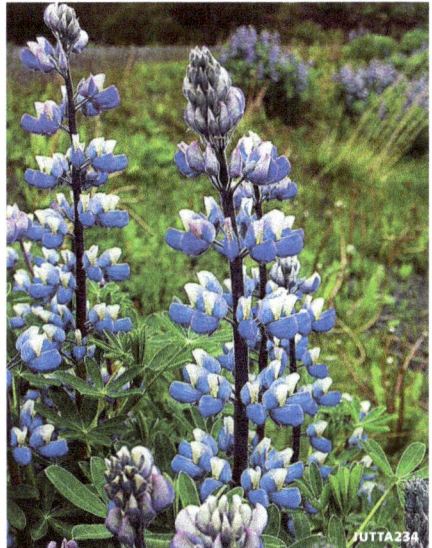
Lupinus nootkatensis NOOTKA LUPINE

Oxytropis LOCOWEED

(Greek, sharp keel; the keel of the flower in *Oxytropis* always have a pointed tip.)

1 Stipules leaf-like; pods drooping; plants with short, leafy stems. . . . . *O. deflexa*
1 Stipules not leaf-like; pods spreading to erect; plants without leafy stems 2
2 Plants more or less glandular-viscid *O. borealis*
2 Plants not glandular-viscid 3
3 Stipules chestnut brown; flowers yellow. . . . . .
. . . . *O. maydelliana*
3 Stipules papery white or yellow; flowers various
. . . . 4
4 Leaflets (or at least some of them) in whorls of 3 or 4 . . . . *O. campestris*
4 Leaflets opposite or alternate. 5
5 Leaflets 1 or 3 (sometimes 5) . . *O. mertensiana*
5 Leaflets 5 to many 6
6 Dwarf species with loosely tufted or compact habit; flowers purple. 7
6 Plants taller, loosely tufted . . . . . *O. campestris*
7 Loosely tufted . . . . *O. scammaniana*
7 Plants densely tufted or cushion-forming 8
8 Pods short, less than 2 times longer than wide; flowers 1 (rarely 2) per peduncle . . . .
. . . . *O. huddelsonii*
8 Pods elongate; usually at least 3 times longer than broad; flowers 2 or 3 (rarely 1) per peduncle . . . . *O. bryophila*

Oxytropis borealis BOREAL LOCOWEED

♦*Oxytropis borealis* DC. BOREAL LOCOWEED
Oxytropis viscida Nutt.

Habit tufted perennial herb, from a taproot and much-branched base; stems glandular and leafless, 10–20 cm tall. Leaves pinnately compound; leaflets numerous, 25–51, glabrous to hairy, often glandular. Flowers 5–10 in a head-like cluster, pale blue; calyx gray-hairy and glandular (separating this species from our other *Oxytropis*). Fruit a finely hairy pod, 1–2 cm long, with a hooked beak.

Where Found occasional in rocky places in subalpine and alpine areas, including gravel bars, and especially on south-facing slopes.

♦*Oxytropis bryophila* (Greene) Jurtzev
YUKON LOCOWEED
Oxytropis nigrescens subsp. *bryophila* (Greene) Hultén

Habit small, cushion-forming perennial herb; plants only a few centimeters high from a long taproot; stem-base covered in gray-hairy persistent stipules. Leaves pinnately compound; leaflets 5–15, sparsely covered in long white or gray hairs. Flowers generally in pairs (sometimes single), at end of a stalk not much higher than the leaves; corolla purple; calyx black-hairy. Fruit a pod, 3–3.5 cm long, densely covered in gray or black hairs.

Where Found common in well-drained tundra and rocky areas on both sides of Alaska Range in Denali, and is common in alpine tundra along Denali Park Road.

Similar Species can be identified by its small, cushion-forming habit, purple flowers, and its brown stipules with gray hairs. *O. scammaniana* is similar, but has hairless straw-colored stipules and usually blue flowers.

♦*Oxytropis campestris* (L.) DC.
FIELD LOCOWEED
Habit densely tufted perennial herb, from a

Oxytropis bryophila YUKON LOCOWEED

taproot and branching stem-base (which is often covered with old stipules), stems 5–30 cm tall; one of the first plants to green-up in spring. Leaves pinnately compound; leaflets 15–35, long-hairy on both sides. Flowers many in a raceme, tightly clustered when young and elongating when mature; corolla pale yellow to cream-colored, 10–12 mm long; calyx covered with dark and light hairs. Fruit a pod, 12–18 mm long, covered in black hairs.

Where Found occasional on subalpine flood-plains and sandy river terraces.

♦ *Oxytropis deflexa* (Pall.) DC.
DEFLEXED LOCOWEED

Habit tufted perennial herb, from a strong taproot and branching stem-base; stems few to several, decumbent to erect, to 15–30 cm long, hairy. Leaves pinnately compound; leaflets 15–41, sparsely to densely soft-hairy on both surfaces or glabrous above. Flowers 5–25, in a compact to elongate raceme 5–15 cm long; corolla usually bluish or purple; calyx with dark, stiff hairs; flowers at first upright but soon nodding and often arranged on one side of the raceme. Fruit a drooping, oblong pod, 10–25 mm long, with short dark hairs.

Where Found in gravelly or sandy soils, often on lakeshores or along rivers.

Oxytropis huddelsonii A.E. Porsild
HUDDELSON'S LOCOWEED

Habit tufted or cushion-forming perennial herb, from a stout taproot and branching stem-base covered with persistent stipules,

to 4 cm tall. Leaves basal, pinnately compound, the leaf axis purple, white soft-hairy; leaflets 7–13, soft-hairy on upper surface, nearly glabrous below, margins inrolled. Flowers 1–2; corolla pink-purple; calyx with appressed dark hairs. Fruit an elliptic pod, 1–2 cm long, with hooked beak, 1-chambered, lying on ground when mature.

Where Found uncommon on alpine ridges, heathlands, frost boils.

♦ *Oxytropis maydelliana* Trautv.
MAYDELL LOCOWEED

Habit tufted perennial herb, from a branching, densely hairy stem-base covered with old, reddish brown leaf-stalks and stipules; stems leafless, two or more, to 20 cm tall. Leaves mostly basal, pinnately compound, leaflets 11–21 elliptic, margins entire. Flowers 5–9, in a compact raceme; corolla yellow or cream; calyx with dense black (or white) hairs. Fruit a long-hairy pod, 1.5–2 cm long, tipped by a bent beak.

Where Found subalpine to alpine tundra.

Similar Species distinguished from other *Oxytropis* by its yellow flowers and conspicuous persistent reddish stipules at base of plant.

Traditional Uses roots of *Oxytropis maydelliana* were traditionally eaten in Nunavut, either raw or fried in seal oil (Aiken et al. 2003), but like others members of the genus, can be harmful if ingested in quantity.

Oxytropis campestris FIELD LOCOWEED

Oxytropis deflexa DEFLEXED LOCOWEED

Oxytropis mertensiana Turcz.
MERTENS' LOCOWEED

Habit perennial herb, from a branching stem-base covered with persistent stipules; stems less than 10 cm tall, white-pubescent below, becoming black-pubescent above. Leaves single to 3-parted; leaflets ciliate on margins. Flowers 1–3, corolla purple; calyx black-woolly. Fruit a black-hairy pod, 1–2 cm long

Where Found uncommon on moist alpine slopes, gravel bars.

Oxytropis scammaniana Hultén
SCAMMAN LOCOWEED

Habit tufted perennial herb, from a taproot and branching stem-base covered with persistent straw-colored stipules; stems erect, to 10 cm long, covered in long white hairs. Leaves pinnately compound; leaflets 9–13. Flowers typically 3; corolla blue to purple; calyx black-hairy. Fruit a black-hairy pod, 1–2 cm long.

Where Found common in moist to wet alpine tundra (including snowbeds).

Similar Species separated from other cushion-forming, blue-flowered *Oxytropis* by upright flowering stems, and the straw-colored, stipules that are hairless on upper surface.

Note Named in honor of Edith Scammon (1882–1967), a botanist who collected thousands of plants in the Denali region and throughout Alaska; *Claytonia scammaniana* is also named after her.

Trifolium CLOVER
(Latin three, and leaf.)

1 Flowers 1–2 cm long, reddish . . . . . *T. pratense*
1 Flowers small, about 1 cm long, white or pink 2
2 Stems erect-ascending . . . . *T. hybridum*
2 Stems creeping, rooting at nodes . . . . *T. repens*

Trifolium hybridum L.
ALSIKE CLOVER

Habit perennial herb, from a taproot; stems several, ascending to erect, 10–40 cm tall,

Oxytropis mertensiana MERTENS' LOCOWEED

Oxytropis maydelliana MAYDELL LOCOWEED

Oxytropis scammaniana SCAMMAN LOCOWEED

rarely rooting at nodes, slightly hairy. Leaves palmately compound; leaflets 3. Flowers a dense, globe-shaped head; corolla pink or white. Fruit an oblong pod; seeds 1–3.

Where Found uncommon in disturbed places; introduced from Eurasia.

Trifolium pratense L.
RED CLOVER

Habit perennial or biennial herb, from a taproot; stems several, ascending to sprawling, soft-hairy, 20–70 cm tall. Leaves palmately compound; leaflets 3 (rarely 4), often with a white, crescent-shaped spot towards base, soft-hairy. Flowers 50–200, in a dense, globe-shaped head; corolla rose-red; calyx hairy. Fruit an ovate pod, about 2 mm long; seeds 2.

Where Found disturbed places; introduced from Europe.

Trifolium repens L.
WHITE CLOVER

Habit creeping perennial herb, from a slender taproot; stems branching from base, often rooting at nodes, glabrous or sparsely hairy. Leaves palmately compound; leaflets 3, ovate, with a notch at tip, often with a pale blotch; margins finely toothed. Flowers numerous, in a dense, globe-shaped head; corolla creamy white to pinkish; calyx glabrous, the tube white with green veins. Fruit an oblong pod, about 5 mm long; seeds 1 to 4.

Where Found uncommon on disturbed sites; introduced from Europe.

Vicia VETCH
(The classical Latin name.)

Vicia cracca L.
COW-VETCH

Habit perennial herb; stems climbing or trailing, to 1 m long, finely short-hairy to glabrous, angled and somewhat grooved. Leaves alternate, pinnately compound; leaflets 8 to 24, linear to lance-elliptic, abruptly narrowed to a pointed tip, 1–3 cm long; tendrils well-developed, branching; stipules entire to toothed. Flowers 20–70, in an axillary, long-stalked, crowded raceme; flowers pea-like, drooping; corolla blue to reddish purple, two-toned dark and pale; calyx half as long as corolla. Fruit a glabrous pod, 2–3 cm long, with 4–8 seeds.

Where Found uncommon in disturbed places, roadsides; an Eurasian introduction.

GENTIANACEAE
Gentian Family

1	Corolla tubular or funnel-like 2
1	Corolla rotate (flat and spreading) 6
2	Flowers large, 2–5 cm long; corolla lobes fringed . . . . *Gentianopsis*
2	Flowers smaller; corolla lobes not fringed. . . . 3
3	Corolla with folds in the sinuses . . . . . *Gentiana*
3	Corolla without folds in the sinuses 4
4	Corolla not fringed in the throat . . *Gentianella*
4	Corollas fringed in the throat 5
5	Flowers solitary, terminal; flower stalks longer than the adjacent internodes . . . . . *Comastoma*
5	Flowers few to several, axillary and terminal; flower stalks shorter than the adjacent internodes . . . . *Gentianella*
6	Rhizomatous perennial; leaves mainly basal . . . . *Swertia*
6	Taprooted annual with; leaves mainly along stem . . . . *Lomatogonium*

Comastoma LAPLAND GENTIAN
(Greek: hair, mouth, the corolla fringed.)

◆*Comastoma tenellum* (Rottb.) Toyok.
LAPLAND GENTIAN, SLENDER GENTIAN
Gentianella tenella (Rottb.) Börner

Habit Annual herb from a taproot; stems ascending to erect, several, branched or sim-

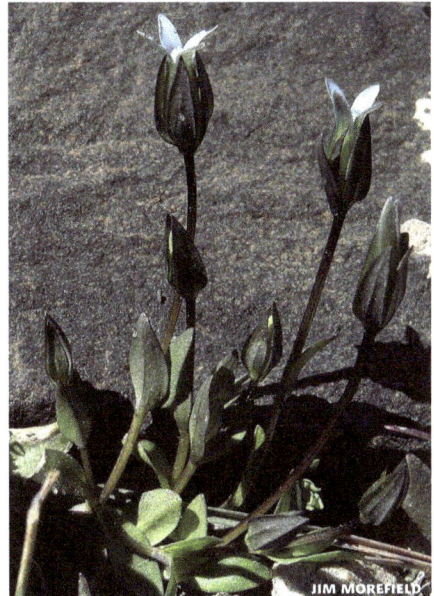

Comastoma tenellum LAPLAND GENTIAN

ple, 4–12 cm tall. Leaves basal and along stem; basal leaves a pair, or more numerous in a rosette, ovate to elliptic; stem leaves opposite, lanceolate to elliptic, not joined (except for the lower ones). Flowers solitary, terminal, long-stalked; corolla blue to white, to about 1 cm long, tubular, 4-lobed (sometimes 5-lobed); calyx 4–10 mm long, 4–5-lobed; stamens shorter than the corolla tube. Fruit a narrowly ovate capsule, slightly longer than the persistent corolla; seeds ovate, slightly flattened, wingless, yellow to light brown.

Where Found uncommon in dry, gravelly alpine areas.

Gentiana GENTIAN

(Gentius, king of Illyria, who used roots of some species to treat malaria.)

1 Plants annual, from slender taproots 2
1 Plants perennial, from rhizomes 3
2 Plants prostrate to ascending, simple or branched from base; flowers solitary, terminal. . . . . *G. prostrata*
2 Plants erect or ascending, branched throughout or simple; flowers terminal and axillary, often more than one . . . . *G. douglasiana*
3 Flowers 3–5 cm long, cream to yellowish green with blue-purple spots or stripes; leaves linear to narrowly oblong . . . . *G. algida*
3 Flowers 1.5–2 cm long, blue to yellowish green, rarely white; leaves oval to elliptic . . . *G. glauca*

♦ *Gentiana algida* Pall. WHITISH GENTIAN
Habit small perennial herb; stems 3–15 cm tall from a short branching stem-base. Leaves basal and opposite along the stem, shiny yellow-green, linear or oblong, margins entire. Flowers 1–3, large, trumpet-shaped; petals fused, white to cream to pale greenish with dark blue patches, 3.5–5 cm long, folded into sinuses. Fruit an elliptic capsule, 2–3 cm long, splitting open by two valves to release the seeds.

Where Found occasional in upper elevation moist meadows, openings in mossy shrub tundra, and alpine tundra.

Similar Species No other species in Denali has similar folded, large, blue-marked white flowers and opposite leaves.

Gentiana douglasiana Bong.
SWAMP GENTIAN
Habit annual herb from a taproot; stems erect, several, freely branching, angled, 10–

20 cm tall. Leaves basal and along stem; basal leaves few in a rosette, ovate to elliptic, to 1 cm long; stem leaves shorter, fused at base. Flowers solitary, or more usually in a loose terminal cluster; corolla white with purplish streaks, 8–12 mm long, tubular with 5 pointed lobes, the lobes blue on back; calyx 4–6 mm long, half the length of corolla; stamens shorter than the corolla tube. Fruit an obovate, wing-margined capsule; seeds dark brown, spindle-shaped, 1.5 mm long.

Where Found uncommon in bogs, wet meadows.

♦ *Gentiana glauca* Pall. GLAUCOUS GENTIAN
Habit perennial herb from a slender rhizome; stems erect, solitary, simple, yellow-green, glabrous, to 15 cm tall. Leaves basal and along stem, pale yellow-green, slightly fleshy; basal leaves in a rosette, spatulate to obovate, stem leaves elliptic to orbicular, in 1–3 oppositely arranged pairs, margins entire. Flowers blue-green, closed, in a cluster at top of stem, sometimes with more flowers in leaf axils below; calyx and corolla (petals) fused into tubes, calyx usually bluish and half the length of corolla; corolla deep blue or blue-green, 1–2 cm long, folded (plicate). Fruit a long capsule, splitting open to release many wing-margined seeds.

Where Found common in alpine snowbeds, meadows and heath tundra, especially on north-facing slopes.

Similar Species No other plant in Denali has deep blue, closed flowers, and fleshy yellow-green leaves.

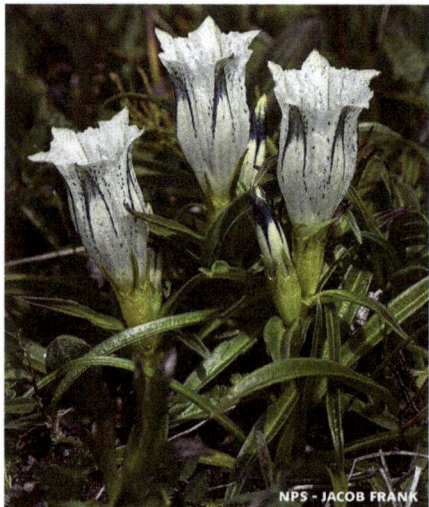

Gentiana algida WHITISH GENTIAN

♦ *Gentiana prostrata* Haenke
MOSS GENTIAN, PYGMY GENTIAN

Habit small, annual creeping herb from a slender taproot; stems prostrate or ascending, few to many branched from the base, glabrous, to 7 cm long. **Leaves** in opposite pairs along stem, elliptic-ovate, margins entire; lowermost bract scalelike. **Flowers** single and terminal, blue; calyx green, with acute lobes; petals fused, with usually 4 (sometimes 5) main triangular lobes, only opening in sunlight. **Fruit** a long-stalked capsule; seeds not wing-margined.

Where Found common in alpine areas, especially on steep, east- or west-facing slopes.

Similar Species *Gentianella propinqua* also with pale flowers, but that species upright, with multiple lilac to pale purple flowers on each stem.

Gentianella DWARF GENTIAN
(Latin, little *Gentiana*.)

1   Corolla mostly less than 15 mm long, the lobes fringed with hairs at base within . . *G. amarella*
1   Corolla mostly more than 15 mm long, the lobes naked at base within . . . . *G. propinqua*

♦ *Gentianella amarella* (L.) Börner
AUTUMN DWARF-GENTIAN

Habit Annual herb from a taproot; stems ascending to erect, several, simple or branched, 10–40 cm tall. **Leaves** basal and along stem; basal leaves oblanceolate but soon deciduous; stem leaves opposite, lanceolate to ovate, 1–6 cm long, somewhat purplish. **Flowers** few to several, stalked, in axillary or terminal clusters; corolla bluish purple or pink to yellow-green, 10–15 mm long, tubular, 5-lobed, the lobes fringed in the throat; calyx long, 5-lobed; stamens shorter than corolla tube. **Fruit** a cylindric capsule.

Where Found uncommon in open woods, meadows, streambanks.

Gentiana glauca GLAUCOUS GENTIAN

Gentiana prostrata MOSS GENTIAN

Gentianella amarella AUTUMN DWARF-GENTIAN

◆ *Gentianella propinqua* (Richardson) J.M. Gillett **FOUR-PART DWARF GENTIAN**

Habit small annual herb, from a taproot; stems several, ascending to erect, to 10 cm tall, simple or branched from base. **Leaves** basal and along stem; stem leaves opposite (sometimes whorled), lanceolate to oblong. **Flowers** 3–5, in a terminal cluster and single in leaf axils; petals fused, pale purple (rarely white), 1–2 cm long, with four small lobes; calyx fused, with acute teeth. **Fruit** an elongate capsule.

Where Found common in well-drained grassy places, floodplains, dry slopes, and open soil, from lowlands to the lower alpine.

Similar Species *Gentiana prostrata,* but that species smaller, grows prostrate on ground, and its flowers solitary and pale blue; *G. prostrata* also restricted to tundra environments and is less common in Denali.

Traditional Uses the entire aboveground plant was boiled to make a tea for coughs and colds by Tetlin-area Natives (Kari 1995).

Gentianopsis **FRINGED-GENTIAN**
(Greek, resembling *Gentiana*.)

◆ *Gentianopsis detonsa* (Rottb.) Ma **YUKON FRINGED-GENTIAN**
Gentiana detonsa Rottb., *Gentianella detonsa* (Rottb.) G. Don

Habit annual or biennial taprooted herb; stems erect, 10–30 cm tall, simple or sparingly branched from near the base. **Leaves** basal and along stem; basal leaves spatulate to oblanceolate; upper stem leaves narrower, 2–5 cm long; **Flowers** solitary, at ends of branches; corolla tubular, blue, 2–4 cm long, the lobes narrow, fringed on margins; calyx 4-lobed. **Fruit** a cylindric capsule.

Where Found uncommon in alpine tundra, meadows, woods.

Lomatogonium **MARSH FELWORT**

◆ *Lomatogonium rotatum* (L.) Fries **MARSH FELWORT, STAR GENTIAN**

Habit annual herb from a small taproot; stems erect or ascending, 10–30 cm tall, occasionally simple but usually with erect or ascending branches. **Leaves** basal and along stem; basal leaves oblanceolate, soon deciduous; stem leaves opposite, narrowly lanceolate, 1–3 cm long. **Flowers** on long slender stalks, in an open cluster, terminal or axillary from upper leaves; corolla blue or white, 4–

ALFRED COOK

Gentianella propinqua
FOUR-PART DWARF GENTIAN

NPS - DIANE RENKIN

Gentianopsis detonsa YUKON FRINGED-GENTIAN

5-lobed, the lobes cleft nearly to base, often purple-veined; calyx deeply 4–5-lobed, about 4/5 length of corolla; stamens nearly half the length of corolla. Fruit a cylindric capsule, 1–2 cm long, slightly longer than corolla; seeds wingless.

Where Found uncommon in wet places: streambanks, shores, marshes, bogs.

Swertia FELWORT
(Emanuel Swert was a German herbalist.)

♦ *Swertia perennis* L. FELWORT
Habit glabrous perennial herb, from a thick short rhizome; stems solitary, simple, erect, 10–60 cm tall. Leaves basal and along stem; basal leaves ovate to oblong-elliptic, 5–12 cm long; stem leaves opposite, reduced except at the first 2-3 nodes. Flowers 1 to several, long-stalked, in terminal and sometimes axillary clusters; corolla bluish purple to whitish with streaks of green, deeply 5-lobed, often

Lomatogonium rotatum MARSH FELWORT

Swertia perennis FELWORT

toothed at tip; calyx 5-lobed, just over half as long as corolla; stamens 2/3 length of the corolla. Fruit a compressed capsule, slightly longer than calyx; seeds winged on margin.

Where Found occasional in moist meadows, streambanks.

GERANIACEAE
Geranium Family

Geranium CRANE'S-BILL
(Greek, crane, from beak of fruit.)

♦ *Geranium erianthum* DC.
WOOLLY CRANE'S-BILL
Habit perennial herb from a thick stem-base or rhizome; stems ascending to erect, 20–50 cm tall, branched hairy with the hairs pointed downward. Leaves in opposite pairs on the stem, deeply and repeatedly-lobed, with long petioles, margins roughly toothed. Flowers 1–5 in a terminal branched inflorescence; sepals densely woolly; petals five, lilac-purple, obovate with round tips, hairy on inside at base, with several prominent veins of darker violet; stamens 10, anthers purple, surrounding the single pistil. Fruit an elongate seed capsule, 2.5–3 cm long, splitting along four seams, expelling the tiny seeds.

Where Found common in moist meadows and forest edges at low- to mid-elevations, much more common on southern slopes of Alaska Range than in interior areas of Denali.

Traditional Uses The Aleut traditionally prepared geranium leaves as a sore throat gargle, Kodiak Island natives chewed the roots to treat tuberculosis, and the Dena'ina used an infusion for a variety of external and internal ailments (Garibaldi 1999).

Geranium erianthum WOOLLY CRANE'S-BILL

GROSSULARIACEAE
Currant Family

Ribes CURRANT, GOOSEBERRY
(Arabic, for plants of this genus.)

1 Plants with spines or prickles at nodes, and often along internodes . . . . *R. lacustre*
1 Plants without spines or prickles 2
2 Leaves and ovaries with yellowish, unstalked, crystalline glands. . . . . *R. hudsonianum*
2 Leaves and ovaries without yellowish, unstalked glands. 3
3 Leaves primarily 3–5-lobed; ovary glabrous, sepals as wide as long . . . . *R. triste*
3 Leaves 5–7-lobed; ovary hairy or with stalked glands; sepals longer than wide. 4
4 Petals red to purplish; berries blue-black . . . . *R. laxiflorum*
4 Petals white to pink; berries dark red . . . . *R. glandulosum*

♦ ***Ribes glandulosum*** Weber SKUNK CURRANT
Habit deciduous shrub, with a fetid odor, loosely branched, 0.5–1 m tall; stems spreading, unarmed; bark brownish. **Leaves** alternate, mapleleaf-shaped, 3–8 cm wide, 5–7-lobed slightly over half their length, glabrous; petioles about equal to or slightly longer than blades. **Flowers** 6–15, in an erect raceme; flower stalks not jointed below the flowers, with stalked glands; petals white to pink, 1–1.5 mm long, ovate; calyx white to rose; styles hairy, about equaling the stamens. **Fruit** a nearly round, dark red berry, with stalked glands.

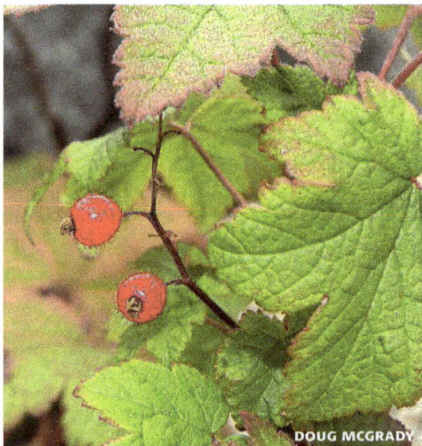
Ribes glandulosum SKUNK CURRANT

Where Found uncommon in woods and thickets.
Similar Species Similar to *Ribes laxiflorum* in habit and leaf characters.

♦ ***Ribes hudsonianum*** Richardson
HUDSON BAY CURRANT
Habit deciduous shrub, loosely branched, 0.5–1 m tall; stems erect, sparsely bristly, with yellow glands. **Leaves** alternate, mapleleaf-shaped, 2–12 cm wide, 3-lobed less than half their length, also with two lower, smaller unequal lobes, usually yellowish glandular; margins coarsely double-toothed. **Flowers** 6–15, in a spreading to erect raceme shorter than the leaves; flower stalks 3–8 mm long, jointed below the flowers; petals white; calyx white, crisp-hairy. **Fruit** a black and more or less glaucous berry, smooth or with unstalked glands, scarcely edible.
Where Found occasional in moist woods and thickets.

♦ ***Ribes lacustre*** (Pers.) Poir.
SWAMP GOOSEBERRY
Habit deciduous shrub, loosely branched, 0.5–1 m tall; stems erect to spreading, finely short-hairy and bristly with slender, sharp prickles and usually larger, 6–12 mm long spines at leaf nodes; bark reddish brown. **Leaves** alternate, 5-lobed more than half their length, 2–7 cm wide, glabrous or sparsely short-hairy along veins, rarely glandular; margins coarsely toothed. **Flowers** 5–15, in a drooping raceme; flower stalks jointed just

Ribes hudsonianum HUDSON BAY CURRANT

below flower; petals pinkish; calyx pale yellowish green to dull reddish brown, glandular-hairy. Fruit a dark purple berry, stalked, glandular-hairy; fruit used to a limited extent.

Where Found uncommon in moist woods and thickets.

◆ *Ribes laxiflorum* Pursh
TRAILING BLACK CURRANT

Habit deciduous shrub, loosely branched, 0.5–1 m long; stems spreading to decumbent, unarmed, finely short-hairy and with sparse, nearly unstalked glands; bark purplish red. Leaves alternate, maple leaf-shaped, 4–10 cm wide, usually 5-lobed nearly half their length, glabrous on upper surface, short-hairy and glandular below (at least on veins); margins toothed. Flowers 6–12, in an erect to

Ribes lacustre SWAMP GOOSEBERRY

Ribes laxiflorum TRAILING BLACK CURRANT

ascending raceme much shorter than the leaves; flower stalk jointed just below flower; petals red to purplish; calyx greenish white to deep red or purplish, hairy on back and sparsely glandular. Fruit a purplish black, glaucous berry, with glandular bristles.

Where Found uncommon in woods and thickets.

Traditional Uses berry has a fetid odor but can be eaten or preserved.

◆ *Ribes triste* Pall. SWAMP RED CURRANT

Habit deciduous shrub, loosely branched, 60–90 cm tall; stems ascending to decumbent, glabrous to crisp-hairy, unarmed, sometimes rooting at nodes; bark straw-colored to purplish brown, shedding in strips. Leaves alternate, shallowly three- or five-lobed, margins toothed. Flowers 6–15, in drooping racemes; petals pinkish, alternating with five white anthers; calyx five-lobed, larger than petals; pedicels dotted with white glands, with a bract at base, jointed, and persisting on stem after fruits have fallen. Fruit a translucent bright red berry, hairs absent.

Where Found common in shady forests and alder thickets at low- to mid-elevations.

Similar Species Other less common currants in Denali are *Ribes hudsonianum*, with glandular hairs on lower leaf surface and black fruit, and *Ribes glandulosum*, which lacks shedding bark and has red berries covered in glandular hairs.

Traditional Uses fruit eaten, and bark used by Native peoples to make tea, or chewed for respiratory illnesses, a tonic for general sickness, and as a wash or poultice for eye problems (Garibaldi 1999).

Ribes triste SWAMP RED CURRANT

HALORAGACEAE
Water-Milfoil Family
Myriophyllum WATER-MILFOIL
(Greek, myriad-leaved.)

1 Upper bracts entire or nearly so . . *M. sibiricum*
1 Upper bracts pinnately divided *M. verticillatum*

◆ *Myriophyllum sibiricum* Kom.
SIBERIAN WATER-MILFOIL
Myriophyllum exalbescens Fernald
  Habit perennial aquatic herb, from a short rhizome, stems to 1.5 m long, simple or forked, purplish, becoming white when dry. Leaves in whorls of 3 or 4 mostly 1 cm or more apart, pinnate with 11 or fewer segments; winter buds well-developed, 1–4 cm long. Flowers in emergent, erect spikes, to about 15 cm long; in whorls, lowermost female, upper male, bright pink-red; bract leaves shorter than flowers and fruits; petals about 2.5 mm long; stamens 8. Fruit a nearly round mericarp, 2–3 mm long, smooth or slightly wrinkled.
  Where Found ponds, slow-moving streams.

Myriophyllum verticillatum L.
SPIKE WATER-MILFOIL
  Habit perennial aquatic herb, from a rhizome, wholly submersed, or with spike and upper leaves sometimes emersed; stems simple or with a few long branches to 2 m long. Leaves submersed and sometimes emersed; submersed leaves to 45 mm long, with opposite or alternate pairs of narrow, flaccid segments; emersed leaves and bracts smaller, with coarser divisions or merely pinnately comb-like; winter buds well-developed at end of growing season, 1–4 cm long, club-shaped. Flowers in whorls of 4–6, perfect or the lower ones female and the upper male; female flower petals spoon-shaped or rudimentary, about 2 mm long; stamens 8. Fruit a nearly round mericarp, about 2 mm long, smooth or with tiny bumps.
  Where Found ponds, slow-moving streams.

LAMIACEAE
Mint Family
Scutellaria SKULLCAP
(Latin, tray, from the calyx dome or ridge.)

◆ *Scutellaria galericulata* L.
MARSH SKULLCAP
  Habit perennial herb from slender rhizome or stolons; stems mostly erect, 20–70 cm tall, simple or branched, 4-angled, with short, stiff downward pointing hairs, especially along the angles, sometimes glabrous. Leaves along stem, opposite, oblong-lanceolate, 2–5 cm long, short-petioled, sessile near the top of the stem, margins entire to blunt-toothed. Flowers solitary in axils of slightly reduced leaves, on stalks 2–4 mm long; corolla tubular, blue, 15–20 mm long, 2-lipped, the upper lip hoodlike, shorter than lower lip; lower lip 3-lobed, the broad central lobe papillate, not hairy, marked with white; calyx 2-lipped. Fruit a brown nutlet, in a cluster of four.

Myriophyllum sibiricum
SIBERIAN WATER-MILFOIL

Scutellaria galericulata MARSH SKULLCAP

Where Found uncommon on streambanks, pond margins, thickets, bogs.

LENTIBULARIACEAE
Bladderwort Family

1 Plants of moist to wet places; leaves entire. . . .
. . . . *Pinguicula*
1 Plants aquatic, submerged; leaves dissected. . .
. . . . *Utricularia*

Pinguicula BUTTERWORT
(*Pinguis*, fat, in allusion to the greasy leaves.)

1 Flower stem with short hairs; corolla less than 10 mm long. . . . . *P. villosa*
1 Flower stem smooth, corolla 12–25 mm long . .
. . . . *P. vulgaris*

◆*Pinguicula villosa* L. HAIRY BUTTERWORT

Habit insect-eating perennial herb, from thin fibrous roots; stems erect, simple, solitary to few, to 10 cm tall, densely long glandular-hairy. Leaves basal, elliptic, 2–5 mm long, succulent, with a sticky-slimy upper surface, margins inrolled; leaves with two types of glands used to catch insects: stalked glands produce droplets of a sticky substance, which attracts and traps insects; second set of glands are sessile to the leaf; once an insect is trapped, both sets of glands release digestive enzymes, and nutrients from the insect are absorbed. Flowers solitary, bilaterally symmetrical, nodding; petals blue-purple, with darker veins and a yellow center,

Pinguicula villosa HAIRY BUTTERWORT

6–10 mm long, spurred. Fruit a round capsule, 3–5 mm long.

Where Found occasional in lower elevation bogs and muskeg, almost always in sphagnum moss.

Similar Species *Pinguicula vulgaris* not densely glandular-hairy.

◆*Pinguicula vulgaris* L.
COMMON BUTTERWORT

Habit insect-eating perennial herb, from a fibrous root; stems erect, simple, solitary to few, to 15 cm tall, glabrous or nearly so. Leaves basal, 5–7, simple, entire, fleshy, lance-elliptic, 1.5–5 cm long, upper surface glabrous or slimy-glandular (where small insects are digested), underside glabrous, margins inrolled. Flowers single; corolla funnel-like, dark violet-blue, rarely white, 15–25 mm long, spurred; calyx lobed, 3–5 mm long. Fruit an erect capsule, 4–6 mm long.

Where Found occasional on moist shores and meadows; mossy seeps.

Utricularia BLADDERWORT
(*Utriculus*, a little bladder.)

1 Bladders and leaves on separate branches; leaf segments flat . . . . *U. intermedia*
1 Bladders and leaves not on separate branches; leaf segments threadlike. 2

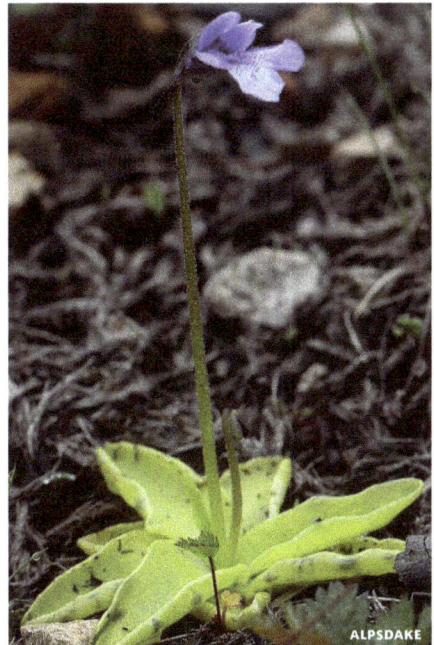

Pinguicula vulgaris COMMON BUTTERWORT

2   Bladders 3–5 mm long; leaves 2–5 cm long . . .
. . . . *U. macrorhiza*
2   Bladders to 2 mm long; leaves less than 1 cm
long . . . . *U. minor*

Utricularia intermedia Hayne
FLAT-LEAF BLADDERWORT

Habit perennial aquatic herb without roots; stems very slender, floating, submerged or creeping along bottom, leafy, to 50 cm long. **Leaves** alternate, numerous, to 2 cm long, divided into 3 parts at base, and then again 1–3 times into 20 or more thread-like segments; bladders usually on separate, leafless branches. **Flowers** 2–4, in a lax raceme on stem 6–20 cm long; corolla yellow, 10–15 mm long, lower lip 8–12 mm long. **Fruit** a capsule, on a nearly erect stalk.

Where Found occasional in ponds and lakes.

◆ *Utricularia macrorhiza* LeConte
GREATER BLADDERWORT
Utricularia vulgaris L. p.p.

Habit perennial aquatic herb without roots; stems submerged, very leafy. **Leaves** 2–3-pinnately dissected; bladders 2–4 mm long. **Flowers** 5–10, in a lax raceme on stem 10–30 cm long; corolla bright yellow, spur hornlike, slightly curved **Fruit** a capsule on a recurved stalk.

Utricularia macrorhiza **GREATER BLADDERWORT**

Where Found occasional in ponds and lakes, floating bog mats.

Utricularia minor L. **LESSER BLADDERWORT**

Habit perennial aquatic herb without roots; stems very slender, floating, submerged or creeping along the bottom, leafy, to 75 cm long. **Leaves** alternate, numerous, to 1 cm long, divided into 3 parts at base, and then again 1–3 times into 5 flattened, ultimate segments; bladders few, 1–2 mm wide, borne on leaves. **Flowers** 3–9, in a lax raceme at end of stem to 15 cm long; corolla pale yellow, spur sac-like, poorly developed as a hump below lower lip; bracts ear-like at base of flower. **Fruit** a capsule on a recurved stalk.

Where Found uncommon in shallow ponds.

LINACEAE
Flax Family

Linum **FLAX**
(Classical Latin name.)

◆ *Linum lewisii* Pursh **BLUE FLAX**

Habit perennial herb with blue flowers, from a woody base and a taproot; stems erect, usually several, simple, glabrous, 10–60 cm tall. **Leaves** alternate, linear, 1–3 cm long, 1–3 mm wide, sharply acute at tip. **Flowers** saucer-shaped, in a loose terminal cluster; petals blue, 15–20 mm long, soon deciduous; sepals rounded at tip, 4–7 mm long, the margins membranous, entire; styles heterostylic (of varying lengths). **Fruit** a more or less round capsule, 10-celled, 5–8 mm long; seeds 3.5–4.5 mm long.

Where Found uncommon on sandy or gravelly soils, streambanks, meadows.

Linum lewisii **BLUE FLAX**

MENYANTHACEAE
Buckbean Family

Menyanthes BUCKBEAN

(Greek, disclosing, and flower, from flowers opening in succession in inflorescence.)

◆ *Menyanthes trifoliata* L. BUCKBEAN

Habit perennial wetland herb from a thick rhizome covered with old leaf bases; stems prostrate or ascending, glabrous, 10–30 cm long. Leaves basal, alternate, divided into 3 elliptic, glabrous leaflets, 1–5 cm wide, margins coarsely toothed, petioles 10–30 cm long, crowded near base of flowering stem. Flowers many, in a simple or compound terminal cluster; corolla white tinged with purple, 5–6 lobed; calyx divided into 5 lobes. Fruit an oval, many-seeded capsule; seeds brownish yellow, smooth, shiny, buoyant.

Where Found occasional in shallow water of bogs, wet meadows, ponds.

MONTIACEAE
Candy-Flower Family

1　Perennial herbs, with slender rhizomes or stolons 2

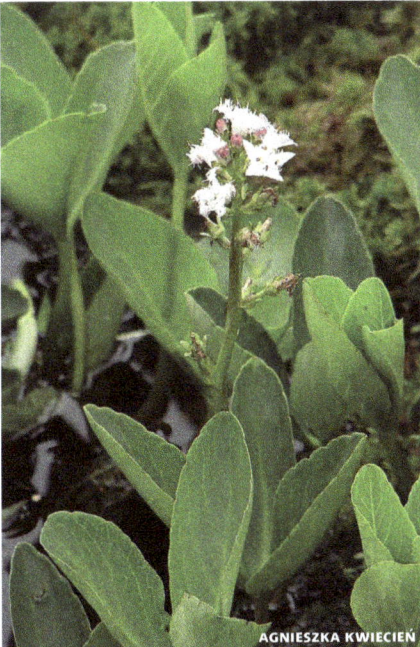

Menyanthes trifoliata BUCKBEAN

1　Perennial herbs, with thickened taproots or corms 3
2　Basal leaves narrowly oblong-spatulate to linear, with conspicuously sheathing membranous base . . . . *C. scammaniana*
2　Basal leaves broadly elliptic to ovate or spatulate, tapering to the petiole and not conspicuously sheathing at base . . . . *C. sarmentosa*
3　Plants from a short, thick, deep-seated corm; basal leaves 1–few, or absent . . . . . *C. tuberosa*
3　Plants from a fleshy thickened taproot; basal leaves several to many, with membranous sheathing base . . . . *C. acutifolia*

Claytonia SPRINGBEAUTY

(In honor of John Clayton, 1686-1773, physician and plant collector in Virginia.)

◆ *Claytonia acutifolia* Pall. ex Willd.
GRASSLEAF SPRINGBEAUTY
Claytonia eschscholtzii Cham.

Habit perennial herb; stems usually several, 5–15 cm tall, arising directly from a thick fleshy root. Leaves basal and along stem; basal leaves narrowly lanceolate to linear, arising directly from the crown of the root, stem leaves similar but smaller. Flowers 2–5, in racemes; petals usually white, rarely pink, 12–15 mm long; sepals 2. Fruit a rounded-oval seed, nearly 3 mm in diameter.

Where Found uncommon on moist tundra and heath.

◆ *Claytonia sarmentosa* C.A. Mey.
ALASKA SPRINGBEAUTY
Montia sarmentosa (C.A. Mey.) B.L. Rob.

Habit loosely matted perennial herb, from threadlike rhizomes and stolons; stems erect, simple, 1–several from tip of rhizome, to 15 cm tall. Leaves basal and along stem;

Claytonia acutifolia GRASSLEAF SPRINGBEAUTY

basal leaves elliptic or lanceolate, long-petioled; stem leaves opposite, ovate, sessile. Flowers in a raceme; petals five, pink, or white with pink veins; sepals two. Fruit a small green capsule which splits open to release the seeds.

Where Found common in moist, rich areas such as meadows and tundra snowbeds in alpine and subalpine zones.

Similar Species distinguished from *Claytonia scammaniana* by its broader leaves and its habitat: *Claytonia sarmentosa* occurs in meadows and moist places; *C. scammaniana* primarily on barren, loose scree-slopes.

Traditional Uses entire plant edible, either raw or cooked.

♦ *Claytonia scammaniana* Hultén
SCAMMAN'S SPRINGBEAUTY
Montia scammaniana (Hultén) S.L. Welsh

Habit delicate perennial herb with pink flowers; stems 4–6 cm high, arising from a threadlike rhizome. Leaves basal and along stem; basal leaves linear to oblanceolate, fleshy; stem leaves opposite, sessile and narrowly elliptical. Flowers 1–2, with 5 purplish to pink glossy petals and 2 sepals. Fruit a dry green capsule, splitting along seams to release seeds.

Where Found uncommon on steep, alpine rocky scree-slopes and slide-rock.

Similar Species the other pink-flowered *Claytonia* in Denali is *C. sarmentosa,* found in moister meadow habitats, with generally broader leaves.

Claytonia sarmentosa ALASKA SPRINGBEAUTY

Claytonia tuberosa Pall. ex Schult.
TUBEROUS SPRINGBEAUTY

Habit perennial herb from a spherical underground corm with fibrous roots, the corm 1–1.5 cm wide; stems erect, simple, solitary, 4–15 cm tall. Leaves basal and along stem; basal leaves 1–2 arising from the corm, elliptic to oblong, 2–6 cm long; stem leaves narrowly elliptic to oblanceolate, 1.5–6 cm long. Flowers 3–8 in a round-topped raceme, with one bract subtending lowermost flower; petals white or pink, fused at base, 9–15 mm long; sepals 2. Fruit a capsule, 4–6 mm long; seeds 2–6, reddish brown, 2 mm long.

Where Found uncommon in moist alpine tundra and heath.

Claytonia scammaniana
SCAMMAN'S SPRINGBEAUTY

MYRICACEAE
Bayberry Family

Myrica SWEETGALE
(Ancient name of the tamarisk.)

♦ *Myrica gale* L. SWEETGALE
Habit shrub, 0.5–2 m tall, spreading by suckers; stems finely hairy when young, glabrous when mature, loosely branched, bark dark reddish. Leaves alternate, deciduous, oblanceolate, 3–6 cm long, to 2 cm wide, entire to coarsely toothed above the middle, strongly dotted with yellow wax-glands, aromatic. Flowers either male or female, in spikes on separate plants; male spikes 1–2 cm long, the male flowers with 3–5 stamens; female spikes 1 cm long, yellow-waxy. Fruit a cone-like nutlet, about 3 mm long, glabrous except for wax glands.

Where Found common on lake margins, streambanks, bogs.

NYMPHAEACEAE
Water-Lily Family

1   Sepals petal-like, yellow; petals small, scalelike; leaf blade to 25 cm long from sinus to tip . . . . *Nuphar*

1   Sepals green; petals white; leaf blade to 6 cm long from sinus to tip . . . . *Nymphaea*

Nuphar POND-LILY
(Ancient Arabic or Persian name.)

♦ *Nuphar polysepala* Engelm.
YELLOW POND-LILY
Nuphar lutea subsp. *polysepala* (Engelm.) Beal

Habit perennial aquatic herb from a thick large rhizome; stems thick, fleshy, submerged or emersed, 1–2 m long. Leaves floating or submerged; blade heart-shaped, 10–30 cm long, 10–20 cm wide, leathery, the sinus narrow or closed. Flowers solitary, large, waxy, floating, on long stalks arising from the rhizome; petals yellow (with reddish or greenish tinges), 10–20, smaller than the sepals and the numerous yellow or reddish purple stamens; sepals usually 6 or 9, 2.5–6 cm long, the outer greenish and shorter than the inner yellow sepals. Fruit a berry-like oval capsule; seeds 4–5 mm long, numerous in a jelly-like mass.

Where Found occasional in ponds.

Nymphaea WATER-LILY
(Greek, nymphe, goddess of mountains, waters, meadows, and forests.)

♦ *Nymphaea tetragona* Georgi
PYGMY WATER-LILY
Habit perennial aquatic herb from a thick rhizome; stems slender. Leaves arising from the rhizome, long-stalked, without blotches or dots, heart-shaped; blades floating, 5–10 cm long, 3–7 cm wide, the sinus open. Flowers showy, opening in morning, closing in afternoon, 3–6 cm wide; petals white, equal to the sepals; sepals greenish, 2–3 cm long; stamens yellow. Fruit a berry-like, many-seeded capsule, with a jelly-like seed mass; seeds ovate, 2–3 mm long.

Where Found occasional in lakes and ponds.

ONAGRACEAE
Evening-Primrose Family

1   Flowers 2-merous, fruit a bristly, one-seeded capsule . . . . *Circaea*

1   Petals 4, stamens 8, fruit a many-seeded capsule . . . . *Epilobium*

NPS - JACOB FRANK

Nuphar polysepala YELLOW POND-LILY

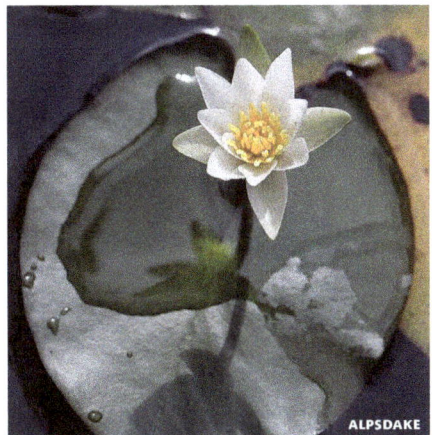

ALPSDAKE

Nymphaea tetragona PYGMY WATER-LILY

OLE HUSBY

Myrica gale SWEETGALE

Circaea
ENCHANTER'S-NIGHTSHADE
(Circe of mythology was an enchantress.)

♦ *Circaea alpina* L.
SMALL ENCHANTER'S-NIGHTSHADE
Habit perennial herb, from a slender, tuber-tipped rhizome; stems erect, 10–30 cm tall, simple or branched, glabrous or appressed short-hairy. Leaves opposite, cordate to ovate, 2–6 cm long, sharp-toothed to more or less entire, short-hairy on lower surface; petiole 1.5–4 cm long, narrowly winged. Flowers 8–12, in terminal clusters, often with 1 or 2 linear bracts at base; flower stalks spreading to erect, becoming reflexed; petals 2, white to pale pink, 1–1.5 mm long, deeply notched; sepals 2, 1–2 mm long, bent downward; stigmas 2-lobed. Fruit a top- or pear-shaped hairy capsule, about 2 mm long; seeds 1.

Where Found uncommon in moist woods.

Epilobium WILLOWHERB
(Greek *epi*, upon, and *lobos*, a pod or capsule, as the flower and capsule appear together, the corolla borne on end of ovary.)

1 Stigma 4-lobed. 2
1 Stigma entire or slightly 4-angled 4
2 Petals notched at tip; floral tube prolonged above ovary; flowers regular; leaves opposite below inflorescence . . . . *E. luteum*
2 Petals rounded at tip; floral tube absent; flowers slightly irregular; leaves alternate throughout 3
3 Plants rhizomatous, usually more than 1 m tall; leaves 10–20 cm long; floral bracts linear, much smaller than leaves; inflorescence usually with at least 15 flowers . . . . *E. angustifolium*
3 Plants clumped, usually less than 40 cm tall; leaves less than 6 cm long; floral bracts broad, leaf-like; inflorescence usually with less than 12 flowers . . . . *E. latifolium*

Circaea alpina SMALL ENCHANTER'S-NIGHTSHADE

4 Plants grayish, with short appressed hairs (at least in inflorescence); leaves linear to narrowly lanceolate, usually less than 3 mm wide 5
4 Plants usually glabrous or predominantly glandular-hairy, not gray and short appressed-hairy; leaves usually broader, lanceolate to oblong (more than 3 mm wide) 6
5 Capsule glabrous, or becoming so; leaf margin flat, not rolled under, often finely sharp-toothed; plants usually 5–20 cm tall; plants with basal rosettes; stolons with fleshy bulblets absent. . .
. . . . *E. davuricum*
5 Capsule with short appressed hairs; leaf margin rolled under, plants usually at least 30 cm tall; basal rosettes absent, forming stolons with condensed fleshy bulblets at tips (these often absent in pressed specimens). . . . . *E. palustre*
6 Plants not clumped (or only loosely so), with leafy basal rosettes . . . . *E. ciliatum*
6 Plants clumped, with short, leafy, aboveground stolons 7
7 Stems to about 20 cm tall; stem leaves nearly entire; capsules 2–4 cm long . *E. anagallidifolium*
7 Stems 10–50 cm tall; stem leaves toothed (rarely entire); capsules 4–10 cm long. 8
8 Petals white; inflorescence mostly nodding in bud . . . . *E. lactiflorum*
8 Petals pink to rose-purple; inflorescence mostly erect in bud . . . . *E. hornemannii*

♦ *Epilobium anagallidifolium* Lam.
PIMPERNEL WILLOWHERB
Habit perennial herb, from a fibrous root, tufted, somewhat mat-forming, with short stolons; stems ascending to erect, 10–20 cm tall, green or reddish tinged, sparsely short stiff-hairy in decurrent lines below, with some glandular hairs above, often with basal offshoots. Leaves opposite, simple, elliptic to oblong, to 2.5 cm long, glabrous, margins entire. Flowers 1–3 in a nodding raceme; petals pink to rose-purple; stamens eight. Fruit an upright dehiscent capsule, 2–3 cm long; seeds with a tuft of long silky hairs to aid in dissemination by wind.

Where Found occasional at low- to high-elevations in moist, rich meadows and tundra.

Similar Species distinguished from other small-flowered, short-statured *Epilobium* by having sessile, unwinged lower leaves (or with petioles to 3 mm long), nodding buds and glabrous inflorescences; most similar to *E. hornemannii* but that species generally larger and stouter, with serrated leaves and a glandular inflorescence.

◆ *Epilobium angustifolium* L.
COMMON FIREWEED
Chamerion angustifolium (L.) Scop.

Habit Tall perennial herb, with a spike of bright pink flowers from widely spreading rhizome-like roots; stems erect, 1–2 m tall, usually simple, glabrous except for fine hairs in inflorescence. **Leaves** alternate, simple, lanceolate, glabrous, distinctly veined, 5–20 cm long; margins entire. **Flowers** many, in a dense spike; petals 4, pink to magenta, 10–12 mm long, alternating with narrow dark pink sepals; lower flowers opening first and develop into fruit as uppermost flowers bloom. **Fruit** a stalked, elongate dehiscent capsule; seeds with a tuft of silky hair to aid in wind-dispersal.

Where Found abundant at all elevations along roadsides, in meadows, floodplains, around animal burrows, and in recently burned areas.

Similar Species dwarf fireweed (*Epilobium latifolium*) has similar flowers, but is much smaller and without the many-flowered spike, found growing on gravelly terraces.

Traditional Uses common fireweed is one of the most recognizable plants of the north. Many residents of Alaska use fireweed stalks to track the progress of summer, because the flowers open sequentially from the bottom of the spike upwards over a period of many weeks; the flowering of the top-most flowers signals the coming end of summer. Young stems and leaves are edible, either raw or cooked; roots can be eaten raw or cooked, or dried and ground in a flour. When abundant, a valuable nectar source for honeybees. *E. angustifolium* has also been used in traditional medicine in a variety of forms such as a tea, infusion or topical ointment; the Alutiiq used a tea for constipation or to stimulate milk production (Birket-Smith in Garibaldi 1999) or a poultice of roots was placed on boils (Wennekens 1985 in Garibaldi 1999). The Dena'ina used stems for treatment of boils (Kari 1995). Some Yup'ik boiled leaves in a tea as use in stomach troubles (Garibaldi 1999).

Epilobium ciliatum Raf.
FRINGED WILLOWHERB

Habit perennial herb, from basal rosettes or fleshy bulblets, rhizomes absent; stems 20–90 cm tall, usually branched, pubescent above, glandular in the inflorescence. **Leaves** opposite (or alternate above), mostly lance-olate, the middle ones short-petioled, 3–8 cm

Epilobium anagallidifolium
PIMPERNEL WILLOWHERB

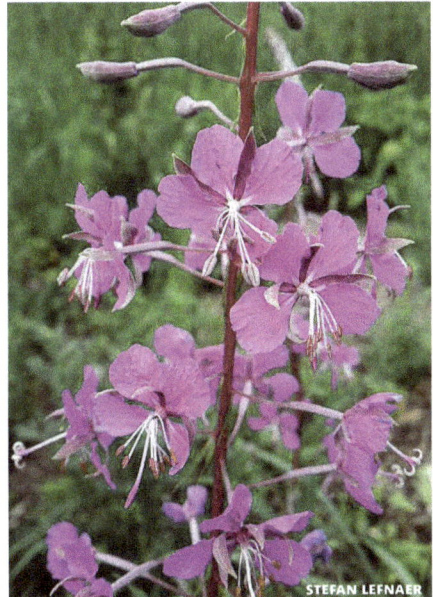
Epilobium angustifolium
COMMON FIREWEED

long; margins finely sharp-toothed to almost entire. Flowers in a terminal, leafy-bracted panicle or raceme, finely stiff-hairy, with some spreading and glandular hairs; petals rose-purple to white, 2–5 mm long, notched at tip; sepals often reddish; stamens less than or equal to length of pistil; stigmas club- or head-shaped. Fruit capsule, 3–8 cm long, with a tuft of white hairs from tip.

Where Found moist woods, thickets, roadsides.

Epilobium davuricum Fisch. ex Hornem.
SWAMP WILLOWHERB

Habit perennial herb, from a short rhizome, stolons absent; stems erect, to 30 cm tall, simple, single or a few together, green or sometimes reddish, upper internodes with fine curved hairs in lines. Leaves basal and along stem; basal leaves in a compact rosette; stem leaves opposite on lower stem, alternate above, linear, 2–5 cm long; margins entire or somewhat toothed, fringed with hairs. Flowers few, nodding when young; petals 2–4 mm long, whitish; sepals glabrous. Fruit an erect capsule, 3–5 cm long; seeds 1–2 mm long, with a tuft of dingy hairs.

Where Found moist woods, bogs, along streams.

Epilobium hornemannii Rchb.
HORNEMANN'S WILLOWHERB

Habit perennial herb, from short, leafy stolons; stems unbranched, to 35 cm tall, loosely clumped, glandular short stiff-hairy in inflorescence. Leaves alternate, simple, lanceolate, elliptic or ovate (upper leaves usually narrower), to 6 cm long and 3 cm wide; margins sparsely toothed. Flowers in a terminal raceme, either nodding or erect in flower; petals rose to pink, to 10 mm long. Fruit an elongated dehiscent capsule, 3–5 cm long; seeds with a tuft of silky white hairs to aid in wind-dispersal.

Where Found occasional in floodplains, rocky slopes, rich meadows and moist tundra, mostly in subalpine and alpine areas.

Similar Species most similar to *Epilobium anagallidifolium,* but that species lower growing and matted, and with a glabrous inflorescence and entire leaves.

Epilobium lactiflorum Hausskn.
WHITE-FLOWER WILLOWHERB

Habit perennial herb, from leafy stolons; stems 15–50 cm tall, often clumped, densely short stiff-hairy in lines below, glandular-hairy and short stiff-hairy in inflorescence. Leaves elliptic or narrowly ovate to lanceolate, glabrous, margins short stiff-hairy, finely-toothed; petioles of lower leaves winged, upper leaves unstalked. Flowers in an inflorescence usually nodding in bud; petals white (or sometimes pinkish or with red veins), notched at tip; sepals sparsely glandular-hairy; ovaries densely glandular-hairy. Fruit a glandular-hairy capsule; seeds with a white tuft of hairs.

Where Found streambanks, wet meadows.

Epilobium latifolium L.
DWARF FIREWEED, RIVER-BEAUTY
Chamerion latifolium (L.) Holub

Habit tufted perennial herb, from a stout stem-base, often forming colonies; stems ascending, 15–40 cm long, simple to freely branched, leafy, grayish green and often with a waxy bloom; stems and leaves hairless. Leaves alternate or opposite, fleshy, broadly lanceolate to elliptic, margins entire. Flowers large and axillary, with 4 bright pink to purple petals alternating with 4 narrowly lanceolate purple sepals. Fruit an elongated capsule, opening when mature to release the seeds; seeds with a tuft of silky white hair to aid in wind-dispersal.

Where Found abundant at all elevations on gravel bars along streams, scree-slopes.

Epilobium lactiflorum
WHITE-FLOWER WILLOWHERB

Similar Species common fireweed (*Epilobium angustifolium*) has similar flowers, but is taller, with a large, many-flowered spike; dwarf fireweed foliage has a characteristic whitish tinge not evident in *E. angustifolium*.

Traditional Uses leaves, stems and flowers are edible, either raw or cooked.

Note the national flower of Greenland.

Epilobium leptocarpum Hausskn.
SLENDER-FRUIT WILLOWHERB

Habit perennial herb, from a taproot; stems erect or decumbent at base, 5–30 cm tall, slender, simple or branched, often reddish, with fleshy winter bulblets at base; young vegetative buds often present in leaf axils. Leaves mostly opposite, lanceolate, to 25 cm long, tapering to blunt tip, finely toothed, glabrous or hairy on the margins; short-stalked. Flowers few, in a nodding to almost erect, few terminal inflorescence; petals 2–6 mm long, whitish to pink; sepals glabrous to short-hairy; stigmas broadly club-shaped. Fruit a more or less glabrous capsule, 1–5 cm long; seeds with a tuft of tawny hairs.

Where Found moist meadows, streambanks.

Epilobium luteum Pursh
YELLOW WILLOWHERB

Habit perennial herb, from widespread rhizomes, sometimes with basal winter bulblets; stolons short and leafy or compact; stems erect, 15–70 cm tall, simple or branched above. Leaves mostly opposite, sessile, spatulate to ovate, 2.5–8 cm long, 1.2–3.5 cm wide, glandular-toothed. Flowers 2–10, in upper leaf axils, nodding in bud, densely glandular and short stiff-hairy; petals 1–2 cm long, yellow or cream-colored, wavy-margined, notched at tip; sepals densely glandular; ovaries densely glandular; styles usually noticeably longer than petals; stigmas 4-lobed. Fruit an erect, linear capsule, 4–8 cm long, glandular-hairy; seeds with a tuft of rust-colored hairs.

Where Found streambanks, lakeshores, seeps.

◆ *Epilobium palustre* L.   MARSH WILLOWHERB

Habit perennial herb, from a slender rhizome, with long, threadlike, aboveground runners that end in fleshy bulblets at base of stem; stems erect, to 35 cm tall, simple or branched. Leaves alternate, simple, linear to lance-shaped, to 7 cm long and 2 mm wide, margins entire to slightly toothed. Flowers few to many in a nodding (or erect in bud) inflorescence with short stiff hairs; petals pink to

Epilobium latifolium DWARF FIREWEED

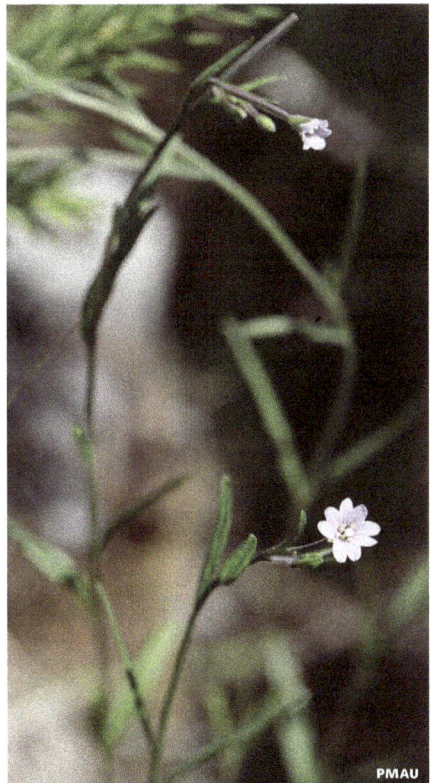

Epilobium palustre MARSH WILLOWHERB

white, 2–9 mm long. Fruit an elongated dehiscent capsule, 3–8 cm long; seeds with a tuft of silky white hair to aid in wind-dissemination.

Where Found occasional in lowland and montane zone moist lakeshores, depressions, marshes.

Similar Species distinguished from other *Epilobium* by long threadlike runners at base of plant.

Traditional Uses leaves and young shoots edible.

OROBANCHACEAE
Broom-Rape Family

1 Plant without green leaves and stems; parasitic on roots of other plants . . . . *Boschniakia*
1 Plants with green leaves and stems 2
2 Annual herbs 3
2 Biennial or perennial herbs. 5
3 Corolla 3–4 mm long . . . . *Euphrasia*
3 Corolla longer 4
4 Calyx flattened, conspicuously inflated in fruit . . . . *Rhinanthus*
4 Calyx not flattened . . . . *Pedicularis*
5 Leaves entire or pinnatifid; upper leaves bractlike and usually highly colored . . . . *Castilleja*
5 Leaves dissected or toothed; upper leaves green . . . . *Pedicularis*

Boschniakia GROUNDCONE
(Boschniak was a Russian botanist.)

♦ *Boschniakia rossica* (Cham. & Schltdl.) B.Fedtsch. NORTHERN GROUNDCONE
Habit Parasitic, non-photosynthetic herb, from a coarse fleshy root and thickened stem base; stems single or clustered, short glandular-hairy, stout (to 1.5 cm thick), dark purple-brown, 10–15 cm tall, often with flowers on its entire length. Leaves alternate, triangular, lowermost bract scalelike. Flowers with fused petals; upper lip 8–13 mm long, shallowly divided, giving each flower a hooded appearance; stamens extending outside the corolla. Fruit a capsule; one flowering stalk can produce thousands of tiny seeds.

Where Found occasional in shrub thickets and wooded places; parasitic on roots of alders and other woody plants.

Similar Species Looking like an elongated pine-cone emerging from the ground, no

other plant in Denali can be confused with this distinctive plant.

Traditional Uses root was used by the Tlingit to treat sores, presumably as a poultice.

Castilleja INDIAN-PAINTBRUSH
(In honor of Domingo Castillejo, Spanish botanist, 1744—1793.)

1 Bracts yellowish to yellowish green . . *C. pallida*
1 Bracts violet-purple to reddish or pink . . . . *C. elegans*

♦ *Castilleja elegans* Malte
ELEGANT INDIAN-PAINTBRUSH
Habit perennial herb, partially parasitic on the roots of other plants, with several stems grow from a branching taproot; stems dark brown-purplish, sparsely hairy at base, becoming long-woolly upwards. Leaves alternate near base, linear-lanceolate; upper leaves often with two narrow lobes from the middle. Flowers in a dense spike; bracts and sepals cream-pink to dark red; bracts subtending the flowers ovate in outline, sometimes lobed; sepals fused, with four lobes,

Boschniakia rossica NORTHERN GROUNDCONE

shorter than the yellow-green petals; corolla of two lips: the innermost longer, the lower three-lobed, inconspicuous compared to the colorful calyx and bracts. Fruit a dry capsule, 6–10 mm, which splits along one seam to release many small seeds.

Where Found occasional in alpine tundra and rocky places primarily on the north side of Alaska Range; common on dry ridges along the Park Road and in the Kantishna Hills.

Similar Species the only red-flowered Indian paintbrush in Denali.

Note *Castilleja* are hemi-parasites: they produce their own sugars, but also form connections to the roots of other plants to obtain nutrients.

♦ *Castilleja pallida* (L.) Spreng.
PORT CLARENCE INDIAN-PAINTBRUSH
Castilleja caudata (Pennell) Rebrist.

Habit tufted perennial herb, partially parasitic on the roots of other plants, from a taproot, with a spike of pale yellow flowers; stems red-purple, unbranched, 20–40 cm tall; lower half of plant hairless, inflorescence with long white hairs. Leaves alternate, without petioles, lower leaves narrowly lanceolate, becoming broader and shorter upwards on stem. Flowers yellow, several in a terminal cluster; bracts below the flowers entire to deeply cleft into narrow segments, greenish or reddish in color, subtending the four-lobed, yellow calyx nearly as long as the petals; petals two-lipped, the upper lip more than 5 times longer than lower lip. Fruit a dry capsule, 9–10 mm long, which splits along one seam to release numerous seeds.

Where Found occasional at lower elevations on exposed floodplains and open soil on well-drained slopes.

Similar Species This is the only pale yellow-flowered paintbrush in Denali, the other member of the genus, *C. elegans,* is usually magenta-flowered and found in alpine tundra.

Euphrasia   EYEBRIGHT
(Greek, delight, good cheer.)

1   Inflorescence a more or less rounded head; corolla 4–5 mm long; leaves ovate to orbiculate
. . . . *E. mollis*

1   Inflorescence more elongate; corolla 3–4 mm long; leaves oblanceolate to broadly ovate . . . .
. . . . *E. subarctica*

Castilleja elegans ELEGANT INDIAN-PAINTBRUSH

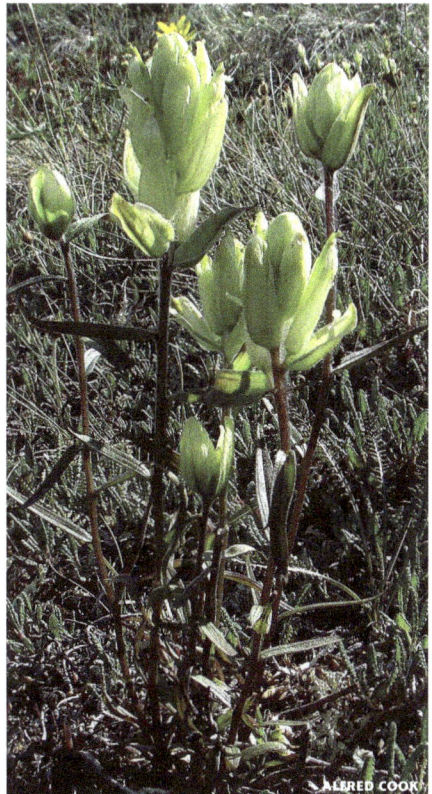

Castilleja pallida
PORT CLARENCE INDIAN-PAINTBRUSH

Euphrasia mollis (Ledeb.) Wettst.
SUBALPINE EYEBRIGHT
Euphrasia arctica var. *mollis* (Ledeb.) Welsh

Habit annual herb; stems simple, rarely branched, 4–12 cm tall, pubescent. **Leaves** opposite, ovate to nearly round, 4–8 mm long. **Flowers** small, in a compact head; corolla yellow, calyx densely hairy. **Fruit** a small capsule, 4–5 mm long.

Where Found uncommon on streambanks, in bogs and seeps.

♦ *Euphrasia subarctica* Raup
ARCTIC EYEBRIGHT

Habit annual herb, from a taproot; stems slender, erect, 3–30 cm tall, simple or branched from below the middle, minutely hairy and sometimes glandular-hairy above. **Leaves** opposite, unstalked, few, ovate to oblanceolate, 2–6 mm long, palmately veined, prominently 7–11-toothed, sparsely hairy; bracts resembling the leaves but with more pointed teeth. **Flowers** small, from the axils of leafy bracts in a terminal spike; corolla whitish with purple markings and a yellow spot, 2-lipped, the upper lip with 2 lobes, the lower lip spreading, with 3 shallowly notched lobes; calyx bell-shaped, hairy

ALFRED COOK
Euphrasia subarctica **ARCTIC EYEBRIGHT**

or glandular-hairy, almost as long as the corolla, 4-toothed; stamens 4. **Fruit** an oblong, flattened capsule, 3–6 mm long, more or less hairy; seeds numerous, narrowly winged.

Where Found uncommon on streambanks, pond and lake margins.

Pedicularis LOUSEWORT
(Latin, lice, from belief that ingestion by stock promoted lice infestation.)

1 Stems branched; annual or biennial or short-lived perennial herbs. 2
1 Stems simple; evidently perennial herbs 3
2 Flowers yellow, sometimes splotched or tinged with red, in few-flowered spikes. *P. labradorica*
2 Flowers purple, in short spikes, or solitary in leaf axils . . . . *P. parviflora*
3 Stem leaves verticillate . . . . *P. verticillata*
3 Stem leaves alternate or absent 4
4 Corolla predominantly yellow. 5
4 Corolla pink or purple 6
5 Inflorescence headlike, few-flowered; corolla creamy-yellow, sometimes tinged with red. . . . . *P. capitata*
5 Inflorescence spikelike; corolla bright yellow with tip of upper lip darker . . . . *P. oederi*
6 Upper lip dark purple; plants with a branching rhizome; stem leaves absent or 1–2. *P. sudetica*
6 Upper lip pink; plant with a distinct taproot . . 7
7 Spike densely white-wooly . . . . *P. lanata*
7 Spike glabrous or nearly so . . . . . *P. langsdorfii*

♦ *Pedicularis capitata* Adams
CAPITATE LOUSEWORT

Habit perennial herb, with a few hooded yellow flowers, from a slender branched rhizome; stems single, erect, 5–15 cm tall, unbranched, usually short-hairy or long-hairy in the inflorescence. **Leaves** green, sometimes with white marks on margins; pinnate, each leaflet pinnately cleft; leaflets angled horizontally from the vertical leaf. **Flowers** 2–5, subtended by several pinnatifid bracts; two-lipped, upright, pale cream to yellow or pink-suffused; upper petal curved; lower lip three-cleft, shorter than upper lip; calyx hairy; stamens four, within the upper petal. **Fruit** a many-seeded capsule.

Where Found common in subalpine to alpine willow-shrub and dwarf-shrub tundra.

Similar Species *Pedicularis oederi* is also unbranched and yellow-flowered but that plant has stem leaves and many more flowers; unlike other members of the genus, *Pedicularis capitata* is often found without a flowering stem, identified by its leaves alone.

◆ *Pedicularis labradorica* Wirsing
LABRADOR LOUSEWORT

Habit annual, biennial or short-lived perennial herb, with yellow flowers, from a spindly taproot; stems ascending to erect, 10–30 cm tall, one to several, usually branched, white-hairy typically in lines below the leaf bases. **Leaves** green, often purple on edge; lower leaves pinnatifid, upper leaves merely toothed; leaves hairless or short-pubescent. **Flowers** in short, 5–20 flowered axillary clusters, with yellow leaf-like bracts, petals 13–17 mm long, the upper petal with two teeth, sometimes reddish tinged; lower petal three-lobed. **Fruit** a capsule.

Pedicularis capitata CAPITATE LOUSEWORT

Pedicularis labradorica LABRADOR LOUSEWORT

Where Found common in forests to shrubby tundra, especially in the subalpine.

Similar Species No other lousewort has highly branched stems and yellow flowers.

◆ *Pedicularis lanata* Cham. & Schltdl.
WOOLLY LOUSEWORT

Habit perennial herb, with a cylindric spike of pink flowers, from a thick yellow taproot; stems usually single, erect, 5–25 cm tall, unbranched, densely long-hairy to white-woolly, especially in the inflorescence; when young, plants appear like a conical cotton-ball with a few leaves sticking out. **Leaves** pinnatifid, green-purple; stem leaves many, lower leaves with long broad petioles, petioles of upper leaves shorter. **Flowers** pink (rarely white); upper petal hooded, the tip blunt and untoothed; lower petal with three rounded lobes; stamens 4, with white filaments and black-yellow anthers. **Fruit** a capsule. **Flowering** early in the season; inflorescence elongating in flowering and continuing to elongate in fruit.

Where Found common in alpine tundra.

Similar Species distinguished from Denali's other hairy, pink-flowered lousewort, *Pedicularis langsdorffii*, by the dense woolly hairs covering the stem and the toothless upper petal.

◆ *Pedicularis langsdorffii* Fisch. ex Steven
LANGSDORF'S LOUSEWORT

Habit perennial herb, from a stout yellow taproot surmounted by a somewhat woody stem-base; stems one to several, erect, 5–20 cm tall, unbranched, nearly smooth to somewhat long-woolly (not densely woolly-hairy

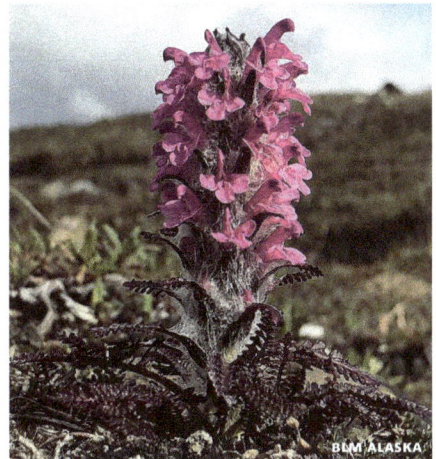

Pedicularis lanata WOOLLY LOUSEWORT

as in *P. lanata*). Leaves green with purplish edges (sometimes wholly purple), with a broad central vein; stem leaves several below the inflorescence (distinguishing it from *P. sudetica*); long bracts intermixed with the flowers. Flowers purple; upper petal with two small teeth; lower petal paler pink, with three rounded lobes; calyx fused, with 5 triangular teeth. Fruit a many-seeded dry capsule, 12–15 mm long. Flowering early to mid-summer; the inflorescence elongates when in fruit.

Where Found occasional in alpine tundra (often where steep), and moist to dry meadows.

◆ *Pedicularis oederi* Vahl
OEDER'S LOUSEWORT

Habit perennial herb, from thickened, spindle-shaped roots; stems usually single, erect, 5–20 cm tall, unbranched, nearly smooth to long-woolly, especially in the inflorescence. Leaves at base pinnatifid, toothed and purplish on margins; stem leaves similar but interspersed with the flowers. Flowers bright yellow, in a terminal spike; corolla two-lipped, upper petal (the galea) upward facing and curved, brownish at tip, with red blotches on either side below; bottom petal with three rounded lobes, usually a paler yellow than the galea; style and anthers exserted. Fruit a many-seeded dry capsule, 11–16 mm long.

Where Found occasional in wet to moist alpine tundra.

Similar Species *Pedicularis capitata* is the other yellow-flowered, unbranched lousewort species in Denali, but that species usually with only two or three pale yellow or whitish flowers in a capitate cluster.

Pedicularis parviflora Sm.
MUSKEG LOUSEWORT
Pedicularis macrodonta Richards.

Habit annual or biennial herb, from a spindly taproot; stems single, ascending to erect, 10–40 cm tall, simple or more commonly branched, smooth except sometimes minutely hairy in the inflorescence. Leaves alternate, unstalked, lance-oblong, 1–5 cm long, pinnately cleft to lobed, the segments usually toothed; basal leaves small or absent; bracts similar to the leaves but reduced upwards. Flowers solitary in upper axils or in a loose, several-flowered terminal spike; corolla purple or two-toned pinkish and purple, 2-lipped, the upper lip slightly arched, hoodlike, beakless, with or more often without a pair of slender teeth near the tip, the lower lip 3-lobed; calyx 2-lobed, the lobes jaggedly toothed; stamens 4, the filaments long-hairy. Fruit an ovate capsules, partly enveloped by the dry expanded calyx.

Where Found uncommon in wet meadows, bogs, muskegs.

Pedicularis langsdorffii
LANGSDORF'S LOUSEWORT

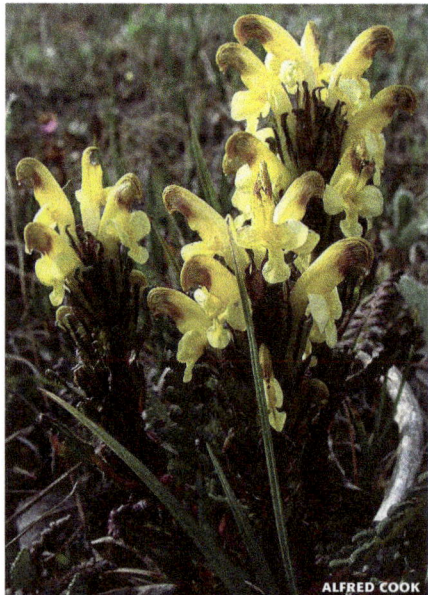

Pedicularis oederi OEDER'S LOUSEWORT

⬧ *Pedicularis sudetica* Willd.
SUDETIC LOUSEWORT
Pedicularis interior (Hultén) Molau & D.F. Murray

Habit perennial herb, with two-lipped magenta flowers in a pyramidal inflorescence, from a stout branched rhizome; stems usually single, erect, 10–40 cm tall (alpine plants shorter), unbranched, often purplish, long-woolly in the inflorescence. Leaves mostly basal, hairless, pinnatifid and serrate; flowering stem with a single leaf or leaves absent, with many leaf-like bracts interspersed with the flowers. Flowers in a terminal, compact, pyramid-shaped inflorescence, densely white-woolly, less than a third the length of stem during flowering period; calyx tubular; upper lip of petal purple or magenta, lower lip often paler; inflorescence elongating as fruits mature. Fruit a many seeded, beaked capsule; seeds with a papery outer coat.

Where Found occasional at all elevations but most common in the subalpine in moist areas along streams, and in moist to wet tundra.

⬧ *Pedicularis verticillata* L.
WHORLED LOUSEWORT

Habit perennial herb, from a taprooted, branching stem-base; stems one to several, clustered, erect to ascending, 10–35 cm tall, long-hairy to woolly in the inflorescence. Leaves mostly basal, pinnatifid with dentate margins, from long petioles; stem leaves similar but petioles much reduced or absent.

Flowers verticillate (arranged around the stem in whorls), purple-magenta, with darker veins; petals two, the upper hooded and without teeth, the lowering flaring into three wide lobes; sepals fused into a small tube, covered with hairs. Fruit a dry capsule, splitting open to release many seeds.

Where Found occasional in high-elevation floodplains, meadows and moist tundra.

Similar Species Whorled lousewort the only member of the genus with whorled leaves and axillary flowers.

Rhinanthus YELLOW-RATTLE
(Greek, nose-flower, from the beaked corolla.)

⬧ *Rhinanthus groenlandicus* Chabert
NORTHERN YELLOW-RATTLE
Rhinanthus borealis (Sterneck) Chabert, *Rhinanthus minor* subsp. *groenlandicus* (Chabert) Neuman

Habit annual herb; stems erect, 10–80 cm tall, simple or few-branched, somewhat 4-angled, nearly smooth to thinly soft-hairy at nodes and in lines down 2 of the 4 sides. Leaves opposite, lanceolate to oblong, 1–5 cm long, prominently toothed, rough flattened-hairy; petioles absent. Flowers in a leafy-bracted, terminal, spikelike cluster of several to many, nearly unstalked flowers; corolla yellow, 2-lipped, upper lip hoodlike and usually with a pair of short, broad, often purplish teeth near tip; lower lip 3-lobed; calyx membranous, much inflated in fruit, like a flattened net-veined balloon, 4-toothed; stamens 4. Fruit a nearly globe-shaped, flat-

Pedicularis sudetica SUDETIC LOUSEWORT

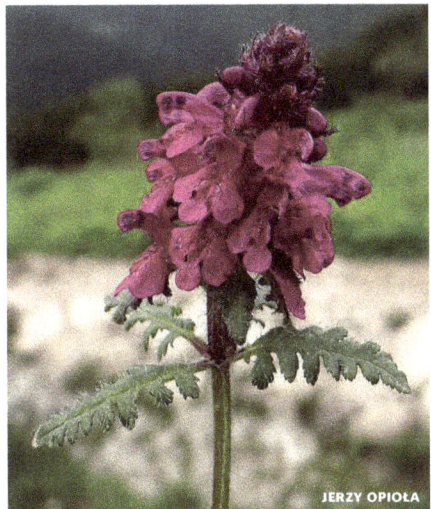

Pedicularis verticillata WHORLED LOUSEWORT

tened capsule, enveloped by the calyx; seeds several, 3–6 mm in diameter, flat, narrow-winged.

Where Found uncommon on dry gravelly soils.

PAPAVERACEAE
Poppy Family

1 Flowers regular; stamens many (rarely as few as 3); petals 4 . . . . *Papaver*
1 Flowers irregular; stamens 6; petals 4 . . . . *Corydalis*

Corydalis FUMEWORT
(Greek, crested lark.)

1 Perennial herb, from a small deeply buried tuber; flowers blue or purple, in a few-flowered raceme; leaves 3-parted . . . . *C. pauciflora*
1 Annual or biennial herb, from a weak taproot; flowers in an elongate raceme; leaves pinnately divided 2
2 Corolla yellow; plants low-growing; stems much-branched, spreading . . . . *C. aurea*
2 Corolla pink with yellow tip; plants taller, erect; stems simple or branched above . . . . *C. sempervirens*

Rhinanthus groenlandicus
NORTHERN YELLOW-RATTLE

♦ *Corydalis aurea* Willd. GOLDEN CORYDALIS
Habit Annual or biennial herb from a tap-root; stems spreading to prostrate, freely branched, glabrous, 10–50 cm long. Leaves alternate, divided several times, blue-green, usually with a waxy bloom. Flowers several, in axillary and terminal racemes; corolla yellow, 12–18 mm long, the spur one-third to one-fourth of its entire length. Fruit a curved, drooping capsule, 2–3 cm long, constricted between the seeds; seeds 2 mm long, black, shiny.

Where Found open woods, hillsides, sometimes where disturbed.

♦ *Corydalis pauciflora* (Stephan) Pers.
FEW-FLOWER FUMEWORT
Corydalis arctica Popov
Habit perennial herb from a tuberous root; stems usually solitary, erect, glabrous, 5–15 cm tall. Leaves 2–5, clustered at stem-base; ternately divided, leaflets lobed. Flowers usually 2 or 3, in a terminal cluster; petals fused into a bluish purple tubular corolla with a 6–10 mm long spur, which is abruptly bent at top. Fruit a drooping capsule 1–2 cm long.

Where Found moist to wet meadows, shrub-

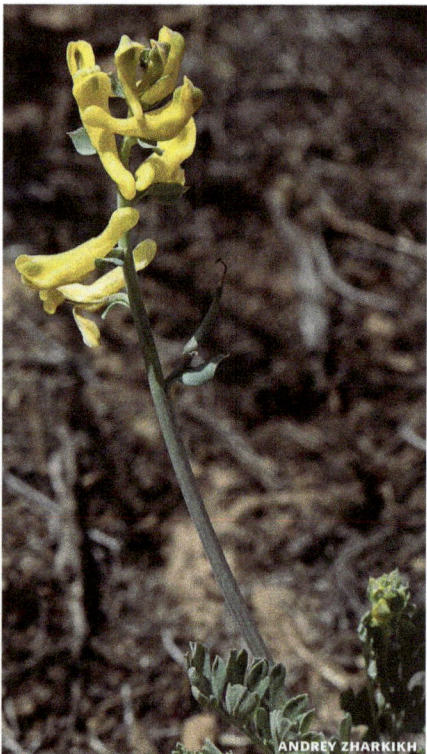

Corydalis aurea GOLDEN CORYDALIS

lands and tundra mostly in the alpine zone, on both sides of Alaska Range crest.

Similar Species Other plants with bilaterally symmetric flowers and lobed leaves include monkshood (*Aconitum delphinifolium*) and larkspur (*Delphinium glaucum*); these separated from *Corydalis* by their much different flower-shape.

◆ *Corydalis sempervirens* (L.) Pers.
PINK CORYDALIS

Capnoides sempervirens (L.) Borkh.

Habit Biennial herb from a fleshy taproot; stems 1 to several, erect, branched above, glabrous, 20–80 cm tall. Leaves alternate, long-stalked, divided 3–5 times, glabrous, with a waxy bloom. Flowers 3–10, in a terminal raceme; corolla rose or purplish with yellow tip, 10–15 mm long; spur less than one-third length of body. Fruit a capsule, 3–5 cm long, curved or somewhat twisted; seeds black, shiny.

Where Found open woods, thickets.

Papaver POPPY
(Latin name of the poppy.)

1   Plants low-growing; flower stems to 15 cm tall
    2
1   Plants taller 4
2   Leaves bipinnate; capsule with distinct central
    projection . . . . *P. mcconnellii*

Corydalis pauciflora FEW-FLOWER FUMEWORT

2   Leaves less dissected; capsule flat, arched, or
    acute. 3
3   Flowers large; capsule longer than wide, broadest at middle . . . . *P. macounii*
3   Flowers smaller; capsule broadest at top. . . . . .
    . . . . *P. lapponicum*
4   Plants mostly more than 25 cm tall; petals yellow or white; capsule club-shaped, with many rays; flowers large . . . . *P. nudicaule*
4   Plants less than 25 cm tall; flowers various. . . 5
5   Petals white to rose-pink; capsule pear-shaped to elliptical, or nearly spherical . *P. lapponicum*
5   Petals yellow; capsule much longer than wide .
    . . . . *P. macounii*

◆ *Papaver lapponicum* (Tolm.) Nordh.
PALE POPPY

Papaver alboroseum auct. non Hultén p.p.

Habit perennial herb, from a taproot and a cluster of cleft basal leaves; stem-base with brown decaying leaf bases; stems decumbent to erect, simple, spreading stiff-hairy, to 15 cm tall; flowering stalks one to a few, leafless, with a single, terminal flower. Leaves gray-green, divided into three leaflets, each leaflet 2–5 lobed; leaf blades white-bristly. Flowers with four white to rose-pink petals, yellow at center, broader and blunt at tip; anthers 10 or more; stigma disk with 5 or 6 yellow lobes; when in bud, flower covered by two sepals, these shed once flower opens. Fruit an ovate to globose, stiff-bristled capsule, longer than broad; opening at top by many pores to release numerous tiny seeds. Flowering early in the season.

Where Found uncommon in alpine talus and gravelly places.

Similar Species other poppies in Denali are yellow-flowered, and have capsules with dark colored hairs; flowers of pale poppy are

Corydalis sempervirens PINK CORYDALIS

white and the capsule is covered with stiff, light-colored hairs.

♦ *Papaver macounii* Greene
MACOUN'S POPPY

Habit perennial herb, loosely cushion-forming, stems to 25 cm tall; usually one leafless stem per plant (sometimes several), each with a single yellow flower; stems, leaves and sepals hairy (or sometimes nearly hairless), the hairs light brown. **Leaves** basal, ovate in outline, pinnately cleft, the segments often divided again; dark green on upper surface, paler below. **Flowers** with four yellow petals; disk on top of pistil with 4–6 yellow stigma lobes; anthers numerous. **Fruit** a capsule 4 times longer than broad, narrower at base than the top, with a slight projection at the tip; capsules dehisce through small openings at top of capsule, releasing out many tiny seeds. **Flowering** early in the season.

Where Found occasional in alpine meadows, open treeline areas, and damp places in tundra; the most common poppy in Denali.

Similar Species Distinguished by its long and thin (4 times longer than broad), club-shaped capsule.

♦ *Papaver mcconnellii* Hultén
MCCONNELL'S POPPY

Habit small-statured perennial herb, forming loose cushions and tufts; flowering stalks to 20 cm tall; stem-base with many persistent dead leaves. **Leaves** basal, gray-blue, sparsely hairy, long-petioled; highly dissected into small, narrowly ovate segments. **Flowers** solitary on leafless stalks, somewhat flexuose; large, 3–6 cm in diameter, with yellow petals; pistil globose, with 5–6 stigmatic lobes in a disk at top; anthers numerous, yellow. **Fruit** a capsule, as long as broad, opening by pores at top to release many small seeds.

Flowering early in the season.

Where Found occasional in sparsely vegetated alpine areas such as scree-slopes, gullies, and rock outcrops.

Similar Species distinguished from other poppies by its blue-green, bipinnate leaves, and capsule as long as broad.

Papaver nudicaule L.
ICELANDIC POPPY

Habit perennial herb, from a taproot, with a stem-base covered with brown decaying leaf bases; stems erect, simple, bristly-hairy, 20–40 cm tall. **Leaves** basal, 8–20 cm long, the petioles two-thirds the leaf length, deeply dissected into lanceolate or strap-shaped segments, with 3–4 pairs of primary lateral lobes, nearly smooth or white bristly-hairy above, gray-green below, green above. **Flowers** solitary on bristly-hairy stalks; petals yellow or white, 15–30 mm long. **Fruit** a nearly round to elliptic capsule, conspicuously ribbed, 10–15 mm long, 1.5–2.5 times longer than wide, bristly-hairy.

Papaver macounii MACOUN'S POPPY

Papaver lapponicum PALE POPPY

Papaver mcconnellii MCCONNELL'S POPPY

Where Found may be present in Denali in dry rocky openings in the boreal forest.

Note a cultivated, non-native 'Icelandic poppy,' *Papaver croceum* Ledeb., sometimes escapes from cultivation to roadsides and disturbed areas in Alaska; it has petals varying from red or orange, as well as white and yellow.

PHRYMACEAE
Lopseed Family
Erythranthe MONKEY-FLOWER
(Formerly placed in *Mimulus*, Latin, a buffoon, from the grinning corolla.)

♦*Erythranthe guttata* (DC.) G.L. Nesom
YELLOW MONKEY-FLOWER,
SEEP MONKEY-FLOWER
Mimulus guttatus DC.

Habit perennial herb, from rhizomes or creeping stolons, sometimes an annual with fibrous roots; stems stout and erect, to sometimes weak and trailing and rooting at nodes, 10–70 cm tall, simple or branched, smooth or sparsely hairy above. Leaves opposite, broadly oval to ovate, 1–10 cm long, coarsely and irregularly toothed, palmately 3–7-veined from base, lower leaves stalked, upper leaves sessile or clasping. Flowers several to many, in a loose, terminal raceme, or sometimes one to several long-stalked flowers in axils of upper leaves; corolla broadly funnel-shaped, yellow with maroon markings in the flaring throat, 1–3 cm long, strongly 2-lipped, upper lip 2-lobed, lower lip 3-lobed, densely yellow-hairy at the throat; calyx bell-shaped, green dotted or tinged with red, 5-toothed, the upper tooth larger than the others; stamens 4. Fruit a broadly oblong capsule, rounded at tip, narrowed to a short-stalked

Erythranthe guttata YELLOW MONKEY-FLOWER

base, 7–12 mm long; seeds numerous.
Where Found uncommon on wet streambanks and near seeps.

PLANTAGINACEAE
Plantain Family
Now includes several former members of Scrophulariaceae.

1	Plants aquatic, or in wet soil or mud 2
1	Plant of drier habitats, not aquatic 3
2	Leaves generally opposite . . . . *Callitriche*
2	Leaves in whorls of 6–12 . . . . *Hippuris*
3	Stamens 2. 4
3	Stamens 4 . . . . *Linaria*
4	Leaves opposite (alternate in *Veronica alaskensis*), all cauline; bracts sometimes foliose and alternate . . . . *Veronica*
4	Leaves alternate or basal; stem leaves absent or much reduced in size upwards 5
5	Leaves basal and along stem, leathery . *Lagotis*
5	Leaves all in a basal rosette, not leathery; flower stems naked . . . . *Plantago*

Callitriche WATER-STARWORT
(Greek, beautiful hair.)

1	Plants dark green; leaves all linear; fruit conspicuously winged . . . . *C. hermaphroditica*
1	Plants light green; leaves both linear and oblanceolate; fruit wingless or barely wing-margined above 2
2	Submersed leaves linear-oblanceolate. . . . . *C. palustris*
2	Submersed leaves linear, narrower than stems. . . . . *C. heterophylla*

Callitriche hermaphroditica L.
AUTUMN WATER-STARWORT
Callitriche autumnalis L.

Habit aquatic or semi-aquatic perennial, rooting in mud; stems slender, 5–15 cm long, with widely spaced internodes. Leaves opposite, linear, 10–15 mm long, clasping at base, single-nerved. Flowers tiny, inconspicuous, without bracts, stalkless or shortly-stalked. Fruit 4, achene-like, winged, each 1-seeded, 1–2 mm long.

Where Found uncommon in shallow water of ponds.

Callitriche heterophylla Pursh
GREATER WATER-STARWORT
Callitriche anceps Fernald

Habit aquatic or semi-aquatic perennial, rooting in mud; stems leafy, 5–40 cm long. Leaves opposite; submerged leaves linear, single-veined, notched at tip, 5–25 mm long; floating and emergent leaves broadly ovate or oblanceolate, 3-veined, to 1 cm wide. Flowers tiny, inconspicuous, with a pair of tiny bracts, stalkless or short-stalked. Fruit achene-like, 4, each 1-seeded.

Where Found shallow water of ponds.

♦ *Callitriche palustris* L.
VERNAL WATER-STARWORT
Callitriche verna L.

Habit aquatic or semi-aquatic perennial, rooting in the mud; stems slender, 5–20 cm long, submerged, partially floating or stranded on mud, leaf bases joined by small, winged ridges. Leaves opposite; submerged leaves linear, 5–20 mm long, thin, single-nerved, notched at tip; floating and emergent leaves broadly spoon-shaped, 5–10 mm long, 3-nerved. Flowers tiny, with bracts; female flowers stalkless or shortly-stalked. Fruit achene-like, 4, each 1-seeded.

Where Found uncommon in shallow ponds.

Hippuris MARE'S-TAIL
(Greek, horse and tail.)

1   Stems to 10 cm high and to 0.5 mm thick . . . . .
. . . . *H. montana*
1   Stems much longer and thicker . . . . *H. vulgaris*

Hippuris montana Ledeb. ex Rchb.
MOUNTAIN MARE'S-TAIL

Habit perennial, semi-aquatic or terrestrial herb, from a slender creeping rhizome; stems erect, simple, glabrous, 0.5 mm wide, 4–10 cm tall. Leaves 5–8 per whorl, linear, unstalked, 3–8 mm long, 0.5–1 mm wide,

Callitriche palustris VERNAL WATER-STARWORT

pointed at tip, stiff above water but limp underwater. Flowers tiny, single, inconspicuous, in several whorls in axils of leaf whorls, mostly unisexual, with male flowers below female flowers; petals absent. Fruit a nutlet, about 1 mm long; seeds 1.

Where Found uncommon along alpine streams.

♦ *Hippuris vulgaris* L. COMMON MARE'S-TAIL

Habit perennial aquatic emergent herb, from an extensive creeping rhizome; stems erect, simple but sometimes short-branched from lower nodes, 1.5–5 mm wide, 5–40 cm tall, partly above water. Leaves 8–12 per whorl, linear, pointed at tip, 6–35 mm long, 1–2 mm wide. Flowers tiny, mostly bisexual, in several whorls in axils of leaf whorls; petals absent. Fruit a nutlet, 2–2.5 mm long; seeds 1.

Where Found occasional in shallow ponds, mud flats.

Lagotis WEASELSNOUT
(Greek, hare's-eared.)

♦ *Lagotis glauca* Gaertn. WEASELSNOUT

Habit perennial glabrous herb, with relatively large basal leaves and stout stems, bearing a dense cluster of striking dark blue flowers; stems fleshy, unbranched, to 20 cm tall, growing from a rhizome. Leaves both basal and along stem; basal leaves 2–17 cm long, leathery, elliptic or oblanceolate, mar-

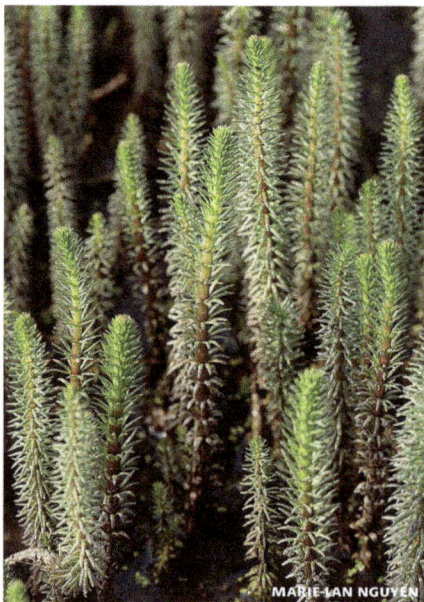

Hippuris vulgaris COMMON MARE'S-TAIL

gins with widely spaced teeth; stem leaves similar but smaller. Flowers in a terminal cylindric spike, with leafy bracts; small and bilaterally symmetric, consisting of two fused sepals and a two-lipped corolla; sepals green, ciliate; corolla dark blue-violet, the lower lip cleft; style exerted, the two stamens fused to the petals. Fruit a 2-seeded capsule.

Where Found occasional in wet meadows, seeps and streambanks in alpine areas.

Similar Species Weaselsnout could be confused with *Veronica alaskensis,* but that plant is densely woolly and its leaves orbicular to reniform (not elliptic and lobed); also, Veronica alaskensis flowers much earlier in spring, and grows on dry rocky slopes and ridges, not in the moist meadows typical of weaselsnout.

Linaria BUTTER-AND-EGGS
(Latin, flax, from flax-like leaves of some species.)

Linaria vulgaris P. Mill. BUTTER-AND-EGGS
Habit perennial herb, from a long creeping rhizome; stems erect, 10–80 cm tall, sometimes branched above, smooth, glaucous, with milky juice (when stems or leaves broken). Leaves alternate or the lowermost nearly opposite, unstalked, linear to narrowly lanceolate, 2–8 cm long, margins entire. Flowers numerous, short-stalked, in a long termi-

nal, spikelike cluster, at first dense, elongating in age; corolla bright yellow with an orange throat, 20–35 mm long including the long straight basal spur (about as long as rest of corolla), 2-lipped, the upper lip 2-lobed, the lower lip 3-lobed; calyx deeply 5-lobed; stamens 4. Fruit an ovate capsule, 5–10 mm long; seeds numerous, about 2 mm long.

Where Found uncommon weed of waste places; Eurasian introduction.

Plantago PLANTAIN
(The Latin name.)

1 Leaves lanceolate, gradually tapering to petiole . . . . *P. canescens*
1 Leaves oval, with blade abruptly tapering to narrow petiole. . . . . *P. major*

Plantago canescens Adams HAIRY PLANTAIN
Habit perennial herb, from a stout taproot; stems erect, several, simple, 5–30 cm tall. Leaves basal, lanceolate to oblanceolate, to 15 cm long and 2.5 cm wide, entire, 3–5-veined, with long or short petioles; margins entire or few-toothed. Flowers in a dense bracteate spike, the spike elongate, 1.5–8 cm long; corolla greenish, 4-lobed, the lobes 1.5–2 mm long, spreading; bracts ovate, shorter than the sepals, fringed; stamens conspicuous. Fruit an ovate capsule, about 3–3.5 mm

Lagotis glauca WEASELSNOUT

long; seeds 4, brown to black, 1–2 mm long.

Where Found may be present in Denali in open rocky or gravelly places.

Plantago major L.
COMMON PLANTAIN

Habit perennial herb, from a fibrous root; stems erect, several, simple, smooth or stiff-hairy, 5–50 cm tall. Leaves basal, oval or ovate, 5–15 cm long, on petioles of same length or less, 5–7-ribbed, margins entire or irregularly toothed. Flowers in a dense, narrow, bracteate spike, the spikes 5–20 cm long; corolla greenish, 4-lobed; stamens inconspicuous. Fruit an ovate capsule, about 3 mm long; seeds 5–25, black or brown, 1 mm long.

Where Found uncommon weed of waste places; introduced from Eurasia.

Veronica SPEEDWELL
(Named for St. Veronica.)

1 Leaves alternate . . . . *V. alaskensis*
1 Leaves opposite 2
2 Racemes axillary 3
2 Racemes terminal 4
3 Leaves sessile, linear to lanceolate, margin entire . . . . *V. scutellata*
3 Leaves petioled, lanceolate to oblong or elliptic, margin toothed . . . . *V. americana*
4 Leaves conspicuously sharp-toothed, 4–8 cm long . . . . *V. longifolia*
4 Leaves entire or obscurely toothed 5
5 Leaves sessile; capsule longer than wide . . . . *V. wormskjoldii*
5 Lower leaves short-petiolate; capsule wider than long . . . . *V. serpyllifolia*

♦ *Veronica alaskensis* M.M. Mart. Ort. & Albach
NORTHERN KITTENTAILS
Synthyris borealis Pennell

Habit short, woolly, perennial herb, with a dense cluster of blue flowers; stems thick, 5–15 cm tall from a rhizome. Leaves both basal and alternate along stem, with stiff white hairs (stem leaves hidden by the flowers early in season); basal leaves rounded or reniform, lobed, the divisions toothed; last year's leaves often persistent and visible beneath the new growth; stem leaves much smaller, ovate or fan-shaped, toothed at tip. Flowers in a dense spikelike raceme, with woolly bracts between the flowers (nearly covering the petals); petals blue; corolla (fused petals) two-lipped, upper lip slightly

longer with one notch, lower lip 2-notched; stamens 2, exerted at top of flowers; style and filaments also blue, anthers with yellow pollen. Fruit a heart-shaped capsule, opening along top to release the round seeds. Flowering late May and early June (soon after snowmelt); when in bloom, plants often not much taller than a few centimeters, elongating during fruiting.

Where Found uncommon in dry alpine tundra and gravelly places, mostly north of Alaska Range crest.

Similar Species Weaselsnout (*Lagotis glauca*) also an alpine plant with a dense spike of bilaterally symmetric blue flowers, but that species is taller, lacks the dense wooliness, and does not have reniform leaves; also, *Lagotis* occurs in moist meadow habitats, *V. alaskensis* is found on barren rocky sites or sparse Dryas tundra.

♦ *Veronica americana* (Raf.) Schwein. ex Benth.
AMERICAN BROOKLIME

Habit perennial amphibious herb, from a shallow creeping rhizome, smooth throughout; stems usually decumbent and rooting at base, 10–60 cm long, rooting at lower nodes, simple or branched, somewhat fleshy. Leaves opposite, short-stalked, lanceolate to ovate, 2–6 cm long, usually distinctly toothed. Flowers 5–25, in opposite racemes from axils of upper leaves; flower stalks much longer than the linear bracts; corolla blue, saucer-shaped, 5–10 mm across, irregularly 4-lobed, the lobes much longer than the short tube; calyx 2–5 mm long, deeply 4-lobed; styles exserted; stamens 2. Fruit an orbicular capsule, barely notched at tip, 3–4 mm long, a little wider than long, plump, somewhat

Veronica alaskensis NORTHERN KITTENTAILS

globe-shaped; seeds numerous, flattened, about 0.5 mm long.

Where Found uncommon along streams and muddy places, marshy areas, seeps, springs.

♦ *Veronica scutellata* L.
GRASS-LEAF SPEEDWELL

Habit perennial amphibious herb, from a shallow creeping rhizome, smooth throughout or sometimes sparingly hairy; stems slender, weak, 10–40 cm long, rooting at the lower nodes, simple to much-branched at the base, somewhat fleshy, often purple-tinged. Leaves opposite, unstalked and slightly clasping, linear to narrowly lanceolate, 2–6 cm long, 2–6 mm wide, often purple-tinged; margins nearly entire. Flowers 5–20 in lax, stalked racemes from axils of upper leaves, the thread-like flower stalks spreading at maturity, much longer than the reduced, linear bracts; corolla blue or white with purple lines, saucer-shaped, 6–10 mm across, irregularly 4-lobed, the lobes much longer than the short tube; calyx deeply 4-lobed; styles exserted; stamens 2. Fruit a capsule, 3–4 mm long, distinctly wider than long, flattened, broadly notched at tip; seeds 5 to 9 per chamber.

Where Found uncommon on lakeshores, bogs, wet thickets, marshy areas.

Veronica serpyllifolia L.
THYME-LEAF SPEEDWELL
Veronica tenella All.

Habit perennial herb, from a creeping rhizome; stems ascending, 10–30 cm long, often decumbent or creeping at base and rooting at nodes, smooth or short-hairy. Leaves opposite, often short-stalked below,

unstalked above, elliptic to broadly ovate, 1–2 cm long, margins entire or with a few blunt teeth. Flowers several to many in a terminal bracted raceme, at first compact then elongating and lax; flower stalks finely short-hairy and often also glandular, shorter than the bracts; corolla bright blue or pale blue to white with darker blue lines, saucer-shaped, 4–8 mm across, irregularly 4-lobed, the lobes much longer than the short tube; calyx short-hairy or glandular-hairy, deeply 4-lobed; stamens 2, exserted. Fruit a flattened, heart-shaped capsule, 3–4 mm long, wider than long, distinctly notched at tip, with sparse glandular hairs.

Where Found uncommon in moist soil of streambanks, seeps, marshy areas.

♦ *Veronica wormskjoldii* Roem. & Schult.
AMERICAN ALPINE SPEEDWELL

Habit perennial herb, from a shallow branching rhizome; stems erect or decumbent at base; 10–30 cm tall, simple, long wavy-hairy. Leaves opposite, elliptic to ovate, short-petioled, 1–4 cm long, margins slightly sharp-toothed. Flowers in a small terminal inflorescence of several deep-blue flowers; bracts and calyx covered in glandular hairs; raceme compact at first, elongating later; corolla fused at base, divided into four blue-violet lobes, the lowest lobe narrower than the others; calyx four-lobed; stamens 2, style white. Fruit a dry, flattened, rounded capsule, notched at top.

Where Found occasional in meadows and turfy places in subalpine and alpine tundra, much more common south of Alaska Range crest than north.

Similar Species the most common *Veronica* in Denali, distinguished from other speedwells by its terminal cluster of flowers.

JOSHUA MAYER

Veronica americana AMERICAN BROOKLIME

GERTJAN VAN NOORD

Veronica scutellata GRASS-LEAF SPEEDWELL

POLEMONIACEAE
Phlox Family

1 Leaves pinnately compound . . . . . *Polemonium*
1 Leaves simple . . . . *Phlox*

Phlox PHLOX
(Greek, flame.)

Phlox richardsonii Hook.
RICHARDSON'S PHLOX

Habit low, loosely tufted perennial herb; base well-branched, somewhat woody. Leaves opposite, narrow, linear, boat-shaped and sharp-tipped, to 2 cm long and about 2 mm wide, with a groove along upper surface midvein; margins fringed with hairs. Flowers solitary, unstalked, very fragrant; corolla 5-lobed about 1 cm in diameter, pale lavender or pale blue; sepals narrow, sharp-pointed. Fruit an ovate capsule with several seeds.

Where Found uncommon in sandy or gravelly alpine tundra.

Veronica wormskjoldii
AMERICAN ALPINE SPEEDWELL

Polemonium JACOB'S-LADDER
(Greek, perhaps from Polemon, Athenian philosopher, or polemos, strife or war.)

1 Leaves glabrous; corolla lobes fringed with hairs
. . . . *P. villosum*
1 Leaves glandular-hairy; corolla lobes not fringed with hairs 2
2 Corolla 15–20 mm long . . . . *P. boreale*
2 Corolla shorter, 10–12 mm long . . . .
. . . . *P. pulcherrimum*

♦ *Polemonium boreale* M.F. Adams
NORTHERN JACOB'S-LADDER

Habit perennial herb, from a rhizome and branching stem-base; stems single or several, loosely tufted, erect or ascending, spreading-hairy to glandular-hairy, 10–15 cm tall; entire plant (apart from petals) densely white pubescent. Leaves pinnately compound, leaflets elliptic; most Leaves basal, with a few on stem. Flowers in a terminal cyme; petals fused, the throat yellow on inside, with 5 violet-purple lobes, 15–20 mm long (as opposed to the smaller petals of the uncommon *P. pulcherrimum*); petal tips rounded (in contrast to triangular petals of *P. villosum*). Fruit a dry capsule with a few small seeds.

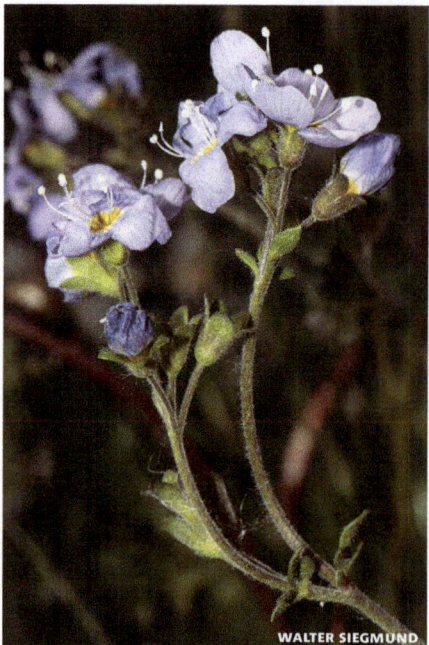

Polemonium boreale
NORTHERN JACOB'S-LADDER

Where Found occasional at high-elevations in tundra and scree.

♦ ***Polemonium pulcherrimum*** Hook.
PRETTY JACOB'S-LADDER
Habit tufted perennial herb, from a branched woody rootstock; stems 1–many, loosely erect to sprawling, often branched, 5–30 cm tall, glandular-hairy especially in the inflorescence, sometimes nearly smooth elsewhere, foul-smelling if rubbed. Leaves basal and along stem; basal leaves pinnately compound with 11 to 25 orbicular to ovate, opposite leaflets, glandular-hairy when young; stem leaves few, reduced. Flowers long-stalked, crowded in a terminal head; corolla blue, rarely white, with yellow centers, bell-shaped, the 5 rounded lobes equal to or nearly twice as long as tube; calyx 5-lobed. Fruit a 3-chambered capsule.

Where Found uncommon on gravelly hillsides and open woods.

♦ ***Polemonium villosum*** Rudolph ex Georgi
TALL JACOB'S-LADDER
Polemonium acutiflorum Willd. ex Roem. & Schult.

Habit perennial herb, from a rhizome; stems single, erect from a decumbent base, glandular-hairy especially above, 15–35 cm tall. Leaves pinnately divided, the segments lanceolate or elliptic, glabrous (or nearly so), the margins dark. Flowers several, light purple, from leaf axils or tip of stem; corolla

fused, broadly bell-shaped, throat white lined with purple veins; the bell flared into five lobes; stigmas with three curled lobes; stamens five with bright yellow anthers. Fruit a dry capsule with a few small seeds.

Where Found common in subalpine to alpine areas in moist to wet meadows; and in alder, birch, and willow communities.

Similar Species the shape of the petals distinguishes tall Jacob's-ladder from Denali's other species of *Polemonium*.

POLYGONACEAE
Buckwheat Family

1 Sepals 3; tiny alpine annual herb (often only a few centimeters high), with slender, simple or branched stems . . . . *Koenigia*
1 Sepals more than 3; plants larger. 2
2 Stigma tufted; sepals 4 or 6 3
2 Stigma capitate; sepals 5, often petal-like 4
3 Leaves kidney-shaped; sepals 4. . . . . *Oxyria*
3 Leaves not kidney-shaped; sepals 6 . . . . *Rumex*
4 Perennial herbs 5
4 Annual herbs, often weedy. 6
5 Stems simple, unbranched; terrestrial plants from a short rhizome; inflorescence spikelike . . . . *Bistorta*
5 Stems freely branching; aquatic or wetland plants. . . . . *Persicaria amphibia*
6 Stems twining; leaves ovate-sagittate . . . . *Fallopia convolvulus*

Polemonium pulcherrimum
PRETTY JACOB'S-LADDER

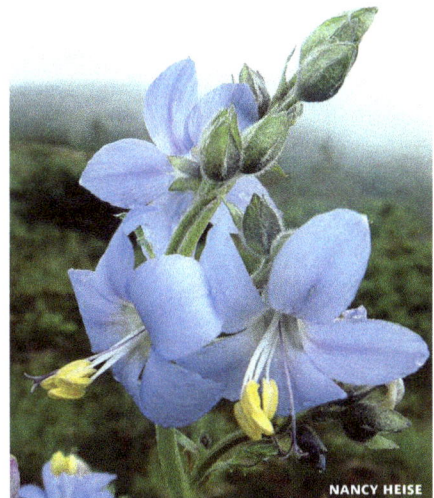
Polemonium villosum TALL JACOB'S-LADDER

6 Stems erect-ascending or prostrate; leaves lance-olate or elliptic-oblong 7

7 Inflorescence of terminal or axillary spikes . . . .
. . . . *Persicaria lapathifolia*

7 Inflorescence of small axillary clusters. . . . .
. . . . *Polygonum aviculare*

Bistorta BISTORT

(Latin, *bi-*, twice, *tortus*, twisted, alluding to contorted rhizomes.)

1 Spikes narrow, of white or pinkish flowers in upper part, bulblets in lower part . . . .
. . . . *B. vivipara*

1 Spikes wider, usually over 1 cm thick, short-cylin-dric, bulblets absent; flowers often deep pink .
. . . . *B. plumosa*

◆ *Bistorta plumosa* (Small) Greene
PLUMED BISTORT
Polygonum plumosum Small

Habit perennial deciduous herb, with a dense spike of pink flowers; stems 15–30 cm tall from a thick rhizome, single to several per plant. Leaves alternate, simple, elliptic to oblong, dark green above, paler below; peti-oles winged, margins entire. Flowers numer-ous, small, pink, in a terminal compact spike usually more than 1 cm wide. Fruit a 3-angled, pale brown, lustrous achene.

Where Found in moist peaty areas from low-elevation muskeg to alpine tundra.

Similar Species a distinctive member of the flora; no other species has a similar broad spike of tightly-packed small pink flowers.

Traditional Uses leaves can be used as a spinach substitute.

◆ *Bistorta vivipara* (L.) Delarbre
ALPINE BISTORT, SERPENT-GRASS
Polygonum viviparum L.

Habit perennial deciduous herb, with basal leaves and bulblets at base of the spike of white flowers, from a short, thick, often con-torted rhizome; stems erect, solitary, simple, 5–15 cm tall. Leaves basal and alternate on stem; dark green above, shiny grayish below, narrowly oblong-lanceolate; stem leaves with long brown sheaths around stem. Flow-ers small, in a terminal spike 2–10 cm long; tepals 5, white; at base of spike flowers re-placed by bulblets, and sometimes more bul-blets than flowers present (bulblets sometimes sprouting while still attached to stem). Fruit a 3-angled, pale brown achene, but seldom ripening.

Where Found peaty sites and tundra in the subalpine to alpine.

Similar Species bulblets below the spike of white flowers are diagnostic; leaves some-what resemble those of *Bistorta plumosa*, but are usually much narrower.

Traditional Uses all parts of plant edible, ei-ther raw or cooked.

ALFRED COOK

Bistorta plumosa PLUMED BISTORT

JERZY STRZELECKI

Bistorta vivipara ALPINE BISTORT

Fallopia BLACK-BINDWEED
(In honor of Gabriele Fallopio, 1523--1562, Italian professor of anatomy and botany, and for whom the Fallopian tubes also named.)

Fallopia convolvulus (L.) Á. Löve
BLACK-BINDWEED
Polygonum convolvulus L.

Habit Annual herb, from a taproot; stems erect when young, soon prostrate or climbing, branched, smooth, 20-100 cm long. Leaves arrowhead-shaped to ovate, dull green, blades 2-5 cm long, petioles long; stipules funnel-shaped, usually brownish membranous, soon deciduous. Flowers few to several, in axillary and terminal racemes; perianth green, about 4 mm long, 5-lobed. Fruit a 3-angled, black achene.

Where Found disturbed places; introduced from Eurasia.

Koenigia FLEECEFLOWER
(In honor of botanist Charles Dietrich Eberhard Konig, 1774–1851.)

---

1   Tall perennial herb of lower elevations . . . .
. . . . *K. alaskana*
1   Small annual herb of moist alpine habitats . . . .
. . . . *K. islandica*

◆ *Koenigia alaskana* (Small) T.M. Schust. & Reveal
ALASKA FLEECEFLOWER, ALASKA WILD-RHUBARB
Aconogonon alaskanum (Small) Soják, *Polygonum alaskanum* (Small) W. Wight ex Hultén, *Polygonum alpinum* subsp. *alaskanum* (Small) S.L. Welsh

Habit tall perennial herb, with open panicles of white to cream-colored flowers; stems to 2 m tall, hollow, simple or branching, from a thick woody root. Leaves ovate to lanceolate with an acute tip, 5-20 cm long, margins crisped. Flowers numerous, in terminal or axillary panicles, loosely ascending; tepals small, greenish or white. Fruit an achene.

Where Found spruce forests, open soil of recent landslides, burned areas, and disturbed places, at low- to mid-elevations.

Similar Species Alaska fleeceflower readily recognizable by its height, the many small white flowers, and its long, lanceolate leaves.

Traditional Uses All parts edible, either cooked like rhubarb or raw, though it should not be eaten in large quantities; raw roots and stem bases were traditionally used by Dena'ina to treat coughs and colds (Kari 1985).

◆ *Koenigia islandica* L.
KOENIGIA, ISLAND-PURSLANE
Habit annual herb, from a slender taproot; stems ascending, slender, simple or branched, several, 2-6 cm long, often reddish or crimson. Leaves basal and along stem; basal leaves few, somewhat fleshy, smooth, elliptic to lanceolate, 2-9 mm long, usually unstalked; stem leaves similar, few, alternate or opposite; sheathing stipules wax-papery. Flowers few- to several, in terminal or axillary umbel-like clusters; perianth greenish, whitish, or reddish, 1-2 mm long. Fruit a 3-angled achene, to 1 mm long.

Where Found uncommon on sandy shores or in wet, mossy places.

Koenigia alaskana ALASKA FLEECEFLOWER

Koenigia islandica KOENIGIA

Oxyria MOUNTAIN-SORREL

(Greek, sour, in reference to the acid leaves.)

♦ *Oxyria digyna* (L.) Hill MOUNTAIN-SORREL

Habit perennial herb, with many fleshy, rounded basal leaves, and a branching reddish raceme, from a long, stout, fleshy taproot and branched crown; stems erect, few to many, to 30 cm tall, leafless, smooth, often reddish tinged, strongly acrid-juiced. **Leaves** long-petioled, kidney-shaped, often reddish; margin somewhat wavy. **Flowers** in branching racemes; petals absent, replaced by four green to reddish tepals surrounding 6 stamens. **Fruit** a lens-shaped achene with a broad membranaceous red wing.

Where Found occasional in slide rock, meadows and moist, shady sites.

Similar Species the kidney-shaped leaves and petal-less red raceme distinguish this species.

Traditional Uses The sour leaves are edible; traditionally (and to present day) Alaskan Natives eat the leaves raw, boil them in water, or preserve the leaves in seal oil; the leaves still highly valued as a wild green.

Oxyria digyna MOUNTAIN-SORREL

Persicaria SMARTWEED

(Latin, *persica*, peach, and *-aria*, alluding to resemblance of leaves of some species.)

1   Flowers rose-colored, usually confined to 1 or 2 terminal or subterminal spikelike inflorescences . . . . *P. amphibia*
1   Flowers white, greenish-white, or pink, usually borne in 2 to many contracted panicles . . . . *P. lapathifolia*

♦ *Persicaria amphibia* (L.) S.F. Gray
WATER SMARTWEED
Polygonum amphibium L.

Habit variable perennial herb, from a rhizome or stolon; stems prostrate and freely rooting to ascending, several, simple; flowering branches 30–80 cm long. **Leaves** in aquatic form (with floating stems) smooth, glossy, tinged with red, oblong or elliptic; in amphibious form (with upright stems) lanceolate, with stiff pubescence; petioles to half as long as blades; stipules smooth to hairy, cylindric, 1–2 cm long. **Flowers** in 1 or 2 spikelike panicles, 1–8 cm long, 1–2 cm wide; perianth rose-colored, 4–5 mm long, 5-lobed. **Fruit** a lens-shaped achene, brown to black, shiny or sometimes dull, 2–3 mm long.

Where Found shallow water of ponds, muddy shores.

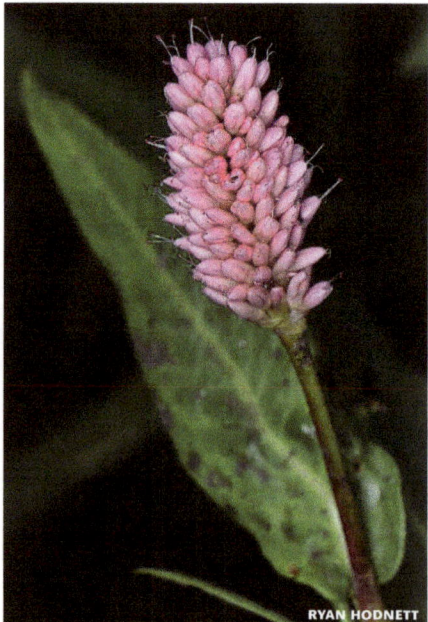

Persicaria amphibia WATER SMARTWEED

Persicaria lapathifolia (L.) Delarbre
DOCK-LEAF SMARTWEED
Polygonum lapathifolium L.

Habit annual herb, from a taproot; stems erect (sometimes prostrate), solitary, usually freely branched, 20–80 cm long. Leaves alternate, lanceolate or oblong-lanceolate, smooth or more often hairy or glandular below, blades 5–20 cm long, petioles short, margins fringed with hairs; stipules 5–20 mm long, brownish, fringed with bristly hairs at top. Flowers in a loose, often drooping cluster of spikelike racemes 1–6 cm long; perianth greenish white to pink, distinctly veined, 4–5-lobed nearly to the base; flower stalks with stalked glands. Fruit a lens-shaped, dark brown, shiny achene, 2–3 mm long.

Where Found lakeshores, disturbed areas.

Polygonum KNOTWEED

(Greek, many, and knee, from the swollen joints of many species.)

♦*Polygonum aviculare* L.
COMMON KNOTWEED

Habit annual herb, from a taproot; stems prostrate to erect, 10–100 cm long, several, branched. Leaves alternate, widely linear to lanceolate-oblong, mostly bluish green, blades 1–3 cm long, often crisped on margin, slightly reduced upwards; branch leaves smaller than stem leaves; sheathing stipules brown, ragged, 3–6 mm long. Flowers of 2–6, in a axillary clusters; sepals green with whitish or pinkish margins, 5-lobed more

Polygonum aviculare COMMON KNOTWEED

than half the distance to the base. Fruit a 3-angled, dark brown achene, 2–3 mm long.

Where Found disturbed areas; both native and introduced forms reported for Alaska.

Rumex DOCK

(The ancient Latin name.)

1 Leaves arrowhead-shaped; flowers dioecious (male and female flowers on separate plants) . . . . *R. alpestris*
1 Leaves oblong to lanceolate; flowers perfect (with both male and female parts). 2
2 Valves distinctly toothed . . . . *R. fueginus*
2 Valves entire or only slightly fringed *R. arcticus*

♦*Rumex alpestris* Jacq. LAPLAND SORREL
Rumex acetosa subsp. *alpestris* (Scop.) A. Löve

Habit dioecious perennial herb; stems ridged, with sheathing stipules, 30–60 cm high from a short rhizome. Leaves both basal and on stem; basal leaves long-petioled, stem leaves shorter, alternate; leaves hastate, the base with two triangular lobes pointing

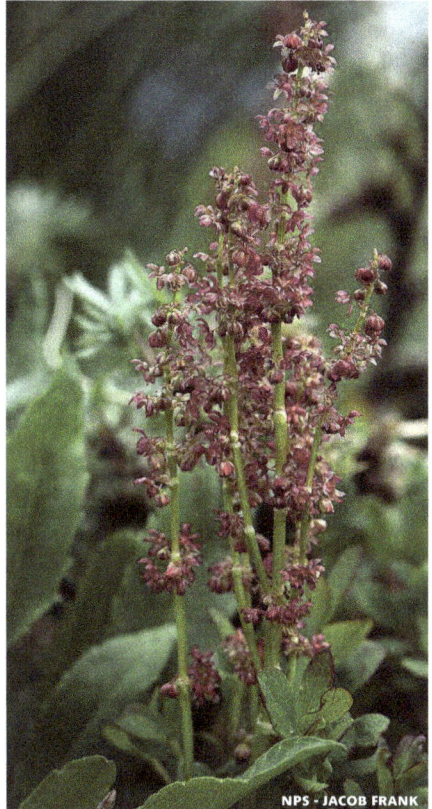

Rumex alpestris LAPLAND SORREL

out. Flowers in an open, branched, terminal inflorescence; flowers tiny, reddish, with 6 tepals; male flowers shed soon after flowering. Fruit a winged, red seed, 2-3 mm long.

Where Found occasional in mid- to high-elevation meadows and shrub tundra.

Similar Species Plants similar to *Rumex arcticus*, but that species does not have hastate leaves and if found in wet areas.

Traditional Uses leaves edible, with a sour taste.

♦ *Rumex arcticus* Trautv. ARCTIC DOCK
Habit tall perennial herb, with small reddish flowers; stems 30-10 dm tall, from a stout rhizome, typically reddish, longitudinally ribbed. Leaves vary from dark green to red-margined or entirely red; basal leaves fleshy, long-petioled, oblong to lanceolate; stem leaves alternate, narrow, acute. Flowers in a terminal, open, branched raceme; tepals small, reddish. Fruit a winged seed, 1-2 mm long.

Where Found common in wet meadows from low- to high-elevations.

Similar Species *Rumex alpestris*, but leaves of

Rumex arcticus oblong, not hastate.

Traditional Uses leaves and stem of Rumex arcticus edible, either raw or cooked; used extensively by indigenous people, and often preserved for winter use; the rhizomatous root is usually boiled and mixed with seal oil or added to stews; leaves and stems are boiled in water to make a drink similar to lemonade; root has been used as a tonic, laxative and to treat gastrointestinal problems (Garibaldi 1999); juice from the stem can be used to relieve the sting from mosquito bites or stinging nettles.

♦ *Rumex fueginus* Phil. GOLDEN DOCK
Rumex maritimus subsp. *fueginus* (Phil.) Piper & Beattie
Habit annual or biennial herb, from a taproot; stems erect, 20-60 cm tall, solitary, freely branched, finely hairy. Leaves alternate, narrowly oblong to lanceolate, blades 4-10 cm long, reduced upwards, underside usually slightly hairy, margins somewhat crisped. Flowers numerous, in tight whorls in a large and leafy panicle, golden brown when mature; flower stalks jointed near their base; perianth segments 1-2 mm long at flowering, enlarging to 3-7 mm long including the long-tapering sharp tip, each segment with 2-4 slender teeth and also usually with a prominent, narrow, grain-like swelling (tubercle). Fruit a brown, smooth, shiny achene, 1-2 mm long.

Where Found uncommon on margins of lakes, ponds, streams; marshy areas.

Rumex arcticus ARCTIC DOCK

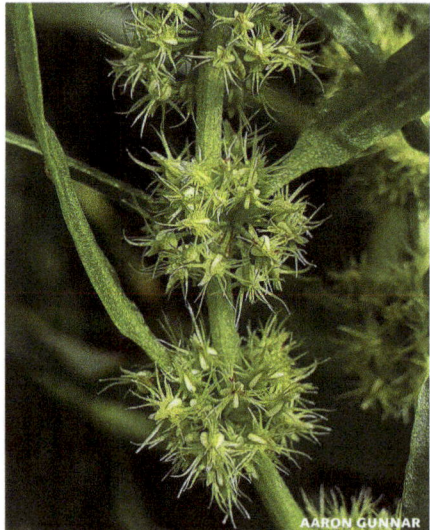
Rumex fueginus GOLDEN DOCK

PRIMULACEAE
Primrose Family

1 Leaves all basal 2
1 Plants with leafy stems 5
2 Plants densely tufted or with a dense rosette of leaves; flowers solitary, and short-pediceled or sessile in a few-flowered umbel. . . . .
. . . . *Androsace alaskana*
2 Plants with basal rosettes; flowers in terminal umbels 3
3 Corolla lobes reflexed; calyx deeply cleft. . . . . .
. . . . *Primula*
3 Corolla lobes spreading; calyx tubular. 4
4 Throat of corolla constricted; style short . . . . . .
. . . . *Androsace*
4 Throat of corolla not constricted; style elongate
. . . . *Primula*
5 Leaves opposite . . . . *Lysimachia thyrsiflora*
5 Lower leaves small and alternate, with upper ones larger and whorled *Lysimachia europaea*

Androsace DWARF-PRIMROSE
(Greek, *andros*, male, and *sakos*, shield, alluding to anther shape.)

1 Plants densely tufted or with a dense rosette of leaves; flowers solitary, and short-pediceled or sessile in a few-flowered umbel. 2
1 Plants with basal rosettes; flowers in terminal umbels 3
2 Plants with a single basal rosette. . *A. alaskana*
2 Plants with multiple rosettes or tufted cushions
. . . . *A. constancei*
3 Perennial herb; flower stalk villous with simple hairs. *A. chamaejasme*
3 Annual or biennial herb; flower stalk glabrous or with minute branched hairs. *A. septentrionalis*

♦*Androsace alaskana* Coville & Standl. ex Hultén ALASKA DWARF-PRIMROSE
Douglasia alaskana (Coville & Standl. ex Hultén) S. Kelso
Habit annual or biennial herb, from a taproot; flower stems several, 1- or 2-flowered, to 15 cm long. Leaves basal, in a dense rosette, to 25 mm long, 3-lobed at tip, upper surface more or less pubescent, margins ciliate. Flowers sessile with one lanceolate bract at base of each flower; corolla white, 4–5 mm long; slightly longer than calyx. Fruit a capsule 5–6 mm long; seeds dark brown, angular, about 2 mm long.

Where Found uncommon on rocky alpine tundra.

♦*Androsace chamaejasme* Wulfen
SWEET-FLOWER ROCK-JASMINE
Habit small perennial herb, with yellow-centered white flowers, from a branched stem-base, to 10 cm tall, growing singly or in mats of basal rosettes growing from rhizomes. Leaves sessile, strap-like to oblong, variably hairy, 3–15 mm long, margins entire. Flowers 3–6, in an umbel, on leafless, often reddish stalks; petals fused at base, five-lobed, white, yellow at base, each lobe 2–5 mm long. Fruit a five-valved capsule.

Where Found occasional in alpine areas on steep, rocky slopes and tundra.

Similar Species *Androsace chamaejasme* has long unbranched hairs, the somewhat similar *Androsace septentrionalis* is an annual or

Androsace alaskana
ALASKA DWARF-PRIMROSE

Androsace chamaejasme
SWEET-FLOWER ROCK-JASMINE

biennial (not perennial) plant, hairless or with short unbranched hairs.

Note fragrant flowers give the plant the name of rock jasmine, although *Androsace* is unrelated to true jasmine.

♦*Androsace constancei* Wendelbo
GORMAN'S DWARF-PRIMROSE
Douglasia gormanii Constance

Habit cushion-forming perennial herb, with large pink to magenta flowers, from a branched stem-base; stems single at ends of branches, erect, densely hairy with branched and forked hairs, only several cm high. Leaves semi-evergreen, oblanceolate to linear, 1–10 mm long, layered in small overlapping rosettes; covered on both sides with long hairs, margins with branched hairs; many dead leaves may persist at base of plant. Flowers on pedicels just above leaves, sometimes appearing sessile; petals 5, bright pink; corolla tube 3–4 mm long, lobes 1–2 mm long; calyx with five triangular lobes; pedicels elongating in fruit, to 3 cm long. Fruit a dry rounded capsule, with 1–4 seeds. Flowering one of the first alpine plants to flower, blooming in early to mid-May.

Where Found uncommon on steep, alpine scree-slopes, fellfields, and gravelly tundra.

Similar Species Other cushion-forming alpine plants with pink flowers include alpine azalea (*Kalmia procumbens*), whose flowers are star-shaped and leaves with revolute margins; *Silene acaulis*, which does not have leaves in tight rosettes; and *Saxifraga oppositifolia*, whose petals are separate at base and the flowers with two fused carpels.

♦*Androsace septentrionalis* L.
PYGMY-FLOWER ROCK-JASMINE

Habit annual or biennial herb, with a basal rosette of leaves and several narrow umbels of tiny white flowers, taprooted; stems erect,

leafless, 1–5 per plant, usually of unequal heights, nearly smooth to moderately hairy with branched hairs (these sometimes glandular), 5–20 cm tall. Leaves lanceolate, often reddish green, 0.5–5 cm long, margins entire or slightly toothed. Flowers 5–20, in an umbel (many flowers radiating from one point); petals fused into a five-lobed bell, 3–5 mm long, white at tip with a yellow center. Fruit a rounded 5-valved capsule. Flowering shortly after snowmelt.

Where Found occasional in dry, open soil, usually on south-aspect slopes, from mid-elevations to the subalpine.

Similar Species differs from *Androsace chamaejasme* by the absence of long, unbranched hairs.

Androsace constancei
GORMAN'S DWARF-PRIMROSE

Androsace septentrionalis
PYGMY-FLOWER ROCK-JASMINE

Lysimachia LOOSESTRIFE
(Greek *lysis*, dissolve, and *mache*, strife, alluding to soothing properties.)

1 Leaves opposite; corolla yellow . . *L. thyrisiflora*
1 Upper leaves in a whorl; corolla white. . . . . . .
 . . . . *L. europaea*

◆ *Lysimachia europaea* (L.) U. Manns & Anderb.
ARCTIC STARFLOWER
Trientalis europaea L.
 Habit small perennial herb, with a whorl of leaves and small white flowers, from a slender rhizome, and a scarcely enlarged horizontal tuber; stems 10-20 cm tall; peduncle (1 or a few per plant) grows from the center, longer than the leaves. Leaves in a whorl around stem tip, obovate, 2-6 cm long. Flowers with 5-9 petals per flower (typically 6-7), white (sometimes pale pink); sepals green, linear-lanceolate; stamens 5-9, with yellow anthers and white filaments. Fruit a rounded capsule opening by 5 (-7) valves.
 Where Found occasional at low- to mid-elevations in humus-rich soils, more common south of Alaska Range crest than north.
 Similar Species the only wildflower in Denali with whorled leaves and flowers with 5 or more petals.

◆ *Lysimachia thyrsiflora* L.
TUFTED YELLOW-LOOSESTRIFE
 Habit perennial herb, finely dark-purplish or blackish spotted almost throughout, from a creeping rhizome; stems erect, 20-70 cm tall, solitary, simple, smooth. Leaves opposite, unstalked, upper leaves linear to lanceolate, to about 10 cm long; lowermost leaves reduced to scales. Flowers in short, dense, slender, spikelike clusters in axils of two or three larger leaves near mid-stem, on peduncles 1-3 cm long; individual flowers crowded and nearly unstalked; corolla pale yellow, dotted with red or purplish black spots, deeply 5-lobed; calyx 5-lobed, spotted. Fruit a capsule, 2-3 mm long; seeds few.
 Where Found uncommon on wet shores, marshy areas.

Primula
PRIMROSE, SHOOTINGSTAR
(Latin, first, from the early blooming habits of some species.)

1 Corolla lobes reflexed; calyx deeply cleft. . . . . .
 . . . . *P. frigida*
1 Corolla lobes spreading; calyx tubular 2
2 Flowers large (about 2 cm long); corolla lobes nearly entire . . . . *P. eximia*
2 Flowers much smaller; corolla lobes deeply notched 3
3 Leaves ovate to elliptical or wedge-shaped. . . .
 . . . . *P. cuneifolia*
3 Leaves narrower 4
4 Flowers 6–8 mm wide; calyx lobes fringed with glandular hairs . . . . *P. egaliksensis*
4 Flowers 8–15 mm wide; calyx with capitate glands . . . . *P. mistassinica*

Lysimachia europaea ARCTIC STARFLOWER

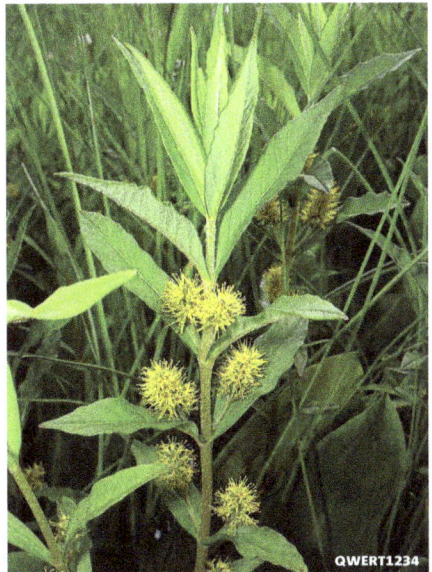
Lysimachia thyrsiflora
TUFTED YELLOW-LOOSESTRIFE

♦ *Primula cuneifolia* Ledeb. PIXIE-EYES

Habit small alpine perennial herb, roots fibrous; stems 2–10 cm tall, leafless and relatively stout, bearing 1–4 flowers. **Leaves** all basal, oblanceolate to wedge-shaped, 1–8 cm long; upper margins toothed. **Flowers** 1–9, in an umbel; homostylous (stamens and styles of same length); petals 5, pink, 1–2 cm wide; calyx with triangular lobes. **Fruit** a nearly round capsule, shorter than the calyx.

Where Found uncommon in moist alpine tundra and meadows.

Similar Species Pixie-eyes is the most common primrose in Denali, distinguished by its very small stature and oblanceolate leaves with toothed upper margin; plants also without farina (a powdery-white covering), a diagnostic character for some members of the genus.

♦ *Primula egaliksensis* Wormsk.
GREENLAND PRIMROSE

Habit perennial herb; stems glabrous to sparsely glandular-hairy, not whitish mealy, 5–15 cm tall. **Leaves** basal, oval or lance-ovate, narrowed into winged petioles, not succulent, entire to wavy-margined (sometimes slightly toothed), glabrous, 0.5–5 cm long. **Flowers** mostly 1–3, in an umbel; involucral bracts lanceolate, sac-shaped at base, homostylous (stamens and styles of same length); corolla lavender to white, with a yellow throat; calyx green, often striped with purple. **Fruit** a narrowly cylindric capsule, more than twice as long as calyx.

Where Found uncommon on moist soils, streambanks, lakeshores, marshy areas.

♦ *Primula eximia* Greene ARCTIC PRIMROSE
Primula pumila (Ledeb.) Pax

Habit small perennial herb, from short rhizomes with fibrous roots; stems naked, 10–40 cm tall. **Leaves** basal, slightly fleshy, broadly oblanceolate, tapering toward base, toothed at tip; dead leaves numerous and persistent at base of plant. **Flowers** usually 3–6, in an umbel; homostylous (stamens and styles of same length), corolla tube white, with five magenta to pink petals; calyx of five fused teeth, green-black. **Fruit** a many-seeded capsule.

Where Found uncommon in moist to wet alpine tundra and meadows.

Similar Species plants initially covered with white 'farina' (powder), distinguishing it from several other primrose species, but this diminishes with age, except on the calyx.

Primula cuneifolia PIXIE-EYES

Primula egaliksensis GREENLAND PRIMROSE

◆ *Primula frigida* (Cham. & Schltdl.) A.R. Mast & Reveal WESTERN ARCTIC SHOOTINGSTAR
Dodecatheon frigidum Cham. & Schltdl.

Habit perennial herb with broad basal leaves and showy flowers with strongly re-flexed pink petals, from a woody stem-base; stems erect, solitary, simple, finely glandular-hairy, 5–30 cm tall. Leaves basal, ovate, 4–10 cm long, margins wavy. Flowers 2–5 in a compact inflorescence at end of leafless stem; petal lobes five, magenta to lavender, center of corolla yellow or white; calyx lobed with sharp points, inconspicuous in flower, but persistent in fruit; heads nodding downwards. Fruit a cylindric capsule, opening by at tip to release many tiny seeds. Flowering summer; the heads turning upwards when fruiting in late-summer.

Where Found common in alpine and sub-alpine meadows and heath tundra.

Similar Species no other herbaceous plant in Denali has reflexed pink flowers.

◆ *Primula mistassinica* Michx.
LAKE MISTASSINI PRIMROSE

Habit perennial herb; stems glabrous or sometimes yellowish mealy when young, 5–15 cm tall. Leaves oblanceolate to spade-shaped, tapering to narrowly winged petiole, margins wavy to shallowly toothed (sometimes entire), sometimes inrolled. Flowers 1–5, in an umbel; heterostylous (stamens and styles of unequal lengths); corolla pink to lavender with yellow throat; calyx green, glandular; pedicels slender, flexuous to erect, 5–20 mm long. Fruit a cylindric capsule, slightly longer than calyx.

Where Found uncommon in moist meadows, lakeshores, streambanks.

RANUNCULACEAE
Buttercup Family

1   Fruit berrylike; flowers small, white or greenish, in a dense cylindrical raceme . . . . *Actaea*
1   Fruit not berrylike 2
2   Fruit a follicle, opening along one side 3
2   Fruit a dry achene clustered into a head, or a short-cylindric spike 6
3   Flowers regular, yellow or white 4
3   Flowers irregular, blue 5

Primula frigida WESTERN ARCTIC SHOOTINGSTAR

Primula eximia ARCTIC PRIMROSE

Primula mistassinica LAKE MISTASSINI PRIMROSE

4 Follicles sessile; leaves more or less entire . . . .
. . . . *Caltha*

4 Follicles on short stalks; leaves 3-parted . *Coptis*

5 Upper sepal hooded; flowers few, in an open
raceme. . . . . *Aconitum*

5 Upper sepal with long spur; flowers numerous,
in a spikelike raceme. . . . . *Delphinium*

6 Petals normally present; sepals 3 or 5 . . . .
. . . . *Ranunculus* (also see *Halerpestes*)

6 Petals absent, sepals petal-like. 7

7 Flowers small and numerous . . . . . . *Thalictrum*

7 Flowers large and showy, 1 to several 8

8 Styles long and plumose; sepals purple or blue
. . . . *Pulsatilla*

8 Styles short, not plumose; sepals yellow, white,
or pale blue 9

9 Achenes woolly hairy . . . . *Anemone*

9 Achenes smooth, not woolly hairy . . . .
. . . . *Anemonastrum*

Aconitum MONKSHOOD

(Ancient Greek name.)

◆*Aconitum delphiniifolium* DC.
LARKSPUR-LEAF MONKSHOOD

Habit perennial herb, with distinctive purple hooded flowers and deeply lobed leaves, from a tuberous taproot; stems erect, slender, 20–50 cm tall, smooth to nearly so below, spreading recurved-hairy above. Leaves alternate, palmately lobed and deeply cleft into narrow segments, round in outline; upper stem leaves two-lobed or linear. Flowers 1–5, in an open raceme, bilaterally symmet-

Aconitum delphiniifolium
LARKSPUR-LEAF MONKSHOOD

ric, deep purple, strongly veined, with five petal-like sepals and two small petals hidden within; uppermost sepal helmet-like, positioned above two vertically aligned sepals; petals long-clawed, beaked at tip, paler purple. Fruit usually 3–5 follicles, 1.5–2 cm long, with many black seeds.

Where Found common in moist places, from shady lowland woods to alpine meadows.

Similar Species larkspur (*Delphinium*) also has deeply lobed leaves and bilaterally symmetric blue-purple flowers; however, the flowers of larkspur have an elongate spur in the back, rather than a hoodlike flower.

Traditional Uses the entire plant contains aconitine, a neurotoxin, and should never be eaten.

Actaea BANEBERRY

(Greek, aktea, ancient name for the elder, perhaps because of similar leaves.)

◆*Actaea rubra* (Aiton) Willd. RED BANEBERRY

Habit shrub-like perennial herb, with clusters of white flowers maturing to scarlet red berries, from a stout, branched, woody stembase and fibrous roots; stems 1 to several, erect, 3–10 dm tall, usually branched, pubescence of stems and leaves variable. Leaves alternate, large, divided into pinnate segments, the segments ovate or deltoid in outline, green on upperside, paler below, margins sharply serrate. Flowers many, in a terminal pyramidal inflorescence; petals five, white, 2–3.5 mm long; stamens white, longer than the petals. Fruit a bright red (or less often white) berry about 5 mm wide, each berry with 9 to 16 seeds; stigma long-persistent, leaving a black dot on tip of berry.

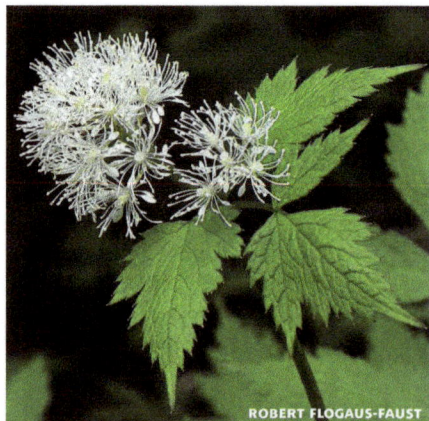

Actaea rubra RED BANEBERRY

Flowering late May to early June; fruit set in June and July.

Where Found occasional in low-elevation forests, woodlands and meadows.

Similar Species potentially confused with highbush cranberry (*Viburnum edule,* with edible berries), but leaves of that plant opposite (not alternate), lobed (not pinnate), and the berries less numerous in clusters below the leaves, not in a terminal pyramidal spike.

Traditional Uses entire plant is slightly poisonous (with the toxins most concentrated in roots and berries); however, in the past, dilute preparations of baneberry were used as a medicinal treatment by Alaska Natives.

Anemonastrum THIMBLEWEED
(Somewhat like *Anemone.*)

1 Plants rhizomatous; flowers solitary; sepals yellow. . . . . *A. richardsonii*
1 Plants tufted; flowers solitary to several in an umbel; sepals white or blue-tinged . . . . *A. sibiricum*

♦*Anemonastrum richardsonii* (Hook.) Mosyakin YELLOW THIMBLEWEED
Anemone richardsonii (Hook.) Starod.

Habit perennial creeping herb, from a slender rhizome; stems erect, 5–20 cm tall, hairy above. Leaves single, long-petioled, arising from the rhizome, and also opposite and paired below the flower; basal leaves palmately lobed, round in outline, margins

Anemonastrum richardsonii
YELLOW THIMBLEWEED

toothed; stem leaves 3-cleft, toothed, sessile. Flowers solitary, with about 6 yellow tepals (looking like petals); stamens 25–55, yellow, surrounding a cone-shaped compound ovary with many styles. Fruit a rounded head of many dry fruits (achenes); the achene hairless with a long curved beak, which is also hooked at tip.

Where Found common on streambanks, moist thickets and moist meadows, from lowlands to alpine zones.

Similar Species the only yellow-flowered thimbleweed in Alaska, also our only *Anemone* with hooked, hairless achenes.

♦*Anemonastrum sibiricum* (L.) Holub
SIBERIAN FALSE THIMBLEWEED
Anemone narcissiflora var. *alaskana* (Hultén) B.Boivin, *Anemone sibirica* L.

Habit tufted perennial herb; stems 20–40 cm tall. Leaves basal, long-petioled, hairy when young, becoming hairless, divided in threes, each leaflet further lobed; small, sessile leafy bracts present below flower. Flowers 1–8, in an umbel, each flower stem radiating from the same point of attachment; tepals 5–9 (looking like petals), white or blue-tinged, ovate to elliptic. Fruit in rounded heads of elongate, hairless, narrowly winged achenes; the achene shiny black, with a narrow, curved or recurved beak.

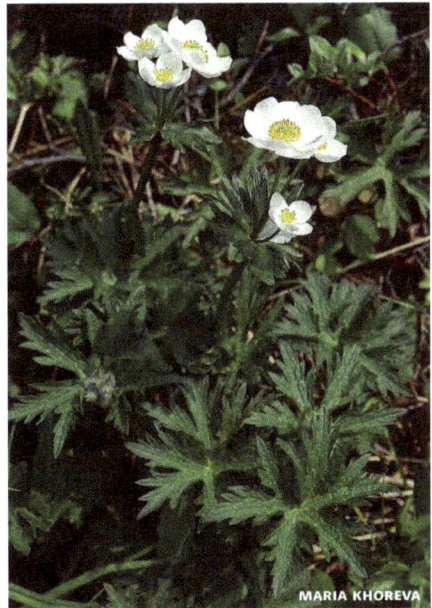

Anemonastrum sibiricum
SIBERIAN FALSE THIMBLEWEED

Where Found common in open alpine tundra and rocky slopes, less commonly at low- to mid-elevations.

Traditional Uses *Anemone* species contain anemonin, a toxin. Tea made from thoroughly boiled roots was used by the Aleut to treat hemorrhages (Bank 1953, 1971, in Garibaldi 1999).

Anemone
THIMBLEWEED, WINDFLOWER
(Greek, *anemos*, wind.)

1 Plants rhizomatous; sepals white . *A. parviflora*
1 Plants tufted 2
2 Plant usually less than 20 cm high; flowers solitary; sepals white or blue-tinged . . . . *A. drummondii*
2 Plants 20–40 cm high; flowers 1–3; sepals mostly creamy white (or tinged with purple . . . . *A. multifida*

♦*Anemone drummondii* S. Watson
DRUMMOND'S ANEMONE
Habit small tufted perennial herb, with large white flowers with a bluish blush, from a branching woody stem-base; stems erect, 10–20 cm tall; leaves and flower stems silky-haired when young, hairless when mature. Leaves 3–4 times palmately cleft, the leaflets further lobed into linear segments; basal leaves long-petioled, stem leaves sessile and opposite; bracts below flower (looking like stem leaves) are 2 times 3-parted (as opposed to once 3-parted bracts of Anemone multifida). Flowers solitary, long-stalked, 2–3 cm wide; sepals petal-like, 6–9, ovate, appressed-hairy on outer surface, white or blue-tinged, forming a cup; stamens 80–100,

yellow. Fruit in a cone-shaped head of many achenes; styles unhooked, persisting on achene, and covered in long hairs, allowing achene to be dispersed by wind. Flowering early summer (soon after snowmelt).

Where Found uncommon on rocky slopes and dry tundra at mid- to high-elevations.

Similar Species can be difficult to distinguish from other *Anemone* species, but it is one of only two species with hairy achenes with an unhooked style; *Anemone multifida* has similar fruits, but its leaf segments more linear, and plants typically taller (20–40 cm), and rarer, generally occurring at lower elevations in Denali.

♦*Anemone multifida* Poir.
CUT-LEAF ANEMONE, RED WINDFLOWER
Habit perennial herb, from a woody stem-base; stems 1 to many, erect, 10–30 cm tall, sparsely to densely long-hairy. Leaves basal, 3 to 6, palmately 1- or 2-times 3-parted, margins incised on upper 1/3, smooth to long-hairy on upper surface, long-hairy on underside; petioles 4–10 cm long. Flowers solitary or less often 2–3, on long, erect stalks; petals absent; sepals usually 5 to 9, petal-like, cream-colored, or tinged with blue, purple, or red, especially on outer surface, hairy on outside, smooth inside; sta-

Anemone drummondii DRUMMOND'S ANEMONE

Anemone multifida CUT-LEAF ANEMONE

mens 50–80, whitish; styles white. Fruit a densely woolly achene, many in a subglobose or ovate head; achene beak more or less straight, curved or hooked at tip.

Where Found uncommon in meadows, gravelly slopes, woodland openings, mostly at low- to mid-elevations.

♦ *Anemone parviflora* Michx.
SMALL-FLOWER THIMBLEWEED

Habit small perennial herb, with white flowers and divided leaves, from a short woody stem-base on widespread, slender, horizontal rhizomes; stems erect, 5–20 cm tall; nearly smooth to densely soft-hairy. Leaves basal and several along stem, glabrous and shiny dark green; leaf blade rounded in outline, divided by threes into wedge-shaped segments; stem leaves arranged like a collar below the flower, similar to basal leaves but smaller and sessile. Flowers single at end of a long villous stalk; petals absent; sepals petal-like, cream to white, blue-tinged on underside, appressed hairy; stamens 70–80, yellow. Fruit a spherical to ovate head of achenes; achenes white-woolly. Flowering typically one of the first flowers of the spring.

Where Found common at low- to high-elevations on rocky slopes, meadows and tundra.

Similar Species distinguished from other species of *Anemone* by its woolly achenes and broad leaf segments.

Traditional Uses *Anemone* species contain anemonin, a toxin. Leaves of A. parviflora were used as a poultice for skin abrasions (McKenna 1965 in Garibaldi 1999), or powdered and brewed into a 'peppery' tea for treating tuberculosis.

Caltha MARSH-MARIGOLD
(Greek name for some yellow-flowered plant.)

1	Stems erect, naked or with a single leaf; sepals white . . . . *C. leptosepala*
1	Stems ascending or decumbent, floating or creeping 2
2	Stems ascending or decumbent; sepals yellow; carpels 6–12 . . . . *C. palustris*
2	Stems floating or creeping; sepals white; carpels about 30 . . . . *C. natans*

♦ *Caltha leptosepala* DC.
MOUNTAIN MARSH-MARIGOLD

Habit perennial herb, from a short, thick stem-base with fibrous roots; stems erect, 5–40 cm tall, leafless or with a single leaf; plants smooth, fleshy. Leaves basal, waxy green, ovate to circular or kidney-shaped with a narrow sinus at base, 2–12 cm long, margins wavy toothed or nearly entire; petioles long (2–25 cm). Flowers 1–2, 2–4 cm wide; petals absent; sepals 6 to 12, white or greenish, purple tinged on outside; stamens 50 or more. Fruit a spreading follicle, 10–20 mm long; beak straight or curved 1 mm long; seeds brown, about 2 mm long.

Where Found uncommon in wet alpine meadows and streams.

♦ *Caltha natans* Pallas ex Georgi
FLOATING MARSH-MARIGOLD

Habit perennial herb, from a fibrous root; stems leafy, slender, floating or creeping, rooting at nodes, 30–100 cm long; plants smooth. Leaves often floating, ovate to kid-

Anemone parviflora
SMALL-FLOWER THIMBLEWEED

Caltha leptosepala MTN. MARSH-MARIGOLD

ney- or heart-shaped, with a narrow sinus at base, 3–5 cm wide, margins nearly entire; bract leaves reduced. Flowers solitary or in a loose cluster of 2 to 6, terminal or from leaf axils; petals absent; sepals 5 or 6, white or pinkish; stamens about 20, shorter than carpels. Fruit a globe-shaped head of widely spreading follicles about 4 mm long with a very short beak; seeds brown.

Where Found occasional in shallow water and on shores.

♦ *Caltha palustris* L. YELLOW MARSH-MARIGOLD
Habit wetland or aquatic perennial herb, with yellow flowers, from a short, thick stem-base with fibrous roots; stems floating, erect, or ascending, 10–50 cm long; plants smooth. Leaves basal and along stem; basal leaves petioled, rounded, often kidney-shaped, to 20 cm wide, margins entire or crenate; stem leaves smaller, short-petioled to nearly sessile. Flowers one to several flowers grouped together; tepals five, 2–5 cm wide, bright yellow; stamens many, yellow. Fruit a follicle, which splits open to release several seeds; seeds about 2 mm long.

Where Found uncommon in wetlands, lakeshores, and ponds at low- to high-elevations.

Similar Species A few similar-looking species of *Ranunculus* can be found in similar wet habitats, but none with as large yellow flowers or with as broad kidney-shaped leaves.

Traditional Uses plants contain protoanemonin and aconite, poisonous compounds. Tea brewed from the leaves was used by the Yup'ik to treat diarrhea or constipation (Lantis 1959 in Garibaldi 1999) to re-

move toxic compounds, water had to be changed several times (Jernigan et al. 2015).

Coptis GOLDTHREAD
(Greek, *kopto*, to cut, referring to the dissected leaves.)

♦ *Coptis trifolia* (L.) Salisb.
THREE-LEAF GOLDTHREAD
Habit perennial herb, from a yellow to orange rhizome; stems erect, threadlike, 3–12 cm tall, not elongating in fruit, minutely-hairy above. Leaves basal, shining and evergreen, stalked, 3-parted; leaflets ovate, 1–2 cm long, slightly lobed, toothed, wedge-shaped at base; involucral bracts tiny. Flowers solitary, erect, on stalks 1–4 cm long; petals 5–7, half the length of sepals, club-shaped, fleshy; sepals usually 5, whitish (often pink-tinged) with yellow base; stamens 30–60. Fruit 3 to 7 spreading follicles, 4–8 mm long, on stalks equal to or longer than fruit; beak straight but hooked at tip, 2–4 mm long; seeds dark, about 1 mm long, wrinkled.

Where Found uncommon in alpine tundra, woods, muskegs, bogs, moist meadows.

Delphinium LARKSPUR
(Latin, *delphin*, dolphin, from some resemblance in the flower.)

Coptis trifolia THREE-LEAF GOLDTHREAD
SUPERIOR NF

Caltha natans FLOATING MARSH-MARIGOLD
ALFRED COOK

Caltha palustris YELLOW MARSH-MARIGOLD
JOSHUA MAYER

1   Flowers few, about 2 cm long; follicles densely hairy . . . . *D. brachycentrum*
1   Flowers many, 1–1.5 cm long; follicles glabrous or nearly so . . . . *D. glaucum*

◆ *Delphinium brachycentrum* Ledeb.
NORTHERN LARKSPUR

Habit perennial herb, with many dark blue flowers and deeply divided leaves; stems 10–40 cm high, growing from a rhizome; entire plant covered with short, soft, white hairs; base of the stem usually reddish. **Leaves** alternate, long-petioled, palmately much-divided, the smallest segments linear, dark green, paler on underside, with deeply impressed veins on upper surface. **Flowers** 5–18, in an open raceme; bilaterally symmetric; tepals blue-purple, uppermost tepal spurred. **Fruit** a hairy follicle.

Where Found uncommon in alpine tundra, meadows and scree, especially on south-aspect slopes north of Alaska Range crest.

Similar Species very similar to the more common *Delphinium glaucum;* northern larkspur smaller, restricted to alpine areas, with distinctly larger flowers (2 cm instead of 1–1.5 cm) and hairy fruit (glabrous in *D. glaucum*).

Traditional Uses all parts of the plant poisonous and should never be consumed.

◆ *Delphinium glaucum* S. Watson
MOUNTAIN LARKSPUR

Habit tall perennial herb, with spurred deep-purple flowers, from a thick, tough rootstock; stems one or more, hollow, erect, 50–120 cm tall, green or reddish purple, mostly smooth with a waxy bloom. **Leaves** alternate, palmately divided, the segments further divided into pointed segments; dark green above and lighter below, with visible veins on upper surface. **Flowers** many in a terminal raceme; each flower on a 1–3 cm long pedicel, with a prominent spur extending backwards; sepals blue to dark purple. **Fruit** 2–3 purple-veined follicles; splitting along one seam to release winged seeds.

Where Found common in moist, rich areas in forests, thickets, meadows and streambanks from lowlands to the alpine zone.

Similar Species another plant in Denali with bilaterally symmetric blue flowers and much-dissected leaves is *Aconitum delphinifolium*, but that species has only a few rounded, helmet-like flowers, not a spikelike raceme of spurred flowers.

Traditional Uses the whole plant contains a toxic alkaloid; the Dena'ina used an infusion of the root to wash away lice, or drank it to treat tuberculosis (Kari 1995).

Delphinium brachycentrum
NORTHERN LARKSPUR

Delphinium glaucum **MOUNTAIN LARKSPUR**

Halerpestes ALKALI BUTTERCUP

♦ *Halerpestes cymbalaria* (Pursh) Greene
ALKALI BUTTERCUP, SHORE BUTTERCUP
Ranunculus cymbalaria Pursh

Habit perennial stoloniferous herb, from fibrous roots; flowering stems erect or ascending and 5–30 cm tall, decumbent to prostrate stems (stolons) rooting at nodes, 10–40 cm long. **Leaves** basal and along stem; basal leaves simple, undivided, oblong to heart-shaped or circular, shallowly to deeply round-toothed, somewhat fleshy; stem leaves alternate, few, much reduced; lowermost bract scalelike. **Flowers** 1–5, on stalks 2–6 cm long; petals usually 5, distinct, yellow, oblanceolate to spoon-shaped, 2–7 mm long; sepals 5, spreading, early deciduous, greenish yellow; stamens 15–30; pistils 50–200. **Fruit** an achene, many in a cylindric or ovate head, 6–12 mm long; achenes ovate, about 2 mm long, with a short, straight beak to 0.2 mm long.

Where Found moist meadows, muddy shores.

Pulsatilla PASQUEFLOWER

♦ *Pulsatilla nuttalliana* (DC.) Bercht. & J. Presl
AMERICAN PASQUEFLOWER
Anemone nuttalliana DC., *Pulsatilla ludoviciana* (Nutt.) Heller, *Pulsatilla patens* subsp. *nuttalliana* (DC.) Grey-Wilson

Habit tufted perennial herb, with large, lavender-blue blossoms, from a woody, taprooted stem-base covered in old leaf bases; stems one to many, erect, short early in the season (10–15 cm), elongating in flower to 25–35 cm; the whole plant densely white-woolly in bud. **Leaves** basal and along stem (basal leaves long-petioled, developing after flowering), three-parted, deeply cleft into narrow, linear segments; stem leaves sessile. **Flowers** pale blue to deep lavender; tepals ovate and pointed, with long white appressed hairs on outer side; each flower with 150–200 yellow stamens, surrounding many white-styled pistils. **Fruit** in a head of many densely hairy achenes; styles plumose, to 2–3 cm long in fruit. **Flowering** one of the first wildflowers of the spring; flower buds emerge shortly after snowmelt and before the basal leaves grow.

Where Found open woods, slopes at mid-elevations.

Similar Species Denali's only spring-flowering plant with large purple blossoms and silky-haired stems.

Ranunculus BUTTERCUP

(Latin *rana*, frog, *unculus*, little, from the wet habitats of many species.)

1 Plants stoloniferous, rooting at nodes; flowers yellow or white 2
1 Plants tufted, terrestrial or in wetlands, with erect or ascending stems 7
2 Aquatic or amphibious plants, with creeping or floating stems 3
2 Terrestrial plants; flowers yellow 5
3 Aquatic plants, with white flowers; leaves finely dissected . . . . *R. trichophyllus*
3 Amphibious plants; flowers yellow 4
4 Leaves lobed, the primary divisions of leaves entire . . . . *R. hyperboreus*
4 Leaves lobed, the lobes again divided; floating leaves firm; submersed leaves flaccid . . . . *R. gmelinii*

Halerpestes cymbalaria ALKALI BUTTERCUP

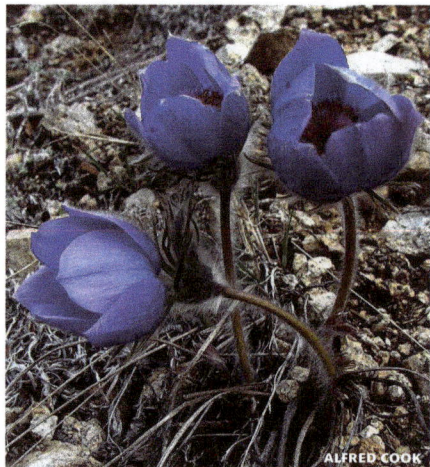
Pulsatilla nuttalliana AMERICAN PASQUEFLOWER

5 Flowers on a naked stalk; sepals 3 . . . .
. . . . *R. lapponicus*

5 Flowers on short peduncles with small bracts; plants decumbent, rooting at nodes or with threadlike runners; sepals 5 6

6 Achenes 50-200, in a cylindric or long-ovate head . . . . *Halerpestes cymbalaria*

6 Achenes less than 60, in a more or less globular head . . . . *R. reptans*

7 Plants glabrous or very nearly so 8

7 Plants distinctly hairy, especially on leaf petioles; lowland species 15

8 Stems hollow; plant of lower elevation wetlands . . . . *R. sceleratus*

8 Stems firm; alpine plants 9

9 Petals shorter than sepals; dwarf species . . . 10

9 Petals longer than sepals 11

10 Leaf segments 3-lobed . . . . *R. pygmaeus*

10 Leaf segments again 3-parted . . . . *R. grayi*

11 Basal leaves 3-lobed 12

11 Basal leaves deeply incised; flower peduncles hairy 14

12 Sepals with sparse pale yellowish hairs . . . .
. . . . *R. eschscholtzii*

12 Sepals densely brown or black hairy 13

13 Receptacle glabrous . . . . *R. nivalis*

13 Receptacle with reddish brown hairs . . . .
. . . . *R. sulphureus*

14 Leaves pubescent . . . . *R. occidentalis*

14 Leaves glabrous . . . . *R. arcticus*

15 Terminal or middle segment of basal leaves not stalked . . . . *R. macounii*

15 Terminal or middle segment of basal leaves stalked 16

16 Petals shorter than sepals; fruiting head cylindric-oblong . . . . *R. pensylvanicus*

16 Petals as long or longer than sepals; fruiting head globose . . . . *R. macounii*

Ranunculus arcticus Richardson
NORTHERN BUTTERCUP

Ranunculus pedatifidus subsp. *affinis* (R.Br.) Hultén

Habit tufted perennial herb; stems 10–30 cm high, few to several, erect, slender, simple or slightly forking. Leaves basal and along stem; basal leaves long-petioled, cordate to reniform in outline, cleft nearly to the centre into 5–9 entire, linear or lobed segments; lowermost stem leaves sessile or short-petioled, similar to basal leaves; upper stem leaves 3-cleft into linear segments. Flowers solitary; petals 5 obovate or almost orbicular, from pale to bright yellow, 5–10 mm long;

sepals 5, greenish, thinly gray-hairy on the back. Fruit a glabrous achene about 2 mm long, in an ovoid or short-cylindric head; beak curved, readily deciduous, to 1 mm long.

Where Found alpine tundra, sandy or gravelly meadows.

◆ *Ranunculus eschscholtzii* Schltdl.
ESCHSCHOLTZ'S BUTTERCUP

Habit small perennial herb, with yellow flowers and palmately divided leaves, from a compact, stem base covered with withered leaf bases, with a cluster of fibrous roots; stems 1 to several, erect, 5–25 cm tall, not hollow; stems and leaves hairless. Leaves basal and along stem (or stem leaves absent), rounded or heart-shaped, each leaf with three segments, these shallowly lobed and rounded at tip; stem leaves alternate, 1–3. Flowers solitary (rarely 2); petals five, shiny yellow, 7–12 mm long, widest toward tip; sepals reddish, with short yellow hairs; stamens yellow. Fruit a glabrous achene, in cylindric heads; beak to 1 mm long.

Where Found moist to wet rivulets, seeps, and snowflush gullies in alpine and subalpine zones.

Similar Species distinguished from other buttercups by its tufted habit, lobed leaves, and yellow-hairy sepals.

◆ *Ranunculus gmelinii* DC.
LESSER YELLOW WATER BUTTERCUP

Habit aquatic or amphibious perennial herb, rooting from nodes of lower stems; stems slender, simple to branched, floating or trailing, to 50 cm long, hollow. Leaves alternate, kidney-shaped to circular, 3-lobed or -parted, bases heart-shaped, the segments 1-3-times lobed to dissected, entire or round-

Ranunculus eschscholtzii
ESCHSCHOLTZ'S BUTTERCUP

toothed; submerged leaves sometimes dissected into linear or thread-like segments. Flowers solitary, from leaf axils, sometimes few-flowered in a terminal cyme; petals 5 or more, ovate, yellow, 3–7 mm long; sepals 4 or 5, spreading or bent back from base, early deciduous; stamens 10–45; pistils 20–70. Fruit an ovate, slightly flattened achene, many in an ovate to globe-shaped head; beak persistent, lanceolate to thread-like, straight, about 0.5 mm long.

Where Found shallow water of ponds, lakeshores, mud flats.

Ranunculus grayi Britt.
ARCTIC BUTTERCUP
Ranunculus gelidus subsp. *grayi* (Britt.) Hultén

Habit tufted perennial herb, with yellow flowers, from a short, thickened stem base with fibrous roots; stems erect or ascending to decumbent, 5–15 cm tall, smooth below, minutely-hairy above, not hollow. Leaves at base long-petioled, rounded or heart-shaped in outline, three-parted and divided into elliptic segments; flowering stems with leaves only at base. Flowers solitary on each stem, less often branched and with 2–3 flowers; petals 5, yellow, 3–5 mm long, barely longer than sepals. Fruit a round-ovate achene, beak short, curved.

Where Found alpine talus and scree (especially on south-facing slopes), and in open pockets of soil in alpine tundra.

Similar Species distinguished from other *Ranunculus* species by its pubescent flowering stems, petals equal to sepals, and the twice-ternately divided leaves.

◆ Ranunculus hyperboreus Rottb.
FAR-NORTHERN BUTTERCUP

Habit aquatic or amphibious perennial herb, with yellow flowers, rooting at nodes; roots fibrous; stems slender, floating or trailing, smooth. Leaves kidney-shaped or semicircular in outline, broader than long, 3–5-lobed. Flowers tiny, from axils of leaf buds; petals 5, yellow, 2–4 mm long, slightly larger than the green sepals; stamens many, yellow. Fruit an achene, clustered in a globose head; beak short, hooked at tip.

Where Found at low- to mid-elevations, in seasonally wet areas and along small waterbodies.

Similar Species the small size, leaf shape, and preference for wet or aquatic sites, help identify arctic buttercup.

◆ Ranunculus lapponicus L.
LAPLAND BUTTERCUP
Coptidium lapponicum (L.) Gand. ex Rydb.

Habit creeping perennial herb, with yellow flowers; stems prostrate, slender, rooting at nodes; flower stems 3–20 cm tall. Leaves basal and single or few-together, with long petioles; blade rounded or kidney-shaped, twice cleft into three coarsely toothed segments.

Ranunculus hyperboreus
FAR-NORTHERN BUTTERCUP

Ranunculus lapponicus LAPLAND BUTTERCUP

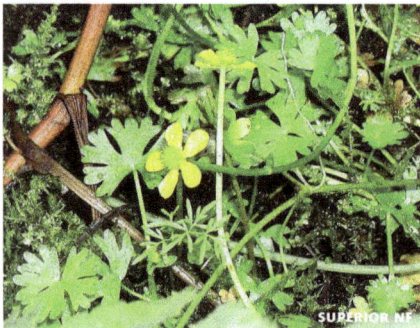
Ranunculus gmelinii
LESSER YELLOW WATER BUTTERCUP

Flowers single, about 1 cm wide, borne on leafless stems; petals 6–10, pale yellow or white; sepals 3. Fruit an achene, clustered into a rounded head; beak to 2 mm long, curved.

Where Found low-elevation boggy wetlands.

Similar Species the creeping habit, leafless flowering stems, and three sepals distinguish this species from other buttercups.

Ranunculus macounii Britt.
MACOUN'S BUTTERCUP

Habit perennial herb, from thick and somewhat fleshy roots; stems nearly erect to prostrate, often rooting at nodes, 20–60 cm long, long-hairy (rarely glabrous), hollow. Leaves basal and along stem; basal leaves persistent, heart- to kidney-shaped, leaflets 3-lobed or 3-parted, petioles to 30 cm long; stem leaves 1–2; bracts much-reduced. Flowers few, in terminal cymes, the flower stems to 6 cm long; receptacle long-hairy; petals 5, ovate, yellow; sepals 5, spreading or bent back about 1 mm above base, soon deciduous; stamens 20–40; pistils 20–60. Fruit an elliptic to ovate achene about 3 mm long, many in a globe-shaped to ovate head; beak persistent, lanceolate, 1 mm long, straight or nearly so.

Where Found wet meadows, shores, streambanks, thickets.

♦ *Ranunculus nivalis* L. SNOW BUTTERCUP

Habit perennial herb, with glossy yellow petals, from short rhizomes with clusters of fibrous roots; stems stout, fleshy, reddish, erect, 5–15 cm tall, smooth or sparsely-hairy; stem-base wrapped in brown, old leaf sheaths. Leaves basal and along stem, 3–5-

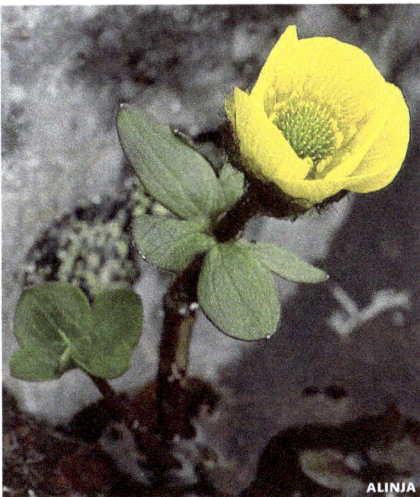

Ranunculus nivalis SNOW BUTTERCUP

lobed with entire margins; basal leaves long-petioled; stem leaves several, sessile. Flowers single at end of stem; petals 5, shiny dark yellow, twice as long as sepals; sepals 5, densely black-brown hairy; blunt-tipped. Fruit an achene, grouped in rounded to cylindric heads; beak short, straight. Flowering early, soon after snowmelt.

Where Found alpine snowbeds, meadows, moist gullies.

Similar Species dark hairy sepals, the hairless receptacle, and lobed leaves help identify *Ranunculus nivalis*.

Ranunculus occidentalis Nutt.
WESTERN BUTTERCUP

Habit perennial herb, from a cluster of fibrous roots; stems 1 to several, erect or nearly so, 15–40 cm tall, more or less hollow; plants variously hairy. Leaves basal and along stem; basal leaves broadly ovate or semi-circular to kidney-shaped, deeply 3-lobed or 3-parted, the segments 1–2-times incised, petioles 1 to several times length of blade; stem leaves alternate, more deeply dissected, shorter-stalked; upper bracts entire. Flowers few to many, in terminal cymes; petals usually 5, oblong to narrowly ovate, yellow; sepals 5, bent back 2–3 mm from base, early deciduous, greenish or pinkish tinged, stiffly hairy; stamens 30–60; pistils 5–20. Fruit an achene, several to many in a hemispheric head; beak persistent, straight or curved.

Where Found moist alpine meadows and heathlands.

Ranunculus pensylvanicus L. f.
BRISTLY BUTTERCUP,
PENNSYLVANIA BUTTERCUP

Habit annual or short-lived perennial herb, from a cluster of fibrous roots; stems single, erect, 30–60 cm tall, hollow; plants stiffly hairy. Leaves basal and along stem; basal leaves persistent, heart-shaped, 3-parted, the leaflets usually deeply cleft, the ultimate segments coarsely sharp-toothed; petioles to 15 cm long; stem leaves alternate, 3 to 8, transitional to upper 3–5-lobed and toothed bracts. Flowers few in terminal cymes; receptacle stiffly hairy; petals 5, yellow, broadly ovate; sepals 5, bent back about 1 mm above base, deciduous, more or less stiffly hairy; stamens 15–25; pistils 50–80. Fruit an elliptic to ovate achene, grouped into a cylindric head; beak persistent, broadly lanceolate, straight or nearly so, to 1 mm long.

Where Found wet meadows; open places,

sometimes where disturbed.

◆ *Ranunculus pygmaeus* Wahlenb.
PYGMY BUTTERCUP

Habit perennial herb, from fibrous roots; stems slender, erect or ascending, to 15 cm tall, not hollow. **Leaves** basal and along stem; basal leaves persistent, kidney-shaped to semicircular, deeply 3-lobed, the lateral segments lobed, petioles very slender, to 4 cm long; stem leaves few, with shorter petioles; bracts usually of 3 linear to narrowly lanceolate lobes, 5–10 mm long. **Flowers** usually solitary (sometimes 2); petals 5, distinct, yellow, ovate; sepals 5, early deciduous, spreading, greenish; stamens 10–20; pistils 25–50. **Fruit** an ovate achene, several to many in a globe-shaped to cylindric head; beak persistent, slender, awl-shaped, straight or slightly hooked at tip.

Where Found alpine tundra, often near snowbeds.

◆ *Ranunculus reptans* L. CREEPING SPEARWORT
Ranunculus flammula L.

Habit amphibious perennial herb, usually with stolons and rooting from nodes, roots fibrous; stems decumbent to prostrate, creeping, to 50 cm long, simple to few branched near base, smooth or sparsely stiff short-hairy, somewhat hollow. **Leaves** alternate (in clusters at stem nodes), simple, linear, lanceolate, or thread-like, the blade scarcely distinguishable from the petiole; margins usually entire. **Flowers** solitary or several, on stalks to 10 cm long; petals 5 or 6, ovate, pale yellow; sepals 5, spreading or weakly bent back; stamens 10–50; pistils 5–50. **Fruit** an ovate achene, several to many in a globe-shaped head; beak persistent, straight or curved.

Where Found shallow water of ponds; wet shores, wet meadows.

Ranunculus sceleratus L.
CELERY-LEAF BUTTERCUP, CURSED BUTTERCUP

Habit amphibious annual or short-lived perennial herb, from slender, fleshy roots; stems 1 to several, erect, 15–50 cm tall, usually branched, smooth, hollow and somewhat fleshy. **Leaves** basal and along stem; kidney-shaped to semi-circular, deeply 3-lobed or 3-parted, the segments again lobed or parted, sometimes undivided, margins lobed or with rounded teeth, petioles 2–4-times length of blade; stem leaves alternate, more deeply lobed and divided than basal leaves. **Flowers** few to many, in terminal cymes, flower stalks stout, 1–3 cm long; petals 3–5, ovate, yellow; sepals 3–5, yellowish, bent back from near base, early deciduous; stamens 15–20. **Fruit** an ovate, slightly flattened achene, many in an elliptic to cylindric head; beak short, stout, triangular, usually straight.

Where Found shallow water of ponds, mud flats, streambanks.

◆ *Ranunculus sulphureus* Sol.
SULPHUR BUTTERCUP

Habit tufted perennial herb, with slender fibrous roots; stems stout, erect, 5–25 cm tall, sparsely-hairy with brown hairs or smooth; stems thick, with a few alternate leaves, red-greenish, hairy, with a single-flower. **Leaves** basal and along stem; basal leaves several, thick, waxy, kidney-shaped to rounded, evenly lobed; stem leaves more deeply divided, sessile. **Flowers** with five shiny yellow petals; sepals densely reddish brown hairy, much shorter than the petals. **Fruit** an achene, many in an ovoid head; beak short, straight

Ranunculus pygmaeus PYGMY BUTTERCUP

Ranunculus reptans CREEPING SPEARWORT

or curved. Flowering early, soon after snowmelt.

Where Found uncommon in snowbeds, meadows, and moist gullies in the mountains.

Similar Species the shallowly lobed leaves and red-hairy receptacles are distinctive.

◆ *Ranunculus trichophyllus* Chaix
WHITE WATER-CROWFOOT
Ranunculus aquatilis var. *capillaceus* (Thuill.) DC.

Habit aquatic perennial herb, rooting from nodes of lower stems; stems weak, few-branched, creeping or floating, 20–80 cm long, often mat-forming, smooth. Leaves alternate, of two types: floating and submerged (or leaves all submerged); floating leaves usually kidney-shaped, 3-parted, margins often notched; submerged leaves 3- to 5-times 3-dissected, segments thread-like. Flowers solitary, white; petals about 5 mm long. Fruit an ovate, flattened achene, 10 to

Ranunculus sulphureus SULPHUR BUTTERCUP

Ranunculus trichophyllus
WHITE WATER-CROWFOOT

20 in an ovate to globe-shaped head; beak persistent, thread-like, to 1 mm long.

Where Found shallow water of ponds and streams.

Thalictrum MEADOW-RUE
(Ancient Greek name for some plant mentioned by Dioscorides.)

1 Low-growing alpine plant; stems naked . . . . . .
. . . . *T. alpinum*
1 Taller plant of lower elevations; stems leafy . . .
. . . . *T. sparsiflorum*

◆ *Thalictrum alpinum* L. ALPINE MEADOW-RUE
Habit small perennial herb, with distinctive dark green divided leaves and subtle purple flowers, from slender rhizomes; stems single, erect or nearly so, to 20 cm tall (usually shorter); plants smooth, with a whitish bloom. Leaves small, all basal, and divided into three sets of trifoliate segments, held only a few centimeters off the ground; leaflets 2–10 mm long, with a shiny, waxy cast and visible veins. Flowers few, in a terminal raceme on long leafless stems, the heads nodding downwards; petals ovate, white or purplish, 1–3 mm long; stamens two or three times longer than petals, with purple filaments and yellow anthers; petals quickly shed. Fruit 2–4 achenes; achene broader at tip than base, with a curved persistent style at tip. Flowering early summer; petals quickly shed from the flowers.

Where Found common in alpine meadows and tundra.

Similar Species recognizable by its highly reduced flowers; and small, waxy, dark green, trifoliate leaflets.

Thalictrum alpinum ALPINE MEADOW-RUE

♦*Thalictrum sparsiflorum* Turcz. ex Fisch. & C.A.Mey. FEW-FLOWER MEADOW-RUE

Habit tall perennial herb, with divided leaves and inconspicuous white flowers, from a rhizome; stems erect, slender, 20–50 cm tall, simple or branched above, smooth. Leaves once or twice divided into rounded leaflets 10–20 mm long; upper surface with a conspicuous network of veins, margins shallowly notched. Flowers few from upper leaf axils; petals white, reflexed; stamens many, long, white; at flower center is a cluster of ovaries with short, beak-like styles. Fruit a cluster of achenes, splitting along one seam to release their seeds. Flowering early summer.

Where Found common in moist boreal meadows and forests.

Similar Species Unlike the more common *Thalictrum alpinum*, the leaves are on stems and do not have the same glossy appearance; also, these two species have very different habitats.

Traditional Uses the Alutiiq traditionally made tea from of the leaves to treat pneumonia, and from the roots for tuberculosis (Wennekens 1985 in Garibaldi 1999).

ROSACEAE
Rose Family

1 Ovary inferior; fruit a pome 2
1 Ovary superior; fruit an achene, follicle, drupe, or many fused drupelets 3

ALEXEY YAKOVLEV

Thalictrum sparsiflorum
FEW-FLOWER MEADOW-RUE

2 Leaves pinnately compound . . . . *Sorbus*
2 Leaves simple . . . . *Amelanchier*
3 Fruit fleshy; a drupe or cluster of fused drupelets . . . . *Rubus*
3 Fruit dry; an achene or follicle (achenes on a fleshy receptacle in *Fragaria*) 4
4 Leaves simple, at most lobed or divided 5
4 Leaves compound 7
5 Plants an erect shrub . . . . *Spiraea*
5 Plants herbs or prostrate shrubs 6
6 Flowers solitary; achenes feathery-hairy . *Dryas*
6 Flowers in cymes or racemes; achenes not feathery-hairy . . . . *Luetkea*
7 Leaves compound with 3 leaflets 8
7 Leaves pinnately or palmately compound; leaflets more than 3 9
8 Corolla conspicuous; petals usually greater than 5 mm long, longer than calyx-lobes; stamens often more than 10 . . . . *Potentilla*
8 Corolla inconspicuous; petals less than 5 mm long, equal to or shorter than calyx lobes; stamens 5 . . . . *Sibbaldia*
9 Achenes enclosed in hypanthium at maturity 10
9 Achenes not enclosed in hypanthium at maturity 11
10 Shrubs; stems prickly or bristly; petals showy; hypanthium fleshy at maturity . . . . *Rosa*
10 Herbs, stems not prickly or bristly; petals absent; hypanthium not fleshy at maturity *Sanguisorba*
11 Styles persistent, elongating after blooming, feathery-hairy or jointed . . . . *Geum*
11 Styles usually deciduous, not elongating after blooming 12
12 Petals reddish-purple . . . . *Comarum*
12 Petals yellow to whitish 13
13 Shrubs; achenes hairy . . . . *Dasiphora*
13 Herbs; achenes smooth . . . . *Potentilla*

Amelanchier SERVICEBERRY
(The Savoy name of the medlar shrub.)

Amelanchier alnifolia (Nutt.) Nutt. ex M. Roem. SASKATOON SERVICEBERRY

Habit shrub, 1–2 m tall; stems and twigs smooth, reddish brown; sometimes spreading by rhizomes or stolons and forming small colonies. Leaves deciduous, alternate, oval to nearly round, glabrous above, woolly hairy below when young, margins saw-toothed on top half. Flowers 3–20, on slender stalks, in drooping to erect, leafy or bracted, terminal racemes at ends of branches; corolla, petals 5, white, linear to lanceolate; calyx 5-lobed, the lobes lance-triangular, often densely woolly; stamens about 20. Fruit a berry-like pome (like a miniature apple), crowned with the persistent calyx, round to ovate, dull red when young, becoming purple to nearly black, with a white bloom.

Where Found may occur in Denali in open woods, dry slopes, and thickets.

Comarum MARSHLOCKS

(Greek *komaros,* strawberry-tree, alluding to similarity of fruit.)

♦ *Comarum palustre* L.
MARSH CINQUEFOIL, PURPLE MARSHLOCKS
Potentilla palustris (L.) Scop.

Habit perennial herb of wet places, with deep-red flowers, from a long-creeping (sometimes floating), somewhat woody rhizome; stems prostrate to ascending, 30–60 cm long, smooth and often reddish below, becoming hairy and glandular above. Leaves basal and alternate on the stem; palmately divided into five segments (upper stem leaves with 3 segments), with long petioles; dark green above and paler below, with stipules at base that sheath stem, margins serrate in upper half. Flowers few, terminal; petals 5, sepals 5, both tinged red-purple; sepals large (appearing to be the petals), glandular hairy on their back; petals much smaller; carpels numerous, with straight red styles, forming a thimble-shaped structure at flower center; stamens about 20, with red filaments and black-purplish anthers. Fruit a cluster of many fleshy achenes, similar to a raspberry.

Where Found common from low-elevations to the subalpine zone, sometimes emergent in standing water.

Similar Species Denali's only wetland species with deep red flowers and palmately divided leaves.

Traditional Uses In Chevak and on Nelson Island, leaves formerly made into a tea (Jernigan et al. 2015).

Dasiphora SHRUBBY CINQUEFOIL

(Greek, alluding to referring to hairy achenes.)

♦ *Dasiphora fruticosa* (L.) Rydb.
SHRUBBY CINQUEFOIL, TUNDRA-ROSE
Potentilla fruticosa L.

Habit low to medium shrub, 0.3–1 m tall (smaller at high-elevations); stems spreading to erect, freely branched; young branches silky-hairy but becoming smooth; older branches with brown, shredding bark. Leaves

Comarum palustre MARSH CINQUEFOIL

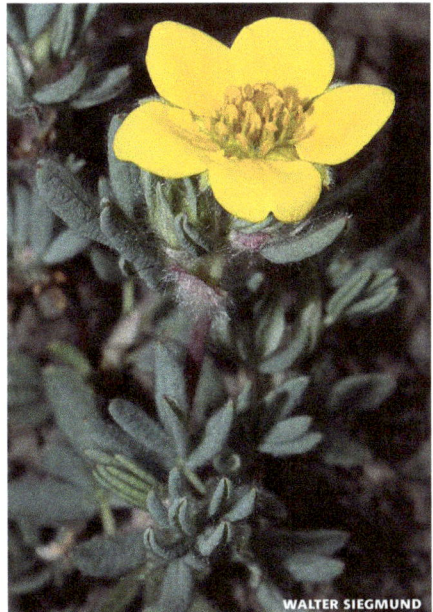

Dasiphora fruticosa SHRUBBY CINQUEFOIL

small, short-petioled or sessile, five-foliate (sometimes with 3 or 7 leaflets); leaflets narrowly elliptic, about 1 cm long, gray-green above and silvery below, both sides sparsely silky-hairy, margins entire. Flowers 2–3 cm wide, solitary, from leaf axils, or few in a cyme, petals 5, yellow; sepals broadly triangular; stamens yellow; pistils numerous. Fruit a white-hairy achene, with a single seed.

Where Found abundant from low- to high-elevations (most common at mid-elevations), on rocky slopes, dry tundra, riverbanks, lake meadows and snowbed tundra.

Similar Species Denali's only yellow-flowered shrub.

Traditional Uses stems or entire plant were used by the Alutiiq to brew a tea for colds, sore throats, respiratory and gastrointestinal illnesses, including tuberculosis and pneumonia; the Dena'ina also made a tea of the stems and leaves (Garibaldi 1999).

Dryas MOUNTAIN-AVENS
(Latin name of a Greek wood nymph.)

1   Petals yellow; filaments hairy; flowers nodding in anthesis . . . . *D. drummondii*
1   Petals white; filaments glabrous; flowers erect in anthesis 2
2   Midvein on leaf underside with gland-tipped hairs bearing tufts of white or brown hairs. . . . . *D. octopetala*
2   Midvein on leaf underside with naked gland-tipped hairs or hairs absent 3
3   Midvein on leaf underside with gland-tipped hairs . . . . *D. alaskensis*
3   Midvein on leaf underside often hidden under tomentum and without stalked gland-tipped hairs 4
4   Leaf margins inrolled, base of leaf cordate or truncate . . . . *D. integrifolia*
4   Leaf margins flat, not inrolled; base of leaf rounded . . . . . . *D. integrifolia* subsp. *sylvatica*

Dryas alaskensis Porsild
ALASKA MOUNTAIN-AVENS
Dryas octopetala subsp. *alaskensis* (Porsild) Hultén

Habit dwarf shrub, forming dense, low mats underlain by persistent dead leaves, with single white to cream flowers atop a leafless, white-hairy stem. Leaves semi-evergreen (lasting several seasons), oblong to lanceolate, quite leathery, dark green above, green-gray and short hairy below; midvein on underside with gland-tipped hairs (rarely

hairless), a distinguishing character of the species. Flowers 2–3 cm wide; petals 8, white; sepals 8–10, with both white and glandular hairs; stamens many, yellow; pistils greenish. Fruit a group of unfused achenes, with long styles covered in feathery white hairs; styles twisted together when the fruits develop, opening into a dandelion-like head when mature. Flowering a snowbed species, flowering as soon as the snow melts.

Where Found common in alpine tundra, meadows and snowbed areas, also in open patches of subalpine shrub tundra.

Similar Species *Dryas* is easily distinguished from any other genus, but identifying species relies on minute hair and gland characters of the leaves; to distinguish this species from the more common *Dryas octopetala*, *D. alaskensis* leaves are longer and more oblong, and without the rusty-colored scales with tufts of white hair on the leaf midveins; however, hybrids between the two species occur, with intermediate leaf characters.

◆*Dryas drummondii* Richardson ex Hook.
YELLOW MOUNTAIN-AVENS

Habit dwarf densely matted shrub, with yellow flowers; stems trailing, freely branching and rooting, often forming large colonies; leaf bases and flowering stalks from the earlier season often persistent. Leaves semi-evergreen, leathery, elliptic, sometimes oblong or obovate, dark green above, densely white hairy (tomentose) below, margins inrolled,

Dryas drummondii YELLOW MOUNTAIN-AVENS

wavy-crenate; leaf base wedge-shaped as opposed to rounded or notched as in other Dryas. Flowers with 8–10 yellow petals; sepals densely glandular-hairy; stamens yellow, numerous, with hairy filaments; styles many, plumose; when in bloom, flowers appear half-closed and nodding. Fruit a group of unfused achenes, with long styles covered in feathery white hairs, the styles initially twisted together; when in fruit the heads face upwards.

Where Found common in gravelly floodplains, streambeds, and moraines, from lowlands (most often) to lower alpine zone; sites almost always nearly level.

Similar Species yellow mountain-avens (the only yellow-flowered *Dryas*) easy to recognize when in flower, but more difficult to identify when fruiting; it is almost always found in dense mats on early successional floodplains, whereas other *Dryas* species usually occur in tundra (or open forest), and the leaf base of yellow mountain-avens is a different shape.

♦ *Dryas integrifolia* Vahl
ENTIRE-LEAF MOUNTAIN-AVENS
Dryas octopetala subsp. *integrifolia* (Vahl) Hartz

Habit mat-forming or densely tufted dwarf shrub; stems trailing, freely branching and rooting; buds glandular and red-hairy. Leaves

Dryas integrifolia **ENTIRE-LEAF MOUNTAIN-AVENS**

semi-evergreen, lanceolate, 3 times longer than broad, the base truncate or rounded, upper surface dark green, lower surface white-hairy; underside midvein typically covered in hairs; margins entire or with a few teeth toward base, the edges inrolled. Flowers 1–3 cm wide, single atop a leafless, hairy stem; petals 8 (to 10), white, broadly ovate or elliptic, hairy; sepals narrowly triangular with woolly white hairs and many dark red glandular hairs; stamens and pistils numerous; styles initially twisted together before opening into a dandelion-like head. Fruit a single-seeded achene with attached feathery style.

Where Found common in well-drained alpine tundra and on gravelly slopes.

Similar Species separated from other Dryas by its lanceolate leaves with mostly smooth (toothless) margins.

Dryas integrifolia subsp. ***sylvatica*** (Hultén) Hultén **FOREST MOUNTAIN-AVENS**
Dryas sylvatica (Hultén) A.E. Porsild

Habit low-growing dwarf shrub; plants form low, dense mats, with persistent dead leaves attached to the woody stems. Leaves semi-evergreen, thick, dark green on top and white-hairy below, margins only slightly inrolled (unlike *D. integrifolia* subsp. *integrifolia* above); leaves of this subspecies particularly long, on long petioles, with rounded tips (in contrast to the more pointed tips of *D. integrifolia* subsp. *integrifolia*); leaves flat and smooth, in contrast to other subspecies of *D. integrifolia;* margins only narrowly revolute (if margins inrolled at all). Flowers on slender, leafless stalks; petals 8–10, white; sepals hairy; stamens and pistils many. Fruit in a head with many small achenes with long, feathery styles.

Where Found woods, meadows, and shrublands from low-elevations into the lower alpine, most common on river terraces north of Alaska Range crest.

Similar Species this is a subspecies of the circumpolar *D. integrifolia* complex.

♦ *Dryas octopetala* L.
WHITE MOUNTAIN-AVENS

Habit low-growing dwarf shrub; stems trailing, freely branching and rooting, forming dense mats with many persistent dead leaves on the branches. Leaves semi-evergreen, leathery, oblong-elliptic, upper surface dark green, lower surface white-hairy, margins inrolled, crenate to toothed; midvein on leaf underside has characteristic reddish scales with a tuft of long white hairs, distinctive to the species and known as 'octopetala scales' (these visible with a hand lens). Flowers on leafless, white-hairy stalks; petals white; sepals white-hairy and with black glandular hairs. Fruit a single-seeded achene with a long feathery style, the styles initially twisted together in early fall before opening into a dandelion-like head.

Where Found abundant, especially in alpine tundra, and in the northern part of Denali.

Similar Species the rusty brown scales on the midvein of the leaf distinguish this species from other mountain-avens, though hybrids are known to occur.

Note some authors consider *Dryas octopetala* to be restricted to Greenland and northern Eurasia (and absent from North America); Denali (and Alaskan) plants would then be split among *D. alaskensis* and *D. integrifolia*.

Geum AVENS
(The ancient Latin name.)

1   Terminal leaflet largest, shaped differently than other leaflets . . . . *G. macrophyllum*
1   Leaflets all more or less alike 2
2   Leaves and stems conspicuously long-hairy; flowers 4–5 cm in diameter . . . . *G. glaciale*

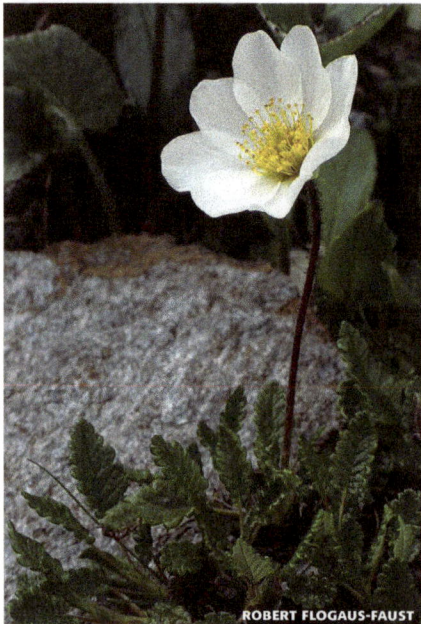

Dryas octopetala WHITE MOUNTAIN-AVENS

2   Leaves and stems glabrous or nearly so; flowers 2–3 cm in diameter . . . . *G. rossii*

♦ ***Geum glaciale*** Adams ex Fisch.
GLACIER AVENS

Habit densely tufted plant; from a stout, somewhat woody base. Leaves mainly basal, short-petioled, pinnate, with 5–7 pairs of entire or lobed leaflets; leaflets mostly 8–12 mm long (the terminal leaflet somewhat larger), tipped with long hairs, glabrous above, underside (and petiole and flowering stem) densely villous with soft, yellowish white hairs; stem leaves few, small. Flowers solitary, 3–4 cm wide; petals 5–8, light yellow, oval, 1.5–2 cm long. Fruit a hairy achene, with 2–3 cm long plumose styles.

Where Found uncommon on rocky alpine tundra, heath.

Geum macrophyllum Willd.
LARGE-LEAF AVENS

Habit tall perennial herb, from a short rhizome and stout stem-base; stems erect, 30–70 cm tall, simple, one to several, with coarse spreading hairs. Leaves basal and on stem; basal leaves lyrate-pinnate with serrate margins, the large apical lobe deeply cleft, lower opposite segments much smaller; stem leaves few, trifoliate. Flowers terminal in a small, branched head; petals five, ovate, yellow, widely spaced. Fruit in a round head with several achenes with hooked styles, each achene 7–10 mm long.

Where Found low-elevation meadows, lakeshores, riverbanks.

Similar Species distinguished from other *Geum* by the leaf shape (*G. rossii* and *G. glaciale* have evenly pinnate leaves), its tufted habit, and its presence at higher elevations.

***Geum glaciale* GLACIER AVENS**

♦ *Geum rossii* (R.Br.) Ser. ROSS' AVENS

Habit tufted perennial herb, from a thick scaly rhizome and stout stem-base covered with remains of old leaves; stems erect, 10–25 cm tall, simple, sparsely long-hairy. Leaves all basal, divided into many segments; each segment 2- or 3-lobed, glossy green on upper side, paler below; flowering stalks leafless except for a few bracts just below the flower; leaves hairless or sparsely hairy. Flowers one to several on each stem; petals five, yellow, about 1 cm long. Fruit a hairy achene, 5–7 mm long, gradually tapering to a straight style, each achene containing a single seed. Flowering shortly after snowmelt.

Where Found occasional in alpine wet places, meadows, snowbeds, and mossy ericaceous tundra.

Similar Species may be confused with *Geum glaciale,* which is quite rare in Denali and is much hairier with larger flowers; or with *G. macrophyllum,* which is a taller plant of lower elevations with large, lobed leaflets at tips of leaves.

Luetkea PARTRIDGEFOOT

(In honor of Count F. P. Luetke, commander of a Russian exploring expedition.)

♦ *Luetkea pectinata* (Pursh) Kuntze
PARTRIDGEFOOT

Habit prostrate, mat-forming, semi-shrub with a spike of white flowers, from a rhizome and branching stolons; flowering stem erect or nearly so, 5–15 cm tall, reddish, smooth or sparsely soft-hairy in grooves along stem; can form dense colonies. Leaves basal and along stem, evergreen; basal leaves in a rosette, wedge-shaped, palmately divided into many linear segments; stems leaves sim-

ilar but smaller. Flowers in a compact raceme that elongates in fruit; petals five, white, 3–5 mm long, alternating with five short triangular sepals; stamens about 20; pistils five. Fruit a follicle (a capsule splitting open at one seam), 4–5 mm long, each partition containing four linear seeds. Flowering immediately after snowmelt.

Where Found uncommon in moist areas of the subalpine, and in alpine tundra, snowbeds and meadows, particularly in maritime-influenced areas south of Alaska Range crest.

Similar Species distinctive and not likely to be confused with any other plant.

Potentilla CINQUEFOIL

(Latin, powerful, from medicinal properties of some species.)

1 Plants with long, slender, freely rooting stolons; flowers solitary . . . . *P. anserina*
1 Plants without stolons; flowers 1 or more. . . . 2
2 Basal leaves pinnate; leaflets 5 or more . . . . *P. pensylvanica*
2 Basal leaves 3-foliate or palmately compound; leaflets 5 or more 3
3 Plants annual or biennial herbs. . . *P. norvegica*
3 Plants perennial herbs 4
4 Basal leaves 5- or 7-parted . . . . *P. glaucophylla*

Geum rossii ROSS' AVENS

Luetkea pectinata PARTRIDGEFOOT

4 Basal leaves 3-parted. 5
5 Leaflets divided to base into linear lobes. . . . . .
. . . . *P. biflora*
5 Leaflets toothed. 6
6 Flowers 2–3 cm in diameter; leaflets leathery, dark gray-green above, tomentose and distinctly ribbed below . . . . *P. villosula*
6 Flowers smaller; leaflets not leathery, not distinctly ribbed below 7
7 Leaflets soft-hairy on underside . . *P. hyparctica*
7 Leaflets woolly-hairy on underside 8
8 Plants densely tufted or matted, with long, silky hairs; flowers solitary or rarely 2 or 3 . . . .
. . . . *P. subgorodkovii*
8 Plants loosely tufted; lower surface of leaves woolly-hairy; flowers several to many in terminal clusters . . . . *P. nivea*

Potentilla anserina L.
SILVERWEED

Habit perennial herb, with long, stolons or runners, rooting and producing tufted clusters of leaves at nodes, stolons spreading-silky. **Leaves** basal, 5–25 cm long, stalked, ascending; pinnately compound, with 7 to 21 main leaflets interspersed with smaller leaflets, whitish silky-woolly on both surfaces (upper surface sometimes greenish and sparsely hairy); margins coarsely saw-toothed. **Flowers** single, on long naked stalks from leafy stolon nodes; corolla yellow, petals 5, 6–12 mm long; calyx 5-lobed, silky-hairy. **Fruit** an achene, about 2 mm long.

Potentilla biflora **TWO-FLOWER CINQUEFOIL**

Where **Found** may occur in Denali (common in most of Alaska) on gravelly or sandy lakeshores and riverbanks.

♦ Potentilla biflora D.F.K. Schltdl.
TWO-FLOWER CINQUEFOIL

Habit dwarf cushion-forming perennial herb, from a branched stem-base covered with shiny brown remains of leaf-bases; stems densely tufted, ascending to erect, to 15 cm tall, leafless apart from two leaf-like stipules below the flower. **Leaves** trifoliate, each leaflet deeply divided into several linear segments, with a few long hairs; margins inrolled. **Flowers** on stems tipped with one or two flowers; petals five, yellow, 5–8 mm long (longer than the sepals); receptacle densely white-hairy; sepals five, narrowly triangular. **Fruit** a hairless achene.

Where **Found** uncommon in alpine tundra and rocky slopes.

Similar Species distinguished from other *Potentilla* by its three-parted leaves which are lobed into linear segments.

♦ Potentilla glaucophylla Lehm.
MOUNTAIN-MEADOW CINQUEFOIL
Potentilla × diversifolia Lehm.

Habit perennial herb, from a short stout rhizome and branched stem-base; stems usually several, tufted, spreading to erect, 10–40 cm tall, smooth toward base, appressed-hairy above. **Leaves** mostly basal, long-stalked, palmately or pinnately compound; leaflets 5 to 7, oblong-lanceolate to ovate, greenish or often glaucous blue-green on upper surface, generally appressed-hairy below; margins toothed mostly above the middle; stem leaves alternate, 1 or 2. **Flowers** stalked, few to several (less than 20), in an open terminal cluster; petals 5, yellow, shallowly notched at tip; calyx silky-long-hairy, 5-lobed, alternating with 5 shorter, narrowly

Potentilla glaucophylla
MOUNTAIN-MEADOW CINQUEFOIL

lanceolate bractlets; stamens 20. Fruit a brown achene.

Where Found uncommon in moist alpine meadows, heathlands.

◆ *Potentilla hyparctica* Malte
ARCTIC CINQUEFOIL

Habit small, loosely cushion-forming perennial herb, with relatively large (for its size) yellow flowers; plants 5–25 cm tall from a branched stem-base. Leaves trifoliate, appressed hairy; margins toothed. Flowers on stems with one to three flowers; petals five, yellow, shallowly notched at tip; sepals lanceolate, hairy, shorter than petals; stamens 15–25, yellow; pistils 20–45. Fruit a single-seeded achene.

Where Found occasional in alpine zone of Denali, in moist tundra and snowbeds, on both sides of Alaska Range crest.

Similar Species *Potentilla nivea* and *P. subgorodkovii* similar, but those species densely hairy on leaf underside, not soft-pubescent as in arctic cinquefoil.

◆ *Potentilla nivea* L. SNOW CINQUEFOIL
Potentilla hookeriana auct. non Lehm. p.p.

Habit annual to biennial herb, from a taproot; stems erect to ascending, 10–30 cm tall, often branched above, reddish, coarsely stiff-spreading-hairy with often pustular-based hairs. Leaves basal and along stem; basal leaves few, long-stalked, palmately compound; leaflets 3, ovate to oblong, coarsely hairy on both sides, margins coarsely round-toothed; stem leaves alternate, similar, several. Flowers several to many, in a compact, leafy-bracted, terminal cluster; petals 5, yellow or whitish yellow, broadly ovate, shorter than calyx-lobes; calyx hairy, 5-lobed, the lobes lanceolate, alternating with 5 narrower bractlets about same length as calyx-lobes; stamens usually 20. Fruit a brown, wrinkled achene.

Potentilla hyparctica ARCTIC CINQUEFOIL

Where Found alpine gravelly or rocky slopes and outcrops.

◆ *Potentilla norvegica* L.
NORWEGIAN CINQUEFOIL

Habit annual to biennial herb, with small yellow flowers, from a taproot; stems erect to ascending, 20–60 cm tall, sometimes branched above, leafy, coarsely stiff-spreading-hairy with often pustular-based hairs, often reddish. Leaves a few at base, more leaves alternate on stem; three-parted, the leaflets obovate and strongly toothed, long-hairy. Flowers several, in a terminal cyme; petals 5, yellow, widely spaced, flat or notched at tip; calyx lobes triangular and

Potentilla nivea SNOW CINQUEFOIL

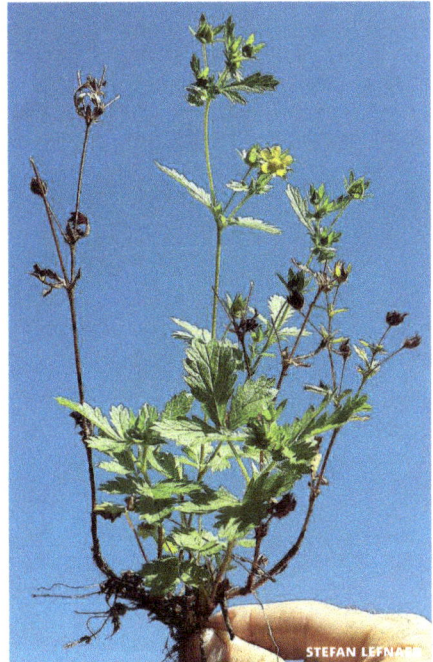

Potentilla norvegica NORWEGIAN CINQUEFOIL

longer than or equal to petals. Fruit a single-seeded achene.

Where Found occasional in moist to wet areas at low-elevations, often where disturbed.

Similar Species Unlike many other cinquefoils, most leaves on stem and not in a basal cluster.

♦ *Potentilla pensylvanica* L.
PENNSYLVANIA CINQUEFOIL
Potentilla litoralis Rydb., *Potentilla virgulata* A. Nelson

Habit perennial herb, with yellow flowers, from a simple or branched stem-base covered with brown remains of old leaves; stems slender, single to several, tufted, spreading to erect, 10–40 cm tall, simple or branched above, hairy and usually also thinly woolly. Leaves mostly basal, with several smaller stem leaves; pinnately divided into 5–9 strongly toothed segments; leaflets green above, white-hairy below. Flowers several, in a terminal cyme; petals 5, bright yellow, obovate, and not overlapping one another; sepals acute, hairy, about as long as petals; stamens and pistils many. Fruit a single-seeded achene with a long style, many produced per flower.

Where Found uncommon on warm, dry sites on slopes or river terraces.

Similar Species one of the few Denali cinquefoils with pinnately divided leaves.

Potentilla subgorodkovii Jurtzev
ONE-FLOWER CINQUEFOIL
Potentilla uniflora auct. non Ledeb. p.p.

Habit densely to loosely tufted perennial herb; stem-base covered with brown or blackened old leaves; stems erect-ascending, 5–15 cm tall, simple or branched. Leaves basal and along stem; basal leaves 3-parted, petioles long silky-pubescent; leaflets with 5–7 teeth, green and more or less pubescent above, white-tomentose and long silky-hairy below; stem leaves smaller. Flowers 1–2; petals 5, yellow; sepals silky hairy. Fruit a single-seeded achene.

Where Found alpine gravelly slopes, rock outcrops.

Potentilla villosula Jurtzev
VILLOUS CINQUEFOIL

Habit perennial herb, with branched stem-base thickly covered with dark brown stipules; stems 5–25 cm high, erect, with long spreading hairs. Leaves basal and along stem; 3-parted, terminal leaflet obovate, coarsely toothed at tip, entire and wedge-shaped at base; upper surface grayish green; lower surface with white woolly and strongly ribbed. Flowers one to several; petals 5, broadly obcordate, yellow; calyx lobes ovate-triangular; bractlets elliptic to ovate, about as long as calyx lobes. Fruit a single-seeded achene.

Where Found alpine tundra, rocky alpine slopes.

Rosa ROSE
(The Latin name.)

♦ *Rosa acicularis* Lindl. **PRICKLY ROSE**

Habit deciduous pink-flowered shrub, mostly 3–12 dm tall, spreading by extensive rhizomes and sometimes forming thickets; stems erect to arching, usually covered with straight, bristly prickles of various sizes; mature stems reddish to grayish brown. Leaves pinnately divided into 5 or 7 leaflets; each leaflet elliptic, slightly hairy on underside,

ALFRED COOK

Potentilla pensylvanica
PENNSYLVANIA CINQUEFOIL

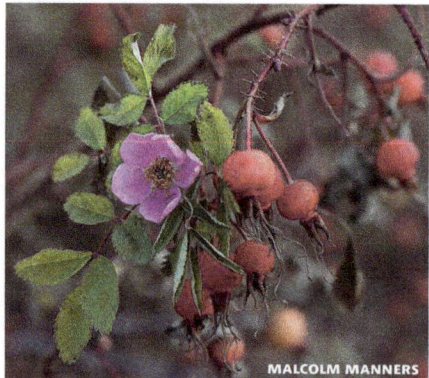

MALCOLM MANNERS

Rosa acicularis **PRICKLY ROSE**

margins serrate. Flowers with five, deep pink petals; and five narrowly triangular, green, hairy sepals. Fruit a dark red rosehip, below the persistent sepals.

Where Found abundant in forest understory, from low-elevations to the subalpine.

Similar Species the only species of rose known in Denali.

Traditional Uses The Dena'ina prepared a tea from the bark and used in treating colds, flu, fever, eye problems, stomach troubles, and menstrual problems (Garibaldi 1999). Stems and leaves are eaten by hares and other wildlife, the fruits eaten by birds and small mammals.

Rubus BLACKBERRY, RASPBERRY
(Latin, *ruber*, red.)

1	Plants with bristles or broad-based prickles . . . . *R. idaeus*
1	Plants unarmed, bristles absent 2
2	Stems erect, woody; petals pink to red . . . . *R. spectabilis*
2	Stems trailing, not woody 3
3	Plants dioecious (male and female flowers on separate plants); leaves round or kidney-shaped, shallowly lobed. . . . . *R. chamaemorus*
3	Plants with perfect flowers; leaves mostly compound 4
4	Leaves 3-parted; petals pink to reddish, 8–18 mm long; plants without stolons . . . . *R. arcticus*
4	Leaves mostly 5-parted; petals white, mostly less than 8 mm long; plants with stolons *R. pedatus*

◆ *Rubus arcticus* L. NAGOONBERRY
Habit perennial herb (rarely somewhat woody at base), with pink flowers that develop into a red berry, from a slender rhizome; annual flowering shoots erect, 5–15 cm tall, leafy, unarmed, finely soft-hairy.

Rubus arcticus NAGOONBERRY

Leaves alternate, 3-parted (occasionally just lobed), light green and more or less hairy on both sides, usually especially hairy on underside veins, margins toothed. Flowers 1–3 above the leaves; petals five, deep to light pink; sepals narrow, hairy; stamens numerous with pink filaments, initially curved inward toward styles. Fruit raspberry-like, red, about 1 cm wide. Flowering mid-summer; leaves turning dark red in fall.

Where Found abundant in moist shrub thickets, floodplains, and poplar forests, at low- to high-elevations (most common in alpine zone).

Similar Species distinguished from Denali's other small *Rubus*, cloudberry (*Rubus chamaemorus*), by leaf shape and flower color: cloudberry has five-parted leaves and white flowers, nagoonberry has 3-parted leaves and pink flowers.

Traditional Uses berries tasty and commonly picked and eaten.

◆ *Rubus chamaemorus* L. CLOUDBERRY
Habit perennial dioecious herb, with white flowers and large pink-yellow berries, from a

Rubus arcticus NAGOONBERRY

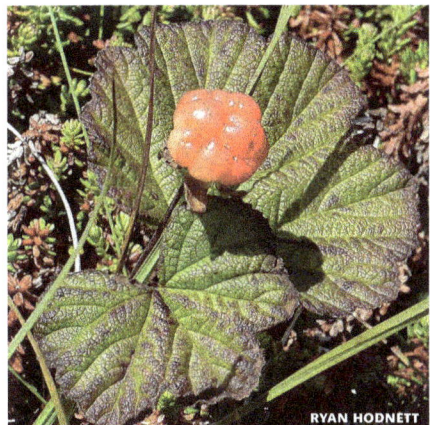

Rubus chamaemorus CLOUDBERRY

slender creeping rhizome; stems erect, 5–30 cm tall, unbranched, unarmed, hairy and often glandular (or sometimes nearly smooth), the lowest nodes with stipules only. Leaves alternate, 1–3 along stem, slightly leathery, dark green and net-veined, with five shallow lobes, margins toothed. Flowers single at end of stem; pedicels white-hairy; both male and female flowers with five white petals and five green, hairy, triangular sepals; petals slightly fringed at tip; flowers with either many stamens or many pistils; male flowers slightly larger than female. Fruit a raspberry-like fruit, typically orange or salmon-colored, sometimes red.

Where Found abundant in black spruce muskegs, bogs, and tussock tundra from the lowlands to the subalpine zone of Denali.

Similar Species similar to Denali's other small, berry-producing *Rubus* in the park, nagoonberry (*R. arcticus*); that plant has three-parted leaves (not five-parted), pink flowers (not white) and red fruit (never salmon-colored).

Traditional Uses The sweet, juicy, aromatic berries are some of the most flavorful wild fruits in Alaska; however, in central Alaska, cloudberry usually not abundant enough to be gathered in large quantities. Cloudberry fruit has been used by the Yup'ik for treating diarrhea and hives.

Rubus idaeus L. AMERICAN RASPBERRY

Habit medium shrub, 0.5–1 m tall, with white flowers and red berries, perennial with biennial stems (canes); stems erect to ascending, almost unarmed to prickly and bristly, often glandular-hairy; bark shredding. Leaves alternate, pinnately divided into three to five segments; terminal leaflet often three-lobed; leaflets toothed, with incised veins. Flowers at top of a leaning cane, in a branched raceme; petals 5, white; sepals 5;

stamens and pistils numerous. Fruit a red raspberry, 0.5–1 cm across.

Where Found found in meadows and forest openings, often establishing after fire; once established, can form thickets of many canes.

Similar Species easily recognized by the unbranched, prickly stems and raspberries in fall.

Traditional Uses berries picked and eaten or turned into jam.

♦ *Rubus pedatus* Sm.
CREEPING RASPBERRY, STRAWBERRY-LEAF RASPBERRY

Habit perennial herb, with white flowers, from slender, long-creeping (to 1 m) stolons or runners, rooting at nodes, with short (10 cm or less), erect flowering shoots with 1 to 4 leaves; unarmed, finely hairy to nearly smooth. Leaves alternate, deciduous (some persisting through winter), long-stalked, palmately compound; leaflets usually 5, sometimes 3, lateral leaflets divided nearly to base, 1–3 cm long, margins coarsely toothed or cleft, smooth except for hairy veins beneath. Flowers single, long-stalked, on erect leafy shoots; petals 5, white, spreading or bent back; calyx smooth or sparsely hairy, 5-lobed; stamens numerous. Fruit a drupelet, 1 to 6 more or less joined in a small red raspberry-like cluster about 1 cm wide, remaining attached to the receptacle.

Where Found uncommon in moist woods, heath.

♦ *Rubus spectabilis* Pursh SALMONBERRY

Habit medium to tall shrub, 1–2 m tall, with reddish flowers, from extensive rhizomes, often thicket-forming; stems erect to arching, unarmed to strongly bristly, especially below, the bristles short and straight; bark yellowish brown, shredding. Leaves alternate, deciduous; divided into 3 shallowly lobed leaflets, sharply long-pointed at tip, greenish on both surfaces, smooth to sparsely hairy above, underside paler and hairy on veins; margins double saw-toothed; stipules linear, 5–10 mm long. Flowers 1 or 2, stalked, nodding, on short, leafy, lateral branches; petals 5, pink to red; calyx 5-lobed, hairy; stamens 75 to 100. Fruit a drupelet, more or less joined in a yellow or salmon to dark red cluster that separates from the receptacle (raspberry-like), the berries 1.5–2 cm long.

Where Found uncommon in woods and thickets.

ALPSDAKE

Rubus pedatus CREEPING RASPBERRY

Traditional Uses the fruit has a poor flavor when fresh but can be made into a fine jelly.

Sanguisorba BURNET

(Latin, blood and absorb, apparently alluding to traditional uses to stop external or internal bleeding, suggested by dark red flowers of some species and medieval doctrine of signatures.)

1 Spikes oblong 1–1.5 cm long, flowers purple; stamens not or barely exserted ..... *S. officinalis*
1 Spikes cylindrical, 3–10 cm long; stamens exserted, longer than the sepals, ... 2
2 Flowers purplish .... *S. menziesii*
2 Flowers greenish or whitish .... *S. canadensis*

♦ *Sanguisorba canadensis* L.
CANADIAN BURNET

Habit perennial herb, with narrow spikes of white flowers; stems 20–80 cm tall from a thick stem-base. Leaves basal and along stem; basal leaves 10–50 cm long, with 9–15 pinnate leaflets; leaflets oblong-ovate, with rounded tip and notched base, long-petioled, margins toothed; stem leaves much reduced, sessile, with few leaflets. Flowers in a terminal cylindric spike 3–10 cm long, high above the basal leaves, flowering from the base up; petals absent; sepals four, greenish white; stamens many, giving the flowering head a bottle-brush appearance. Fruit an achene. Flowering mid-summer; leaves turning purple-red in the fall.

Where Found common in moist subalpine to alpine meadows and shrub thickets.

Similar Species the only species in Denali with pinnately compound, toothed leaves, and a bottle-brush spike of white flowers.

Sanguisorba menziesii Rydb.
SMALL-HEAD BURNET

Habit perennial herb, with reddish purple flowers, from a stout rhizome, smooth; stems erect to ascending, 20-80 cm tall, sometimes branched above. Leaves basal and along stem; basal leaves several, 15-40 cm long, pinnately compound, with stipules fused to base of long leaf-stalks and forming membranous margins; leaflets 9 to 15, coarsely saw-toothed; stem leaves alternate, 1 or 2, reduced, with leaflet-like stipules. Flowers in a dense, cylindric, long-stalked spike of numerous small flowers; petals absent; calyx reddish purple to pink, 4-lobed; stamens 4. Fruit an achene, enclosed in the 4-angled, winged hypanthium.

Where Found woods, meadows.

Note possibly of hybrid origin from *Sanguisorba canadensis* and *S. officinalis*.

Rubus spectabilis SALMONBERRY

Sanguisorba canadensis CANADIAN BURNET

♦ *Sanguisorba officinalis* L. GREAT BURNET

Habit perennial herb, with dark red-purple flowers, from a thick short rhizome; stems erect, 20 to 90 cm tall, smooth, usually glaucous, often branched above. Leaves basal and along stem; basal leaves 15–30 cm long, pinnately divided into 7–15 leaflets; leaflets stalked, margins serrate, petioles long; stem leaves 1–2, small. Flowers in a dense, rounded cylinder of flowers, long-stalked above the leaves; each flower with four maroon sepals, and no petals; stamens four, not much extended out from the flowers, filaments red. Fruit a single-seeded achene. Flowering midsummer; leaves turn purple red in fall before being shed.

Where Found at mid-elevations on wet to moist gravelly riverbanks, marshes, and lakeshores.

Similar Species differentiated from the more common *Sanguisorba canadensis* by its red flowering heads, and its wetland habitat.

Sibbaldia SIBBALDIA

(In honor of Robert Sibbald, 1642–1722, a Scotch professor of medicine.)

**♦ *Sibbaldia procumbens* L.
CREEPING SIBBALDIA**

Habit dwarf perennial herb, with yellow flowers, from a rhizome and branched woody stem-base; stems spreading to prostrate, tufted or mat-forming, 2–15 cm long, with stiff, appressed hairs. Leaves 3-parted, each leaflet wedge-shaped with three teeth at the wide tip; lower surface hairy (as are stem and calyx). Flowers in a dense few-flowered cyme; petals five, yellow, much narrower and shorter than sepals; sepals prominent, with five triangular lobes; stamens five; pistils several. Fruit a small achene.

Where Found occasional in moist alpine areas such as snowbeds and meadows, most commonly south of Alaska Range crest.

Similar Species the 3-parted leaves with wedge-shaped, three-toothed leaflets are diagnostic.

Sorbus MOUNTAIN-ASH

(The ancient Latin name for the pear or service-tree.)

**♦ *Sorbus scopulina* Greene
CASCADE MOUNTAIN-ASH**

Habit shrub or small tree, 1–4 m tall; stems several, erect to spreading, freely branched, reddish brown to yellowish; winter buds and young growth sticky, somewhat white- or gray-hairy. Leaves alternate, deciduous, pinnately compound; leaflets 9 to 13, 2–8 cm long, usually short-tapering to a sharp tip, smooth, finely saw-toothed almost to base. Flowers numerous (70 to 200 or more), in a flat-topped to somewhat rounded, branched cluster, the branches more or less white-hairy; petals 5, white to cream, 4–6 mm long; calyx 5-lobed, white-hairy; stamens 15–20. Fruit a berry-like pome (like a miniature apple), nearly globe-shaped, 7–10 mm long, orange to scarlet, not glaucous, 2- to 5-chambered; seeds 1 or 2 per chamber.

Where Found woods, thickets, moist alpine slopes.

Sanguisorba officinalis GREAT BURNET

Sibbaldia procumbens CREEPING SIBBALDIA

Spiraea SPIREA, MEADOWSWEET

(Greek, to twist, referring to the follicles of some species, or to flexible branches suitable for wreaths.)

◆ *Spiraea stevenii* (C.K.Schneid.) Rydb.
BEAUVERD SPIREA

Habit low shrub, with rounded heads of white flowers, 20–60 cm tall (sometimes taller), from long creeping rhizomes; stems erect to spreading, with thin, wiry, reddish brown branches, the young growth hairy. **Leaves** alternate, ovate to blunt-elliptic, margins toothed along upper half. **Flowers** in a rounded to flat-topped corymb (a branched cluster, the flowers all more or less at same height); petals 5, white (often pink in bud); sepals fused, with five triangular lobes, reddish or green; stamens many, long and slender, giving the inflorescence a fuzzy appearance. **Fruit** an aggregated follicle.

Where Found abundant in lowland forest and muskeg ranging into subalpine meadows and thickets.

Sorbus scopulina CASCADE MOUNTAIN-ASH

Spiraea stevenii BEAUVERD SPIREA

Similar Species easily identified, as Denali's only shrub with ovate, crenate-margined leaves, and many small white flowers.

RUBIACEAE
Madder Family

Galium BEDSTRAW

(Greek, milk, from use of some species for curdling.)

1	Leaves in whorls of 6, broadly lanceolate, tipped with a small sharp awn; fruit with hooked bristles . . . . *G. triflorum*
1	Leaves in whorls of 4 or 6, blunt or acute at tip; fruit without hooked bristles 2
2	Flowers many, in showy axillary and terminal infloresences; plants stout, upright, tufted, from a slender rhizome. . . . . *G. boreale*
2	Flowers single or several, in small axillary or terminal inflorescences; plants weak and slender, often matted . . . . *G. trifidum*

◆ *Galium boreale* L. NORTHERN BEDSTRAW

Habit perennial herb, from a creeping rhizome; stems erect or ascending, simple or few-branched, short-hairy below the nodes, angled (square), 20–40 cm long. **Leaves** lanceolate-elliptic, sessile, in whorls of four,

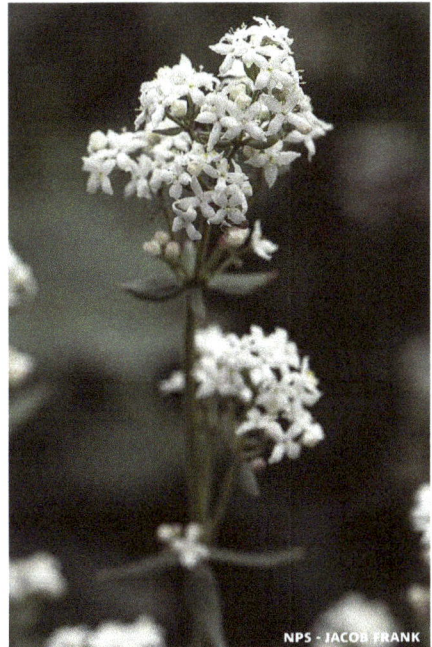

Galium boreale NORTHERN BEDSTRAW

with three prominent veins, margins entire. Flowers in a branched inflorescence, both terminal and from leaf axils; flowers small, with four white petals and four stamens. Fruit a pair of round, densely hairy achenes, fused at center.

Where Found common in open woods, forest edges, and meadows, particularly following fire; also in moist subalpine meadows.

Similar Species the only other plant in Denali with whorled leaves and many small white flowers is the related *Galium trifidum;* that plant is much smaller and its flowers have 3, not 4, petals.

Traditional Uses a poultice of this plant was traditionally used by some Athabaskans for aches and pains (Kari 1995).

♦ *Galium trifidum* L.
SMALL BEDSTRAW, THREE-PETAL BEDSTRAW
Galium brandegeei A. Gray

Habit small perennial herb, from a rhizome; stems simple to loosely branched, 10–50 cm long, sprawling and often forming tangled clumps. Leaves in whorls of four at each node, narrowly elliptic, with rounded tip; margins with backward-pointing bristly hairs. Flowers 1-3 from axils or in a terminal cyme; petals 3.

Galium trifidum SMALL BEDSTRAW

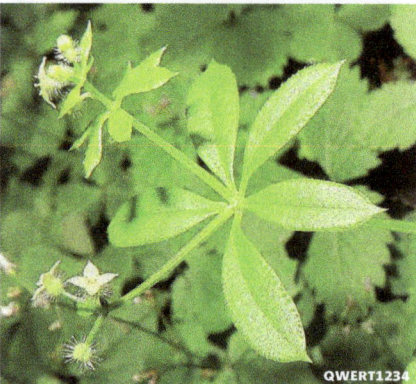
Galium triflorum FRAGRANT BEDSTRAW

Fruit a pair of smooth capsules, fused at center.

Where Found low- to mid-elevations in wetlands and moist woods.

Similar Species flowers with 3 petals and smooth fruit, distinguishing it from the more common *Galium boreale* with 4 petals and hairy fruit.

♦ *Galium triflorum* Michx.
FRAGRANT BEDSTRAW

Habit perennial herb, from a creeping rhizome; stems prostrate to ascending or climbing, 20-80 cm long. several, shining, branched, square in cross-section, short-hairy on the angles, the hooked hairs pointed downwards, Leaves in whorls of 6 (sometimes 4 or 5 on smaller branches), narrowly elliptic to oblanceolate, 1-veined, unstalked, short-hairy on margins and with hooked bristles on veins beneath, the hairs pointed forward; basal leaves few, soon deciduous. Flowers stalked, usually 3, in a loose axillary or terminal cluster; corolla whitish, 4-lobed. Fruit a pair of capsules, 2-2.5 mm long, with short, hooked bristles.

Where Found moist woods.

SALICACEAE
Willow Family

1 Mainly shrubs or small trees; catkins erect-ascending; each flower with 1–4 basal glands; winter buds covered by a single scale . . . . *Salix*
1 Trees; catkins soon drooping; each flower arising from a basal cup-shaped disc; winter buds covered by several scales . . . . *Populus*

Populus COTTONWOOD, POPLAR
(The ancient Latin name.)

1 Leaf blade nearly round, less than 5 cm long; petiole flattened . . . . *P. tremuloides*
1 Leaf blade longer than wide, 6–12 cm long; petiole round in section. 2
2 Leaf underside pale green and brownish; seed capsule pointed, hairless, 2-parted . . . . *P. balsamifera*
2 Leaf underside whitish; seed capsule rounded, hairy, 3-parted . . . . *P. trichocarpa*

◆*Populus balsamifera* L. BALSAM POPLAR

Habit dioecious, deciduous tree, to 20 m tall (in Denali, however, most trees much smaller); not colony-forming; bark gray, smooth when young, becoming deeply furrowed at base when older; branches brown the first year, turning gray later; twigs smooth or sparsely hairy; buds of leaves and flowers covered in a sticky, aromatic resin, the source of the name 'balsam'; winter buds 1–3 cm long, long-pointed, shiny red-brown, resinous. **Leaves** ovate, pointed at tip, shiny dark green above, pale green with rusty brown veins below, margins finely crenate. **Flowers** either male or female and borne on separate trees; male catkins (aments) with many staminate flowers, 20–30 red-purple stamens per flower; female catkins 5–9 cm long, with many small flowers, each having round disks beneath two fused carpels and broad stigmas. **Fruit** a green capsule opening along two seams (as opposed to three seams in black cottonwood); each seed attached to many long white hairs. **Flowering** in spring before the leaves; after pollen release, male catkins wither and drop from the tree; leaves develop after peak flowering; seeds released from capsules in mid-summer, seed-dispersal lasting about two weeks.

Where Found common on gravel bars, fire-disturbed sites, and open soil of steep slopes; quick to establish following disturbance.

Similar Species distinguished from quaking aspen by the much larger, lanceolate and glossy leaves, petioles round in cross-section, older trees with furrowed bark, and difference in habitat. Alaska birch can at first glance look similar, but the bark of balsam poplar is never papery, and the leaf margins not serrated.

Traditional Uses sometimes used as lumber or firewood; the resin was widely used by Alaska Natives as a balm; cottonwood buds have been collected in spring and used to make a tincture for an all-purpose healing salve, used on skin, and to treat toothaches, congestion, and sore throats (Garibaldi 199); cambium of young trees has also been used as a laxative.

Note Balsam poplar has the widest geographic distribution of any Alaskan tree (even found on floodplains of the Arctic slope).

Populus balsamifera subsp. ***trichocarpa***
(Torr. & Gray ex Hook.) Brayshaw
BLACK COTTONWOOD
Populus tristis Fisch., *Populus trichocarpa* Torr. & Gray ex Hook.

Habit dioecious, deciduous tree; bark smooth and greenish when young, becoming deeply furrowed and gray in age; branches pubescent. **Leaves** broadly ovate to ovate-lanceolate, cordate to rounded at base, 6–12 cm long, pale beneath, margins finely crenate-serrate. **Flowers** either male or female and borne on separate trees; in catkins 5–12 cm long, or in fruit up to 20 cm long. **Fruit** a 3-valved capsule.

Where Found occasional on river floodplains and shores.

◆*Populus tremuloides* Michx.
QUAKING ASPEN

Habit dioecious, deciduous tree, 6–12 m tall; forming colonies; bark smooth, yellow-green, with dark branch scars (bark with chlorophyll, allowing trees to begin photosynthesis prior to leaf growth); twigs green-

Populus balsamifera BALSAM POPLAR

Populus tremuloides QUAKING ASPEN

ish white, smooth; winter buds ca. 6 mm long, long-pointed, shiny red-brown. Growing clonally from roots, one genetic individual can eventually dominate an entire hillside. Leaves round-ovate, 3–5 cm long, with a short pointed tip, light green with white veins, turning yellow in the fall, lighter in color below than above; petiole flattened near base of leaf blade, causing leaves to 'quake' or 'tremble' in the wind; margins serrate. Flowers in catkins, male or female, and on separate trees; catkins covered in long gray hairs; male catkins with many staminate flowers, 6–12 red stamens per flower; female catkins with numerous small flowers, each having round disks beneath two fused carpels. Fruit a cone-shaped capsule, maturing from green to brown, and opening along two seams; each capsule releases 5–7 tiny seeds attached to long silky hair to aid their dispersal via wind. Flowering early May, prior to bud-burst; leaves begin opening between 5 and 16 days after flowering, in mid-May; leaf yellowing begins in mid- to late-August, leaf-fall occurs in late August to mid-September.

Where Found abundant on south-facing slopes, river terraces, and burned areas in the boreal zone; establishing early in the succession process.

Similar Species potentially confused with Alaska birch and balsam poplar; Alaska birch has white, papery bark, and serrate leaf margins; balsam poplar has larger, longer leaves that are glossy green and have a pungent smell; quaking aspen the only tree in Denali with flattened petioles.

Traditional Uses The wood is occasionally used for firewood or lumber, but is not as desirable as other trees; the Dena'ina used the inner bark to treat coughs and colds (Garibaldi 1999).

Salix WILLOW

As willow flowers and fruit are typically short-lived, the following key uses primarily vegetative features for identification of each species. (Latin name for willow.)

1 Low, prostrate shrubs less than 30 cm high .. 2
.... (Group I)
1 Erect shrubs or trees, more than 30 cm high. 11
.... (Group II)

GROUP I
Low shrubs less than 30 cm high.

2 Creeping shrubs with long prostrate branches 10–30 cm long, often rooting at nodes, but with branches ascending; leaves more than 2.5 cm long 3
2 Matted or creeping shrubs, usually less than 10 cm tall, usually in compact mats without long creeping branches; leaves entire, less than 2.5 cm long 8
3 Leaf margins toothed, green on both surfaces, or sometimes lighter green on underside 4
3 Leaves entire, or toothed only on lower half, green above, whitish (glaucous) on underside 5
4 Leaves bluish green, leathery or fleshy, 3–4 times longer than wide, tapering gradually to base .. .. *S. setchelliana*
4 Leaves not bluish green, oval, not tapering to base, thin................... *S. myrtillifolia*
5 Leaves dark green above, conspicuously net-veined, round, with long red petiole .... *S. reticulata*
5 Leaves not conspicuously net-veined, more than 2 times as long as broad, petiole green...... 6
6 Leaves fleshy, 3–4 times longer than wide, tapering to base, bluish green; in dry gravelly places .... *S. setchelliana*
6 Leaves not fleshy or bluish green, 2 times longer than wide, not tapering to base; in bogs or alpine tundra........................ 7
7 Trailing shrub with long branches rooting at nodes, leaves finely glandular toothed on lower half; usually in boggy places..... *S. fuscescens*
7 Leaves entire, forming dense mats from short branches; mostly in dry alpine sites .. *S. arctica*
8 Leaves green above, whitish (glaucous) on underside..................... *S. stolonifera*
8 Leaves green on both sides................ 9
9 Shrubs forming loose mats, usually with long trailing buried branches; stems pale yellow, thin; leaves to 2.5 cm long, usually smaller *S. polaris*
9 Shrubs densely matted, often from a central taproot; leaves less than 2 cm long; stems brown to reddish brown 10
10 Shrub mat with abundant dead leaves persistent; leaves 1–2 cm long.......... *S. phlebophylla*
10 Shrubs with few or no dead leaves persisting; leaves 4–10 mm long .... *S. rotundifolia*

GROUP II
Erect shrubs or trees, more than 30 cm high.

11 Upright shrubs usually less than 1 m high .. 12

11 Tall shrubs or trees 1–7 m or more in height. 19

12 Leaves with hairs on lower surface, gray or silvery 13

12 Leaves without conspicuous hairs 15

13 Leaves linear to lanceolate, 5–7 times longer than wide, densely woolly-hairy on underside; uncommon bog shrub . . . . *S. candida*

13 Leaves broader, not densely woolly on underside 14

14 Leaves with dense straight hairs, often oriented in vertical plane; petioles green, yellow, or brown; low compact shrub with thick branches; bud scales giving off yellow waxy substance when plant is dried . . . . *S. barrattiana*

14 Leaves with scattered hairs; petioles reddish; upright shrub with slender branches; buds not giving off waxy substance . . . . *S. niphoclada*

15 Leaves fleshy, bluish green, 3–4 times longer than wide, tapering gradually to base . . . . *S. setchelliana*

15 Leaves thin, green, oval 16

16 Stipules, if present, persisting less than one year 17

16 Stipules persistent for several years 18

17 Leaves toothed around margin, lower surface light green, not whitish (glaucous) . . . . *S. myrtillifolia*

17 Leaves toothed only on basal half with fine glandular teeth, lower surface whitish (glaucous) . . . . *S. fuscescens*

18 Stipules broad at base and glandular toothed along margins; twigs coarse, brown to black, with dense hairs persistent for several years . . . . *S. richardsonii*

18 Stipules linear, narrow at base, without glandular teeth; twigs fine, usually reddish brown and shiny, without dense hairs after one year . . . . *S. pulchra*

19 Leaves linear, 4–10 cm long, and 6 mm wide, with scattered small teeth; usually growing on river alluvium . . . . *S. interior*

19 Leaves broader 20

20 Mature leaves with hairs on lower surface . . 21

20 Mature leaves without hairs on lower surface 30

21 Lower surface of leaves with dense hairs, appearing silvery, white, or gray 22

21 Lower surface of leaves visible through less dense hairs 25

22 Lower surface of leaves with dense white woolly hairs 23

22 Lower surface of leaves with dense straight hairs 24

23 Leaves long and narrow, lance-shaped, 5–10 cm long and only 6–15 mm wide; low shrubs seldom exceeding 1.2 m in height; uncommon in bogs . . . . *S. candida*

23 Leaves broader, 5–10 cm long, and 12–40 mm wide; tall shrub or tree to 9 m . . . . *S. alaxensis*

24 Lower surface silky hairy, upper surface green, with scattered hairs; tall shrub or tree to 6 m high . . . . *S. sitchensis*

24 Lower surface dull gray hairy, upper surface greenish gray, without hairs; shrub usually less than 3 m high . . . . *S. glauca*

25 Margins of leaves distinctly toothed 26

25 Margins of leaves not toothed or with a few teeth on basal half 27

26 Leaves light green on both surfaces, not shiny, oval, about 2 times longer than wide; shrub 1–2 m high . . . . *S. commutata*

26 Leaves dark green and shiny above, whitish (glaucous) beneath, 3–4 times longer than wide; shrub 3–4.5 m tall, with slender branches . . . . *S. arbusculoides*

27 Hairs on lower surface short and stiff, at least some red, giving a reddish hue . *S. scouleriana*

27 Hairs denser, longer, not reddish 28

28 Tall shrubs or trees 3–7 m tall; twigs diverging at nearly right angles from the main stem . . . . *S. bebbiana*

28 Medium shrubs, usually under 3 m high; twigs usually branching at 45° angle or less 29

29 Petioles 3–10 mm long, yellow, leaves obovate to oblong, acute to obtuse . . . . *S. glauca*

29 Petioles less than 3 mm long, reddish, leaves strap-shaped, rounded or blunt . *S. niphoclada*

30 Stipules persistent on twigs several years . . . 31

30 Stipules not persisting more than one year . . 32

31 Stipules broad at base and glandular toothed along margin; twigs coarse, brown to black, densely hairy, even after several years . . . . *S. richardsonii*

31 Stipules linear, narrow at base, without glandular teeth; twigs, fine, usually reddish brown, shiny, without dense hairs at 1 year . *S. pulchra*

32 Leaves with teeth around margin 33

32 Leaves entire, or with teeth only on lower part 37

33 Leaves 3–4 times longer than wide; tall shrubs or trees 34

33 Leaves less than 3 times longer than wide .. 35

34 Leaves large, 7–10 cm long, lance-shaped, with long tapering tip; young twigs woolly . . . .
. . . . *S. lasiandra*

34 Leaves smaller, 5–8 cm long, not lance-shaped, short-pointed; young twigs not woolly . . . .
. . . . *S. arbusculoides*

35 Leaves whitish (glaucous) beneath 36

35 Leaves light green, not whitish beneath . . . . .
. . . . *S. pseudomyrsinites*

36 Leaves broadly lance-shaped to oval, usually narrowing to small projection at tip (apiculate), often reddish when young *S. pseudomonticola*

36 Leaves ovate, blunt at tip; not reddish when young . . . . *S. barclayi*

37 Tall shrubs or trees, 3–7 m tall . . . . *S. bebbiana*

37 Smaller shrubs, to 3 m tall (occasionally taller).
. . . . 38

38 Leaves strap-shaped, grayish; petioles reddish, stipules absent . . . . *S. niphoclada*

38 Leaves oval, green, petioles green or yellow, stipules usually present. 39

39 Upper leaf surface light green, not shiny. . . . . .
. . . . *S. hastata*

39 Upper leaf surface dark green, usually shiny. . .
. . . . *S. barclayi*

◆ *Salix alaxensis* (Andersson) Coville
FELTLEAF WILLOW, ALASKA WILLOW

Habit shrub or small tree, 1–4 m tall, not colonial; branches erect, sometimes gnarled and semi-prostrate, flexible at base; twigs brownish, velvety hairy. **Leaves** narrowly ovate to oblanceolate, 4–9 cm long; upper surface dark green, underside woolly hairy, margins entire, inrolled, petioles yellowish; stipules persistent, densely hairy. **Flowers** (female) in sessile catkins, appearing before the leaves; female catkins relatively large (6–15 cm); floral bracts long-hairy, acute, black tipped. **Fruit** a 2-valved hairy capsule. **Flowering** catkins generally appear mid-April to mid-May; leaves appear in early May.

Where Found abundant in Denali at low- to high-elevations on floodplains, gravel bars, scree slopes, ravines.

Similar Species recognizable by its large leaves dark green above, and covered with felt-like hairs below .

Traditional Uses *Salix alaxensis* has a wide variety of traditional uses as food, medicine, construction material, and firewood. Like all willows, the fresh bark of *S. alaxensis* contains salicin, a precursor to aspirin and has traditionally been used as a pain and fever reliever. The fresh inner bark has long been a food source for indigenous peoples throughout its range; young buds and shoots are said to be sweet and have a watermelon or cucumber taste. Willow suckers (long straight branches) have long been used to make baskets, crab pots, and furniture. Above the northern treeline, *S. alaxensis* is the largest (living) source of firewood. *S. alaxensis* has been used for streambank restoration as cuttings can be directly planted and will root.

◆ *Salix arbusculoides* Andersson
LITTLE-TREE WILLOW

Habit narrow-leafed tall shrub or tree, 1–6 m tall, not colonial; branches erect, flexible at base; twigs red-brown, shiny, smooth to sparsely hairy. **Leaves** long, narrow, 5–7 cm long; elliptic-lanceolate, glossy green, silky hairy underneath, margins finely glandular-serrate; stipules absent. **Flowers** (female) in loosely flowered catkins about 5 cm long. **Fruit** a gray-hairy capsule, 4–5 mm long. **Flowering** catkins and leaves develop together in mid-May; seeds released by mid-June.

Where Found common along streams and in moist forests at low-elevations.

Similar Species the smooth reddish twigs, lack of stipules, hairy catkins and narrow, serrated leaves with gland-tipped teeth help identify this willow.

Salix alaxensis FELTLEAF WILLOW

Note This is one of several species that can form 'diamond willow' when attacked by a canker.

Salix arbusculoides LITTLE-TREE WILLOW

♦ *Salix arctica* Pall. ARCTIC WILLOW

Habit creeping dwarf shrub, 3–15 cm tall, layering; branches decumbent, trailing or ascending, flexible at base, sometimes strongly glaucous; twigs yellow-brown to violet, hairless. **Leaves** ovate (but variable), 2.5–7 cm long; dark green above, pale below, with a silky 'beard' at leaf tip, margins entire; stipules absent. **Flowers** (female) in catkins 3–7 cm long, borne on leafy branchlets, appearing woolly due to long hairs on the brown bracts. **Fruit** a 2-valved short-hairy capsule. **Flowering** leaves and catkins develop together, generally appearing early to mid-June.

Where Found abundant in the alpine in dry tundra and rocky areas.

Similar Species distinguished from other common dwarf willows in the park by the pale underside of the leaf and the beard of hairs at the tip of the leaf.

Traditional Uses like all willows, the fresh bark of arctic willow contains salicin, a precursor to aspirin and has traditionally been used as pain and fever reliever. Leaves and young twigs are edible.

♦ *Salix barclayi* Andersson BARCLAY'S WILLOW

Habit thicket-forming, medium-sized shrub, 0.5–2 m tall; branches erect, flexible at base; twigs yellow-green, hairy. **Leaves** elliptic or obovate, 3–8 cm long; hairless, green above, glaucous below, margins finely glandular-serrate; stipules broad. **Flowers** (female) in catkins to 7 cm long, borne on leafy

RAGNHILD & NEIL CRAWFORD

Salix arctica ARCTIC WILLOW

branches; pistils hairless and green, often maturing to a reddish color. Fruit a glabrous capsule, 5–6 mm long. Flowering leaves and catkins develop together, generally appearing mid-May to mid-June.

Where Found occasional in the subalpine to alpine on glacial moraines, hillsides, lakeshores, fens, and along streams.

Similar Species some key characters are the long, leafy catkin peduncles and the long styles (1–2 mm).

Note This species can have 'willow rose' galls stimulated by insect parasites.

♦ *Salix barrattiana* Hook. BARRATT'S WILLOW

Habit thicket-forming shrub, with oily buds and stipules, 0.3–1.5 m tall; branches erect or decumbent, flexible at base; twigs red-brown to violet, coarsely and densely gray-hairy. Leaves oblanceolate, 3–9 cm long; densely appressed hairy above; gray silky below (plants appear gray from a distance), margins entire or minutely serrate; stipules leafy, oily, glandular-margined. Flowers (female) in upright catkins, 4–7 cm long; pistils densely gray-hairy. Fruit a 2-valved gray-silky capsule. Flowering catkins appear before leaves in late spring.

Where Found occasional at mid- to high-elevations on gravel floodplains, and subalpine and alpine meadows.

Similar Species oily stipules and buds and gray appearance of the leaves distinguish this willow.

♦ *Salix bebbiana* Hook. BEBB'S WILLOW

Habit much-branched shrub or tree, reaching 10 m in height (our largest willow species), not colonial; branches erect, flexible or somewhat brittle at base; twigs red-brown, woolly to almost hairless. Leaves elliptic to obovate, 2.5–6 cm long; upper side green with impressed veins, underside pale green, both surfaces with scattered, curled, long white hairs (or becoming smooth with age), margins entire to crenate; stipules shed early in the season. Flowers (female) in loose, long-stalked female catkins, 3–5 cm long, on leafy stalks; pistils elongate, green and hairy. Fruit a gray-hairy capsule. Flowering male and female catkins appear at the same time from mid-June to mid-July; seeds released in midsummer, and withered female catkins often persist over winter.

Salix barclayi BARCLAY'S WILLOW

Salix barrattiana BARRATT'S WILLOW

Where Found common in northern boreal regions of Denali, occurring in a range of habitats from floodplains to conifer forests to boggy areas.

Similar Species the loosely-flowered female catkins with very long peduncles are distinctive in this species and visually separate it from other willows; leaves with deeply impressed veins, pale undersides, and long curled white hairs are also diagnostic for *Salix bebbiana*. However, this species can hybridize with other local willows, sometimes making identification difficult.

⧫ *Salix candida* Flüggé ex Willd. SAGE WILLOW
Habit shrub, to 1 m tall, layering; branches erect, flexible at base; twigs yellow- to gray-brown, densely hairy. Leaves narrowly ovate to lanceolate, 3–8 cm long; upper surface dull or shiny, sparsely hairy or woolly; lower surface glaucous, densely white-woolly; margins entire, inrolled; stipules leaflike. Flowers (female) in catkins, 2–4 cm long, on short leafy stalks. Fruit a white-woolly capsule. Flowering catkins appear as leaves emerge (or just before the leaves).

Where Found uncommon in fens, pond margins.

⧫ *Salix commutata* Bebb UNDERGREEN WILLOW
Habit shrub, 0.2–3 m tall, not colonial; branches erect, flexible at base; twigs yellow-

ish to red-brown, sparsely to densely hairy. Leaves narrowly oblong to elliptic, 3–7 cm long; upper surface yellow-green, dull, smooth or long soft-hairy, lower surface smooth to long soft-hairy, margins entire to finely glandular-serrate; petioles without glandular dots at top; stipules leaflike. Flowers (female) in catkins, 3–6 cm long, on leafy stalks. Fruit a glabrous, reddish capsule. Flowering catkins appear as leaves emerge.

Where Found alpine meadows, glacial moraines, rocky slopes, gravelly river terraces.

Salix candida SAGE WILLOW

Salix bebbiana BEBB'S WILLOW

Salix commutata UNDERGREEN WILLOW

◆ *Salix fuscescens* Andersson
ALASKA BOG WILLOW
Habit dwarf to low shrub; branches creeping in moss, with many adventitious roots from the reddish brown, shiny, glabrous stems and branches. **Leaves** obovate to elliptic, to 2 cm long; glossy dark green above, paler and glaucous below, margins toothed at leaf base, usually inrolled; stipules absent. **Flowers** (female) in upright catkins, 3–5 cm long, on leafy stalks. **Fruit** a long-beaked, reddish brown capsule. **Flowering** typically flowers in early summer (mid-May), the catkins developing with the leaves; seeds disseminated mid-July.

Where Found uncommon in wet bogs and fens at low- to mid-elevations on both sides of Alaska Range crest.

Similar Species identified by its creeping habit, leaves toothed at base, and preference for very wet habitats.

◆ *Salix glauca* L. **GRAY-LEAF WILLOW**
Habit highly variable shrub, 0.3–5 m tall, with late-developing white-woolly catkins; erect or decumbent, not colonial; branches flexible at base; twigs reddish brown, sparsely to densely hairy. **Leaves** oblanceolate, 3–5 cm long; dull green above, glaucous and hairy below; petioles yellowish, margins entire; stipules linear, small, not persistent. **Flowers** (female) in catkins, 3–5 cm long, on leafy stalks; pistils densely white-hairy. **Fruit** a densely gray-hairy capsule. **Flowering** one of the last willows to flower; catkins appearing

Salix glauca GRAY-LEAF WILLOW

Salix fuscescens ALASKA BOG WILLOW

with, or soon after the leaves, remaining on the plant over winter, releasing seeds the next spring.

Where Found one of the most common willows in Denali, mostly at mid-elevations and in various habitats including gravel bars, spruce forest, subalpine slopes, and occasionally in alpine tundra.

Similar Species often confused with *Salix niphoclada,* but that species has shorter petioles, the stipules are almost absent, and the leaf tips usually not pointed.

◆ *Salix hastata* L. HALBERD WILLOW

Habit thicket-forming shrub, 1–3 m tall; branches reddish brown, covered with hook-shaped hairs. **Leaves** elliptic to obovate, 3–7 cm long; green above, paler below, generally hairless except for characteristic reddish hairs on the upper midrib (which distinguishes it from *Salix barclayi*), margins entire; stipules leaf-like. **Flowers** (female) in catkins, 2.5–5 cm long, on leafy stalks; pistils hairless, reddish green. **Fruit** a capsule, reddish at base. **Flowering** catkins appear with the leaves, usually around early June.

Where Found riparian areas, open woodlands and shrublands in upland and subalpine terrain, most common north of Alaska Range crest.

Similar Species *Salix pseudomyrsinites,* but that willow has toothed leaves; a useful character for recognizing *Salix hastata* are reddish hairs on midrib of upper leaf surface.

◆ *Salix interior* Rowlee SANDBAR WILLOW

Habit upright colony-forming shrub, rarely over 2 m high; branches with smooth brown or grayish bark; branchlets reddish brown, sparsely pubescent, becoming nearly hairless. **Leaves** linear, 4–11 cm long, about 10 times longer than wide, nearly hairless; mar-

gins usually with small, widely spaced teeth. **Flowers** (female) in catkins, 5–8 cm long, on leafy branches, the catkins spreading or somewhat drooping. **Fruit** a yellowish brown, glabrous capsule. **Flowering** catkins appear with the leaves in spring.

Where Found colonizer of sand and gravel bars, mud flats.

◆ *Salix lasiandra* Benth. PACIFIC WILLOW

Habit shrub or tree, 1–10 m tall, not colonial; branches erect, flexible at base; twigs brownish, smooth or sparsely to densely hairy. **Leaves** narrowly elliptic to lanceolate, 6–12 cm long, tip long and tail-like; upper surface glossy, smooth or becoming so, lower surface soft-hairy, becoming nearly smooth; mar-

Salix interior SANDBAR WILLOW

Salix hastata HALBERD WILLOW

Salix lasiandra PACIFIC WILLOW

gins serrate; petioles usually with two glandular dots at top; stipules leaflike. Flowers (female) in catkins, 5-10 cm long, on leafy stalks. Fruit a glabrous capsule. Flowering catkins appear with the opening of leaves in spring.

Where Found occasional on sand and gravel bars, riverbanks.

◆ *Salix myrtillifolia* Andersson
BLUEBERRY WILLOW

Habit low shrub, 10-60 cm tall, layering; stems decumbent or erect, flexible at base; twigs yellow- to red-brown, sparsely hairy. Leaves narrowly elliptic to broadly ovate, 2-5 cm long; upper surface satiny, smooth, lower surface slightly paler; margins finely toothed; petioles without glandular dots at top; stipules small, rarely leaflike. Flowers (female) in catkins, 2-4 cm long, on leafy twigs. Fruit a glabrous, yellow-green capsule. Flowering catkins appear as leaves emerge.

Where Found occasional in mossy fens, muskegs, streambanks, lakeshores.

◆ *Salix niphoclada* Rydb.
BARRENGROUND WILLOW

Salix brachycarpa subsp. *niphoclada* (Rydb.) Argus, *Salix lingulata* Andersson

Habit shrub, 0.3-1.5 m tall, not colonial; branches erect, decumbent, or trailing, flexible at base; twigs violet to yellow-brown, densely hairy. Leaves narrowly oblong to lanceolate or ovate, glaucous, densely hairy beneath, less so above, margins entire; petiole reddish, 2-5 mm long; stipules tiny or absent. Flowers (female) in catkins, 2-4 cm long; pistils short, densely hairy. Fruit a gray-hairy capsule. Flowering catkins and leaves develop together around late-May; catkins mature in mid-June.

Where Found occasional in alpine meadows, floodplains, shrub tundra, and scree-slopes.

Similar Species often confused with *Salix glauca,* but differs in having shorter petioles, stipules and stipes, and rounded leaf tips.

◆ *Salix phlebophylla* Andersson
SKELETON-LEAF WILLOW

Habit matted, creeping dwarf shrub, only 1-7 cm tall, with many persistent 'skeletonized' dead leaves; branches reddish brown, glossy, glabrous. Leaves firm and leathery, elliptic to obovate, mostly less than 1 cm long, glossy green above, underside glossy, not glaucous, margins entire; dead leaves persist on the plant for many years, becoming skeletonized so that only veins remain. Flowers (female) in upright, densely flowered catkins, 1.5-2.5 cm long; pistils usually hairy, purplish. Fruit a glabrous to sparsely hairy capsule. Flowering leaves and catkins appear together.

Salix myrtillifolia BLUEBERRY WILLOW

Salix niphoclada BARRENGROUND WILLOW

Where Found uncommon in alpine tundra and rocky places.

Similar Species this species known to hybridize with *S. rotundifolia,* another tiny alpine willow; *Salix polaris* is a similar dwarf willow, but that species lacks ciliate leaf margins and the many persistent dead leaves.

♦ *Salix polaris* Wahlenb. **POLAR WILLOW**

Habit creeping dwarf shrub, to 10 cm tall, with small elliptic leaves, forming rhizomatous mats; branches erect, flexible at base, weakly to strongly glaucous; twigs yellowish brown, smooth. **Leaves** ovate to elliptic, mostly 1–1.5 cm long, thin, lustrous and fresh green above and below, underside with prominent veins; margins entire, often reddish. **Flowers** (female) in catkins, 2–4 cm long; pistils hairy. **Fruit** a hairy to glabrous, red-purple capsule. **Flowering** leaves and catkins appear together.

Where Found occasional in the alpine moist tundra and gravels, seeps, snowbeds and meadows, often on steep slopes.

Similar Species distinguished from other willows by the leaves, which are green (not glaucous) on both sides, the entire, not-hairy leaf margins, and the pubescent pistils.

♦ *Salix pseudomonticola* Ball
FALSE MOUNTAIN WILLOW
Salix barclayi var. *pseudomonticola* (Ball) L. Kelso, *Salix monticola* Bebb

Habit shrub, 1–6 m tall, not colonial; branches erect, flexible at base; twigs yellow-

green, smooth or densely hairy. **Leaves** alternate, simple, elliptic to broadly ovate, 4–6 cm long; upper surface green and glabrous, lower surface glaucous, with prominent veins; margins finely glandular-toothed; petioles without glandular dots at top; stipules leaflike. **Flowers** (female) in catkins, 4–9 cm long, unstalked on the twig. **Fruit** a glabrous capsule. **Flowering** catkins appear before leaves emerge.

Where Found fens, floodplain thickets, muskegs and moist woods.

Salix pseudomyrsinites Andersson
FIRM-LEAF WILLOW
Salix myrtillifolia var. *pseudomyrsinites* (Andersson) C.R. Ball ex Hultén, *Salix novae-angliae* Andersson

Habit shrub, 1–4 m tall, not colonial; branches erect, flexible at base; twigs yellow- to red-brown, sparsely to densely hairy. **Leaves** narrowly elliptic to obovate, 3–6 cm

Salix polaris **POLAR WILLOW**

Salix phlebophylla **SKELETON-LEAF WILLOW**

long; young leaves reddish; mature leaves green above, with white and rusty hairs on midrib, underside pale green, glossy; margins finely toothed (with glands on the teeth); stipules 1–5 mm long. Flowers (female) in catkins, 2–4 cm long, on leafy peduncles; pistils green, hairless. Fruit a green, glabrous capsule. Flowering catkins and leaves appear together in early summer.

Where Found at low- to mid-elevations in floodplains and terraces, muskegs, lakeshores.

Similar Species distinguished from *Salix myrtillifolia* by its larger size, and longer leaves and stipules.

♦ *Salix pulchra* Cham.
DIAMOND-LEAF WILLOW, TEA-LEAF WILLOW
Salix planifolia subsp. *pulchra* (Cham.) Argus

Habit highly branched shrub, to 3 m tall (shorter at high elevations), with glossy-green diamond-shaped leaves; not colonial; branches erect, flexible at base; twigs brownish, smooth and often shiny. Leaves usually di-

amond-shaped in outline, 3–5 cm long; upper surface dark green, satiny; underside glaucous; margins entire or with few teeth; stipules linear, persistent on the plant for several years (old, red leaves sometimes also persistent). Flowers (female) in sessile catkins, 2–6 cm long; pistils hairy. Fruit a sparsely hairy, tan or greenish capsule. Flowering catkins appear before the leaves; leaves form from end of May to early June; seeds disseminated by mid-summer (mid-June to early July).

Where Found abundant at low- to high-elevations, and one of Denali's most widespread willows, occurring in forests, bogs, floodplains, forming thickets in subalpine and alpine tundra.

Similar Species the combination of reddish twigs, narrow elliptic hairless leaves, and persistent, linear stipules identify *Salix pulchra*.

Traditional Uses has been used medicinally to treat mouth sores, as an analgesic, and as an eye medicine (Moerman 1998). Young leaves and shoots can be eaten as food either raw, cooked, or mixed with seal oil; it is reportedly high in vitamin C. It is an important browse plant for moose.

♦ *Salix reticulata* L. **NET-LEAF WILLOW**
Habit dwarf, creeping shrub, 3–10 cm tall, with characteristic, rounded, net-veined leaves; branches trailing, flexible at base; twigs yellow- to red-brown, smooth. Leaves round-elliptic, 1–6 cm long, leathery; dark glossy green with deeply embossed veins above, pale glaucous below; margins nearly

Salix pseudomonticola FALSE MOUNTAIN WILLOW

Salix pulchra DIAMOND-LEAF WILLOW

entire; petioles 10–25 mm long. Flowers (female) in catkins, 1–5 cm long, atop a leafless, hairy stalk; pistils densely hairy. Fruit a hairy, reddish capsule. Flowering catkins and leaves appear together shortly after snowmelt.

Where Found abundant in moist to wet areas in the alpine zone, from meadows to tundra and steep slopes.

Similar Species the round leaves with deeply impressed veins distinguish this dwarf willow from others in the park; the leaves at first glance may be confused with the leathery leaves of *Arctous rubra* or *A. alpina,* but net-leaf willow has rounder leaves, and catkins instead of flowers or berries.

◆ *Salix richardsonii* Hook.
RICHARDSON'S WILLOW

Salix lanata subsp. *richardsonii* (Hook.) A.K. Skvortsov

Habit shrub, 0.3–3 m tall, with leafy, toothed stipules at the base of the leaf; not colonial; branches erect, flexible at base; twigs red- to yellow-brown, sparsely to densely hairy, often covered with old dried stipules giving it a shaggy look. Leaves elliptic, 3–6 cm long; sparsely hairy and shiny above, less hairy and glaucous below, margins entire to glandular-serrate; stipules large, linear to ovate, usually persist for several years. Flowers (female) in catkins, 4–9 cm long, on leafy stalks. Fruit a hairless capsule. Flowering catkins develop well before the leaves and appear during or immediately after snowmelt.

Where Found abundant at low- to high-elevations on floodplains and terraces, meadows and slopes.

Similar Species the leafy stipules with glandular teeth persistent for multiple years identifies this willow, along with the fuzzy, white-hairy young twigs.

Traditional Uses Native Americans made a tea from boiled bark of Richardson's willow

for sore throats and tuberculosis, while flexible shoots were woven into baskets and furniture; also an important browse plant for moose.

◆ *Salix rotundifolia* Trautv.
ROUND-LEAF WILLOW, TIMBERLINE WILLOW

Habit dwarf, mat-forming shrub, to 20 cm tall, with yellow-brown, glabrous, mostly subterranean branches; branches can have persistent dead leaves. Leaves round to elliptic, 5–14 mm long, hairless, glossy green on both sides with 3 distinct veins; margins entire, inrolled, and reddish. Flowers (female) in few flowered catkins (2–12 capsules per catkin), 1–2 cm long, on a stalk with two leaves. Fruit a glossy, reddish brown capsule. Flowering leaves and catkins develop together early to mid-summer.

Where Found in alpine tundra, gravelly and rocky places, exposed ridges, often on steep slopes.

Salix richardsonii RICHARDSON'S WILLOW

Salix reticulata NET-LEAF WILLOW

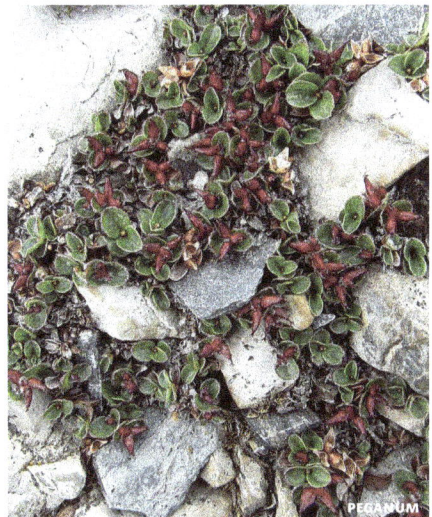

Salix rotundifolia ROUND-LEAF WILLOW

Similar Species differentiated from other dwarf willows by its size, its round leaves (lacking deeply impressed net-veins), and its few-flowered catkins with hairless pistils.

♦ *Salix scouleriana* Barratt ex Hook.
SCOULER'S WILLOW

Habit shrub or small tree, 3–20 m tall, not colonial; branches erect, flexible at base; twigs yellow-green to yellow-brown, sparsely to densely velvety-hairy. Leaves obovate to narrowly elliptic, 4–8 cm long; upper surface hairy, becoming nearly smooth (midrib remaining hairy); lower surface glaucous, silky to woolly hairy, becoming sparsely so, the hairs white and rust-colored; margins entire or toothed; petioles without glandular dots at top; stipules small. Flowers (female) in unstalked or short-stalked catkins, 2–5 cm long. Fruit a woolly-hairy, black capsule. Flowering catkins open before leaves emerge in spring.

Where Found well-drained woods, muskegs, willow thickets.

♦ *Salix setchelliana* Ball SETCHELL'S WILLOW

Habit creeping dwarf shrub, to 25 cm tall, forming colonies by root shoots; branches decumbent or erect, flexible at base; twigs reddish, densely white-woolly. Leaves

oblanceolate, leathery, 2.5–6 cm long; upper surface light green, hairless, with impressed veins; lower surface glabrous, pale yellow-green; margins entire to glandular-serrate. Flowers (female) in densely flowered, dark red catkins, 1.5–2.5 cm long, on leafy stalks. Fruit a dark red to gray-brown, hairless capsule. Flowering leaves and catkins develop together in mid-June.

Where Found uncommon at low- to mid-elevations on large glacial floodplains adjacent to large rivers, lakeshores, and moraines.

Similar Species Denali's only willow with fleshy, light green leaves and fleshy, hairless capsules, usually found creeping along river gravel bars.

♦ *Salix sitchensis* Sanson ex Bong. SITKA WILLOW

Habit shrub or small tree, 1–3 m tall, not colonial; branches erect, flexible at base; twigs yellow- to red-brown, densely hairy. Leaves elliptic to obovate, 4–8 cm long, upper surface bright green, dull, sparsely long soft-

Salix scouleriana SCOULER'S WILLOW

Salix setchelliana SETCHELL'S WILLOW

hairy to nearly smooth; lower surface densely silky or woolly, the hairs white; margins entire or sparsely glandular-serrate; petioles without glandular dots at top; stipules small. Flowers (female) in catkins, 3–7 cm long, on leafy twigs. Fruit a hairy capsule. Flowering catkins open as leaves emerge (or just before the leaves).

Where Found uncommon on gravel bars, thickets, forest openings.

Salix sitchensis SITKA WILLOW

Salix stolonifera CREEPING WILLOW

♦*Salix stolonifera* Coville CREEPING WILLOW
Habit dwarf shrub, to 10 cm tall, forming rhizomatous mats; branches trailing or erect, flexible at base; twigs brownish, smooth. Leaves elliptic to nearly circular, 15–40 mm long; upper surface glossy, glabrous; lower surface glaucous, sparsely hairy, becoming nearly smooth; margins entire or irregularly toothed in lower half of leaf; petioles without glandular dots at top; stipules small. Flowers (female) in catkins, 2–4 cm long, on leafy stalks. Fruit a glabrous capsule. Flowering catkins appear with the leaves in spring.

Where Found uncommon in alpine tundra, rocky slopes and moraines.

SANTALACEAE
Sandalwood Family

Geocaulon FALSE TOADFLAX
(Greek, referring to the subterranean stems and rhizomes.)

♦*Geocaulon lividum* (Richardson) Fernald
FALSE TOADFLAX
Comandra livida Richardson
Habit perennial parasitic herb from creeping rhizomes; stems erect, one to several in a clump, simple, hairless, 10–20 cm tall. Leaves alternate, elliptic to oval, turning purplish in fall; often infected with a virus that causes the leaves to have a variegated, mottled appearance. Flowers along the stem in clusters of 2–3, with five green tepals; middle flower perfect, the other flowers with stamens only. Fruit a berry-like, orange to red, mealy drupe, with a single seed. Flowering early in season; fruits develop slowly and mature in late fall; foliage turns maroon-red in fall.

Where Found abundant at low-elevations and is parasitic on roots of forest plants such

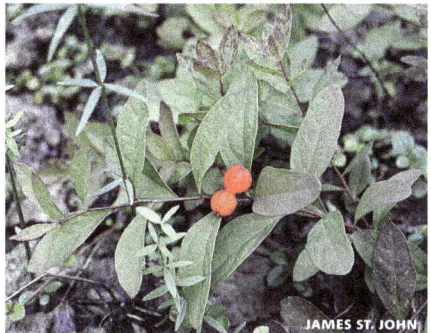

Geocaulon lividum FALSE TOADFLAX

as spruce (*Picea*), birch (*Betula*), willow (*Salix*), alder (*Alnus*) and twinflower (*Linnea borealis*); generally on acidic, nitrogen-poor soils.

Similar Species identified by its orange fruits from leaf axils along stem of an upright herb.

Traditional Uses berries edible, but not necessarily desirable; the Dena'ina used leaves as poultice for cuts, and made a tea of the roots or chewed berries for stomach problems, sore throats, and tuberculosis (Kari 1995).

SAXIFRAGACEAE
Saxifrage Family

1 Stamens 4 or 8; petals absent; flowers small, in a flat-topped inflorescence ... *Chrysosplenium*
1 Stamens 5 or 10; flowers in an elongate inflorescence 2
2 Stamens 10. 3
2 Stamens 5. 5
3 Leaves leathery. . . . . *Leptarrhena*
3 Leaves not leathery 4
4 Leaves both basal and along stem (stem leaves may be reduced) . . . . *Saxifraga*
4 Leaves all basal (or nearly so) . . . . . *Micranthes*
5 Petals pinnately or ternately cleft. . . *Pectiantia*
5 Petals entire. 6
6 Leaves kidney- or heart-shaped. . . . . . *Boykinia*
6 Leaves 3–5-lobed. . . . . *Heuchera*

Boykinia BROOKFOAM
(In honor of Samuel Boykin, 1786-1848, physician and naturalist of Georgia, USA.)

♦ *Boykinia richardsonii* (Hook.) Rothr.
BROOKFOAM, ALASKA BOYKINIA
Habit perennial herb from a thick stembase; stems slender, leafy, 10–50 cm tall, brownish to reddish hairy, often glandular-hairy. Leaves both basal and along stem; kidney-shaped with shallow lobes and irregularly toothed margins; basal leaves 5–10 cm across, shiny green with a stiff, waxy feel, petioles long; base of plant with many persistent, brown, dead leaves; stem leaves similar but sessile and and smaller upwards. Flowers in a crowded terminal spikelike panicle; petals ovate to elliptic, 8–12 mm long, white or pink-veined, often suffused with rose; sepals five, dark red, glandular, narrowly triangular; stamens five, anthers yel-

low; styles two. Fruit a dry capsule, 9–12 mm long, with many smooth brown seeds.

Where Found abundant in meadows, rocky sites, snowbeds, and tundra.

Similar Species No other plant in Denali has similar waxy, kidney-shaped leaves, and a spike of large white-pink flowers.

Chrysosplenium
GOLDEN-SAXIFRAGE
(Greek, golden spleen, from reputed medicinal properties.)

1 Sepals green; petiole glabrous; stamens 4 . . . . *C. tetrandrum*
1 Sepals minutely purple-dotted; petiole usually crinkly-hairy with pale rusty hairs; stamens 8 . . . . *C. wrightii*

♦ *Chrysosplenium tetrandrum* (N. Lund) Th. Fr. **NORTHERN GOLDEN-SAXIFRAGE**
Habit creeping perennial herb, with cup-shaped yellow flowers, from slender leafy stolons; stems succulent, ascending to erect, to 15 cm long, 2- or 3-branched near tip. Leaves alternate, basal and along stem, small (1 cm), round to kidney-shaped with even lobes, pale green (sometimes yellowish), glabrous or sparsely hairy, margins up-

NPS - JACOB FRANK

Boykinia richardsonii BROOKFOAM

turned. Flowers several in a flat-topped terminal cluster; petals absent; sepals 4, fused at base, yellow-greenish, the tips often curved back; stamens four. Fruit a capsule, resembling a bird's nest when splitting to leave one round, cup-like half remaining; seeds few, red-brown.

Where Found occasional in seeps, depressions, streambanks, and other wet areas.

Similar Species distinguished from other members of Saxifrage family by its lack of petals; separated from *Chrysosplenium wrightii* by the number of stamens (4 vs. 8), and the hairless petioles.

Chrysosplenium wrightii Franch. & Sav.
WRIGHT'S GOLDEN SAXIFRAGE

Habit perennial herb, with small clusters of yellow-green flowers, from thick rhizomes; stems succulent, usually erect, 2–10 cm long, simple or branched, sparsely soft-hairy. Leaves mostly basal; rounded to kidney-shaped, toothed and fleshy, sparsely to densely hairy; petioles with rusty brown hairs; flowering stems leafless. Flowers 2–20, in a terminal cluster, subtended by leaf-like bracts; tepals 4, yellow-greenish or purple-mottled; stamens 8; nectary disk prominent, yellow or purple. Fruit resemble a bird's nests: the capsules split, with one round, cup-like half remaining; seeds few, red-brown.

Where Found occasional in moist gravelly sites and scree-slopes in alpine zone.

Similar Species the only other plant in Denali with kidney-shaped, fleshy leaves and petal-less cup-like flowers is *Chrysosplenium tetrandrum;* that species has 4 stamens (not 8), hairless petioles, and is usually found at lower elevations in much wetter areas.

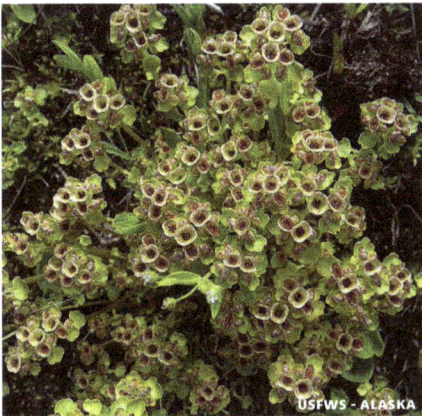

Chrysosplenium tetrandrum
NORTHERN GOLDEN-SAXIFRAGE

Heuchera ALUMROOT
(In honor of Johann Heinrich von Heucher, 1677-1747, Austrian-born medical botanist and professor of medicine.)

◆ Heuchera glabra Willd. ex Schult.
ALPINE ALUMROOT

Habit perennial herb, from well-developed rhizomes, old, brown leaf-bases persistent; stems 1 to several, erect, 15–60 cm tall, smooth to finely glandular-hairy below, strongly glandular-hairy in inflorescence. Leaves mostly basal, thin and shining, heart-shaped, 4–12 cm long, shorter than wide, palmately 5-lobed, smooth above, sparsely glandular-hairy below; margins doubly toothed; stem leaves small, 1 or 2. Flowers many, in an open panicle, the branches and flower-stalks thread-like; petals 5, white, clawed; calyx 5-lobed, greenish yellow, glandular-hairy; stamens 5, longer than calyx lobes. Fruit an ovate capsule, 5–6 mm long; seeds brown.

Where Found rocky woods and slopes, streambanks.

Leptarrhena
LEATHERLEAF SAXIFRAGE
(Greek, delicate and male, probably referring to the slender stamens.)

◆ Leptarrhena pyrolifolia (D. Don) Ser.
LEATHERLEAF SAXIFRAGE

Habit perennial herb, with a small terminal cluster of white flowers, from spreading rhizomes; stems erect, reddish, 10–25 cm tall, glandular-hairy above. Leaves leathery, evergreen, mostly basal; ovate and evenly toothed, in a cluster parallel to the ground; stems with 1–2 leaves, close to the base, with a bract below inflorescence; leaves turn dark red in fall, re-greening in spring. Flowers many, in a dense terminal cyme; petals white, linear, 1–2 mm long, alternating with

Heuchera glabra ALPINE ALUMROOT

the similarly colored stamens; anthers orange. Fruit two carpels fused at base; seeds light brown, 2–3 mm long, with tail-like ends 2–3 times as long as the seed.

Where Found occasional alpine plant, rare on north side of Alaska Range in Denali, more common south of the crest.

Similar Species resembles other members of Saxifrage family, such as *Micranthes reflexa*, but distinguished by its shiny, leathery, evergreen leaves, and at a distance, the inflorescence has a fuzzy appearance.

Leptarrhena pyrolifolia LEATHERLEAF SAXIFRAGE

Micranthes SAXIFRAGE

(Greek *mikros*, small, and *anthos*, flower.)

1 Inflorescence with all or some flowers replaced by bulblets. . . . . *M. foliolosa*
1 Inflorescence without bulblets 2
2 Ovary inferior to about one-half inferior (sometimes appearing more superior in fruit) 3
2 Ovary more or less superior (to at most one-half inferior) 8
3 Leaf margin toothed near tip; pistils joined for more than half their length 4
3 Leaf margin entire (or nearly so), toothed throughout, or toothed on upper two-thirds of blade; pistils joined for less than half their length 5
4 Leaves oblanceolate to narrowly spatulate; inflorescence branches glabrous. . . . . *M. razshivinii*
4 Leaves wider, fan-shaped to nearly round; inflorescence branches densely long-hairy . . . . *M. calycina*
5 Petals pink to purple, or 1–5 and white to greenish white or cream, or absent. . *M. hieraciifolia*
5 Petals 5, white to greenish white, cream, or, rarely, purple, sometimes pink or purplish tinged 6
6 Petals white or margins pink with age; stems with tangled white hairs . . . . *M. nivalis*

6 Petals reddish to purple; stem hairs not as above 7
7 Stems with a mix of long, tangled white and brown hairs; fruiting inflorescence raceme-like or panicle-like . . . . *M. rufopilosa*
7 Stems hairless (or nearly so), or with short white glandular hairs; fruiting inflorescence corymblike . . . . *M. tenuis*
8 Pistils joined for half their length or more. . . . 9
8 Pistils distinct almost to their base. . *M. reflexa*
9 Capsules dark purple or purple-black 10
9 Capsules green to yellow and purple-tinged, purple, or upper half purple. 12
10 Filaments club-shaped . . . . *M. nelsoniana*
10 Filaments linear, flattened 11
11 Leaves oblanceolate to narrowly oblanceolate; inflorescence branches glabrous. *M. razshivinii*
11 Leaves fan-shaped; inflorescence branches with dense, long, tangled hairs. . . . . *M. calycina*
12 Leaves round, kidney-shaped, or spatulate to obovate; filaments club-shaped 13
12 Leaves elliptic to oblanceolate, obovate, or spatulate; filaments linear, flattened . . *M. foliolosa*
13 Leaves spatulate to obovate, wedge-shaped at base. . . . . *M. lyallii*
13 Leaves round to ovate or kidney-shaped, heart-shaped to truncate at base 14
14 Inflorescence cone-shaped to globular; petals white to pinkish, rarely orange-spotted; filaments club-shaped . . . . *M. nelsoniana*
14 Inflorescence spikelike; petals cream to yellowish; filaments only narrowly club-shaped . . . . *M. spicata*

Micranthes calycina (Sternb.) Gornall & H. Ohba
ALASKA SAXIFRAGE
Saxifraga calycina Sternb., *Saxifraga davurica* subsp. *grandipetala* (Engl. & Irmsch.) Hultén

Habit tufted perennial herb; flower stems 5–15 cm tall, leafless, somewhat glandular-hairy. Leaves all basal, ascending, oblanceolate or wedge-shaped at base, coarsely several-toothed above, glabrous or nearly so, 1–4 cm long. Flowers several in a loose cluster; petals white, to 3–4 mm long; sepals about 2 mm long, purple, reflexed; Fruit a dark red capsule, 6–8 mm long.

Where Found occasional in alpine tundra and heathlands.

♦ *Micranthes foliolosa* (R.Br.) Gornall
LEAFY-STEM SAXIFRAGE
Saxifraga foliolosa R. Br.

Habit tufted perennial herb, often with leafy stolons ending in a leafy rosette; flower stems 5–20 cm tall, simple or branched, glandular-hairy. Leaves basal, wedge-shaped to oblanceolate, to 2 cm long, with 3–5 teeth at tip; margins fringed with hairs. Flowers solitary at end of stem and often single at end of branch, bulblets or tufts of small leaves also often present; petals white, 4–5 mm long; sepals 1–2 mm long. Fruit a capsule, 4–5 mm long.

Where Found uncommon in moist to wet alpine tundra, often along small streams.

♦ *Micranthes hieraciifolia* (Waldst. & Kit. ex Willd.) Haw. **STIFF-STEM SAXIFRAGE**
Saxifraga hieraciifolia Waldst. & Kit. ex Willd.

Habit perennial herb, with green-purple flowers; flowering stem single, stout, 10–50 cm tall, reddish, finely hairy. Leaves in a basal rosette, elliptic or oblong-lanceolate, underside often reddish, margins slightly round-toothed or entire. Flowers several to many in a spikelike cluster (sometimes few-branched), petals and sepals 2–3 mm long, purplish. Fruit a red, two-beaked capsule.

Where Found occasional in moist to wet areas of tundra and meadows at high-elevations, much more common north of Alaska Range than south.

Similar Species distinguished from other *Micranthes* by its spikelike inflorescence and greenish purple petals.

♦ *Micranthes lyallii* (Engl.) Small
RED-STEM SAXIFRAGE
Saxifraga lyallii Engl.

Habit tufted perennial herb, with white or pinkish flowers, from well-developed rhizomes; flowering stems one to several, red, leafless, 4–20 cm tall. Leaves mostly basal, diamond- or fan-shaped on long petioles, margins strongly toothed at tip; stem leaves absent or few, very small. Flowers several in a branched, open panicle; petals white or pinkish, clawed and yellow-spotted, and just longer than the green-purple sepals; stamens with filaments broad at base and red anthers. Fruit a red, two-beaked capsule.

Where Found occasional along brooks, in seeps, and in moist alpine meadows, on both sides of Alaska Range.

Micranthes foliolosa LEAFY-STEM SAXIFRAGE

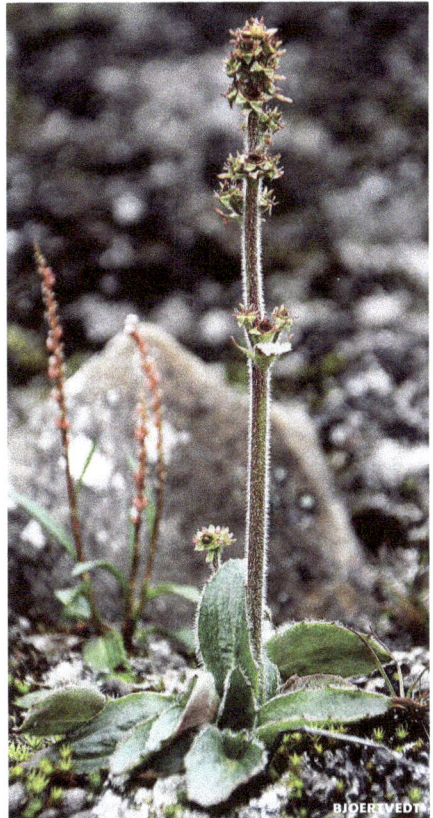

Micranthes hieraciifolia STIFF-STEM SAXIFRAGE

♦*Micranthes nelsoniana* (D.Don) Small
HEART-LEAF SAXIFRAGE
Micranthes porsildiana (Calder & Savile) Elven & D.F. Murray, *Saxifraga nelsoniana* D. Don

Habit perennial herb, with open panicles of small white flowers, from a rhizome; stems green or red, leafless, long-hairy, 5–40 cm high. **Leaves** all basal, round or reniform in outline, somewhat fleshy, covered with fine hairs, purple on underside, petioles long; margins strongly toothed. **Flowers** 10 or more, in a compact to open panicle; petals white or pinkish; sepals 1–2 mm long, reflexed; stamens with orange anthers at end of club-shaped filaments. **Fruit** a two-beaked, reddish capsule.

Where Found common on alpine stream-banks, snowbeds, seeps.

Similar Species this species distinguished by its reniform (kidney-shaped) leaves.

Note *Micranthes porsildiana* sometimes treated as separate from the *M. nelsoniana* complex of closely related taxa.

♦*Micranthes nivalis* (L.) Small
SNOW SAXIFRAGE
Saxifraga nivalis L.

Habit tiny perennial herb, with small white flowers, from short, stout rhizomes and black, fibrous roots; flowering stems single, leafless, purple, glandular-hairy, 4–12 cm tall. **Leaves** leathery, purple-tinged, in a basal rosette, oblanceolate to spatulate, reddish hairy on underside; margin toothed. **Flowers** 10–40, in a dense cluster; petals five, white, 2–4 mm long, surrounded by shorter purple sepals; stamens 10. **Fruit** a red or purple (when mature) capsule, with two divergent beaks.

Micranthes nelsoniana **HEART-LEAF SAXIFRAGE**

Micranthes lyallii **RED-STEM SAXIFRAGE**

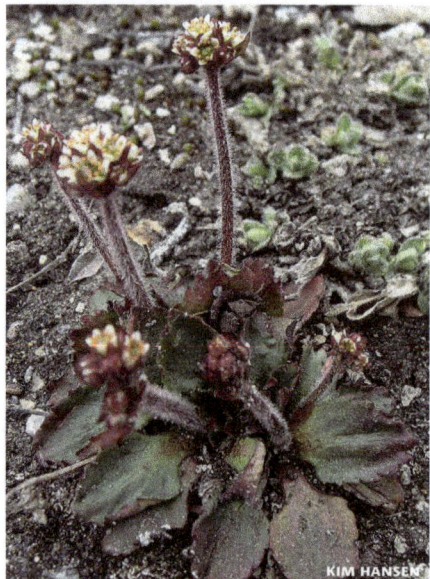

Micranthes nivalis **SNOW SAXIFRAGE**

Where Found uncommon in moist sheltered places, gravelly areas, and frost boils in the alpine zone.

Similar Species distinguished from *Micranthes nelsoniana* by shape of its leaves (oblong-oblanceolate, not reniform); *M. hieraciifolia* with a spikelike inflorescence, not a branching cyme; *M. lyallii* with fan-shaped leaves and club-shaped filaments; *M. reflexa* with leaves hairy on both sides (not just underside), and sepals reflexed backwards at maturity.

♦ *Micranthes razshivinii* (Zhmylev) Brouillet & Gornall RAZSHIVIN'S SAXIFRAGE
Saxifraga razshivinii Zhmylev

Habit perennial herb, with spatulate leaves and white flowers, from a branching rhizome; flowering stem, branching towards tip, 3–15 cm tall. Leaves basal (and with a few small leaves on stem), slightly fleshy, gradu-

ally widening from base, hairless on both sides, 2–5 cm long, margins with sparse hairs, toothed at tip. Flowers in a terminal cluster; petals white or sometimes purplish, petals slightly longer than the reflexed calyx; stamens 10, filaments threadlike. Fruit a purplish black, two-beaked capsule, 6–10 mm long.

Where Found in snowbeds, gravelly places, and small streams of alpine zone.

Similar Species inflorescence branches hairless, distinguishing it from closely related *Micranthes calycina*; also similar to *M. lyallii*, separated by its narrow filaments (instead of club-shaped).

♦ *Micranthes reflexa* (Hook.) Small
YUKON SAXIFRAGE
Saxifraga reflexa Hook.

Habit perennial herb, with white flowers, from a short stem-base and black fibrous roots; flowering stem single, reddish, stout, glandular-hairy, to 25 cm tall. Leaves all basal, thick, ovate with a broad petiole, leaf underside purplish, both sides densely hairy, margins toothed. Flowers many in an open, branched cyme, petals 5, white, 2–3 mm long; sepals half as long as petals, at maturity reflexed backwards. Fruit a two-beaked capsule.

Where Found occasional in open, dry areas on slopes, ridges and floodplains, from boreal uplands to alpine zone.

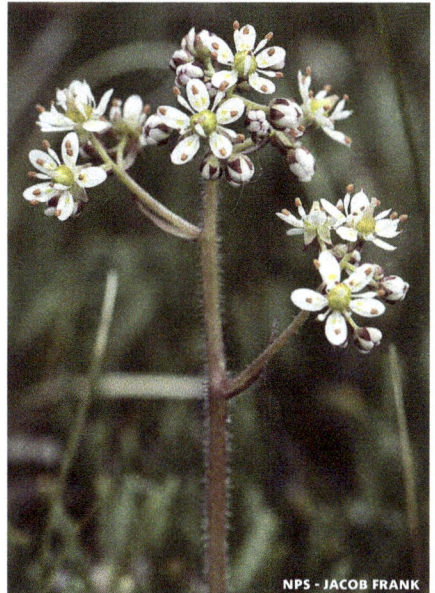

NPS - JACOB FRANK

Micranthes razshivinii RAZSHIVIN'S SAXIFRAGE

NPS - JACOB FRANK

Micranthes reflexa YUKON SAXIFRAGE

Similar Species differentiated from other *Micranthes* species by the reflexed sepals and hairs on both sides of the leaves.

Micranthes rufopilosa (Hultén) D.F. Murray & Elven REDHAIR SAXIFRAGE
Saxifraga rufopilosa (Hultén) A.E. Porsild

Habit tufted perennial herb, with black fibrous roots; flower stem erect, slender, solitary or few together, to 10 cm tall, purplish, glandular-hairy. Leaves all basal, 0.5–2 cm long, oblanceolate to ovate, wedge-shaped at base; green above, green splotched with purple and rust-colored hairs below; margins toothed. Flowers in dense clusters, each flower subtended by a small bract; petals narrowly obovate, about 2 mm long, pink or pale purplish; sepals about as long as petals, purple, glandular-hairy. Fruit a purple capsule, about 3 mm long.

Where Found alpine turf, rocky slopes; endemic to Alaska and the Yukon.

Micranthes spicata (D.Don) Small SPIKE SAXIFRAGE
Saxifraga spicata D. Don.

Habit tufted perennial herb, from short, stout rhizomes; stems 2–6 dm tall, leafless, glandular-hairy. Leaves basal, ascending, with long petioles, blades kidney-shaped to nearly round, cordate at base, 2–5 cm long, margins with gland-tipped teeth; stem leaves absent or several and bractlike. Flowers in a slender, spikelike panicle; petals yellowish, about 4 mm long; sepals about 2 mm long, reflexed. Fruit a capsule, 6–10 mm long.

Where Found uncommon in moist alpine tundra, moist rocky slopes.

Micranthes tenuis (Wahlenb.) Small SLENDER SAXIFRAGE
Saxifraga nivalis var. *tenuis* Wahlenb.

Habit tufted perennial herb; flower stem single, leafless, pubescent with dark or reddish hairs. Leaves all basal, thick, green and glabrous above, purple and more or less densely pubescent below; margins toothed, fringed with hairs. Flowers several in a loose terminal cluster; petals white or reddish, slightly longer than calyx lobes. Fruit a capsule, with reflexed beaks.

Where Found alpine slopes.

Pectiantia MITREWORT
(Latin, comb, from petals; opposing, for stamens opposite petals in *P. pentandra*.)

♦ *Pectiantia pentandra* (Hook.) Rydb. ALPINE MITREWORT
Mitella pentandra Hook.

Habit perennial herb from slender rhizomes, sometimes with stolons; stems erect, 10–30 cm tall, glandular-hairy to almost smooth. Leaves basal, ovate, heart-shaped at base, 2–5 cm wide, shallowly lobed, nearly smooth to stiffly hairy, margins toothed; stem leaves absent or with 1 small leaf. Flowers 6–25, in a spikelike cluster, often in pairs; flower stalks 2–7 mm long; petals greenish, 2–3 mm long, divided into 5–9 threadlike segments; calyx 5-lobed; stamens 5, opposite petals. Fruit a capsule; seeds black, veiny-pitted.

Where Found moist woods, streambanks, subalpine and alpine meadows.

Saxifraga SAXIFRAGE
(Latin, rock and to break, referring to the habitat of many of the species.)

1 Leaves opposite and overlapping on stem; plants low-growing with trailing branches and solitary purple flowers on short leafy stalks . . . . *S. oppositifolia*
1 Leaves alternate. 2
2 Flowering stems naked . . . . *S. eschscholtzii*
2 Flowering stem leafy. 3
3 Basal leaves sessile, petiole absent 4

Pectiantia pentandra ALPINE MITREWORT
ANDREY ZHARKIKH

3 Basal leaves with petioles; blade kidney-shaped, heart-shaped or wedge-shaped, 3- to 5-lobed; flowers white or pale pinkish 8
4 Petals yellow; leaves not persistent 5
5 Plant with long, whiplike, leafless stolons terminating in a rooting offset. . . . . *S. flagellaris*
5 Plants without long stolons 6
6 Leaves small, linear, fleshy . . . . . *S. serpyllifolia*
6 Leaves oblanceolate (at least basal leaves), with petioles; flowering stem usually 1-flowered . . . . *S. hirculus*
4 Petals white or cream-colored; leaves leathery, withering but persistent 7
7 Leaves elliptic to spatulate, tipped with a small sharp point; petals clawed at base. . . . . *S. bronchialis*
7 Leaves narrowly wedge-shaped, reddish, shiny, sharply 3-toothed; petals rounded or truncate at base . . . . *S. tricuspidata*
8 Bulblets present in inflorescence or at base of flowering stem 9
8 Bulblets absent 10
9 Inflorescence of one terminal and functional flower, and reddish or black bulbils in axils of upper stem leaves . . . . *S. cernua*
9 Inflorescence of normal flowers; bulblets rarely present at base of flowering stem, often replaced by short rooting stolons . . . . *S. rivularis*
10 Plants densely matted or tufted; leaves green and somewhat clammy . . . . *S. cespitosa*
10 Plants from tiny, reddish green rosette . . . . *S. adscendens*

♦ *Saxifraga adscendens* L.
WEDGE-LEAF SAXIFRAGE
Habit tufted perennial herb, from a taproot; stems erect, simple or branched, 2–8 cm tall; plants glandular-hairy. Leaves basal and along stem; basal leaves overlapping in a rosette, oblanceolate to ovate, 5–15 mm long, entire to toothed or shallowly lobed at tip, often reddish purple; stem leaves alternate, usually entire. Flowers several in a loose spikelike cluster; petals white, deciduous, 2–3-times length of calyx lobes, clawed; calyx 5-lobed, reddish purple; stamens 10. Fruit a capsule, 3–5 mm long.
Where Found uncommon on alpine gravels and rocks, glacial moraines.

♦ *Saxifraga bronchialis* L.
SPOTTED SAXIFRAGE
Saxifraga funstonii (Small) Fedde
Habit cushion-forming, evergreen, perennial herb, with yellow-spotted flowers, from a branched stem-base; stems slender, often reddish or yellow, 4–15 cm long. Leaves in a tight basal rosette, elliptic with a sharp tip, 3–15 mm long, margins fringed with stiff hairs; stem leaves few, alternate, linear, often yellowish; lowermost bract scalelike. Flowers one to several in a terminal, branching inflorescence; petals five, 5–8 mm long, white or cream, with yellow (to red-purple) spots. Fruit a capsule with two long, divergent beaks.

Saxifraga adscendens **WEDGE-LEAF SAXIFRAGE**

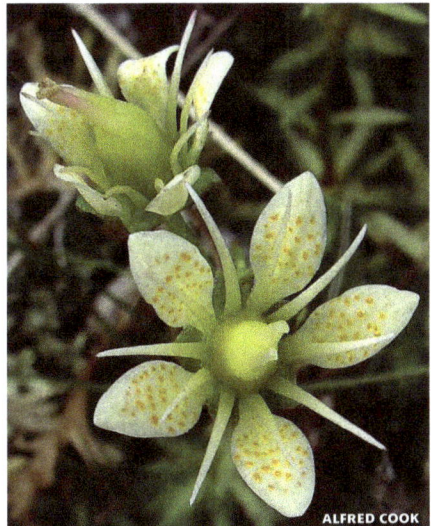
Saxifraga bronchialis **SPOTTED SAXIFRAGE**

Where Found occasional in well-drained alpine tundra and talus slopes.

Similar Species *Saxifraga tricuspidata* has similar flowers and basal rosettes of leaves, but its basal leaves are tipped with three teeth.

◆ *Saxifraga cernua* L. NODDING SAXIFRAGE

Habit perennial deciduous herb, from dense, fibrous roots; with one or more leafy flowering stems, 10–20 cm tall, glandular-hairy, with red vegetative bulblets below a single white flower; the reddish stem often angled in different directions at each node, giving a zig-zag appearance. Leaves basal (these sometimes absent) and along stem; broad, 3–5 lobed or toothed, lower leaves long-petioled, stem leaves short-petioled to sessile, becoming smaller upwards. Flowers either solitary or absent, white and relatively large; petals five, 5–12 mm long; sepals small, green. Fruit a two-beaked capsule.

Where Found uncommon at high-elevations on sparsely vegetated scree and rock outcrops.

Similar Species leaf shape, presence of stem leaves, and the unbranched stem can be used to distinguish it from *Micranthes foliolosa*, which is also single-flowered with many bulblets; also, *M. foliolosa* is a plant of moist to wet meadows, whereas *S. cernua* usually occurs in dry rocky places.

Note the scientific name 'cernua' is Latin for 'nodding,' referring to the drooping habit of the flower when first in bloom.

◆ *Saxifraga cespitosa* L.
TUFTED ALPINE SAXIFRAGE

Habit densely tufted perennial herb, from branched stem-base; flowering stems 3–15 cm tall, glandular-hairy. Leaves basal and along stem; basal leaves usually 3-lobed, the lobes linear to lanceolate, lightly glandular-fringed to soft-hairy, crowded on sterile shoots; stem leaves smaller, 2–5, alternate, entire or lower ones lobed. Flowers several in a terminal, somewhat flat-topped cluster; petals creamy white, deciduous, ovate to broadly wedge-shaped, the tip rounded, sometimes notched; calyx 5-lobed, purplish, glandular-hairy; stamens 10. Fruit a capsule, 5–10 mm long.

Where Found uncommon on talus slopes, alpine meadows, cliffs.

Saxifraga eschsholtzii Sternb.
CUSHION SAXIFRAGE

Also spelled *Saxifraga eschscholzii*.

Habit cushion-forming perennial herb, with yellow flowers, sometimes mistaken for a

Saxifraga cernua NODDING SAXIFRAGE

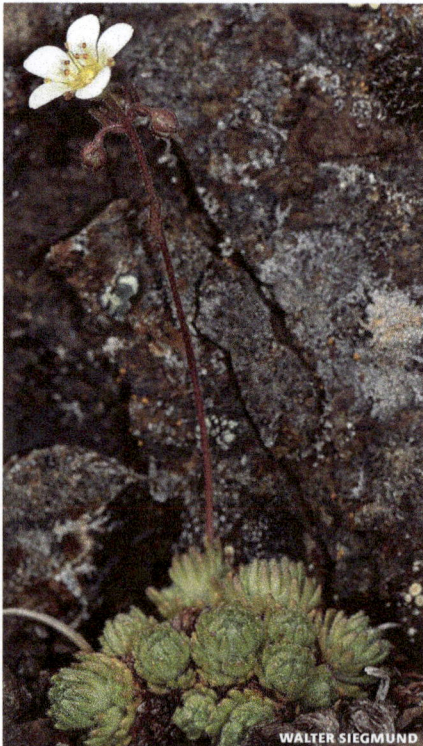
Saxifraga cespitosa TUFTED ALPINE SAXIFRAGE

moss due to its small, compact form; flower stems absent or to about 1 cm above the cushion of leaves. Leaves alternate along stem, 1–3 mm long, entire, tightly overlapping; margins hairy; dead leaves persistent, gray in color. Flowers inconspicuous, solitary, less than 5 mm wide, sessile or raised on short peduncles; petals five, yellow, 1 mm long, surrounded by sepals of similar length. Fruit a reddish capsule with two divergent beaks. Flowering very early in the season.

Where Found uncommon in alpine rock crevices, tundra fell-fields, and frost boils.

Similar Species once identified as a vascular plant rather than a moss, *Saxifraga eschscholtzii* is hard to confuse with other species.

♦ *Saxifraga flagellaris* Willd. ex Sternb.
WHIPLASH SAXIFRAGE
Saxifraga setigera Pursh

Habit reddish perennial herb, with yellow flowers, from dense fibrous roots and many long reddish runners (stolons); stems 3–15 cm tall, purplish glandular-hairy; stolons threadlike, leafless, to 10 cm long, with small, rooting rosette of leaves at end; the slender stolons lead to the common name of 'whiplash saxifrage'. Leaves basal and along stem, evergreen; basal leaves fleshy, oblong-lanceolate, covered in coarse hairs; stem leaves smaller, alternate, and sessile. Flowers 1–3, in a terminal, leafy, hairy, slightly branched inflorescence; petals five, bright yellow, sometimes with darker yellow spots near the center; sepals shorter, green. Fruit a capsule, 8–10 mm long, with two divergent beaks.

Where Found occasional in tundra on north side of Alaska Range.

Similar Species No other plant in Denali has yellow flowers and red runners.

♦ *Saxifraga hirculus* L.
YELLOW MARSH SAXIFRAGE

Habit perennial herb, with a single yellow flower, from a freely branched stem-base and fibrous roots; flowering stems several, erect, 5–20 cm tall, brownish or yellowish hairy, at least above. Leaves basal and several along stem; lanceolate to spatulate, hairless; stem leaves smaller. Flowers single, initially nodding, atop an upright, leafy, hairy stalk; petals bright yellow, broadly ovate, often orange-spotted near base; sepals green; stamens 10. Fruit a capsule with two beaks.

Where Found occasional at mid- to high-elevations in seeps, rivulets, and wet meadows.

Similar Species distinguished from other saxifrage by its yellow flowers, long linear leaves and several alternate stem leaves.

♦ *Saxifraga oppositifolia* L.
PURPLE MOUNTAIN SAXIFRAGE

Habit cushion-forming perennial herb, with pink flowers, from highly branched, trailing stems; flowering stems several cm tall; plants generally smooth but bristle-fringed on

Saxifraga flagellaris WHIPLASH SAXIFRAGE

Saxifraga hirculus YELLOW MARSH SAXIFRAGE

leaves and calyx. Leaves leathery, clasping, lowermost bract scalelike; opposite on stem. Flowers single, terminal; petals five, bright pink to lilac (rarely white); sepals green-purplish, hairy; stamens 10. Fruit a capsule with two beaks. Flowering early in the season.

Where Found occasional in alpine tundra, gravelly areas, fellfields, talus.

Similar Species not easily mistaken with any other *Saxifrage,* but could be confused with other pink-flowered cushion-forming alpine plants; the tight basal rosettes of leaves and two fused carpels inside the flower are distinctive.

◆ *Saxifraga rivularis* L.
ALPINE BROOK SAXIFRAGE

Habit tufted perennial herb; stems 2–10 cm tall, glabrous or finely glandular-hairy; bulblets often present in axils of basal leaves. Leaves fan-shaped or reniform, 3–5-lobed, 3–10 mm wide, glabrous; stem leaves smaller, sometimes entire. Flowers 1–5; petals white or purplish, nearly twice as long as sepals. Fruit a capsule with two widely divergent beaks.

Where Found uncommon in alpine tundra, moist gravelly soils, cliffs.

◆ *Saxifraga serpyllifolia* Pursh
THYME-LEAVED SAXIFRAGE

Habit small cushion-forming or matted perennial herb, with yellow flowers, from long, somewhat rhizomatous, branched stem-bases; flowering stems several, 2–6 cm

tall, with stalked glands. Leaves evergreen, shiny, leathery, in a tiny circular basal rosette, blunt-tipped, 3–10 mm long; stems with only a few scalelike bracts. Flowers about 1 cm in diameter; petals ovate, bright yellow, with darker yellow spots; sepals smaller, purplish; stamens 10. Fruit a capsule.

Where Found uncommon in alpine tundra, gravelly sites, and scree, on both sides of Alaska Range.

Similar Species *Saxifraga hirculus* is another saxifrage with solitary yellow flowers, but that species has well-developed stem leaves.

Saxifraga rivularis ALPINE BROOK SAXIFRAGE

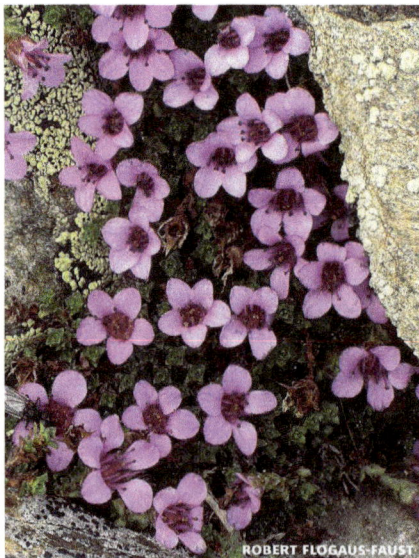

Saxifraga oppositifolia
PURPLE MOUNTAIN SAXIFRAGE

Saxifraga serpyllifolia THYME-LEAVED SAXIFRAGE

♦ *Saxifraga tricuspidata* Rottb.
PRICKLY SAXIFRAGE
Habit cushion-forming perennial herb, with yellow or white flowers, from branched stem-base; flowering stems numerous, 3–10 cm tall, minutely glandular-hairy to smooth, with a few small, opposite leaves. Leaves mostly in rosettes of leathery brown-green leaves, with reddish, persistent, dead leaves below, evergreen and turning red in fall; leaves elongate, with 3 sharp teeth at tip. Flowers 3–10, in an open, unbranched terminal cyme; petals five, ovate, yellow or white, often with yellow spots at base and orange spots at tip; stamens 10. Fruit a two-beaked capsule. Flowering early to mid-summer.
Where Found in dry disturbed sites on slopes and gravel bars, most often at high-elevations.
Similar Species can be distinguished from the similar *Saxifraga bronchialis* by the toothed leaves.

URTICACEAE
Nettle Family
Urtica NETTLE
(Latin *urtica*, nettle; derived from Latin *uro*, to burn.)

♦ *Urtica dioica* L. STINGING NETTLE
Habit perennial herb from strong rhizomes; stems erect, to about 1 m tall simple or branched, solitary, smooth except for a few stinging hairs and bristles. Leaves opposite, narrowly lanceolate to ovate, blades 5–12 cm long, coarsely toothed, stalked; stipules 5–15 mm long. Flowers greenish, either male or female in an axillary panicle on same (female flowers usually uppermost) or different plants; corolla absent; sepals 4. Fruit an ovoid, flattened achene, 1–1.5 mm long.
Where Found uncommon in rich moist soil of thickets, open woods, streambanks.
Note plants covered with irritating hairs.

VIBURNACEAE
Arrow-Wood Family

1 Small perennial herb	*Adoxa*
1 Shrubs	2
2 Leaves simple	*Viburnum*
2 Leaves compound	*Sambucus*

Adoxa MUSKROOT
(Greek, without glory, i.e. insignificant.)

♦ *Adoxa moschatellina* L. MUSKROOT
Habit inconspicuous perennial herb, from a fleshy-scaled rhizome; stems erect, 5–15 cm tall; flowering stalks slender, unbranched, with and a terminal inflorescence; plants with a musky odor. Leaves two, opposite, at

NPS - JACOB FRANK
Saxifraga tricuspidata PRICKLY SAXIFRAGE

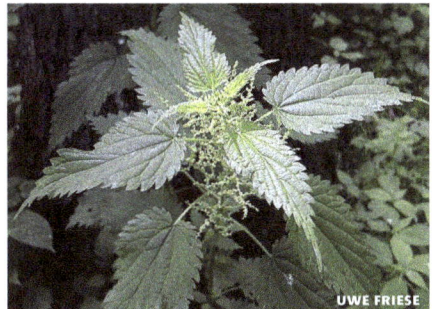
UWE FRIESE
Urtica dioica STINGING NETTLE

base of stem, long-petioled, divided into deeply lobed leaflets with entire margins, dark green above, paler below. Flowers in an inflorescence of five yellowish green flowers: one four-petaled flower facing upwards, and four smaller five-petaled flowers surrounding it, giving the flowering head a box-like appearance; topmost flower with 4 styles and 4 deeply divided anthers, the other four flowers with 5 styles and anthers. Fruit a dry drupe with 4–5 nutlets. Flowering early spring, fruits in mid-summer.

Where Found occasional in moist thickets, most often on south-aspect slopes.

Similar Species no other Denali plant has the distinctive box-like arrangement of its flowers.

Sambucus ELDERBERRY
(Latin name of the elder.)

♦ *Sambucus racemosa* L. **RED ELDERBERRY**

Habit deciduous, erect shrub, 1–4 m tall; twigs thick, soft, pithy, usually somewhat glaucous; bark dark reddish brown, warty. Leaves opposite, stalked, large, compound, pinnately divided into 5–7 elliptic to lanceolate leaflets, often asymmetric at base, abruptly sharp-pointed at tip, margins sawtoothed. Flowers numerous, in an ovate to conical cluster, 4–8 cm across; petals white or cream, fused at base into a short tube, 5-lobed at tip, the lobes longer than tubes. Fruit a red, berrylike, globose drupe, 5–6 mm wide, not glaucous, with 3 small, smooth to wrinkled stones, each enclosing a seed.

Where Found thickets, woods, hillsides, streambanks.

Viburnum SQUASHBERRY
(Ancient Latin name.)

♦ *Viburnum edule* (Michx.) Raf.
SQUASHBERRY, HIGHBUSH-CRANBERRY

Habit deciduous, sprawling to erect shrub, to 2 m tall, spreading from rhizomes and by layering; twigs glabrous; bark smooth, reddish to gray. Leaves opposite, 3-lobed; leaf underside hairy along veins; margins toothed. Flowers in flat-topped cymes from lateral branches, each with 20–40 small blossoms; each flower about 6–8 mm wide; corolla fused, the five petals lobed nearly to base; stamens five, style short, with 3 stigma lobes. Fruit a juicy berry-like drupe, to 1 cm wide; drupes typically bright red, with several in a cluster; each drupe with a single large, flat seed. Flowering early to mid-summer; fruits mature in autumn, the leaves turning red when the plants are in fruit.

Where Found common in productive spruce and mixed forests and also occurring in boreal and subalpine meadows

Traditional Uses the fruits are tart, but have a pleasant flavor, and are used for preserves and beverages, particularly jelly, cranberry-like sauce, and tea; because of the large seed, the berries are usually juiced first, not cooked or eaten plain; berries are often picked after the first frost.

Sambucus racemosa **RED ELDERBERRY**

Adoxa moschatellina **MUSKROOT**

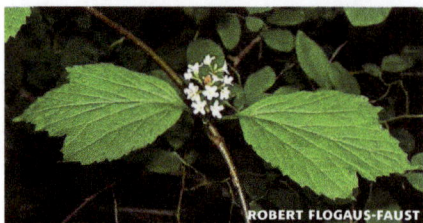

Viburnum edule **SQUASHBERRY**

VIOLACEAE
Violet Family

Viola VIOLET
(The Latin name.)

1   Flowers yellow. 2
1   Flowers violet, blue, or white 3
2   Sepals fringed with hairs in upper half, and with a conspicuous purple-black stripe; style head smooth . . . . *V. biflora*
2   Sepals not fringed with hairs, without a purple-black stripe; style head bearded . . . *V. glabella*
3   Flowers white . . . . *V. renifolia*
3   Petals violet or blue. 4
4   Plants with obvious leafy stems at flowering time 5
4   Plants without obvious leafy stems at flowering time 6
5   Stipules ragged or sharp-toothed (at least basally), reddish-brown or greenish with reddish brown flecks . . . . *V. adunca*
5   Stipules wax-papery, white or greenish, more or less entire . . . . *V. langsdorfii*
6   Plants with stolons. . . . . *V. epipsila*
6   Plants without stolons. 7
7   Stipules joined to petiole; petals not bearded; leaves hairy on upper surface . . . . . . *V. selkirkii*
7   Stipules not joined to petiole; at least the 2 lateral petals bearded; leaves essentially smooth 8
8   Stipules jagged or sharp-toothed (at least basally), reddish-brown or greenish, often with reddish brown flecks; flowers small, 5–15 mm long . . . . *V. adunca*
8   Stipules entire, white or greenish; flowers larger, 16–25 cm long . . . . *V. langsdorfii*

Viola adunca Sm. HOOK-SPUR VIOLET
Habit perennial herb from a rhizome, without stolons; stems lacking in spring but developing as season progresses, usually hairy, 2–10 cm tall. **Leaves** basal and along stem; basal leaves ovate to heart-shaped, blades 1–4 cm long, smooth or hairy, margins with blunt teeth; stem leaves similar; stipules jagged or sharp-toothed, reddish-brown or greenish, 3–10 mm long. **Flowers** single, axillary; petals 5, blue to deep violet, lower petal to 15 mm long including the 4- to 8-mm long spur; lowest 3 petals often whitish with purple markings, lateral pair white-bearded; sepals 5, lanceolate. **Fruit** a smooth capsule, 6–10 mm long; seeds dark brown.

Where Found may be present in Denali in moist woods, thickets, meadows.

♦ *Viola biflora* L. ARCTIC YELLOW VIOLET
Habit creeping perennial herb, with yellow flowers, from a rhizome and fibrous roots, without stolons; stems ascending to erect, 5–15 cm tall, smooth, leafless except on uppermost section. **Leaves** basal, round or kidney-shaped, with crenate margins. **Flowers** single to several on a slender stalk; petals yellow with brown-purple stripes; sepals green, lanceolate. **Fruit** a capsule, opening by three valves to release numerous seeds.

Where Found occasional in and near the mountains in meadows, rocky slopes, shrublands and tundra.

Similar Species Only one other yellow-flowered violet occurs in Denali (*Viola glabella*, which is less common and only found in wetter areas on south side of Alaska Range), in that species the leaf tips are distinctly pointed.

Traditional Uses violets are edible either raw or cooked.

♦ *Viola epipsila* Ledeb. DWARF MARSH VIOLET
Habit perennial herb, with pale purple flowers; plants stemless, leaves and flowers growing from a long thin rootstock and long stolons. **Leaves** basal, thin, heart-shaped to ovate, hairless, the margins toothed. **Flowers** solitary, on slender peduncles directly from the rootstock, the peduncles with a single

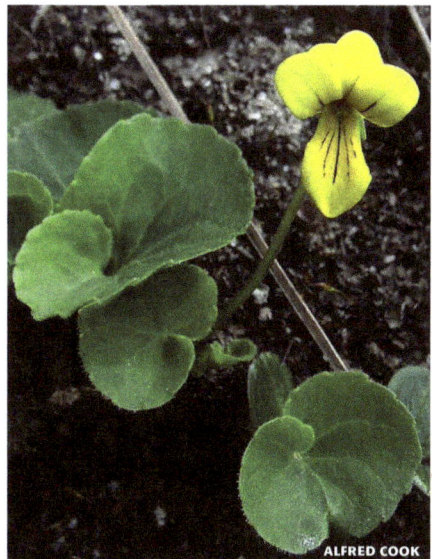

Viola biflora ARCTIC YELLOW VIOLET

bract; petals five, pale purple with dark veins on lower petals. Fruit a capsule opening by three valves to release numerous seeds.

Where Found occasional in riparian areas, meadows and shrub thickets

Similar Species this species very similar to the more common blue-flowered violet, *Viola langsdorffii;* that species has longer petals, a stout rootstock, and a short leafy stem; other similar violets are *Viola selkirkii,* which has hairy leaves, and *V. renifolia* which has white flowers with purple stripes.

Traditional Uses violets are edible either raw or cooked.

♦ *Viola glabella* Nutt. STREAM VIOLET

Habit perennial herb, from a scaly, fleshy rhizome, without stolons; ascending to erect, smooth, 5–30 cm tall. Leaves basal and along stem; basal leaves heart-shaped to kidney-shaped, with blades 5–9 cm long and 4–8 cm wide, margins toothed; stem leaves similar. Flowers single, axillary; petals 5, deep yellow, the lower petal 8–14 mm long including the 1–2 mm long spur; lower petals with purplish markings on inner side, the lateral pair bearded; sepals 5, lanceolate. Fruit a smooth capsule; seeds brown to black.

Where Found uncommon in moist woods to alpine tundra.

♦ *Viola langsdorffii* Fisch. ex Ging.
ALEUTIAN VIOLET

Habit perennial herb, from a rhizome, without stolons; stems erect, smooth or sometimes sparsely hairy, 5–15 cm long, with large stipules. Leaves basal, hairless, ovate to kidney-shaped, with a pointed tip; margins with rounded teeth. Flowers single at end of a long, leafless stalk; petals five, bluish violet, bearded, 15–25 mm long. Fruit a capsule opening by three valves to release numerous seeds.

Where Found occasional in rich subalpine meadows and turfy alpine tundra; much more common south of the Alaska Range crest than to the north.

Similar Species the other purple-flowered violets in Denali are *Viola selkirkii,* which has hairy leaves, and the uncommon *V. renifolia,* which has white flowers with purple stripes.

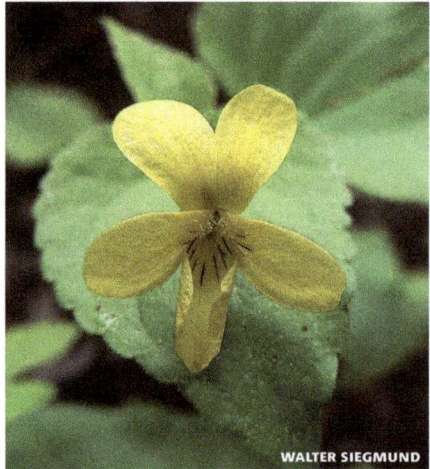

WALTER SIEGMUND

Viola glabella STREAM VIOLET

ALFRED COOK

Viola epipsila DWARF MARSH VIOLET

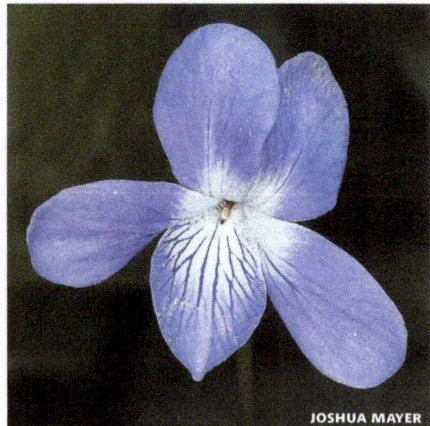

JOSHUA MAYER

Viola langsdorffii ALEUTIAN VIOLET

Viola epipsila also similar, with blue flowers with shorter petals (9-16 mm), and no stems.

Traditional Uses violets are edible either raw or cooked.

Viola renifolia Gray
KIDNEY-LEAF WHITE VIOLET

Habit perennial herb, from a short rootstalk, without stolons, plants to 15 cm tall; stems absent. Leaves basal, heart- to kidney-shaped; blades 1.5-3.5 cm long, 2-6 cm wide, petioles hairy, margins toothed; stipules lanceolate, toothed. Flowers single, axillary; petals 5, white, the lower petal 10-15 mm long including the 1-2 mm spur; lower 3 petals beardless, with purplish markings; sepals 5, lanceolate. Fruit a nearly globe-shaped capsule, usually purple; seeds brown.

Where Found may be present in Denali in moist woods.

◆ *Viola selkirkii* Pursh ex Goldie
GREAT-SPUR VIOLET

Habit perennial herb, from a slender, elongate rootstock, without stolons, plants 5-10 cm tall; stems lacking. Leaves basal, heart-shaped to ovate, with a narrow sinus, 1-3 cm long, 1-3 cm wide; upper surface hairy, especially along veins, underside glabrous; margins with rounded teeth; petioles 1.5-5 cm long. Flowers single, axillary on a naked stalk; petals 5, pale violet, the lower petal 8-13 mm long including the 3-5 mm long spur; sepals 5, lanceolate. Fruit a nearly round capsule, seeds pale brown.

Where Found uncommon in moist woods, thickets.

Viola selkirkii GREAT-SPUR VIOLET

AMARYLLIDACEAE
Daffodil Family

Allium WILD ONION
(Latin name of garlic.)

◆ *Allium schoenoprasum* L. WILD CHIVES

Habit perennial herb, from an oblong-ovate, scaly bulb, the bulbs clustered; flowering stems erect, 20-50 cm tall, stout, cylindric, smooth. Leaves all basal, linear, sheathing bulb and lower stem, round in cross-section, becoming hollow towards the tips. Flowers in a rounded umbel, with many tightly clustered small pink-purple flowers; petals fused, with six lobes, light pink to purple with dark purple midveins; in bud, the whole umbel enclosed in two overlapping papery bracts, pale purple in color, faded but persistent during flowering. Fruit a capsule, releasing numerous black seeds.

Where Found uncommon along streams and in meadows near eastern boundary of park.

Similar Species No other plant in Denali has lilac-colored flowers in a dense umbel, with linear, onion-like basal leaves.

Traditional Uses related to domestic onions and garlic, and plants have an onion-like scent; leaves used as a kitchen herb, fresh or dried.

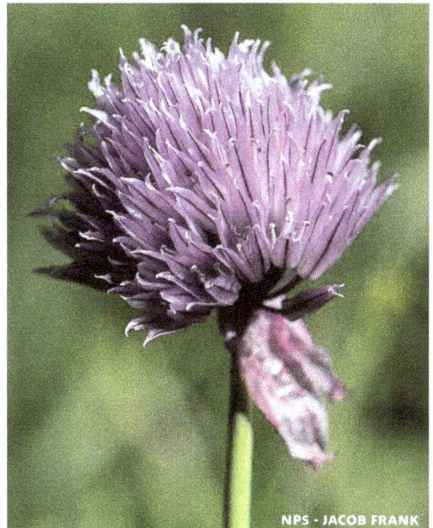

Allium schoenoprasum WILD CHIVES

ARACEAE
Arum Family

1 Tiny aquatic plant floating on water surface . . .
. . . . *Lemna*
1 Larger plant of wetlands, with a showy white
spathe . . . . *Calla*

Calla WATER ARUM
(Ancient name.)

◆ *Calla palustris* L.
WATER ARUM, WATER-DRAGON
Habit perennial aquatic herb from a long,
creeping rhizome; stems solitary, 10–20 cm
tall. Leaves basal, blades ovate to broadly
heart-shaped, entire, 5–12 cm long, 4–11 cm
wide; petioles 1–3 dm long. Flowers numerous,
densely packed, in a cylindric spike 2–3 cm
long, the spike subtended by a bract (spathe)
similar to the leaves in shape but white colored and smaller. Fruit berry-like, ovate, red,
5 mm long; seeds 6 to 8.
Where Found occasional in shallow water of
bogs and ponds.

Lemna DUCKWEED
(Greek, in allusion to the swamp habitat.)

Lemna trisulca L.
IVY-LEAF DUCKWEED
Habit tiny aquatic annual herb; fronds usually submerged with several generations attached to each other, oblong, 6–10 mm long,
2–3 mm wide, obscurely 3-nerved, often
without rootlets; young plants produced
from pouches on either side near the junction of the stalk and the plant body
Where Found uncommon in in ponds and
quiet water.

ASPARAGACEAE
Asparagus Family

Maianthemum
FALSE SOLOMON'S-SEAL
(Greek, May and flower, referring to the sea-
son of flowering.)

◆ *Maianthemum stellatum* (L.) Link
STARRY FALSE SOLOMON'S-SEAL
Smilacina stellata (L.) Desf.
Habit perennial herb from a slender, pale
rhizome; stems erect to arched-ascending
more or less flexuous above, 20–50 cm tall,
finely hairy. Leaves 5 to 11, alternate (often in
2 rows), flat to folded, lanceolate, 5–15 cm
long, 2–4 cm wide, tapering to a sessile,
somewhat clasping base, short-hairy on underside, margins entire. Flowers an unbranched, 2–7 cm long, terminal cluster of
5–10 (15), spreading, stalked flowers, the
stalks at least as long as the flowers; flowers
creamy-white, star-shaped, of 6 similar, distinct tepals, the tepals 4–7 mm long, narrowly oblong to lanceolate, spreading;

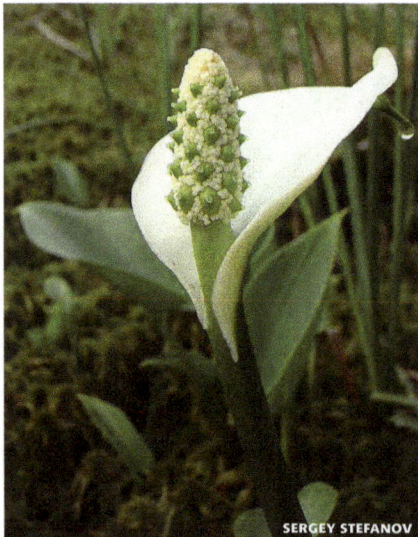

SERGEY STEFANOV
Calla palustris WATER ARUM

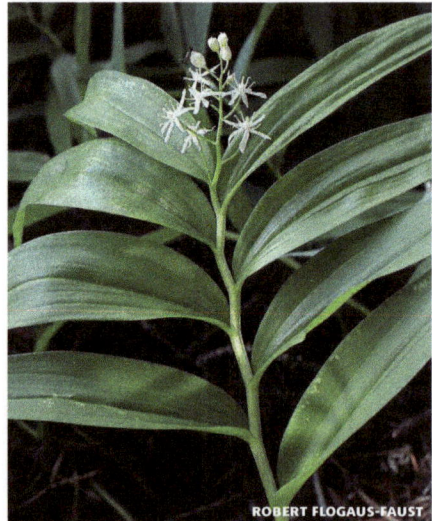

ROBERT FLOGAUS-FAUST
Maianthemum stellatum
STARRY FALSE SOLOMON'S-SEAL

stamens 6, shorter than tepals; pistil 1, 3-chambered. Fruit a globe-shaped berry, 7–10 mm wide, at first greenish yellow with darker stripes, when mature dark blue to reddish black; seeds usually 1 or 2.

Where Found occasional in open woods.

CYPERACEAE
Sedge Family

1 Flowers either male or female; achene enclosed in a flask-shaped perigynium subtended by open scales . . . . *Carex*
1 Flowers mostly perfect; achene not enclosed in a perigynium; perianth bristle-like. 2
2 Spikes with 1 (rarely 2) achenes. *Rhynchospora*
2 Spikes with several to many achenes. 3
3 Styles thickened toward base, persistent to form a conspicuous tubercle atop achene. *Eleocharis*
3 Styles not thickened (but achenes may be abruptly sharp-pointed) 4
4 Perianth bristles 10 or more. . . . . . . *Eriophorum*
4 Perianth bristles 8 or fewer 5
5 Spikes with subtending, leafy bracts 6
5 Spikes with lower scales slightly modified, not leafy 7
6 Involucral bract solitary, not leaflike or spreading, appearing as an extension of stem; stems round in cross-section . . . . *Schoenoplectus*
6 Involucral bracts 2 or more, some of them leaflike and more or less spreading; stems rounded-triangular in cross-section . . . . *Scirpus*
7 Lower scales of the spikes short, not more than half as long as spikes. . . . . *Eleocharis*
7 Lower scales of the spikes long, nearly as long as or longer than the spikes . . . . . . *Trichophorum*

Carex SEDGE
(Greek, to cut, on account of the sharp-edged leaves.) Key adapted from Hultén (1968).

KEY TO CAREX GROUPS
1 Perigynia open, with unsealed margins, merely wrapped around achene (former *Kobresia*). . . . . Group I
1 Perigynia closed, except at tip 2
2 Spike single, terminal . . . . Group II
2 Spikes more than 1 (in Group 2, often densely congested into headlike inflorescence) 3
3 Spikes sessile, with both male and female flowers . . . . Group III

3 Spikes stalked, usually either male or female, sometimes with both male and female flowers 4
4 Stigmas 2, perigynia plano-convex or biconvex . . . . Group IV
4 Stigmas 3, perigynia mostly trigonous (3-angled) 5
5 Beak of perigynia with truncate mouth. . . . . Group V
5 Beak of perigynia with more or less bidentate mouth. . . . . Group VI

GROUP I
1 Spike linear, with numerous small 2-flowered spikelets. . . . . *C. myosuroides*
1 Spike oval-oblong, with several spikelets 2
2 Spikelets with 1 staminate and 2–3 pistillate flowers; scales 4–5 mm long . *C. borealipolaris*
2 Spikelets either male or female, 1- to 2-flowered; upper spikelets staminate, lower spikelets pistillate; scales shorter . . . . *C. simpliciuscula*

GROUP II
1 Male and female flowers on different plants . 2
1 Male and female flowers on same spike 3
2 Stigmas 2; perigynia smooth. . . . . *C. gynocrates*
2 Stigmas 3; perigynia pubescent . . *C. scirpoidea*
3 Stigmas 2 4
3 Stigmas 3 6
4 Stems straight, slender; spike globular, apiculate . . . . *C. capitata*
4 Stems shorter, mostly curved; spike oblong . . 5
5 Perigynia slender, spreading or reflexed at maturity; female scales shed early . . *C. micropoda*
5 Perigynia short and broad. . . . . *C. nardina*
6 Perigynia with short beak or beakless. 7
6 Perigynia lanceolate, with long beak. 9
7 Perigynia beakless, flat. . . . . *C. leptalea*
7 Perigynia with short beak, trigonous. 8
8 Perigynia ovate, shiny, dark brown. *C. obtusata*
8 Perigynia obovate . . . . *C. rupestris*
9 Perigynia reflexed; pistillate scales falling early 10
9 Perigynia not reflexed. 11
10 Perigynia 6–7 mm long; stems triangular in cross section, curved at base . . . . *C. pauciflora*
10 Perigynia mostly shorter; stems circular in cross section, straight at base . . . . . . *C. microglochin*
11 Spike slender, scales light brown with pale midvein . . . . *C. anthoxanthea*
11 Spike ovate, dark, with dark-brown scales. . . . . *C. nigricans*

GROUP III

1 Spikes with female flowers at base, male flowers at tip 2

1 Spikes with male flowers at base, female flowers at tip 3

2 Rhizome long, creeping . . . . . . *C. chordorrhiza*

2 Rhizome short; plant tufted . . . . *C. diandra*

3 Margin of perigynia more or less winged 4

3 Margin of perigynia not winged 7

4 Spikes aggregate, forming dense head . . . . *C. phaeocephala*

4 Spikes not distinctly aggregated into one head 5

5 Perigynia lanceolate or ovate-lanceolate . . . . *C. crawfordii*

5 Perigynia ovate 6

6 Beak of perigynia terete, not margined toward tip . . . . *C. praticola*

6 Beak of perigynia flattened, serrulate and margined to tip . . . . *C. foena*

7 Perigynia white-puncticulate, beakless or with short, not decidedly bidentate beak 8

7 Perigynia not white-puncticulate, with long, bidentate beak 15

8 Plant loosely tufted, with stolons; spikes few, few-flowered; perigynia beakless or very short-beaked 9

8 Plants tufted, stolons absent; spikes usually several, densely flowered; perigynia beaked (beak sometimes very short) 11

9 Spikes with male flowers at top, female flowers at base; perigynia slightly inflated, biconvex, abruptly short-beaked, with promment nerves. . . . . *C. disperma*

9 Spikes with female flowers at top, male flowers below; perigynia compressed, beakless 10

10 Spikes aggregated at top of stem; perigynia obovate-oval, with slightly prominent nerves . . . . *C. tenuiflora*

10 Spikes separated from one another; perigynia slightly conical at tip, with prominent nerves . . . . *C. loliacea*

11 Spikes 2–4, aggregate . . . . *C. lachenalii*

11 Spikes 4–8, the lower separated from others 12

12 Beak of perigynia scabrous on margins 13

12 Beak of perigynia smooth . . . . *C. lapponica*

13 Beak and upper part of perigynium with distinct hyaline-margined suture . . . . . . *C. brunnescens*

13 Beak sometimes slightly cleft at tip, but lacking distinct suture along body of perigynium . . . 14

14 Perigynia less than 2 mm long; heads small, few-flowered, subglobose; scales dark-colored . . . . *C. bonanzensis*

14 Perigynia 2–3 mm long; heads (usually) larger, elongated, many-flowered; scales yellowish or yellowish brown . . . . *C. canescens*

15 Perigynia tapering toward base, more or less appressed . . . . *C. laeviculmis*

15 Perigynia broadest near base, spreading 16

16 Leaves flat, soft, 2–4 mm broad . . . . *C. arcta*

16 Leaves grooved, rigid, 1–3 mm broad 17

17 Stems straight, about 40 cm tall, longer than leaves . . . . *C. interior*

17 Stems shorter, curved, often shorter than leaves . . . . *C. echinata*

GROUP IV

1 Perigynia long-beaked . . . . *C. saxatilis*

1 Perigynia beakless or very short-beaked 2

2 Inflorescence nearly flat-topped, of 3–5 dark spikes at top of stem; lowest bract with sheath . . . . *C. eleusinoides*

2 Inflorescence otherwise 3

3 Lowest bract with sheath; perigynia almost beakless 4

3 Lowest bract sheathless or very short-sheathed 6

4 Sheath of lowest bract 2–4 mm long, with black auricles at mouth . . . . *C. bicolor*

4 Sheath of lowest bract lacking black auricles . 5

5 Perigynia fleshy, translucent when ripe; terminal spike mostly male . . . . *C. aurea*

5 Perigynia dry; terminal spike female above . . . . *C. garberi*

6 Lowest bract shorter than inflorescence . . . . *C. bigelowii*

6 Lowest bract as long as inflorescence or longer 7

7 Stems aphyllopodic (lower leaves reduced to scales or sheaths); spikes drooping . *C. lyngbyei*

7 Stems phyllopodic (but sterile shoots often aphyllopodic); spikes erect 8

8 Perigynia nerved, ovate; sheaths brown or yellowish-brown . . . . *C. kelloggii*

8 Perigynia nerveless, rounded; sheaths purplish . . . . *C. aquatilis*

GROUP V

1 Bracts without sheaths, or with only very short sheaths 2

1 Bracts with distinct sheath 16

2 Spikes small, short, few-flowered, aggregated, sessile; plant low-growing, with narrow leaves 3

2 Spikes larger, with more numerous flowers; plant mostly taller 4

3 Perigynia glabrous; beak cylindrical. . *C. supina*

3 Perigynia pubescent . . . . *C. deflexa*

4 Terminal spike male (rarely with 1–2 undeveloped perigynia at base) 5

4 Terminal spike with female flowers at top. . . 10

5 Female scales broad, obovate, small, 1.5–2.5 mm long; perigynia small; spikes approximate; leaves narrow . . . . *C. stylosa*

5 Female scales larger, acute; spikes more or less remote; leaves wider 6

6 Scales tipped with a long bristle . . . .
. . . . *C. macrochaeta*

6 Scales blunt, acute, or short-acuminate 7

7 Perigynia ciliate-serrulate in margin . . . .
. . . . *C. atrofusca*

7 Perigynia smooth in margin 8

8 Stems aphyllopodic (lower leaves reduced to scales or sheaths), with short, scalelike leaves below, and well-developed stem leaves 9

8 Stems phyllopodic, lacking stem leaves . . . .
. . . . *C. microchaeta*

9 Scales obtuse, with midvein obscure toward apex
. . . . *C. podocarpa*

9 Scales light colored, with excurrent midvein . . .
. . . . *C. spectabilis*

10 Female scales awned, or at least cuspidate . . 11

10 Pistillate scales not awned or cuspidate 12

11 Perigynia beakless; lower scales shorter than perigynia . . . . *C. adelostoma*

11 Perigynia short-beaked; lower scales longer than perigynia . . . . *C. buxbaumii*

12 Perigynia 5 mm long, much longer than scales, membranous, broad, light green-yellowish, abruptly contracted into very narrow beak; spikes numerous, cylindrical; stems nearly winged . . . . *C. mertensii*

12 Perigynia shorter, dull green to brown when ripe; stems not winged 13

13 Scales with conspicuous white-hyaline margins
. . . . 14

13 Scales lacking conspicuous white-hyaline tip or margins . . . . *C. atrosquama*

14 Stems slender; scales small, shorter than perigynia; perigynia somewhat inflated, with slightly serrulate beak . . . . *C. media*

14 Stems stiff; scales about as long as perigynia 15

15 Scales obtuse, rounded, reddish-brown, with hyaline margin and green midvein *C. parryana*

15 Scales somewhat acute, purplish-black, with hyaline tip and margin . . . . *C. albonigra*

16 Perigynia pubescent . . . . *C. concinna*

16 Perigynia glabrous 17

17 Leaves narrow, 0.2–1 mm broad, grooved or involute 18

17 Leaves broader, flat (or grooved in *C. limosa*) 19

18 Lowest bract with awl-like blade; scales purplish-black . . . . *C. glacialis*

18 Lowest bract without blade; scales yellowish-white . . . . *C. eburnea*

19 Female spikes drooping, more or less densely flowered 20

19 Female spikes erect, loosely flowered 23

20 Lowest bract leaflike, over-topping spikes; scales narrower than perigynia, long-acuminate . . . . .
. . . . *C. magellanica*

20 Lowest bract subulate, not over-topping spikes
. . . . 21

21 Female spike mostly solitary; leaves grooved . .
. . . . *C. limosa*

21 Female spikes 2–3; leaves flat 22

22 Female spikes 2–10-flowered; perigynia 3–3.5 mm long; stems obtusely triangular *C. rariflora*

22 Female spikes 10–25-flowered; perigynia 4–4.5 mm long; stems sharply triangular *C. pluriflora*

23 Leaves glaucous; perigynia elliptic, nearly beakless . . . . *C. livida*

23 Leaves green; perigynia ovate, long-beaked . . .
. . . . *C. vaginata*

GROUP VI

1 Leaves without swollen cross-partitions 2

1 Leaves with swollen cross-partitions 9

2 Perigynia flat, ciliate-finely toothed on margin 3

2 Perigynia trigonous, not ciliate-finely toothed on margin; scales light brown or hyaline 5

3 Terminal spike with male flowers at top; plants with slender rhizomes . . . . *C. petricosa*

3 Terminal spike with pistillate flowers at top; plants tufted or with ascending stolons 4

4 Perigynia with rounded base, about as long as scales, beak with indistinctly bidentate mouth; scales purplish-black . . . . *C. atrofusca*

4 Perigynia narrowly lanceolate, long-beaked, longer than scales; beak distinctly bidentate; scales dark-brown . . . . *C. fuliginosa*

5 Spikes on threadlike stalks, drooping when ripe; beak indistinctly bidentate, hyaline-margined 6

5 Spikes short, erect, on stout stalks; beak distinctly bidentate 8

6 Terminal spike with female flowers at top . . . . .
. . . . *C. krausei*

6 Terminal spike male 7

7 Leaves flat; perigynia nerveless except for marginal nerve; beak ciliate on margin *C. capillaris*

7 Leaves bristle-like, involute; perigynia with few nerves; beak smooth . . . . *C. williamsii*

8 Lower perigynia deflexed; beak curved, about as long as body . . . . *C. flava*

8 Lower perigynia not deflexed; beak nearly straight, distinctly shorter than body *C. viridula*

9 Perigynia firm, somewhat leathery; teeth of beak awl-like, 1 mm long or longer . . . . *C. atherodes*

9 Perigynia membranaceous; teeth of beak shorter 10

10 Perigynia pubescent . . . . *C. lasiocarpa*

10 Perigynia glabrous 11

11 Leaves involute, narrow; plant with long stolons . . . . *C. rotundata*

11 Leaves flat, broader; long stolons absent . . . 12

12 Plant tall; female spikes 5–12 cm long; perigynia and scales yellowish green 13

12 Plants shorter; female spikes 1–2 cm long; scales purplish-black 14

13 Plants with folded leaves 2–4 mm wide, with silica pimples on upper surface; female spikes dense; perigynia horizontally spreading, rounded, ovate or flask-shaped, abruptly contracted into abbreviated beaks; stems triangular above (the angles rounded) . . . . *C. rostrata*

13 Plants with flat leaves 4–12 mm wide, without silica pimples on upper surface; female spikes loose; perigynia divergent, gradually tapering into short beaks; stems sharply triangular above . . . . *C. utriculata*

14 Spikes long-stalked, drooping . . . . . *C. saxatilis*

14 Spikes sessile, erect . . . . *C. membranacea*

Carex adelostoma V.I. Krecz.
CIRCUMPOLAR SEDGE
Habit perennial sedge, from rhizomes; stems 15–35 cm tall. **Leaves** flat, 2–3 mm wide; sheaths purplish red, blades on lower sheaths absent. **Flowers** in 3–4 erect to nodding spikes; terminal spike gynaecandrous (with both female and male flowers, the female flowers uppermost), or sometimes staminate; lateral spikes pistillate, sessile, the lowermost separated from the upper ones; female scales about as long as the perigynia, ovate, brown with a green median stripe. **Perigynia** elliptic, rounded at base and tip, grayish green; beak absent; stigmas 3. **Where Found** uncommon in moist to wet places.

♦Carex albonigra Mackenzie
BLACK-AND-WHITE SEDGE
Habit tufted perennial sedge, from short rhizomes; stems 10–30 cm tall, much ex-

ceeding the leaves. **Leaves** flat with revolute margins, 2–5 mm wide; lower leaves not much reduced; sheaths reddish toward base; bract subtending the spikes leaflike, about equal to or shorter than the spikes. **Flowers** in usually 3 spikes, the terminal spike with both female and male flowers, the female flowers uppermost; the lower 1 or 2 spikes of female flowers; female scales broadly ovate, about as long as and wider than the perigynia, pointed at tip, reddish black, roughly pimpled, with white translucent margins and tips. **Perigynia** ovate, flattened, reddish black, margins translucent; beak short, less than 0.4 mm long; stigmas 3.

Where Found uncommon in dry to moist alpine turf.

Carex anthoxanthea J. & C. Presl
GRASSY-SLOPE ARCTIC SEDGE
Habit perennial sedge, from creeping scaly rhizomes; stems 5–35 cm tall, roughened above, equaling the leaves or nearly so. **Leaves** 2 to 4 from near base, flat, 1–3 mm wide, erect or recurved; lower leaf blades absent or reduced; sheaths short, whitish green; bract subtending the spike absent. **Flowers** in a solitary spike, with both female and male flowers, the male flowers uppermost (androgynous), or sometimes of all female or all male flowers, 1–3 cm long; female scales lanceolate, dark brown with 1–3-nerved green centers; lower scales awn-tipped, upper scales round-tipped. **Perigynia** lanceolate to narrowly elliptic, yellowish green to straw-colored; beak about 1 mm long; stigmas 3 (or rarely 2).

Where Found occasional in bog and wet meadows.

♦Carex aquatilis Wahlenb. WATER SEDGE
Habit tufted perennial sedge, from yellow to brown, cord-like, creeping rhizomes; stems sharply angled, with smooth edges, sur-

Carex albonigra BLACK-AND-WHITE SEDGE

rounded by old dried leaves and sheaths, to about 1 m tall. Leaves mostly basal, flat to channeled, 3–8 mm wide, glabrous, nearly as long as stem; lowest bract leaf-like, equaling or exceeding inflorescence. Flowers either male or female in separate spikes (but on same stem); terminal spikes (2–4) erect, male, 1–2 cm long; lateral spikes (2–7) erect, female, 1–10 cm long; female scales ovate to oblong-ovate, sharp-pointed, reddish to purplish brown with a pale midvein, usually much narrower than the perigynia. Perigynia obovate, often flattened, pale green; beak very short; stigmas 2.

Where Found abundant in shallow water of ponds, fens, wet meadows, from low- to high-elevations; may form nearly pure stands.

Similar Species *Carex bigelowii* similar, but in that species, scales blunt-tipped, spikes not longer than 3 cm, and the lowest bract is not taller than the inflorescence.

Carex arcta Boott
NORTHERN CLUSTER SEDGE

Habit densely tufted perennial sedge, from elongate fibrous roots; stems 30–60 cm tall, about as long as the leaves, sharply triangu-

lar, scabrous in upper part. Leaves many, about as long as stem, flat, 2–3 mm wide, glaucous, borne on lower part of stem; sheaths tight; lowermost bract awnlike, about 0.5–2 cm long. Flowers in 5–15 spikes in a 3–5-cm long, dense, cylindric or narrowly ovate head, occasionally with a few spikes separate below, with both female and male flowers, the female flowers uppermost, the male flowers inconspicuous; female scales ovate, covering about half of the perigynia, pointed, nearly colorless to brownish, with green midribs and hyaline margins. Perigynia ovate, green, dark green or brownish, minutely white-dotted; beak about 1 mm long; stigmas 2.

Where Found uncommon in bogs and marshes where it may form large tussocks.

♦ Carex atherodes Spreng.
AWNED SEDGE, SLOUGH SEDGE

Habit loosely tufted perennial sedge, from long-creeping rhizomes or stolons; stems 3–15 dm tall, exceeding the leaves, smooth, reddish tinged at the bases. Leaves flat, 3–10 mm wide, smooth or often stiff-hairy on underside near base of blade; lower sheaths breaking into threads, middle to upper sheaths with long hairs; bracts subtending the male spikes small or absent, those subtending female flowers leaflike, well-developed, and longer than the inflorescence. Flowers in 4–10 spikes, the upper 2–6 spikes with male flowers, separate, unstalked, erect, narrowly linear, the lower 2–4 spikes with female flowers, widely separated, short-

Carex aquatilis WATER SEDGE

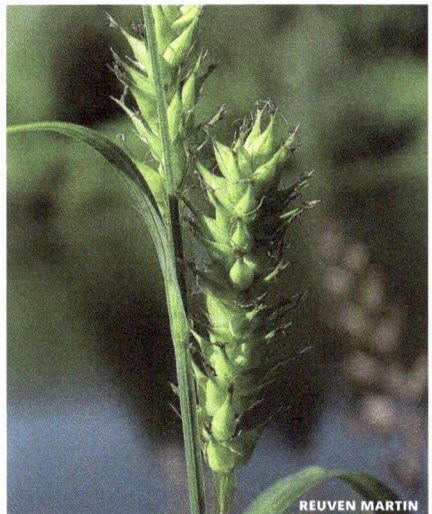

Carex atherodes AWNED SEDGE

stalked, erect, narrowly cylindric; female scales narrowly ovate, awn-tipped, the awns nearly as long as the scales, dull reddish brown with 3-nerved green centers. Perigynia lanceolate to broadly ovate, yellowish green or light brown, somewhat inflated, strongly ribbed; beak toothed; stigmas 3.

Where Found uncommon on shores, wet meadows.

Carex atrofusca Schkuhr
DARK-BROWN SEDGE

Habit tufted perennial sedge, also with stolons; stems 1–3 dm tall, obtusely triangular, usually nodding. Leaves clustered at base, 2–4 mm wide; lowest bract long-sheathing. Flowers in a terminal spike with both female and male flowers, the female flowers uppermost, and in 2–3 lateral spikes drooping on slender peduncles; scales black with somewhat lighter margins and midribs. Perigynia ovate-lanceolate, dark with lighter base, tapering to long, hyaline-margined beak; stigmas 3.

Where Found occasional in wet places in alpine tundra.

♦ *Carex atrosquama* Mackenzie
BLACK-SCALE SEDGE

Habit tufted perennial sedge, with a prominent black-colored spike, from short rhizomes; stems scabrous, 20–80 cm tall, much exceeding the leaves. Leaves 2–5 mm wide; sheaths reddish; lowest bract leaflike, more or less equal in length to the inflorescence.

Flowers in 3–4 erect, clustered, short-stalked spikes, the inflorescence 2.5–3 cm long; terminal spike with the female flowers above, male flowers below; lateral spikes with only female flowers; female scales black, lanceolate, shorter than the perigynia. Perigynia elliptic, green (maturing to brown), papillose; beak purple; stigmas 3.

Where Found occasional in floodplains and meadows in the subalpine zone north of the Alaska Range crest.

Similar Species *Carex media* is similar; in that species the female scales have a transparent margin, and the spikes and perigynia are smaller.

♦ *Carex aurea* Nutt. **GOLDEN-FRUIT SEDGE**

Habit loosely tufted perennial sedge, from long rhizomes or stolons; stems 5–35 cm tall, arising singly or a few together, shorter than the leaves. Leaves 3 to 6 per stem, flat, 2–4 mm wide, borne on lower third of stem; sheaths tight; bracts subtending female spikes leaflike, the lower over-topping the inflorescence. Flowers in 3–5 spikes, the terminal spike of male flowers (occasionally with a few perigynia), the lower 2–4 spikes of female flowers, stalked, the stalks to 4 cm long; female scales ovate, shorter and narrower than the perigynia, reddish brown, with greenish midribs and translucent margins. Perigynia globe-shaped, inflated, bright orange with a powdery surface, beakless; stigmas 2 (or rarely 3).

Where Found occasional in wet meadows, fens, shores.

Carex atrosquama BLACK-SCALE SEDGE

Carex aurea GOLDEN-FRUIT SEDGE

◆ *Carex bicolor* Bellardi ex All.
TWO-COLOR SEDGE

Habit loosely tufted perennial sedge, from short rhizomes or stolons; stems 5–20 cm tall, roughened above, longer than the leaves. **Leaves** 3 to 6 per stem, flat, 3–6 cm long, 1–3 mm wide, borne on lower third of stem, lower leaves reduced; sheaths tight; bracts subtending female spikes scalelike, the lowermost barely reaching the top of the inflorescence. **Flowers** in 3–5 spikes clustered at top of stem, the terminal spike with both female and male flowers, the female flowers uppermost; lateral spikes of female flowers; female scales ovate, shorter and narrower than perigynia, purplish black to reddish brown, with greenish midribs and translucent margins. **Perigynia** ovate, inflated, dull green to bluish white with a powdery surface, beakless; stigmas 2.

Where Found occasional on wet sands and silty shores.

◆ *Carex bigelowii* Torr. ex Schwein.
BIGELOW'S SEDGE
Carex lugens Holm

Habit tufted perennial sedge (sometimes forming large tussocks in the lowlands) or rhizomatous, with sharply angled, stiff stems 10–40 cm tall, exceeding the leaves, slightly rough below inflorescence. **Leaves** mostly basal, flat to revolute, 2–4 mm wide; lowest bract scale- or leaf-like, shorter than inflorescence. **Flowers** in erect spikes, with usually a single terminal male spike and 2–3 lateral female spikes; female scales purplish black to black, equal or shorter than the perigynia, unawned. **Perigynia** green, spotted or mottled purple-black on upper half; beak short; stigmas 2 (or rarely 3).

Where Found abundant at low-elevations to the alpine zone in Denali, usually in poorly drained sites on acidic, peaty soil such as bogs, muskeg and tussock tundra.

Similar Species *Carex microchaeta* superficially similar, but has three stigmas (not two), the pistillate spikes are often peduncled and nodding, and the scales are acute-tipped.

Carex bonanzensis Britt. **YUKON SEDGE**

Habit tufted perennial sedge; stems 25–40 cm tall, stiff, sharply 3-angled, scabrous near tip. **Leaves** 2–3 mm wide, flat, rough-margined, shorter than stems; lowest bract 15–30 mm long, the upper scalelike. **Flowers** in 7–10 spikes, the lower distant, with both female and male flowers, the female flowers uppermost; staminate flowers conspicuous in terminal spike; scales thin, keeled. **Perigynia** small, about 1.5 mm long, exceeding the scales, dark straw-colored, sharp-edged; stigmas 2.

Where Found occasional on river terraces, shores, seeps.

Carex borealipolaris S.R. Zhang
SIBERIAN BOG SEDGE
Kobresia sibirica (Turcz.) Boeckeler

Habit densely tufted perennial sedge, from grayish hairy fibrous roots; stems wiry, 10–30 cm tall. **Leaves** numerous, linear to thread-like, about 1 mm wide, shorter than stems; sheaths brownish, persistent, crowded, shredded; involucral bracts solitary, scalelike. **Flowers** in a solitary, terminal, erect spike, the spikelets each with 1 male and 2 or 3 female flowers, the male flower above the female flowers; scales brown, the margins broadly translucent. **Fruit** a 3-angled achene; stigmas 3.

Carex bicolor TWO-COLOR SEDGE

Carex bigelowii BIGELOW'S SEDGE

Where Found uncommon in dry sphagnum mats and heathy tundra.

Carex brunnescens (Pers.) Poir.
BROWNISH SEDGE

Habit somewhat tufted perennial sedge, from short rhizomes; stems lax, 10–60 cm tall, usually longer than the leaves. Leaves numerous, borne on lower part of stem, flat, 1–2.5 mm wide, roughened toward tip; lowermost leaves often reduced; sheaths tight; lowest bract prolonged, the upper lowermost bract scalelike. Flowers in 5–10 spikes in a 3–5 cm, narrow, interrupted inflorescence; spikes with both female and male flowers, the female flowers uppermost, the male flowers inconspicuous; female scales ovate, covering about 2/3 of the perigynia, white-hyaline with greenish center and usually more or less tinged with brown. Perigynia ovate, dark green or brownish, minutely white-dotted, beak about 0.5 mm long; stigmas 2.

Where Found occasional in meadows, subalpine slopes, muskegs.

♦ *Carex buxbaumii* Wahlenb.
BROWN BOG SEDGE, BUXBAUM'S SEDGE

Habit loosely tufted perennial sedge, from slender, creeping rhizomes or stolons; stems 20–80 cm tall, exceeding the leaves. Leaves 2–4 mm wide, flat, with revolute margins and channeled toward base; lower leaves reduced; sheaths purplish red toward base, shredding; bracts subtending the spikes leaflike, about equaling the inflorescence. Flowers in 2–5 spikes, the terminal spikes with both female and male flowers, the female uppermost; the lower spikes 1–4, of female flowers, short-stalked, erect; female scales lanceolate, narrower than the perigynia, awn-tipped, dark with light center. Perigynia elliptic, bluish green; beak tiny, less than 0.3 mm long; stigmas 3.

Where Found occasional in bogs, fens, wet meadows and shores.

♦ *Carex canescens* L. **SILVERY SEDGE**

Habit loosely to densely tufted perennial sedge, from elongate fibrous roots; stems 10–50 cm tall, sharply triangular, rough below the inflorescence, about as long as the leaves. Leaves flat, soft, 2–4 mm wide, glaucous green; subtending bract absent. Flowers in 4–8 unstalked spikes, these either male and female and in the same spike, female flowers

Carex buxbaumii BROWN BOG SEDGE

Carex canescens SILVERY SEDGE

above the male; uppermost spikelets bunched together, the lower more widely spaced; female scales ovate, whitish, translucent. Perigynia ovate, gradually tapering to beak with scabrous margins, light green to straw-colored, becoming brown; stigmas 2.

Where Found bogs, fens, pond margins, beaver impoundments.

Similar Species *Carex brunnescens* and *Carex lapponica* superficially look very similar; *C. brunnescens* has two-beaked perigynia, *C. lapponica* is not tufted, and the perigynia beak is smooth.

♦ *Carex capillaris* L. HAIR-LIKE SEDGE

Habit densely tufted perennial sedge, from fibrous roots; stems to 40 cm tall. Leaves flat, firm, 1–4 mm wide, much shorter than stem; lowest bract leaf-like, of variable length. Flowers male or female and in separate spikes; terminal spike male, more or less erect; lateral spikes female, drooping; female scales ovate, light brown, wider and shorter than the perigynia. Perigynia ovate, brown, gradually tapering to a transparent beak 2–3 mm long; stigmas 3.

Where Found occasional in moist to wet places, especially on lowland to subalpine gravel bars and meadows, more rarely in moist to wet areas in the alpine zone.

Similar Species *C. krausei* is closely related (but less common), and varies in having a terminal spike with female flowers above male flowers (instead of a staminate terminal spike) and more needle-like leaves.

Carex capitata Sol. CAPITATE SEDGE

Habit loosely tufted perennial sedge, from short ascending rhizomes; stems 10–35 cm tall, equaling or much longer than leaves. Leaves 2 to 4 per stem, from near base, thread-like and involute, less than 1 mm wide; lower leaves absent or reduced to scales. Flowers in a solitary, erect, ovate spike, with both female and male flowers, the male flowers up-

permost; bractless; female scales ovate, slightly shorter than the perigynia, dark brown, margins translucent. Perigynia ovate to nearly globe-shaped, pale green, flattened; beak about 0.5 mm long; stigmas 2.

Where Found occasional in shrubby open woods, muskegs, meadows, tundra.

♦ *Carex chordorrhiza* L.f. ROPE-ROOT SEDGE

Habit creeping perennial sedge, with several erect stems arising from horizontal cord-like stolons, these usually buried in wet moss, or in standing water; stems 10–35 cm tall, arising singly, branched at base into several sterile shoots much longer than the leaves. Leaves 1–3 mm wide, shorter than stem; sheaths purplish; lowest bract reduced to a scale. Flowers in 2–8 sessile, few-flowered spikes; spikes with male flowers above, female below; female scales ovate, usually longer than the perigynia, brown with translucent margins and a pale midvein. Perigynia ovate, with prominent veins, brown; stigmas 2.

Where Found occasional on wet shores and shallow water of ponds (sometimes locally abundant, forming patches by means of its creeping stolons).

Similar Species distinctive because of its cordlike stems and aquatic habitat.

Carex capillaris HAIR-LIKE SEDGE

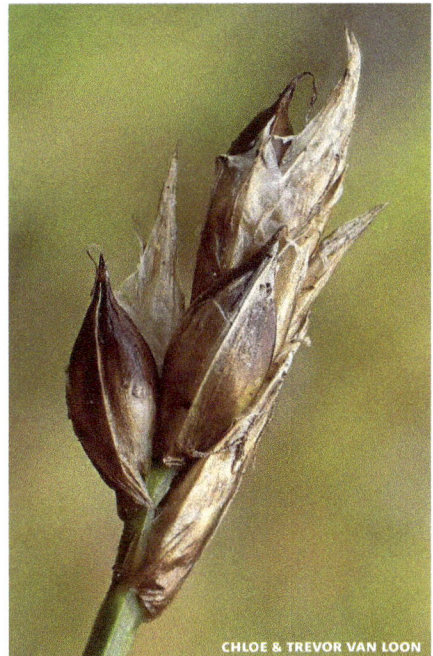

Carex chordorrhiza ROPE-ROOT SEDGE

♦ *Carex concinna* R. Br. LOW NORTHERN SEDGE

Habit loosely tufted perennial sedge, from slender, scaly rhizomes; stems 10–20 cm tall, arching. **Leaves** basal, flat, dark green, 1–3 mm wide, about half the height of stem; sheaths purplish. **Flowers** in a tightly clustered inflorescence, with a single terminal male spike, and 2–3 sessile, lateral female spikes; female scales reddish brown with a greenish midrib and transparent-ciliate margins. **Perigynia** green, twice as long as the scales (giving spikes a bicolored appearance), distinctly hairy; stigmas 3 (or rarely 2).

Where Found common in well-drained spruce forests, river terraces, and warm, open slopes mostly in the lowlands but extending into the lower alpine zone in Denali.

Similar Species the sheathing bracts and pubescent perigynia help distinguish this species from other sedges.

♦ *Carex crawfordii* Fern. CRAWFORD'S SEDGE

Habit densely tufted perennial sedge, from fibrous roots; stems stiff, 10–60 cm tall, longer than the leaves. **Leaves** flat, 1–3 mm wide, borne on lower third of stem; sheaths tight; bracts subtending the spikes reduced, inconspicuous. **Flowers** in 3–12 spikes, grouped into a compact, narrow head, with both female and male flowers, the female uppermost; female scales elliptic, light brown with greenish center, somewhat shorter and narrower than perigynia. **Perigynia** narrowly lanceolate, pale green or straw-colored, more or less flattened, margins narrowly winged nearly to base; beak 1 mm long; stigmas 2.

Where Found uncommon in moist, open woods and slopes.

♦ *Carex deflexa* Hornem. NORTHERN SEDGE

Habit loosely tufted perennial sedge, from slender branched rhizomes; stems very slender, densely clustered, 5–25 cm tall, longer than or sometimes equaling the leaves, purple-tinged at base. **Leaves** short, flat, channeled toward base, 1–2 mm wide, smooth or somewhat rough, borne on lower third of stem; sheaths tight, persistent; bracts subtending the female spikes leaflike, longer than the inflorescence, upper bracts smaller. **Flowers** in 2–8 spikes; terminal spike of male flowers; lower spikes few-flowered, of female flowers, 2 to 4 of these located near the terminal male spike, and one or more usually near base of stem; female scales ovate, usually shorter and somewhat wider than perigynia, purplish brown, with lighter midribs and translucent margins. **Perigynia** elliptic to broadly ovate, greenish to straw-colored, finely short-hairy; beak short, to about 0.5 mm long; stigmas 3.

Where Found uncommon in open woods, especially where sandy or gravelly, or on mats of lichen.

CHLOE & TREVOR VAN LOON

Carex concinna LOW NORTHERN SEDGE

RYAN DURAND

Carex deflexa NORTHERN SEDGE

♦ *Carex diandra* Schrank
LESSER PANICLED SEDGE
Habit somewhat tufted perennial sedge, from fibrous roots; stems stiff, 30–70 cm tall, roughened on the angles, longer than the leaves. Leaves 3 or 4 per stem, mostly near base, flat, 1–3 mm wide, margins inrolled; sheaths conspicuously red-dotted with glandular projections on side nearest stem; bracts inconspicuous, similar to the female scales. Flowers in numerous spikes, erect or mostly ascending, in a brownish head 2–5 cm long, with both female and male flowers, the male flowers uppermost; female scales ovate, equaling or slightly longer than the perigynia, brown, the margins translucent. Perigynia broadly ovate, straw-colored to usually dark brown, shining; beak as long as body; stigmas 2.
Where Found occasional in marshes, wet meadows, and in water on floating bog margins.

♦ *Carex disperma* Dewey **SOFT-LEAF SEDGE**
Habit loosely tufted perennial sedge, from rhizomes and elongated, light brown stolons; stems 10–60 cm tall, slender and weak, shorter than or about as long as the leaves. Leaves numerous, soft, thin, 1–2 mm wide, borne on lower part of stem; sheaths tight; bracts reduced, awl-like. Flowers in 2–4 separated, ascending spikes, the uppermost closer together; with both female and male flowers, the male flowers uppermost but inconspicuous; female scales ovate, shorter or longer than perigynia. Perigynia elliptic, light green, minutely whitish dotted, beakless; stigmas 2.
Where Found occasional in mossy muskegs, shores, bogs, wet meadows.

Carex eburnea Boott **BRISTLE-LEAF SEDGE**
Habit tufted perennial sedge, from long rhizomes; stems 10–30 cm tall, arising singly or a few together, longer than the leaves, reddish tinged at the bases. Leaves 3 to 6 per stem, inrolled, 0.5 mm wide, often recurved-spreading, borne on lower third of stem;

Carex diandra **LESSER PANICLED SEDGE**

Carex disperma **SOFT-LEAF SEDGE**

sheaths tight; bracts subtending female spikes tubular-sheathing, bladeless. Flowers in 3–5 spikes, the terminal spike stalked, 4–8 mm long, of male flowers; lower spikes 2–4, erect, long-stalked, of female flowers; female scales ovate, shorter than the perigynia, whitish with green midrib, often tinged yellowish brown, margins translucent. Perigynia ovate to elliptic, dark green to black, shining; beak short, to 0.3 mm long, translucent at tip; stigmas 3.

Where Found uncommon in moist to dry woods and slopes.

♦ *Carex echinata* Murray
STAR SEDGE, STELLATE SEDGE

Habit densely tufted perennial sedge, from fibrous roots; stems wiry, 10–35 cm tall, about equaling the leaves, roughened above. Leaves 2 to 4 per stem, flat or channeled, 1–2 mm wide, borne on lower half of stem; lower leaves reduced; sheaths tight, more or less red-dotted on front; bracts subtending female spikes short to prolonged and hairlike, to 2 cm long. Flowers in 2–7 spikes; terminal spike unstalked, 4–10 mm long, with both male and female flowers, the female flowers uppermost; lower spikes 1–4, ascending, of female flowers; female scales ovate, shorter than perigynia, light brown with wide hyaline margins and green midrib. Perigynia ovate, greenish yellow to brownish; beak 1–1.5 mm long; stigmas 2.

Where Found uncommon in bogs and fens.

Carex echinata STAR SEDGE

♦ *Carex eleusinoides* Turcz. ex Kunth
GOOSEGRASS SEDGE

Habit loosely tufted perennial sedge; stems 25–35 cm tall, erect, exceeding the leaves, somewhat flattened. Leaves flat or channeled, about 2 mm wide; uppermost bract equal to inflorescence, lower bract typically longer. Flowers in usually four, erect, cylindric spikes, 1–2 cm long; terminal spike with both female and male flowers, the female flowers uppermost; the lateral female but generally with a few staminate flowers at tip; scales black with conspicuous greenish midvein. Perigynia flattened on one side, nerveless, pale grayish green; beak very short; stigmas 2.

Where Found occasional on gravelly or sandy streambanks and terraces.

Carex foenea Willd. **BRONZE SEDGE**
Carex aenea Fern.

Habit tufted perennial sedge, from fibrous roots; stems 30–80 cm tall, exceeding the leaves. Leaves flat, weak, 2–4 mm wide, borne on lower half of stem but not crowded at base; sheaths tight; bracts subtending the spikes reduced and inconspicuous. Flowers in 4 to 10 unstalked spikes, with both female and male flowers, the female flowers uppermost; the male portion often elongated; lower spikes remote; scales acute, yellowish brown, with translucent margins and three-ribbed green center. Perigynia ovate, light green to straw-colored or brownish, more or less flattened, abruptly contracted into the beak; stigmas 2.

Where Found dry, sandy slopes.

♦ *Carex fuliginosa* Schkuhr **SHORT-LEAF SEDGE**
Carex misandra R. Br.

Habit densely tufted perennial sedge, from fibrous roots; stems single, smooth, 10–30 cm tall, much longer than the leaves. Leaves curved, 1–3 mm wide, yellowish green; sheaths light-brown; lowest bract leaf-like or

Carex eleusinoides GOOSEGRASS SEDGE

reduced, shorter than inflorescence. Flowers in 3–4, drooping, long-stalked spikes; terminal spike with female flowers above, male flowers below; lateral spikes of only female flowers; female scales brown or black with pale green midvein and papery margins, shorter than the perigynia. Perigynia lanceolate, pale brown, margins ciliate, beaked, darker toward tip; stigmas 3.

Where Found occasional in alpine turf, seeps, and well-drained tundra (primarily north of Alaska Range crest).

Similar Species *Carex podocarpa* is another alpine sedge with drooping spikes, but its perigynia are black (not brown) and not two-beaked.

♦ *Carex garberi* Fernald ELK SEDGE
Habit loosely tufted perennial sedge, from long rhizomes or stolons; stems 5–60 cm tall, longer than leaves. Leaves 3 to 6 per stem, flat above, channeled below, 2–4 mm wide, borne on lower third of stem, lower leaves reduced; sheaths tight; bracts subtending female spikes short-sheathing, leaflike, the lowermost equal to or slightly longer than inflorescence. Flowers in 3–5 spikes; terminal spike entirely of male flowers or with a few female flowers at top; lateral spikes 2–4, of female flowers on long, rough peduncles; female scales ovate, slightly shorter and narrower than the perigynia, brown with prominent light center and translucent margins. Perigynia globe-shaped, inflated, bluish

gray-green with a powdery surface, beakless; stigmas 2.

Where Found occasional in moist mud of shores and wet meadows.

Carex glacialis Mack. GLACIAL SEDGE
Habit densely tufted perennial sedge, from short fibrous roots; stems wiry, stiff, 5–15 cm tall, longer than the leaves. Leaves 3 to 8 per stem, stiff, recurved, flat at base, channeled above, about 1 mm wide, borne on lower half of stem; lower leaves reduced; sheaths straw-colored to purplish brown; bracts subtending female spikes inconspicuous, scalelike. Flowers in 2–4 spikes; terminal spike unstalked, 2–6 mm long, of male flowers; lower spikes 1–3, 2–5 mm long, of female flowers; female scales ovate to elliptical, about as long as the perigynia, brownish, with greenish to straw-colored midrib and translucent margin. Perigynia ovate to lanceolate, yellowish green to straw-colored; beak short, to 0.5 mm long, translucent; stigmas 3.

Where Found may be present in Denali on gravelly or sandy alpine tundra.

♦ *Carex gynocrates* Wormsk. ex Drejer
NORTHERN BOG SEDGE
Carex dioica subsp. *gynocrates* (Nyman) Hultén
Habit perennial sedge from long, slender rhizomes or stolons; stems stiff, obtusely triangular, 5–30 cm tall, single or a few together, longer than the leaves. Leaves 3 to 5

Carex fuliginosa SHORT-LEAF SEDGE

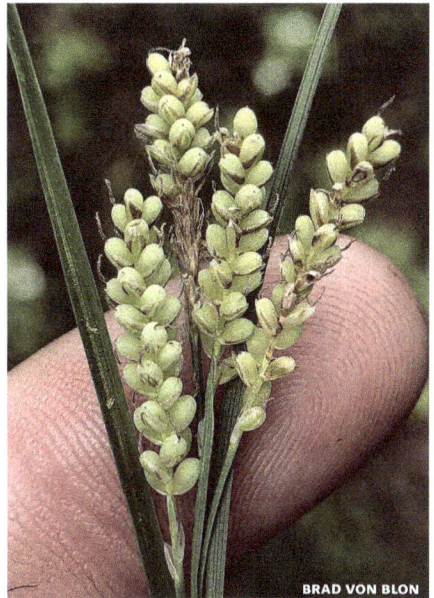

Carex garberi ELK SEDGE

per stem, about 0.5 mm wide, involute, stiff, borne on lower half of stem; lower leaves reduced, persisting; sheaths tight; bracts absent. Flowers in a solitary spike, usually with both female and male flowers, the few male flowers uppermost (or sometimes spikes with all male or female flowers); female scales ovate, shorter but wider than perigynia, reddish brown to brown, lighter at center. Perigynia ovate, yellowish to brownish black, inflated, shiny, reflexed when ripe; beak about 0.5 mm long; stigmas 2.

Where Found occasional in fens, streambanks, wet meadows; often where calcareous.

Carex incurviformis Mack.
CURVED-SPIKE SEDGE
Carex maritima var. *incurviformis* (Mackenzie) Boivin

Habit loosely tufted perennial sedge, from long-creeping, scaly rhizomes; stems 2–10 cm tall, arising singly, shorter than the leaves. Leaves mostly basal, 4 to 7 per stem, flat at base, inrolled above, to 1.5 mm wide; sheaths tight, translucent; bract absent. Flowers in 3–5 spikes, densely clustered into a broadly ovate head; with both female and male flowers, male flowers uppermost; female scales broadly ovate, shorter than perigynia, brown, lighter at center, margins translucent. Perigynia ovate, brown, shiny; beak short, about 1 mm long; stigmas 2.

Where Found uncommon on shores, bogs, alpine tundra, heathlands.

♦ Carex interior L.H. Bailey INLAND SEDGE
Habit densely tufted perennial sedge, from ascending dark-colored rhizomes; stems slender, wiry, 15–50 cm tall, usually longer than the leaves, roughened above on the angles. Leaves about 3 per stem, a fresh green color, flat or slightly channeled, 1–3 mm wide, scabrous in upper part, borne on lower half of stem; lower leaves reduced; sheaths tight; bracts scalelike, inconspicuous. Flowers in 2–6 spikes; terminal spike with both male and female flowers, the female flowers uppermost (sometimes almost all male or almost all female); lower spikes 1 to 5, ascending to widely spreading, of female flowers only; female scales broadly ovate, shorter than perigynia, yellowish brown, with greenish midrib and whitish, translucent margins. Perigynia ovate to deltoid, greenish or pale brown; beak 1/3 to 1/4 length of the body; stigmas 2.

Where Found uncommon in muskegs, bogs, seeps.

Carex kelloggii W. Boott KELLOGG'S SEDGE
Carex lenticularis var. *lipocarpa* (Holm) L.A.Standl.

Habit perennial tufted sedge, with very short ascending stolons; stems slender, 2–7 dm tall. Leaves flat or channeled, 1.5–3 mm wide; sheaths straw-colored to reddish brown; lowest bract leaflike, upper bracts reduced. Flowers in 4–6 spikes; terminal spike male, 1–4 cm long; lateral spikes 3–5, female, 15–35 mm long; scales dark with hyaline margins and lighter center. Perigynia flattened biconvex, light green, granular, beak usually black-tipped; stigmas 2.

Where Found wet meadows, lake and river shores, gravel bars.

Carex gynocrates **NORTHERN BOG SEDGE**

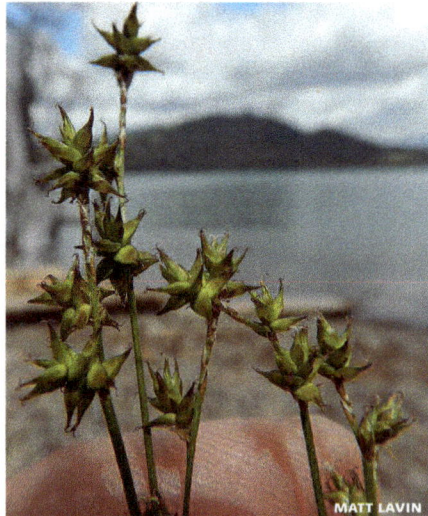

Carex interior **INLAND SEDGE**

Carex krausei Boeckeler **KRAUSE'S SEDGE**
Carex capillaris subsp. *krausei* (Boeckl.) Böcher

Habit tufted perennial sedge, from fibrous roots; stems 10–40 cm tall. Leaves flat, 1–4 mm wide, borne on lower third of stem, nearly as long as stems, sometimes longer; sheaths tight, brownish to straw-colored; bracts subtending female spikes leaflike, the upper bract smaller. Flowers in 4–7, erect to ascending spikes, with both female and male flowers, female flowers uppermost; female scales ovate, rounded to pointed, brownish, with green centers, with translucent margins, shorter but often wider than the perigynia. Perigynia lanceolate to ovate, green to greenish brown; beak about 0.5 mm long; stigmas 3.

Where Found uncommon on lakeshores, streambanks, muskegs, tundra, open woods.

Similar Species resembles the more common *Carex capillaris* but *C. krausei* much smaller, the terminal spike has both female and male flowers (female flowers uppermost), the perigynia with shorter beaks which are finely spinulose on margins.

♦ ***Carex lachenalii*** Schkuhr
ARCTIC HARE-FOOT SEDGE

Habit tufted perennial sedge, from elongate fibrous roots; stems stiff, curved, dark green, 10–30 cm tall, longer than leaves; lowest bract reduced to a scale and inconspicuous. Leaves 1–2 mm wide; sheaths brownish; bract lowermost bract scalelike. Flowers in 2–5, sessile, clustered, compact spikes; female flowers above and male flowers below; female scales oblong-ovate, shorter than the perigynia, brown with a pale center. Perigynia lanceolate with scabrous margins, brownish green when young, yellow-brown when mature; stigmas 2.

Where Found occasional in alpine snowbeds and poorly drained places on both sides of Alaska Range crest in Denali (and usually on north-facing slopes).

Carex lachenalii **ARCTIC HARE-FOOT SEDGE**

Similar Species the female flowers above the male, the compact head, and the tufted habit help identify this sedge.

Carex laeviculmis Meinsh.
SMOOTH-STEM SEDGE

Habit densely tufted perennial sedge, from short slender rhizomes; stems 30–70 cm tall, longer than the leaves, roughened above. Leaves 3 to 5 per stem, flat, weak, 1–2 mm wide, borne on lower half of stem; lower leaves reduced; sheaths tight; bracts of lowest spike hairlike, to 5 cm long, upper bracts smaller. Flowers in 3–8 spikes; terminal spike unstalked, 4–7 mm long, with both male and female flowers, the female flowers uppermost; lower spikes 2 to 7, ascending to widely spreading, of female flowers only; female scales ovate, sharply keeled, shorter than perigynia, yellowish brown, with conspicuous green midrib. Perigynia ovate, plano-convex, greenish brown to light green; beak 1/3 to 1/4 length of the body; stigmas 2.

Where Found uncommon in wet woods and muskegs, open gravelly slopes.

Carex lapponica O. Lang **LAPLAND SEDGE**

Habit somewhat tufted perennial sedge, from short fibrous rhizomes; stems 15–30 cm tall, longer than the leaves. Leaves several, flat, 1–3 mm wide, borne on lower part of stem; sheaths tight; lowermost bract awl-like, about 0.5–2 cm long. Flowers in 3–7 well-separated spikes; with both female and male flowers, female flowers uppermost, male flowers inconspicuous; female scales ovate, covering about 3/4 of perigynia, pale brown with greenish midrib. Perigynia ovate, light green, minutely whitish dotted, biconvex; beak about 0.2 mm long; stigmas 2.

Where Found wet meadows, bogs.

Similar Species resembles *Carex canescens* but is less distinctly tufted, stems and leaves more slender, spikes smaller and fewer-flowered, and perigynia smooth and not serrulate on margins.

♦ ***Carex lasiocarpa*** Ehrh.
SLENDER SEDGE, WOOLLY-FRUIT SEDGE
Carex lanuginosa Michx.

Habit loosely tufted perennial sedge, from long, creeping rhizomes; stems slender, smooth, obtuse-angled, to 1 m tall, single or a few together, wine-red at base. Leaves 2 to 5 per stem, flat at base, strongly inrolled above, 1–2 mm wide, borne on lower 3/4 of stem; lower leaves reduced; sheaths tight, cross-wrinkled, yellowish to brownish tinged, the lowest sheaths breaking into threads; bracts subtending lowest spike leaflike, usually longer than the inflorescence. Flowers in 3–5 spikes; terminal 2 (sometimes 1), long-stalked, with many male flowers; lower 2–3 spikes cylindric, female, unstalked to short-stalked, erect; female scales lanceolate to narrowly ovate, long-pointed or awned, more or less fringed, narrower than perigynia, purplish brown, with a broad pale mid-vein and dull translucent margins. Perigynia ovate to nearly globe-shaped, dull brownish green, somewhat inflated, densely soft-hairy; beak 0.8–1.2 mm long, deeply biden-tate; stigmas 3.

Where Found bog margins, shallow pools.

Carex leptalea Wahlenb.
BRISTLE-STALKED SEDGE

Habit densely tufted perennial sedge, from slender rhizomes; stems filiform 10–50 cm tall, slightly shorter to longer than the leaves. Leaves 2 to 3 per stem, flat or channeled, very narrow (about 1–2 mm wide), borne on lower 1/4 of stem; sheaths tight; bract absent. Flowers in a solitary spike, male flowers above female; female scales much shorter than

perigynia, brownish with a greenish mid-section. Perigynia cylindric or elliptic, yellowish green to pale green, shining, beakless; stigmas 3.

Where Found occasional in mossy woods, bogs, lakeshores.

♦*Carex limosa* L. **SHORE SEDGE**

Habit perennial sedge, from long, creeping rhizomes or stolons, and rusty-reddish roots; stems 15–50 cm tall, arising singly or a few together, much longer than the leaves, usually reddish at base. Leaves 1 to 3 per stem, 1–2 mm wide, deeply channeled, borne on lower third of stem; lower leaves reduced; sheaths tight, sometimes breaking into threads at base; bracts subtending lowest spike leaflike, 2–6 cm long, shorter than the inflorescence. Flowers in 2–4 spikes; terminal spike male, long-stalked; lower 1–3 spikes female, drooping on slender peduncles; female scales ovate, about as long and wide as perigynia, light to dark brown, with lighter center. Perigynia compressed-triangular, glaucous-green, densely pimpled; stigmas 3.

Where Found occasional in sphagnum bogs, fens, wet meadows.

♦*Carex livida* (Wahlenb.) Willd. **LIVID SEDGE**

Habit perennial sedge, from slender, creeping rhizomes; stems 10–50 cm tall, arising singly or a few together, shorter or longer than the leaves. Leaves 6 to 12 per stem, to 3 mm wide, bluish green involute, borne on lower third of stem; sheaths smooth, thin, lower sheaths persisting; bracts subtending lowest female spikes sheathing, leaflike, sometimes longer than the inflorescence; upper bracts smaller. Flowers in 2–4 spikes; terminal spike of male flowers; lower 1–3 spikes of female flowers, the lower more or less remote and long-stalked, the upper un-stalked or short-stalked; female scales ovate, equal to or slightly shorter than perigynia, purplish brown, pale green at center, the margins wide, translucent. Perigynia ovate,

MATT LAVIN

Carex lasiocarpa SLENDER SEDGE

YOAN MARTIN

Carex limosa SHORE SEDGE

glaucous-green, densely pimpled, beakless; stigmas 3.

Where Found occasional in fens, wet meadows, often calcareous.

Carex loliacea L. RYEGRASS SEDGE

Habit loosely tufted perennial sedge, with elongated stolons; stems slender, weak, 15–40 cm tall, about as long as leaves or longer. Leaves numerous, flat, soft, 1–2 mm wide, borne on lower part of stem; sheaths tight; lowermost bract awnlike, about 0.5–1 cm long; upper bracts reduced. Flowers in 2–5 spikes, widely separated on top of stem; female flowers above the inconspicuous male flowers; female scales ovate, keeled, covering about half of the perigynia, whitish green, with green midribs. Perigynia narrowly elliptic, pale green, dark green or brownish, beakless; stigmas 2.

Where Found muskegs, sphagnum bogs, streambanks, seeps.

Carex livida LIVID SEDGE

♦ *Carex lyngbyei* Hornem. LYNGBYE'S SEDGE

Habit perennial sedge, from long, creeping rhizomes or stolons; stems 1–10 dm tall, arising singly or in small clumps, longer than the leaves, purple-red or brownish at base. Leaves 4 to 8 per stem, flat, 2–12 mm wide, margins inrolled, borne on lower half of stem, lower leaves reduced, persistent; sheaths tight; bracts subtending lowest spike leaflike, longer than the inflorescence. Flowers in 4–7 spikes; terminal 2–3 linear, long-stalked, of male flowers; lower 2–4 spikes narrowly cylindric, of female flowers (or some with male flowers above female), short-stalked, drooping on slender peduncles; female scales lanceolate to ovate, long-pointed or awned, narrower and longer than the perigynia, brownish or blackish with light center and narrow, translucent margins. Perigynia elliptic to broadly ovate, glaucous-green or brownish, somewhat inflated, 2-ribbed; beak short, to 0.3 mm long; stigmas 2.

Where Found wet meadows, bogs.

Carex macloviana d'Urv. THICK-HEAD SEDGE

Habit tufted perennial sedge, from fibrous roots; stems sharply triangular, 20–50 cm tall, exceeding the leaves. Leaves flat, 2–4 mm wide, borne on lower third of stem; sheaths tight; bracts subtending spikes reduced, inconspicuous. Flowers in 5–10 spikes, clustered into a dense head; female flowers above male flowers; female scales elliptic, brown, with broad translucent margins, somewhat shorter and narrower than the perigynia. Perigynia ovate, dark green to brown, with copper-brown edges, the margins winged nearly to base, and upper half fringed with teeth; beak to 1 mm long; stigmas 2.

Where Found bogs, gravelly shores, moist meadows.

Carex lyngbyei LYNGBYE'S SEDGE

Carex macrochaeta C.A. Mey.
LONG-AWN SEDGE

Habit loosely tufted perennial sedge, from short, matted rhizomes; stems 10-60 cm tall, as long as or longer than the leaves, reddish tinged at base. **Leaves** 2 to 5 per stem, flat with slightly inrolled margins, 2-4 mm wide; borne on lower half of stem; sheaths tight; bracts subtending lowest spike leaflike, the others reduced. **Flowers** in 3-5 spikes; terminal spike male; lower 2-4 spikes female, long-stalked, erect or drooping on slender peduncles; female scales ovate, with awns 3-5 mm long, as wide as the perigynia, dark with light whitish midrib excurrent as a serrulate awn 2-10 mm long. **Perigynia** narrowly ovate, usually light green, beakless to short-beaked, to 0.2 mm long; stigmas 3.

Where Found alpine meadows, heathlands.

♦ *Carex magellanica* Lam. **BOREAL BOG SEDGE**
Carex paupercula Michx.

Habit loosely tufted perennial sedge, from short or long rhizomes, the roots yellowish woolly; stems 10-40 cm tall, longer than the leaves, reddish brown at base. **Leaves** 3 to 9 per stem, 2-4 mm wide, flat with slightly inrolled margins, borne on lower half of stem; lower leaves reduced; sheaths thin, red-dotted below; bracts subtending lowest spike leaflike, 2-10 cm long, longer than the inflorescence, the others reduced. **Flowers** in 3-5 spikes; terminal spike of male flowers; lower 2-4 spikes of female flowers (or sometimes with a few male flowers below), drooping on slender peduncles; female scales lanceolate to narrowly ovate, usually longer and narrower than the perigynia, light to dark brown, usually with lighter, greenish center. **Perigynia** compressed triangular, pale or glaucous-green, densely pimpled, conspicuously

AARON GUNNAR

Carex magellanica BOREAL BOG SEDGE

few-nerved, beakless or short-beaked, the beak 0.5-1 mm long; stigmas 3.

Where Found occasional in bogs, fens, and muskegs.

♦ *Carex media* R. Br. SCANDINAVIAN SEDGE

Habit tufted perennial sedge, from short rhizomes and fibrous roots; stems single, 15-40 cm tall, exceeding the leaves. **Leaves** 2-4 mm wide, margins inrolled; sheaths reddish to brown; lowest bract leaf-like, about equal in length to inflorescence; lowermost bract leaflike to awl-shaped. **Flowers** in 2-5 spikes; terminal spike with female flowers above, male flowers below; lateral spikes 2-5, female, two-colored (green-purple to black); female scales brown, with light green transparent margins, lanceolate to ovate, shorter than the perigynia. **Perigynia** elliptic, green (maturing brown), papillose; stigmas 3.

Where Found occasional in forests, shrublands, and meadows, frequently on floodplains and stream terraces.

Similar Species *Carex atrosquama* is similar but its female scales lack a transparent margin, and the spikes and perigynia are larger.

♦ *Carex membranacea* Hook. FRAGILE SEDGE

Habit perennial sedge, with inflated black perigynia, from long-creeping rhizomes; stems 10-50 cm tall, arising singly, rough

RYAN DURAND

Carex media SCANDINAVIAN SEDGE

below inflorescence. Leaves about same length as stems, flat to V-shaped, 3–6 mm wide, margins somewhat inrolled; lowermost bract leaflike. Flowers in 2–6 spikes; male spikes 1–3, terminal, narrow; female spikes 1–3, lateral, sessile or on a short, upright stalk; female scales ovate to lanceolate, black, shorter and narrower than the perigynia. Perigynia shiny, black, membranaceous; stigmas 3.

Where Found common in moist to wet places at low- to high-elevations, especially in the subalpine zone.

Similar Species *Carex rotundata* and *C. saxatilis* have similar large, black spikes; *C. rotundata* is distinguished by its rounded stems; *C. saxatilis* has 2 stigmas, and the pistillate spikes are long-peduncled.

Carex mertensii J.D. Prescott ex Bong.
MERTENS' SEDGE

Habit tufted perennial sedge, from short, stout rhizomes or stolons; stems sharply triangular, rough, 20–100 cm tall, exceeding the leaves. Leaves flat, 3–6 mm wide, flat with revolute margins; lower leaves much reduced; sheaths purplish red toward base; bracts subtending spikes leaflike, longer than inflorescence. Flowers in 5–10 spikes; terminal spike with female flowers uppermost,

male flowers below; lower 4–9 spikes of female flowers, drooping on slender peduncles; female scales lanceolate, much shorter and narrower than the perigynia, reddish black with light center, with light brown margins. Perigynia broadly ovate, pale yellow or light brown, often dark-spotted near tip; beak short, less than 0.5 mm long; stigmas 3.

Where Found uncommon on open slopes, woods, meadows.

♦ *Carex microchaeta* Holm
ALPINE-TUNDRA SEDGE

Habit tufted perennial sedge, with wide basal leaves, from short, stout rhizomes; stems 10–35 cm tall, exceeding the leaves. Leaves all basal, flat or V-shaped, 3–6 mm wide; lowest bract leaflike or lowermost bract scalelike; shorter than inflorescence. Flowers in 2–5 spikes; 1–2 terminal male spikes, and 1–3 lateral drooping female spikes on long peduncles; female scales reddish brown to purple, with a light colored midrib. Perigynia brown to blackish, papillose, typically concealed by the scales; stigmas 3.

Where Found abundant in Denali's alpine tundra (where the most common sedge), especially north of Alaska Range crest.

Similar Species *Carex podocarpa* is similar, but that plant has stem rather than basal leaves.

Carex membranacea FRAGILE SEDGE

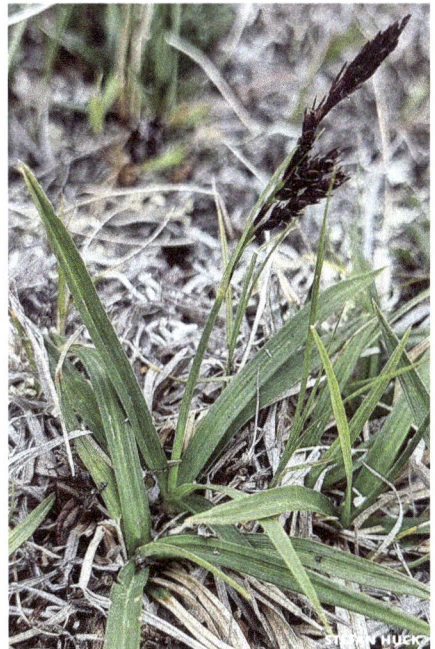
Carex microchaeta ALPINE-TUNDRA SEDGE

♦ *Carex microglochin* Wahlenb.
FEW-SEEDED FEN SEDGE

Habit perennial sedge from slender rhizomes; stems 1 to 3, stiff, erect, 5–25 cm tall, much longer than the leaves. **Leaves** 4 to 8, about 1 mm wide, involute, stiff, erect to ascending, light green with blunt tip, clustered near base; sheaths tight, brown at base; lowermost bract scalelike, deciduous. **Flowers** in a solitary spike, 5–12 mm long, with female flowers below the male flowers; female scales narrowly ovate, wider than and about half as long as the perigynia, early deciduous, light chestnut-brown, the margins lighter. **Perigynia** narrowly lanceolate, pale green, brownish green or straw-colored, soon reflexed; beak not differentiated from body; stigmas 3.

Where Found occasional on wet shores, streambanks.

Carex micropoda C.A. Mey. **PYRENEAN SEDGE**
Carex pyrenaica subsp. *micropoda* (C.A.Mey.) Hultén

Habit densely tufted perennial sedge, from fibrous roots, stems slender, 5–25 cm tall, exceeding the leaves. **Leaves** flat, channeled, to 2 mm wide, borne on lower third of stem; lowermost leaves reduced to scales; sheaths tight; lowermost bract scalelike. **Flowers** in 5–10 spikes, clustered into a dense head, female flowers below inconspicuous male flowers in each spike; scales elliptic, somewhat shorter and narrower than the perigynia, blackish chestnut to straw-colored, with translucent margins. **Perigynia** ovate, light green, straw-colored, or light brown, shining, margins winged nearly to base; beak to 1.5 mm long; stigmas 2.

Where Found occasional in moist alpine tundra, often near snowbeds.

Carex myosuroides Vill. **PACIFIC BOG SEDGE**
Kobresia myosuroides (Vill.) Fiori

Habit densely tufted perennial sedge, from smooth, fibrous roots; stems slender, wiry, more or less circular in cross-section, 10–40 cm tall, usually longer than the leaves. **Leaves** somewhat wiry and thread-like, often nearly as tall as flowering stem; sheaths light brown, persistent on plant for many years. **Flowers** in a solitary spike; spikelets several, each with a male flower above, female below, in axil of scale; scales brown with pale midvein and margins. **Fruit** an achene about 2 mm long.

Where Found occasional in dry turfy places and sloping meadows on tundra and in the subalpine zone, primarily north of the Alaska Range crest.

Similar Species Formerly placed in genus *Kobresia* (with achene enclosed in a scale open on one side unlike the fully closed perigynia in *Carex*), but that genus now treated as part of *Carex*. This species can be distinguished from other, less common former species of *Kobresia* (in Denali, *Carex borealipolaris* and *C. simpliciuscula*) by its narrow spike versus ovate flowering heads in those two species.

♦ *Carex nardina* (Hornem.) Fr. **SPIKENARD SEDGE**
Carex hepburnii Boott.

Habit densely tufted perennial sedge, from fibrous roots; stems 2–15 cm tall, shorter than to slightly longer than the leaves. **Leaves** 1 to 2 per stem, stiff, wire-like, about 0.5 mm wide, erect or recurved, persistent, borne on lower 1/4 of stem; sheaths conspicuous, persistent; bract below inflorescence absent. **Flowers** in a

Carex microglochin **FEW-SEEDED FEN SEDGE**

Carex nardina **SPIKENARD SEDGE**

2d

solitary erect spike, the male flowers uppermost, female below; female scales ovate, about equaling the perigynia, reddish brown with straw-colored center. Perigynia lanceolate to ovate; beak short; stigmas 2 or 3.

Where Found uncommon on grassy or rocky slopes, ridges, sandy or gravelly terraces.

♦*Carex nigricans* C.A. Mey. BLACK ALPINE SEDGE

Habit loosely tufted perennial sedge, from stout, creeping rhizomes; stems 5–35 cm tall, longer than the leaves. Leaves 4 to 9 per stem, flat or channeled, 1–2 mm wide, borne on lower 1/4 of stem; sheaths tight; bract below inflorescence absent. Flowers in a solitary erect spike, the male flowers uppermost, female below (rarely the spikes with all male or all female flowers); staminate scales persistent, reddish brown, becoming straw-colored; female scales lanceolate to ovate, much shorter than the perigynia, deciduous, dark brown, the midrib pale. Perigynia compressed-triangular, yellowish to brownish, appressed when young, spreading and reflexed when mature; beak short; stigmas 3.

Where Found alpine meadows, mountain slopes.

♦*Carex obtusata* Lilj. BLUNT SEDGE

Habit perennial sedge, from slender, creeping, purple-black rhizomes; stems 10–20 cm

tall, arising singly or a few together, longer than the leaves. Leaves basal, about 1 mm wide; sheaths purplish; bract below inflorescence absent. Flowers in a solitary spike; male flowers above female flowers; scales acute, brownish with transparent margins, enclosing the perigynia. Perigynia obovate, dark brown, slightly beaked; stigmas 3.

Where Found uncommon in warm, dry places in the mountains, including turfy sites in sloping meadows and tundra, mostly north of Alaska Range crest.

Similar Species *Carex rupestris,* but that species is shorter, the rhizome is brown (not purplish) and the perigynia are a dull yellowish brown, not shiny dark brown.

Carex parryana Dewey PARRY'S SEDGE

Habit loosely tufted perennial sedge, from creeping rhizomes; stems 10–40 cm tall, exceeding the leaves. Leaves stiff, flat, with revolute margins, 2–4 mm wide, the lower leaves not reduced; sheaths purplish red toward base; bracts subtending spikes bristlelike to scalelike, shorter than inflorescence. Flowers in 3–6 spikes; terminal spike of male flowers, often with female flowers at tip or throughout; lower 2–5 spikes erect, of female flowers; female scales lanceolate to ovate, nearly as long and wide as perigynia, tip sometimes extended into a short awn, reddish black, with green midrib and light

Carex nigricans BLACK ALPINE SEDGE

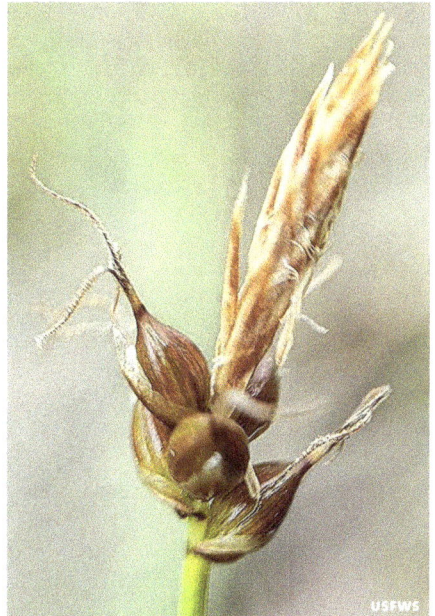

Carex obtusata BLUNT SEDGE

brown margins. Perigynia obovate, straw-colored (or purplish toward tip); beak short, less than 0.3 mm long; stigmas 3.

Where Found uncommon in marshes, wet meadows, shrub thickets.

♦ *Carex pauciflora* Lightf. FEW-FLOWER SEDGE

Habit perennial sedge from slender rhizomes; stems solitary, arising singly or a few together, stiff, erect, 10–50 cm tall, longer than the leaves. Leaves 1 to 3, involute or channeled, 1–2 mm wide, smooth or sometimes with roughened margins, ascending, the tips long-pointed; sheaths brownish, tight; bracts absent. Flowers in a solitary spike, the few male flowers uppermost, the lower 1–6 flowers female; female scales lanceolate, short-awned, as wide as or slightly wider and shorter than perigynia, brownish, early deciduous, with greener midstripes, the margins often translucent. Perigynia narrowly lanceolate, pale green (becoming brownish green or straw-colored), soon reflexed, nearly round in cross-section, beak not differentiated from body; stigmas 3.

Where Found bogs, fens, muskegs.

Carex petricosa Dewey
ROCK-DWELLING SEDGE

Habit densely tufted perennial sedge, from scaly rhizomes or stolons; stems 10–35 cm tall, longer than leaves. Leaves flat or channeled, 2–3 mm wide, margins inrolled, grayish green, somewhat curly, shorter than stems; lower leaves reduced; sheaths tight; bracts subtending lowest spike leaflike, the blade much shorter than the inflorescence. Flowers in 4–7 spikes; upper 1–3 spikes of male flowers (sometimes with a few female flowers below); lower 1–4 spikes separate, erect to ascending or spreading, of all female flowers, or sometimes with male flowers above the female; female scales ovate, slightly shorter than the perigynia, dark brown, the centers paler, the margins translucent. Perigynia lanceolate to ovate, short-hairy or only a fringe of hairs on margins, beak short; stigmas 3.

Where Found uncommon on gravelly slopes and rock outcrops, often where calcareous.

♦ *Carex phaeocephala* Piper
MOUNTAIN HARE SEDGE

Habit tufted perennial sedge, from matted, fibrous roots; stems stiff, 10–30 cm tall, exceeding the leaves; bracts subtending spikes inconspicuous. Leaves folded or involute, 1–2 mm wide, borne on lower third of stem; sheaths tight. Flowers in 3–6 spikes, clustered into a rather compact head; female flowers uppermost in each spike, conspicuous male flowers below; female scales longer and wider than perigynia, brown with narrow translucent margins and lighter midvein. Perigynia ovate, straw-colored to dark brown; margins winged nearly to base; beak to 1 mm long; stigmas 2.

Where Found uncommon on rocky alpine slopes and meadows.

♦ *Carex pluriflora* Hultén MANY-FLOWER SEDGE

Habit loosely tufted perennial sedge, from creeping, dark or purplish black rhizomes or stolons, the roots yellow-woolly; stems 10–50 cm tall, arising singly or a few together, equaling the leaves, reddish tinged at the

Carex pauciflora FEW-FLOWER SEDGE

Carex phaeocephala MOUNTAIN HARE SEDGE

bases. Leaves 3 to 5 per stem, 2–4 mm wide, flat with slightly inrolled margins, finely and densely white-pimpled below, borne on lower half of stem; lower leaves much reduced; sheaths loose; bracts subtending spikes membranaceous and whitish at base, the tip bristlelike, shorter than the spikes; upper bracts reduced. Flowers in 2–4 spikes; terminal spike male, long-stalked; lower 1–3 spikes female, separate, on long threadlike peduncles, nodding; staminate scales reddish brown with translucent margins; female scales broadly ovate, usually awn-tipped, narrower and longer than perigynia, black to dark brown, the centers lighter, tending to wrap around the perigynia. Perigynia ovate to narrowly ovate, glaucous-green, later blackish brown, densely pimpled, beakless; stigmas 3.

Where Found bogs, muskegs, wet meadows, pond margins.

♦ *Carex podocarpa* R. Br. SHORT-STALK SEDGE

Habit tufted perennial sedge, from short, stout rhizomes; stems sharply 3-angled, 15–60 cm tall, exceeding the leaves. Leaves 2–4 mm wide, abruptly pointed, with scarious tips; subtending bract shorter than inflorescence. Flowers in 2–5 spikes; terminal spikes (1–2) erect, male, lateral spikes (1–3) female, drooping on long peduncles; female scales black, acute, nearly as long as perigynia. Perigynia elliptic, blackish, with an abrupt beak; stigmas 3.

Where Found common in moist subalpine and alpine meadows on both sides of Alaska Range.

Similar Species *Carex microchaeta* similar, but its leaves all basal, not along stem.

Note *Carex podocarpa* is 'aphyllopodic,' meaning it has no basal cluster of leaves, but instead these are reduced in size, with increasingly well-developed leaves up the stem; however, clusters of sterile basal leaves, connected by underground rhizomes, are produced.

♦ *Carex praticola* Rydb.
NORTHERN MEADOW SEDGE

Habit tufted perennial sedge from fibrous roots; stems 20–70 cm tall, exceeding the leaves. Leaves flat, light green, 1–3 mm wide, borne on lower third of stem; sheaths tight; bracts subtending spikes reduced, inconspicuous. Flowers in 3–7 spikes, clustered into a loose head, female flowers above the male flowers; female scales elliptic, longer and wider than the perigynia, yellowish brown, with broad translucent margins and lighter centers. Perigynia narrowly ovate, straw-colored to dark brown; margins winged nearly to base; beak to 1 mm long; stigmas 2.

Where Found open woods, muskegs, meadows, streambanks.

Carex podocarpa SHORT-STALK SEDGE

Carex pluriflora MANY-FLOWER SEDGE

Carex praticola NORTHERN MEADOW SEDGE

◆ *Carex rariflora* (Wahlenb.) Sm.
LOOSE-FLOWER ALPINE SEDGE
Habit loosely stoloniferous perennial sedge, roots with rust-colored hairs; stems 10–35 cm tall. Leaves 1.5–2.5 mm wide, on lower 1/3 of stem; lower leaf blades very short or absent; bracts colored at base, blade awl-like to leaflike. Flowers in 2–3 spikes; terminal spike male; lateral spikes 1–2, female, nodding; scales purplish black with lighter center. Perigynia ovate to elliptic, greenish to straw-colored; stigmas 3.

Where Found wet, peat-rich alpine tundra and heath; bogs, shallow ponds, shores.

G. CARTER

Carex rariflora **LOOSE-FLOWER ALPINE SEDGE**

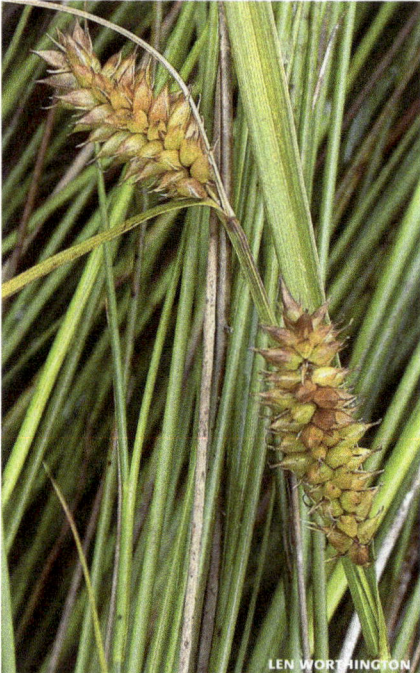
LEN WORTHINGTON

Carex rostrata **BEAKED SEDGE**

◆ *Carex rostrata* Stokes **BEAKED SEDGE**
Habit tufted perennial sedge, from creeping rhizomes or stolons; stems 30–80 cm tall, smooth except slightly rough below inflorescence, slightly longer than the leaves. Leaves 4 to 8 per stem, borne on lower half of stem, 2–10 mm wide, folded or channeled, with papillae on upper surface, margins revolute; lower leaves reduced, persistent; sheaths tight; bracts subtending lowest spike leaflike, the lowest bract longer than the inflorescence. Flowers in 3–8 spikes; the terminal 1–2 (sometimes 3–4) linear, long-stalked, with many male flowers; lower 2–4 spikes cylindric, short-stalked, of female flowers, the lowermost spikes spreading; female scales lanceolate to ovate, rarely awned, narrower and shorter than the perigynia, yellowish to chestnut-brown, with lighter centers and narrow, translucent margins. Perigynia ovate, yellowish green to reddish brown, somewhat inflated, shiny, strongly nerved, rather abruptly contracted into a beak 1.5–2 mm long; stigmas 3.

Where Found occasional on floating bog mats and pool-edges in fens and bogs.

◆ *Carex rotundata* Wahlenb.
ROUND SEDGE, PUMPKIN-FRUIT SEDGE
Habit perennial sedge, from pale, cordlike stolons; stems slender, 10–40 cm tall, in small clusters. Leaves basal, narrow, 1–3 mm wide, as long as or longer than stem; lowermost bract leaflike. Flowers in 2–4 spikes; terminal spike male, lateral spikes female, widely spaced; female scales ovate, brown to black, shorter and narrower than the perigynia. Perigynia inflated, shiny dark brown or black, with a bidentate beak; stigmas 3.

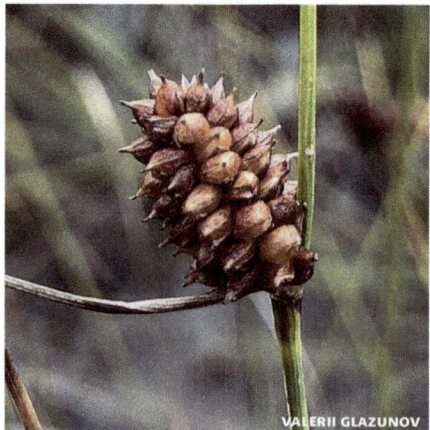
VALERII GLAZUNOV

Carex rotundata **ROUND SEDGE**

Where Found common in boreal zone wetlands, especially sphagnum bogs and pond margins in peatlands, also occasional in marshes and fens.

Similar Species This species looks highly similar to *Carex membranacea,* but that species has angled, not rounded, stems.

♦ *Carex rupestris* All. CURLY SEDGE

Habit small, tufted, perennial sedge, from creeping rhizomes; stems 6–15 cm tall, slightly scabrous, single or a few together; subtending bract absent. Leaves flat or involute, scabrous, about as long as stem, the tips often curled and scarious; lowermost bract scalelike. Flowers in a solitary, erect spike, male flowers at tip, and a few female flowers below; female scales dark brown with a translucent margin, wider than and about as long as perigynia. Perigynia light brown, short-beaked; stigmas 3.

Where Found occasional in dry turfy alpine tundra and rubble slopes, primarily north of Alaska Range crest, often where calcareous.

Similar Species no other alpine sedge in Denali has a single spike with distinctly curly leaves; however, could be confused with *Carex scirpoidea,* but that plant is dioecious (spikes composed entirely of staminate or pistillate flowers); *Carex obtusata* similar, but that species taller, with a purplish rhizome

and shiny dark brown perigynia.

♦ *Carex saxatilis* L. RUSSET SEDGE
Carex physocarpa J. & C. Presl

Habit perennial sedge, from creeping rhizomes; stems 10–80 cm tall, arising singly, triangular, rough below the inflorescence, longer than the leaves. Leaves 4 to 8 per stem, flat, 2–5 mm wide, the margins inrolled, borne on lower half of stem, lower leaves reduced, persistent; sheaths tight; bracts subtending lowest spike leaflike, longer than the inflorescence. Flowers in 4–7 spikes; terminal 1–3 spikes linear, long-stalked, with many male flowers; lower 1–4 spikes cylindric, with female flowers (or some with male flowers above female), spreading or drooping on slender peduncles; female scales purplish black with lighter midrib and prominent translucent tip. Perigynia elliptic to broadly ovate, yellowish green or brown to purplish black, usually dark tinged above, somewhat inflated, shiny, 2-ribbed, beak short, to 0.3 mm long; stigmas 2 (or rarely 3).

Where Found occasional in wet, springy tundra, or in shallow water at pool edges.

♦ *Carex scirpoidea* Michx. SINGLE-SPIKE SEDGE

Habit dioecious perennial sedge, rhizomatous or tufted; stems to 35 cm tall, sharply 3-angled and stiffly erect, single or a few

Carex rupestris CURLY SEDGE

together, equaling or longer than the leaves. Leaves flat, 3–4 mm wide, scabrous; lowest bract awl-like to leaflike. Flowers solitary, either male or female and found on separate plants (dioecious); female spikes linear and 2–3 cm long; male spikes shorter, with exserted stamens; female scales purple-black, ciliate, shorter than perigynia, with papery margins. Perigynia distinctly hairy, brown or green, beaked; stigmas 3.

Where Found common from lowlands to the alpine in a variety of usually rocky habitats: woodlands, shrublands, meadows, and alpine tundra, on both sides of the Alaska Range.

Similar Species the only other sedge in Denali that is sometimes dioecious with single spikes is the uncommon *Carex gynocrates;* that species smaller, less densely tufted, with narrower leaves, shorter spikes, brown (not black) scales, and the perigynia not hairy.

Carex simpliciuscula Wahlenb.
SIMPLE BOG SEDGE
Kobresia simpliciuscula (Wahl.) Mack.
Habit tufted perennial sedge, from smooth fibrous roots; stems 7–35 (50) cm tall. Leaves

linear, 0.5–1.5 mm wide; sheaths brown to yellowish brown, persistent, with conspicuous dried blades from previous year; bracts solitary, scalelike or leaflike, bristle-tipped. Flowers in 3–10 erect spikes, in a head 10–35 mm long, which sometimes appears spikelike; spikelets usually each with 1 male and 1 female flower, male flower above female flower; scales brownish, with broad, translucent margins. Fruit a compressed, 3-angled achene; stigmas 3.

Where Found uncommon in moist gravelly alpine tundra, heathlands, pond shores.

Similar Species stems and leaves similar to *Carex myosuroides,* also formerly placed in *Kobresia.*

Carex spectabilis Dewey **SHOWY SEDGE**
Habit tufted perennial sedge, from matted, stout rhizomes; stems slender, 15–60 cm tall, exceeding the leaves. Leaves 2–5 mm wide, flat with revolute margins; lower leaves much reduced; sheaths purplish red toward base; bracts subtending spikes bristlelike or

Carex saxatilis RUSSET SEDGE

Carex scirpoidea SINGLE-SPIKE SEDGE

leaflike, shorter than or sometimes longer than the inflorescence. Flowers in 3–9 spikes; terminal spike male; lower 2–8 spikes female, erect, except lowermost spike often long-stalked and nodding; female scales lanceolate, nearly as long as and narrower than perigynia, tips extended into short awns, reddish black, with lighter or whitish midrib and light brown margins. Perigynia ovate, yellow-green, or brown to purple-black, the beak short, to 0.5 mm long; stigmas 3.

Where Found uncommon in marshes, wet meadows, and other wet places.

♦ *Carex stylosa* C.A. Mey. VARIEGATED SEDGE
Habit tufted perennial sedge, from short, stout rhizomes; stems 15–40 cm tall, exceeding the leaves. Leaves 2–4 mm wide, flat with revolute margins or channeled toward base; lower leaves not reduced; sheaths purplish red toward base; bracts subtending the spikes bristlelike to scalelike, shorter than inflorescence. Flowers in 3–5 spikes; terminal spike male; lower 2–4 spikes female, erect; female scales lanceolate, shorter and narrower than perigynia, very dark, with lighter midrib and light brown margins; styles prominently exserted. Perigynia ovate, yellowish brown tinged purplish black, the beak tiny; stigmas 3.

Where Found uncommon in muskegs and bogs.

♦ *Carex supina* Willd. ex Wahlenb.
WEAK ARCTIC SEDGE
Habit loosely tufted perennial sedge, from reddish brown rhizomes; stems 8–15 cm tall,

roughened, longer than the leaves. Leaves basal, narrow (to 1.5 mm wide); margin scabrous; lowermost bract awl-shaped. Flowers in 2–3 spikes; terminal spike male, lateral spikes female (but sometimes spikes tightly clustered and appearing as one); female scales ovate, reddish brown with papery margins and a pale midvein. Perigynia ovate, shiny brown, with a prominent beak; stigmas 3.

Where Found occasional in dry alpine sites north of the Alaska Range crest, including rocky places and discontinuous tundra.

Similar Species Another small alpine sedge is Carex rupestris, that species is smaller, has a single spike with both male and female flowers, and usually has strongly curled leaves.

♦ *Carex tenuiflora* Wahlenb.
SPARSE-FLOWER SEDGE
Habit loosely tufted perennial sedge, from slender rhizomes; stems somewhat arching, 10–50 cm tall, longer than the leaves. Leaves narrow, about 1 mm wide, flat or with thin parallel channels, grayish green. Flowers in 2–4 spikes, closely clustered at end of stem; female spikes above male; female scales about the same size as the perigynia, transparent, papery, with 3 green nerves. Perigynia elliptic, green, faintly veined, beakless; stigmas 2.

Where Found peatland bogs, pond margins, and other wet areas in the boreal zone on both sides of Alaska Range crest.

Similar Species Carex tenuiflora similar to the less common C. loliacea, but spikes more widely spaced in that species and the perigynia strongly veined.

♦ *Carex utriculata* Boott.
NORTHWEST TERRITORY SEDGE
Habit tufted perennial sedge, from creeping rhizomes; stems to 1 m or more long, sharply 3-angled, smooth except slightly rough below the inflorescence, about equal in length to the leaves. Leaves 4 to 8 per stem, yellow- or olive-green, cross-walled, 5–12

Carex stylosa VARIEGATED SEDGE

Carex supina WEAK ARCTIC SEDGE

Carex tenuiflora SPARSE-FLOWER SEDGE

mm wide, flat, margins scabrous, borne on lower half of stem; lower leaves reduced, persistent; sheaths tight; bracts subtending lowest spike leaflike, longer than the inflorescence. Flowers in 4–7 spikes; terminal 2 or 3 spikes male, long-stalked; lower spikes 2–4, female (or some with male flowers above female flowers), cylindric, long-stalked, lowermost spikes drooping; female scales lanceolate to ovate, narrower and shorter than perigynia, brown with lighter midvein and margins. Perigynia elliptic, yellowish green to reddish brown, somewhat inflated, shiny, strongly nerved, contracted into long beak 1.5–3 mm long, the beak bidentate with straight teeth; stigmas 3.

Where Found occasional on margins of lakes, ponds and streams.

♦ *Carex vaginata* Tausch SHEATHED SEDGE

Habit perennial sedge, from slender, creeping scaly rhizomes or stolons; stems stiff, smooth, 15–20 cm tall, arising singly or a few together, longer than the leaves. Leaves basal, much shorter than stem, flat, yellowish green, 1–4 mm wide; lowest bract shorter than inflorescence. Flowers in 1–3 spikes; terminal spike male; lateral spikes 1–2, female, and usually separated from the terminal spike; female scales shorter than perigynia, light brown with a broad green midrib. Perigynia light-green, beaked; stigmas 3.

Where Found common in riparian areas, muskegs, meadows, shrub tundra, and into the lower alpine zone on both sides of Alaska Range crest.

Similar Species the uncommon *Carex livida* similar, but that plant taller, its leaves a glaucous green, its perigynia unbeaked, and it occurs in much wetter sites than typical for *C. vaginata*.

♦ *Carex viridula* Michx. GREEN SEDGE
Carex oederi subsp. *viridula* (Michx.) Hultén

Habit densely tufted perennial sedge, from fibrous roots; stems 10–30 cm tall, longer than the leaves. Leaves 4 to 8 per stem, 1–3 mm wide, channeled, borne on lower half of stem, lower leaves reduced; sheaths pale below; bracts subtending female spikes conspicuous, leaflike, 4–9 cm long, much exceeding the inflorescence; upper bracts shorter. Flowers in 3–7 spikes; terminal spike male (rarely some female flowers); lower spikes 2 to 6, erect, cylindrical, of female flowers (sometimes the upper with male flowers at tip), unstalked or nearly so; female scales ovate, short-awned at tip, shorter than perigynia, reddish, with greenish midrib and narrow translucent margins; stigmas 3. Perigynia ovate to elliptic, yellowish green to green, several-nerved, the beak shortly bidentate, about 1/3 as long as body of perigynium.

Where Found uncommon in wet meadows, lakeshores.

Carex vaginata SHEATHED SEDGE

Carex utriculata NORTHWEST TERRITORY SEDGE

Carex williamsii Britt. WILLIAMS' SEDGE

Habit tufted sedge; stems 3-20 cm tall. Leaves bristlelike, channeled or rolled; sheaths purple-brown; lowest bract 1-4 cm long. Flowers in 2-5 spikes, erect or more or less nodding; terminal spike male; lateral spikes female, few-flowered; female scales shorter than perigynia, yellowish brown, margins translucent. Perigynia lanceolate, greenish to reddish brown, prominently few-nerved, bent outwards toward tip; stigmas 3. Where Found sandy soil, often on hummocks by edge of small ponds.

Eleocharis SPIKE-RUSH

(Greek *heleios*, dwelling in a marsh, and *charis*, grace.)

1	Stems short, 3-12 cm long	*E. acicularis*
1	Stems taller, stouter, 12 cm tall or more	2
2	Achene lens-shaped; basal scale shorter than half the length of spike	*E. palustris*
2	Achene 3-sided; basal scale half as long as spike, or longer	*E. quinqueflora*

♦ ***Eleocharis acicularis*** (L.) Roem. & Schult.
NEEDLE SPIKE-RUSH

Habit perennial, usually densely tufted spike-rush, from slender rhizomes, forming dense mats; stems thread-like, erect to ascending, 3-12 cm tall. Leaves with pale sheaths, sometimes purplish below; blades absent. Flowers 3-15, in a solitary, terminal spike; perianth bristles 3-4, equaling or longer than achene, rarely reduced or lacking; stigmas 3. Fruit an ovate, more or less 3-angled achene, white to pale gray or pale yellow, about 1 mm long including the conic-triangular tubercle (about one-fourth as long as achene).

Where Found in shallow water and muddy shores.

♦ ***Eleocharis palustris*** (L.) Roem. & Schult.
COMMON SPIKE-RUSH

Habit perennial spike-rush, from branching rhizomes; stems scattered or in small clusters, circular in cross-section, mostly 10-70 cm tall. Leaves with firm, reddish brown sheaths, purplish or reddish below; blades absent. Flowers in a solitary, terminal spike, lanceolate or narrowly ovate, 5-20 mm long, light to dark brown or chestnut, several-flowered; perianth bristles 4 (sometimes 5 or 6), slightly longer than achene, or rarely reduced or lacking, with fine barbs directed backwards; stigmas 2. Fruit a lens-shaped, yellow to medium brown achene, 1.5-2.5 mm long (including the well-differentiated tubercle), the pyramid-shaped tubercle separated from the achene body by a constriction.

Where Found in wet mud of marshes, and lake, pond and stream margins.

Eleocharis acicularis NEEDLE SPIKE-RUSH

Carex viridula GREEN SEDGE

Eleocharis palustris COMMON SPIKE-RUSH

Eleocharis quinqueflora (Hartmann) O. Schwarz **FEW-FLOWER SPIKE-RUSH**

Habit perennial spike-rush, from short, stout rhizomes and more longer, slender stolons with thickened terminal buds; stems clustered, thread-like, grooved, 10–30 cm tall. **Leaves** cylindric, sheaths brownish to straw-colored below; blades absent. **Flowers** in a solitary terminal spike, lanceolate to ovate, 4–8 mm long, 3–9-flowered, somewhat flattened; perianth bristles 4–6, equaling or surpassing the achene, or more or less reduced; stigmas 3. **Fruit** a 3-angled, grayish brown achene, 2–2.5 mm long (including the short, barely differentiated tubercle).

Where Found uncommon on shores, in marshes and muskegs.

Eriophorum COTTONGRASS

(Greek *erion,* wool or cotton, and *phoros,* bearing.)

1 Spikes solitary, not subtended by leafy bracts . **2**
1 Spikes several, drooping or clustered, subtended by 1 or 2 leafy bracts **6**
2 Plants stoloniferous. **3**
2 Plants tufted **4**
3 Anthers minute (1 mm long, or less); fruiting head globose . . . . *E. scheuchzeri*
3 Anthers 1.5 mm long, or longer; fruiting head oblong. . . . . *E. chamissonis*
4 Scales monochrome, without pale margins, not spreading or reflexed at maturity; fruiting heads obovate; anthers 1–2 mm long **5**
4 Scales pale-margined, divergent or spreading at maturity; fruiting spikes globose; bristles dull white; anthers 2–3 mm long . . . . *E. vaginatum*
5 Stems slender, 30–60 cm high; uppermost sheath mostly above middle of culm; anthers more than 1 mm long; mature bristles dull white. . . . . *E. brachyantherum*
5 Stems stout and stiff, 20–30 cm high; uppermost sheath often below middle of culm; anthers not more than 1 mm long; mature bristles with a sheen, mostly pure white . . . . *E. callitrix*
6 Leaves linear, 3-angled, 1–1.5 mm broad; bract usually only one. . . . . *E. gracile*
6 Leaves broader, flat, folded or involute; bracts 2 or 3. . . . . **7**
7 Midrib of scales prominent, extending to very tip . . . . *E. viridicarinatum*
7 Midrib of scales slender, not reaching tip . . . . *E. angustifolium*

◆ *Eriophorum angustifolium* Honck. **TALL COTTONGRASS**

Habit perennial multi-headed cottongrass, from creeping rhizomes; stems 10–80 cm tall. **Leaves** linear, dark green; blades flat, triangular at tip (tip often reddish or withered); involucral bracts (leaves near the spikes) 2–3, longer than inflorescence. **Flowers** in several spikes hanging from flat peduncles.

Where Found abundant from low- to high-elevations in bogs, muskegs, tundra, shallow water.

Similar Species distinguished from other species of cottongrass by its rhizomatous habit (instead of forming dense tufts), having many drooping heads, and flat rather than linear leaves.

Traditional Uses Alaska Natives traditionally collect and eat the stem-bases of *Eriophorum angustifolium,* and would raid vole caches of stored cottongrass rhizomes in the fall. The 'cotton' of this and other *Eriophorum* species was used as stuffing, as a fire-starter, or placed on boils or sores (Jernigan et al. 2015).

Eriophorum brachyantherum Trautv. & C.A. Mey. **CLOSED-SHEATH COTTONGRASS**

Habit perennial, densely tufted cottongrass, with solitary white heads formed by the bristles surrounding the flowers, from fibrous roots; stems slender, round in cross-section, 30–60 cm tall. **Leaves** basal, threadlike, basal sheaths gray-brown. **Flowers** in a dense solitary white head; flowers subtended by scales, the scales opaque, blackish; bristles yellowish white.

Where Found bogs, wet meadows, shallow ponds, at mostly low-elevations; primarily in

FRANZ XAVER

Eriophorum angustifolium TALL COTTONGRASS

permafrost-influenced areas north of Alaska Range.

Similar Species may be mistaken for the more abundant (and larger) tussock-forming *Eriophorum vaginatum;* to separate the two, check whether the flowering head scales are opaque (*E. brachyantherum*) or translucent (*E. vaginatum*).

Eriophorum callitrix Cham. ex C.A. Mey.
ARCTIC COTTONGRASS

Habit perennial tufted cottongrass, from small, solitary, compact tufts; stems stiff, slender, 6–20 cm tall. Leaves stiff, thread-like, folded, stem leaves usually lacking or solitary, located below the middle of the stem; basal sheath usually one, close to the base, brownish, cross-wrinkled, persistent; involucral bracts absent. Flowers in a solitary, terminal spike, at least some of them drooping; scales blackish or yellowish, midrib not reaching the tip; perianth bristles numerous, pure white with a silky sheen, many times longer than the achene.

Where Found bogs, wet peaty slopes.

◆ *Eriophorum chamissonis* C.A. Mey.
CHAMISSO'S COTTONGRASS
Eriophorum russeolum Fr.

Habit perennial cottongrass, with solitary, cotton-like flowering heads formed by bristles surrounding the flowers, from creeping rhizomes or stolons, forming extensive colonies; stems slender, round in cross-section, 20–50 cm tall. Leaves threadlike and channeled; basal sheaths gray-brown. Flowers in a dense, round solitary head, the small flowers subtended by scales; scales grayish black, ovate-lanceolate; bristles rusty-white.

Where Found bogs, shores, wet meadows, alpine tundra.

Similar Species This cottongrass differentiated by its growth form (rhizomatous, not tussock-forming), and the rust-colored bristles.

◆ *Eriophorum gracile* W.D.J. Koch
SLENDER COTTONGRASS

Habit perennial, loosely tufted or turf-forming cottongrass, from slender, much-branched rhizomes; stems arising singly, triangular in cross-section (at least above), 20–60 cm tall. Leaves basal or 2–3 along stem, shorter than the stem, narrow and folded towards tip or triangular in cross-section, not over 2 mm wide, uppermost leaves with reduced blades; basal sheaths brownish to reddish brown, cross-wrinkled, persistent; involucral bracts several but only one green and leaflike, usually shorter than the inflorescence, not purplish at base. Flowers in 2–8 terminal spikes; scales blackish green to greenish brown, the slender midrib not reaching the tip; perianth bristles numerous, white or whitish, 15–25 mm long, many times longer than achene.

Where Found bogs, lakeshores.

Eriophorum chamissonis
CHAMISSO'S COTTONGRASS

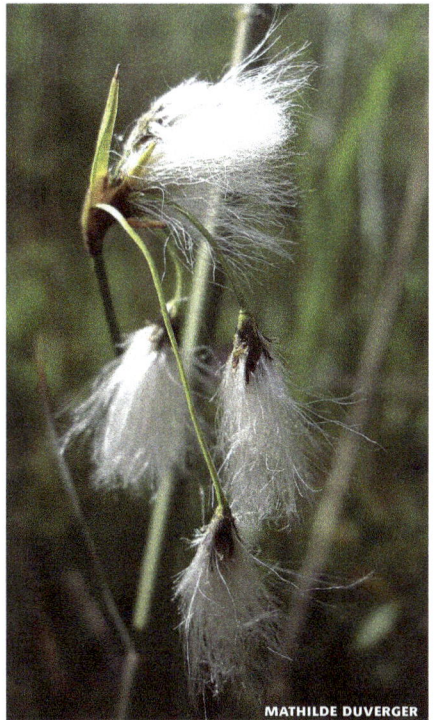

Eriophorum gracile SLENDER COTTONGRASS

♦ *Eriophorum scheuchzeri* Hoppe
WHITE COTTONGRASS

Habit perennial single-head cottongrass, from creeping rhizomes, extensively colonial (and not forming dense tussocks like the more abundant *Eriophorum vaginatum*); stems mostly solitary, stiff, with persistent sheaths at base, 5–35 cm tall. **Leaves** channeled, about 1 mm wide. **Flowers** in a solitary, round spike; scales blackish gray to dark green, without a transparent margin; bristles numerous, white.

Where Found common in wetlands from low elevations to the alpine zone, most often in the large basin lowlands north of Alaska Range.

Similar Species Another cottongrass with a single upright flowering head and a rhizomatous habit is *E. chamissonis;* in that species, the scales have a transparent margin and the bristles are rust-colored.

♦ *Eriophorum vaginatum* L.
TUSSOCK COTTONGRASS

Habit perennial cottongrass, forming large, dense tussocks made up of many persistent dead leaves; stems 10–60 cm tall or more, as the tussock can raise the whole plant higher (making walking difficult). **Leaves** thread-like, triangular in cross-section; involucral bracts absent. **Flowers** in a solitary, upright spike, round to ovoid-oblong in shape; scales subtending the flowers dark gray at center with pale or transparent margins (distinguishing it from related tussock-forming *E. brachyantherum* and *E. callitrix*); bristles numerous, white.

Where Found abundant in low-lying, nearly flat, moist to wet areas with acidic soils underlain by permafrost.

Traditional Uses The cottony flowering head traditionally used by Alaska Natives as stuffing or as a fire-starter.

Note One of the most abundant and distinctive plants across Alaska, and dominant across large areas of suitable wet habitat.

Eriophorum viridicarinatum (Engelm.) Fernald THIN-LEAF COTTONGRASS

Habit perennial cottongrass, from thin rhizomes; stems 30–100 cm tall. **Leaves** mainly basal, flat except at tip, stem leaves 2 or more; basal sheaths persistent, brownish, cross-wrinkled; involucral bracts 2–3, usually the longest ones surpassing the inflorescence. **Flowers** in 4–10 terminal, loosely clustered spikes, on drooping stalks stalks to 5 cm long; scales blackish green, the conspicuous paler midrib extending to the tip (and sometimes beyond); perianth bristles numerous, creamy-white or slightly yellowish, many times longer than the achene.

Where Found sphagnum moss bogs.

Schoenoplectus CLUB-RUSH

(Greek *schoinos,* a rush, and *plectos,* woven, in reference to uses of the stems.)

♦ *Schoenoplectus tabernaemontani* (C.C. Gmel.) Palla SOFT-STEM BULRUSH
Scirpus validus Vahl

Habit Perennial rush, from long rhizomes; stems nearly round in cross-section, tapered, smooth, spongy and easily crushed between the fingers, 50–200 cm tall or more. **Leaves**

Eriophorum scheuchzeri WHITE COTTONGRASS

Eriophorum vaginatum TUSSOCK COTTONGRASS

few, all near base of stem, to about half the length of stem; sheaths brown to straw-colored or reddish near base; blades usually absent; involucral bracts solitary, erect, not leaflike, C-shaped to nearly circular in cross-section, tapered, to as much as 7 cm long and appearing like an extension of the stem. Flowers in several to many terminal, reddish brown spikelets 5–12 mm long, clustered in a branching inflorescence, the branches lax, sometimes drooping; perianth bristles 6, brown, about equal to or longer than achene; achene about 2 mm long, not completely concealed by the scale when mature.

Where Found uncommon in shallow water of ponds, fens, and marshes.

Scirpus BULRUSH
(Latin name for the bulrush.)

♦ **Scirpus microcarpus** J. & C. Presl
SMALL-FRUIT BULRUSH

Habit perennial bulrush, from well-developed creeping rhizomes; stems single or a few together, obscurely triangular in cross-section, to about 1 m tall. Leaves Several, both basal and along stem; sheaths tinted reddish purple or straw-colored to greenish, cross-wrinkled; blades flat, grass-like, 7–15 mm wide, to 1 m long; involucral bracts several, conspicuous, leaflike, 10–30 cm long. Flowers numerous in 3–4 mm long spikelets, spikelets clustered in an umbel-like cyme; perianth bristles 4–6, finely barbed, about as long as the whitish achene (but not longer than the scale); stigmas 2.

Where Found lakeshores, riverbanks, marshes.

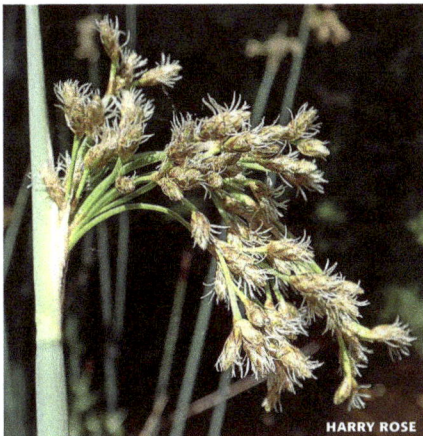
Schoenoplectus tabernaemontani
SOFT-STEM BULRUSH

Trichophorum
LEAFLESS BULRUSH
(Greek, *tricho-*, hair, and *phorum*, stalk.)

1 Stems sharply triangular in cross-section, rough on the angles; at maturity, perianth bristles forming a silky white tuft extending 1–2.5 cm beyond the spikes . . . . *T. alpinum*
1 Stems round in cross-section, smooth; perianth bristles barely, if at all, longer than the spikes . . . . *T. cespitosum*

♦ **Trichophorum alpinum** (L.) Pers.
ALPINE BULRUSH
Eriophorum alpinum L., *Scirpus hudsonianus* (Michx.) Fernald

Habit perennial sedge, from short rhizomes; stems more or less densely clustered in rows, sharply triangular in cross-section, rough on the angles, 10–30 cm tall. Leaves scalelike at base of stem, with 1–2 more normally-developed leaves above the base; sheaths straw-colored to brownish, not cross-wrinkled; involucral bracts absent. Flowers many in a terminal solitary spike, medium or light brown. Fruit a purplish brown, 3-angled achene; perianth bristles 6, white, 10–25 mm long at maturity.

Where Found uncommon in sphagnum moss bogs and muskegs.

♦ **Trichophorum cespitosum** (L.) Hartman
TUFTED BULRUSH
Scirpus cespitosus L.

Habit densely tufted perennial sedge (forming small tussocks), from fibrous roots, with stems 10–40 cm tall topped by small, inconspicuous flowers; the many flowering stems in a tuft are round, wiry, and grooved. Leaves reduced to a brownish sheath and very short

Scirpus microcarpus SMALL-FRUIT BULRUSH

bladelike bract. Flowers in a terminal spike of 2-5 flowers, above a single scalelike bract nearly as long as the spike. Fruit a 3-angled achene with 6 white bristles, 3-5 mm long (about twice as long as the achene).

Where Found occasional in poorly drained wet bogs and fens, including boreal and subalpine areas on both sides of the Alaska Range crest.

Similar Species this genus can be distinguished from other sedges in Denali by the terminal, solitary spike and mostly bladeless leaves (species of the genus *Eleocharis* are less common, and have no leaf blade at all); the only other *Trichophorum* species in the Park, *T. alpinum,* grows from short rhizomes, not in dense cushions.

HYDROCHARITACEAE
Tape-Grass Family

Najas WATERNYMPH
(Greek Naias, a water-nymph.)

Najas flexilis (Willd.) Rostk. & Schmidt
WAVY WATERNYMPH

Habit perennial aquatic herb, from fibrous roots; stems much branched, submersed, 30-150 cm long, about 1 mm thick. Leaves along the stem, linear, 1-3 cm long, about 0.5 mm wide, in nearly opposite pairs, the base more or less sheathing, the margins minutely toothed. Flowers solitary or paired, unstalked (or nearly so), in an axillary inflorescence of single-sex flowers; perianth parts lacking. Fruit an achene, spindle-shaped, about 3 mm long, smooth.

Where Found uncommon in low- to mid-elevation ponds.

IRIDACEAE
Iris Family

Iris IRIS
(Greek *iris*, rainbow.)

♦ *Iris setosa* Pall. ex Link BEACH-HEAD IRIS
Habit tall perennial herb, with showy purple flowers, from a short rhizome with many fibrous roots, forming clumps or extensive colonies; stems once or twice branched, 30-70 cm tall remains of last season's leaves and flowering stems often persistent. Leaves mainly basal, long and sword shaped, paral-

Trichophorum alpinum ALPINE BULRUSH

Trichophorum cespitosum TUFTED BULRUSH

Iris setosa BEACH-HEAD IRIS

MONOCOTS

lel-veined, upright; stem stem leaves alternate. Flowers of 6 tepals, violet-blue, the center white and yellow with purple veins; the three prominent tepals with a narrow base and round, broadly expanded tips, to 2 cm long; smaller tepals with finely lobed edges. Fruit a dry capsule which splits open by three valves to release many large seeds.

Where Found occasional at low-elevations on wetland flats and river bars.

Similar Species the only native iris in Alaska.

Traditional Uses the root of *Iris setosa* was made into a tea used by Aleutian islanders as a laxative, chewed by the Dena'ina to treat colds or to place on sores, and used medicinally by the Tlingit (Garibaldi 1999). Irises contain toxins such as irisin, iridin, or irisine, which are typically concentrated in the roots. Consumption can cause vomiting and fevers (or death if enough is consumed); incidental contact can cause allergic reactions in some people.

JUNCACEAE
Rush Family

1 Leaves stiff, smooth; leaf-sheaths open; capsule many-seeded . . . . *Juncus*
1 Leaves flexible, usually hairy on margins near their base; leaf-sheaths closed; seeds 3 . *Luzula*

Juncus RUSH
(Latin, *jungo*, to bind, alluding to use of these plants for withes.)

1 Involucral bract resembling an extension and continuation of stem; inflorescence appearing as if on side of stem. 2
1 Involucral bract not forming an extension or continuation of stem; inflorescence terminal 4
2 Flowers usually only 2 or 3; seeds with tail-like appendages on each end . . . . . . *J. drummondii*
2 Flowers several or numerous; seeds cylindrical without tail-like appendages 3
3 Stems finely grooved; sheaths dull, light brown; involucral bract nearly as long as or longer than stem; inflorescence located about halfway between the tip of involucral bract and base of stem; perianth greenish or whitish . *J. filiformis*
3 Stems smooth; sheaths shiny brown; involucral bract shorter than stem; inflorescence located closer to upper part of plant; perianth brownish green to red-brown. . . . . *J. arcticus*

4 Leaf blades without cross-walls, or with cross-walls only near tip. 5
4 Leaf blades with prominent cross-walls. 9
5 Plants annual. . . . . *J. bufonius*
5 Plants perennial. 6
6 Leaves all basal; plants less than 20 cm tall. . . 7
6 Leaves along stem in addition to basal leaves; stems often more than 25 cm tall. 8
7 Capsule distinctly notched; inflorescence usually 2-flowered . . . . *J. biglumis*
7 Capsule blunt to pointed; inflorescence 3- to 5-flowered. *J. albescens*
8 Capsule 6–8 mm long, chestnut brown; anthers 1–1.5 mm long; plants with stolons and rhizomes . . . . *J. castaneus*
8 Capsule 5–6 mm long, pale brown; anthers 0.4–0.7 mm long; plants without stolons or rhizomes . . . . *J. stygius*
9 Early leaves threadlike, flaccid, usually submerged; stems decumbent, rooting at nodes; inflorescence often viviparous (bearing young small plants) . . . . *J. supiniformis*
9 Early leaves stiff, not threadlike; plants erect or decumbent, but not rooting at nodes; inflorescence not viviparous 10
10 Heads many-flowered, more or less globe-shaped. . . . . *J. mertensianus*
10 Heads with few flowers, cone-shaped. 11
11 Capsule twice as long as perianth, over 5 mm long . . . . *J. supiniformis*
11 Capsule less than twice as long as perianth, less than 5 mm long . . . . *J. alpinoarticulatus*

Juncus albescens (Lange) Fernald
THREE-FLOWER RUSH
Juncus triglumis subsp. *albescens* (Lange) Hultén

Habit tufted rush, with a solitary head of 3–5 flowers; stems 15 cm or more tall, from a short rootstock, leafless apart from 2–3 dark, short, lowermost bract scalelike; bracts below inflorescence. Leaves basal, shorter than the stems, filiform (uniformly narrow along entire leaf); sheaths reddish brown. Flowers (and capsule) dark reddish brown with age; capsule about one-third longer than tepals.

Where Found occasional in mountainous areas on wet or saturated soil, usually growing in a mineral rather than organic substrate.

Similar Species similar to *Juncus biglumis*, but with more flowers and a single leaf-like bract below the inflorescence is not present.

♦ *Juncus alpinoarticulatus* Chaix
NORTHERN GREEN RUSH
Juncus alpinus Vill.

Habit loosely tufted perennial rush, from short rhizomes; stems erect, 15–45 cm tall. Leaves 1–2, on lower part of stem, nearly circular in cross-section, tapered, the early leaves stiff, with prominent cross-walls; sheaths open. Flowers 3–10 in terminal, panicled heads; branches few, erect; perianth segments brown or purplish brown, 2–3 mm long; involucral bracts usually shorter than inflorescence. Fruit a capsule, rounded at top, about as long as the perianth segments (or slightly longer); seeds lacking appendages.
Where Found sandy and gravelly shores.

Juncus arcticus Willd. **ARCTIC RUSH**
Habit perennial rush, from long, creeping rhizomes; stems arising singly, not in dense clusters, round, usually straight, smooth, wiry, erect, 15–60 cm tall. Leaves reduced to small sheaths at base of stem; sheaths shiny brown. Flowers 3–12, in a crowded head; branches 1–7 cm long, appearing as if on the side of the stem (in upper third of stem); perianth segments dark with translucent margins, red-brown, 4–5 mm long, the outer slightly longer than the inner ones; involu-

cral bract 2–20 cm long, cylindrical, resembling a continuation of stem. Fruit a blunt-tipped capsule, about equal to the perianth segments; seeds lacking tail-like appendages.
Where Found lake shores, wet meadows.

Juncus biglumis L. **TWO-FLOWER RUSH**
Habit tufted perennial rush, from a short rhizome; stems erect, 5–15 cm tall, leafless apart from one leaf-like bract more or less same height as inflorescence. Leaves basal, round in cross-section, almost as long as stem. Flowers in a terminal inflorescence with two dark brown flowers arranged vertically. Fruit a dark brown capsule, notched on its tip, protruding from the tepals.
Where Found occasional in open wet soil in seeps, along rivulets and streams, in pond margins and depressions usually in mountainous areas in Denali.
Similar Species distinguished from other species of *Juncus* in Denali by its two-flowered, terminal inflorescence with a short, leaf-like bract.

♦ *Juncus bufonius* L. **TOAD RUSH**
Habit low, much-branched annual rush, from fibrous roots; stems erect or sprawling, 5–25 cm tall. Leaves on lower part of stem, narrow and involute, the lower up to 5 cm long, the upper short, nearly circular in cross-section, cross-walls absent. Flowers in an open, terminal inflorescence, commonly much branched, forming about 1/2 to 3/4 of the plant height, with many single flowers; perianth segments green, about equal; lower bract leaflike, nearly circular in cross-section, tapered, usually shorter than inflorescence. Fruit a capsule, shorter than the perianth segments; seeds lacking tail-like appendages.

Juncus alpinoarticulatus **NORTHERN GREEN RUSH**

Juncus bufonius **TOAD RUSH**

Where Found uncommon in moist, sandy meadows, pond margins, along trails and old roads, and other moist to wet places.

◆*Juncus castaneus* Sm. CHESTNUT RUSH

Habit perennial rush, with one or more small clusters of brown flowers, from long, creeping scaly rhizomes or stolons; stems erect, 10–30 cm tall. **Leaves** basal, erect, flat or slightly channeled, often as tall as stems; the lower leafy bract longer than inflorescence. **Flowers** in an inflorescence of 1–3 heads, each head with 4–10 flowers; typically with a central cluster and 1–2 stalked, smaller clusters; flowers chestnut brown, sepals brownish black and as long as or longer than the narrow obtuse petals. **Fruit** a purplish black capsule, about 6 mm long, longer than the tepals.

Where Found common at low- to high-elevations in wetlands and riparian areas, from small thermokarst pits and depressions to large meadows.

Similar Species separated from other *Juncus* by its multi-headed inflorescence and flat, channeled leaves.

◆*Juncus drummondii* E. Mey. DRUMMOND'S RUSH

Habit densely tufted perennial rush, from short, matted rhizomes; stems wiry, erect,

10–40 cm tall. **Leaves** reduced to sheaths base of the stem, or uppermost basal sheath with blade less than 1 cm long; involucral bract 1–3 cm long, cylindrical, resembling a continuation of stem. **Flowers** in a loose head with 1 to 4, nearly terminal flowers, appearing as if on side of stem; perianth segments green to brown. **Fruit** a notched capsule, longer than perianth segments; seeds with long, tail-like appendages at each end.

Where Found occasional in alpine snowbeds, wet slopes, moist meadows.

◆*Juncus filiformis* L. THREAD RUSH

Habit perennial rush, from creeping rhizomes; stems arising singly, not in dense clusters, round, finely grooved, 10–50 cm tall. **Leaves** reduced to small sheaths at base of stem; sheaths dull, light brown; involucral

Juncus drummondii DRUMMOND'S RUSH

Juncus castaneus CHESTNUT RUSH

Juncus filiformis THREAD RUSH

bract 7–20 cm long, erect, resembling a continuation of the stem. Flowers in a head-like cluster, with numerous flowers on branches 0.5–3 cm long, appearing as if on the side of the stem, located about halfway between tip of involucral bract and base of the stem; perianth segments pale green or whitish, 3–4 mm long. Fruit a globe-shaped capsule, about as long as the perianth segments.

Where Found occasional in wet meadows and sandy shores.

♦*Juncus mertensianus* Bong. MERTENS' RUSH
Habit loosely tufted perennial rush, from elongated rhizomes; stems erect, 10–25 cm tall. Leaves 2–3 on lower part of stem, occasionally longer than stem, nearly circular in cross-section, tapered, the early leaves stiff, with prominent complete cross-walls; sheaths open, with rounded, ear-shaped lobes; involucral bract solitary, short, as long as or longer than inflorescence. Flowers numerous, in single, terminal, hemispheric heads; perianth segments dark brown; Fruit a cylindric to ovate capsule, slightly shorter than the perianth segments; seeds lacking tail-like appendages.

Where Found occasional in alpine meadows, bogs, muskegs, shores.

Juncus stygius L. MOOR RUSH
Habit loosely tufted perennial rush; stems erect, 10–20 cm tall. Leaves 1–3 on lower part of stem, erect or ascending, nearly circular in cross-section, tapered, lacking cross-walls; involucral bract leaflike, usually slightly longer than inflorescence. Flowers 2–5, in usually one (to three) terminal heads; perianth segments green or light brown with wide translucent margins. Fruit a blunt capsule, 1.5 times longer than the perianth segments,

pale brown to straw-colored; seeds with tail-like appendages at each end.

Where Found uncommon on margins of bog pools, wet mossy places.

Juncus supiniformis Engelm.
HAIRY-LEAF RUSH
Habit loosely tufted perennial rush, from short rhizomes; stems erect or spreading, 10–30 cm long, often submerged, rooting at nodes, often also viviparous (producing plantlets in the inflorescence). Leaves 2–4 on lower part of stem, nearly circular in cross-section, tapered; early leaves threadlike, flaccid; older leaves firm and erect, usually submerged, with crosswalls; sheaths open, with conspicuous hyaline margins and auricles (ear-shaped lobes); involucral bract shorter than inflorescence. Flowers 3–10, in 2 to 6 terminal heads, the branches ascending; perianth segments dark brown or reddish brown. Fruit a narrowly cylindric, dark brown to black capsule, often twice as long as perianth segments; seeds without tail-like appendages.

Where Found uncommon in swamps, pond margins, bogs.

Luzula WOODRUSH
(Latin, *lux*, light, suggested by leaves shining with dew.)

1 Flowers single, at end of ultimate branches of paniculate or umbellate, somewhat drooping inflorescence; branches threadlike 2
1 Flowers crowded, in few- to many-flowered glomerules or spikes 5
2 Inflorescence umbel-like.........*L. rufescens*
2 Inflorescence a loose compound cyme 3
3 Bracts entire to slightly ciliate; bractlets entire to lacerate but never strongly ciliate; stem leaves usually 4 or more ....*L. parviflora*
3 Bracts and bractlets strongly long-ciliate.....4
4 Lowest bract 0.4–1 cm long; stem leaves 2, thin, more or less shiny green; seeds dark brown ...
.........................*L. wahlenbergii*
4 Lowest bract 1.5–2.5 cm long; stem leaves 3, thick, dull bluish to grayish green; seeds pale yellowish brown.....................*L. piperi*
5 Leaves involute 6
5 Leaves flat 7
6 Inflorescence spikelike, drooping....*L. spicata*
6 Inflorescence often of several glomerules, on erect or spreading stiff branches....*L. confusa*

Juncus mertensianus MERTENS' RUSH

7 Bracts of inflorescence usually conspicuous, longer than inflorescence; inflorescence often dense and glomerate, occasionally with smaller lateral and stalked glomerules . . . *L. multiflora*

7 Bracts of inflorescence short and inconspicuous
. . . . 8

8 Leaves 2–3 mm wide, with thin attenuate tips; stems slender; inflorescence of several few-flowered, drooping glomerules on threadlike branches . . . . *L. arcuata*

8 Leaves 3–5 mm wide, with blunt, callous tips . 9

9 Inflorescence capitate . . . . *L. nivalis*

9 Inflorescence of several erect-ascending, stalked glomerules . . . . *L. kjellmaniana*

◆ *Luzula arcuata* (Wahlenb.) Sw.
CURVED WOODRUSH

Habit loosely tufted perennial rush, with drooping clusters of flowers borne on long peduncles, from short rhizomes; stems slender, arched, 10-25 cm tall, with 1-3 small leaves. **Leaves** mostly basal, flat, narrow (2-3 mm wide), shorter than stems; sheaths purple-brown. **Flowers** in an open cyme of 2-10 drooping branches, with terminal clusters of 3-5 flowers; tepals 6, light brown with hairy margins. **Fruit** a capsule with 3 small seeds.

Where Found in snowbeds, heath tundra, scree-slopes, and other alpine habitats, on both sides of Alaska Range crest.

Similar Species *Luzula parviflora* also has drooping inflorescence branches, but that species with only one flower at end of a branch.

◆ *Luzula confusa* Lindeb.
NORTHERN WOODRUSH

Habit loosely tufted perennial rush, with small, dense clusters of flowers, from short rhizomes and fibrous roots; stems stiff and upright, 10-25 cm tall, with deep purple-brown, shiny bases. **Leaves** basal and along stem, with reddish sheaths; basal leaves narrow and involute, and can persist on the plant for a number of years; stem leaves alternate, 1 or 2 per stem. **Flowers** in an inflorescence of 1–4 erect, stalked clusters of 2-5 flowers, or sometimes clusters packed together and appear to be a single cylindric spike; tepals 6, dark brown. **Fruit** a capsule with 3 small seeds.

Where Found common in alpine tundra and shrublands, fellfields, and open gravelly areas.

Similar Species separated from other *Luzula* species by its involute leaves, and densely clustered flowers.

Luzula kjellmaniana Miyabe & Kudô
TUNDRA WOODRUSH

Habit loosely tufted perennial rush, from fibrous roots; stems upright, 10-25 cm tall, with 1-3 alternate leaves. **Leaves** basal and along stem; basal leaves flat, wide (4–8 mm), abruptly pointed at tip, shorter than stems and with gray-brown sheaths; often with many persistent dead leaves. **Flowers** in an open raceme of 2-5 clusters, each with 3-8

Luzula arcuata CURVED WOODRUSH

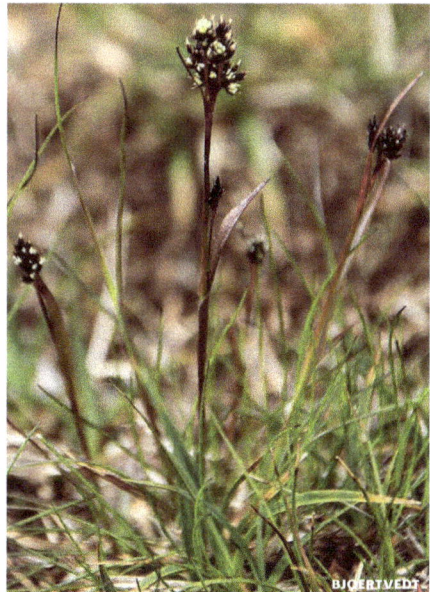

Luzula confusa NORTHERN WOODRUSH

flowers; some clusters on thin, arched branches, some sessile; tepals 6, brown and somewhat translucent. Fruit a chestnut brown capsule, shorter than the tepals, opening by three valves to release three small seeds.

Where Found occasional in alpine tundra, snowbeds, and sparsely vegetated areas; most common on steep, north-facing slopes.

Similar Species tundra woodrush recognized by its wide, pale leaves and pale inflorescence.

♦ *Luzula multiflora* (Ehrh.) Lej.
COMMON WOODRUSH

Habit densely tufted perennial rush, from fibrous roots; stems 10–35 cm tall. Leaves basal and along stem; basal leaves flat, 2–4 mm wide, with white-ciliate margins; stem leaves 2–3, alternate; leafy bract longer than inflorescence. Flowers in a raceme of 2–5 clusters of 8–16 flowers; there is often one large sessile head and a few smaller, lateral, stalked heads; tepals 6, brown with pale margins Fruit a capsule slightly shorter than the tepals, splitting open by three valves to release 3 small seeds.

Where Found common in woodlands, shrublands, gravel bars, and (less frequently) tundra.

Similar Species the white-ciliate leaf margins separate this species from other members of the genus *Luzula* in Denali.

Luzula nivalis (Laest.) Spreng.
ARCTIC WOODRUSH
Luzula arctica Blytt

Habit densely tufted perennial rush, with a single terminal cluster of flowers, from fibrous roots; stems stiff, brown at base, 8–20 cm tall. Leaves mostly basal (stems sometimes with a single leaf), grass-like, flat, 3–5 mm wide, sometimes purple-tinged, often persisting on plant for many years; stems with only a few leaves; inflorescence subtended by a small red-brown bract. Flowers superficially in a single head (but actually a cluster of 1–3 smaller heads); flowers with 6 tepals, 6 stamens, and 3 stigmas. Fruit a capsule with 3 small seeds.

Where Found snowbeds, heath tundra, *Dryas* tundra, fellfields, and moist gravelly places in the mountains.

Similar Species the flat leaves of this species help distinguish it from *Luzula confusa* and the uncommon *L. spicata*; *L. multiflora* can also have a very dense inflorescence (though typically it has several distinct heads), but that species distinguished by its copious long-white hairs along the leaf margin.

♦ *Luzula parviflora* (Ehrh.) Desv.
SMALL-FLOWER WOODRUSH

Habit loosely tufted perennial rush, from elongate rhizomes, with a loose, drooping inflorescence and wide leaves; stems 20–50 cm tall, green or slightly reddish at base. Leaves basal and along stem; basal leaves nu-

Luzula multiflora COMMON WOODRUSH

Luzula parviflora SMALL-FLOWER WOODRUSH

merous, flat, 6–10 mm wide; stem leaves usually 3–5, 5–7 mm wide. Flowers in a loose, drooping cyme with a single flower at end of each branch; tepals green or brown, about as long as the capsule. Fruit a shiny brown capsule, with three seeds.

Where Found occasional in meadows, shrub thickets and tundra in moist sites across Denali, but most common in the mountains, particularly in subalpine meadows.

Similar Species similar to *Luzula arcuata,* another rush with drooping inflorescence branches, but that species with several flowers clustered together at end of a branch.

Luzula piperi (Coville) M.E. Jones
PIPER'S WOODRUSH

Habit loosely tufted perennial rush, from short rhizomes; stems bluish green, 20–30 cm tall. Leaves mostly basal, flat, dull bluish to grayish green, sparsely fringed with fine hairs only around the sheaths, 5–10 cm long, 3–4 mm wide, with sharp tips, shorter than the stems; stem leaves 3, linear, to 5 mm wide. Flowers in loose, open, nodding inflorescence; flowers borne singly or in 2-flowered clusters; perianth segments dark brown with distinct midribs, lanceolate; stamens 6; bracts and bractlets fringed with long, curly hairs. Fruit a brown elliptic capsule, longer than the perianth segments.

Where Found alpine meadows and slopes.

Luzula rufescens Fisch. ex E.Mey.
HAIRY WOODRUSH

Habit loosely tufted perennial rush, with an umbel of dark reddish flowers, from elongated rhizomes; stems 10–30 cm tall. Leaves both basal and along stem, with reddish sheaths; basal leaves narrow, 1–4 mm wide, with ciliate margins; lowest bract half the length of inflorescence. Flowers in an umbel-like inflorescence; umbel branches thin, each bearing a single flower; tepals brown, scarious margined. Fruit a capsule with 3 seeds.

Where Found occasional in woodlands, meadows, shores, including recently burned areas on the north side of Denali, from the boreal zone into the subalpine.

Similar Species the umbel-like inflorescence distinguishes this *Luzula* from other woodrush species.

♦ *Luzula spicata* (L.) DC. SPIKED WOODRUSH

Habit densely tufted perennial rush, from fibrous roots; stems erect, 10–30 cm tall. Leaves narrow, channeled, sparsely fringed

with fine hairs, about 5–15 cm long, 1–3 mm wide, with sharp tips; sheaths brown to purplish. Flowers in a drooping, spikelike head with 5 to 10 clusters, each cluster with 3 to 6 flowers; perianth segments brown with paler tips, 2–3 mm long, lanceolate, tapering into long awns; stamens 6. Fruit an elliptic, pointed capsule, shorter than the perianth segments.

Where Found uncommon in alpine tundra and open slopes.

Luzula wahlenbergii Rupr.
WAHLENBERG'S WOODRUSH

Habit tufted perennial rush; stems erect, 10–35 cm tall. Leaves mostly basal, usually not more than 3 mm wide. Flowers solitary (but often two to four close together), in a diffuse inflorescence; branches very slender, curved; perianth segments acute, brown with hyaline tips. Fruit an ovoid capsule about equaling the perianth.

Where Found alpine slopes, moist meadows, streambanks.

JUNCAGINACEAE
Arrow-Grass Family

Triglochin ARROW-GRASS
(Greek, *treis,* three, and *glochis,* a point.)

1 Large plants with ovate, 6-parted capsules; leaf blades compressed in cross-section *T. maritima*
1 Smaller plants with linear club-shaped, 3-parted capsules; leaf blades more or less round in cross-section . . . . *T. palustris*

♦ *Triglochin maritima* L.
SEASIDE ARROW-GRASS

Habit perennial wetland herb from a rhizome; stems to about 60 cm tall. Leaves all basal, tufted, linear, 10–50 cm long, 2–3 mm wide, flat. Flowers many, in a leafless, spikelike raceme, usually longer than the leaves;

Luzula spicata SPIKED WOODRUSH

pedicels 2–4 mm long, ascending in fruit; perianth parts usually 6; stamens usually 6; fertile ovaries 6. Fruit a dry, oblong to ovate capsule, splitting into 6 carpels at maturity; seeds 1 per carpel.

Where Found uncommon in wet soil, muskegs, river banks.

♦ *Triglochin palustris* L.
MARSH ARROW-GRASS

Habit perennial wetland herb from a rhizome; stems 15–50 cm tall. Leaves all basal, tufted, linear, tapering to a sharp point, 10–30 cm long, 0.5–2 mm wide. Flowers many, in a leafless, spikelike raceme, usually longer than the leaves; pedicels slender, 2–6 mm long, erect in fruit; perianth parts usually 6; stamens usually 6; fertile ovaries 3. Fruit a dry, linear to club-shaped capsule, 6–7 mm long, splitting into 3 carpels when mature; seeds one per carpel.

Where Found uncommon on wet soil, shores, fens, muskegs.

Triglochin maritima **SEASIDE ARROW-GRASS**

LILIACEAE
Lily Family

1	Stem leaves whorled	*Fritillaria*
1	Stem leaves not whorled	2
2	Flowers axillary, 1 or 2 together	*Streptopus*
2	Flowers single, terminal	*Gagea*

Fritillaria FRITILLARY
(Latin, checkered, from the checkered marking of the perianth of some species.)

♦ *Fritillaria camschatcensis* (L.) Ker. Gawl.
KAMCHATKA FRITILLARY, BLACK LILY

Habit perennial herb, from a bulb of several larger, fleshy scales subtended by numerous small, rice-grain bulblets; stems stout, smooth, 20–60 cm tall. Leaves usually in 2 or 3 main whorls of 5 to 10 on upper part of stem, with a few scattered and alternate leaves near tip, lanceolate, 5–10 cm long, 0.5–2.5 cm wide, smooth. Flowers usually several, spreading to nodding, in axils of upper leaves; bronze to purplish brown or nearly black, rarely yellowish green, rarely mottled, narrowly bell-shaped; of 6 similar, distinct tepals, oblong-lanceolate to elliptic or ovate, 2–3 cm long, ridged lengthwise on inner surface; stamens 6; pistil 1, 3-chambered. Fruit an erect, barrel-shaped capsule, bluntly 6-angled, 2–3.5 cm long; seeds numerous, flattened.

Where Found uncommon in moist subalpine meadows.

Triglochin palustris **MARSH ARROW-GRASS**

Gagea ALP-LILY

(In honor of English naturalist Sir Thomas Gage, 1791-1820.)

◆ *Gagea serotina* (L.) Ker Gawl. ALP-LILY
Lloydia serotina (L.) Rchb.

Habit delicate perennial herb, from a small, oblong, grayish, fibrous-coated bulb at end of a rhizome; flowering stems smooth, 5-15 cm tall. Leaves mostly basal, grass-like, entire-margined, waxy to the touch, almost as tall as the flowering stem; stems leaves similar but shorter, opposite. Flowers single at end of stem; tepals 6, cream colored, with prominent dark purplish veins; stamens 6, pistil 1. Fruit a rounded capsule which splits open by three valves. Flowering mid- to late-summer (the epithet 'serotina' means 'late-flowering').

Where Found common at high-elevations in tundra, rocky areas, and meadows.

Similar Species the purple-veined white flowers, with 6 petals are distinctive; it can also be recognized by the thread-like, waxy leaves alone, but plants are inconspicuous when not flowering.

Streptopus TWISTEDSTALK

(Greek, twisted stalk, referring to the stem.)

◆ *Streptopus amplexifolius* (L.) DC.
CLASPING TWISTEDSTALK

Habit perennial herb, with white flowers, from a thick, short rhizome covered with fibrous roots; stems erect, 15–80 cm tall, branched, twisting at each node (zigzag), smooth throughout or coarsely hairy on lower third. Leaves opposite, ovate, with acuminate tip and noticeable parallel veins, base of leaf clasping stem. Flowers from leaf axils, pendent; tepals white, fused at base, divided into six, acuminate, upturned lobes; stamens 6, pistil 1. Fruit an elongate red berry with watery flesh. Flowering early summer; fruits ripening mid- to late-July.

Where Found occasional in moist, herb-rich meadows, forested areas, and shrub thickets; relatively rare north of the Alaska range crest, but common on south slopes of the range, especially in the subalpine zone.

Similar Species the twisted stem and clasping leaves are distinctive; it could potentially be confused with *Veratrum viride* (uncommon on south side of Alaska Range), but that species does not have red berry-like fruit, dangling white flowers, or a kinked stalk.

Gagea serotina ALP-LILY

Fritillaria camschatcensis
KAMCHATKA FRITILLARY

Streptopus amplexifolius
CLASPING TWISTEDSTALK

MELANTHIACEAE
False Hellebore Family

1 Leaves linear; plants from a bulb . . . . . *Anticlea*
1 Leaves broad; plants from a short rhizome . . . .
 . . . . *Veratrum*

Anticlea DEATHCAMAS
(Greek, yoke and gland, referring to the pair of glands in some species.)

♦ *Anticlea elegans* (Pursh) Rydb.
MOUNTAIN DEATHCAMAS
Zigadenus elegans Pursh

Habit perennial herb, with long linear leaves and 6-parted white or pale yellow flowers, from a deep, scaly, narrowly ovate bulb 2–3 cm long; flowering stems smooth, glaucous, 10–60 cm tall. Leaves 1–3, all basal, narrow and linear with parallel venation and a keeled midrib, 10–30 cm long, gray-green and somewhat glaucous, margins entire. Flowers 10–40, in a terminal, branched or unbranched raceme; tepals 6, white to yellow-green, each with a green gland at base; stamens 6; pistil with 3 styles. Fruit a 3-parted capsule. Flowering early, one of the first herbs to emerge in the spring, appearing on sunny, south-facing, rocky slopes soon after snowmelt.

Where Found common in well-drained, open situations at low- to high-elevations, in open

woods, meadows, rocky tundra, floodplains, dry slopes.

Similar Species no other species in Denali has grass-like leaves and numerous six-parted pale flowers.

Note Not to be eaten as the plant is highly poisonous.

Veratrum FALSE-HELLEBORE
(Ancient name of the Hellebore.)

♦ *Veratrum viride* Aiton
GREEN FALSE-HELLEBORE, CORN LILY
Veratrum eschscholtzii A. Gray

Habit perennial herb, from a short, stout rhizome; flowering stems robust, erect, to 2 m tall, often clustered, unbranched, leafy and short-hairy to woolly throughout or smooth in lower half. Leaves numerous along stem, round-oval to ovate-lanceolate, 10–35 cm long, 5–15 cm wide, becoming smaller and narrower upwards, prominently ribbed (accordion-pleated), smooth above, densely hairy beneath, unstalked or nearly so, clasping at base, margins entire; basal leaves absent. Flowers numerous, stalked, in a branched terminal panicle; the branches densely hairy, at least the lower drooping; the stalks 2–3 mm long, turning up as the flowers open; flowers pale green or yellow-green, with dark green centers, star-shaped, of 6 similar, distinct tepals, the tepals narrowly lanceolate to oblong-elliptic, 6–13 mm long, about twice as long as the 6 stamens; pistil 1, 3-chambered. Fruit a barrel-shaped, 3-lobed, mostly smooth capsule; seeds numerous, flat, broadly winged.

Where Found occasional in meadows and open woods at upper elevations.

Note not to be eaten as plants highly poisonous.

Anticlea elegans MOUNTAIN DEATHCAMAS

Veratrum viride GREEN FALSE-HELLEBORE

ORCHIDACEAE
Orchid Family

1 Plants saprophytic, without green stems and leaves. . . . . *Corallorhiza*

1 Plants not saprophytic, with green stems and leaves 2

2 Lip a large inflated sac more than 1 cm long. . 3

2 Lips not saclike, or if so, less than 1 cm long. . 4

3 Leaves one (basal); lip hairy . . . . *Calypso*

3 Leaves two or more (either basal or on flowering stem); lip smooth. . . . . *Cypripedium*

4 Flowers with a distinct spur projecting downward from the base of lip 5

4 Flowers not spurred 7

5 Flowers white to pale pink, spotted with dark red . . . . *Galearis*

5 Flowers white to green, not spotted 6

6 Lip three-lobed at tip; bracts greatly exceeding flowers . . . . *Dactylorhiza*

6 Lip not lobed at tip; bracts usually not exceeding flowers. . . . . *Platanthera*

7 Leaves basal. 8

7 Leaves (at least some of them) along the stem 11

8 Leaves fleshy and evergreen, mottled or veined with white; plants without bulb-like corms. . . . . *Goodyera*

8 Leaves membranous, not evergreen and not mottled or veined with white; plants with bulb-like corms. 9

9 Flowers and mature capsules about 1 cm long . . . . *Neottia*

9 Flowers and mature capsules less than 0.5 cm long 10

10 Plants small, leaves 2 or 4 . . . . *Hammarbya*

10 Plants larger, leaves 1 or 2 . . . . *Malaxis*

11 Leaves 2, opposite and unstalked . . . . . *Neottia*

11 Leaves several, alternate. . . . . *Spiranthes*

Calypso FAIRY-SLIPPER ORCHID
(Greek god, Calypso, whose name signifies concealment.)

♦ *Calypso bulbosa* (L.) Oakes
FAIRY-SLIPPER ORCHID
Habit perennial herb, with a solitary flower above a leafless stem, and one basal leaf, from a fleshy, cylindric or globe-shaped corm; stems to 15 cm tall, smooth but with 2 to 4 sheathing brown bracts. **Leaves** single, ovate, parallel veined, shiny green, 3–6.5 cm long. **Flowers** solitary; sepals and upper petals narrow, pink, 12–23 mm long; lip inflated, slipper-like, bearded, with dark red spots and a yellow center. **Fruit** an elliptic capsule, longitudinally ridged, containing hundreds of tiny seeds.

Where Found uncommon in mossy woods and open areas at low- to mid-elevations; although showy, this small, uncommon orchid is easily overlooked.

Similar Species the other orchid in Denali with a single large, spotted flower is *Cypripedium guttatum;* however, that species has two large basal leaves (not one), the lip is not bearded, and the flower lacks narrow upper pink petals.

Corallorhiza CORALROOT
(Greek, meaning coral and root.)

♦ *Corallorhiza trifida* Châtel.
EARLY CORALROOT, YELLOW CORALROOT
Habit perennial saprophytic herb, from coral-like rhizomes; stems 10–30 cm tall, pale yellow-green, smooth, with a few brown, transparent sheaths but no leaves. **Leaves** absent. **Flowers** 3–18, small, with green petals and sepals and a white lip; lip obovate, slightly lobed. **Fruit** an ellipsoid capsule, 5–15 mm long, with hundreds of minute seeds.

Where Found occasional in mossy forests and thickets, from lowlands to subalpine zone of Denali.

Similar Species no other orchid in Denali completely lacks leaves.

Note yellow coral root is dependent on mycorrhizal fungi for its food because it derives

JASON HOLLINGER

Calypso bulbosa FAIRY-SLIPPER ORCHID

little from photosynthesis and lacks fully developed leaves. The rhizome is thick and twisted, the source of the generic and common name, 'coralroot'.

Cypripedium LADY'S-SLIPPER
(Greek, Venus and shoe.)

---

1   Leaves 2, more or less opposite on lower third of stem; flower solitary, lip white, spotted with purple; plant turns black when dried . *C. guttatum*

1   Leaves 3–5; flowers 1–3, lip white . . . . *C. passerinum*

◆ *Cypripedium guttatum* Sw.
SPOTTED LADY'S-SLIPPER

Habit medium-sized perennial herb, with inflated, purple-spotted flowers, from long rhizomes; stems 10–20 cm tall, sometimes found in clusters; the whole plant covered in tiny hairs. **Leaves** two per stem, alternate to nearly opposite, clasping stem, ovate to elliptic, 2–8 cm wide and 2–15 cm long. **Flowers** single, with an upright leaf-like bract clasping the stem below the flower; petals and sepals white with red-purple blotches; upper sepal forms a hood; lower sepals fused behind the lip and leaf-like; lip large, inflated, sac-like, about 2 cm long; the spotting and coloration

of the flowers varies widely, even within local populations. **Fruit** a capsule with many minute seeds.

Where Found uncommon in mid-elevation woods, heathlands, and ridges.

Similar Species *Cypripedium passerinum* has more than two stem leaves; another orchid species with solitary spotted flowers is *Calypso bulbosa,* but that species has only one leaf and a differently shaped flower.

◆ *Cypripedium passerinum* Richardson
SPARROW-EGG LADY'S-SLIPPER

Habit perennial herb, with white, conspicuously inflated flowers, from slender rhizomes and coarse fibrous roots; stems long soft-hairy, 10–40 cm tall. **Leaves** several, alternate on stem, clasping at base, elliptic to ovate-lanceolate, sparsely long-hairy. **Flowers** one (rarely two); lower lip slipper-like, inflated, purple-speckled inside; upper sepal green and leaf-like; lateral sepals white. **Fruit** a capsule containing hundreds of minute seeds.

Where Found uncommon in mossy forests and river terraces in Denali.

Similar Species in fruit, sparrow's egg lady slipper can be confused with spotted lady's-slipper (*Cypripedium guttatum*), but that species has only two more or less opposite leaves, not several alternate leaves up the stem; both species are rare in Denali.

Corallorhiza trifida **EARLY CORALROOT**

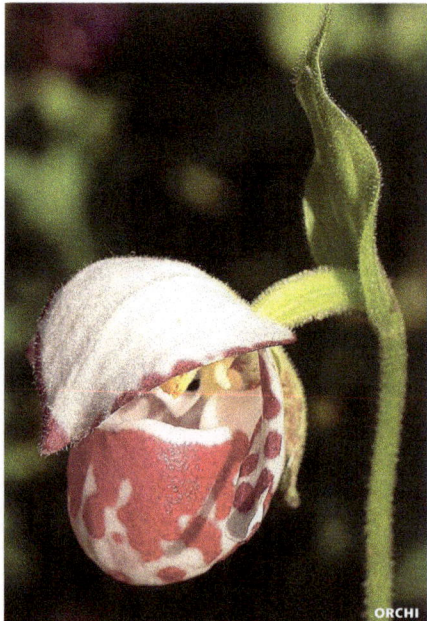

Cypripedium guttatum **SPOTTED LADY'S-SLIPPER**

Dactylorhiza FROG ORCHID

(Greek *dactylos,* finger, and *rhiza,* root, in reference to the fingerlike tubers of some species.)

♦ *Dactylorhiza viridis* (L.) R.M. Bateman, Pridgeon & M.W. Chase LONG-BRACT FROG ORCHID
Coeloglossum viride (L.) Hartm.

Habit perennial herb, with a compact spike of greenish flowers, from fleshy roots, smooth throughout; stems leafy, 15–30 cm tall. Leaves alternate, sheathing the stem, obovate to lanceolate, parallel veined, margins entire. Flowers up to 40 per stem, in a dense raceme; the lowest petal (lip) elongate, 2- or 3-lobed at tip, forming a sac-like nectar spur; the other two petals are linear, inconspicuous beneath the hooding sepals; the whole flower is greenish, sometimes blushed brown or purplish (particularly on the lip). Fruit a capsule, 7–14 mm by 4–5 mm, containing many tiny seeds.

Where Found occasional in moist meadows and snowmelt swales in the mountains.

Similar Species other orchids with multiple green flowers and several leaves include *Platanthera dilatata,* which lacks a lobed lip, and *Listera borealis,* with the lip much longer than the other petals and with a prominent central indent.

Galearis SHOWY ORCHID

(Latin galea, helmet.)

♦ *Galearis rotundifolia* (Banks ex Pursh) R.M. Bateman ROUND-LEAF ORCHID
Amerorchis rotundifolia (Banks ex Pursh) Hultén, *Orchis rotundifolia* Banks ex Pursh

Habit perennial herb, with a single basal leaf and purple- or pink-spotted white flowers, from short rhizomes and fleshy, fibrous roots; stems leafless, smooth, 10–20 cm tall. Leaves single, rounded to elliptic, simple, entire-margined, 3–7 cm long. Flowers 2–4; sepals and lateral petals white to violet-pink; lip prominent, lobed, white with purple spots, 5–10 mm long, the spur 3–7 mm long.

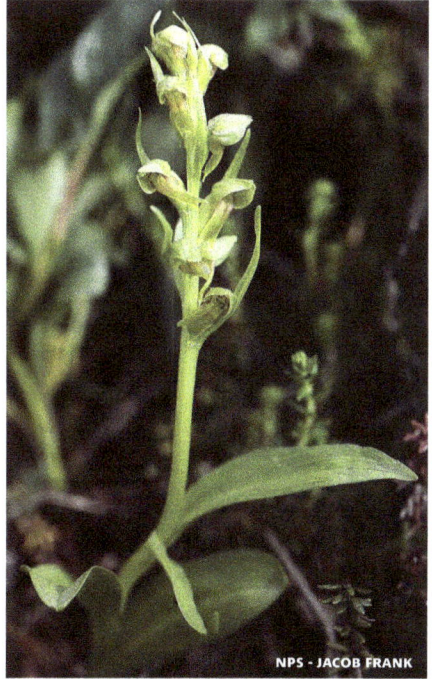

NPS - JACOB FRANK

Dactylorhiza viridis LONG-BRACT FROG ORCHID

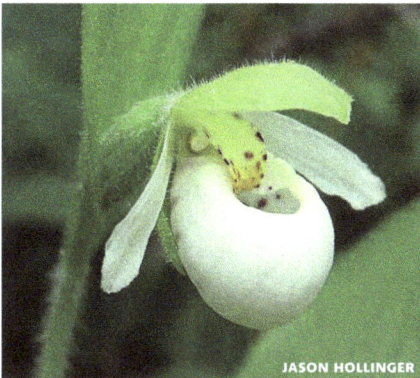

JASON HOLLINGER

Cypripedium passerinum
SPARROW-EGG LADY'S-SLIPPER

CEASOL

Galearis rotundifolia ROUND-LEAF ORCHID

Fruit an ellipsoid capsule containing many tiny seeds.

Where Found uncommon in subalpine woodlands, meadows, and along streambanks.

Similar Species round-leaf orchid could be confused with other orchids. However, in other orchids with spotted flowers (such as *Calypso bulbosa* and *Cypripedium guttatum*), the flower is much larger and solitary. The genus *Platanthera* has members in Alaska with several small flowers and a single leaf, but the flowers are never violet-spotted.

Goodyera
RATTLESNAKE-PLANTAIN
(Greek, referring to the pouch-like lip.)

♦ *Goodyera repens* (L.) R. Br.
DWARF RATTLESNAKE-PLANTAIN

Habit Evergreen white-flowered perennial herb, from slender creeping rhizomes; stems single, leafless but with several bracts, glandular-hairy, 10–25 cm tall. Leaves low to the ground in a rosette, the blade ovate and net-

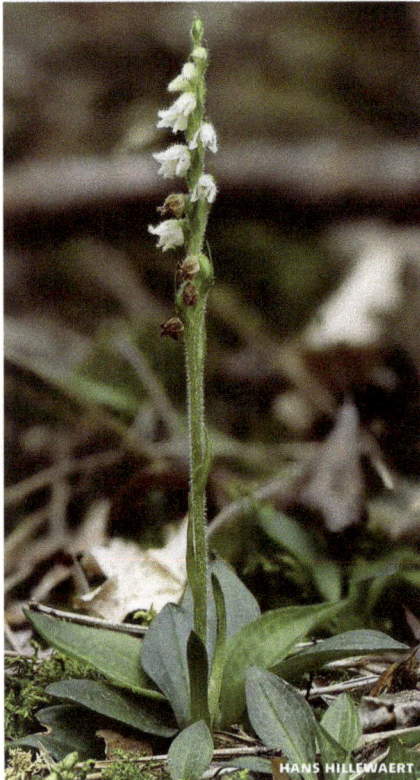

Goodyera repens
DWARF RATTLESNAKE-PLANTAIN

veined; sometimes leaves conspicuously variegated with white veins. Flowers usually fewer than 12, on one side of flowering stem, appearing somewhat twisted; composed of three petals and three sepals, all white-hairy; lowermost petal (lip) inflated; upper petals and upper sepal forming a hood. Fruit a capsule containing many tiny seeds.

Where Found occasional in mossy understory of Denali's lowland boreal forests; sites moist to wet.

Similar Species multiple white flowers and an inflated lip separate this species from other Denali orchids.

Hammarbya
BOG ADDER'S-MOUTH
(Named after Hammarby, the summer home of Linnaeus.)

♦ *Hammarbya paludosa* (L.) Kuntze
BOG ADDER'S-MOUTH ORCHID
Malaxis paludosa (L.) Sw.

Habit perennial herb, from a bulblike base (corm), with a few fibrous roots; stems 5–15 cm tall, leafless, slender, glabrous, angled above. Leaves 2–5, in a basal cluster, ovate, 1–3 cm long, pale green, the base broadly

Hammarbya paludosa
BOG ADDER'S-MOUTH ORCHID

sheathing the stem. Flowers several to many, on ascending pedicels, in a terminal, spike-like raceme; small (about 6 mm long), yellowish green; sepals 2–2.5 mm long, the middle one drooping, the lateral 2 erect; petals 1–1.5 mm long; lip erect, 1–3 mm long, triangular, green-veined; column about 0.3 mm long. Fruit an ovate capsule, 3–5 mm long.

Where Found uncommon in sphagnum moss of bogs and muskegs.

Malaxis
ADDER'S-MOUTH ORCHID
(Greek, in reference to soft texture of leaves.)

Malaxis monophyllos
WHITE ADDER'S-MOUTH ORCHID

♦ *Malaxis monophyllos* (L.) Sw.
WHITE ADDER'S-MOUTH ORCHID

Habit perennial herb, from bulblike base (corm), with a few fibrous roots; stems leafless, glabrous, pale green, 10–20 cm tall. Leaves single (rarely two and nearly opposite), near base, ovate to elliptic, 2–8 cm long, 1–4 cm wide, light green, keeled on back, the sheathing stalk 2–3 cm long. Flowers in a loose, terminal, spikelike raceme; small, greenish white, the flower stalks (pedicels) about 2.5 mm long; sepals 1–2 mm long; petals 1–2 mm long, linear, bent back, pointed at tip; lip drooping, 2 mm long, broadly triangular; column less than 1 mm long. Fruit an erect, elliptic capsule, 4–5 mm long.

Where Found uncommon in open woods, meadows.

Neottia TWAYBLADE
(Greek, nest, a reference to the tangled roots of orchids in this genus.)

1 Flowers purplish; lip narrow, deeply cleft; leaves ovate-cordate or deltoid . . . . *N. cordata*
1 Flowers green; lip broad, slightly cleft or notched at tip; leaves ovate-elliptic . . . . *N. borealis*

♦ *Neottia borealis* (Morong) Szlach.
NORTHERN TWAYBLADE
Listera borealis Morong

Habit perennial herb, with two stem leaves and green flowers with large, flattened lips, from fleshy fibrous roots; stems 5–20 cm tall, glandular-hairy above. Leaves simple, ovate-elliptic, with parallel veins and entire margins. Flowers 2–20 on short pedicels, green, in an open spike; sepals and upper petals narrow, 2–3 mm long, strongly bent back from the column and lip, 3–6 mm long; lip flattened into an oblong flap, expanded into two rounded auricles at its tip, and with an elongate dip in the middle. Fruit an ellipsoid capsule, containing many tiny seeds.

Where Found uncommon in meadows, forest and woodlands (and is most frequent in mossy sites on river terraces).

Similar Species *Neottia borealis* can be distinguished from *Neottia cordata* by the color of the flowers (green instead of purple) and the shape of the flower lip: oblong in *N. borealis* and deeply cleft in *N. cordata*; also, *N. cordata* occurs only south of the Alaska Range in Denali.

Note The common name 'twayblade' refers to the two leaves opposite each other on the stem, often above the stem midpoint.

◆ *Neottia cordata* (L.) Rich.
HEARTLEAF TWAYBLADE
Listera cordata (L.) R. Br.

Habit perennial herb, from slender rhizomes, with fibrous roots; stems 7–25 cm tall, with 2 leaves, smooth except slightly hairy just above the leaves. Leaves two, usually below middle of stem, opposite, broadly ovate to kidney-shaped, 1–4 cm long, 1–4 cm wide, smooth, heart-shaped at base, abruptly pointed at tip. Flowers 4–20, in a terminal raceme, purplish or maroon; sepals 2–3 mm long, ovate; petals similar to sepals; lip 3–6 mm long, linear to oblong, deeply cleft into 2 linear-lanceolate lobes, with 2 awl-like teeth at base; column 0.5–1.5 mm long. Fruit a spreading, ovoid capsule, 4–6 mm long.

Where Found occasional in moist woods, streambanks, bogs.

Platanthera BOG ORCHID
(Greek *platys*, broad, and *anthera*, anther.)

1 Stem naked . . . . *P. obtusata*
1 Stem leafy 2
2 Spur broadly club-shaped to saccate; stem with numerous scalelike bracts . . . . *P. stricta*
2 Spur cylindrical; stem with a few leaflike bracts 3
3 Flowers greenish, lip not conspicuously dilated at base . . . . *P. aquilonis*
3 Flowers pure white; lip conspicuously dilated at base . . . . *P. dilatata*

◆ *Platanthera aquilonis* Sheviak
BOG ORCHID
Platanthera hyperborea auct. non (L.) Lindl.

Habit perennial herb, with a slender spike of delicate greenish white flowers and several stem leaves, with a few fibrous roots; stems to 35 cm tall, thick, soft, leafy. Leaves several, alternate, linear-lanceolate, sheathing the stem, gradually reduced upwards to bracts. Flowers many in a dense, terminal, cylindric spike; greenish or white; each flower with three petals and three sepals; the upper two petals and centermost sepal form a hood over the flower, the two lateral sepals spread to the side, the lower petal (or lip) has a spur at the back, is narrowly triangular in shape, and not dilated at base. In Alaska, the flowers are reported to be odorless (Sheviak 1999). Fruit a cylindric capsule.

Neottia borealis NORTHERN TWAYBLADE

Neottia cordata HEARTLEAF TWAYBLADE

Where Found occasional in moist meadows and floodplains.

Similar Species similar to *Platanthera dilatata,* usually differing in flower color and shape of the lip; however, the species hybridize, and it can be difficult to clearly distinguish the two.

◆ *Platanthera dilatata* (Pursh) Lindl. ex L.C. Beck
SCENTBOTTLE, WHITE BOG ORCHID

Habit spicy-sweet scented perennial herb, with a few fibrous roots; stems 15–40 cm tall, leafy. **Leaves** several, alternate on the stem, broadly linear-lanceolate; uppermost leaves reduced to bracts. **Flowers** in a compact cylindrical spike; petals and sepals pure white, 4–11 mm long; each flower with a spurred lower lip, two spreading lateral sepals, and two petals and an uppermost sepal forming a hood over the flower. **Fruit** a cylindric capsule.

Where Found uncommon in bogs and other wetlands at low-elevations to the subalpine.

Similar Species the base of the lip is expanded, with two rounded lobes from the sides, unlike other *Platanthera* in Denali.

◆ *Platanthera obtusata* (Banks ex Pursh) Lindl.
BLUNT-LEAF ORCHID

Habit perennial herb, with delicate greenish flowers and a single basal leaf, from a few fleshy-tuberous roots; stems 10–35 cm tall, without leaves. **Leaves** solitary, sheathing the stem at base of plant, the blade elliptic or oblanceolate with a rounded tip. **Flowers** 3–15, in an open terminal spike, greenish white in color; bilaterally symmetric and small (less than 1 cm wide); tepals narrow, the lateral tepals curved back towards the stem; lip 3–8 mm long, narrowly triangular, curved outward at tip, with a narrow spur at base. **Fruit** a cylindric capsule containing many tiny seeds.

Platanthera dilatata SCENTBOTTLE

Platanthera aquilonis BOG ORCHID

Platanthera obtusata BLUNT-LEAF ORCHID

Where Found occasional in mossy forests and shrublands, often on river terraces.

Similar Species Denali's only *Platanthera* with a solitary basal leaf.

♦ *Platanthera stricta* Lindl.
SLENDER BOG ORCHID
Habenaria saccata Greene, *Habenaria stricta* (Lindl.) Rydb.

Habit perennial herb, with greenish flowers, from a tuberous stem-base, with a few fibrous roots; stems 30–80 cm tall, stout, leafy. **Leaves** near base lanceolate, obtuse; upper leaves smaller, acute; reduced to bracts below inflorescence; leaves generally widely diverging from stem. **Flowers** in a slender, open spike, small, green, usually lightly scented, bracted; bracts of lower flowers 2–5 cm long, leaflike, much reduced in upper flowers; lateral sepals 4–6 mm long, broadly lanceolate, thin, 3-veined, spreading; upper sepal ovate, slightly hooded at tip, 3–5 mm long; petals lanceolate to ovate, fleshy, often purplish tinged, asymmetric, in close contact with upper sepal to form a hood; lip narrowly oblong or linear, 5–8 mm long; spur generally shorter than lip, inflated, scrotum- or sac-shaped, only slightly, if at all curved; column short and thick, about 2 mm long. **Fruit** an erect capsule, to 15 mm long.

Where Found uncommon in open woods, thickets, meadows, muskegs.

Spiranthes LADIES'-TRESSES
(Name from the spiral arrangement of the flowers.)

♦ *Spiranthes romanzoffiana* Cham.
HOODED LADIES'-TRESSES
Habit perennial herb, with a spiraled spike of delicate white flowers; from long, fleshy, tuberous roots (and a few fibrous roots); stems 10–30 cm tall. **Leaves** basal and along stem; basal leaves few, linear; stem leaves sheathing and alternate; upper leaves highly reduced bracts. **Flowers** in a dense cylindrical spike, arranged in spirals of four; white at tip, becoming greenish at base; upper petal and the two sepals fused to form a curved hood, the lower lip curving back towards the stem. **Fruit** a cylindric capsule containing many tiny seeds.

Where Found occasional in wet meadows in boreal zone on both sides of Alaska Range.

Platanthera stricta SLENDER BOG ORCHID

Spiranthes romanzoffiana
HOODED LADIES'-TRESSES

Similar Species potentially confused with *Platanthera dilatata*, another orchid with a spike of spiraled white flowers; in that species, flowers with elongate, wing-like petals; *Spiranthes romanzoffiana* has a much thicker, tightly spiraled inflorescence, and the flowers are more tubular.

POACEAE
Grass Family

KEY TO POACEAE GROUPS

1   Spikelets on short stalks, forming a panicle or raceme 2
1   Spikelets sessile (or nearly so), in spikes or spike-like racemes 5
2   Spikelets 1-flowered . . . . Group I
2   Spikelets 2- to many-flowered 3
3   Spikelets with 1 perfect terminal floret, and 2 lateral male or sterile florets. . . . . *Anthoxanthum*
3   Spikelets normally with only bisexual flowers   4
4   Lemmas with a bent awn arising from the back; glumes usually as long as spikelet . . . . Group II
4   Lemmas awnless or with an apical awn; glumes shorter than first floret . . . . Group III
5   Spikelets on one side of rachis; spikes usually more than 1 . . . . *Beckmannia*
5   Spikelets on opposite sides of rachis; spike mostly solitary and terminal . . . . Group IV

GROUP I

1   Inflorescence cylindrical or ovoid, spikelike. . . 2
1   Inflorescence not spikelike 3
2   Glumes awnless . . . . *Alopecurus*
2   Glumes awned . . . . *Phleum*
3   Inflorescence narrow and short; glumes minute, much shorter than lemma; fruit at maturity loosely enclosed in lemma. . . . . *Phippsia*
3   Inflorescence paniculate or racemose; fruit at maturity adherent to lemma 4
4   Spikelet disarticulating below glumes; broad-leaved forest species . . . . *Cinna*
4   Spikelet disarticulating above glumes 5
5   Lemmas surrounded at base by a tuft of stiff hairs, in some species reaching to tip of lemma; lemmas awned dorsally . . . . *Calamagrostis*
5   Lemmas lacking tuft of hairs at base 6
6   Glumes shorter than lemma . . . . . *Arctagrostis*
6   Glumes longer than lemma; lemma with or without dorsal awn. 7
7   Paleas present, at least 1/2 as long as lemma. . . . . *Podagrostis*

7   Paleas absent, or if present then less than 1/4 as long as lemma . . . . *Agrostis*

GROUP II

1   Lemmas bifid at tip, with a flat bent awn attached between lobes. . . . . *Danthonia*
1   Lemmas merely toothed at tip, awned from back of body 2
2   Lemmas convex, awned from below the middle . . . . *Deschampsia*
2   Lemmas keeled, awned from above the middle 3
3   Awn long-exserted, scabrous. . . . . *Trisetum*
3   Awn barely exserted, smooth. . . . . . . *Vahlodea*

GROUP III

1   Lemmas bifid at tip, awned from notch or just below 2
1   Lemmas not bifid at tip; if awned the awn apical 3
2   Callus of floret bearded . . . . *Schizachne*
2   Callus of floret not bearded . . . . *Bromus*
3   Glumes nearly as long as lowermost floret . . . 4
3   Glumes shorter than lowermost floret. 5
4   Tall marsh plants from a creeping rhizome; leaves broad and flat, yellowish green or purplish; ligules lacerate. . . . . *Arctophila*
4   Dwarf terrestrial tufted plants with crinkly roots; leaves flat or folded, yellowish green with a metallic luster; ligules entire . . . . *Puccinellia*
5   Lateral nerves of lemma arched or converging; lemmas awnless, acuminate or awned 6
5   Lateral nerves of lemma parallel; lemmas awnless, with blunt or rounded tip 8
6   Lemmas distinctly rounded on the back 7
6   Lemmas distinctly keeled; tip blunt or erose. . . . . *Poa*
7   Lemmas awned or with acuminate tip . *Festuca*
7   Lemmas awnless; tip blunt or erose . . . . . . *Poa*
8   Lemmas prominently nerved . . . . *Glyceria*
8   Lemmas obscurely nerved; glumes minute much shorter than lowermost lemma . . . . *Puccinellia*

GROUP IV

1   Spikelets single at each node . . . . *Elymus*
1   Spikelets in groups of 2 or more at each node   2
2   Spikelets 1-flowered . . . . *Hordeum*
2   Spikelets 2- to 9-flowered 3
3   Leaf blades stiff, harsh . . . . *Leymus*
3   Leaf blades soft . . . . *Elymus*

Agrostis BENTGRASS
(Greek, referring to the field habitat of many of these species.)

1 Mature inflorescence more or less open, the branches spreading and visible . . . *A. hyemalis*
1 Mature inflorescence more or less constricted, the branches mostly appressed to the central axis
. . . . 2
2 Inflorescence dense, the branches barely visible, covered with spikelets to their base. *A. exarata*
2 Inflorescence loose, the branches visible, with fewer spikelets (these mostly above middle of branch) . . . . *A. mertensii*

Agrostis exarata Trin.
SPIKE BENTGRASS, SPIKE REDTOP
Agrostis alaskana Hultén

Habit tufted perennial grass, from fibrous roots; stems 2–10 dm tall. Leaves flat, 4–15 cm long, 1–8 mm wide; ligule 2–4 mm long; sheath smooth to rough-hairy. Spikelets in a spikelike inflorescence, 4–20 cm long; branches ascending or appressed, barely visible and densely covered with spikelets to their base; spikelets numerous, crowded; glumes acuminate or awn-pointed, 2–4 mm long, scabrous, especially on the keel; lemma about 2 mm long, often with an awn.

Where Found moist meadows, open woods.

◆Agrostis hyemalis (Walter) B.S.P.
ROUGH BENTGRASS, TICKLEGRASS
Agrostis scabra Willd.

Habit densely tufted perennial grass, from fibrous roots; stems 2–7 dm tall. Leaves mostly basal, flat, usually narrow or awl-like, 4–14 cm long, 1–3 mm wide, finely rough short-hairy; ligule 2–5 mm long; sheath smooth. Spikelets in a large open panicle, 10–30 cm long, about as wide as long, diffuse with hair-like, lax branches, these frequently detaching when mature, branched 1 or 2 times above the middle; spikelets few, broadly separated at tips of branches; glumes usually purplish, 2–3 mm long, rough short-hairy on the keels; lemma shorter than the glumes, awnless or rarely awned, the awn to 2 mm long, more or less straight. At maturity the whole panicle breaks away and may roll in the wind.

Where Found occasional on riverbanks, sandy thickets, roadsides.

◆Agrostis mertensii Trin.
ARCTIC BENTGRASS, NORTHERN BENTGRASS
Agrostis borealis Hartman

Habit tufted perennial grass, from fibrous roots; stems 10–40 cm tall. Leaves mostly basal, flat, 5–10 cm long, 1–3 mm wide; ligule 2–3 mm long; sheath smooth. Spikelets in an open, loose to more or less constricted panicle, 3–10 cm long; branches ascending or appressed; spikelets sparse, borne mostly above midpoint of branch, 2–3 mm long; lemmas slightly shorter than the glumes, awned, the awn 3–4 mm long, exserted, bent.

Where Found alpine tundra streambanks and slopes.

Alopecurus MEADOW-FOXTAIL
(Greek, fox plus tail.)

1 Panicle ovoid to short-cylindric; stems erect; spikelets densely woolly . . . . . *A. magellanicus*
1 Panicle narrowly cylindricaal; stems erect or decumbent; spikelets not densely woolly . . . .
. . . . *A. aequalis*

Agrostis hyemalis ROUGH BENTGRASS

Agrostis mertensii ARCTIC BENTGRASS

♦*Alopecurus aequalis* Sobol.
SHORT-AWN FOXTAIL

Habit tufted perennial grass, from fibrous roots; stems erect or decumbent, freely rooting at nodes (especially when growing in standing water), 20–60 cm tall. **Leaves** lax to firm, 2–4 mm wide; minutely roughened (at least on upper surface); ligule jagged or entire, sharp-pointed, 4–8 mm long; sheath open. **Spikelets** in a pale green, cylindric panicle, 2–7 cm long; spikelets about 2 mm long (excluding the awn); glumes more or less silky over the back, the nerves fringed with long, fine hairs; lemmas awned, the awns inserted at or just below mid-length, straight, 2–3 mm long, scarcely exserted or exserted up to 1 mm longer than glumes.

Where Found uncommon in water of shallow ponds, on streambanks.

Alopecurus magellanicus Lam.
ALPINE FOXTAIL
Alopecurus alpinus Sm.

Habit tufted perennial grass, from short rhizomes; stems often decumbent at base, 10–60 cm tall. **Leaves** flat, 3–6 mm wide, roughly short-hairy; ligule jagged, 1–3 mm long; sheath open, glabrous, often inflated. **Spikelets** in a short panicle, 1–3 cm long; glumes very woolly; lemmas villous on upper portion, awn attached below middle, usually exserted.

Where Found uncommon in moist tundra, riverbanks, pond margins, bogs.

Anthoxanthum
SWEET VERNAL GRASS
(Greek, yellow blossom, referring to color of mature spikelets.)

1 Stems from short rhizomes, often appearing densely tufted; lemma of second male floret with a long geniculate and twisted awn . . . . *A. monticola*
1 Stems solitary, from a creeping rhizome; awn absent . . . . *A. hirtum*

♦*Anthoxanthum hirtum* (Schrank) Y. Schouten & Veldkamp **SWEETGRASS, VANILLA GRASS**
Anthoxanthum nitens auct. non (Weber) Y. Schouten & Veldkamp, *Hierochloe odorata* (L.) P. Beauv.

Habit perennial grass, from creeping rhizomes; stems 2–6 dm tall. **Leaves** 2–6 mm wide, those of the sterile shoots elongate. **Spikelets** in an open panicle 4–12 cm long; spikelets about 5 mm long; lemmas awnless or nearly so, brown-pubescent.

Where Found occasional in moist meadows, streambanks; less often in drier alpine tundra.

♦*Anthoxanthum monticola* (Bigelow) Veldkamp **ALPINE SWEETGRASS**
Hierochloe alpina (Sw. ex Willd.) Roem. & Schult.

Habit rhizomatous perennial grass (may appear tufted); stems 10–30 cm tall. **Leaves** at base narrow and involute with purplish sheaths; stem leaves shorter and wider; ligule 1 mm long, fringed. **Spikelets** in a small panicle, 3-flowered, the terminal floret perfect, the others staminate.

Where Found can be abundant in the alpine zone, particularly in heath tundra and along gravelly ridgetops.

CHLOE & TREVOR VAN LOON

Alopecurus aequalis SHORT-AWN FOXTAIL

MATT LAVIN

KRZYSZTOF ZIARNEK

Anthoxanthum hirtum SWEETGRASS

Similar Species a sweet smell is characteristic of the genus; stems with a pleasant, vaguely vanilla taste; often the first grass to flower in spring.

Arctagrostis POLARGRASS
(Latin, arctic and *Agrostis*.)

♦ *Arctagrostis latifolia* (R.Br.) Griseb.
POLARGRASS

Habit coarse perennial grass, from rhizomes; stems solitary or forming tufts, hollow, sometimes reaching 1.5 m tall. Leaves have open sheaths with rough flat blades, 4–15 mm wide; ligule jagged and often suffused with red or purple at base. Spikelets in a narrow, somewhat open panicle, 7–30 cm long; spikelets 1-flowered, 3–6 mm long; glumes unequal, usually shorter than the awnless lemmas.

Where Found common from boreal lowlands to the high alpine, in a variety of moist to wet habitats including streambanks, meadows, woodlands, early successional sites, and tundra.

Similar Species the only common grass with relatively wide leaves, and awnless, single-flowered spikelets.

Arctophila PENDANT GRASS
(Greek, north plus love, a reference to its Arctic distribution.)

♦ *Arctophila fulva* (Trin.) Rupr. ex Andersson
PENDANT GRASS
Dupontia fulva (Trin.) Röser & Tkach

Habit perennial grass, from long creeping rhizomes; stems smooth, erect or decumbent at base, 2–8 dm tall. Leaves flat, pungent-pointed or sometimes obtuse, 5–25 cm long, 5–8 mm wide, smooth; ligule 1–6 mm long, membranous, the margins jagged; sheaths closed about half their length, smooth. Spikelets in an open panicle, 5–15 cm long, the branches stiff to pendulous; spikelets 4–6 mm long; glumes shorter than adjacent lemmas, broadly lanceolate to ovate, translucent; lemmas 3–4 mm long, ovate, smooth; calluses with a few stiff hairs.

Where Found occasional in shallow water or mud of shores and streambanks.

Arctagrostis latifolia POLARGRASS

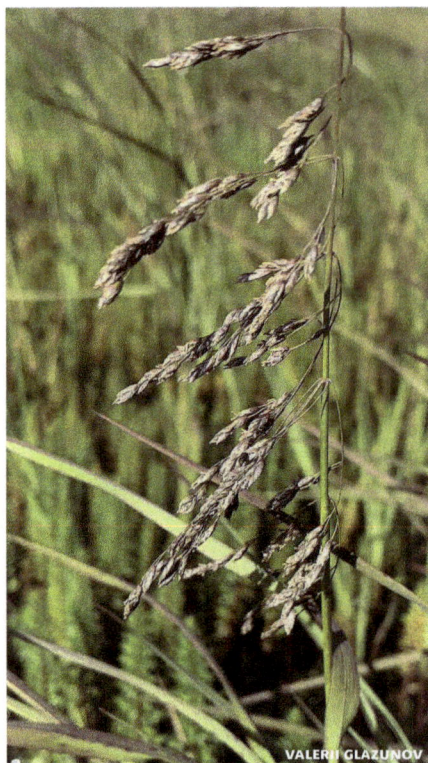

Arctophila fulva PENDANT GRASS

Beckmannia SLOUGH-GRASS
(In honor of Johann Beckmann, 1739–1811,
natural history professor in St. Petersburg.)

◆ *Beckmannia syzigachne* (Steud.) Fernald
AMERICAN SLOUGH-GRASS
Habit annual grass, often with stolons;
stems erect, hollow, to 1 m tall. Leaves flat,
mostly 4–8 mm wide; ligule 6–11 mm long,
pointed, entire or often with jagged margin,
sheath open. Spikelets numerous, appressed
to ascending, in a narrow, crowded spike, 10–
25 cm long; spikelets 1-flowered, articulating
below glumes, closely aggregated in two
rows on one side of the rachis; glumes
strongly compressed and inflated, semi-circular, 3-nerved, abruptly pointed, about 3
mm long; lemmas lanceolate, much narrower than glumes, somewhat long-pointed.
Where Found uncommon in shallow water or
mud of ponds, streams, and muskegs.

Bromus BROME
(Greek, an ancient name of the oat.)

1 Plants tufted, creeping rhizomes absent; lemmas
   pubescent only on margins . . . . *B. ciliatus*
1 Plants with creeping rhizomes 2
2 Lemmas glabrous; awns 1–2 mm long. . . . .
   . . . . *B. inermis*
2 Lemmas pubescent, especially toward margins;
   awns 1–6 mm long . . . . *B. pumpellianus*

Beckmannia syzigachne
AMERICAN SLOUGH-GRASS

Bromus ciliatus L. FRINGED BROME
Habit perennial grass, from fibrous roots;
stems usually hairy at nodes but sometimes
smooth, 50–100 cm tall. Leaves flat, lax, 5–10
mm wide, upper surface smooth to soft-
hairy; ligule minutely jagged and fringed
with fine hairs, 0.5–1 mm long; sheath usually open for 1–2 cm, smooth to thickly soft-
hairy. Spikelets in an open panicle, 15–25 cm
long; branches drooping; spikelets 2–3 cm
long; lemmas nearly glabrous on back, pubescent along the lower half to three-quarters of the margins, about 12 or 13 mm long;
awn 3–5 mm long.
Where Found uncommon in moist woods
and meadows.

Bromus inermis Leyss. SMOOTH BROME
Habit perennial grass, from creeping rhizomes; stems erect, smooth to hairy, 6–10
dm tall. Leaves flat, 4–10 mm wide, usually
smooth; ligule minutely jagged or more or
less fringed with fine hairs, 0.5–2.5 mm long;
sheath smooth to stiff- or soft-hairy. Spikelets
in a narrow panicle, to 20 cm long, the
branches ascending to erect; spikelets often
strongly purplish tinged, nearly circular in
cross-section to somewhat compressed, 1.5–
3 cm long; glumes lanceolate, narrowly to
broadly translucent-margined; lemmas
smooth to hairy or rough, rounded on the
backs, the tips blunt, only shallowly bidentate, unawned or with an awn 1 or 2 mm long.
Where Found roadsides, waste places; introduced as a forage grass from Eurasia.

◆ *Bromus pumpellianus* Scribn.
ARCTIC BROME
Habit perennial grass, with creeping rhizomes, stems 5–10 dm tall. Leaves 1–2 dm
long, 5–10 mm wide, upper surface scabrous
or pubescent, underside smooth; Spikelets 2–
3 cm long, in an often purplish panicle, 1–2
dm long, with short, spreading to erect or ascending branches; lemmas 10–12 mm long,
pubescent along margin and across the back
at base; awn 2–3 mm long.
Where Found occasional in meadows, open
woods, gravel bars, rock outcrops, streambanks.

Calamagrostis REEDGRASS
(Greek, signifying reedgrass.)

1 Awn longer than glumes, twisted and bent when
   dry . . . . *C. purpurascens*

1 Awn shorter than or equaling glumes, straight (or twisted less than once), only slightly geniculate (bent) 2

2 Panicle stiff, erect, its branches appressed except at flowering time; callus hairs one-third to almost as long as lemma . . . . *C. stricta*

2 Panicle usually open and lax; callus hairs not tufted, as long as lemma. 3

3 Panicle branches 3–8 cm long, sparsely to densely flowered along upper half; stems with 3–8 nodes, often branched in upper part; glumes 3–6 mm long . . . . *C. canadensis*

3 Panicle branches shorter, to 4 cm long; stems with 2 or 3 nodes, unbranched; glumes 4–5 mm long . . . . *C. lapponica*

◆ *Calamagrostis canadensis* (Michx.) P. Beauv.
BLUEJOINT REEDGRASS
Habit tufted perennial grass, arising from rhizomes; stems smooth, often branching above, 60–150 cm tall.
Leaf blades usually flat, scabrous, 3–8 mm wide. Spikelets often purplish, in an open, drooping panicle, 5–30 cm long; glumes narrow; lemma awn contained within the glumes; callus hairs as long as the lemma.
Where Found abundant in a variety of habitats (usually in wet to moist situations), from boreal lowlands into lower alpine areas.

Calamagrostis lapponica (Wahlenb.) Hartm.
LAPLAND REEDGRASS
Habit loosely tufted perennial grass, from fibrous roots and rhizomes; stems 30–90 cm tall, unbranched. Leaves flat, scabrous, 5–15 cm long, 2–4 mm wide; ligule membranous, 1.5–4 mm long with entire margins. Spikelets in a loose panicle, 5–15 cm long, sometimes purplish brown with age; glumes 4–5 mm long, with an acute tip; lemmas slightly shorter than glumes with a short awn; callus hairs numerous and as long as lemma.
Where Found occasional in heath and shrub tundra from uplands into the subalpine zone in (most frequently north of Alaska Range crest).
Similar Species distinguished from other local *Calamagrostis* species by the long, narrow panicle and the narrow glumes, more than 3 times longer than broad.

◆ *Calamagrostis purpurascens* R. Br.
PURPLE REEDGRASS
Habit loosely tufted perennial grass, from a stout rhizome; stems erect, scabrous and stiff, 20–70 cm tall; old, dried leaf blades persisting at base of plant. Leaves scabrous, flat, becoming involute with age, 2–4 mm wide, much shorter than the stems. Spikelets in a

Calamagrostis canadensis BLUEJOINT REEDGRASS

Calamagrostis purpurascens PURPLE REEDGRASS

Bromus pumpellianus ARCTIC BROME

purplish, spikelike, compact panicle, 6–8 cm long; spikelets with a single floret; the two glumes of different lengths; lemma with a long (4–8 mm), exserted, geniculate (bent) awn attached at the base of the lemma; callus hairs shorter than lemma.

Where Found occasional in well-drained areas in Denali, from the boreal zone into alpine areas (primarily north of Alaska Range crest), including gravel bars, open soil on slopes, grassy meadows, and stony south-facing tundra.

Similar Species the geniculate awn separates this species from other Denali *Calamagrostis*.

Calamagrostis stricta R. Br.
NORTHERN REEDGRASS
Calamagrostis inexpansa Gray

Habit loosely tufted perennial grass, from fibrous roots and rhizomes; stems unbranched, 20–100 cm tall. Leaves 5–30 cm long, more or less involute (2–5 mm wide), smooth to scabrous; ligule membranous, 1–3.5 mm long with more or less entire margins. Spikelets in a narrow, spikelike, purplish panicle, 5–15 cm long; spikelets 2–4.5 mm long, containing one flower; glumes 2–6 mm long, and less than 3 times long as broad, with an acute tip; lemmas slightly shorter than the glumes, with a short awn; callus hairs numerous and shorter than the lemma.

Where Found occasional in wet to moist areas and meadows on both sides of the Alaska Range, most commonly in boreal lowlands.

Similar Species distinguished from other local *Calamagrostis* by the long, narrow panicle, the callus hairs shorter than the lemma, and the glumes that are less than 3 times as long as broad.

Cinna WOOD-REED
(Greek name for some grass.)

♦*Cinna latifolia* (Trevir. ex Göpp.) Griseb.
NODDING WOOD-REED

Habit perennial grass, from rhizomes; stems hollow, 50–150 cm tall. Leaves flat, lax, 5–15 mm wide; ligule 3–8 mm long, membranous, hairy, the margins usually more or less strongly torn; sheaths open, smooth or minutely rough. Spikelets in a large, loose panicle 15–30 cm long, the branches spreading to drooping, very thin; spikelets about 4 mm long, flattened; glumes 3–4 mm long, strongly keeled; lemmas 2–3 mm long,

strongly compressed, short-hairy over the backs, unawned or awned (sometimes in the same panicle), when present the awn to nearly 1 mm long.

Where Found Streambanks, talus slopes, meadows, moist woods.

Danthonia OAT-GRASS
(In honor of Etienne Danthione, an early 19th century French botanist.)

♦*Danthonia intermedia* Vasey
TIMBER OAT-GRASS

Habit tufted perennial grass, from fibrous roots; stems not disarticulating at the nodes, 10–50 cm tall. Leaves somewhat inrolled, or those on stem flat, 5–10 cm long, 1–4 mm wide, smooth or slightly soft-hairy, not curled with age; blades long-hairy at throat and collar; ligule less than 1 mm long, fringed with short hairs; sheath usually smooth. Spikelets few-flowered, purplish, in a narrow, congested panicle; branches appressed, the

Cinna latifolia NODDING WOOD-REED

Danthonia intermedia TIMBER OAT-GRASS

lower branches with 2 or 3 spikelets; spikelets 12-15 mm long; lemmas 7-10 mm long, smooth over the back, densely soft-hairy along margins, awned from back, the awns abruptly bent, 7-8 mm long.

Where Found uncommon in open meadows.

Deschampsia HAIRGRASS

(In honor of Louis Auguste Deschamps (1765-1842), French physician and botanist.)

♦ *Deschampsia cespitosa* (L.) P.Beauv.
TUFTED HAIRGRASS
Habit densely tufted perennial grass, from fibrous roots, stems numerous, erect, 20-100 cm tall. Leaves rather stiff, usually folded or inrolled, 2-3 mm wide; with a few, prominent, raised veins, upper surface rough, lower surface smooth to rough; ligule entire but often split, hairy, 4-8 mm long; sheath open, smooth to rough. Spikelets in an open to narrow, sometimes nodding panicle, 1-3 dm long; branches spreading or drooping (sometimes erect); spikelets usually glistening, purplish to tawny; glumes narrow; lemmas 5-nerved, awned from base, the awns straight or bent, about as long as, or slightly longer than the lemma; callus hairs about 1 mm long.

Where Found uncommon on shores, gravel bars, wet meadows, bogs.

Note a wide-ranging, circumboreal species, and a number of subspecies and varieties have been defined.

Elymus WILD RYE

(Greek, an ancient name for a kind of barley.)

1 Lemmas with awns longer than body . . . .
. . . . *E. violaceus*
1 Lemmas with awns shorter than body 2

2 Glumes narrowly lanceolate or elliptic, gradually tapering from middle toward tip, with narrow translucent-papery margin 3
2 Glumes usually narrowly obovate or broadly oblanceolate, with broad papery margins; margins conspicuously wider near tip 5
3 Anthers 4-5 mm long; plants with long, creeping, yellowish, wiry rhizomes . . . . *E. repens*
3 Anthers shorter; plants tufted or occasionally with short rhizomes 4
4 Glumes about one-half the length of spikelet, usually 3-ribbed . . . . *E. macrourus*
4 Glumes about three-quarters the length of spikelet. . . . . *E. violaceus*
5 Glumes large, only slightly shorter than spikelet; stem nodes glabrous. . . . . *E. violaceus*
5 Glumes one-half to two-thirds length of spikelet; stem nodes hairy . . . . *E. alaskanus*

♦ *Elymus alaskanus* (Scribn. & Merr.) Á. Löve
ALASKA WILDRYE
Habit tufted perennial grass, from fibrous roots or short rhizomes; stems 20-80 cm tall, sometimes decumbent at base, the nodes pubescent. Leaves flat or involute, 3-7 mm wide, scabrous on both sides; ligule membranous, to 0.5 mm long; sheath smooth to rough or finely hairy. Spikelets in a spike, 6-10 cm long, with 1 spikelet per node; spikelets 9-15 mm

Deschampsia cespitosa TUFTED HAIRGRASS

Elymus alaskanus ALASKA WILDRYE

long; glumes 3/4 as long as lemmas, awnless or short-awned; lemmas 8-11 mm long, smooth or hairy, unawned or awned, the awns to 7 mm long.

Where Found sandy and gravelly bars and shores, open slopes.

Elymus macrourus (Turcz. ex Steud.) Tzvelev
THICK-SPIKE WILDRYE

Habit tufted perennial grass, occasionally with short rhizomes; stems 35-100 cm high. Leaves flat, 3-8 mm wide, glabrous or scabrous on upper surface. Spikelets in an erect, loose spike, 5-20 cm long; spikelets 12-20 mm long; glumes with narrow hyaline margins; lemmas short-hairy especially in lower part, awnless or with awns to 7 mm long.

Where Found in tundra and wooded areas on shores, gravel bars, terraces, open slopes.

Elymus repens (L.) Gould QUACKGRASS
Agropyron repens (L.) P. Beauv.

Habit perennial grass, from extensive rhizomes; stems erect to decumbent, 50-100 cm long, smooth. Leaves flat, 5-10 mm wide, upper surface rough along the nerves, undersides smooth; ligule 0.25-1.5 mm long, membranous; sheath smooth or hairy. Spikelets in an erect spike, 5-15 cm long, with 1 spikelet per node; spikelets 10-27 mm long; glumes unequal, 7-10 mm long, with transparent edges along the upper half; lemmas about 8 mm long, acute or awned, the awn, when present, may be nearly as long as the lemma body.

Where Found disturbed places, roadsides; introduced from Eurasia.

♦ *Elymus violaceus* (Hornem.) J. Feilberg
HIGH WILDRYE
Elymus trachycaulus (Link) Gould

Habit tufted perennial grass, from fibrous roots; stems 0.4-1 m tall. Leaves flat, 2-5 mm

Elymus violaceus HIGH WILDRYE

wide; ligule membranous. Spikelets sessile in a narrow spike, 8-25 cm long, with one spikelet per rachis node; glumes about 3/4 the length of the lemmas, with awns 11-17 mm long; lemmas awnless or with awns to 5 mm long.

Where Found occasional in disturbed places, gravel bars, rocky areas, sloping meadows.

Similar Species the sessile spikelets, short-awned lemmas, the glumes 3/4 as long as the lemmas, and one spikelet per rachis node, help identify this grass.

Festuca FESCUE
(Classical Latin name for a weedy grass.)

1	Plants rhizomatous 2
1	Plants tufted 3
2	Lemma 6–7 mm long, roughened toward tip . . . . *F. rubra*
2	Lemma 4–6 mm long, densely pilose to partially pubescent. . . . . *F. richardsonii*
3	At least upper florets with leaflike proliferations . . . . *F. viviparoidea*
3	All florets perfect. 4
4	Plants tall, usually more than 40 cm. . *F. altaica*
4	Plants usually shorter than 40 cm 5
5	Anthers 2–3 mm long . . . . *F. lenensis*
5	Anthers shorter 6
6	Upper part of stems finely hairy, with short upwardly curved hairs. . . . . *F. baffinensis*
6	Stems glabrous or nearly so 7
7	Blade of flag leaf usually more than 1 cm long; sheaths of flag leaf (first leaf below the inflorescence) hardly if at all inflated . . *F. brachyphylla*
7	Blade of flag leaf shorter; sheaths of flag leaf distinctly or at least somewhat inflated . . . . *F. brevissima*

♦ *Festuca altaica* Trin. ROUGH FESCUE

Habit densely tufted perennial grass, sometimes forming tussocks 25 to 50 cm in diameter, from fibrous roots; stems 20-70 cm tall. Leaves mainly basal, folded, narrow, stiff and scabrous, to 4 mm wide when flattened. Spikelets in an open, loose panicle, roughly triangular in outline, with lax branches; spikelets 10-15 mm long; lemmas 5-nerved with short awns to 0.7 mm long.

Where Found abundant in Denali from low- to high-elevations, but most common in the alpine zone.

Similar Species separated from other fescues by its size (relatively tall and stout), open panicle (as opposed to closed and spikelike), narrow folded leaves, and short awns.

Festuca baffinensis Polunin BAFFIN FESCUE

Habit small, densely tufted, perennial grass, from fibrous roots; stems 5–15 cm tall, densely hairy within and just below the panicle. Leaves basal, shorter than the stems, thread-like (less than 1 mm wide), folded, scabrous. Spikelets in a dense, spikelike panicle, 2–4 cm long, often dark purple in color; glumes lanceolate and glabrous; lemmas awned from tip, the awn to 3 mm long.

Where Found uncommon in rocky sites, snowbeds, and tundra in the alpine zone, primarily north of the Alaska Range crest.

Similar Species separated from other members of *Festuca* by its hairy stems.

Festuca brachyphylla Schult. & Schult. f.
ALPINE FESCUE

Habit small, densely-tufted, perennial grass, from fibrous roots; stems mostly smooth, 5–35 cm tall. Leaves mainly basal, soft, folded, under 3 mm wide; ligule membranous. Spikelets in a cylindric, compact panicle 1.5–4 cm long; spikelets purplish with several florets; glumes shorter than the included florets; lemmas 5-nerved, with a prominent awn 1–3 mm long.

Where Found occasional in well-drained alpine tundra and rocky or gravelly sites.

Festuca altaica ROUGH FESCUE

Similar Species distinguished from other narrow-spiked fescues by its hairless stems and short anthers (0.5–1 mm long).

Festuca brevissima Jurtzev ALASKA FESCUE

Habit densely tufted perennial grass, with numerous leaf sheaths of dead leave at bases; stems 5–12 cm tall. Leaves one- to two-thirds as long as flowering stems, minutely scabrous on the inrolled margins. Spikelets less than 8 in a narrow panicle, 1–2 cm long; branches with a single spikelet; glumes acute, finely ciliate on margins; lemmas with awns 0.5–2.5 mm long.

Where Found uncommon in alpine tundra.

◆*Festuca lenensis* Drobow TUNDRA FESCUE

Habit small, densely tufted perennial grass; stems slightly scabrous, 10–30 cm tall. Leaves basal, shorter than stems, folded and thread-like (less than 1 mm wide), bluish gray, scabrous. Spikelets in a narrow panicle 1–3 cm long; spikelets green tinged with purple; glumes lanceolate, glabrous; lemmas awned (to 3 mm long) from their tip.

Where Found uncommon on dry, southern exposure tundra and rocky slopes, in subalpine to alpine zones of Denali.

Similar Species key characters include its tufted habit, short height, threadlike leaves, and long anthers (ca. 2–4 mm long).

Festuca richardsonii Hook.
RICHARDSON'S FESCUE
Festuca rubra subsp. *richardsonii* (Hook.) Hultén

Habit rhizomatous, or rarely loosely tufted perennial grass; stems 10–40 cm tall. Leaves all basal, shorter than stems, narrow (about 1 mm wide); ligule membranous. Spikelets densely hairy, often dark purple, in a spike-

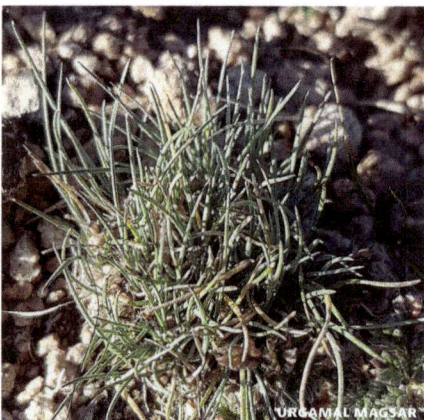

Festuca lenensis TUNDRA FESCUE

like panicle 3–7 cm long; spikelets typically purplish; glumes lanceolate, hairy; lemmas distinctly hairy and awned (up to 2 mm long) from their tip.

Where Found occasional in floodplains and stony slopes, mostly in or near the mountains.

Similar Species sometimes considered a subspecies of closely related *Festuca rubra; F. richardsonii* is distinguished by its densely hairy lemmas.

Festuca rubra L. RED FESCUE

Habit loosely tufted perennial grass; stems glabrous and curved at base, 15–60 cm tall. Leaves mainly basal, involute and less than 3 mm wide, stem leaves often withering; ligule membranous. Spikelets in a narrow panicle when young, becoming pyramidal during flowering; spikelets 6–11 mm long, greenish or purplish; lemmas 5-nerved, with awns 0.5 to 3 mm long.

Where Found common in floodplains and open soil and gravels on slopes and ridges, from boreal to alpine zone.

Similar Species the closely related *Festuca richardsonii* (sometimes considered a subspecies) is distinguished by its densely hairy lemmas; that species is rhizomatous rather than densely tufted, as in most other local fescues.

Festuca viviparoidea Krajina ex Pavlick NORTHERN FESCUE

Festuca vivipara subsp. *glabra* Frederiksen

Habit densely tufted perennial grass; stems to 30 cm high. Leaves inrolled, glabrous or somewhat scabrous toward tip, one-third to one-half as long as stems. Spikelets in a panicle, 1–6 cm long; branches ascending, scabrous; spikelets with at least upper florets viviparous (with leaflike clusters), and with lower florests sometimes fertile.

Where Found alpine tundra, rocky slopes.

Glyceria MANNAGRASS

(Greek, sweet, the seed of the type species being sweet.)

---

1 Spikelets linear, nearly round in cross-section, 10 mm long (or more); panicle narrow, erect. . . . .
. . . . *G. borealis*
1 Spikelets ovate or oblong, rarely more than 5 mm long; panicle lax and often nodding. 2
2 First glume less than 1 mm long; lemmas small, prominently nerved. . . . . *G. striata*
2 First glume 1–1.5 mm long. 3
3 Plants stout, often more than 1 m high, with a large compound panicle . . . . *G. grandis*
3 Plants slender, rarely more than 50 cm high; panicle less than 20 cm long, few-flowered. . . . . . .
. . . . *G. pulchella*

◆ *Glyceria borealis* R. Br.
NORTHERN MANNAGRASS

Habit perennial grass, from conspicuous rhizomes, freely rooting; stems erect to more or less decumbent, hollow, glabrous, 60–150 cm long. Leaves usually folded, 1–2 dm long, 2–4 mm or more wide, more or less pimpled on upper surfaces; ligule pointed, entire but usually splitting, 5–10 mm long; sheath somewhat flattened, smooth or slightly scabrous, open for 1–4 cm. Spikelets in a narrow panicle, 2–4 dm long, the branches ascending-appressed; spikelets linear, tapered at tip, 10–15 mm long; lemmas prominently 7-nerved, smooth except on the scabrous nerves.

Where Found pond and stream margins, wet meadows, bogs.

◆ *Glyceria grandis* S. Watson
REED MANNAGRASS, AMERICAN MANNAGRASS

Habit perennial grass, from conspicuous rhizomes; stems erect to more or less decumbent, stout, hollow, glabrous, 1–1.5 m long.

Glyceria borealis NORTHERN MANNAGRASS

Leaves flat, firm, 15–35 cm long, 6–15 mm wide, upper surface minutely rough, smooth on lower surface; ligule blunt, nearly entire, 4–9 mm long; sheaths smooth, closed or open for about 1 cm. Spikelets in an open, loose panicle, 20–35 cm long; branches numerous, spreading; spikelets ovate, flattened slightly, 5–8 mm long; glumes lanceolate; lemmas purplish, prominently 7-nerved.

Where Found wet meadows, pond and stream margins, bogs.

Glyceria pulchella (Nash) K.Schum.
SLENDER MANNAGRASS,
MACKENZIE VALLEY MANNAGRASS

Habit perennial grass, from rhizomes, often rooting at lower nodes; stems erect, stout, smooth, 40–60 cm tall. Leaves crowded, flat, 15–30 cm long, 2–5 mm wide, minutely rough on both surfaces; ligule 2–4 mm long; sheath rough, the hairs angled backwards, open at least near top. Spikelets in a loose open panicle, 15–25 cm long, the branches ascending to spreading-ascending; spikelets ovate to cylindric, compressed, 4–6 mm long; glumes brownish or purplish, scarious-margined, obtuse, much shorter than lemmas; lemmas usually purplish, prominently 7-nerved.

Where Found uncommon in marshes, streambanks and shores, muskegs.

Glyceria striata (Lam.) Hitchc.
FOWL MANNAGRASS

Habit tufted perennial grass, from rhizomes; stems erect to more or less decumbent, hollow, 20–60 cm tall. Leaves 2–5 mm wide, flat or folded, mostly erect, minutely rough; ligule blunt, 2–3 mm long; sheath somewhat flattened, minutely rough, usually closed to the top and often split. Spikelets in a loose panicle, about 10 cm long, the branches slender, usually ascending; spikelets about 3 mm long; glumes ovate, usually more or less fringed with fine hairs; lemmas broad, firm, barely 2 mm long, prominently 7-nerved.

Where Found uncommon in marshes and fens.

Hordeum BARLEY
(Classical Latin name for barley.)

♦*Hordeum jubatum* L. FOXTAIL BARLEY

Habit tufted perennial grass, from fibrous roots, smooth to densely soft-hairy; stems 20–50 (60) cm tall. Leaves 2–4 mm wide, scabrous; ligule to 0.6 mm long, blunt, more or less entire; sheaths open. Spikelets in a nodding spike, 5–10 cm long (including awns), the rachis disarticulating; glumes awnlike, 4–7 cm long; lemma of central spikelet 6–8 mm long with awn as long as the glumes; lemmas of lateral spikelets reduced almost to a short awn.

Where Found disturbed areas, roadsides, riverbanks.

Glyceria grandis REED MANNAGRASS

Hordeum jubatum FOXTAIL BARLEY

Koeleria JUNEGRASS
(In honor of German botanist Goerg Ludwig Koeler, 1765-1807.)

♦ *Koeleria spicata* (L.) Barberá, Quintanar, Soreng & P.M. Peterson SPIKE TRISETUM
Trisetum spicatum (L.) K. Richt.

Habit tufted perennial grass, from fibrous roots; stems rough or short-hairy, 10–50 cm tall. Leaves flat, 1.5–4 mm wide; ligule fringed, hairy. Spikelets in a compact, narrow, spike-like panicle, 2–15 cm long, often purple to copper or silvery in color; glumes unequal, 6–8 mm long; lemmas with two teeth at tip, and a bent awn, 4–6 mm long, giving the inflorescence a slightly 'fuzzy' look.

Where Found common in a variety of habitats at low- to high-elevations, occurring most frequently in the mountains (on both sides of Alaska Range) on well-drained sandy to rocky soils in alpine tundra, gravel bars, cliffs, lakeshores, open woods, and disturbed areas.

Similar Species This is the only *Koeleria* reported from Denali; the hairy stem below the tightly-packed flowering head and exserted awns are distinctive.

Leymus LYME GRASS
(Anagram of *Elymus*.)

♦ *Leymus innovatus* (Beal) Pilg.
DOWNY RYEGRASS
Elymus innovatus Beal

Habit large, usually tufted, perennial grass, from rhizomes; stems usually slightly hairy below nodes and inflorescence, 30–80 cm tall. Leaves mostly basal, 2–6 mm wide, stiff and involute; ligule membranous; stem leaves short. Spikelets in a purplish 'fuzzy' spike, with two spikelets per node; flowers

reduced to a series of bracts with each spikelet of 2–3 florets (with one often undeveloped); glumes unequal, broadest at base; lemmas longer than glumes, with an attached short awn, 2–4 mm long; anthers purple.

Where Found common in floodplains and sandy terraces at low-elevations on the north side of the Alaska Range crest.

Similar Species similar grasses in Denali include species of *Elymus*, which have soft leaves and glumes broader above their base.

Phippsia ICE-GRASS
(In honor of Arctic navigator John Constantine Phipps, 1744–1792.)

♦ *Phippsia algida* (Sol.) R. Br. ICE-GRASS

Habit low, tufted, glabrous perennial grass; stems to about 15 cm tall (often shorter), barely over-topping the leaves. Leaves flat or folded, soft, narrow, prow-like at tip, yellowish green; sheaths inflated. Spikelets in a narrow, crowded panicle 3–4 cm long; spikelets about 1 mm long; glumes unequal, much shorter than lemma; lemma yellowish green or sometimes purplish, glabrous or slightly pubescent.

Where Found moist to wet alpine slopes and streambanks.

Koeleria spicata SPIKE TRISETUM

Leymus innovatus DOWNY RYEGRASS

Phleum TIMOTHY
(Greek, a kind of reed.)

◆*Phleum alpinum* L. MOUNTAIN TIMOTHY
Habit tufted perennial grass, from fibrous roots; stems from a decumbent base, rooting at nodes, not bulbous at base, 15–50 cm long. **Leaves** flat, 2–10 cm long, 3–7 mm wide, the margins rough; ligule blunt, nearly entire, 1–3 mm long; sheaths smooth. **Spikelets** in a short-cylindric panicle, 1–4 cm long; glumes hairy on the sides, fringed with long, bristle-like hairs on the keels, abruptly narrowed to stout awns about 2 mm long; lemmas short-hairy, toothed by the 5 nerves.
Where Found moist alpine meadows.

Phippsia algida ICE-GRASS

Phleum alpinum MOUNTAIN TIMOTHY

Poa BLUEGRASS
(Greek, for a grass.)

1 Plants rhizomatous 2
1 Plants tufted 4
2 Stems conspicuously flattened; introduced species . . . . *P. compressa*
2 Stems round in cross-section, or at most very slightly flattened; native species 3
3 Surface between nerves of palea finely hairy . . . . *P. arctica*
3 Surface between nerves of palea glabrous . . . . *P. pratensis*
4 Anthers less than 1 mm long 5
4 Anthers more than 1 mm long 6
5 Lemmas distinctly webbed at base. . . . . *P. paucispicula*
5 Lemmas not distinctly webbed at base . . . . *P. pseudoabbreviata*
6 Lemmas distinctly webbed at base. 7
6 Lemma not distinctly webbed at base 9
7 Spikelets usually glaucous; stems with 2 or rarely 3 nodes; uppermost stem leaf short, below middle of stem . . . . *P. glauca*
7 Spikelets not glaucous; stems with 4 or 5 nodes (some nearly basal) 8
8 Panicle usually flexuose; upper ligules wider than long. *P. nemoralis*
8 Panicle rigid and open; upper ligules mostly 2–3 mm long, longer than wide . . . . *P. palustris*
9 Lemma without long woolly hairs between keel and marginal nerves . . . . *P. glauca*
9 Lemma with long woolly hairs between keel and marginal nerve 10
10 Surface between nerves of palea finely hairy . . . . *P. arctica*
10 Surface between nerves of palea glabrous . . . . *P. alpina*

◆*Poa alpina* L. ALPINE BLUEGRASS
Habit densely tufted perennial grass, from fibrous roots; stems 10–40 cm tall; viviparous plants (plants with small bulblets instead of flowers) are known to occur. **Leaves** short, wide (2–5 mm), flat, and abruptly pointed, blue-green with persistent white sheaths; mostly basal, with 1–2 stem leaves. **Spikelets** in an open, oval or pyramidal panicle, as wide as long, greenish or purplish; spikelets compressed; glumes ovate; lemmas ovate, pubescent on keel but without cobwebby hairs, awnless.
Where Found common from low-elevation meadows on floodplains to high alpine tun-

dra and scree on both sides of Alaska Range crest; most common at high-elevations.

Similar Species *Poa arctica*, but in that species the palea is hairy between nerves.

Poa arctica R. Br. ARCTIC BLUEGRASS

Habit densely to loosely tufted perennial grass, from fibrous roots and rhizomes; stems usually decumbent (less often upright), 10–30 cm long; usually with 2 nodes along each stem. Leaves mostly basal, short, often narrow and thin, flat to inrolled; ligule membranous. Spikelets in an open pyramidal panicle, the branches often flexuose; glumes of equal length; lemmas long-hairy between the nerves, with a basal tuft of cobwebby hairs.

Where Found primarily in subalpine and alpine areas in a variety of habitats: from muskeg to dwarf shrub to sparsely vegetated alpine slopes.

Similar Species the long-hairy lemma helps to distinguish this species from other *Poa* species in the park.

Poa compressa L. CANADA BLUEGRASS

Habit perennial tufted grass, pale bluish green, from fibrous roots and long rhizomes; stems often decumbent, 15–60 cm long with stems and nodes distinctly compressed, some lowermost nodes exserted from sheaths of stem leaves. Leaves flat, 1–4 mm wide; ligule 1–3 mm long, the tip rounded, the back and margins rough; sheaths distinctly compressed. Spikelets in an erect panicle, 2–10 cm long, often interrupted, the short branches usually in pairs, distinctly rough on the angles; spikelets laterally compressed, 4–7 mm long; glumes 2–3 mm long; lemmas lanceolate, the tips sharp-pointed, keel and marginal nerves short silky-hairy; callus hairless or more often cobwebby.

Where Found may occur in Denali on roadsides or in disturbed or waste places; introduced, native of Eurasia.

♦ *Poa glauca* Vahl GLAUCOUS BLUEGRASS

Habit densely tufted, glaucous perennial grass, from fibrous roots; stems erect to spreading, stiff, wiry, straight or slightly decumbent, 15–30 cm tall. Leaves flat or folded, 0.5–1 mm wide, glaucous and shorter than the stem; ligule membranous. Spikelets in a narrow panicle, 3–12 cm long, with stiff, short scabrous branches; spikelets compressed; glumes broadly lanceolate; lemmas scabrous, with pubescence on the keel, cobwebby hairs at base absent.

Where Found common in a variety of low- to high-elevation, well-drained, sandy or rocky habitats including: hummocks, snow beds, alpine tundra, river terraces, streambanks, animal burrows, ridges, and slopes.

Similar Species the long anthers, lack of cobwebby hairs and scabrous lemma help identify this grass.

Poa nemoralis L. WOOD BLUEGRASS

Habit tufted perennial grass, from fibrous roots, green or glaucous; stems mostly erect or ascending, 20–70 cm tall. Leaves more or less flat, 1–3 mm wide; ligule membranous, about 1 mm long. Spikelets in a drooping, open panicle; spikelets green, somewhat laterally compressed; glumes lanceolate, 3-nerved; lemmas acute, lanceolate, with pubescence on the keel.

Where Found at low- to high-elevations in moist shady woods and meadows, usually where well-drained.

Similar Species very similar to *Poa palustris* but differentiated by the drooping panicle and ligules wider than long.

Poa alpina ALPINE BLUEGRASS

Poa glauca GLAUCOUS BLUEGRASS

Poa palustris L. FOWL BLUEGRASS
Habit densely to loosely tufted perennial grass, from fibrous roots, sometimes with stolons; stems erect or decumbent, 30–80 cm long, sometimes branching above base, with 4–6 nodes, uppermost node above middle. **Leaves** rough, flat, 1–2 mm wide; ligule 3–5 mm long. **Spikelets** in an open, upright, pyramid-shaped panicle; glumes 2–3 mm long, lanceolate with acute tip; lemmas lanceolate, purple-tinged, with pubescence on the keel.
Where Found at low- to high-elevations (especially on south-facing slopes), in lowland forests, lakeshores, meadows, gravel bars.
Similar Species *Poa nemoralis* similar but differs in having a drooping panicle and ligules wider than long.

Poa paucispicula Scribn. & Merr.
ALASKA BLUEGRASS
Habit tufted perennial grass, from fibrous roots; stems 15–30 cm tall. **Leaves** slightly scabrous and narrow (1–3 mm wide); ligule membranous, 1–2 mm long with a rounded tip. **Spikelets** in an open panicle of paired thread-like branches, with 1–3 spikelets per branch; branches flexuose and drooping; spikelets laterally flattened, 4–6 mm long and purple; glumes lanceolate; lemmas lanceolate with a pointed tip, hairy on back; callus hairs cobwebby.
Where Found uncommon at low- to high-elevations in moist to wet meadows, snowbeds, seeps, and tundra.
Similar Species key identifying features of *Poa paucispicula* include the short anthers (less than 1 mm long), the pairs of drooping panicle branches, and the cobwebby callus hairs.

◆***Poa pratensis*** L. KENTUCKY BLUEGRASS
Habit densely to loosely tufted perennial grass, from fibrous roots and rhizomes; stems erect or decumbent, 30–70 cm long. **Leaves** folded or flat, 1–4 mm wide with prow-shaped tips; ligule membranous and short (1–2 mm) with rounded tip. **Spikelets** in an open, pyramid-shaped panicle 3–15 cm long, with 3–5 panicle branches at lower nodes; spikelets flattened, purple-blue; glumes equal in length, lanceolate to ovate, shorter than lemmas; lemmas 5-nerved with numerous hairs at base; callus hairs cobwebby.
Where Found in a variety of habitats: gravel bars, riparian forest, meadows, shrublands, tundra.

Similar Species distinguished by its cobwebby callus hairs, a creeping rhizome and the 3–5 panicle branches at the lower nodes.

Poa pseudoabbreviata Roshev.
POLAR BLUEGRASS
Habit densely tufted perennial grass, from fibrous roots; stems 5–20 cm tall, glabrous. **Leaves** linear, much shorter than the stems; ligule membranous. **Spikelets** in an open, ovate to pyramidal panicle, with long (1.5–5 cm) scabrous branches; spikelets with 2–4 flowers; glumes purple and keeled; lemmas purple, lanceolate, short-hairy on the keel, basal cobwebby tuft of hairs absent.
Where Found uncommon in alpine scree-slopes, fellfields, and rocky tundra.
Similar Species long panicle branches and short anthers (0.2-0.7 mm long) separate this species from other Denali bluegrasses.

Podagrostis FALSE BENT
(Greek, foot, -*Agrostis*, spikelets resembling that genus, but with prolonged rachilla.)

1 Plants of lowland and montane zones, often more than 30 cm tall; anthers 0.8–1.5 mm long . . . . *P. aequivalvis*
1 Plants of subalpine and alpine zones, usually less than 30 cm tall; anthers 0.6-0.8 mm long . . . . *P. humilis*

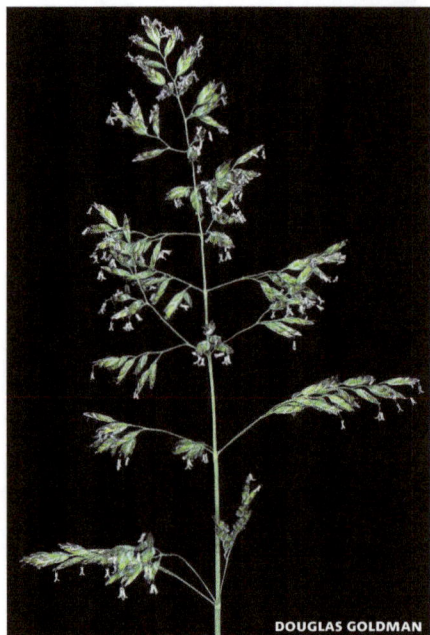
DOUGLAS GOLDMAN
Poa pratensis KENTUCKY BLUEGRASS

Podagrostis aequivalvis (Trin.) Scribn. & Merr.
ARCTIC FALSE BENT
Agrostis aequivalvis (Trin.) Trin.

Habit loosely tufted perennial grass, from short rhizomes; stems 20–60 m tall, ascending from a spreading base. Leaves flat, 4–18 cm long, 1–3 mm wide; ligule 0.5–2 mm long, slightly rough on outside; sheaths smooth Spikelets in an open, loose, often drooping, purplish panicle, 5–15 cm long, the lower branches more or less spreading; spikelets sparse; lemmas awnless, callus hairs absent or sparse, to 0.1 mm long.

Where Found uncommon in bogs, lakeshores.

♦ ***Podagrostis humilis*** (Vasey) Björkman
ALPINE FALSE BENT
Agrostis thurberiana Hitchc., *Podagrostis thurberiana* (Hitchc.) Hultén

Habit perennial tufted or matted grass, from fibrous roots; stems 5–30 cm tall. Leaves 2–15 cm long, 1–3 mm wide, flat or inrolled; ligule 1–3 mm long, slightly rough short-hairy on the outside; sheaths smooth. Spikelets in an open panicle (becoming more or less constricted when mature), to 10 cm long, the branches spreading or appressed; spikelets numerous; lemmas awnless; callus hairs absent or sparse, to 0.5 mm long.

Where Found uncommon in moist alpine meadows.

Podagrostis humilis ALPINE FALSE BENT

Puccinellia ALKALI GRASS
(In honor of Italian botanist Benedetto Luigi Puccinelli,1808-1850.)

Puccinellia vahliana (Liebm.) Scribn. & Merr.
VAHL'S ALKALI GRASS
Colpodium vahlianum (Liebm.) Nevski, *Phippsia vahliana* (Liebm.) Á. & D. Löve

Habit densely tufted perennial grass; roots pale, fibrous; stems stout, erect, 10–25 cm tall, with 2–3 leaves. Leaves yellowish green, lax, flat, with a metallic luster; ligule about 1 mm long, somewhat pointed, broader than long; leaf sheaths soft, early decaying. Spikelets in a contracted panicle 1.5–5 cm long; branches in twos or threes, ascending, bearing only a few spikelets; spikelets lanceolate, 6–7.5 mm long, dark purple, shining; glumes and lemmas thin, translucent, their tips ragged in age; glumes more or less equal; lemmas densely hairy near base.

Where Found mountain seeps and tundra.

Schizachne FALSE MELIC GRASS
(Greek, schizein, to split, achne, chaff, referring to teeth of the lemma.)

♦ ***Schizachne purpurascens*** (Torr.) Swallen
FALSE MELIC GRASS
Habit perennial, loosely tufted grass, from fibrous roots; stems decumbent at base, 30–60 cm tall. Leaves usually smooth, 2–4 mm wide, folded or loosely inrolled; ligule 0.5–1.5 mm long; sheath closed almost to top. Spikelets in a zig-zagged or loosely erect panicle, about 1 dm long, the branches more or less drooping, bearing 1 or 2 spikelets; spikelets 3–6-flowered; glumes pointed, purplish; lemmas with 7–9 prominent nerves, tips bidentate, awned, the awn arising below tip, as long or longer than lemma body, twisted and spreading or slightly abruptly bent; callus stiff-hairy.

Where Found woods.

Vahlodea ARCTIC HAIRGRASS
(Jens Laurentius Vahl, 1796-1854, Danish plant collector.)

♦ ***Vahlodea atropurpurea*** (Wahlenb.) Fr.
MOUNTAIN HAIRGRASS
Deschampsia atropurpurea (Wahlenb.) Scheele

Habit perennial, loosely tufted grass, purplish at base, from fibrous roots; stems erect, 20–60 cm tall. Leaves smooth to soft hairy, blade flat (rarely inrolled), 2–6 mm wide, to 30 cm long with prow-like tip; ligule rounded to blunt, 1–3.5 mm long, the margin often jagged; lower sheath usually stiff-hairy, the hairs angled backwards. Spikelets mostly purplish, in an open to contracted panicle, to 15 cm long; spikelets 4–7 mm long with 2 florets; glumes purplish, smooth or rough-hairy on the keel and marginal nerves; lemmas awned, awn attached at about middle, bent, 2–4 mm long; callus with hairs about half the lemma length.

Where Found occasional in alpine and sub-alpine meadows (often below snowbeds).

POTAMOGETONACEAE
Pondweed Family

1 Stipules free, not united to leaf base . . . .
. . . . *Potamogeton*
1 Stipules united with leaf base or petiole; leaves 1- to 3-nerved . . . . *Stuckenia*

Schizachne purpurascens FALSE MELIC GRASS

Vahlodea atropurpurea MOUNTAIN HAIRGRASS

Potamogeton PONDWEED
(Greek, *potamos*, river, and *geiton*, neighbor.)

1 Floating leaves present, submerged leaves always present on young plants, sometimes disintegrating with age. 2
1 Floating leaves absent. 5
2 Submerged leaves narrowly linear, more than 20 times longer than wide. 3
2 Submerged leaves lanceolate to linear-lanceolate or oblong, less than 15 times longer than wide
. . . . 4
3 Floating leaves cordate to rounded at base; petioles with brownish, curved, jointlike portion at junction with blade; submerged leaves nearly terete, linear, soon shed . . . . *P. natans*
3 Floating leaves cuneate or tapering at base; petioles without jointlike portion at junction with blade; submerged leaves 2–10 mm wide, ribbon-like, flat, flaccid, and translucent. . *P. epihydrus*
4 Submerged leaves obtuse at tip, with margin entire; floating leaves gradually tapering into petioles; plant suffused with red . . . . *P. alpinus*
4 Submerged leaves acute to sharp-pointed at tip, with 1-celled, translucent denticles in margin (at least when young); floating leaves cuneate to rounded at base; plant greenish . . *P. gramineus*
5 Plants with all leaves linear, less than 10 mm wide, the sides parallel, unstalked. 6
5 Plants with at least some leaves lanceolate or ovate, the larger leaves more than 9 mm wide.
. . . . 14
6 Leaves with two translucent bands along the midveins, the bands more than 2 cells wide . . 7
6 Leaves without translucent bands along midveins or with translucent bands only 1 or 2 cells wide 8
7 Translucent bands of submersed leaves forming about 1/3 of the leaf width; leaves 2-ranked; stems flattened. . . . . *P. epihydrus*
7 Translucent bands of the submersed leaves forming less than 1/3 of the leaf width; leaves not 2-ranked; stems round in cross-section *P. pusillus*
8 Submersed leaves with 9 to 35 veins. 9
8 Submersed leaves with 1 to 7 veins. 11
9 Leaves attached about 5–10 mm above the nodes, with distinct ear-shaped lobes at the bases . . . . *P. robbinsii*
9 Leaves attached at the nodes, without ear-shaped lobes at the bases. 10
10 Plant bright green; leaves 2–4 mm wide, 15- to 35-nerved. . . . . *P. zosteriformis*
10 Plant dull green or tawny, leaves 1.5–2 mm wide, 9- to 17-nerved. . . . . *P. sibiricus*

11 Stipules coarsely fibrous, whitish, the older tending to disintegrate into shreds; bases of winter buds hard and strongly ribbed . . . . *P. friesii*

11 Stipules delicate, not fibrous, greenish or brownish; base of winter buds soft and smooth . . . 12

12 Leaves 2–4 mm wide, rounded at the tips; fruits 3–4 mm long . . . . *P. obtusifolius*

12 Leaves to 3 mm wide, tapered to pointed tips or abruptly slender-tipped; fruits 2–3 mm long. 13

13 Fruit with distinct keels on back; veins on stipules evident as ridges running the entire length of stipule; glands at base of stipule either lacking or poorly developed . . . . *P. foliosus*

13 Fruit without keels on back; veins on stipule obscure and faint; glands at base of stipule usually well-developed . . . . *P. pusillus*

14 Submersed leaves nearly round in cross-section, tapered . . . . *P. natans*

14 Submersed leaves flat 15

15 Submersed leaves ribbon-like with parallel sides, 5–10 mm wide; parallel-sided median translucent band several cells wide and comprising 1/4 or more of total leaf width; stems compressed . . . . *P. epihydrus*

15 Submersed leaves lanceolate to ovate in outline; translucent bands absent or less than 1/4 blade width; stems nearly round in cross-section . . 16

16 Submersed leaves clasping stem 17

16 Submersed leaves not clasping stem 18

17 Leaves cylindrical to ovate in outline, mostly 10–20 cm long, with hood-shaped tips; fruit more than 4 mm long . . . . *P. praelongus*

17 Leaves lanceolate to ovate in outline, 1–10 cm long, without hood-shaped tips; fruit less than 3.5 mm long . . . . *P. richardsonii*

18 Stems and leaves with reddish tinge, stems usually not branched; floating leaves, if present, not markedly different from the submersed . . . . *P. alpinus*

18 Stems and leaves greenish, stems freely branched; floating leaves markedly different from submersed . . . . *P. gramineus*

Potamogeton alpinus Balb.
ALPINE PONDWEED

Habit perennial, reddish tinged aquatic herb, from strong rhizomes; stems simple or sparingly branched, nearly round in cross-section, to 1.5 m long. Leaves submersed and floating; submersed leaves flat, thin, oblong to linear-lanceolate, 4–10 cm long, 5–20 mm wide, with 7 to 9 veins, unstalked, not clasping stem; stipules 1.5-2.5 cm long, thin, membranous, persistent; floating leaves (sometimes absent), oblanceolate or spatu-

late, 4–10 cm long, 2–5 cm wide, gradually tapered at base. Flowers in a spikelike inflorescence, the spikes 1–3.5 mm long, with 5 to 10 whorls, the stalks thick. Fruit an ovoid, lenticular achene, about 3 mm long, beak long, often curved, with a sharp middle keel, the lateral keels obscure.

Where Found lakes, ponds, slow-moving streams.

Potamogeton epihydrus Raf.
RIBBON-LEAF PONDWEED

Habit perennial aquatic herb, from strong rhizomes; stems to 1 m long, flattened, usually unbranched. Leaves submersed and floating; submersed leaves ribbon-like, thin, the sides parallel, whitish green, to 20 cm long, 3–7 mm wide, unstalked, pointed at tip, with broad translucent bands along midveins (equaling about 1/3 of leaf width), 5-nerved, the outer nerves nearly marginal; stipules 0.5-3 cm long, inconspicuous; floating leaves 2–7 cm long, 0.5–2 cm wide, leathery, long-stalked, lanceolate to elliptic, pointed at tip, narrowed at base. Flowers in a spikelike inflorescence, the spikes 2–4 cm long, with 5 to 12 whorls of flowers, the stalks thin. Fruit an achene, almost globe-shaped, 2.5-4.5 mm long, 2–3 mm wide, flattened, beakless, the keels pronounced, winged.

Where Found lakes, ponds, streams.

Potamogeton foliosus Raf.
LEAFY PONDWEED

Habit perennial aquatic herb, from fine, tufted roots; stems to 1 m long, branched. Leaves all submersed, linear, the sides parallel, thin, green, 1–9 cm long, 0.5–2.5 mm wide, usually with 3 veins, unstalked, pointed at tip; stipules 0.5–1 cm long, delicate, not fibrous, greenish or brownish. Flowers in a spikelike inflorescence, spikes 0.5-1.5 cm long, with 2 to 5 whorls, the stalks thin. Fruit an ovoid achene, 1.5-2.5 mm long, widest at middle, beak short-stubby, keels well-developed, winged.

Where Found lakes, ponds, streams.

Potamogeton friesii Rupr.
FLAT-STALK PONDWEED

Habit perennial aquatic herb, from fine, tufted roots; stems to 1 m long, sparsely branched. Leaves all submersed, linear, the sides parallel, rigid, light to olive-green, 2.5-7 cm long, 1.2-3.5 mm wide, usually with 5 to 7 veins and narrow translucent bands (1 or 2 cells wide) along midveins; stipules 0.5-2 cm long, coarsely fibrous, whitish, shredding at tip; basal glands present. Flowers in a spikelike inflorescence, spikes 0.5–1.5 cm long, with 2 to 5 whorls, the stalks often thicker than stem. Fruit an ovoid achene, 1.5–2.5 mm long, widest above middle, beak short, keels low and rounded.

Where Found lakes, ponds.

◆ *Potamogeton gramineus* L.
GRASSY PONDWEED

Habit perennial aquatic herb, from strong rhizomes; stems to 1.5 m long, freely branched, nearly round in cross-section. Leaves submersed and floating; submersed leaves narrowly lanceolate, thin, flat, green, 2–7 cm long, 0.5–2.5 cm wide, unstalked, not clasping stem, rounded or pointed at tip; stipules 0.5–3 cm long; floating leaves usually present, distinctly different from submersed leaves, oval, thick and leathery, 2–10 cm long, 1–4 cm wide, long-stalked, pointed at tip, tapering at base. Flowers in a spikelike inflorescence, spikes 1–3 cm long, with 5 to 10 whorls, the stalks thin. Fruit an achene, almost globe-shaped, 2–3 mm long, beak short, keels sharp and prominent.

Where Found lakes, ponds, streams.

Potamogeton natans L.
BROAD-LEAF PONDWEED

Habit perennial, aquatic herb, from strong rhizomes; stems to 1.5 m long, simple or sparingly branched. Leaves submersed and floating; submersed leaves reduced to narrow, firm, dark green cylindric stalks without blades, growing from the main stem but not persisting, 10–20 cm long; stipules 4–9 cm long, fibrous; floating leaves ovate, 4–10 cm long, leathery, long-stalked, rounded at tip, notched at bases. Flowers spikelike inflorescence, with 6–10 whorls of flowers, the stalks thick. Fruit a broadly ovoid achene, 3.5–5 mm long, beak cylindrical; keel obscure, present in upper half of achene.

Where Found lakes, ponds.

◆ *Potamogeton obtusifolius* Mert. & W.D.J. Koch **BLUNT-LEAF PONDWEED**

Habit perennial aquatic herb, from fine, tufted roots; stems to 1 m long, sparsely branched. Leaves all submersed, linear, the sides parallel, soft, 3–8 cm long, 2–4 mm wide, usually with 3 to 5 veins, rounded at tip; stipules 0.5–2 cm long, delicate, not fibrous, greenish or brownish, not shredding at tips. Flowers in a spikelike inflorescence, 3–5 cm long, with 3 to 8 whorls, the stalks thin. Fruit an ovoid achene, 3–4 mm long, widest above middle; beak short; keel absent.

Where Found lakes, ponds.

◆ *Potamogeton praelongus* Wulfen
WHITE-STEM PONDWEED

Habit perennial aquatic herb, from strong rhizomes; stems white, flexuous, branched or unbranched, slightly flattened in cross-section, to 2 m long. Leaves all submersed, linear-lanceolate, thin, flat, light green fading to white, 10–20 cm long, 1–3 cm wide, with 3–5 main nerves, clasping stem, rounded or hood-shaped at tip; stipules 3–10 cm long, fibrous or stringy. Flowers in a spikelike inflorescence, 3–5 cm long, with 6 to 12 whorls, the stalks inflated. Fruit a broad ovoid achene, 4–5 mm long; beak prominent, widely triangular; slightly keeled.

Where Found lakes, ponds.

Potamogeton gramineus GRASSY PONDWEED

Potamogeton obtusifolius
BLUNT-LEAF PONDWEED

◆ *Potamogeton pusillus* L.
SMALL PONDWEED

Habit perennial aquatic herb; stems thread-like, to 100 cm long, sparingly branched. Leaves all submersed, linear, the sides parallel, thin, green, 2–6 cm long, 1–1.5 mm wide, unstalked, with strong midrib and usually inconspicuous side veins, pointed at tip; stipules 0.5–1 cm long, delicate, not fibrous, greenish or brownish; basal glands at nodes small but well-developed. Flowers in a spikelike inflorescence, the spikes 0.5–1.5 cm long, with 2 to 5 whorls of flowers, the stalks thin; bases of the winter buds soft, smooth. Fruit an achene, almost rounded, about 2 mm long, widest above middle; beak short, stubby; keel absent.

Where Found lakes, ponds.

Potamogeton richardsonii (A. Benn.) Rydb.
CLASPING-LEAF PONDWEED

Habit perennial aquatic herb, from strong rhizomes; stems to 150 cm long, branched. Leaves all submersed, lanceolate, thin, dark green, 3–10 cm long, 1–3 cm wide, the tips blunt, clasping stem; stipules 1–3 cm long,

Potamogeton praelongus
WHITE-STEM PONDWEED

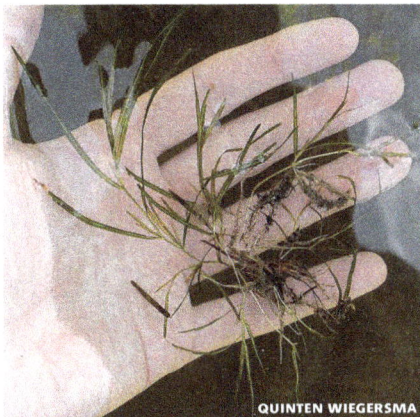

Potamogeton pusillus SMALL PONDWEED

coarse, disintegrating into persistent whitish fibers. Flowers in a spikelike inflorescence, 1–4 cm long, with 6 to 12 whorls, the stalks inflated, club-shaped. Fruit a nearly rounded achene, 2.5–3 mm long, beak prominent, keel absent.

Where Found lakes, ponds, streams.

Potamogeton robbinsii Oakes
ROBBINS' PONDWEED

Habit perennial aquatic herb, from strong rhizomes; stems to 100 cm long, branched. Leaves all submersed, 2-ranked, linear-lanceolate, the sides parallel, dark green, stiff, unstalked, 2–10 cm long, 4–8 mm wide, pointed at tip, margins toothed; stipules 0.5–2 cm long, light green or whitish, shredded at tip. Flowers in an often branched, spikelike inflorescence, 2.5–4 cm long, with 3 to 5 whorls. Fruit an achene, but rarely developed.

Where Found may be present in Denali in lakes and ponds.

Potamogeton sibiricus A. Benn.
SIBERIAN PONDWEED
Potamogeton subsibiricus Hagstr.

Habit perennial aquatic herb, with thread-like stems, simple or slightly branched in upper part. Leaves all submersed, linear, 2–8 cm long, with a prominent median nerve, tapered to tip; stipules 1–2 cm long, free from leaf, not fused, whitish. Flowers in 3–4 whorls, in a short-stalked, cylindric spike. Fruit oblong-ovoid, 3–4 mm long; beak 0.3–0.5 mm long.

Where Found lakes, ponds.

Potamogeton zosteriformis Fernald
FLAT-STEM PONDWEED

Habit perennial aquatic herb; stems to 130 cm long, strongly flattened, branched. Leaves all submersed, linear, the sides parallel, stiff, olive green, 10–20 cm long, 2–5 mm wide, usually with 7 to 15 veins, tapering to pointed tips; stipules 1.5–3.5 cm long. Flowers in a spikelike inflorescence, 1.5–3 cm long, with 5 to 9 whorls. Fruit an ovoid achene, 4–5 mm long, beak conspicuous, keel winged.

Where Found lakes, ponds.

Stuckenia FALSE PONDWEED
(Probably in honor of German botanist Wilhelm Adolf Stucken, 1852-1901.)

1   Spike with 5–12 whorls of flowers; stipular sheaths prominent, 2–5 cm long; leaves blunt .
.... *S. vaginata*

1 Spike with 2–6 whorls of flowers; stipular sheaths inconspicuous, less than 2 cm long .. **2**

2 Leaves sharp pointed at tip; fruit 3–4 mm long. . . . . *S. pectinata*

2 Leaves obtuse or blunt at tip; fruit 2–3 mm long . . . . *S. filiformis*

Stuckenia filiformis (Pers.) Börner
SLENDER-LEAF PONDWEED
Potamogeton filiformis Pers.

Habit perennial aquatic herb, from long rhizomes; stems 10–100 cm long, to 1 mm in diameter, branched at base. Leaves all submersed, linear, thread-like, 5–10 cm long, 0.2–1.5 mm wide, with 1 vein, tip rounded to blunt; stipules 0.5–1 cm long, fused, forming a tight sheath around the stem. Flowers in a spikelike inflorescence, 1.5–2.5 cm long, with 2–8 whorls. Fruit an achene, 2–3 mm long, widest above middle, beak and keel absent.
Where Found lakes, ponds, streams.

♦ *Stuckenia pectinata* (L.) Börner
SAGO PONDWEED
Potamogeton pectinatus L.

Habit perennial aquatic herb; stems to 1 m long, repeatedly forked. Leaves all submersed, linear, thin, green, 5–10 cm long, to 1 mm wide, with 1 to 3 veins, tip sharp-pointed; stipules 0.5–2 cm long. Flowers in a spikelike inflorescence, 1.5–2.5 cm long, with 2 to 5 whorls. Fruit an achene, 3–4 mm long, widest above middle, with a short prominent beak, keel absent.
Where Found ponds, lakes.

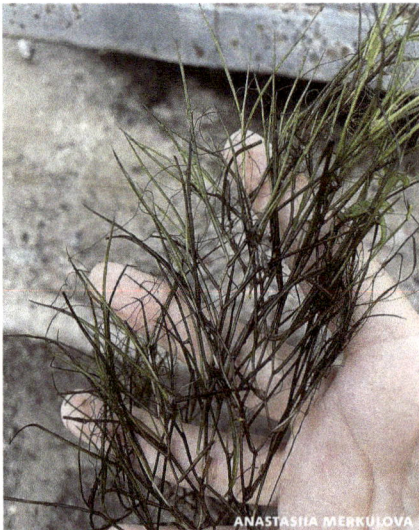

Stuckenia pectinata SAGO PONDWEED

Stuckenia vaginata (Magnin) Holub
SHEATHED PONDWEED
Potamogeton vaginatus Turcz.

Habit perennial aquatic herb, from long rhizomes; stems to 120 cm long, unbranched or sparsely branched. Leaves all submersed, linear, thread-like, to 20 cm long, the lower ones to 2 mm wide, with 1 vein, tips round to blunt or notched, firm, dark green; stipules 2–5 cm long, joined with inflated sheath. Flowers in a spikelike inflorescence, 3–5 cm long, with 3–12 whorls. Fruit an achene, 2.5–3 mm long, widest above middle, beak and keel absent.
Where Found lakes, ponds, streams.

SCHEUCHZERIACEAE
Scheuchzeria Family

Scheuchzeria SCHEUCHZERIA
(In honor of Swiss botanist Johann Jakob Scheuchzer, 1672-1733.)

♦ *Scheuchzeria palustris* L.
SCHEUCHZERIA, RANNOCH-RUSH

Habit perennial wetland herb, from long rhizomes, rooting at the nodes; stems 10–30 cm tall. Leaves basal and along stem; basal leaves linear, 10–40 cm long, parallel-lined, sheathing, persistent; stem leaves reduced upwards. Flowers 3–12 in a terminal raceme, greenish white, on stalks to 2.5 cm long; perianth segments 6; stamens 6. Fruit a beaked follicle, 5–9 mm long; seeds 4–5 mm long.
Where Found sphagnum bogs, lakeshores.

TOFIELDIACEAE
Featherling Family

1 Stems glandular-hairy, at least in inflorescence . . . . *Triantha*

1 Stems smooth throughout . . . . *Tofieldia*

Tofieldia FALSE-ASPHODEL
(In honor of English botanist Thomas Tofield, 1730–1779.)

1 Flowers greenish-white; stems leafless or at most with one small bract. . . . *Tofieldia pusilla*

1 Flowers purplish; stems with one or more leaves . . . . *Tofieldia coccinea*

♦ *Tofieldia coccinea* Richardson
NORTHERN FALSE-ASPHODEL

Habit small perennial herb, with a short purplish stem, 4–12 cm tall, topped by one or two tight clusters of small purple to red flowers, from a short rhizome. Leaves mostly basal, 5-nerved, stiff and sword-shaped, arranged like a fan through which the stem rises; stem leaves single (rarely two), with a small bract just below the inflorescence. Flowers in tightly-packed clusters when young, opening somewhat later; usually purple to deep red but can be pink or yellowish; tepals six; stamens six; pistil with 3 styles. Fruit a dry, spherical capsule, with 15 to 30 seeds.

Where Found occasional in subalpine to alpine areas north of the Alaska Range crest, on calcium-rich gravel bars, tundra, and meadows.

Similar Species this species usually stouter than *Tofieldia pusilla,* which is thinner and more lax, does not have stem leaves, has usually 3-nerved basal leaves, and grows more frequently in boggy sites; *Tofieldia coccinea* prefers calcium-rich gravelly situations and tundra.

♦ *Tofieldia pusilla* (Michx.) Pers.
SCOTCH FALSE-ASPHODEL

Habit small perennial herb, with greenish white flowers, from a short rhizome; flowering stems erect, leafless, 5–20 cm tall, very slender, smooth. Leaves all basal, 3-nerved, stiff and sword-shaped, arranged like a fan through which the stem rises. Flowers usually in one, sometimes two, terminal clusters, at first tightly-packed, later more open; greenish white or yellowish (never red or purple); tepals 6, stamens 6, pistil with 3 styles. Fruit a dry, spherical capsule, with 15 to 30 seeds.

Where Found occasional in moist to wet areas at low to high-elevations; bogs, alpine seeps, moist meadows.

Similar Species *Tofieldia pusilla* is less stout (with narrower leaves) than *Tofieldia coccinea,* and lacks a stem leaf.

Triantha FALSE-ASPHODEL

(Greek *tris,* three-, and *anthos,* flower, alluding to aggregation of flowers in threes.)

Scheuchzeria palustris RANNOCH-RUSH

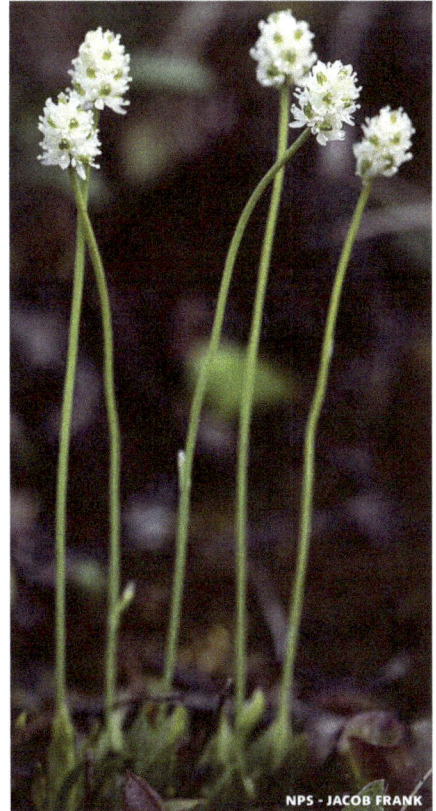

Tofieldia coccinea NORTHERN FALSE-ASPHODEL

◆ *Triantha occidentalis* (S. Watson) R.R. Gates
WESTERN FALSE-ASPHODEL
Tofieldia glutinosa subsp. *occidentalis* (S. Watson) C.L.
Hitchc., *Tofieldia occidentalis* S. Watson

Habit perennial herb, from a short, strong rhizome; flowering stems 10–20 cm tall, smooth or viscid with black, stalked glands below the inflorescence. Leaves basal and along stem; basal leaves several, tufted, broadly linear, 5–20 cm long, 2–4 mm wide, smooth, sheathing at base, margins entire; stem leaves smaller often one, sometimes 2 to 3 (or absent). Flowers in a compact, spike-like, terminal cluster, 2–6 cm long, in bunches of 2 or 3 at each node of inflorescence; flowers white to greenish yellow, cup-shaped; tepals 6; stamens 6, the anthers often purplish and conspicuous; pistil 3-chambered. Fruit a 3-lobed erect ovoid capsule, 5–7 mm long; seeds numerous, about 1 mm long.

Where Found uncommon in moist meadows, lakeshores.

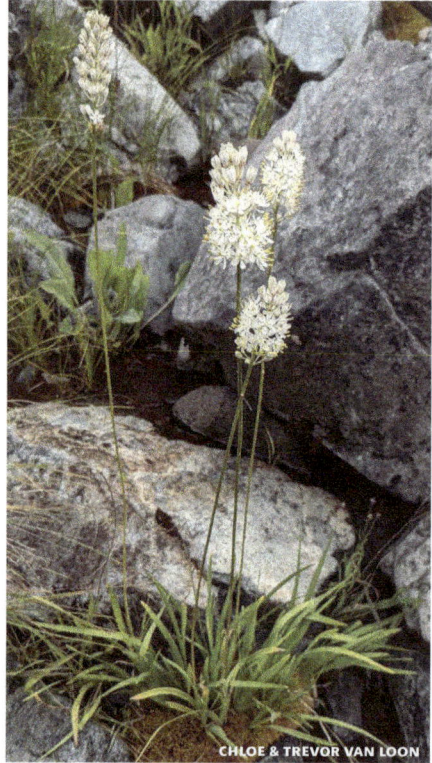

CHLOE & TREVOR VAN LOON

Triantha occidentalis WESTERN FALSE-ASPHODEL

CHRISTIAN BERG

Tofieldia pusilla SCOTCH FALSE-ASPHODEL

TYPHACEAE
Cat-Tail Family

Family now includes genus *Sparganium* from former family Sparganiaceae.

1 Female flowers in one to several spherical heads; perianth of greenish sepals; leaves strongly keeled (3-angled in cross-section). *Sparganium*
3 Female flowers in an elongate densely flowered spike; perianth of white hairs; leaves flat-elliptic in cross-section . . . . *Typha*

Sparganium BUR-REED
(From Greek, diminutive of *sparganon*, a swaddling band.)

1 Male head single; beak of fruit 0.5-1.5 mm long 2
1 Male heads 2 or more; fruit with longer beak. . . . . *S. angustifolium*
2 Fruiting heads axillary; fruit with conical beak . . . . *S. natans*
2 Fruiting heads (at least upper ones) on stalks; fruit nearly beakless. . . . . *S. hyperboreum*

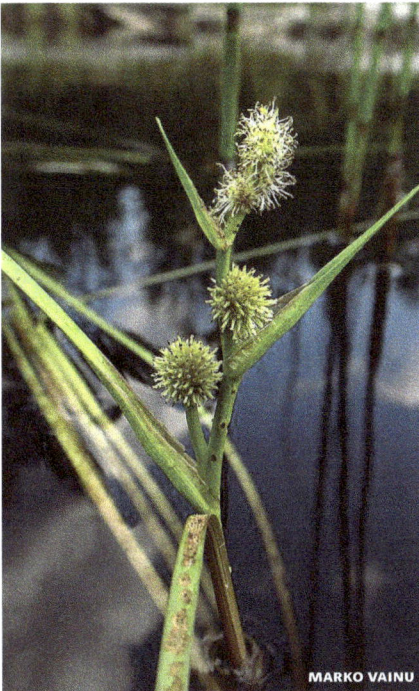

Sparganium angustifolium
NARROWLEAF BUR-REED

◆ *Sparganium angustifolium* Michx.
NARROWLEAF BUR-REED
Habit perennial aquatic herb, from long rhizomes; stems usually floating, 30–40 cm long. Leaves floating, mostly 2–3 mm wide, often wider at base. Flowers in an unbranched inflorescence; female heads 1–3, shiny, about 2 cm wide, the lowest stalked, the upper female heads stalkless; male heads 2–6, close together above female heads. Fruit a spindle-shaped achene, 5–7 mm long, dull brown except at the red-brown base, abruptly contracted to a beak 1–3 mm long.
Where Found shallow water of lakes and ponds.

◆ *Sparganium hyperboreum* Buerling ex. Laest. NORTHERN BUR-REED
Habit perennial aquatic herb, from weak rhizomes; stems floating, 20–80 cm long. Leaves flat, linear with sheathing bases, limp, floating, 1–5 mm wide. Flowers in an unbranched inflorescence of 1 to 4 female heads below and 1 (rarely 2) male heads above, the heads globe-shaped, at least some borne above the leaf axils; the heads unstalked above, stalked below. Fruit an achene, 2–5 mm long, constricted at middle, beaked or beakless, the beak less than 0.5 mm long.
Where Found shallow water of lakes and ponds.

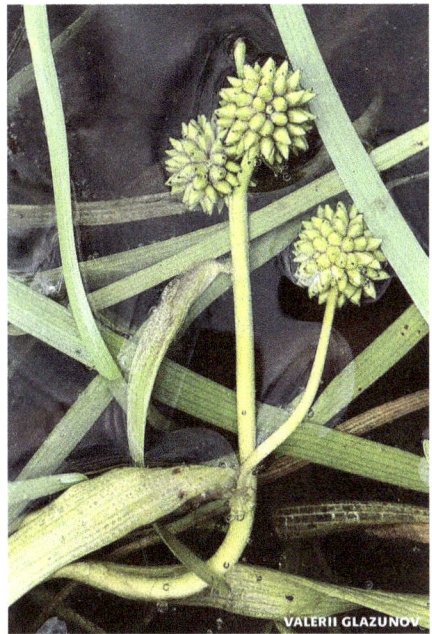

Sparganium hyperboreum
NORTHERN BUR-REED

♦ *Sparganium natans* L. SMALL BUR-REED
Sparganium minimum (Hartman) Wallr.

Habit perennial aquatic herb; stems usually long and floating, sometimes shorter and upright, 10–40 dm or more long. Leaves linear, dark green, thin, flat, 2–6 mm wide. Flowers in an unbranched inflorescence; female heads 2–3, from bract axils, stalkless or the lowest sometimes short-stalked, 1 cm wide when mature; male heads usually 1 (rarely 2). Fruit a broadly oval achene, 3–4 mm long, dull green-brown, the beak 1–2 mm long.

Where Found shallow water, shores.

Typha CAT-TAIL
(Greek name for cat-tail.)

♦ *Typha latifolia* L. COMMON CAT-TAIL

Habit Perennial emergent herb; stems erect, 1–2.5 m long. Leaves upright, linear, mostly 1–2 cm wide. Flowers either male or female the male and female portions of spike normally contiguous (rarely separated by 3–4 mm); male portion 5–15 cm long and 1.5–2 cm wide at flowering time; female portion of spike dark brown, 10–15 cm long and 2–3 cm wide when mature. Fruit a dry follicle, 1 cm long, with many white, linear hairs from its base.

Where Found Uncommon in marshes, lakeshores, and pond margins, usually in shallow water.

Sparganium natans SMALL BUR-REED

Typha latifolia COMMON CAT-TAIL

MOSSES

Mosses form an important part of Denali's flora and its ecosystems, with about 500 species known from the region; described below are the most common species.

AULACOMNIACEAE

♦ *Aulacomnium palustre* (Hedw.) Schwägr.
RIBBED BOG MOSS, GLOW MOSS
Key Characters plants in clumps, bright yellow-green; their bright color sometimes gives ribbed bog moss an almost incandescent appearance, leading to one of its common names of glow moss; stems 3-10 cm long, mostly unbranched, reddish-brown, and covered in dense red-brown rhizoids, looking like a layer of felt; leaves acute-tipped, distinguishing it from *Aulacomnium turgidum*.
Where Found in bogs, fens, swamps, moist, acidic forests; also common in arctic tundra.

♦ *Aulacomnium turgidum* (Wahlenb.) Schwägr.
TURGID BOG MOSS, HOODED GLOW MOSS
Key Characters plants bright yellow-green; stems typically unbranched, 3-12 cm long, grow in mats or cushions, and covered in dense red-brown rhizoids, looking like a layer of felt; leaves concave, blunt-tipped, distinguishing it from *Aulacomnium palustre*.
Where Found in arctic tundra and heath, spruce woods.

HYLOCOMIACEAE

♦ *Hylocomium splendens* (Hedw.) Schimp.
SPLENDID FEATHER MOSS, STAIRSTEP MOSS
Key Characters plants green-gold to reddish yellow, grow in wide loose patches, and often form mats; it is recognized by its red stems, twice-branched branches and a growth pattern which produces 'stair-steps' along the stem (each step approximately one year's growth; stems red and covered with tiny reddish hairs (paraphyllia).
Where Found by far the most abundant moss in Denali (and one of the most abundant plants in the state), most commonly found in forests of white and black spruce.
Similar Species superficially similar to the also abundant *Pleurozium schreberi*, but that species lacks the stair-step pattern, is not twice-pinnate, and its red stems do not have paraphyllia; *Pleurozium schreberi* is also shinier when dried.
Traditional Uses long used for chinking log structures in Alaska (and to present-day); the

Aulacomnium turgidum TURGID BOG MOSS

Hylocomium splendens SPLENDID FEATHER MOSS

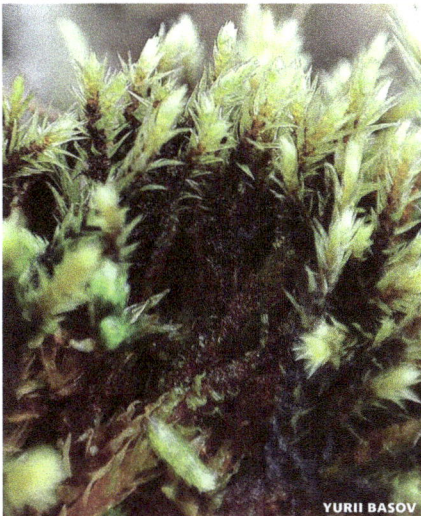
Aulacomnium palustre RIBBED BOG MOSS

wet moss is pressed into cracks between logs using a wooden chisel; when the moss is dry, it remains compressed and stays green for the life of the cabin.

♦ *Pleurozium schreberi* (Willd. ex Brid.) Mitt.
SCHREBER'S BIG RED STEM MOSS

Key Characters plants yellow to green and may form large mats; stems 5-10 cm long, with irregularly pinnate branches; leaves concave, ovate and blunt-tipped, loosely overlapping, and cover the red stem.

Where Found the second-most abundant moss in Denali, found in forests of white and black spruce, and continuing into the alpine zone.

Similar Species *Hylocomium splendens,* but *Pleurozium schreberi* without the stair-step growth pattern of that species; big red stem also has a satiny sheen when dry, while *H. splendens* is dull.

Traditional Uses similar to splendid feather moss, this species also used for chinking log structures.

HYPNACEAE

♦ *Ptilium crista-castrensis* (Hedw.) De Not.
KNIGHT'S PLUME MOSS

Key Characters plants are perfectly pinnate (similar to a feather), shiny yellow-green, and often form dense mats; stems 3-10 cm long with a somewhat wiry central spine; lateral branches are evenly spaced and taper to a point; other mosses in Denali lack the wiry stem and perfect feather-like appearance.

Where Found forests of black and white spruce.

POLYTRICHACEAE

♦ *Polytrichum juniperinum* Hedw.
JUNIPER HAIRCAP MOSS

Key Characters plants grow singly or form large hummocks; plants have a single stem, 3-4 cm long; leaves 1 cm long, held out in all directions, giving an overall bristly appearance, similar to a bottlebrush or conifer seedling; when dry, leaves tightly inrolled, leading to a long white line along the center of the leaf (visible with a handlens); reproductive structures often present: either a stalked capsule with a hairy cap (female) or a brown cup-like structure at the tip of the plant (male).

Where Found dry, acidic spruce forests, heathlands, and dwarf-shrublands; common on open, south-facing hillsides and recently burned areas.

♦ *Polytrichum strictum* Menzies ex Brid.
BOG HAIRCAP MOSS

Key Characters forms very dense hummocks, the plants intertwined by white to brown woolly hairs; plants have a single stem, 6-12 cm long; leaves 2-5 mm long, held out in all directions, giving an overall bristly appearance, similar to a bottlebrush or conifer seedling; leaf margins folded over, creating a long line along the center of the leaf (visible with a handlens); reproductive structures often present: either a stalked capsule with a hairy cap (female) or a brown cup-like structure at the tip of the plant (male).

Where Found sphagnum moss bogs, wet tundra, muskeg, sedge meadows, on fallen trees in wet spruce forests.

Similar Species *Polytrichum juniperinum* lacks the dense covering of felty hairs.

Pleurozium schreberi
SCHREBER'S BIG RED STEM MOSS

Ptilium crista-castrensis
KNIGHT'S PLUME MOSS

RHYTIDIACEAE

♦ *Rhytidium rugosum* (Hedw.) Kindb.
PIPECLEANER MOSS
   Key Characters one of the largest mosses in interior Alaska; plants have a main stem and irregular lateral branches; color varies from yellow-green to orange-brown; leaves glossy, concave and very wrinkled (under magnification), closely overlapping one another on the stem.
   Where Found usually in dry, rocky situations, such as boulder fields and exposed ridgelines, often where calcareous.

SPHAGNACEAE

♦ *Sphagnum* spp.
SPHAGNUM MOSS, PEAT MOSS
   Key Characters sphagnum mosses are important shapers of wetland environments, with plants forming cushions, hummocks, or lawns, and over time (as plants are very slow to decay), leads to the development of deep mats which insulate soil from heat and protect the permafrost; *Sphagnum* also acidifies its environment, allowing for only a handful of bog-adapted species to co-habitate with it; currently, 24 species of *Sphagnum* are reported from Denali, and worldwide, nearly 400 species have been described; *Sphagnum* species vary in color from bright green, to shades of pink red, and purple; branches in clusters, some hanging down along the stem and some ascending; at the top of the stem, branches are compressed into a tufted head ('capitulum'); leaves have two types of cells: those that photosynthesize, and dead cells that serve only to absorb water (plants are natural sponges, holding up to 30 times their weight in water); spore releasing capsules (only rarely produced), are dark, round and on short stalks above the leafy branches; capsules open via a pressure-driven mechanism (similar to a 'pop-gun'), spraying spores into the wind. Individual species are identified by branching patterns, growth form, color, and leaf cell characteristics, and can be quite challenging!
   Where Found the dominant moss of peat bogs; also common in wet conifer forests and moist arctic tundra.
   Traditional Uses sphagnum mosses used as an insulating material, soil conditioner when dried and milled, and as a bacterial-inhibiting dressing for wounds.

Polytrichum strictum BOG HAIRCAP MOSS

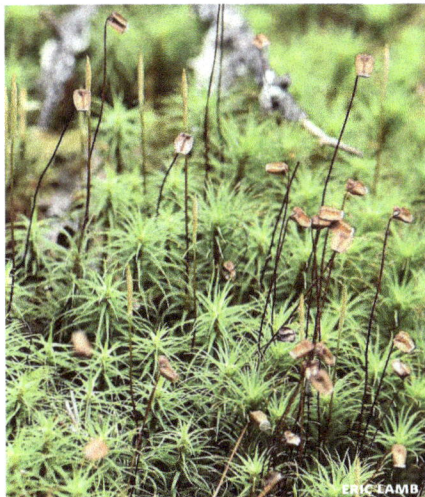

Polytrichum juniperinum JUNIPER HAIRCAP MOSS

Rhytidium rugosum PIPECLEANER MOSS

Sphagnum rubellum

Sphagnum fallax

LICHENS

Lichens are the result of a symbiotic relationship between an algae (or cyanobacteria) and a fungal host. In Denali, over 450 species of lichens have been recorded. Lichens play an important role in weathering rock and contributing nitrogen and other nutrients to the soil; individual lichens can be more than a thousand years old.

Examples of the most conspicuous lichens found in Denali are described below; these lichens are classified as either foliose or fruticose. **Foliose lichens** have two easily distinguishable sides; that is, there is a recognizable top and bottom surface; they can be very flat and leafy like lettuce, or convoluted with many ridges. **Fruticose lichens** have a form like that of a miniature shrub, with branches that are generally not flat in cross-section. Another type of lichen, **crustose lichens** (not included below), are, as the name implies, crust-forming over a surface, such as on a boulder or a tree trunk; and occur in many colors, from yellow and orange to gray or green.

CLADONIACEAE

◆ *Cladonia rangiferina* (L.) Weber ex F.H.Wigg.
REINDEER LICHEN
Cladina rangiferina (L.) Nyl.
Key Characters a much-branched fruticose lichen; thalli (vegetative tissue) 4-12 cm long, branched, grayish, often with a pale brown or pinkish cast, brownish at base; branches round in cross-section, becoming finer with brownish tips, and all bent in one direction.
Where Found open woodlands and dry alpine tundra.
Similar Species *Cladonia stygia* is also gray and has a similar habit (branches bent in one direction), but base of thallus is blackened.
Traditional Uses an important forage for caribou in the winter; however, this lichen contains many chemicals which are mildly toxic, but caribou are able to safely excrete these compounds. In times of food shortages, Native peoples would collect reindeer lichen, boiling them many times to remove toxins before eating.

◆ *Cladonia stellaris* (Opiz) Pouzar & Vězda
POPCORN LICHEN
Cladina stellaris (Opiz) Brodo
Key Characters a fruticose lichen, with clusters of branches forming round puffs; thalli 4-10 cm long, white to pale yellow-green; branching mainly in fours and fives, the branches round in cross-section, with open holes at tips; branches obscure the central main stem. Other species of reindeer lichen lack the even, rounded tufts typical of *C. stellaris*.
Where Found open, drier woodlands and tundra.

Cladonia rangiferina REINDEER LICHEN

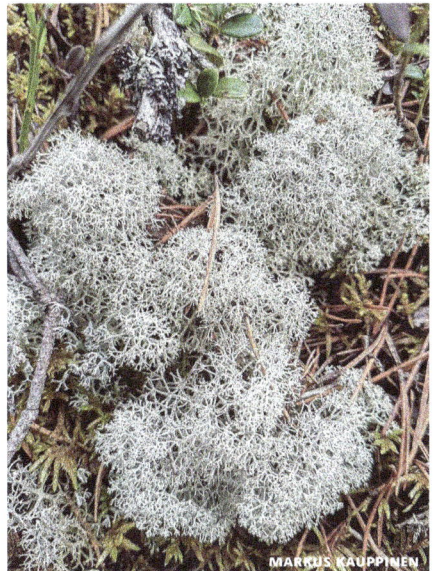

Cladonia stellaris POPCORN LICHEN

ICMADOPHILACEAE

♦ *Thamnolia vermicularis* (Sw.) Ach. ex Schaer.
WHITE WORM LICHEN
Key Characters a distinctive, common lichen in Denali, with many whitish, cylindric (hollow on inside) long, slender branches, these sometimes with short spurs; it is believed to spread only by fragmentation.
Where Found arctic and alpine tundra, rocky slopes, open woodlands.

PARMELIACEAE

♦ *Dactylina arctica* (Hook. f.) Nyl.
FINGER LICHEN, DEAD MAN'S FINGERS
Key Characters an upright fruticose lichen, typically unbranched, but sometimes with short spur branches; always hollow, typically upright, 2-7 cm long, and to 1.5 cm wide; thallus pale or dark yellow, often with a brownish base; apothecia (fruiting structure) resemble small brown eyes but are rarely produced.
Where Found tundra, open conifer woodlands.
Similar Species no other lichen in Denali could be confused with *Dactylina arctica;* the other member of the genus present in the region, *Dactylina ramulosa,* is smaller overall, often tinged with purple, and much branched.

♦ *Flavocetraria cucullata* (Bellardi) Kärnefelt & Thell **CURLED SNOW LICHEN**
Cetraria cucullata (Bellardi) Ach.
Key Characters a foliose lichen with upright thalli 2-8 cm tall; thalli pale yellow, often reddish at base, narrowly inrolled and ruffled, 2-6 mm wide, often partially fused into a tube; thallus unbranched to sparsely and irregularly branched; apothecia, when present, large, round, and brown.
Where Found on forest floor and tundra.
Similar Species include the less common *Flavocetraria nivalis,* but that species wider, not tightly inrolled, and has a crinkled appearance; the uncommon *Flavocetraria miniscula* has an nearly identical appearance, but is much smaller (2-3 cm tall and 1-2 mm wide). *Vulpicida* species are the only other yellow, ruffled lichens in Alaska, but they are a bright saffron-orange color, and the most common species (*V. pinastri*) is found on twigs and bark, not on the ground.

♦ *Flavocetraria nivalis* (L.) Kärnefelt & Thell **FLATTENED SNOW LICHEN**
Cetraria nivalis (L.) Ach.
Key Characters a foliose lichen with upright or spreading thalli 2-5 cm tall and 2-6 mm wide; thallus pale yellow, with short lateral branches, the dying base is yellow or brown (never red).

JERZY OPIOŁA

Thamnolia vermicularis WHITE WORM LICHEN

Where Found moist alpine areas.

Similar Species the whole thallus has a crinkled, netted texture and is never tightly inrolled, distinguishing it from *Flavocetraria cucullata; Asahinea chrysantha,* another yellow foliose alpine lichen, can initially look similar, but it is grows in rounded lobes, and the underside is black.

♦ *Masonhalea richardsonii* (Hook.) Kärnefelt
TUMBLEWEED LICHEN

Key Characters a showy foliose lichen; thallus thin and dichotomously branching, the branches 2-5 mm wide; thalli 4-15 cm long (when lain flat), dark brown on upper surface (brownish-green when wet), with long white patches on underside; apothecia very rarely present.

Dactylina arctica FINGER LICHEN

Flavocetraria cucullata CURLED SNOW LICHEN

Where Found arctic and alpine tundra; when dry, the lichen curls into a loose ball, allowing it to be carried by the wind; when moist, the now reddish-brown thallus spreads out, gripping onto other tundra plants; in swales or depressions, hundreds of individuals may be bunched together.

Similar Species no other lichen in Denali has a similar tumbleweed habit.

PELTIGERACEAE

♦ *Peltigera aphthosa* (L.) Willd.
FRECKLE PELT LICHEN

Key Characters a foliose lichen growing parallel to the ground, the lobes upturned at their edges to show a white undersurface; thalli form rosettes to 10 or 15 cm across in favorable habitats, but are usually smaller; upper surface a bright grassy green (paler gray-green if dry), with dark flecks; the flecks (cephalodia) are pockets of cyanobacteria, a nitrogen-fixing bacterium; thallus underside without a cortex, making it soft-textured; apothecia often present, which are rounded, dark brown to black, extended at edge of thallus.

Where Found common on the forest floor, in thickets, and on tundra.

Similar Species there are many other species of *Peltigera* in Denali, but most lack cephalodia; closely related and abundant *Peltigera britannica* is similar, but the cephalodia form on the surface of the thallus and can be easily removed with a thumbnail.

Flavocetraria nivalis FLATTENED SNOW LICHEN

Peltigera aphthosa FRECKLE PELT LICHEN

Masonhalea richardsonii TUMBLEWEED LICHEN

GLOSSARY

abaxial On the side away from the axis, usually refers to the underside of a leaf (compare with adaxial).

acaulescent Without an upright, leafy stem.

achene A one-seeded, dry, indehiscent fruit with the seed coat not attached to the mature wall of the ovary.

acid Having more hydrogen ions than hydroxyl (OH) ions; a pH less than 7.

acuminate Tapering to a narrow point, more tapering than acute, less than attenuate.

acute Gradually tapered to a tip.

adaxial On the side toward the axis, usually refers to the top side of a leaf (compare with abaxial).

adnate Fused with a structure different from itself, as when stamens are adnate to petals (compare with connate).

adventive Not native to and not fully established in a new habitat.

alkaline Having more hydroxyl ions than hydrogen ions; a pH greater than 7.

alluvial Deposits of rivers and streams.

alternate Borne singly at each node, as in leaves on a stem.

ament Spikelike inflorescence of same-sexed flowers (either male or female); same as catkin.

amphi-Beringian Found on both sides of the Bering straight in Alaska and Siberia.

androgynous Spike with both staminate and pistillate flowers, the pistillate located at the base, below the staminate (compare with gynaecandrous).

angiosperm A plant producing flowers and bearing seeds in an ovary.

annual A plant that completes its life cycle in one growing season, then dies.

anther Pollen-bearing part of stamen, usually at the end of a stalk called a filament.

anthesis The period during which a flower is fully open and functional.

anthocyanic Pigmented with anthocyanins, this usually manifested as a tinging or suffusion of pink, red, or purple.

aphyllopodic Having basal sheaths without blades; with new shoots arising laterally from parent shoot (compare with phyllopodic).

apiculate Coming into an immediate point; usually used when describing the apex of a leaf, petal, and sepal.

apiculus An abrupt, very small, projected tip.

apomixis Clonal reproduction via seeds. Ovules are not fertilized, yet develop into viable seeds that are genetically identical to the mother plant.

apothecia The fruiting body of most lichens; typically an open cup, disk or button-like structure which releases sexually-produced spores. Apothecia are perennial, not shed after a single season; singular apothecium.

appressed Lying flat to or parallel to a surface.

aquatic Living in water.

areole In leaves, the spaces between small veins.

aril A specialized appendage on a seed, often brightly colored, derived from the seed coat.

aristate Tipped with a slender bristle.

armed Bearing a sharp projection such as a prickle, spine, or thorn.

aromatic Strongly scented.

ascending Angled upward.

asymmetrical Not symmetrical.

attenuate Tapering gradually to a prolonged tip.

auricle An ear-shaped appendage to a leaf or stipule.

auriculate Having ear shaped appendages (auricles).

awl-shaped Tapering gradually from a broad base to a sharp point.

awn A thin, pointed appendage often attached at the tip.

axil Angle between a stem and the attached leaf.

barb Sharp, thorn-like projection.

basal From base of plant.

basal rosette Leaves attached to the base of the plant in a circular arrangement; plants with basal rosettes often lack stem leaves.

basic A pH greater than 7.

beak A slender, terminal appendage on a 3-dimensional organ.

beard Covering of long or stiff hairs.

berry Fruit with the seeds surrounded by fleshy material.

biennial A plant that completes its life cycle in two growing season, typically flowering and fruiting in the second year, then dying.

bifid Cleft into two more or less equal parts.

bilateral symmetry Divisible into mirror-image symmetrical halves along one plane, like a face; contrast to 'radial symmetry'.

bipinnate Leaves 2 times pinnately compound.

blade Expanded, usually flat part of a leaf or petiole.

bloom A whitish powdery or waxy coating that can be rubbed away.

bog A wet, acidic, nutrient-poor peatland characterized by sphagnum and other mosses, shrubs and sedges. Technically, a type of peatland raised above its surroundings by peat accumulation and receiving nutrients only from precipitation.

boreal Far northern latitudes.

brackish Salty.

bract A modified leaf (often leaf-like, sometimes scale-like) at the base of a flower or inflorescence; often reduced.

branchlets A small branch.

bristle A stiff hair.

bud An undeveloped shoot, inflorescence, or flower, in woody plants often covered by scales and serving as the overwintering stage.

bulb A group of modified leaves serving as a foodstorage organ, borne on a short, vertical, underground stem (compare with corm).

bulbil A bulb-like structure borne in the leaf axils or in place of flowers.

bulblet Small bulb borne above ground, as in a leaf axil.

ca. About, approximately (Latin circa).

caducous Falling off early, as stipules that leave behind a scar.

caespitose Plants that grow in dense tufts or cushions (also spelled cespitose).

calcareous fen An uncommon wetland type associated with seepage areas, and which receive groundwater enriched with primarily calcium and magnesium bicarbonates.

calciphile Plants that like to grow in lime-rich soils.

calcium-rich Refers to wetlands underlain by limestone or receiving water enriched by calcium compounds.

callosity A hardened thickening.

callus A firm, thickened portion of an organ; the firm base of the lemma in the Poaceae.

calyx The flower whorl that consists of all the sepals, often used when the sepals are fused together.

campanulate Bell-shaped.

canaliculate Grooved or channeled.

capillary Very fine, hair-like, not-flattened.

capitate Abruptly expanded at the apex, thereby forming a knob-like tip.

capsule A dry dehiscent fruit that was derived from more than 1 carpel.

carpel Part of the female reproductive organ, consisting of an ovary, style and stigma; multiple carpels can be fused.

caruncle An appendage at or near the hilum of some seeds.

caryopsis The dry, indehiscent seed of grasses.

catkin Spikelike inflorescence of same-sexed flowers (either male or female); same as ament.

caudex Firm, hardened, summit of a root mass that functions as a perennating organ.

cauline Of or pertaining to the aboveground portion of the stem.

cephalodia Specialized structures in a lichen for containing cyanobacteria.

cespitose Growing in a compact cluster with closely spaced stems; tufted, clumped (also spelled caespitose).

chaff Thin, dry scales; in the Asteraceae, sometimes found as chaffy bracts on the receptacle.

cilia Hairs found at the margin of an organ.

ciliate With hairs along the margin.

circumboreal Refers to a species distribution pattern which circles the earth's boreal regions.

circumpolar Occurring in the arctic around the Northern Hemisphere.

clasping Leaves that partially encircle the stem at the base.

clavate Widened in the distal portion, like a baseball bat.

claw The narrow, basal portion of perianth parts.

cleistogamous Type of flower that remains closed and is self-pollinated.

clumped Having the stems grouped closely together; tufted.

colony-forming A group of plants of the same species, produced either vegetatively or by seed.

column The joined style and filaments in the Orchidaceae.

coma A tuft of fine hairs, especially at the tip of a seed.

composite An inflorescence that is made up of many tiny florets crowded together on a receptacle; members of the Aster Family (Asteraceae).

compound leaf A leaf with two or more leaflets.

concave Curved inward.

conduplicate Folded lengthwise into nearly equal parts.

cone The dry fruit of conifers composed of overlapping scales.

conifer Cone-bearing woody plants.

connate Two like parts that are fused (compare with adnate).

connivent Converging and touching but not actually fused, applies to like organs.

convex Curved outward.

convolute Arranged such that one edge is covered and the other is exposed, usually referring to petals in bud.

cordate With a rounded lobe on each side of a central sinus; heart-shaped.

coriaceous With a firm, leathery texture.

corm A short, vertical, enlarged, underground stem that serves as a food storage organ (compare with bulb).

corolla The flower whorl that consists of all the petals, often used when the petals are fused together.

cortex The upper surface of the thallus of a lichen; it is composed of tough fungal cells, unlike the loosely-structured medulla.

corymb A flat topped cluster of flowers; the lower branches or pedicels have longer stems, leading to the flowers being produced at the same height.

costa (plural costae) A prominent midvein or midrib of a leaflet.

crenate Rounded toothed margins; generally used to describe leaf margins.

crenulate Finely crenate.

crisped An irregularly crinkled or curled leaf margin.

crown Persistent base of a plant, especially a grasses.

culm The stem of a grass or grasslike plant, especially a stem with the inflorescence.

cuneate Tapering to the base with relatively straight, non-parallel margins; wedge-shaped.

cyanobacteria A kind of bacteria that can both photosynthesize and fix nitrogen.

cyme A type of inflorescence in which the central flowers open first.

deciduous Plants that lose their leaves in fall; not evergreen.

decumbent A stem that is prostrate at the base and curves upward to have an erect or ascending, apical portion.

decurrent Possessing an adnate line or wing that extends down the axis below the node, usually referring to leaves on a stem.

dehiscent Opening up at maturity; generally referring to fruit or anthers.

deltate Triangle-shaped.

deltoid Triangular.

dentate Provided with outward oriented teeth.

depauperate Poorly developed due to unfavorable conditions.

dicots One of two main divisions of the Angiosperms (the other being the Monocots); plants having 2 seed leaves (cotyledons), net-venation, and flower parts in 4s or 5s (or multiples of these numbers).

dimorphic Having two forms.

dioecious Bearing only male or female flowers on a single plant.

disarticulation In grasses, spikelets breaking either above or below the glumes when mature, the glumes remaining in the head if disarticulation above the glumes, or the glumes falling with the florets if disarticulation is below the glumes.

disc floret Flowers of the Asteraceae family; with a less prominent fused corolla with 5 lobes; in flowers with both ray florets and disk florets, these are in the center of the flowering head.

discoid In composite flowers (Asteraceae), a head with only disk (tubular) flowers, the ray flowers absent.

disjunct A population of plants widely separated from its main range.

disk In the Asteraceae, the central part of the head, composed of tubular flowers.

dissected Leaves divided into many smaller segments.

disturbed Natural communities altered by human influences.

divided Leaves which are lobed nearly to the midrib.

dolomite A type of limestone consisting of calcium magnesium carbonate.

dorsal Underside, or back of an organ.

drupe A fleshy fruit with a single large seed such as a cherry.

eglandular Without glands.

elliptic Broadest at the middle, gradually tapering to both ends.

emergent Growing out of and above the water surface.

emersed leaf Growing above the water surface or out of water.

endemic A species restricted to a particular region.

entire Margins containing no serrations, smooth.

erect Stiffly upright.

erose With a ragged edge.

escape A cultivated plant which establishes itself outside of cultivation.

evergreen Plant retaining its leaves throughout the year.

excurrent With the central rib or axis continuing or projecting beyond the organ.

exserted Extending beyond the mouth of a structure, such as stamens extending out from mouth of corolla.

falcate Sickle-shaped false

fellfield A slope that due to the snow and wind give these plants characteristic forms; usually references alpine slopes and their respective plants.

fen An open wetland usually dominated by herbaceous plants, and fed by in-flowing, often calcium- and/or magnesium-rich water; soils vary from peat to clays and silts.

fern Perennial plants with spore-bearing leaves similar to the vegetative leaves and bearing sporangia on their underside, or the spore-bearing leaves much modified.

fibrous A cluster of slender roots, all with the same diameter.

filament The stalk of a stamen which supports the anther.

filiform Thread-like.

flexuose A plant or part of the plant that curves, bends, or any combination of the two.

floating mat A feature of some ponds where plant roots form a carpet over some or all of the water surface.

floodplain That part of a river valley that is occasionally covered by flood waters.

floret A small flower in a dense cluster of flowers; in grasses the flower with its attached lemma and palea.

floricane the second-year flowering stem of *Rubus* (compare with primocane).

foliose A growth habit that is primarily two-dimensional, like a leaf with a distinguishable top and bottom (refers to lichens).

follicle A dry fruit that was derived from a single carpel and splits open from a single side.

fruticose A growth habit that has a three-dimensional shape, like a bush (refers to lichens).

gametophyte The haploid reproductive stage of plants, generally much smaller than the diploid life cycle (sporophyte). In ferns and clubmosses, this is an independent plant that produces male and female gametes, and fertilization leads to the larger sporophyte. In conifers and flowering plants, the gametophytes are microscopic and contained within the cones or flowers. Fertilization leads to the production of a seed. In bryophytes (mosses, liverworts, and hornworts) this is reversed, with the gametophyte being the largest and most obvious part of the plant appearing as stem and leaf-like structures.

geniculate An abrupt bending forming a knee at the bend.

genus The first part of the scientific name for a plant or animal (plural genera).

glabrate Nearly glabrous or becoming so.

glabrous Without hair.

gland An appendage or depression which produces a sticky or greasy substance.

glandular Outgrowths that secrete, such as hairs that produce compounds to deter grazing or sticky substances that trap insects.

glaucous With a waxy residue, usually whitish or bluish in color.

glumes A pair of small bracts at base of each spikelet in a grass; the lowermost (or first) glume usually smaller the upper (or second) glume usually longer.

grain The fruit of a grass; the swollen seed-like protuberance on the fruit of some Rumex.

gymnosperm Plants in which the seeds are not produced in an ovary, but usually in a cone.

gynaecandrous In Sedge Family, having both staminate and pistillate flowers on the same spike, the staminate located at the base, below the pistillate (compare with androgynous).

halophyte A plant adapted to growing in a salty substrate.

hardwoods Loosely used to contrast most deciduous trees from conifers.

hastate Shaped like an arrowhead with the bottom lobes facing outwards; compare saggitate.

haustorium A specialized, root-like connection to a host plant that a parasite uses to extract nourishment.

herb A herbaceous, non-woody plant.

herbaceous Like an herb; also, leaflike in appearance.

hilum The scar at the point of attachment of a seed.

hirsute Pubescent with coarse, somewhat stiff, usually curving hairs, coarser than villous but softer than hispid.

hispid Pubescent with coarse, stiff hairs that may be uncomfortable to the touch, coarser than hirsute but softer than bristly.

hummock A small, raised mound formed by certain species of sphagnum moss.

humus Dark, well-decayed organic matter in soil.

hybrid A cross-breed between two species.

hydric Wet (compare with mesic, xeric).

hygroscopic Attracting and absorbing water molecules.

hypanthium A ring, cup, or tube around the ovary; the sepals, petals and stamens are attached to the rim of the hypanthium.

imbricate Overlapping, as shingles on a roof. In flowers with ray and disk florets, these make up the outer margin of the flowering head.

indehiscent Not splitting open at maturity.

indusium In ferns, a membranous covering over the sorus (plural indusia); can be peltate (round attached in the center), linear, or reniform (kidney shaped). Plural indusia.

inferior The position of the ovary when it is below the point of attachment of the sepals and petals.

inflorescence A part of the plant where the flowers are arranged.

insectivorous Refers to the insect trapping and digestion habit of some plants as a nutrition supplement.

internode The space on a stem between each node; see node.

introduced A non-native species.

invasive Non-native species causing significant ecological or economic problems.

involucral bract A single member of the involucre; sometimes called phyllary in composite flowers (Asteraceae).

involucre A whorl of bracts, subtending a flower or inflorescence.

involucrum A whorl of bracts that subtend a flower or inflorescence.

involute Leaf margins rolling inwards towards the upper side of the leaf.

irregular flower Not radially symmetric; with similar parts unequal.

joint A node or section of a stem where the branch and leaf meet.

keel A central rib like the keel of a boat. The length-wise fusion between the lower petals of a flower from the Pea Family (Fabaceae).

laciniate Irregularly dissected into narrow lobes.

lance-shaped Broadest near the base, gradually tapering to a narrower tip.

lanceolate Sword shaped; wider at the base than the tip.

lateral Borne on the sides of a stem or branch.

lax Loose or drooping.

leaf axil The point of the angle between a stem and a leaf.

leaflet One of the leaflike segments of a compound leaf.

lemma In grasses, the lower bract enclosing the flower (the upper, smaller bract is the palea).

lens-shaped Biconvex in shape (like a lentil).

lenticel Blisterlike openings in the epidermis of woody stems, admitting gases to and from the plant, and often appearing as small oval dots on bark.

ligulate Having a ligule; in the Asteraceae, the strap-shaped corolla of a ray floret.

ligule Either the membranous or hairy appendage at the base of a grass leaf; or, the strap-shaped petals of some flowers in the Asteraceae family.

linear Thin and elongate with parallel sides.

lip Upper or lower part of a 2-lipped corolla; also the lower petal in most orchid flowers.

lobed With lobes; in leaves, divisions usually not over halfway to the midrib.

local Occurring sporadically in an area.

lyrate A leaf that is lobed where the terminal lobe is much larger than the lower lobes.

margin The outer edge of a leaf.

marl A calcium-rich clay.

marsh Wetland dominated by herbaceous plants, with standing water for part or all the growing season, then often drying at the surface.

megaspore Large, female spores.

mesic Moist, neither dry nor wet (compare with hydric, xeric).

microspore Small, male spores.

midrib The prominent vein along the main axis of a leaf.

mixed forest A type of forest composed of both deciduous and conifer trees.

moat The open water area ringing the outer edge of a peatland or floating mat.

monocots One of two main divisions of the Angiosperms (the other being the Dicots); plants with a single seed leaf (cotyledon); typically having narrow leaves with parallel veins, and flower parts in 3s or multiples of 3.

monoecious (or monecious) A plant with both male and female flowers on the same plant (imperfect or unisexual flowers) or with flowers have both male and female reproductive parts (perfect or bisexual flowers).

muck An organic soil where the plant remains are decomposed to the point where the type of plants forming the soil cannot be determined.

mucro A sharp point at termination of an organ or other structure.

muskeg Bog dominated by *Sphagnum* mosses with widely spaced spruce trees; a common habitat type in interior Alaska.

mycorrhizae The symbiotic relationship between fungal hyphae and plant roots.

naked Without a covering; a stalk or stem without leaves.

native An indigenous species.

naturalized An introduced species that is established and persistent in an ecosystem.

nectary Where nectar is made; usually a gland at the base of a petal or sepal.

needle A slender leaf, as in the Pinaceae.

nerve A leaf vein.

neutral A pH of 7.

node Where the stem, leaf, and flower (if any) grow on a stem; the joints of a stem.

nutlet The fruit type of mints (Lamiaceae) and borages (Boraginaceae). An ovary that breaks into separate pieces.

obcordate Heart shaped where the attachment is at the narrower end.

oblanceolate Wider at the tip than at the base with attachment at the narrower end; inverse of lanceolate.

oblique Emerging or joining at an angle other than parallel or perpendicular.

oblong Much longer than wide with parallel sides.

obovate Egg shaped with attachment at narrower end.

ocrea A tube-shaped stipule or pair of stipules around the stem; characteristic of the Buckwheat Family (Polygonaceae).

opposite Leaves or branches which are paired opposite one another on the stem.

orbicular More or less circular in outline.

organic Soils composed of decaying plant remains.

oval Elliptical.

ovary The lower part of the pistil that produces the seeds.

ovate Broadly rounded at the base, becoming narrowed above; broader than lanceolate.

palea The uppermost of the two inner bracts subtending a grass flower (the lower bract is the lemma).

palmate Divided into more than three segments with a central point of attachment, like a hand; usually referring to leaves.

panicle An arrangement of flowers consisting of several racemes.

papilla (plural papillae) A short, rounded or cylindrical projections.

pappus The modified sepals of a composite flower which persist atop the ovary as bristles, scales or awns.

parallel-veined With several veins running from base of leaf to leaf tip, characteristic of most monocots.

paraphyllia Tiny, hairlike organs. Singular paraphyllium.

peat An organic soil formed of partially decomposed plant remains.

peatland A wetland whose soil is composed primarily of organic matter (mosses, sedges, etc.); a general term for bogs and fens.

pedicel A stem of a flower in an inflorescence.

peduncle The stem of a solitary flower or an inflorescence.

peltate More or less circular, with the stalk attached at a point on the underside.

pepo A fleshy, many-seeded fruit with a tough rind, as a melon.

perennial Living for 3 or more years.

perfect A flower having both male (stamens) and female (pistils) parts.

perianth Collectively, all the sepals and petals of a flower.

perigynia A flask-like casing that envelops the fruit of a *Carex* species. Singular perigynium.

permafrost a thick subsurface layer of soil that remains frozen throughout the year.

petal An individual part of the corolla, often white or colored.

petiole The stalk of a leaf.

phyllary An involucral bract subtending the flower head in composite flowers (Asteraceae).

phyllode An expanded petiole.

phyllopodic Having the basal sheaths blade-bearing; with new shoots arising from the center of parent shoot (compare with aphyllopodic).

pinna The primary or first division in a fern frond or leaf (plural pinnae).

pinnae The first division of a pinnately compound leaf.

pinnate A leaf regularly divided into segments with leaflets on either side of the axis, resembling a feather.

pinnatifid Pinnately lobed.

pinnule The pinnate segment of a pinna.

pistil The female reproductive organ of a flower, consisting of one or more fused carpels each with a stigma, style, and ovary. Develops into a fruit and contains ovules, which can become seeds if fertilized.

pistillate Flowers imperfect, containing only female reproductive parts. Female flowers.

pith A spongy central part of stems and branches.

pollen The male spores in an anther.

primocane The first-year, vegetative stem in *Rubus* (compare with floricane).

pro sp. When a taxon is transferred from the nonhybrid category to the hybrid category, the author citation remains unchanged, but may be followed by an indication in parentheses of the original category.

prostrate Lying flat on the ground.

pubescence Small hairs that are irregularly arranged and sparse.

pycnidia Specialized structures in lichens which asexually produce spores.

raceme A grouping of flowers along an elongated axis where each flower has its own stalk.

rachilla A small stem or axis.

rachis The central axis or stem of a leaf or inflorescence.

radial symmetry Divisible into symmetric halves along multiple planes, such as in a starfish or a rose flower. In contrast to 'bilateral symmetry'.

radiate heads In composite flowers, heads with both ray and disk flowers (Asteraceae).

ray floret Flowers of the Asteraceae with prominent strap-shaped petals.

ray flower A ligulate or strap-shaped flower in the Asteraceae, where often the outermost series of flowers in the head.

receptacle In the Asteraceae, the enlarged summit of the flower stalk to which the sepals, petals, stamens, and pistils are usually attached.

recurved Curved backward.

regular Flowers with all the similar parts of the same form; radially symmetric.

reniform Kidney shaped.

retuse A shallow notch at the apex.

revolute Leaf margins rolled in towards the underside.

rhizoid A root-like structure which anchors a moss and absorbs nutrients. Not true roots, as they lack vascular tissue.

rhizomatous Spreading by rhizomes (underground stems).

rhizome An underground, horizontal stem.

rib A pronounced vein or nerve.

root nodules Areas on roots of certain plants that house cyanobacteria to fix nitrogen.

rootstock Similar to rhizome but referring to any underground part that spreads the plant.

rosette A crowded, circular clump of leaves.

saggitate Shaped like an arrowhead with the bottom lobes facing downwards; compare hastate.

samara A dry, indehiscent fruit with a well-developed wing.

saprophyte A plant that lives off of dead organic matter.

scale A tiny, leaflike structure; the structure that subtends each flower in a sedge (Cyperaceae).

scape A naked stem (without leaves) bearing the flowers.

scarious Thin and dry in texture, generally not green.

section Cross-section.

secund Flowers mostly on one side of a stalk or branch.

sedge meadow A community dominated by sedges (Cyperaceae) and occurring on wet, saturated soils.

seep A spot where water oozes from the ground.

sepal The outer most whorl of a flower, often leaf-like and initially protecting the flower bud.

serotinous A condition of seed dispersal in some plants needing heat (generally produced by wildfire) to allow opening of fruit or cones to disperse seeds.

serrate tooth like projections along the margin; usually in reference to leaves.

sessile Without a stalk, directly attached.

sheath Tube-shaped membrane around a stem, especially for part of the leaf in grasses and sedges.

shrub A woody plant with multiple stems.

silicle Short fruit of the Mustard Family (Brassicaceae), normally less than 2x longer as wide.

silique Dry, dehiscent, 2-chambered fruit, with a persistent middle septum, of the Mustard Family (Brassicaceae), longer than a silicle.

simple Not compound; a leaf that has not been divided into many leaflets.

sinus The depression between two lobes.

smooth Without teeth or hairs.

sorus Clusters of spore containers (plural sori).

spadix A fleshy axis in which flowers are embedded.

spathe A large bract subtending or enclosing a cluster of flowers.

spatula-shaped Broadest at tip and tapering to the base.

spatulate Spatula-shaped; round at the tip and tapering towards the base.

sphagnum moss A type of moss common in peatlands and sometimes forming a continuous carpet across the surface; sometimes forming layers several meters thick; also loosely called peat moss.

spike A group of unstalked flowers along an unbranched stalk.

spikelet A small spike; the flower cluster (inflorescence) of grasses (Poaceae) and sedges (Cyperaceae). In grasses, the two outermost bracts are called glumes, and each flower inside has two more bracts, the lemma (lower) and palea (upper).

sporangia A case or sac that houses spores.

sporangium The spore-producing structure (plural sporangia).

spore a one-celled reproductive structure that gives rise to the gamete-bearing plant.

sporophore The part of the leaves in the genus *Botrychium* that holds the sporangia; the fertile leaf.

sporophyll A modified, spore-bearing leaf.

sporophyte The diploid part of the plant life cycle consisting of the stems, leaves, and flowers (if any). In bryophytes (mosses, liverworts, and hornworts) the sporophyte stage presents as a capsule on a specialized stalk called a seta.

spreading Widely angled outward.

spring A place where water flows naturally from the ground.

spur A hollow, pointed projection of a flower.

stamen The male reproductive organ, consisting of a filament (stalk-like appendage) and anther, which releases pollen.

staminate Imperfect flowers that contain only stamens; male flowers.

staminode An infertile stamen.

stellate Hairs that arise from a single base; looks star-shaped.

stem The main axis of a plant.

stigma The terminal, often sticky, part of a pistil which receives pollen.

stipe The 'stem' of a fern leaf.

stipule A leaflike outgrowth at the base of a leaf stalk.

stolon A horizontal stem lying on the soil surface that roots and buds into another individual; runners, as in strawberry plants.

stoloniferous Spreading by stolons (aboveground stems).

strobilus A spore-producing cone as in the clubmosses (Lycopodiaceae), but can also reference conifer cones as well. Plural strobilii.

style The stalklike part of the pistil between the ovary and the stigma.

subspecies A subdivision of the species forming a group with shared traits which differ from other members of the species (subsp.).

subtend Attached below and extending upward.

succulent Thick, fleshy and juicy.

superior Referring to the position of the ovary when it is above the point of attachment of sepals, petals, stamens, and pistils.

swale A slight depression.

swamp Wooded wetland dominated by trees or shrubs; soils are typically wet for much of year or sometimes inundated.

taiga boreal forests dominated by trees of black and white spruce and larch; in American usage, often refers to the stunted forests approaching northern limit of tree growth.

talus Fallen rock at the base of a slope or cliff.

taproot A main, downward-pointing root.

tendril A threadlike appendage from a stem or leaf that coils around other objects for support (as in *Vicia*).

tepal Sepals or petals not differentiated from one another.

terete Round in cross section.

terminal Located at the end of a stem or stalk.

ternate In orders of three.

thallus The body of the lichen, containing both algae and fungi. This is the vegetative part of the lichen. Plural thalli.

thicket A dense growth of woody plants.

tomentose Short hairs that are densely packed together.

tomentum A felted covering of rhizoids that appears wooly.

toothed Leaf margin with saw-like indentations.

translucent Nearly transparent.

tree A large, single-stemmed woody plant.

trifoliate Leaf divided into three leaflets.

trophophore The sterile part of the leaf of the genus *Botrychium,* which is green and photosynthetic.

truncate Abruptly cut-off.

tuber An enlarged portion of a root or rhizome.

tubercle Base of style persistent as a swelling atop the achene different in color and texture from achene body.

tundra Treeless plain in arctic regions, having permanently frozen subsoil.

turion A specialized type of shoot or bud that overwinters and resumes growth the following year.

tussock Dense hummock formed by certain grass or sedge species.

umbel A cluster of flowers in which the flower stalks arise from the same level.

umbelet A small, secondary umbel in an umbel, as in the Apiaceae.

upright Erect or nearly so.

urceolate Constricted at a point just before an opening; urn-shaped.

usnic acid A secondary chemical found in many lichens, giving them a characteristic yellowish cast. Usnic acid in lichens is thought to act as a sunscreen and as chemical defense against grazing.

utricle A small, one-seeded fruit with a dry, papery outer covering.

valve A segment of a dehiscent fruit; the wing of the fruit in *Rumex.*

variety Taxon below subspecies and differing from other varieties within the same subspecies (var.).

vein A vascular bundle, as in a leaf.

velum The membranous flap that partially covers the sporangium in *Isoetes.*

venation The pattern of veins on an organ.

ventral Front side.

verrucose Covered with small, wart-like projections.

verticil One whorled cycle of organs.

verticillate Arranged in whorls.

villous Pubescent with long, soft, bent hairs, the hairs not crimped or tangled.

vine A trailing or climbing plant, dependent on other objects for support.

viscid Sticky, glutinous.

viviparous Producing bulbs that begin to develop before becoming detached from the 'mother' plant, often in the place of flowers.

whorl A group of 3 or more parts from one point on a stem.

wing A thin tissue bordering or surrounding an organ.

woody Xylem tissue (the vascular tissue which conducts water and nutrients).

xeric Dry (compare with hydric, mesic).

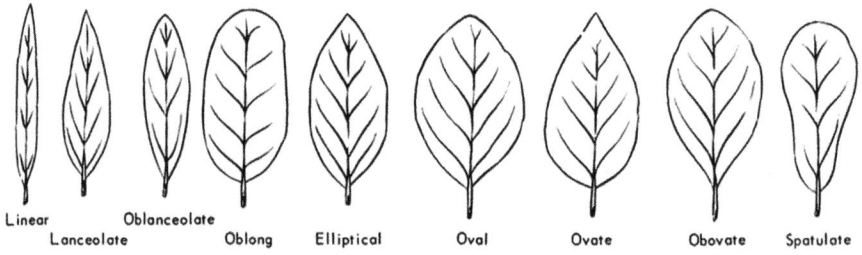

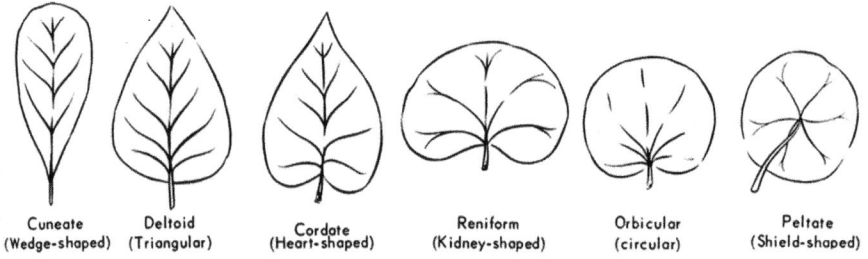

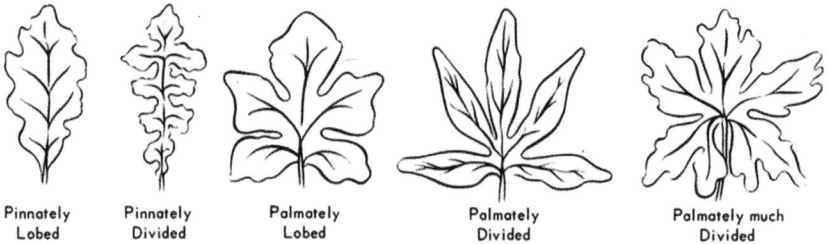

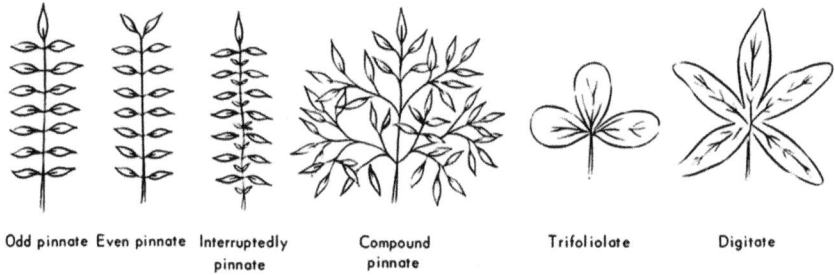

Linear
Lanceolate
Oblanceolate
Oblong
Elliptical
Oval
Ovate
Obovate
Spatulate

Cuneate
(Wedge-shaped)
Deltoid
(Triangular)
Cordate
(Heart-shaped)
Reniform
(Kidney-shaped)
Orbicular
(circular)
Peltate
(Shield-shaped)

Pinnately
Lobed
Pinnately
Divided
Palmately
Lobed
Palmately
Divided
Palmately much
Divided

Odd pinnate Even pinnate Interruptedly
pinnate
Compound
pinnate
Trifoliolate
Digitate

A. C. **BUDD**

Typical leaf shapes.

Flowers not stalked

SPIKE

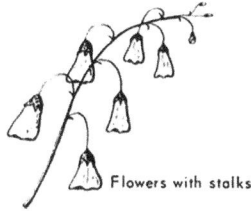

Flowers with stalks

RACEME

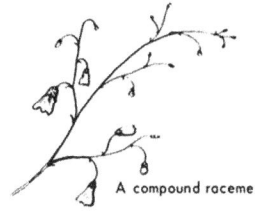

A compound raceme

PANICLE

Flower stalks from a common center

UMBEL

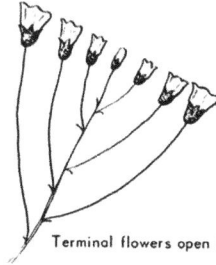

Terminal flowers open last

CORYMB

Terminal flowers open first

CYME

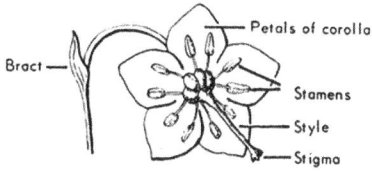

Parts of flower of One-flowered wintergreen

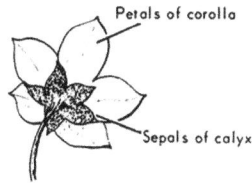

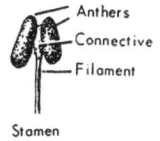

Stamen

Superior ovary

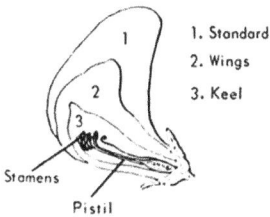

1. Standard
2. Wings
3. Keel

Section of flower of a legume

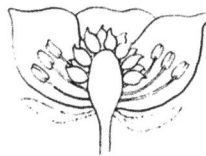

Section of flower of Buttercup

Inferior ovary

A. C. BUDD

Inflorescence types, parts of a flower.

THREE-PETALED
(Arrowhead)

FOUR-PETALED
(Mustard)

FIVE-PETALED
(Chickweed)

MANY-PETALED
(Purple cactus)

URN-SHAPED
(Bearberry)

CYLINDRICAL
(Gentian)

CAMPANULATE
(Harebell)

FUNNELFORM
(Morning-glory)

SALVER-FORM
(Collomia)

ROTATE
(Wild tomato)

(Bittersweet)

REFLEXED PETALS
(Shootingstar)

PAPILIONACEOUS
(Vetchling)

BILABIATE
(Marsh hedge-nettle)

(Monkeyflower)

SPURRED
(Toadflax)

(Violet)

(Low larkspur)

IRREGULAR
(Leafy spurge)

(Lady's-slipper)

A. C. **BUDD**

Types of flowers.

ACORN
(oak)

(American hazel)

NUTS

(Beaked hazel)

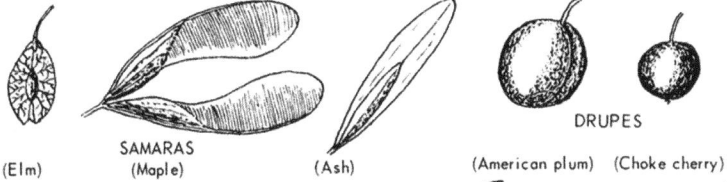

(Elm)

SAMARAS
(Maple)

(Ash)

DRUPES

(American plum)   (Choke cherry)

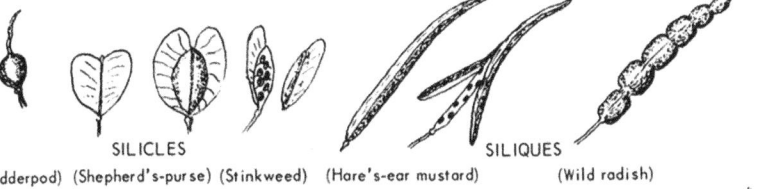

SILICLES

(Bladderpod)   (Shepherd's-purse)   (Stinkweed)   (Hare's-ear mustard)

SILIQUES

(Wild radish)

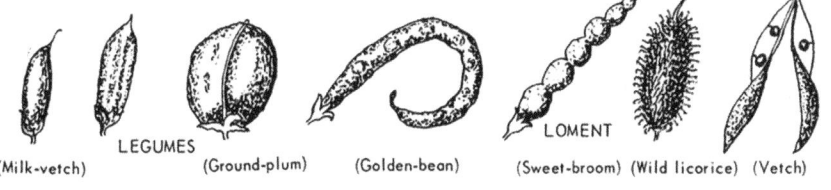

LEGUMES

(Milk-vetch)   (Ground-plum)   (Golden-bean)

LOMENT

(Sweet-broom)   (Wild licorice)   (Vetch)

Violet

(Geranium)   (Fireweed)   (Shootingstar)   (Black henbane)   (Flax)

CAPSULES

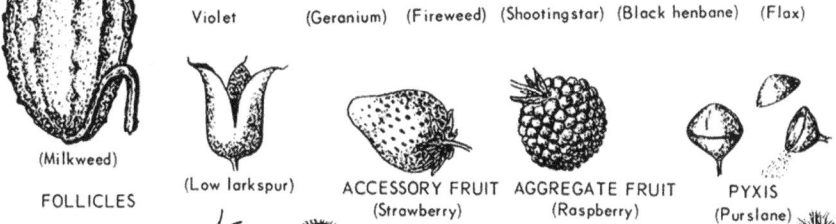

(Milkweed)

FOLLICLES

(Low larkspur)

ACCESSORY FRUIT
(Strawberry)

AGGREGATE FRUIT
(Raspberry)

PYXIS
(Purslane)

SCHIZOCARPS
(cow parsnip)   (Sweet cicely)

BERRIES
(Gooseberry)

BUR
(Cocklebur)

ACHENES
(Various)

A. C. BUDD

Types of fruit.

REFERENCES

PRINT

Anderson, J.P. 1959. *Flora of Alaska and Adjacent Parts of Canada. An illustrated descriptive text of all vascular plants known to occur within the region covered.* Iowa State University Press. Ames, Iowa.

Argus, G.W. 1973. *The Genus Salix in Alaska and the Yukon.* Publications in Botany No. 2. National Museum of Canada. Ottawa, Ontario.

Argus, G.W. 2004. *A Guide to the identification of Salix (Willows) in Alaska, the Yukon Territory, and adjacent regions.* July 2004 workshop on willow identification. Unpublished.

Chadde, S.W. 2020. *Alaska Trees and Shrubs.* Orchard Innovations Books. Mountain View, Arkansas.

Cody, W.J. 2000. *Flora of the Yukon Territory.* Second Edition. National Research Council of Canada Press. Ottawa, Ontario.

Collet, D. 2004. *Willows of Interior Alaska.* U.S. Fish and Wildlife Service.

Douglas, G.W., G.B. Straley, D.V. Meidinger, and J. Pojar. 1998. *Illustrated Flora of British Columbia.* Volumes 1-8. B.C. Ministry of Environment, Land, & Parks and B.C. Ministry of Forests. Victoria, British Columbia.

Flora of North America Editorial Committee (eds.). 1993+. *Flora of North America North of Mexico.* 20+ vols. New York & Oxford.

Garibaldi, A. 1999. *Medicinal flora of the Alaska Natives: a compilation of knowledge from literary sources of Aleut, Alutiiq, Athabascan, Eyak, Haida, Inupiat, Tlingit, Tsimshian, and Yupik traditional healing methods using plants.* Alaska Natural Heritage Program. Univ. of Alaska Anchorage.

Hitchcock, C.L., A. Cronquist, D.E. Giblin, B.S. Legler, P.F. Zika, and R.G. Olmstead. 2018. *Flora of the Pacific Northwest: An Illustrated Manual.* Second Edition. University of Washington Press. Seattle, Washington.

Hultén, E.O. 1968. *Flora of Alaska and Neighboring Territories: A Manual of the Vascular Plants.* Stanford University Press. Stanford, California.

Jernigan, K., O. Alexie, S. Alexie, M. Stover, R. Meier, C. Parker, M. Pete, and M. Rasmussen (eds). 2015. *A Guide to the Ethnobotany of the Yukon-Kuskokwim Region.* University Of Alaska Fairbanks, Alaska Native Language Center.

Kari, P.R. 1995. *Tanaina Plantlore, Dena'ina K'et'una.* Alaska Native Language Center with Alaska Natural History Association and National Park Service.

Moerman, D.E. 1998. *Native American Ethnobotany.* Portland, OR: Timber Press.

Moerman, D.E. 2010. *Native American Food Plants: An Ethnobotanical Dictionary.* Portland, OR: Timber Press.

Roland, C., Stehn, S., Hampton-Miller, C., and Groth, E. 2016. *Ecological Atlas of Denali's Flora.* National Park Service. Available at: ecologicalatlas.uaf.edu.

Sheviak, C.J. 1999. The identities of *Platanthera hyperborea* and *P. huronensis,* with the description of a new species from North America. Lindleyana 14: 193–203.

Skinner Q.D., S.J. Wright, R.J. Henszey, J.L. Henszey, and S.K. Wyman. 2012. *A Field Guide to Alaska Grasses.* Education Resources Publishing: Cumming, GA.

Tande G.F. and R. Lipkin. 2003. *Wetland Sedges of Alaska.* Alaska Natural Heritage Program, Environment and Natural Resources Institute, University of Alaska Anchorage.

Tolmatchev, A.I., J.G. Packer, and G.C.D. Griffiths. 1996. *Flora of the Russian Arctic.* Volumes 1-3. University of Alberta Press. Edmonton, Alberta.

Viereck, L.A., and E.L. Little. 2007. *Alaska Trees and Shrubs.* Second Edition. University of Alaska Press. Fairbanks, Alaska.

Welsh, S.L. 1974. *Anderson's Flora of Alaska and Adjacent Parts of Canada.* Brigham Young University Press. Provo, Utah.

ONLINE

Alaska Center for Conservation Science (ACCS) (*accs.uaa.alaska.edu*).

Alaska Native Plant Society (AKNPS) (*aknps.org*).

Arctic Flora of Canada and Alaska (*arcticplants.myspecies.info*).

Consortium of Pacific Northwest Herbaria (*www.pnwherbaria.org*).

E-Flora British Columbia (*ibis.geog.ubc.ca/biodiversity/eflora*).

Ecological Atlas of Denali's Flora, Denali National Park and Preserve (*ecologicalatlas.uaf.edu*).

Flora of Alaska. (*floraofalaska.org*).

INDEX (Common Name)

INDEX (Scientific Name)

NOTE: Synonyms are listed in *italics*.

www.ingramcontent.com/pod-product-compliance
Lightning Source LLC
Chambersburg PA
CBHW052107030426
42335CB00025B/2879